# LIDC Contributions on Antitrust Law, Intellectual Property and Unfair Competition

More information about this series at http://www.springer.com/series/11817

Bruce Kilpatrick • Pierre Kobel
Pranvera Këllezi
Editors

# Antitrust Analysis of Online Sales Platforms & Copyright Limitations and Exceptions

Springer

*Editors*
Bruce Kilpatrick
Addleshaw Goddard LLP
London, UK

Pierre Kobel
Kobel Avocat Attorney-at-law
Geneva, Switzerland

Pranvera Këllezi
Këllezi Legal
Geneva, Switzerland

ISSN 2199-742X ISSN 2199-7438 (electronic)
LIDC Contributions on Antitrust Law, Intellectual Property and Unfair Competition
ISBN 978-3-030-10053-7 ISBN 978-3-319-71419-6 (eBook)
https://doi.org/10.1007/978-3-319-71419-6



Printed on acid-free paper

This Springer imprint is published by the registered company Springer International Publishing AG part of Springer Nature.
The registered company address is: Gewerbestrasse 11, 6330 Cham, Switzerland

# Preface

On behalf of the LIDC (International League of Competition Law), we are delighted to present the sixth edition of LIDC Contributions on Antitrust Law, Intellectual Property and Unfair Competition, which captures the reports prepared by the international and national reporters at the League's Annual Congress held in October 2017 in Rio de Janeiro, Brazil. This was the first time that the Congress had been hosted in South America, and it was a wonderful way to mark the contribution that new national groups of the League (particularly the Brazilian group) have made to recent Congresses. We would like to thank the organisers of this event and for their dedication and enthusiasm in putting together such a strong programme.

The Congress is, in the editors' opinion, a real 'one of a kind' event, bringing together leading practitioners across the antitrust and intellectual property fields from a wide variety of jurisdictions across the globe, with detailed national reports on two topics chosen by the LIDC's Scientific Committee and an international comparative report on each topic.

It takes a huge amount of work and commitment from the national reports, and particularly the international reporters, to produce their studies, and we would like to thank them for their enormous contribution, which is greatly appreciated. This year's Congress brought together delegates from across the world, with national reports from jurisdictions including Brazil and Australia, as well as from across the European Union. The purpose of this book is to share their learning with a wider audience across the members of the LIDC and its constituent national organisations and with academics, practitioners and students across the world. We hope you enjoy reading it as much as we enjoyed listening to the debate and discussions that took place in Rio.

The League's program in Rio covered the application of competition law to online sales platforms, which is increasingly a focus for antitrust authorities around the world. This year's antitrust topic (Question A) for the Congress was as follows: *What are the major competition/antitrust issues generated by the growth of online sales platforms, and how should they be resolved?* We would like to thank all of the eleven national reporters (Austria, Australia, Belgium, Brazil, France, Germany, Italy, Hungary, Sweden, Switzerland and the United Kingdom) and particularly João Marcelo de Lima Assafim, an attorney from De Lima Assafim Attorneys at Law in Rio de Janeiro, Brazil, for producing an excellent international comparative report on this complex and challenging 'new economy' subject, which remains a focus for policy makers and antitrust enforcement agencies across the globe.

Mr De Lima Assafim's report provides an excellent insight into the application of EU competition both at a national level within the European Union as well as in jurisdictions outside the EU, including in the field of computer algorithms, which can be used to monitor competitors' prices and can give rise to new challenges in the field of antitrust enforcement, as well as the application of competition law to online platforms that possess significant market power. As the report indicates, these issues have been considered in the academic literature and have been investigated by several national competition authorities. The report makes a number of recommendations, in light of the various national reports produced in response to Question A, and at the Congress Mr De Lima Assafim presented these recommendations with a view to finding areas of shared practice for formal adoption as formal League Recommendations.

The second part of the book focuses on the intellectual property question (Question B) that was debated at the Congress, during a further working session. This year's topic was 'To what extent do current exclusions and limitations to copyright strike a fair balance between the rights of owners and fair use by private individuals and others?' The international reporter was Dr Benoit Michaux, from the Université de Namur in Brussels, who reviewed and synthesised comments from twelve national reporters (from Austria, Belgium, Brazil, Czech Republic, France, Germany, Hungary, Italy, Poland, Romania, Switzerland and the UK). Both the international report and the various national reports published in this edition provide an unparalleled comparative analysis of this topic and bring together common themes and contrast the various national provisions dealing with exceptions to copyright, amongst other things. The report examines, in particular, the increasingly complex balance between the interests of copyright owners, on one hand, and the interests of users of their work, on the other, and how this balance has been achieved through national laws and court decisions in the various jurisdictions. The report also captures some of the criticisms levelled at the current systems and identifies potential solutions and mechanisms that might be used to balance these competing interests, including the way in which exceptions and limitations to copyright are framed and interpreted according to national law. It considers a number of key questions in this context, including whether the law should provide for a broad and flexible concept like 'fair use' or any other comparable concept rather than for a list of rigid and well-detailed exceptions and limitations.

The final reports have now been sent to national and supranational competition law enforcers, which have in the past commented very positively on LIDC reports and their value to enforcers. The works of the LIDC have been a well of practical guidance for generations of lawyers, whether or not they are members of the LIDC, and for regulatory authorities.

The editors would like to thank all the authors for their contributions and their patient collaboration during the editing of this book. They would like to express their sincere gratitude to the Members of the Bureau, of the Council and of the Scientific Committee for their kind support and encouragement during the preparation of this book.

London, UK — Bruce Kilpatrick
Geneva, Switzerland — Pierre Kobel
Geneva, Switzerland — Pranvera Këllezi

# Contents

**Part I Anti-trust Analysis of Online Sales Platforms**

1 **International Report** . . . . . . . . . . 3
João Marcelo de Lima Assafim

2 **Australia** . . . . . . . . . . 41
Barbora Jedličková and Julie Clarke

3 **Austria** . . . . . . . . . . 91
Astrid Ablasser-Neuhuber and Gerhard Fussenegger

4 **Belgium** . . . . . . . . . . 107
Steffie De Cock

5 **Brazil** . . . . . . . . . . 127
Pedro Paulo Salles Cristofaro and Luisa Shinzato de Pinho

6 **France** . . . . . . . . . . 139
Linda Arcelin, Nizar Lajnef, Annabelle Lebaudy, Lauren Mechri, Florence Ninane, Michaël Vaz d'Almeida, and Pascal Wilhelm

7 **Germany** . . . . . . . . . . 157
Thomas Hoeren

8 **Hungary** . . . . . . . . . . 187
Álmos Papp and András Horváth

9 **Italy** . . . . . . . . . . 215
Francesca La Rocca

10 **Sweden** . . . . . . . . . . 229
Robert Moldén, Henrik Nilsson, and Dagne Sabockis

11 **Switzerland** . . . . . . . . . . 249
Annemarie Streuli

12 **United Kingdom** . . . . . . . . . . 269
Vineet Budhiraja

## Part II Copyright Limitations and Exceptions

**13 International Report** . . . . . . . . . . 291
Benoit Michaux

**14 Austria** . . . . . . . . . . 329
Valerie Eder

**15 Belgium** . . . . . . . . . . 347
Manon Knockaert

**16 Brazil** . . . . . . . . . . 375
Felipe Barros Oquendo

**17 Czech Republic** . . . . . . . . . . 391
Radka MacGregor Pelikánová

**18 France** . . . . . . . . . . 407
Martina Isola and Guillaume Couet

**19 Germany** . . . . . . . . . . 437
Thomas Hoeren

**20 Hungary** . . . . . . . . . . 463
Zsófia Lendvai

**21 Italy** . . . . . . . . . . 483
Marco Francetti

**22 Poland** . . . . . . . . . . 503
Maria Obara-Piszewska and Filina Sztandera

**23 Romania** . . . . . . . . . . 527
Paul-George Buta

**24 Switzerland** . . . . . . . . . . 567
Sevan Antreasyan

**25 United Kingdom** . . . . . . . . . . 583
Eleonora Rosati

# List of Contributors


**Astrid Ablasser-Neuhuber** bpv Hügel Rechtsanwälte GmbH, Vienna, Austria

**Sevan Antreasyan** Lenz & Staehelin, Geneva, Switzerland

**Linda Arcelin** La Rochelle University, La Rochelle, France

**Felipe Barros Oquendo** Di Blasi, Parente & Associates, Rio de Janeiro, Brazil

**Vineet Budhiraja** Watson Farley Williams LLP, London, UK

**Paul-George Buta** Mușat & Asociații, Bucharest, Romania

**Julie Clarke** Melbourne Law School, The University of Melbourne, Parkville, VIC, Australia

**Guillaume Couet** Association Française d'Etude de la concurrence (AFEC/AFEC Jeunes), Paris, France

**Pedro Paulo Salles Cristofaro** Chediak Lopes da Costa Cristofaro Menezes Cortes Advogados, Rio de Janeiro, Brazil

**Steffie De Cock** Altius, Brussels, Belgium

**Valerie Eder** Gassauer-Fleissner Rechtsanwälte GmbH, Vienna, Austria

**Marco Francetti** Jacobacci & Associati, Milan, Italy

**Gerhard Fussenegger** bpv Hügel Rechtsanwälte GmbH, Vienna, Austria

**Thomas Hoeren** Westfälische Wilhelms-Universität, Münster, Germany

**András Horváth** Hegymegi-Barakonyi and Partner Baker & McKenzie, Budapest, Hungary

**Martina Isola** Association Française d'Etude de la concurrence (AFEC), Paris, France

**Barbora Jedličková** TC Beirne School of Law, The University of Queensland, St Lucia, QLD, Australia

**Manon Knockaert** Centre de Recherche Information, Droit et Société (CRIDS), University of Namur, Namur, Belgium

**Nizar Lajnef** UGGC Avocats, Paris, France

**Francesca La Rocca** Studio Legale Sena e Tarchini, Milan, Italy

**Annabelle Lebaudy** Cabinet Borrel, Paris, France

**Zsófia Lendvai** Hegymegi-Barakonyi and Partner Baker & McKenzie, Budapest, Hungary

**Radka MacGregor Pelikánová** Metropolitan University Prague, Strašnice, Czech Republic

**João Marcelo de Lima Assafim** De Lima Assafim Attorneys at Law, Rio de Janeiro, Brazil

**Lauren Mechri** Cabinet Borrel, Paris, France

**Benoit Michaux** Hoyng Rokh Monegier, Brussels, Belgium

Université de Namur, Namur, Belgium

**Robert Moldén** Front Advokater, Stockholm, Sweden

Stockholm School of Economics, Stockholm, Sweden

**Henrik Nilsson** Wesslau Söderqvist, Stockholm, Sweden

**Florence Ninane** Allen & Overy LLP, Paris, France

**Maria Obara-Piszewska** WKB Kwieciński Wierciński Baehr Law Office, Warsaw, Poland

**Álmos Papp** Bán, S. Szabó & Partners, Budapest, Hungary

**Eleonora Rosati** University of Southampton, Southampton, UK

**Dagne Sabockis** Stockholm School of Economics, Stockholm, Sweden

Wesslau Söderqvist, Stockholm, Sweden

**Luisa Shinzato de Pinho** Novotny Advogados, Rio de Janeiro, Brazil

**Annemarie Streuli** Python, Geneva, Switzerland

**Filina Sztandera** WKB Kwieciński Wierciński Baehr Law Office, Poznań, Poland

**Michaël Vaz d'Almeida** Orrick Rambaud Martel, Paris, France

**Pascal Wilhelm** Wilhelm & Associés, Paris, France

# Abbreviations

| | |
|---|---|
| AUD | Australian dollar |
| Berne Convention | The Berne Convention for the Protection of Literary and Artistic Works of 9 September 1886, as amended |
| Brussels Convention | Brussels Convention Relating to the Distribution of Programme-Carrying Signals Transmitted by Satellite, 1974 |
| BGBl | Bundesgesetzblatt (Germany) |
| BGH | Bundesgerichtshof (Germany) |
| BGN | Bulgarian lev |
| B2B | Business to business |
| B2C | Business to consumers |
| bn | Billion |
| BRL | Brazilian real (reais) |
| c./ca. | Circa |
| cf. | Compare |
| CFI | Court of First Instance of the ECJ (before 1 December 2009) |
| CFREU | The Charter of Fundamental Rights of the European Union, OJ 2010 C 83, p. 389 |
| CHF | Swiss franc |
| CJEU | Court of Justice of the European Union (after 1 December 2009) |
| CMLR | Common Market Law Review |
| $CR_n$ | Concentration ratio measuring the percentage market share held by *n* largest undertakings |
| De minimis Notice | Commission Notice on agreements of minor importance which do not appreciably restrict competition under Article 101(1) of the Treaty on the Functioning of the European Union (de minimis), OJ 2014 C 291, p. 1 |

| | |
|---|---|
| Directive 97/7 | Directive 97/7 of the European Parliament and of the Council of 20 May 1997 on the protection of consumers in respect of distance contracts, OJ 1997 L 144, p. 19 |
| Directive 96/09 or Database Directive | Directive 96/9 of the European Parliament and of the Council of 11 March 1996 on the legal protection of databases, OJ 1996 L 77, p. 20 |
| Directive 2000/31 or Directive on electronic commerce | Directive 2000/31 of the European Parliament and of the Council of 8 June 2000 on certain legal aspects of information society services, in particular electronic commerce, in the internal market, OJ 2000 L 178, p. 1 |
| Directive 2001/21 or InfoSoc Directive | Directive 2001/29 of the European Parliament and of certain aspects of copyright and related rights in the information society, OJ 2001 L 167, p. 10 |
| Directive 2001/83 | Directive 2001/83 of the European Parliament and of the Council of 6 November 2001 on the Community code relating to medicinal products for human use, OJ 2001 L 311, p. 67 |
| Directive 2004/48 | Directive 2004/48 of the European Parliament and of the Council of 29 April 2004 on the enforcement of intellectual property rights, OJ 2004 L 157, p. 45 |
| Directive 2005/29 or Unfair Commercial Practices Directive | Directive 2005/29 of the European Parliament and of the Council of 11 May 2005 concerning unfair business-to-consumer commercial practices in the internal market and amending Council Directive 84/450, Directives 97/7, 98/27 and 2002/65 of the European Parliament and of the Council and Regulation 2006/2004 of the European Parliament and of the Council, OJ 2005 L 149, p. 22 |
| Directive 2006/115 or Rental and Lending Rights Directive | Directive 2006/115 of the European Parliament and of the Council of 12 December 2006 on rental right and lending right and on certain rights related to copyright in the field of intellectual property, OJ 2006 L 376, p. 28 |
| Directive 2009/24 or Software Directive | Directive 2009/24 of the European Parliament and of the Council of 23 April 2009 on the legal protection of computer programs, OJ 2009 L 111, p. 16 |
| Directive 2012/28 or Orphan Works Directive | Directive 2012/28 of the European Parliament and of the Council of 25 October 2012 on certain permitted uses of orphan works, OJ 2012 L 299, p. 5 |
| Directive 2014/104 | Directive 2014/104 of the European Parliament and of the Council of 26 November 2014 on certain rules governing actions for damages under national law for infringements of the competition law provisions of the Member States and of the European Union, OJ 2014 L 349, p. 1 |

| | |
|---|---|
| DKK | Danish krone |
| DM | Deutsche mark |
| e.g. or eg | For example |
| EC | European Community |
| ECHR | Council of Europe, European Convention for Human Rights of 4 November 1950 |
| ECJ | European Court of Justice (before 1 December 2009) |
| ECR | European Court Reports |
| ECtHR | European Court of Human Rights |
| EU | European Union |
| ff | And following |
| GBP | Pound sterling (UK) |
| GC | General Court of the CJEU (after 1 December 2009) |
| GDP | Gross domestic product |
| Guidelines on the effect on trade concept | Commission Notice – Guidelines on the effect on trade concept contained in Articles 81 and 82 of the Treaty, OJ 2004 C 101, p. 81 |
| Guidelines on Vertical Restraints | Guidelines on Vertical Restraints, OJ 2010 C 130, p. 1 |
| ha | Hectare |
| Hague Agreement | Hague Agreement Concerning the International Registration of Industrial Designs, 1925 |
| HRK | Croatian kuna (*hrvatska kuna*) |
| HMT | Hypothetical monopolist test |
| HUF | Hungarian forint (*Magyar forint*) |
| i.e. | Id est (that is) |
| Id./idem | The same as previously mentioned |
| IP | Intellectual property |
| Lisbon Agreement | Lisbon Agreement for the Protection of Appellations of Origin and their International Registration of October 31, 1958, as revised at Stockholm on July 14, 1967, and as amended on September 28, 1979 |
| Locarno (Classification) Agreement | Locarno Agreement Establishing an International Classification for Industrial Designs, 1979 |
| m | Million |
| $m^2$ | Square metre |
| min | Minutes |

| | |
|---|---|
| Madrid Agreement | Madrid Agreement Concerning the International Registration of Marks, 1979 |
| MFN | Most favoured nation |
| NAAT rule | The non-appreciable affectation of trade rule |
| Nice (Classification) Agreement | Nice Agreement Concerning the International Classification of Goods and Services for the Purposes of the Registration of Marks, 1979 |
| Notice on the relevant market | Commission Notice on the definition of relevant market for the purposes of Community competition law, OJ 1997 C 372, p. 5 |
| OECD | Organisation for Economic Co-operation and Development |
| OJ | Official Journal |
| p./pp. | Page(s) |
| para/paras | Paragraph(s) |
| Phonograms Convention | Convention for the Protection of Producers of Phonograms Against Unauthorized Duplication of Their Phonograms, 1971 |
| PTL | Patent Law Treaty, 2000 |
| Paris Convention | Paris Convention for the protection of industrial property, 1883 |
| pt/pts | Point(s) |
| kg | Kilogram |
| R&D | Research and development |
| Regulation 2659/2000 | Commission Regulation 2659/2000 of 29 November 2000 on the application of Article 81(3) of the Treaty to categories of research and development agreements, OJ 2000 L 304, p. 7 |
| Regulation 1400/2002 | Commission Regulation 1400/2002 of 31 July 2002 on the application of Article 81(3) of the Treaty to categories of vertical agreements and concerted practices in the motor vehicle sector, OJ 2002 L 203, p. 30 |
| Regulation 1/2003 | Council Regulation 1/2003 of 16 December 2002 on the implementation of the rules on competition laid down in Articles 81 and 82 of the Treaty, OJ 2003 L 1, p. 1 |
| Regulation 2006/2004 | Regulation 2006/2004 of the European Parliament and of the Council of 27 October 2004 on cooperation between national authorities responsible for the enforcement of consumer protection laws (the Regulation on consumer protection cooperation), OJ 2004 L 364, p. 1 |

| | |
|---|---|
| Regulation 139/2004 | Council Regulation 139/2004 of 20 January 2004 on the control of concentrations between undertakings, OJ 2004 L 24, p. 1 |
| Regulation 110/2008 | Regulation 110/2008 of the European Parliament and the Council of 15 January 2008 on the definition, description, presentation, labelling and protection of geographical indications of spirit drinks, OJ 2008 L 39, p. 16 |
| Regulation 330/2010 | Commission Regulation 330/2010 of 20 April 2010 on the application of Article 101(3) of the Treaty on the Functioning of the European Union to categories of vertical agreements and concerted practices, OJ 2010 L 102, p. 1 |
| Regulation 1151/2012 | Regulation 1151/2012 on quality schemes for agricultural products and foodstuffs, OJ 2012 L 343, p. 1 |
| Regulation 608/2013 | Regulation 608/2013 of the European Parliament and of the Council of 12 June 2013 concerning customs enforcement of intellectual property rights and repealing Council Regulation 1383/2003, OJ 2013 L 181, p. 15 |
| Regulation 1308/2013 | Regulation 1308/2013 of the European Parliament and of the Council of 17 December 2013 establishing a common organisation of the markets in agricultural products and repealing Council Regulations 922/72, 234/79, 1037/2001 and 1234/2007, OJ 2013 L 347, p. 671 |
| Regulation 251/2014 | Regulation 251/2014 of the European Parliament and of the Council of 26 February 2014 on the definition, description, presentation, labelling and the protection of geographical indications of aromatized wine products, OJ 2014 L 84, p. 14 |
| Regulation 316/2014 | Commission Regulation 316/2014 of 21 March 2014 on the application of Article 101(3) of the Treaty on the Functioning of the European Union to categories of technology transfer agreements, OJ 2014 L 93, p. 17 |
| Rome Convention | International Convention for the Protection of Performers, Producers of Phonograms and Broadcasting Organizations, 1961 |
| RON | Romanian leu |
| SEK | Swedish krona |
| Singapore Treaty | Singapore Treaty on the Law of Trademarks, 2006 |
| SMEs | Small and medium-sized enterprises |
| SMP | Significant market power |
| SSNIP | Small but significant and non-transitory increase in price |

| | |
|---|---|
| TEC | Treaty Establishing the European Community |
| TFEU | Treaty on the Functioning of the European Union |
| TLT | Trademark Law Treaty, 1994 |
| TRIPs | Agreement on Trade-Related Aspects of Intellectual Property Rights, Annex 1C of the Marrakesh Agreement Establishing the World Trade Organization, signed in Marrakesh, Morocco on 15 April 1994 |
| UAH | Ukrainian hryvnia |
| UK | United Kingdom |
| US/USA | United States of America |
| v | Versus |
| Vienna (Classification) Agreement | Vienna Agreement Establishing an International Classification of the Figurative Elements of Marks, 1985 |
| WCT/WIPO Copyright Treaty | World Intellectual Property Organization Copyright Treaty, 1996 |
| WPPT | WIPO Performances and Phonograms Treaty, 1996 |

# Part I

# Anti-trust Analysis of Online Sales Platforms

# International Report 1

João Marcelo de Lima Assafim

## 1.1 Introduction

This international report synthesises the eleven national reports[1] answering the questionnaire on the growth of online sales platforms.

Ahead of its October 2017 Congress in Brazil, the International League of Competition Law has gathered information relating to the following *new economy* antitrust question: *What are the major competition/antitrust issues generated by the growth of online sales platforms, and how should they be resolved?*

First, a clarification about the respondents is necessary in this international report. In this survey, as in the past, most of the respondents are Member States of the European Union, and these countries are under the European Union's jurisdiction and therefore must apply competition law in a consistent manner.[2] Some other countries, namely Australia, Brazil and Switzerland, are not part of the European Union. Moreover, at this particular time, there is the further issue of the United Kingdom's decision to leave the EU. This complicated legal and political process is not taken into consideration for the purposes of this report as its implications are unclear, and no comments have been made in the UK report.

The observations and conclusions of this international report are based on the information supplied by the countries that have answered the LIDC questionnaire. Although some major countries with substantial experience in competition policy and legislation are not within the scope of this report, we believe that information

[1] Austria, Australia, Belgium, Brazil, France, Germany, Italy, Hungary, Sweden, Switzerland and United Kingdom.

[2] Articles 3 and 15 of Regulation 1/2003.

J. Marcelo de Lima Assafim (✉)
De Lima Assafim Attorneys at Law, Rio de Janeiro, Brazil
e-mail: joaomarcelo@delimaassafim.adv.br



B. Kilpatrick et al. (eds.), *Antitrust Analysis of Online Sales Platforms & Copyright Limitations and Exceptions*, LIDC Contributions on Antitrust Law, Intellectual Property and Unfair Competition,
https://doi.org/10.1007/978-3-319-71419-6_1

given by the 11 (eleven) respondents is sufficient to lead us to meaningful conclusions.

The challenge of analysing this set of national reports is as complex as analysing any other market relating to vertical agreements or even horizontal agreements, with the difference that in this case the subject is online platforms, which makes the subject matter even more complex.

This issue (the growth of online platforms) is about the effects of the *new economy*[3] on competition law and, more specifically, about Internet-related businesses and enterprises.[4]

All respondents have concerns about the application of competition law to online platforms. This concept is considered, for instance, by the European Commission as a software-based facility *offering multi-sided markets where providers and users of content, goods and services can meet.* Concerns at the supranational, EU level demanded a response by many of the European national policy makers.[5] These concerns are shared in non-EU jurisdictions where competition law deals with online sales platforms as a category of business methods developed through computer software facilities, including *services provided online by online sales platforms, contractual relationships between the online platforms and sellers or buyers, information exchange, power and integration.*[6]

The Australian report indicates that online sales platform *specifically* (they) *may include: algorithms which can coordinate and monitor prices and other business practices among competitors; collecting, exchanging and blocking information and targeting specific customers (consumers or businesses); and creating innovation-driven new monopolistic markets or markets where one online platform possesses significant market power.*

Generally, the reports contributing to this international comparison consider that many specific features of the online sales platforms and their implications have impact on competition policy. Concerns about these phenomena have been raised in the academic literature and investigated by several national authorities. The main issues that arise from these features are predominantly related to the market power of these platforms and the impact of their bargaining power on the interaction between sellers and buyers.

New technology industries are different from traditional industries dedicated to the production and sale of material goods. Antitrust doctrine and practice have developed

---

[3] For competition law purposes, the notion of the 'new economy' covers three specific and related industries. The top element of this set of businesses and companies is the (1) manufacture of computer software; the second is (2) services provided by Internet-based businesses; and, finally, (3) communication service and equipment as production factor for both businesses.

[4] This notion is considered in this International Report as referring to a service based economy from a manufacturing one. It ties in with the idea of Uber being the largest taxi company, but owning no taxis; or AirBnB owning no hotels. However, the issues with 'online sales' are wider than this. Some online platforms – eBay, Amazon Marketplace, Etsy – have stimulated manufacturing.

[5] See *Dynamic Competition in Online Platforms – evidence from five case study markets*, prepared by Europe Economics on behalf of the UK Department for Business, Energy and Industrial Strategy, March 2017, page 6.

[6] See the Australian International Report, Section 1.

standards for the traditional economy, such as automobiles, electricity, clothes, steel, coffee, cigarettes, etc., considering their specific market characteristics. Nevertheless, the outputs of the new economy are different from the output of that first group of traditional industries and from the ordinary sale of material goods through physical (i.e., 'brick and mortar') distribution. In this scenario, intellectual property concepts play a key role. For instance, both Amazon and eBay are very much dedicated to the sale of material goods as they are online sales platforms of 'brick and mortar' retailers (such as online sales platforms of supermarkets). The key is that different forms of distribution are facilitated, avoiding brick-and-mortar retail outlets.

Antitrust literature identifies the features of traditional industries in static competition where it takes place through pricing. Some of these features include multi-plant or multi-firm production, complex industrial organisation, high capital investment, reduced allocation of investment in innovation, stable markets, and limited flux of entry and exit of players.

Nevertheless, the new economy businesses may not share these features. Businesses operating in this new economic environment usually have a broad range of output, in many cases fewer capital requirements,[7] high levels of innovation, fewer barriers to entry, and quick entry and exit into these specialised markets.

These new economy players seem to be born and to die more easily than before in traditional markets. These unstable market conditions demand that these Internet-based industries search for business stability, and for this reason, their business model often includes trying to arrive first in a new market and establish a monopoly or seek cooperation among competitors in standard setting. Here, this international report queries whether we should just focus on evidence-based views. For example, this report could analyse if low start-up costs or cheaper distribution, visibility[8] and direct access to a range of consumers mean that businesses could be set up quickly or not.[9]

This is why network externality is a goal in this kind of business. It is natural that the company that creates a landmark invention or a new business process, establishes a new standard and builds a new market does not tend to let competitors reproduce its methods, products or services so easily. These phenomena also take such discussion to another field, still related to competition, which is the importance of copyright and protection of industrial rights for the new economy and the competitiveness of the Internet-based industries. There are two different points here: (1) network externalities being a feature of platforms as they are multi-sided business models and (2) the importance of IP protection. Even though IP protection is

[7]To some stakeholders high investment costs are a feature of the online businesses. They do not have to invest in brick-and-mortar stores but do have to invest in marketing, software creation. To others, it also allows suppliers to avoid investing in expensive retail distribution systems if they can link up to an established sales platform (eBay/Amazon) or sell through their own website.

[8]To Hungary, *[t]he resulting restrained online visibility affects small and medium-sized dealers more adversely as they usually have limited resources for creating, adequately maintaining and promoting their own online stores than their large rivals.* See Section 4.3. of the Hungarian report.

[9]According to the French report, Section 20: *[I]n a case-by- case effects analysis, a prohibition of sales on marketplaces could be considered as creating a barrier to entry from the point of view of SMEs, which do not necessarily have sufficient resources to develop mobile applications with secure payment systems.*

important to these business methods (as it is to the new economy at all), it is outside of the scope of this paper.

As we know, competition law does not generally forbid a monopoly position acquired through efficiency. On the other hand, competition law does have to define the limits within which a monopolist may compete to keep its monopoly position.

A common aspect of both old and new economies is vertical integration. However, are the standards of antitrust analysis the same for the *old economy* and the *new economy*? The question is: are online sales platforms opposed to the antitrust criteria applicable to the old or traditional economy?

Some authorities' (policy makers') studies have identified what has been considered as two pivotal areas of competition concern: (1) vertical and horizontal integration of online platforms and (2) vertical restrictions, referred to in the study as 'exclusive practices' or 'exclusionary practices'.

Studies[10] identified in the contributions to this survey considered that 'regulatory neutrality'[11] was a key concern for competition policy in the 'sharing economy'.

Some respondents, such as Switzerland,[12] considered that the consumers' behaviour and market features have drastically changed in the last decade, following the development of the 'digital market'. Among the advantages of e-commerce is the reduction of consumers' search cost, the convenience of being able more easily to compare products and prices offered by sellers and ease of access to consumer reviews. These advantages, coupled with an increased number of retailers, lead to stronger intra-brand and inter-brand competition.

On the other hand, among the advantages to distributors is the increase in geographical reach, lower distribution costs and the possibility of developing new business methods.

The countries participating in this comparative study do not have the same culture and legal system. On the contrary, the respondents have distinct history and social and economic characteristics.

Nevertheless, many competition issues are common across all or almost all the countries surveyed. Examples include accommodation booking services. However, the development level of each economy in terms of traditional markets may influence the rules relating to the new economy and more specifically to Internet platforms.

Many of the answers to the questions below about the information highway and high technology industries, as debates on them over the last 20 years show, depend on the definition—or perhaps the redefinition—of the objectives of antitrust law.[13]

---

[10] Deloitte Access Economics, *The sharing economy and the Competition and Consumer Act* (2015, ACCC), available at https://www.accc.gov.au/system/files/Sharing%20Economy%20-%20Deloitte%20Report%20-%202015.pdf ('Deloitte Study').

[11] *In particular, there is concern that, at present, sharing economy providers have fewer regulations applied or enforced* than *traditional businesses and this puts them at competitive disadvantage.* See Australia National Report, Section 1.

[12] Switzerland National Report, Section 1: [t]he use of the Internet as a decisive medium before making any purchase decision is increasing.

[13] For more information see the UNCTAD Intergovernmental Group of Experts on Competition Law and Policy, Fifteenth Session (2016), available at http://unctad.org/en/pages/MeetingDetails.aspx?meetingid=965. Accessed 11 January 2018.

## 1.2 Positive Law

### 1.2.1 The Relevant Competition Rules

#### 1.2.1.1 The Material Law

This international report includes the declarations of the following countries: Austria,[14] Australia,[15] Belgium,[16] Brazil,[17] France,[18] Germany,[19] Italy,[20] Hungary,[21]

---

[14] Austrian Cartel Act 2005 complements the Cartel Act and contains rules on the Federal Competition Authority; EU's Directive 2014/104 on antitrust damages actions; Austrian Unfair Competition Act; Austrian Price Indication Act.

[15] Competition and Consumer Act 2010; Australian Competition and Consumer Commission Misuse of market power guidelines; Australian Competition and Consumer Commission Authorization Guidelines; Australian Competition and Consumer Commission Merger Guidelines; Trade Practices Legislation Amendment Bill 1992, explanatory memorandum, paragraph 12, as cited in Merger.

[16] Guidelines on Vertical Restraints; Treaty on the Functioning of the European Union; Code of Economic Law (CEL); Article 1382 of the Belgian Civil Code.

[17] The Brazilian Antitrust System is structured by Federal Law No. 12,529 of 30 November 2011.

[18] Law of August 6, 2015 for growth, activity and equal economic opportunities (known as the Macron Law); Loi n° 2016-132, 7 October 2016 for a digital Republic; French Consumer Code; Commercial Code; French Code de procédure civile.

[19] Act against Restraints of Competition (GWB); Regulation 139/2004.

[20] Article 101 TFEU; Law 287/1990 on the interpretation of the Italian antitrust norms; Regulation 330/2010.

[21] The competition Act: Act LVII of 1996 on the Prohibition of Unfair Trading Practices and Unfair Competition regulates the entire scope of competition matters; Article 101 and 102 TFEU; Act CXL of 2004 on the General Rules of Administrative Procedures and Services; Act XLVII of 2008 on the Prohibition of Unfair Business-to-Consumer Commercial Practices; Directive 2005/29/EC of the European Parliament and council of 11 May 2005 concerning unfair business-to-consumer commercial practices in the internal market; Act V of 2013 on the Civil Code that contains the general rules for concluding contracts by electronic means; Act CVIII of 2001 on Electronic Commerce and on Information Society Services; Directive 2000/31/EC of the European Parliament and of the Council of 8 June 2000 on certain legal aspects of information society services, in particular electronic commerce, in the Internal Market; Act XXV of 2005 on the financial service contracts concluded as distance contracts. Directive 2002/65/EC of the European Parliament and of the Council of 23 September 2002 concerning the distance marketing of consumer financial services and amending Council Directive 90/619/EEC and Directives 97/7/EC and 98/27/EC; Government Regulation No 45/2014 on the detailed rules of contracts between businesses and consumers; Commission Notice Guidelines on the effect on trade concept contained in Articles 81 and 82 of the Treaty; Council Regulation 1/2003 of 16 December 2002 on the implementation of the rules on competition laid down in Articles 81 and 82 of the Treaty The relationship of EU and national merger control is separately regulated by way of the EU Merger Regulation [Council Regulation 139/2004 of 20 January 2004 on the control of concentrations between undertakings; National laws on B2C unfair commercial practices were fully harmonised by way of the Unfair Commercial Practices Directive; Government Regulation No 205/2011 (X. 7.) on the exemption of certain categories of vertical agreements from the prohibition of restriction of competition; Act XI of 1997 on the Protection of Trademarks and Geographical Indications.

Sweden,[22] Switzerland[23] and the United Kingdom.[24]

None of the respondents considered their jurisdictions to have specific provisions relating to online sales platforms and competition, although issues regarding e-commerce have drawn the attention of the relevant authorities. Rather, broadly drafted antitrust provisions have proved adaptable to the new situations created by the evolution of the market and to new distribution methods in all of the LIDC jurisdictions surveyed.

Countries like Australia and Brazil indicate that they do not have any specific legal antitrust provisions related to online platforms, an issue that is subject to the generic competition and consumer laws. Moreover, to some respondents, there are no different sets of rules for each specific market, neither do they indicate other institutions to enforce competition legal provisions[25] and the competition rules are to be applied to all sectors of the economy (for instance, this is the case in both Austria and Brazil).

All of the respondents stated that there have been no judicial decisions in which the courts have implied or recommended the modification of the existing competition legal provisions related to online platforms.

Some of the respondents have in their legislation a definition of digital platform outside the antitrust system. This is the case of the French legislation,[26] which defines an online platform as follows: *Any natural or legal entity is qualified as operator of on-line platform proposing, professionally, in a paid way or not, a service of communication to the on-line public basing on: 1 ° The classification or the referencing, by means of computing algorithms, of contents, of the goods or services proposed or put on-line by third parties; 2 ° Or the getting in touch of several parties with the aim of the sale of the good, the supply of a service or an exchange or a sharing of a contents, a good or a service.*

It is evident that antitrust goals are not exactly the same among different countries (Europeans and non-Europeans) and among European Union level and its respective state members. As an effort to address such issues, the European

[22] The Swedish Competition Act of 2008 (Konkurrensskadelagen); Swedish Competition Damage Act of 2016; The Act implements the EU Directive 2014/104 of the European Parliament and of the Council of 26 November 2014 on certain rules governing actions for damages under national law for infringements of the competition law provisions of the Member States and of the European Union; Commission Regulation 330/2010 of 20 April 2010 on the application of Article 101(3) of the Treaty on the Functioning of the European Union to categories of vertical agreements and concerted practices; Commission Notice on agreements of minor importance which do not appreciably restrict competition under Article 101(1) of the Treaty on the Functioning of the European Union.

[23] Cartel act on Cartels and Other Restraints of Competition (9RS 251.4) (1) Anticompetitive agreements (Article 5 CartA), (2) abuse of a dominant position (Article 7 CartA) as well as (3) merger control (Articles 9-10 CartA);

[24] Section 26(1) and (2) of the Enterprise and Regulatory Reform Act 2013, with effect from 1 April 2014. Guidelines on Vertical Restraints; Competition Act 1998; Health and Social Care Act 2012.

[25] See Brazilian National Report, Introduction and Section 1.

[26] Law of August 6, 2015 for growth, activity and equal economic opportunities (known as the Macron Law), then was modified in 2016, Loi n° 2016-132, 7 October 2016 for a digital Republic.

Commission has prioritised the matter of a digital single market.[27] Meanwhile, the aim of the Australian bill[28] is to provide what seems to be a political goal when it creates means to protect the PMEs against anticompetitive restrictions especially as it foresees the 'no adverse cost order' *for small business litigation in private cases and to assist with the process of a small business requesting a no adverse cost order.*

In addition to the EU effort, internally, the UK Competition and Markets Authority (CMA) has focused on 'developments in new emerging markets', which have been set as a focus for the CMA by the UK Government itself.[29] On the other hand, the codified law in Germany is in the process of being changed to include specific provisions applicable to two-sided markets in order to assess market power or the dominant position of an undertaking.[30]

Having said that, it is necessary to make some general observations before going deeper in this section.

To start with, because of the wide scope of the antitrust provisions, it is clear that the general provisions of competition law apply to online sales platforms, just as laws applied to commerce in general are applied to e-commerce. All respondents considered this proposition to be true, and it is clearly stated in many reports such as those of, *inter alia*, Austria, Australia, Brazil, France and Germany.

In some cases, consumer law is also applied in coordination with competition law,[31] as is the case in Australia and Hungary. In other countries, consumer welfare is valued and is even an antitrust goal, but its enforcement occurs outside the scope of the application of competition law.

In some countries, competition law is not limited to the prohibition of competition practices and goes further so as to prohibit unfair competition. In this sense, private rights may be considered alongside the market discipline,[32] i.e., the same authorities apply both rules (antitrust and unfair competition).

Nevertheless, in most of the countries surveyed, national competition law and provisions related to the prevention of unfair competition[33] are independent systems

---

[27] UK report, Sec. 2.2. *Vide* also the DSM being one of President Juncker's key objectives. https://ec.europa.eu/commission/publications/president-junckers-political-guidelines_en.

[28] The Australian report (Section 2.1.) states that *reflecting one of the issues discussed in the Harper Report, the Competition and Consumer Legislation Amendment (Small Business Access to Justice) Bill 2017, was introduced as a private members' bill on 16 February 2017 and proposes to address the issue connected with access to justice for small businesses. It recognises that small businesses do not possess the sufficient or significant financial resources necessary for litigating anticompetitive practices. This is particularly an issue for s 46 of the CCA ('misuse of market power') litigation where the accused party possesses significant market (and/or bargaining) power while a potential private plaintiff will in most cases be a much smaller entity.*

[29] Idem.

[30] German report, Section 2.1.2.

[31] This is the case of Australia and Switzerland. Brazil has also a relevant Consumers' Defence Code but not applied to the competition authorities, as it somehow used to happen in the prior competition law (1994).

[32] Austria and Hungary.

[33] In the sense of Paris Union Convention from 1883 (according to the art. 10 of CUP, it is more related to Intellectual Property).

with different laws, and both extend to the emerging business models of the new economy and especially to online platforms (e.g., Austria, Belgium, Brazil, France, Italy, Germany and the UK[34]). In this sense, unfair competition law works much more like some kind of tort or damage compensation provisions and not like justification, 'legal monopoly' or 'automatic exemption' of all kinds of anticompetitive restrictions.[35]

For sure, some points of interaction between both laws are possible in many other situations, e.g. a private action related to a loss raised when an antitrust infringement (which may create distortions in a relevant market structure, a barrier to entry or an exclusionary practice) leads to a free riding[36] or an illicit client deviation. In such case, it is possible to compensate the victim of the antitrust infringement through an unfair competition or a specific damage action[37] to be filed in the civil courts (see forward, Sect. 1.2.7). This is the case of most of the respondents in this survey.

This dichotomy (free competition and unfair competition) happens as in the same way as national jurisdictions of most of the Member States of the European Union where national competition laws are modelled on the EU legislation and apply in a complementary manner.[38]

Moreover, the European influence related to the double aspect (public and private interests) of the competition policy also happens to a degree in the case of Australia, Brazil and Switzerland, even though a certain degree of harmonisation does not mean that the EU law can be applied in these countries.

With some degree of reciprocal influence, national competition laws (especially in European countries) usually prohibit horizontal and vertical agreements and concerted practices as their object or effect is a restriction of competition, such as the classic cartels and exclusive dealings. The EU competition provisions influence the national provision of EU state members. This is the case of Austria, Belgium,

[34] The UK is not normally regarded as having a law of 'unfair competition' (although it does have consumer protection, trade-mark, passing-off laws).

[35] In Brazil, in the 1990s and 2000s, the policy maker used to consider the possession of IPR or related rights as evidence of regular rights use and not subject to the antitrust law. See the Anfape case.

[36] There is an example of an anti-trust infringement leading to free riding when a competitor uses exclusionary practices (like misuse of IPR) to deviate clients of an efficient competitor. They are widely regarded as anticompetitive even though do not involve cooperation between competitor. Probably this practice would be more common more common in concentrated markets, more likely in developing countries. In Brazil, the ShopTour case.

[37] Many systems of competition law provide for damages actions by victims (companies excluded from a market by an exclusionary abuse or customers charged higher prices because of as cartel). That is now true in all EU cases, as well as, eg, the US. In the UK, there is no compensation for 'unfair competition' because they do not have that as a concept.

[38] Is the point that the boundary between competition law and 'unfair competition' law is set in the same place for all EU countries, because in all them the scope of the competition rules is somewhat the same as the competition law and unfair competition are the two sides of the so-called competition policy.

France, Germany, Hungary, Italy and Sweden. For distinct reasons and at different degrees, this influence is also apparent in Brazil, in Switzerland and in the UK.

As well as competition rules relating to the control of commercial agreements, we also need to consider rules relating to unilateral conduct like abuse of dominant position or misuse of market power (e.g., exclusionary practices[39]) and anticompetitive mergers. This is the case in the 2011 Brazilian competition legislation: see Article 36 (I) (agreements and acts restricting competition) and Article 36 (IV) (abuse of dominant position).

Most of the countries surveyed (mainly in the EU) consider that certain types of restrictions in agreements and concerted practices are presumed to be anticompetitive 'by object' (i.e., broadly, *per se*) and are 'directly sanctioned by fines'.[40] For instance, in Austrian national legislation, such restrictions result in voidness. The same seems to happen in some non-European countries, like Australia, where *several forms of anticompetitive practices are expressly subject to* per se *prohibition, meaning that substantial lessening of competition does not have to be proved, but assumed* (in this case, cartels, primary boycotts, certain forms of exclusive dealing—third line forcing—and resale price maintenance). In Brazil, the control of horizontal dealings and concerted horizontal practices (Federal Law No. 12,529 of 30 November 2011, Article 36, paragraph 3, subsections I, II, IV and V) follow the same criterion in the sphere of administrative enforcement by the policy maker (CADE), except vertical agreements, which depend on an analysis of the effects.

As happens in other specific sectors, certain types of conduct that are particularly important to online sales platforms (and which are also common in the distribution sector), such as horizontal agreements, boycotts, passive sales, MFN clause or minimum resale price maintenance, are in some countries *per se* prohibitions.[41]

All the respondents in this survey considered distribution through online sales platform under general provisions of ordinary competition law relating to the control of vertical restraints.

Nevertheless, the importance of law relating to vertical restraints in this field does not mean that other aspects of the competition rules—such as rules on misuse of market power or abuse of dominant position and even prohibitions of hardcore cartels—are irrelevant to digital commerce or to the new business methods created to work through online platforms. Moreover, the application of merger control rules was raised in most of the national reports in this survey, although these are slightly less developed in relation to online sale platforms.

Most respondents indicate that restrictions that are considered not to be a hardcore agreement (such as some aspects of selective distribution systems) are

[39] Whereby a player with market power or dominant position eliminates competitors.

[40] Swiss national report, Section 1.

[41] In the Austrian report, Section 1.5.1.: '*Pioneer was fined in the amount of EUR 350,000 for violating Art 101 TFEU, namely agreeing in vertical price restrictions; Pioneer was also fined for hindering distributors from selling electronic products online. Without referring to a "restriction by object", the Cartel Court considered this concerted practice of being a – literally – "key infringement".*'

reviewable by the competition authorities by a rule of reason analysis or on a case-by-case basis (Italy, Sweden, UK).

In the EU, a block exemption covering vertical agreements grants a 'safe harbour' to recognised competition restrictions (subject to a threshold based on the parties' market share). Some Member States of the EU do not have specific national guidelines to vertical restraints, and the national courts, as in Belgium, apply directly EU rules such as Regulation 330/2010.

Outside the European Union, Australia and Switzerland adopt a similar approach, under which it may be possible to justify an anticompetitive restriction by reference to a public interest consideration. The text of the competition legislation in Brazil, for example, has clearly been inspired by Article 101 (1) and (3) of TFEU, but the policy maker made the administrative option on the rule of reason basis rather than the prohibition/exemptions system for restrictive agreements. The Australian report states that Australian competition law does not adopt a block or a threshold exemption.

The competition rules in general do not enumerate an exhaustive catalogue of prohibited restrictions. In some cases, the broad types of restrictions are set out in a headpiece, followed in the legislative text by an illustrative list of restrictions that may then be developed by administrative guidelines (Australia, Brazil and Switzerland).

In other cases, all that is provided in the legislative text is a general principle (without concepts and examples). But in general, in both cases, the rules are based on broad concepts that allow the policy maker to follow changes in the market and deal more promptly with the problems of online sales growth.

As is the case with all of the respondents, the Australian national report indicates that there is no specific provision relating to online sales platforms and competition, so that general competition law (and consumer law) applies to online sales platforms. That report explains that competition law is under the jurisdiction of the Competition and Consumer Act 2010 (the 'CCA').[42] In 2015, Australian competition law and policy were reviewed extensively by the 'Harper Review', with its final report[43] introducing relevant changes to the Australian competition law.[44] The recommendations of the Australian policy maker led to developments to the Australian system in the following years based on the specific goals of the Australian legislation. The changes introduced by that report are not restricted to competition law itself and carried over to the Competition and Consumer Legislation Amendment (Small Business Access to Justice) Bill 2017. That new bill recognises, for instance,

[42] The Act was previously named the *Trade Practices Act 1974* (Cth). The Australian Constitution, the *Commonwealth of Australia Constitution Act (1900)*, limits the extent to which the federal government can legislate. For that reason, states and territories enacted a 'schedule' version of the Part IV of the CCA, which contains core provisions on competition law. The CCA and the enacted schedule ensure a nationally consistent competition law.

[43] See the 'Harper Report' (2015).

[44] See the Competition and Consumer Amendment (Competition Policy Review) Bill 2017 ('Bill 2017') and the Competition and Consumer Amendment (Misuse of Market Power) Bill 2016 ('Bill 2016').

that small businesses do not possess sufficient or significant financial resources necessary for litigating anticompetitive practices.[45] In a way, this improvement of the Australian competition system recalls the targets of the WIPO (World Intellectual Property Organization) development agenda (which includes some concern related to innovation policies, level of employment, SME (small and medium-sized enterprises) protection against anticompetitive conducts, technology transfer, national authorities' training and promotion of improvements in competition law).

EU countries have their special features. This group of countries are subject to two competition laws applicable within their national jurisdiction. A typical example is the German national antitrust law, codified in the GWB (*Gesetz gegen Wettbewerbsbeschränkungen*), which, like all other Member States of the EU, has its roots in Article 101 ff TFEU and Regulation 139/2004. Both EU and national legal regimes are generally applicable in parallel. The two bodies of law both prohibit restrictions of competition in relation to their respective geographical range and applicable procedural rules. Where conduct qualifies, it can be exempted by an individual or group exemption. EU law provides for several block exemption regulations that apply to different groups of agreements (like technology transfer) or industrial sectors (like automobile distribution). Among them is the EU Commission's Regulation 330/2010.

These exemption regulations are also applicable in solely national cases brought before the national authorities of each state member (for instance, in Germany, according to § 2 (2) GWB; in Belgium; and in Hungary).

Both kinds of regimes (the national and the EU) also prohibit the *abuse of dominant* position (Article 102 TFEU). However, at the same time, all the EU Member States have a national provision equivalent to that EU prohibition (see, e.g., Austrian, Belgian, French, German, Hungarian, Italian and Swedish national reports).

These jurisdictions assess dominance and its abuse according to the TFEU guidance (Article 102), followed by the EU state members (the European Commission's Notice on Enforcement Priorities under Article 102).[46] In this sense, the German national law (§ 18 GWB) serves as guidance when determining whether an undertaking is dominant to that effect by providing rebuttable presumptions and enumerating factors that have to be taken into account when assessing the undertaking's position.

These aspects of the competition rules were developed for traditional economic sectors but also apply to the challenges of the new economy sector. However, other factors are even more relevant for the emerging business models of the new economy sector.

---

[45] Australian National Report, see Section 2.1. *'This is particularly an issue for s 46 of the CCA ("misuse of market power") litigation where the accused party possesses significant market (and/ or bargaining) power while a potential private plaintiff will in most cases be a much smaller entity.'*

[46] In the case of being a reference to the Article 102 case law of the European courts (which is binding, rather than 'guidance' within the EU).

One of the particular issues in the new economy sector is the definition of the relevant market. The respondents considered two or multi-sided markets to be features of online sale platforms. That is why the German legislator will introduce a new sub-paragraph (3a) to § 18 GWB, which will be applicable in particular to two-sided markets. It enumerates factors that are crucial for the examination of an undertaking's position in the new economy sector (e.g., network effects, access to relevant data).

EU competition law is enforced both by the European and by national administrations under the principle of decentralisation of EU competition policy. However, a conflict appears when the two competition systems produce distinct conclusions for the same situation. The European provision prevails if it is stricter. But if the national law is stricter, it prevails: see Article 3 of Regulation 1/2003.

Further, there is the possibility of private lawsuits against an undertaking's conduct that violates antitrust law. If a contractual provision is not in line with antitrust law, the defendant can use that as a defence against an allegation of breach of contract.

The EU legislation may spill over to non-member competition policy. The Swiss national report indicates that the competition framework in Switzerland is the Federal Law on Cartels and Other Restraints of Competition of 6 October 1995, lastly amended in 2014 (CartA or Cartel Act)[47] and the Notices of the Commission. Article 1 establishes the goals of the Swiss competition law to *prevent the harmful economic or social effects of cartels and other restraints of competition and, by doing so, to promote competition in the interests of a liberal market economy*. The content of the Swiss competition law extends to three main objects: (1) anticompetitive agreements (Article 5 CartA), (2) abuse of a dominant position (Article 7 CartA), as well as (3) merger control (Articles 9–10 CartA).

Generally speaking, the first approach of any competition law is related, in the first place, to horizontal agreements. In most of the countries, this is a central concern of competition policy and is occasionally treated as a structural phenomenon. In Brazil, for these reasons, these agreements and practices (cartels), which are object violations, may not be subject to a cease agreement or a consent decree (which assures a decision on the merits to the competition investigation about cartels) but may only be subject to the Brazilian leniency programme under certain circumstances. The horizontal agreements in the field of the online sales platform are unlikely to be out of the range of the policy maker and of competition law enforcement.

The non-EU jurisdictions tend to consider horizontal agreements as a hardcore competition violation and, in some cases, an object violation. For instance, the Swiss legislation establishes that *in horizontal relationships, agreements that aim at directly or indirectly fixing prices, limiting the quantities of goods or services to be produced, purchased or supplied or at allocating markets geographically are considered as hard-core restrictions to competition.*[48]

[47] RS 251.4, available on www.admin.ch.

[48] Swiss National Report, Sec 2. Article 5 para. 3 CartA.

As regards vertical restraints, there are also prohibitions or provisions related to such competition restriction, even though these rules generally consider the features of vertical agreements and the effects of the vertical conduct before declaring it as a violation or before providing an exemption (see, e.g., Australia, Brazil and the UK). As it happens to the franchise businesses, the restriction on intra-brand competition is justified by the increase of inter-brand competition, and these features of the vertical agreements are likely to spill over to the online sales platform. The respondents indicate the following conducts as a competition restriction that relates to *agreements, which set fixed or minimum resale prices as well and/or provide for absolute territorial protections are considered as hard-core restrictions to competition.*[49]

The respondents (Australia, Switzerland and Hungary) brought decisions showing that the so-called hardcore restrictions are considered illegal, regardless of the intensity or scope of the impact on competition.[50] Notwithstanding, the effects of the conduct or agreement must be considered for other restrictions in a case-by-case analysis by the competition authorities.

The control of vertical restraints is not so harmonised outside the EU. The respondents do not provide in their legislation an exhaustive catalogue or a fixed definition of the competition restrictions or dispositions related to the functioning of markets. The broad definition of illegal restraints enables the authorities to develop their competition policies. For this task, in the Swiss report, the main criterion is the intensity of its antitrust effects,[51] ruled by the Commission through guidelines (Notice on the Treatment).

There are situations in which some restrictive agreements are deemed not to be a violation in an anticompetitive perspective, and in this case, they should be exempted. If so, these restrictions are justified as positive effects on competition can outweigh the negative effects. All EU countries (including the UK) and Switzerland have a notification system for vertical agreements, and some of them are the result of custom rather than the legislation provision (Australia). In its former competition law (1994), Brazil used to have a broad notification obligation for all restrictions (agreements and acts), inspired by the EU model and a few times made prestigious by administrative authority. This notification system has been restricted to merger cases by the competition law of 2011,[52] improved from an *ex post* to an *ex ante* obligation.

At a European level, an explanatory statement drafted by the Commission *provided some useful insight on how selective distribution systems and restrictions to*

---

[49] Swiss National Report, Sec 2. Article 5 para. 4 CartA and Article 10 of the Notice on the Treatment of Vertical Restraints.

[50] Swiss Federal Case law 2C_180/2014 dated 28 June 2016, Gaba/WEKO. In this decision, the Federal Tribunal considered that the vertical agreements on territories are considered as hardcore cartels that presumably lead to the elimination of effective competition.

[51] M. Amstutz, B. Carron, M. Reinert, Commentaire Romand, droit de la concurrence, ad. Article 5 CartA para. 2.

[52] Law No. 12.529 of 30 November 2011.

*e-commerce and* the digital commerce might be controlled from an antitrust general perspective.

Under the same legal framework, Article 101 of TFEU (corresponds, e.g., to the Italian provision Article 2 of Law 287/1990 on antitrust and Article 1, paragraph 4, of Law 287/1990) imposes an interpretation of the Italian antitrust norms that conform to the principles of European antitrust and competition legislation. Therefore, the application of national law (like the Italian law in Article 2 of Law 287/1990) would rarely produce different conclusions or outcomes compared to the application of Article 101 TFEU.

Related to this, according to Article 4, let. b), of Regulation 330/2010, the restriction of 'passive sales' into an exclusive territory is considered a hardcore restriction and therefore is forbidden, while the restriction of territory regarding 'active sales' is allowed.

Note that the (1) definition of 'passive sale' is given by the guidelines, which is not entirely clear, and (2) because of the above, only a few cases involving 'passive sales' have been decided by European authorities and judges.

After all, competition law enforcement takes place through investigations grounded on suspicions of horizontal or vertical anticompetitive practices and agreements. In many countries, the competition authorities have not limited their efforts to certain restraint group or categories and have applied their enforcement powers against the restrictive competition practices. Some countries direct their efforts upon a certain category of conducts despite others, e.g. horizontal agreements.

It is difficult for all respondents to obtain data about the markets related to the new economy. A sector inquiry can be a relevant source of information. However, for many countries, like in the Austrian authority's view, *distributors might be hesitant in submitting claims to the respective competition authorities. Hence, in the FCA's view, it might be that competition restraints will not be disclosed in the course of sector inquiries, but only based on investigations, particularly dawn raids.*

### 1.2.1.2 Efficiency, Authorisation and Exemptions

#### General Aspects

All of the respondents considered the importance of 'efficiency' to antitrust enforcement. As happens in other sectors, many types of exemptions from competition law can be found in the new economy and more specifically in the area of online sales.

The European Union adopted through the TCE a competition system specifically created to enable the functioning of the common market (assuring the free movement of goods). The communitarian competition provisions are grounded on a prohibition/exemption system. As a decentralised analysis method, a shortcut has been created to reduce the volume of individual notifications: the block exemptions guidelines.

Some countries have not adopted the prohibition/exemption system, e.g. Brazilian competition law, despite the fact that the law is clearly inspired by Article 101 TFEU. Nevertheless, policy makers have adopted much of the so-called rule of reason as a direct influence of the United States competition policy and scholars' intellectual production (literature).

In these cases, the notion of efficiency is important in situations of authorisation or in cases where either public benefit outweighs any anticompetitive harm or the public benefit is such that the conduct (the restriction of competition) should be allowed. In the Australian system, for example, efficiency can play an important role when considering whether public benefit would prevail over the restriction of competition. The decision *Re Queensland Co-operative Milling Association*[53] states:

> ...[T]he widest possible conception of public benefit [is]... anything of value to the community generally, any contribution to the aims pursued by the society including as one of its principal elements (in the context of trade practices legislation) the achievement of the economic goals of *efficiency* and *progress*. If this conception is adopted, it is clear that it could be possible to argue in some cases that a benefit to the members or employees of the corporations involved served some acknowledged end of public policy even though no immediate or direct benefit to others was demonstrable.[54]

In addition:

> ...the assessment of efficiency and progress must be from the perspective of society as a whole: the best use of society's resources. We bear in mind that (in the language of economics today) efficiency is a concept that is usually taken to encompass "progress"; and that commonly efficiency is said to encompass allocative efficiency, production efficiency and dynamic efficiency.[55]

The Swiss national report informs us that the simple existence of an agreement carrying competition restrictions *is not always in itself unlawful*, so that the competition law *only considers agreements illegal if they eliminate effective competition or restrict competition without being justified on grounds of economic efficiency.* But to fulfil this condition and obtain an exemption, it is necessary to prove benefits such as reduction of production or distribution costs, improvement of products or production processes, dissemination of technical or professional know-how or research development, or a more rational exploitation of the resources, and these achievements will under no circumstances enable the parties involved to eliminate effective competition. The list of pure economic criteria is limited in the legislation,[56] and political and cultural matters might not be taken into account as an argument in rebuttal. The Swiss Competition Commission provided the grounds of economic efficiency in its Notice on the Treatment of Vertical Restraints. For example, the *Commission shall review the market shares: an agreement can be considered as justified on grounds of economic efficiency, if both the supplier's and the purchaser's market shares on the relevant markets are below a 30% threshold within the relevant market.*

---

[53] *Re Queensland Co–operative Milling Association Ltd., Defiance Holdings Ltd. (Proposed Mergers with Barnes Milling Ltd.),* (1976) ATPR ¶40–012.

[54] *Re Queensland Co–operative Milling Association Ltd., Defiance Holdings Ltd. (Proposed Mergers with Barnes Milling Ltd.),* (1976) ATPR ¶40–012, at 17,242 (emphasis added).

[55] *Re 7-Eleven* (1994), ATPR 41-357 at [42,777].

[56] Swiss Report. See Article 5 para. 2 CartA.

The justification of restrictive agreements must be analysed on a case-by-case method, following certain conditions as economic grounds of efficiency, listed as follows: *(1) the protection, for a limited period of time, of investments which aim to open up new products and/or geographical markets, (2) the necessity to insure the uniformity and quality of products (3) the protection of investments linked to a contractual relationship (the hold-up issue) and the (4) free-riding by third entities.*

The national competition authorities of the EU countries reflect the same core position from the European competition (e.g., Belgium, Sweden) about restrictive competition practices, mergers and private enforcement.

#### Efficiency as Justification to Exempt the Repression Against Unfair Competition or Free Rider Conduct

Some of the respondents analysed the question of preventing free riding as an economic and legal justification of a prohibition on online sales.

The issue arises in particular because brick-and-mortar businesses *have a physical presence, as a retail shop in a building, and offer face-to-face customer experiences*. The concern is that online businesses 'free ride' on the information provided by those physical shops, which offer a place to view and sample the product and to obtain detailed advice and information about it: if enough customers then go home (or use their smartphones) to order the products from online retailers that do not have to bear the cost of staff and premises borne by their brick-and-mortar competitors, then in the long run the brick-and–mortar businesses will cease to be viable.

Some respondents referred to decisions that have specifically analysed this hypothesis in relation to brick-and-mortar shops. In those cases, the free rider issue was not a decisive justification. There are some reasons for that conclusion, such as the fact that, in many cases, buyers are professionals and need no professional advice, so that there is no necessary justification for protecting retailers that give that advice. However, plainly some consumers are not professionals and may not have other access to information. In general, the buyer may have access to the stores or physical showroom of the supplier before making the purchase decision.

### 1.2.1.3 The Approach to the Online Sales Raised from Traditional Economy

All of the respondents in this comparative study consider online sales to be pro-competitive. The Internet increases transparency for the consumer and reduces research (or 'shoe leather' costs). At the end, it increases static competition in the sense of fostering price competition among competitors.

The Swiss Competition Commission views online sales as positive for competition as well. It first considers that it is a well-known fact that the Internet increases transparency for consumers. Moreover, the Swiss Commission considers that *online sales may have somewhat of a disciplinary effect on the prices set by brick and mortar shops and it therefore puts pressure on the manufacturer's margins and prices.*[57]

---

[57] DPC/RPW 2011/3 *Behinderung des Online-Handels*, para. 111.

According to the Italian report, 95% of Italians between the age of 25 and 44 use smartphones to surf online, and year by year the use of e-commerce has had a steady growth. However, the Italian report notes that online sales may have a potential negative impact, for example, on luxury brands, due to the fact that indiscriminate access to the sales network of virtual operators can disturb the orders and the traditional dynamics, with undue forms of unfair competition against the traditional physical distributors.

#### 1.2.1.4 The Major Decisions

The respondents indicate that there have been some antitrust cases related to online sales platforms, especially in connection with hotel and real estate sectors, and there is a growing trend of such cases. The respondents considered that the current legal framework (designed for more traditional industries) is sufficient to handle these new cases. In this sense, the respondents indicate that there are no cases in which the court has recognised the existence of a gap or suggested the modification of the existing competition law in the field of online sales platforms. Restrictions related to a total ban on online sales, e.g., have paradigmatic cases such as Amazon and eBay.

In some jurisdictions, like Brazil, there are more cases of mergers in the online sales sector than of infringements in that sector. That may be the reason why the national competition authorities are more likely to deal with market definition in that scenario (mergers) rather than undertake an analysis of individual infringements such as unilateral conduct consisting of exclusionary practices. For most of the respondents, some of the major decisions are related to the general competition issues in the field of vertical restrictions and abuse of dominant position.

Not all countries provide that all vertical restraints are subject to a rule of reason or effects analysis. Swiss case law treats certain categories of vertical restriction as *per se* prohibition, i.e., such hardcore restrictions are considered as illegal, regardless of the intensity or scope of the impact on competition. This is the Swiss Federal Case 2C_180/2014 dated 28 June 2016, *Gaba/Gebro*. In this decision, the Federal Tribunal considered that absolute territorial protection (i.e., prohibition on passive as well as active sales across territories) in vertical agreements is considered a hardcore restriction that is presumed to lead to the elimination of effective competition.

In Belgium, we highlight the *Immoweb* case[58] decided by the national competition authority in November 2016. This case involved the conduct of the leading real estate platform of the country and its potential abuse of dominant position. The authority did not impose any restriction since Immoweb[59] offered commitments and

[58] Belgian Competition Authority (BCA), Case MEDE-I/0-15/0002, Immoweb, 7 November 2016.

[59] According to the Belgian report, 'BCA, Case MEDE-I/0-15/0002, Immoweb, 7 November 2016, §13-14. In this decision, the BCA's Investigation and Prosecution Service stated that 'Most Favoured Customer clauses' inserted in the contracts between Immoweb and developers of software for real estate agencies could be at odds with the prohibition laid down in Article 101 and 102 TFEU and Articles IV.1 and IV.2 of the CEL. However, Immoweb offered commitments and therefore the BCA did not definitively rule on the question of whether the MFC clauses in the contracts between Immoweb and the developers of real estate software infringed Article 101 and 102 TFEU (and their Belgian equivalents, Articles IV.1 and IV.2 of the CEL).'

adjusted its commercial practice. A similar case was also handled in Germany involving Immowelt/Immonet.

The restrictions to competition by the real estate platform involved clauses in the agreements between the platform and developers of software for real estate agencies offering better financial conditions to Immoweb in comparison to its competitors. Due to the network effects related to such business (real estate platform), better prices as the result of reduced charges by software developers to estate agencies would increase the number of visitors (potential buyers or lessees) and attract more sellers or lessors, diminishing the relevance of other platforms.

On online sales antitrust cases, the Hungary report cited the case VJ/55/2013, in which the HCA found that the undertakings concerned restricted competition by creating and operating a rebate system to the detriment of the online retailers of CIBA contact lenses and care products. The HCA imposed a fine on Alcon Services AG Hungarian Branch (HUF 51,356,000–EUR 165,670) and Alcon Hungária Gyógyszerkereskedelmi Kft. (HUF 52,343,000–EUR 168,850).

In Sweden, three recent cases are worth mentioning: (1) Booking.com in 2015,[60] (2) Expedia in 2015[61] and (3) Onlinepizza in 2016.[62]

The cases involving Booking.com and Expedia are similar since both relate to online travel agencies that operate through their online platforms. Materially, their potentially anticompetitive practices concerned the restriction imposed on hotels not to offer lower prices on other platforms (including on hotels' own websites). In Sweden, the cases were resolved by the parties since they offered a set of voluntary commitments to mitigate the negative effects on competition.

The Onlinepizza case was initiated by the Swedish authority based on the potential market foreclosure caused by this platform against its competitor Pizzahero. However, the situation was clarified by Onlinepizza, which confirmed the absence of exclusivity clause in the agreements with restaurants.

Nevertheless, among the most relevant precedents related to abuse of dominant position (and related to market definition) in the new economy, the latest key issue is the Google case in the EU related to Google Shopping, issued on 17 June 2017 (see Sect. 1.2.5 below).

### 1.2.2 Market Definition

The relevant product market is defined by assessing the possibility of substitution between products or services provided to consumers and by actual or potential suppliers. Respondents to the survey confirmed that this approach to market definition in the traditional competition law framework is also applicable to online sales platforms. This is a fundamental criterion for the competition analysis related to

[60] Decision of the Swedish Competition Authority of 15 April 2015, file ref. 596/2013.

[61] Decision of the Swedish Competition Authority of 5 October 2015, file ref. 595/2013.

[62] Decision of the Swedish Competition Authority of 4 April 2016, file ref. 658/2015.

identifying anticompetitive agreements, abuse of dominant position or misuse of market power and to mergers.

In this sense, the general provisions about market structures are central to this issue, mainly in cases that have been prohibited based on a substantial lessening or reduction in competition, and this is 'assessed looking at both market structure and the strategic behaviour of market participants'.[63]

To all of the respondents, market definition remains essential to an assessment. The notion of the relevant market is defined separately in relation to mergers as a market for goods or services (product), which is geographically limited. For all of the respondents, temporal factors and the price relevant markets can both be taken into account in the product market definition analysis on the basis of the substitution possibilities from the consumer's point of view.

The antitrust analysis requires the concept of relevant market in both categories of conduct, i.e., restrictive agreements and abuse of dominant position. The determination of relevant geographic and product markets is a condition (necessary precondition[64]) not only for merger control analysis but also for an analysis of restrictive agreements, exclusionary practices and abuse of dominant position. The respondents recognise the relevant market as a condition for the antitrust analysis.

In the Swiss jurisdiction and the EU Member States, the authorities take into account market shares to determine the impact of a specific agreement in which there are restrictions. In line with the thresholds established by the European block exemption system, such agreements or contracts are not considered to have the effect of appreciably restricting competition, as long as the market share of the parties does not exceed 10%. In the case of vertical agreements, the threshold is 15%. If there is a network of agreements that have a cumulative effect in the market, the relevant threshold falls to 5%. These *de minimis* provisions do not apply where the agreement has the object of restricting competition (as opposed to the effect of restricting competition). Finally, in some countries, the cartel is not *per se illegal* if undertaken by an SME (see Australia).

### 1.2.3 Criterion for Market Power or Dominant Position

Alongside (vertical and horizontal) agreements that restrict free competition, a specific group of unilateral conduct features in various competition laws, namely abuse of a dominant position. A dominant position is inferred on a case-by-case analysis based not only on market structure (market share) but also on other meaningful determinants like barriers to entry, the market share of the competitors and evolution of the structure concentration in the relevant market.

[63] *MMP Framework*, para 4.4.

[64] SHWARTZ, FLYNN and FIRST, Free Enterprise and Economic Organization: Antitrust, Foundation Press, New York, 1983, page 284.

A dominant position is a 'de facto' situation in which its holder can take decisions (about price and commercial conditions) independently of the market. This category of restrictions on free competition relates to the concept of market power.

Legislation in some countries indicates a presumption of market share of 20% (twenty per cent) for the characterisation of a dominant position, as occurs in the case of Brazilian competition law. Notwithstanding, this presumption may be displaced on the ground of efficiency justification. This option coincides to some extent with the 2000 points of the Herfindahl Hirschman Index—HHI criterion (which may be found, e.g., in a relevant market with five competitors with 20% quotas each). But this is a relative presumption (*juris tantum*), and in this sense the Brazilian authority may consider the existence of dominant positions in a case in which the investigated undertaking may possess a share below this level or instead not be held to enjoy a dominant position even above this presumed limit.

Based on the literature, some other systems consider that a share of over 50% can be used as an indication of existence of a dominant position (see the Swiss national report, Sect. 1.4.1). However, some jurisdictions (like Australia and Switzerland) adopt different criteria to delimit the market for the merger cases and abuse of dominant position or misuse of market power.

Most of the national competition legislation does not prohibit a dominant position or the existence of market power but rather prohibits its abuse or misuse. On the other hand, a dominant position acquired by efficiency may not be considered anticompetitive. For instance, the Australian policy maker adopts the notion of misuse of market power. This situation occurs when an enterprise with 'substantial market power' *takes advantage of that power for a prohibited anti-competitive purpose.*

According to most of the policy makers in this survey, there are categories of conducts that may be considered unlawful restrictions of competition. These categories include some classical restrictions like refusal to deal, price and trade conditions fixing, production limitations and imposition of restrictions on contractual conditions that are unacceptable in most circumstances.

According to the Australian report, the misuse of market power may not be further authorised on the ground of public benefits.

Some systems may consider that a market player holding a dominant position or market power may justify restrictive conducts on legitimate business grounds. See, e.g., the Swiss national report (Sect. 1.4.1). Meanwhile, other respondents (see Australian report, Sect. 1.4) consider that competition law should have an economy-wide application and not be driven to any specific sector, and according to this approach there is no possibility of exemption of presumption of legality (safe harbour) to such unilateral conducts (misuse of market power).

### 1.2.4 Types of Infringement

#### 1.2.4.1 General Approach of the Competition Law

According to the results of this survey, there are three main types of infringement in this area: (1) vertical restraints, (2) protection (or overprotection) of IP rights in connection with competition law, (3) a wide range of potentially anticompetitive behaviour involving online sales platforms.

For instance, Australian competition law *prohibits* through a general provision *mergers or acquisitions which have the effect or likely effect of substantially lessening competition and certain other conduct, including exclusive dealing (s 47) and horizontal agreements (s 45),*[65] *where it has the purpose, effect, or likely effect of substantially lessen competition.* The types are cartels,[66] primary boycotts,[67] third line forcing (form of exclusive dealing)[68] and minimum resale price maintenance (including vertical price fixing). All forms of prohibited anticompetitive conduct, with the exception of misuse of market power (section 46), may be authorised in advance[69] on public benefit grounds, rather than a direct assessment of whether the conduct will substantially lessen competition.

In many countries influenced more directly by common law, vertical restrictions are to be considered pro-competitive at first as a result of scale benefits. Nevertheless, in EU Member States, it is possible to consider some restrictions in vertical agreements as hardcore restrictions and, for this reason, unlawful prohibitions.

#### 1.2.4.2 Retail Price Maintenance (RPM) and Refusal to Deal or Supply

An important aspect of the application of competition rules to online platforms is resale price maintenance, which is a prohibited conduct (per se illegal) in most of the countries surveyed and considered as a hardcore competition restriction or violation in some countries. Nevertheless, in the Brazilian competition system (perhaps influenced by the US), the policy makers are not persuaded by the conception in which RPM should be one of the major competition law violations. Most other jurisdictions would consider RPM a significant restriction.

The Australian report brings a concept from the economic studies about online platforms, in which it is recognised that *there are incentives for vertical restraints to be applied in connection with online platforms and the sharing economy.*[70] This

[65] According to the Australian Report: *In theory, s 45 also covers vertical agreements which do not contravene s 47 ('exclusive dealing') and/or s 48 ('resale price maintenance').*

[66] Part IV, Division 1 of the *Competition and Consumer Act 2010* (Cth). This incorporates price-fixing, output restrictions, allocation of customers, suppliers or territories and bid rigging. This conduct is both a criminal offence and subject to civil penalties. Certain joint venture activity is excluded from the scope of the *per se* prohibition, but remains subject to the general prohibition against anticompetitive agreements in s 45.

[67] Section 2.2. of the Australian National Report indicates that [I]f Bill 2017 is passed, third line forcing and primary boycotts will no longer be per se prohibited but will be evaluated under the substantial lessening of competition requirement.

[68] Unlike other forms of exclusive dealing, it is *per se* prohibited, but it is possible for the conduct to be 'notified' and receive immunity on public benefit grounds. This occurs when supply is made on the condition that goods or services are purchased from an unrelated third party (or there is a refusal to supply because of failure to agree to such a condition).

[69] It is not possible for conduct to be retrospectively authorised; approval must be provided in advance of the conduct occurring or it will contravene the Act notwithstanding any demonstrated public benefits.

[70] Australian report, Section 7.

situation includes a hypothesis in which a particular online platform does not have significant market power.

For instance, in the Safeway case, involving the largest supermarket chain and the largest bread retailer in Victoria (Australia's 2nd most populous state), Safeway ceased purchasing bread from producers whose bread was available locally at a discounted price. This refusal to deal was held to constitute a misuse of market power (in this case, also related to RPM and the MFN clauses).

#### 1.2.4.3 IPR Restrictions

The use of intellectual property is one of the main grounds of the business methods created upon a software-based online platform. The net externality effect is an important asset to online platforms, and intellectual property is the centre of these business models, so that the interface between intellectual property rights and competition law is also relevant to online sales platforms. Among these rights are not only copyright but also patents and trademarks and all kinds of protection of IP addressed to innovative goods and services enable to be commercialised through online platforms.

The exhaustion of IPR (and parallel imports) is important to the analysis of conduct as international price discrimination (so-called geo-blocking). Respondents (like Australia) point out that international price discrimination can also be facilitated by restricting parallel imports, which can negatively impact, for instance, online sales platforms such as Amazon and local online retailers.

To some respondents (see Australia[71]), the use of intellectual property prevents the characterisation of the platform as a 'service' and for this reason affects some antitrust criteria created originally for traditional markets, mainly that related to the 'essential facilities'[72] doctrine. This aspect may create difficulties to authorities related to the antitrust control of the 'bottlenecks' (an issue more related to market structures). Some national legislation restricts somehow parallel imports, e.g. the Australian Trade Marks Act (1995) and the Copyright Act (1968).

---

[71] See Australia report, Section 5.4. 'Australia does not apply the essential facility doctrine in the same way as, for instance, the United States of America. In general, s 46 (misuse of market power) deals with situations where a natural monopolist and/or an owner of a bottleneck in a bottleneck industry misuses its market power; for example, in the form of a refusal to supply or provide access. This section has been used successfully in such situations in the past.'

[72] Ibidem; 'the Australian specific law dealing with essential facilities, the national access regime law, will not apply to this example for a number of reasons, including the fact that duplication of an online platform is both possible and not "uneconomical"'. And, in this sense, the report states the following consideration '[I]n the context of online sales platforms, it will be difficult to obtain access via this regime. The primary mechanism for obtaining such access is to have a service "declared", after which negotiation for access can take place. The first hurdle is to establish that there is a service. Although the definition of service in s 44B includes "a communications service or similar service", which could capture online sales platforms, the "supply of goods", "the use of intellectual property" and "the use of a production process" are expressly excluded from the definition of "service" for the purposes of the access regime. As online sales platforms frequently involve the supply of goods, and this is excluded from the scope of the access regime, the circumstances in which the regime will apply are quite limited.'

Generally speaking, there are no static exemptions to the appropriation of IPR itself capable to confer an absolute antitrust immunity as it is a 'patrimonial' asset like any other. On another hand, there are jurisdictions where the local legislation exempts intellectual property rights (IPR), including copyrights, trademarks and licensing from certain provisions of the competition law, other than hardcore restrictions like misuse of market power or abuse of dominant position and resale price maintenance (RPM).[73] Policymakers widely criticise such kind of legal exemption and many have proposed its repeal[74] because it may seriously restrict competition mainly in a field in which there are multiple and competing IPRs. Likely, for this reason, the Australian report says that its legislation leads to IPR overprotection.

#### 1.2.4.4 Other Restraints

The emerging markets generated from the features of the new economy (because of the multi-sided market possibilities) are subject to new restrictions related to the market power of some sales platforms. Even though some of these restrictions come from traditional markets, other vertical restraints like exclusive dealing (non-price vertical restraints), bargaining power (monopsony power[75]) or abuse of buying power may be relevant.

In many countries, such conducts or practices are likely to be prohibited under certain circumstances, like the anticompetitive effect (Brazil) or the effect of 'substantially lessening competition' (Australia). In this sense, some competition laws also consider situations including third-party participation, e.g. the prohibition on 'third line forcing', in which a supplier imposes the acquisition of another good or services from a third party to a purchaser. This practice may have relevance to the online sales markets.

### 1.2.5 Precedents Regarding Abuse of Dominant Position in the Area of Online Sales Platforms

The major cases were referenced in Sect. 1.2.1.4 above, and some relevant aspects will be addressed in this section. There is usually no specific guideline for misuse of market power, but it is widely recognised by the respondents that the meaningful growth of the online platforms may give rise to structural concentration, i.e. players

[73] See Australian National Report, Section 9.

[74] See the Australian National Report, Section 9.

[75] Australia report, sec. 6.1. 'A corporation with significant bargaining power can contravene s 46 by demanding a most favoured nation clause from suppliers. This was demonstrated in the case of *Safeway*. Safeway was the largest supermarket chain and the largest bread retailer in Victoria (the second most populous state in Australia). The relevant market was the market 'for the sale and acquisition of bread by wholesale in Victoria'. Safeway's conduct, which involved refusing to acquire bread from a supplier if the supplier sold bread for less to another buyer, was held to constitute a misuse of market power. In order to find a contravention, the court was required to find that Safeway held substantial market power and that it had taken advantage of that power for an anti-competitive purpose.'

holding substantial market power or dominant position. Considering this hypothesis, there is a list of general principles that can be derived from other cases in order to envisage how competition law might be applied to online platforms.

In Australia, the first task of authorities carrying out an antitrust investigation is to verify if the investigated firm holds 'substantial market power' and after that to demonstrate the connection between the conduct and that extraordinary power (take advantage element). In addition, it is necessary to identify the purpose of restricting the competition.

In Belgium, the *Immoweb* case[76] offers some insight into the competition authority's approach even though the investigation was concluded after the authority accepted commitments offered by the company. As for relevant market definition for online platforms, the authority decided that (1) the relevant product market was online real estate platforms, not competing with websites of real estate agencies, newspapers or street boards, and (2) the relevant geographic market was national. Immoweb had a dominant position (leader player) and applied clauses in the agreements between the platform and developers of software for real estate agencies offering better financial conditions to Immoweb in comparison to its competitors. Such clause—called as most favoured customer—MFC (to be addressed in the following section)—was questioned by the national competition authority and later modified by the platform.

In Sweden, the Booking.com[77] and Expedia[78] cases were related to the MFC issue as well. The type of price parity adopted by both players was similar and was considered as a potential barrier to the entry of new and small platforms that would not have the economic strength to compete with low commission fees (level artificially created due to this practice). It is important to highlight that both companies offered voluntary commitments to change the price parity, and the Swedish authority concluded therefore that there was no threat to competition.

It is possible to identify a trend related to online platforms and competition in Europe, which can be illustrated by the recent Amazon case[79] (European Commission). This goal—fighting against abuse of dominant position by Internet-based companies—was identified in the national cases of Belgium and Sweden, for example.

Among the most relevant precedents related to abuse of dominant position in the new economy, the latest issue is the Google case in the EU. Although this is not a case of online sales itself, this case may establish parameters for the antitrust analysis related to abuse of dominance in an online sales environment.

The recent decision from the European Commission was addressed to Google Inc. and Alphabet Inc., Google's parent company. On 27 June 2017,[80] the European

[76] Belgian Competition Authority (BCA), Case MEDE-I/0-15/0002, Immoweb, 7 November 2016.

[77] Decision of the Swedish Competition Authority of 15 April 2015, file ref. 596/2013.

[78] Decision of the Swedish Competition Authority of 5 October 2015, file ref. 595/2013.

[79] Decision of the European Commission of 4 May 2017. Case No. 40153 (E-book MFNs and related matters – Amazon).

[80] See the release of the EU Commission in http://europa.eu/rapid/press-release_IP-17-1784_en.htm.

Commission announced that it had fined Google €2.42 billion *for abusing dominance as search engine by giving illegal advantage to own comparison shopping service.*[81]

The EU decision follows two prior Statements of Objections sent to Google in April 2015 and July 2016.

The EU authorities are investigating certain of Google's other practices relating to abuse of dominant position in two more cases. One of these cases relates to the Android operating system, in which Google allegedly *stifled choice and innovation in a range of mobile apps and services by pursuing an overall strategy on mobile devices to protect and expand its dominant position in general internet search.* The other case relates to AdSense, in which Google allegedly reduced user's choice by *preventing third-party websites from sourcing search ads from Google's competitors.*[82] The investigation of these two cases is still ongoing.

In the Google case related to the search engine, the European Commission indicated its criteria related to the abuse of dominant position in a multi-sided market. More specifically, it is an antitrust solution to the misuse of market power raised from the network externality effect. At the same time, there are parameters to so-called dynamic competition (which is pending in most of the jurisdictions).

In this case, the network externality effect[83] generated market power. As the EU decision states, *given Google's dominance in general internet search, its search engine is an important source of traffic for comparison shopping services.*

The European Commission found that Google had strategically used its dominance (in general Internet search) to promote its search engine, instead of competing on the merits. This strategy adopted by Google in 2008 for Europe was constructed upon two pillars: (1) the prominent placing by Google of its own comparison shopping service and (2) the demoting of rival comparison shopping services in its search result. The visibility[84] of Google's own comparison shopping

---

[81] In the EU Commission release is possible to access the following Commissioner declaration. *'Commissioner Margrethe Vestager, in charge of competition policy, said: 'Google has come up with many innovative products and services that have made a difference to our lives. That's a good thing. But Google's strategy for its comparison shopping service wasn't just about attracting customers by making its product better than those of its rivals. Instead, Google abused its market dominance as a search engine by promoting its own comparison shopping service in its search results, and demoting those of competitors.*

*What Google has done is illegal under EU antitrust rules. It denied other companies the chance to compete on the merits and to innovate. And most importantly, it denied European consumers a genuine choice of services and the full benefits of innovation.*'

[82] Available at http://europa.eu/rapid/press-release_IP-17-1784_en.htm. Accessed 12 January 2018.

[83] To the Commission, '*[C]omparison shopping services rely to a large extent on traffic to be competitive. More traffic leads to more clicks and generates revenue. Furthermore, more traffic also attracts more retailers that want to list their products with a comparison shopping service.*'

[84] *The evidence shows that consumers click far more often on results that are more visible, i.e. the results appearing higher up in Google's search results. Even on a desktop, the ten highest-ranking generic search results on page 1 together generally receive approximately 95% of all clicks on generic search results (with the top result receiving about 35% of all the clicks). The first result on*

service has grown as a direct result of such strategy in contrast with less visibility of rival comparison shopping services.

The European Commission found that Google is dominant in general Internet search markets in all EEA countries. It found that Google engine search has a dominant position in the 13 countries of the European Economic Area (EEA). The very high market share exceeds 90% in most of the affected national markets. This network effect[85] creates barriers to entry.

Google's market power allowed it to misuse its position in the general market of search engine platforms, i.e. it has abused this market dominance by giving its own service (Google search engine) an anticompetitive advantage.

This platform introduced such practice in all of the 13 EEA countries where Google has launched its service, beginning in January 2008 in Germany and the United Kingdom. After that, it expanded the conduct to *France in October 2010, Italy, the Netherlands, and Spain in May 2011, the Czech Republic in February 2013 and Austria, Belgium, Denmark, Norway, Poland and Sweden in November 2013*. It reached seven countries of this survey.

Moreover, the abuse of dominant position deprived European consumers of genuine choice and innovation. The EU press release indicates that Google is also liable to face civil actions for damages before the courts of the EU Member States instituted by any person or business affected by its anticompetitive conduct. In this sense, the EU Antitrust Damages Directive may facilitate damage actions for the victims of anticompetitive practices to obtain a tort or damage decision.

This decision is a binding precedent (at least as regards antitrust liability) for the national authorities of other EU Member States. The question now is if this approach and criteria may or may not spill over to other jurisdictions around the world.

### 1.2.6 Most Favoured Nation (MFN) Conditions in the Context of Online Sales Platforms

The following investigations raising the issue of the most-favoured-nation clause in France, Italy and Sweden have influenced the revision of this clause in European Union countries and non-European Union countries, e.g. Switzerland. In general, the approach has been based on a finding that this clause interferes directly in the distributor's price formation process.

---

*page 2 of Google's generic search results receives only about 1% of all clicks. This cannot just be explained by the fact that the first result is more relevant, because evidence also shows that moving the first result to the third rank leads to a reduction in the number of clicks by about 50%. The effects on mobile devices are even more pronounced given the much smaller screen size.*

[85] According to de Swiss report: 'This effect occurs when the use of the platform of one group of users depends directly on the participation of the second group of users. For instance, for hotel online booking platforms, the more hotels and end-consumers use the platform, the more said platform becomes attractive for both group of users. This indirect network effect may create a high market concentration with only a few dominant undertakings sharing the market.'

In Switzerland, Sweden and Italy (among other jurisdictions), the competition authorities reviewed the clause applied by online travel booking services, namely the Booking.com, Expedia and HRS platforms.

Nevertheless, the platforms kept their 'narrow MFN'[86] clauses prohibiting hotels from offering lower prices through online services in their own websites. This new narrow MFN clause seems to be less restrictive according to many of the respondents, even though its effect on the market must be reviewed by the policy makers as soon as meaningful empirical data are available. It is interesting to note that the Swiss competition authority refused to settle amicably (avoid a consent decree) on the issue of narrow MFN clauses and is currently monitoring the market, competition law and political developments in Switzerland and abroad.[87]

The first group of Europeans countries (France, Italy and Sweden) through the results of their competition investigations regulated these practices by ordering the removal of the wide MFN or price parity clauses. In such cases, even though the platforms keep the private prohibition barring hotels from announcing rooms with lower prices on their own websites, they may not prevent hotels from offering lower prices in the ordinary channels like travel agencies if these commercial conditions are undisclosed.

As addressed in the precedents related to hotel and real estate industries, this MFN clause can be also called most favoured customer—MFC. It tends to restrict the ability of other platforms to compete by offering better deals to the consumer than the dominant platform. Since the other side of the network (e.g., hotels, landowners) must offer at least as good prices to the dominant platform (according to the MFC clause in their agreements), the other competing platforms cannot compete on price and are hindered from increasing their market share.

In this regard according to the Italian report, in 2014 the Italian Competition Authority took action against the online travel agencies Booking and Expedia in order to examine whether the 'Most Favoured Nation' (MFN) clauses of the contracts concluded by the two online travel agencies (OTA) and their hotel partners in Italy may integrate a vertical restriction in violation of Article 101 TFEU.

[86] 'The online platforms however kept their "narrow MFN clauses" barring hotels from offering lower prices on their own website. With the new narrow MFN clauses, the hotels are however entitled to offer lower prices on their direct distribution channels if those prices are not public and to determine freely their prices, room capacities and other better conditions on competing online platforms. The Swiss Competition Commission mentioned that those new narrow MFN clauses appeared to be less restrictive but considered that their effect on the market still had to be reviewed in the future.' Swiss report, Section 3.2.2.

[87] DPC/RPW 2017/1 Annual Report 2016 of the Competition Commission, p. 62.

### 1.2.7 Compensatory Damages or Unfair Competition Damages in Cases of Antitrust Violations and of Non-compliance with a Consent Decree or Cease-and-Desist Agreement

The respondents confirmed that private enforcement is possible in their jurisdictions, although practical problems still exist in order to make such claims popular.

The EU Damages Directive (Directive 2014/104) has clearly addressed the possibility of damage actions, whether individual or collective, to be proposed in the Member States. The goal of the referred directive was to remove practical obstacles to compensation for all victims of infringements of EU competition law.

An economic agent that intentionally or negligently causes damage by infringing Article 101 or Article 102 TFEU is liable for damages that arise from such conduct. The person harmed by the conduct has the right to full compensation for actual loss and for loss of profit, as well as the payment of interest. Companies taking part in an infringement are jointly and severally liable for the damages, and damages in cartel cases are presumed.

Considering that deadline for transposing the directive into Member States' legal systems expired on 27 December 2016, several respondents are aligned with the European policy for such matter.

Not only the European countries but also other countries (including Brazil, for example) have been influenced by the directive and are discussing how to facilitate private enforcement of competition law and to force companies to compensate for the harm caused due to antitrust violations.

## 1.3 Common Market, Custom Union and Free Trade Market

The main political and economic integration blocks are the European Union (EU), North America Free Trade Area (NAFTA), South Common Market (Mercosur), Andean Pact and Pacific Alliance.

The treaties, which gave rise to these political and economic integrations, have provisions relating to intellectual property rights and free competition, but none of them provides specific provisions or supply general principles about the commerce through online platform. In this survey, the respondents are members of the EU (most of them) and of Mercosur (only one of them).

The respondents indicate that the European Commission attaches great value to the Internet as a sales channel for reaching a wide variety of customers in different countries. The policy maker in the EU recognises that online platforms play a key role in innovation and growth of the digital single market. Through the Commission's communication from 25 May 2016, it stated: *they have revolutionized access to information and have made many markets more efficient by better connecting buyers and sellers of services and goods*. The document was written as a staff working paper accompanying the communication that recognised the benefits of online platforms for consumers, businesses and their general economic and social benefits.

This approach has been confirmed by the Final Report on the E-Commerce Sector Inquiry and its Staff Working Document from 10 May 2017.

The analysis of competition matters in the field of online sales platforms at an EU level is relevant for the national competition authorities of the EU Member States as it expected that the respective policy makers and courts *will follow the guidance offered at the EU level dealing with future cases.*[88]

The discipline of online sales platforms is important to all integrated markets (and to agreements between supranational markets, e.g. European Union–Mercosur Framework Cooperation Agreement[89]) as it influences trade at a supranational level and can prejudice the targets of the related integration treaties and the international trade as a whole. This issue should be the object of further studies.

## 1.4 The Competition Law in the Context of the New Economy

### 1.4.1 Application of General or Specific Criteria to the New Economy

As indicated in the section about substantive law (Sect. 1.2), the respondents of this survey state that their national law does not have specific rules on online sales or related to Internet platforms, which are subject to the general provisions of the competition law. Outside the European Union, this is also the case for Brazil and Switzerland.

### 1.4.2 Applicable Rules and Criteria to Restriction of Online Sales

In some jurisdictions, competition policy adopts a binary test. For example, the Swiss authorities (the Competition Commission), despite the general prohibition related to unlawful restraints on competition on both vertical and horizontal restraints on the relevant market of the statutory Swiss competition law, distinguish two situations: (1) the restriction of passive sales and (2) the general restriction of online sales.

Generally speaking, most of the competition policies of the EU countries consider sales through online platforms to be a sort of passive sale (unless the seller or

[88] Belgian National Report, Section 2.

[89] See the Interregional Framework Cooperation Agreement between the European Community and its Member States, of the one part, and the Southern Common Market and its Party States, of the other part – Joint Declaration on political dialogue between the European Union and Mercosur. According to the UE, the sectors of cooperation include: *trade, standards, customs, statistics and intellectual property; economic cooperation, with the emphasis on industrial, energy, scientific and technological cooperation, telecommunications, the environment and investment promotion.* See the link address http://ec.europa.eu/world/agreements/prepareCreateTreatiesWorkspace/treatiesGeneralData.do?step=0&redirect=true&treatyId=405. Accessed 12 January 2018.

distributor makes serious efforts to reach clients outside the authorised territory or geographical attribution of the distribution contract). In those cases, since restriction of passive sales is generally considered to be an unlawful hardcore restriction subject to penalties, the same treatment is applied to restriction of sales on online sales platforms (Switzerland).

Nevertheless, in some of the countries surveyed, a general ban on online sales is not a hardcore restriction under their competition policy, as long as it is not a tool to attain such objects as price control or a grant of absolute territorial protection (market sharing). In these competition systems, a restriction on online sales does not benefit from an automatic exemption but is a situation subject to a rule of reason so that the authority can, however, still consider it to be unlawful after carrying out an effects analysis. This is the case for Switzerland.[90]

In this case, the policy maker may issue guidance as to its antitrust analysis on a case-by-case basis indicating certain circumstances or features that are likely to amount to serious restrictions of competition. In the Swiss jurisdiction, the authorities have issued new guidance stating that a general ban of online sales can exceptionally be a hardcore restriction when there are 'qualified circumstances', i.e., resale price maintenance.

Most of the respondents consider so-called geo-blocking practices as a competition restriction. These practices prevent the national consumer from accessing websites outside the national territory and employ logic devices processing personal data: these devices prevent the consumer from accessing a page outside of the attributed territory and re-route the consumer to the supplier or a distributor located in his territory. Another similar case is where the distributor is obliged to interrupt the purchase order if it identifies that the consumer is located outside the attributed territory.

#### 1.4.2.1 Bans on Sales Through Third-Party Internet Platforms in Selective Distribution Systems

##### General Aspects of Selective Distribution

Selective distribution agreements are a business method in which the supplier controls distribution by restricting the type of distributor that can be supplied. This system is used in a wide range of markets, e.g., automobiles, luxury, cosmetics, technology and premium brands. In these agreements, the *supplier undertakes to sell its products only to authorised dealers on specific qualitative and quantitative criteria and in which those dealers undertake not to sell the products to unauthorised distributers.*[91]

Exemptions for this type of restriction are usually confined to cases where the nature of the product sold justifies the use of a selective distribution system. Ordinary

[90] See the Swiss guidelines, DPC/PRW2011/3 Behinderung des Online-Handels, para 76 ff.

[91] See Swiss national report Section 3.2.3.1. and Article 4 of the Notice on Treatment of Vertical Restraints.

products (not a luxury or not a technical product) are not entitled to use this kind of distribution method. In this sense, high quality, technology or luxury products may justify the selective distribution system when the intrinsic characteristics of it and the modalities set by the manufacturer demand some kind of limitation of the distribution channels, e.g., obligation to have qualified staff, to respect the trademark identity and to offer after-sales services.

### Anticompetitive Restrictions Related to Online Sales in Selective Distribution Systems

As is the case with the market for traditional newspapers (sale of newspapers/advertising in newspapers), online sales platforms can be characterised as two-sided markets. So an important feature of policy analysis is the existence of network externalities or the 'indirect network effect', as it is termed in the national reports. These indirect externalities arise because software is not priced at marginal cost, and technological evolution of the new economy (including equipment and telecommunications services) creates new standards for consumption. In many cases, it is common to infer these effects spilling over to markets downstream and upstream. As a result, this indirect network effect may under certain circumstances create market power or a dominant position.

In the specific case of the online platforms, this indirect externality effect occurs because one group of users depends directly on a second one.[92] In the same way that a newspaper becomes attractive to advertisers because of its readership, the online platforms also become more attractive to new users as the interdependent user groups are made up of a larger number of people. The point is the fact that an online platform becomes more important to sellers if there are more buyers using it. So more buyers using a platform means more sellers and so more buyers—and there is a virtuous circle that is difficult to break.

This is the reason why the said indirect network effect may create a high concentration market structure with only a few dominant market players.

Most of the respondents indicate that the case law in relation to dominant position of online platforms or even e-companies in general is somewhat scarce.

Generally speaking, Internet sales are considered as passive sales, i.e., a situation in which the buyer searches spontaneously for the supplier. Accordingly, the supplier has not made any commercial active efforts to sell his products beyond the originally attributed territory, as publicity or licensing local distributors. For most respondents (the European competition system), a ban on passive sales to distributors or users is considered a general restriction of competition. This is an important aspect of the phenomena. In many situations, these bans of online (passive) sales not only prohibit a distributor from selling the product to a consumer but also prohibit passive sales to the distributor or retailer. The existence of such extraordinary restriction can be the evidence of a market distortion when it is clear that an authorised dealer must be entitled to sell, both actively and passively, to consumers via

[92] '*For instance, for hotel online booking platforms, the more hotels and end-consumers use the platform, the more said platform become attractive of both group of users.*'

online sales. It does not mean that the sales conditions must be the same in both distribution channels (online and offline). Nevertheless, those conditions must have the same goals and produce comparable results so that the hypotheses of differences between both business methods must be justified upon their features (*different nature of those two modes of distribution*).

The exception to such consideration (anticompetitive character of the ban relating to passive sales) occurs when the seller makes *specific efforts to reach clients established outside the attributed territory*.[93]

Consequently, the restrictions on a specific territory relating to passive Internet sales are considered anticompetitive, i.e. considered unlawful hardcore cartels and subject to fines.

However, in the Swiss competition system, e.g., a general ban of all online sales is not itself a hardcore restriction of competition (applicable only in cases related to resale price fixing and the specific territory granting) and is subject to a so-called rule of reason criterion or a case-by-case scrutiny. However, in certain qualified circumstances, a prohibition or restriction of online sales can also be considered a hardcore agreement. The conduct known as geo-blocking is a type of 'qualified circumstances'.[94]

#### Lawful or Accepted Restrictions Related to the Selective Distribution System Through Online Platform Sales

Some restrictions are generally accepted as long as they are an integral part or are directly related to the business model in which they are used. In this sense, some respondents indicate that authorities permit some manufacturers' restrictions on the distributor. Some of these contractual restrictions are justified on the ground of business feature (such as quality) control relevance, i.e. the manufacturers' right to (search or guarantee) harmonisation of the activities of the authorised distributor and its business methods.

Therefore, if a manufacturer has the right to set a criteria list to be applied to authorised dealers in the online sales, it may affect the characteristics of the respective selective distribution system. For the Swiss Commission, this is *particularly relevant*. The fixation of points of sale and standards must not spill over the product under contract and must be equally applied to all authorised dealers.

[93] Article 2 of the Notice on the Treatment of Vertical Restraints; see also the Explanatory Statement on the Notice on the Treatment of Vertical Restraints, para. 21.

[94] See Swiss Report, Section 3.2. The *geo-blocking practices* are also considered as qualified circumstances. In this case, according to the Competition Commission, territorial agreements are considered to be qualified circumstances if they provide that (1) a distributor will prevent final consumers in Switzerland to have access to its website and/or which will re-route the client automatically towards the webpage of the manufacturer and/or of the Swiss distributors, or that (2) the distributor will stop the transaction if the client's credit card reveals that the client is not from the attributed territory. Explanatory Statement on the Notice on the Treatment of Vertical Restraints para. 20, citing DPC/RPW 2011/3, Behinderung des Online-Handels, 381, para. 74 and DPC 2014/1 Kosmetikprodukte (Dermalogica) 198 para. 142; see also DPC 2014/2, Jura, 413 para. 62.

#### 1.4.2.2 Trademarks and the Use of Third-Party Platforms

There are criteria commonly set in the selective distribution system, but in the online platform, sales may have another meaning related to competition policy, particularly to other brands. In general, imposing any restriction on a dealer regarding the use of third-party trademarks is a serious restriction of competition.

It is important for the player to protect its own brands as it is one of the main elements of consumer research before any purchase decision is made. On the other hand, confusion among competitors leads to free riding and may cause liability issues to the manufacturer responsible for free riding.

One of the tools to keep the identification of the manufacturer clear and his authorised dealer dedicated to online sales is the full disclosure of the respective dealers and of their points of sale, also clearly identified in their websites (clearly mentioned and visible in the dealers' websites). By the way, dealers are entitled to use their own domain names adopting signs that may differ from their trademarks or commercial names, provided that the association of these names is not disadvantageous to the manufacturer's brand.

In this sense, some of the respondents consider that the supplier may impose on the authorised dealer certain quality standards related to a third-party platform and the respective website presentation so that it would be possible for a manufacturer to prohibit the distribution of his products on a third-party platform such as 'eBay'.

There are cases in which branding is used to justify restrictions. Recently, in a German court (the Higher Regional Court Düsseldorf), the 'Asics' case ruled that a general prohibition on distributors using price comparison sites constitutes a competition restriction.[95] In that case, the prohibition is not justified by branding and advisory services. Consumers may not need or want to be advised, in the case of running shoes, or would also be able to get information on the Internet.[96]

This topic was discussed by the EU Member States and resulted in a solid report,[97] which shows the relevance of this matter in the near future of competition.

## 1.5 A Criterion to Structure Definition of Online Platform Markets

None of the countries surveyed have a statutory definition of relevant markets in their respective laws.

[95] Higher Regional Court Düsseldorf, Decision of 5 April 2017, VI Kart 13/15 [V].

[96] Vide also the Austrian Report, sec. 2. '*Interestingly, the question, whether the former distribution system of Asics was also in breach of core antitrust rules because of Asics' prohibition on its distributors to use Google AdWords and third party online marketplaces, was left open. The German Federal Cartel Authority (Bundeskartellamt) had ruled in first instance, and later argued before the Higher Regional Court Düsseldorf, that such a general ban on sales on third-party online sales platforms is a hardcore infringement for its own.*'

[97] Commission (2017) Final Report on the E-commerce Sector Inquiry, http://ec.europa.eu/competition/antitrust/sector_inquiry_final_report_en.pdf.

As in other sectors, the competition authorities define relevant markets (of products or service) by analysing the substitutability for buyers and consumers (adopting the SSNIP test for that) and sometimes examining this 'cross elasticity' in the supply side. It is true that the entry of online platforms affected traditional markets and occasionally market structure analysis and the definition of relevant market.

Among the EU respondents, national authorities closely follow the guidelines and criteria established by the European Commission's notice related to relevant market definition. The policy makers in countries with meaningful national markets like Australia and Brazil also apply a substitutability criterion to define the relevant market. Nevertheless, the growth of online sales platforms induced improvements of the antitrust examination.

The Australian report indicates that through the support of an economic study (from Deloitte), there is a growing trend for online sale platforms to become vertically and horizontally integrated. And the respondent states that *[t]his then 'raise[s] the prospect of any integrated platforms with market power using that market power to force or incentivise their suppliers and/or consumers to support the integrated business model, in order for the platforms to maximize revenues.*

This kind of integration might be considered under the merger rules. In this context, in some jurisdictions, online platforms have been considered as new and 'disruptive' technologies characterised at first by low barriers to entry and the respective mergers subject to approval. There was a relevant incidence of cases in the hotel reservation sector (accommodation booking services) related to mergers. See the Australian Expedia/Wortif case, in which merger was considered by the competition authority to be unlikely to '*impede the degree of dynamic change in the market*'.[98]

## 1.6 Consent Decrees and Cease-and-Desist Agreements

The respondents have statutory provisions related to cease anticompetitive agreements. In many of the online platform cases, the investigations were interrupted or closed by a cessation agreement.

In many cases (see Australia), the cease agreement included not only the payment of a fine but also the admission of a competition law infringement. As usual, the nature of the consent agreement between the authorities and the defendant does not enable us to determine the court's approach to online sales platforms.

[98] *The ACCC observed that barriers for a new entrant to achieve sufficient scale to compete with Expedia, Wotif or Booking.com would be high and would include significant sunk costs in the form of advertising. However, the ACCC observed that recent changes to the market, which included consideration of significant global players, like Amazon, who might have the ability to overcome those barriers, combined with developments in adjacent markets, such as metasearch platforms like TripAdvisor and Google, would ensure the market remained dynamic and there would be significant competitive constraints on OTA incumbents.*

As presented in the cases from Australia, Belgium and Sweden, the main cases related to online platforms were solved after the offering of commitments by the parties being investigated.

In 2016, the Australian competition authority investigated agreements on amending price and availability parity clauses, which Booking.com, Expedia and other online sale platforms reached, or were trying to reach, with Australian hotels and other accommodation providers. The authority was concerned that this conduct restricted price and other competition. During the investigation, the online sales platforms involved agreed to change the parity clauses, which was sufficient to satisfy the authorities' concern so that no further action was taken. It is not clear which provision(s) would have been used if this matter had been litigated[99]; however, sections 45 (anticompetitive agreements) and 48 (resale price maintenance) might have been argued.

Still in Australia, within a universe of 46 cases, only one of them involves online platform sales. In 2011, a consent decision was taken in the *Tiketek* case, in which the defendant admitted that it had violated Australian competition law. In that case, Tiketek agreed that it held a 'large share' of the *Ticketing Related Services Market* and that its conduct operated as a barrier to enter somewhat like bundling practices (very common in integrated two-sided markets). The 'full service' provided by the defendant prevented Venue Operators and Promoters from competing. The fine imposed against Tiketek was reduced to reflect its cooperation with the competition authorities.

## 1.7 Conclusion

This overview of the eleven national reports leads to some significant conclusions.

Despite the convergence that has taken place in telecommunications, online platforms remain under the scope of the antitrust law. Moreover, even given the 'new world' raised from the information highways in the late 1990s, and the subsequent 'boom' of online navigation worldwide, most competition restrictions relating to online platforms seem to be within the scope of competition law.

In this area, it is possible to find all categories of competition restrictions. This wide range of competition problems includes not only agreements between suppliers and distributors but also agreements between competitors, unilateral conduct (e.g., abuse of dominant position) and even mergers. However, the main problems are in the scope of the vertical agreement provisions.

The typical conduct related to abuse of dominant position (or misuse of market power) in online sales platforms is to be assessed using the same provisions related to this same issue in the scenario of the traditional economy.

[99] For further information see, ACCC, 'Expedia and Booking.com agree to reinvigorate price competition by amending contracts with Australian hotels' (Media Release, 2 September 2016) (available at https://www.accc.gov.au/media-release/expedia-and-bookingcom-agree-to-reinvigorate-price-competition-by-amending-contracts-with-australian-hotels).

For these reasons, most jurisdictions have competition laws drafted for situations more like that of the obvious competition markets (e.g., traditional brick-and-mortar shops) rather than the new businesses methods of the so-called new economy, but these broadly drafted provisions are adaptable to the new situations created by the evolution of the market and to new distribution models.

The respondents indicate concerns about the role of online platforms. To Europeans, this issue became especially relevant to national policy makers after the disclosure of concerns related to online platforms by the European Commission (GDVI). For EU competition policy, it is a software-based facility characterised by multi-sided markets. The platforms offer a meeting point to providers and users of content, goods and services enabling several new business methods as a direct result of the respective externalities. Most of the European national policy makers (such as the UK) started off with the EU's concern about online platforms to conduct internal studies and *research addressing the market issues around platforms and come to number of hypotheses about how dynamic competition affects online platforms*.[100]

These approaches have influenced policy to a lower or higher degree depending on the features of the national competition system.

All of the countries in this survey considered that the provisions of their competition laws are able to handle competitive relations on the Internet, including the specific challenges of the online sales platforms. This is also confirmed by the large number of reports that concluded that there is no need for changes in the legislation. However, some countries expect changes in administrative guidelines or notice (e.g., Australia) on the interpretation of the law and application criteria or the result of new studies or at least the observation of more new and robust empirical data (e.g., Switzerland).

Further thinking should be, however, refined on the criteria to be used in antitrust analysis concerning dynamic competition in concentrated markets (considering products, technology, multi-sided and innovation markets). In the Brazilian system, for example, there are some cases related to online platforms that address the relevance of dynamic competition. In many countries, there are no guidelines or notices dealing with restrictions relating to online platforms or any leading case proposing tests or criteria relating to the analysis of dynamic competition in this context. In many of the countries surveyed, there are no specific decisions on the merits concerning online sales platforms, but the policy makers have been gathering efforts to provide the adaptation of the general rules developed prior to the assessment of the anticompetitive restrictions raised in the traditional economy

So it is possible to conclude that general competition in online platforms seems to be functioning well in many aspects. For some respondents, mainly the UK, it is important to consider evidence that *network effects which might otherwise act as a barrier to entry, encourage dynamic competition*.[101] The UK report indicates that

---

[100] See *Dynamic Competition in Online Platforms – evidence from five case study markets*, issue by the UK Department for Business, innovation and Skills in march of 2017.

[101] UK *Dynamic Competition in Online Platforms*, page 6. Available at https://www.gov.uk/govern-

there are three main aspects that may foster dynamic competition: (1) *entry is common and tends to materially affect the market*, (2) *effective entry does not appear to be less likely in more concentrated digital markets* and (3) concentration tends to increase over time in each sector, but competition from other sectors often intensifies. Another question is how a policy maker should act to balance these features related to the dynamic competition.

Another question about online sales platforms is whether and to what extent dynamic competition can produce positive competitive outcomes, despite the lack of traditional or obvious competition. Certainly, it is widely understood that the effect of new business methods and respective practices (in many cases considered as restrictions to competition) can vary on the ground of market characteristics.

Some respondents consider that excessive regulatory control may affect innovation, even though overprotection may do the same.

Innovation itself brings new social demands. There are new issues that will rise and challenge competition as we know it. For example, there is a discussion about whether the value of big data should be taken into account, e.g. merger notification thresholds, due to the relevance of big data to Internet-based businesses.

Of course, there are some difficulties. Most of them come from the fact that different countries have distinct cultures, history, political features and antitrust goals. These difficulties come from the fact that each national competition system pursues a wide range of distinct goals (occasionally even contradictory). For example, a number of countries have included in their competition law or in their unfair competition law a catalogue of per se prohibitions against various business models and practices. It is also possible to identify a close connection of competition law and consumer law in the case of some of the respondents (Australia, Brazil and Switzerland).

In any event, visiting an online sales platform has become a decisive step before making any purchase, and this new consumer behaviour affects traditional markets in many ways, often promoting competition and helping consumers. Even though the authorities tend constantly to monitor—with special attention—the growth of online platforms, and the structure of these multi-sided markets, the existence of market power or dominant position and the possibility of its use, abuse or misuse are still an open matter subject to future scrutiny.

As a general conclusion, it may be considered that under regular conditions, online sales are positive for competition.

Lastly, the changes brought by the so-called new economy raise challenges to the competition authorities across the world, which must keep following up the improvements of the Internet-related business methods in order to secure free competition and consumer welfare.

**Resolution of the LIDC**

Whereas:

---

ment/publications/dynamic-competition-in-online-platforms. Accessed 12 January 2018.

A. competition law allows for the flexible application of established principles to new situations;
B. online sales platforms, which are multi-sided services, are characterised by network effects and can have economies of scale;
C. network effects means that there can be significant barriers to entry, with market power developing quickly;
D. in principle retailers and customers may use a variety of sales routes, including brick-and-mortar stores, online sales platforms, online sales channels, digital sales channels offered in-store;

It is resolved that:

1. network effects are not a new concept and the application of competition law is sufficiently flexible to address issues arising in multi sided markets.
2. market definition must be considered on a case by case basis, taking account of specific consumer and supplier behaviour. Online sales platforms and traditional sales routes may compete with each other or be complements, depending on the sector, consumer behaviour and supplier behaviour.
3. online sales platforms can increase in scale quickly, or can lose market power to competing platforms and technologies. Where competition authorities decide to act, they must act both cautiously and courageously, taking account of the dynamic nature of the features of the market. Competition authorities should also consider providing guidance, where appropriate.

# Australia

# 2

Barbora Jedličková and Julie Clarke

## 2.1 Introduction

Competition law issues arising with regard to online sales platforms centre around computer software, services provided online by online sales platforms, contractual relationships between the online platforms and sellers or buyers, information exchange, power and integration. Specifically, they may include algorithms that can coordinate and monitor prices and other business practices among competitors; collecting, exchanging and blocking information and targeting specific customers (consumers or businesses); and creating innovation-driven new monopolistic markets or markets where one online platform possesses significant market power.

Many specific features of online sales platforms and their implications for competition policy have been identified by academic commentators[1] and have been the

This book chapter reflects the Australian law as understood on 1 July 2017.

[1] See, e.g., A. Ezrachi and M. E. Stucke, *Virtual Competition – The Promise and Perils of the* Algorithm Driven Economy, Harvard University Press 2016; M. Taylor, Competition Law in High Technology Industries: Insights for Australia, Competition Law Conference, Sydney, 30 May 2015.

B. Jedličková (✉)
TC Beirne School of Law, The University of Queensland, St Lucia, QLD, Australia
e-mail: b.jedlickova@law.uq.edu.au

J. Clarke
Melbourne Law School, The University of Melbourne, Parkville, VIC, Australia
e-mail: clarke.j1@unimelb.edu.au



B. Kilpatrick et al. (eds.), *Antitrust Analysis of Online Sales Platforms & Copyright Limitations and Exceptions*, LIDC Contributions on Antitrust Law, Intellectual Property and Unfair Competition,
https://doi.org/10.1007/978-3-319-71419-6_2

subject of study by several competition authorities.[2] Competition issues identified in these studies relate to bargaining power, unfair treatment and market power of the online platforms. They include the following:

- lack of level-playing field;
- lack of choice;
- unfair licensing/parity clauses;
- lack of transparency and non-neutrality of rankings in online searches; and
- contract enforcement.[3]

The Australian Competition and Consumer Commission (the 'ACCC') has also been interested in competition within the digital economy. For example, it commissioned a study on 'The Sharing Economy and the Competition and Consumer Act' (the 'Deloitte Study'),[4] which was reported in 2015. The study identified two pivotal areas of competition concern: (1) vertical and horizontal integration of online platforms and (2) vertical restrictions, referred to in the study as 'exclusive practices'. Importantly, it found that 'regulatory neutrality' was a key concern for competition policy in the 'sharing economy'. In particular, there is concern that, at present, sharing economy providers have fewer regulations applied or enforced than traditional businesses, and this puts the traditional businesses at a competitive disadvantage.[5] For instance, although there are competitive advantages flowing from the 'disruption' caused by ride-sharing platforms, Uber and other emerging innovative technologies,[6] it is clear that Uber is subject to significantly less regulatory restrictions and obligations than its key competitors in the taxi industry.[7]

Other recent Australian official reports, which discuss competition law issues related to online sales platforms and the potential need for modifications to the existing approaches, include the Harper Report on competition policy and the Productivity Commission's 'Digital Disruption' report.[8]

Australia does not have any specific provisions relating to online sales platforms and competition; the generic competition law (and consumer law) apply to online

[2] For example, in May 2016, the European Commission released its study on online platforms: A. Gawer, Study on Online Platforms – Contrasting perceptions of European stakeholders: A qualitative analysis of the European Commission's Public Consultation on the Regulatory Environment for Platforms, (European Commission, DG Communications Networks, Content & technology, 25 May 2016, available at https://ec.europa.eu/digital-single-market/en/reports-and-studies/76009 ('EU Study').

[3] EU Study, pp. 14–15.

[4] Deloitte Access Economics, The sharing economy and the Competition and Consumer Act 2015, ACCC, available at https://www.accc.gov.au/system/files/Sharing%20Economy%20-%20Deloitte%20Report%20-%202015.pdf.

[5] Deloitte Study, p iii.

[6] I. Harper, P. Anderson, S. McCluskey and M. O'Bryan QC, Competition Policy Review: Final Report, March 2015, available at http://competitionpolicyreview.gov.au/final-report/, p 26.

[7] Deloitte Study, pp. 9–11.

[8] Australian Government Productivity Commission, 'Digital Disruption: What do government need to do?' Research Paper, June 2016, p. 61, available at http://www.pc.gov.au/research/completed/digital-disruption. We refer to all these reports and their relevant sections in the text below.

sales platforms. In addition, there have been no cases in which the court has suggested modification of the existing competition law in the context of online sales platforms. In this chapter, we survey the areas of Australian competition and consumer laws relevant to this topic and identify and discuss potential strengths and weaknesses of the existing and proposed law.

After a general introduction of Australian competition law and policy, we explain areas of Australian competition law relevant to online platforms. Later sections of the chapter deal with vertical restraints that could potentially occur in connection with online sales platforms. Then we briefly explain the protection (or overprotection) of IP rights in connection with competition law. In the last section, we explain one of the strengths of Australia's competition law in capturing a wide range of potentially anti-competitive behaviour involving online sales platforms.

## 2.2 Australian Competition Law Legislation: Competition and Consumer Act 2010

### 2.2.1 Legislation and Proposed Amendments

Australian competition law is contained in the *Competition and Consumer Act 2010* (Cth) (the 'CCA').[9] Recently, Australian competition law and policy were reviewed extensively by the 'Harper Review', with its final report, the 'Harper Report' (2015), proposing many changes to the CCA. Currently, two bills, which incorporate many of the recommendations in the Harper Report, have been introduced by the Australian Government:

- Competition and Consumer Amendment (Competition Policy Review) Bill 2017 ('Bill 2017')
- Competition and Consumer Amendment (Misuse of Market Power) Bill 2017 ('Bill 2016')[10]

Another bill, reflecting one of the issues discussed in the Harper Report, the **Competition and Consumer Legislation Amendment (Small Business Access to Justice) Bill 2017,** was introduced as a private members' bill on 16 February 2017 and proposes to address the issue connected with access to justice for small businesses. It recognises that small businesses do not possess the sufficient or significant financial resources necessary for litigating anti-competitive practices. This is

[9] The Act was previously named the *Trade Practices Act 1974* (Cth). The Australian Constitution, the *Commonwealth of Australia Constitution Act (1900)*, limits the extent to which the federal government can legislate. For that reason, states and territories enacted a 'schedule' version of the Part IV of the CCA, which contains core provisions on competition law. The CCA and the enacted schedule ensure a nationally consistent competition law.

[10] Formerly 'Competition and Consumer Amendment (Misuse of Market Power) Bill 2016', the Bill 2016 was introduced into the Parliament in December 2016 and passed the Senate in August 2017. Despite its passing, the amendments in the Bill 2016 will not become law until other amendments in the Bill 2017 (the other Harper-Review bill) are enacted and commence.

particularly an issue for section 46 of the CCA (misuse of market power)—litigation where the accused party possesses significant market (and/or bargaining) power while a potential private plaintiff will in most cases be a much smaller entity. The Harper Report stated in connection with this issue that

> From submissions and consultations with small business, the Panel is convinced that there are significant barriers to small business taking private action to enforce the competition laws. A private action would be beyond the means of many small businesses. In some cases, a small business might not wish to bring a proceeding for fear of damaging a necessary trading relationship.[11]

The aim of the bill is to provide a 'no adverse cost order' for small business litigation in private cases and to assist with the process of a small business requesting a no adverse cost order.

### 2.2.2 Substantial Lessening of Competition

With regard to the current CCA, Australian competition law prohibits mergers or acquisitions that have the effect or likely effect of substantially lessening competition and certain other conduct, including exclusive dealing (section 47) and horizontal agreements (section 45),[12] where it has the purpose, effect or likely effect of substantially lessening competition.

The ACCC approaches this assessment by considering the likely state of competition with and without the relevant conduct. Although efficiencies that bare on the level of competition in the market can be considered, there is no separate 'rule of reason' weighing of efficiencies that can occur as part of the process; in other words, should the conduct produce efficiencies that, despite substantially lessening competition, enhance consumer or total welfare, it will nevertheless contravene the Act.

It is not sufficient that competition be lessened; it must be lessened 'substantially'. This has been interpreted as meaning something 'meaningful or relevant to the competitive process' and is a relative concept.[13] Lessening competition is defined in section 4G of the CCA as including 'references to preventing or hindering competition', and the ACCC has defined it as meaning 'that the field of rivalry is diminished or lessened, or the competitive process is compromised or impacted'.[14] Competition, in turn, 'refers to a process, rather than a situation, and is expressed in

[11] Harper Report, p. 407.

[12] In theory, s 45 also covers vertical agreements which do not contravene s 47 ('exclusive dealing') and/or s 48 ('resale price maintenance'). See below.

[13] ACCC, *Framework for misuse of market power guidelines* (September 2016) ('*MMP Framework*') (https://consultation.accc.gov.au/compliance-enforcement/consultation-on-draft-framework-for-misuse-of-mark/) *('MMP Framework')*, para 4.4. See also *Rural Press Rural Press Limited v Australian Competition and Consumer Commission* [2003] HCA 75 para 41, *Stirling Harbour Services Pty Ltd v Bunbury Port Authority* [2000] FCA 38 para 114, *Universal Music Australia Pty Ltd v ACCC* [2003] FCAFC 193 par 242 and *Australian Competition and Consumer Commission v Cement Australia Pty Ltd* [2013] FCA 909 para 329.

[14] *MMP Framework*, para 4.4.

the form of rivalrous behaviour',[15] is 'a means of protecting the interests of consumers, rather than individual competitors' and is 'assessed looking at both market structure and the strategic behaviour of market participants'.[16]

Several forms of anti-competitive practices are expressly subject to *per se* prohibition, meaning that substantial lessening of competition does not have to be proved,[17] but it is assumed:

- cartels (Part IV, Division 1, sections 44ZZRA–44ZZRV)[18];
- primary boycotts (section 4D, section 45(2)(a)(i) and section 45(2)(b)(i))[19];
- third line forcing (form of exclusive dealing) (section 47(6) and (7))[20]; and
- minimum resale price maintenance (including vertical price fixing) (section 4, section 48, sections 96–100).

If Bill 2017 is passed, third line forcing and primary boycotts will no longer be *per se* prohibited but will be evaluated under the substantial lessening of competition requirement.

### 2.2.3 Immunity and Efficiency

All forms of prohibited anti-competitive conduct, with the exception of misuse of market power (section 46), may be authorised in advance[21] on public benefit grounds, rather than a direct assessment of whether the conduct will substantially lessen competition. In addition, exclusive dealing and collective bargaining can be individually exempted from prohibition through the 'notification' process, which, while also based on a public benefit test, is procedurally less demanding than authorisation.

[15] *MMP Framework*, para 4.4. See also Harper Report, p. 341.

[16] *MMP Framework*, para 4.4.

[17] It is also not required for s 46. Currently, the prohibition on misuse of market power requires demonstration of, in part, a prohibited 'purpose', rather than relying on proof of anti-competitive effect.

[18] Part IV, Division 1 of the *Competition and Consumer Act 2010* (Cth). This incorporates price-fixing, output restrictions, allocation of customers, suppliers or territories and bid rigging. This conduct is both a criminal offence and subject to civil penalties. Certain joint venture activity is excluded from the scope of the *per se* prohibition, but remains subject to the general prohibition against anti-competitive agreements in s 45.

[19] In Australia, these are referred to as 'exclusionary provisions' and are *per se* prohibited where they involve an agreement between competitors having the purpose of preventing, restricting or limiting supply or acquisition to defined persons or classes of persons: ss 45 and 4D of the CCA. Joint ventures benefit from a limited competition defence: s 76C of the CCA.

[20] Unlike other forms of exclusive dealing, it is *per se* prohibited, but it is possible for the conduct to be 'notified' and receive immunity on public benefit grounds. This occurs when supply is made on the condition that goods or services are purchased from an unrelated third party (or there is a refusal to supply because of failure to agree to such a condition).

[21] It is not possible for conduct to be retrospectively authorised; approval must be provided in advance of the conduct occurring or it will contravene the Act notwithstanding any demonstrated public benefits.

A public benefit test has two forms depending on which conduct is the subject of authorisation. Authorisation is granted either if public benefit outweighs any anti-competitive harm or if the public benefit is such that the conduct in question should be permitted. In practice, both tests have been used in a similar way.

The notification process is a faster, cheaper[22] and simpler way of obtaining immunity. It is available only for exclusive dealing conduct and collective bargaining conduct, as discussed below.[23] If Bill 2017 passes, it will also be possible to notify RPM conduct.

One potential public benefit justification for authorisation or notification could be that the conduct was introduced in order to protect brand name. In this respect, 'public benefit' is a broad concept and is capable of including any benefit to the public, not just economic benefits. However, mere protection of brand name has not yet been recognised as a public benefit in authorisation proceedings.[24] It was argued in connection with an RPM case (not a notification/authorisation case),[25] and, although the court expressed some sympathy for the argument that RPM was utilised for this purpose, as RPM is a per se prohibition, it was not able to provide a defence to the proceedings; however, the apparently sympathetic reception from the court suggests that it is an argument that may be successfully invoked in RPM authorisation applications in the future.

Public benefit claims associated with protecting a prestigious or well-known trademark may, however, carry less weight in Australia, given that section 51(3) limits the application of the CCA in connection with trademarks (as further discussed below), which provides that only provisions on misuse of market power and RPM can apply to arrangements between trademark owners and holders.[26] In connection with section 46, such a justification could potentially be relevant when

[22] Fees vary depending on the conduct. For collective bargaining notification the fee is currently AUD 1,000. For exclusive dealing conduct other than third line forcing the fee is AUD 2,500. For third line forcing the fee is AUD 100.

[23] The notification process is also available to price signalling contained in Division 1A of Part IV. However, price signalling provisions apply only to the banking sector and Bill 2017 proposes their repeal.

[24] For instance, the list of potential public benefits contained in *Re ACI Operations Pty Ltd* (1991) ATPR (Com) ¶50-108 does not include the protection of brand names.

[25] *ACCC v Jurlique International Pty Ltd* [2007] FCA 79.

[26] Section 51(b) and (c) provide

(b) the inclusion in a contract, arrangement or understanding authorizing the use of a certification trade mark of a provision in accordance with rules applicable under Part XI of the *Trade Marks Act 1955*, or the giving effect to such a provision; or

(c) the inclusion in a contract, arrangement or understanding between:

(i) the registered proprietor of a trade mark other than a certification trade mark; and

(ii) a person registered as a registered user of that trade mark under Part IX of the *Trade Marks Act 1955* or a person authorized by the contract to use the trade mark subject to his or her becoming registered as such a registered user;

of a provision to the extent that it relates to the kinds, qualities or standards of goods bearing the mark that may be produced or supplied, or the giving effect to the provision to that extent.

defending claims that a corporation 'took advantage' of their market power or did so with a prohibited purpose.

In contrast, efficiency can play an important role when considering whether public benefit would prevail over the restriction of competition. The decision *Re Queensland Co-operative Milling Association*[27] states:

> ...[T]he widest possible conception of public benefit [is]... anything of value to the community generally, any contribution to the aims pursued by the society including as one of its principal elements (in the context of trade practices legislation) the achievement of the economic goals of *efficiency* and *progress*. If this conception is adopted, it is clear that it could be possible to argue in some cases that a benefit to the members or employees of the corporations involved served some acknowledged end of public policy even though no immediate or direct benefit to others was demonstrable.[28]

In addition:

> ...the assessment of efficiency and progress must be from the perspective of society as a whole: the best use of society's resources. We bear in mind that (in the language of economics today) efficiency is a concept that is usually taken to encompass "progress"; and that commonly efficiency is said to encompass allocative efficiency, production efficiency and dynamic efficiency.[29]

Indeed, when referring to efficiency in connection with competition law, it is common that such a reference includes dynamic efficiency arising from innovation.[30] The ACCC summarises the concept of efficiency for the purposes of economic public benefits in its *Authorisation Guidelines* (2013)[31] in the following way:

> Economic efficiency has three aspects:
>
> - allocative efficiency — refers to the allocation of society's scarce resources to their most valuable use. Allocative efficiency is achieved when the price paid for an extra unit of a product (which reflects consumers' willingness to pay or marginal utility) equals the cost of the resources used to produce that product (marginal cost). Allocative efficiency can only be achieved if all the costs and benefits, including externalities, are fully brought into account. Furthermore, allocative efficiency will not be achieved if prices are distorted by market power (which drives a wedge between price and marginal cost).
> - productive efficiency — refers to the production of goods and services using the most cost-effective means.

---

[27] *Re Queensland Co–operative Milling Association Ltd., Defiance Holdings Ltd. (Proposed Mergers with Barnes Milling Ltd.)*, (1976) ATPR ¶40–012.

[28] *Re Queensland Co–operative Milling Association Ltd., Defiance Holdings Ltd. (Proposed Mergers with Barnes Milling Ltd.)*, (1976) ATPR ¶40–012, at 17,242 (emphasis added).

[29] *Re 7-Eleven* (1994), ATPR 41-357 at [42,777].

[30] For instance, the High Court of Australia quoted from the Australian Competition Tribunal decision in *Re Duke Eastern Gas Pipeline Pty Ltd* [2001] ACompT 2 (2001) 162 FLR 1, stating that '...On the basis of many studies and long experience, economists have concluded that the main virtue of competition is that it provides a very powerful means of securing important gains in allocative and especially dynamic efficiency'. *The Pilbara Infrastructure Pty Ltd v Australian Competition Tribunal* [2012] HCA 36.

[31] ACCC, *Authorisation Guidelines* (June 2013), available at https://www.accc.gov.au/system/files/Authorisation%20guidelines.pdf.

- dynamic efficiency — refers to the economically efficient use of resources over time – incorporating process and product innovation in response to changes in the market. For example, arrangements that provide incentives for efficient investment in research and development will promote dynamic efficiency.[32]

The references to efficiency have also been made in connection with other areas of competition law. For instance, enhancing efficiency is relevant when proving that the substantial lessening of competition requirement is not satisfied if, for instance, exclusive dealing restricting intra-brand competition increases inter-brand competition via enhancing of efficiencies.[33] It could also, at least theoretically, assist with an argument that there is no anti-competitive purpose under section 46 and thus no contravention of misuse of market power.[34]

### 2.2.4 'Agreements' Under Section 45 of the CCA

The test of substantially lessening competition also applies in connection with section 45(2) for conduct other than primary boycotts, which are governed by section 45(2)(a)(i) and section 45(2)(b)(i) and prohibited *per se*.[35] It is a general provision, which states:

(a) [a] corporation shall not make a contract or arrangement, or arrive at an understanding, if… a provision of the proposed contract, arrangement or understanding has the purpose, or would have or be likely to have the effect, of substantially lessening competition[36]; or
(b) give effect to a provision of a contract, arrangement or understanding, … if that provision… has the purpose, or has or is likely to have the effect, of substantially lessening competition.[37]

It applies to all horizontal 'agreements' (except for primary boycotts), as well as vertical restraints (in the form of 'agreements'), that are not covered by section 48 (resale price maintenance) or by section 47 (exclusive dealing). It can also apply to cartels, in particular price fixing, territorial or customer allocation, output restriction and bid rigging, which are also prohibited *per se* under the cartel regime in Part IV, Division 1, of the CCA.

In 2016, the ACCC investigated agreements on amending price and availability parity clauses, which Booking.com, Expedia and other online sales platforms reached, or were trying to reach, with Australian hotels and other accommodation

[32] *Authorisation Guidelines* (2013), p. 57.

[33] *Melway Publishing Pty Ltd v Robert Hicks Pty Ltd* (2001) 205 CLR 1 at [20].

[34] S.G. Corones, *Competition Law in Australia* (6th ed., Thomson Reuters Australia, 2014), pp. 494 – 496.

[35] The boycott will not be prohibited anymore and will be governed by the general provision of s 45 if Bill 2017 will amend the CCA.

[36] Section 45(2)(a)(ii) CCA.

[37] Section 45(2)(b)(ii) CCA.

providers. The ACCC was concerned that this conduct restricted price and other competition. During the investigation, the online sales platforms involved agreed to change the parity clauses, which was sufficient to satisfy the ACCC's concern so that no further action was taken. It is not clear which provision(s) would have been used if this matter had been litigated[38]; however, sections 45 (anti-competitive agreements) and 48 (resale price maintenance) might have been argued.

The next part of the chapter will deal with potential issue areas related to online sales platforms and specific provisions of competition and consumer laws that can be (or have been) applied. It will reveal weaknesses and strengths in the relevant Australian regime in the context of this topic. Indeed, there are a number of ways in which Australian competition law (and consumer law) may be applied to address potentially restrictive practices occurring in online sales platforms. These include the following:

- the prohibition of vertical restraints that does not require proof of anti-competitive 'agreement'; rather, they are typically treated as a form of unilateral conduct under section 47 and section 48;
- the fact that, in certain circumstances, agents can be found liable for anti-competitive conduct engaged in with their principals;
- the fact that market power under section 46 may include bargaining power;
- the fact that Australia's broad consumer laws are capable of capturing a range of conduct stemming from market power;
- the possibility for smaller firms to lawfully collectively bargain to overcome or limit the effects of buyer or seller power.

## 2.3 Criterion for Market Definition and Market Power

### 2.3.1 Market Definition

Australia's competition provisions typically require that competition be lessened 'in a market', that power be held in 'a market' or that parties be competitors in 'a market'. As a result, market definition remains essential to an assessment of whether or not the competition provisions have been contravened.

Market is defined as

> a market in Australia and, when used in relation to any goods or services, includes a market for those goods or services and other goods or services that are substitutable for, other otherwise competitive with, the first-mentioned goods or services.[39]

[38] For further information, see ACCC, 'Expedia and Booking.com agree to reinvigorate price competition by amending contracts with Australian hotels' (Media Release, 2 September 2016), (available at https://www.accc.gov.au/media-release/expedia-and-bookingcom-agree-to-reinvigorate-price-competition-by-amending-contracts-with-australian-hotels.

[39] Section 4E CCA.

Market is defined separately in relation to mergers as a market for goods or services in Australia or a state or a territory or a region of Australia.[40]

The meaning of market under Australian law has been 'very stable',[41] with the concept of substitutability as means of defining the market, articulated by the (then) Trade Practices Tribunal in the *QCMA* case in 1976.[42] The Tribunal there defined market as

> the area of close competition between firms or … the field of rivalry between them. … Within the bounds of a market there is substitution—substitution between one product and another and between one source of supply and another, in response to changing prices. So a market is the field of actual and potential transactions between buyers and sellers amongst whom there can be strong substitution, at least in the long run, if given a sufficient price incentive … in determining the outer boundaries of the market we ask a quite simple but fundamental question: if the firm were to 'give less and charge more' would there be, to put the matter colloquially, much of a reaction.[43]

This definition has endured, with this passage from *QCMA* still regularly referenced by the courts. Substitutability, for the purpose of market definition, has been acknowledged to occur along a spectrum; to be considered in the same market, the product or services in question must be 'close' substitutes. Nevertheless, the precise boundaries of the market are always likely to be a matter of contention, with the ACCC acknowledging in its merger guidelines that it is 'rarely possible to draw a clear line around fields of rivalry'.[44]

In the context of mergers,[45] the ACCC focusses on product and geographic market dimensions,[46] starting with 'identifying the products and geographic regions actually or potentially supplied by the merger parties' and then focussing on 'defining markets in areas of activity where competitive harm could occur'.[47] More than one market can, and frequently is, recognised as relevant for the assessment.[48]

When identifying substitutes for purposes of delineating the market, the ACCC focusses on demand side substitution but also considers supply-side substitutes. The hypothetical monopolist (HMT) test is adopted for this assessment, explained by the ACCC as follows:

---

[40] Section 50(6) CCA.

[41] Harper Report, p. 314.

[42] *Re Queensland Co-Op Milling Association Limited and Defiance Holdings Limited* (QCMA) (1976) 8 ALR 481.

[43] *Re Queensland Co-Op Milling Association Limited and Defiance Holdings Limited* (QCMA) (1976) 8 ALR 481, 518.

[44] ACCC, Merger Guidelines (November 2008) ('*Merger Guidelines*'), para 4.10: This is done on a case by case basis, with market definition recognised as 'purposive' (para 4.9).

[45] Although the approach is set out in the *Merger Guidelines*, the ACCC has indicated that this approach to market definition would apply consistently in relation to other competition provisions. For example, in the MMP Framework, the ACCC indicated that the ACCC's approach to market definition would not change for s 46 and the approach is set out in the *Merger Guidelines*.

[46] *Merger Guidelines*, para 4.8.

[47] *Merger Guidelines*, para 4.10: This is done on a case by case basis, with market definition recognised as 'purposive' (para 4.9).

[48] *Merger Guidelines*, para 4.10.

> The HMT determines the smallest area in product and geographic space within which a hypothetical current and future profit-maximising monopolist could effectively exercise market power. In general, the exercise of market power by the hypothetical monopolist is characterised by the imposition of a small but significant and non-transitory increase in price (SSNIP) above the price level that would prevail without the merger, assuming the terms of sale of all other products are held constant.[49]

In making this assessment, the ACCC and courts are alive to the dangers of the cellophane fallacy, as recently highlighted in the *Cement Australia* case,[50] in which the ACCC's expert testimony in relation to market definition considered that the market price for the product in question 'persistently exceeded the competitive price by significantly more than a SSNIP'.[51]

**A Market 'in Australia'**

Both the general definition of market and the merger-specific definition reference a market 'in Australia', although this limitation does not extend to the (relatively new) cartel laws.[52] This reference to 'in Australia', which applies to most of the competition prohibitions, continues to cause some uncertainty in relation to conduct occurring principally outside Australia, but which nevertheless might impact on Australian markets. This issue recently came before Australia's highest court[53] in the context of contracts for the carriage of air cargo. The plurality in that case observed that reconciling the 'abstract notion of a market with the concrete notion of location, so that they work coherently, presents something of a challenge'.[54] Nevertheless, 'the task of attributing to the abstract concept of a market a geographical location in Australia is to be approached as a practical matter of business', and as such it is important that 'any analysis of the competitive processes … is not divorced from the commercial context of the conduct in question'.[55] Importantly, a 'market in Australia does not cease to be so located because it encompasses other places as well'.[56]

In assessing the market, 'it is the substitutability of services as the driver of rivalry between competitors [and] not the circumstances of the act of substitution itself' that is relevant. Consequently, the place where substitution occurs (and contracts are entered) does not necessarily define the geographic market; the rivalry

---

[49] *Merger Guidelines*, para 4.19.

[50] *ACCC v Cement Australia* [2013] FCA 909.

[51] See further Rhonda Smith, 'Market definition and substitution options' (2014) 22 *Competition & Consumer Law Journal* 105 at 117 (although Smith notes that not all cellophane fallacy concerns were recognised in that case (p 118)).

[52] Section 44ZZRD of the CCA, which defines cartel conduct, requires only that parties be 'in competition with each other', without further reference to being in competition in a market in Australia. See also *Norcast S.ár.L v Bradken Limited (No 2)* [2013] FCA 235 (in particular para 228).

[53] The High Court: *PT Garuda Indonesia Ltd v. Australian Competition and Consumer Commission* [2017] HCA 21 (14 June 2017).

[54] Idem, para 14.

[55] Ibidem.

[56] Idem, para 15.

preceding the act of substitution is relevant. In this case, the fact that contracts were arrived at in one jurisdiction (outside Australia) did not preclude the geographic market being in Australia, given that the 'rivalrous behaviour', in which supply was matched with demand, occurred in a market that, geographically, included Australia.[57]

There is no 'effects test' approach to competition jurisdiction in Australia with the result that, absent a finding that there is a market 'in Australia', there will be no contravention of the Act. Notwithstanding concerns that defining an 'Australian' market may fail to give proper consideration to global markets and may result in competition analysis being 'focussed too narrowly',[58] particularly in the case of mergers, the Harper Panel recommended retention of the requirement that a market be in Australia. It is, they concluded, 'necessary and appropriate for the term "market" to be defined as a market in Australia' because 'the CCA is concerned with the economic welfare of Australians' and 'the law is intended to protect competition in Australian markets for the benefit of Australian consumers'.[59]

It appears clear, however, that global or regional markets that include Australia can satisfy this requirement and that when assessing market power and competitive effects, the courts can consider constraints from imports or from other forces external to Australia.[60] In this respect, the Harper Report recommended strengthening the definition of 'competition' to remove any doubt that it includes competition from *potential* as well as existing imports[61]; this recommendation has been accepted and forms part of a current reform bill.[62]

### Two-Sided Markets

The ACCC recognises the two-sided nature of online platforms and their implications, evidenced in the recent review of Expedia's proposed acquisition of Wotif.[63]

---

[57] Idem, para 33.

[58] Harper Report, p. 315. Notably, these comments were made before the recent High Court decision in *Air New Zealand Ltd v ACCC; Pt Garuda Indonesia Ltd v ACCC* [2017] HCA 21, which adopted a broad and pragmatic approach to the concept of 'market in Australia'.

[59] Harper Report, p. 316.

[60] Section 4 of the CCA currently provides that competition 'includes competition from imported goods or from services rendered by persons not resident or not carrying on business in Australia'. The Harper Report stated that 'geographic boundaries of many markets extend beyond Australia' and in those circumstances 'a corporation that competes for the supply of goods or services in Australia does so in the broader geographic market' and any competition assessment 'must take account of those market realities' and has 'been recognised' in decisions of the courts: page 316.

[61] Harper Report, p. 317; recommendation 25.

[62] Bill 2017, Schedule 1, section 1, proposes that s 4 be amended to read: *competition* includes: (a) competition from goods that are, or are capable of being, imported into Australia; and (b) competition from services that are rendered, or are capable of being rendered, in Australia by persons not resident or not carrying on business in Australia'.

[63] Expedia Inc – proposed acquisition of Wotif.com Holdings Limited (ACCC Public Register, reference 55142,http://registers.accc.gov.au/content/index.phtml/itemId/1182044/fromItemId/751046 ('Expedia/Wotif') (accessed 6 June 2017).

The ACCC described the relevant product market in that case as being 'a two-sided market where positive network effects exist'.[64]

Although 'two-sided platforms can create unique challenges for competition agencies', it has been suggested that the existing Australian 'legislative framework has been sufficiently flexible to date in accommodating the consideration of two-sided platforms and the issues they create for market analyses'[65]:

> Issues arising in two-sided markets are assessed by the ACCC and dealt with under the [CCA] using an equivalent approach as toward other markets. This approach involves the ACCC defining the market/s under consideration in terms of product and geographic space and proceeding to consider the competitive constraints on the market.
>
> ... In the case of a two-sided platform, the ACCC first defines markets separately for each customer class, and considers the potential relevance of any indirect network effects as part of the subsequent competition analysis.[66]

### 2.3.2 Market Power

A necessary prerequisite to a contravention of the misuse of market power provision is a finding that the corporation in question has substantial market power. Market power, and changes in market power attributable to certain conduct, is also relevant to competition assessments in other parts of the CCA, particularly in relation to the merger law, where merger-related changes to market power are a particular concern.

Substantial market power for purposes of Australian law does not equate with dominance; importantly, the threshold was lowered to 'substantial market power' from the original threshold of substantial 'control' in 1986.[67] Legislation also makes clear that more than one corporation may have substantial market power in the same market.[68]

Assessment of market power has traditionally required an initial determination of the relevant market (or markets) prior to an assessment of whether or not the corporation in question has substantial market power within it.[69] However, it has

---

[64] ACCC, 'Expedia Inc – proposed acquisition of Wotif.com Holdings Limited', Public Competition Assessment, 13 January 2017, para 43 ('Expedia/Wotif PCA').

[65] OECD, 'Two-Sided Markets', Policy Roundtables, DAF/COMP(2009)20, 17 December 2009, p. 80.

[66] OECD, 'Two-Sided Markets', Policy Roundtables, DAF/COMP(2009)20, 17 December 2009, p. 79.

[67] The change was brought about following a recommendation to 'lower' the threshold. See *The Trade Practices Act: Proposals for Change* (Commonwealth of Australia, Green Paper, 1984) para 29. Section 46(3C) of the Act also makes clear that it is possible for a firm to have substantial market power even though it 'does not substantially control the market' or enjoy 'absolute freedom from constraint' by competitors, potential competitors or persons to whom it suppliers or acquires goods or services.

[68] Section 46(3D) CCA.

[69] See, eg, Rhonda Smith, Market definition and substitution options, (2014) 22 Competition & Consumer Law Journal 105 at 121.

also long been recognised by the courts that, in the context of the misuse of market power provisions, the object is to discover the degree of market power held by the defendant and that '[d]efining the market and assessing the degree of market power within it are part of the same process' and are separated only 'for the sake of simplicity of analysis'.[70] Consequently, although market definition will form an important part of an assessment of market power, it will not always be an essential step towards the court forming a preliminary view about whether or not a firm has substantial market power.[71]

The first High Court case to consider the concept of market power in relation to section 46 of CCA was *QWI*,[72] and the approach adopted in that case has been endorsed in subsequent decisions and by the ACCC, most recently in its MMP Framework (September 2016). Justice Dawson, in *QWI*, stated[73]:

> The term 'market power' is ordinarily taken to be a reference to the power to raise price by restricting output in a sustainable manner…But market power has aspects other than influence upon the market price. It may be manifested by practices directed at excluding competition such as exclusive dealing, tying arrangements, predatory pricing or refusal to deal… The ability to engage persistently in these practices may be as indicative of market power as the ability to influence price. Thus Kaysen and Turner define market power as follows:
>
> A firm possesses market power when it can behave persistently in a manner different from the behavior that a competitive market would enforce on a firm facing otherwise similar cost and demand conditions. …

A range of factors can influence the degree of competitive constraint faced by a firm and are likely to be relevant in assessing whether a firm has a substantial degree of market power. The structural factors considered relevant to this assessment were set out by the Tribunal in early *QCMA* decision:

(i) the number and size distribution of independent sellers, especially the degree of market concentration;
(ii) the height of barriers to entry, that is the ease with which new firms may enter and secure a viable market;
(iii) the extent to which the products of the industry are characterised by extreme product differentiation and sales promotion;
(iv) the character of 'vertical relationships' with customers and with suppliers and the extent of vertical integration; and
(v) the nature of any formal, stable and fundamental arrangements between firms that restrict their ability to function as independent entities.[74]

[70] *Queensland Wire Industries Pty Ltd v Broken Hill Pty Co Ltd* (1989) 167 CLR 177 [15] per Mason CJ and Wilson J.

[71] See, eg, Rhonda Smith, Market definition and substitution options, (2014) 22 Competition & Consumer Law Journal 105 at 121.

[72] *Queensland Wire Industries Pty Ltd v Broken Hill Pty Co Ltd* (1989) 167 CLR 177.

[73] *Queensland Wire Industries Pty Ltd v Broken Hill Pty Co Ltd* (1989) 167 CLR 177 at 200 (footnotes omitted).

[74] *Re Queensland Co-Op Milling Association Limited and Defiance Holdings Limited (QCMA)* (1976) 8 ALR 481, 515[40]; (1976) ATPR 40–012, 17,24.

These factors have regularly been endorsed by the courts, and some have found their way, through legislative amendments, into section 46, which now sets out a number of factors that must be considered when determining whether a corporation has substantial market power.[75]

Although the *QCMA* decision dates back to 1976 and focusses on static market structures, it is clear that the ACCC and courts consider dynamic market characteristics when making competition and market power assessments. For example, in relation to the review of Expedia's acquisition of Wotif, the level and pace of dynamic change in the market was a key factor in the ACCC's decision not to challenge the acquisition. Nevertheless, concerns remain in some quarters that the current approach by the ACCC and courts to market definition and assessment of market power continue to place too much reliance on static market definitions and existing levels of market concentration.[76]

## 2.4 Section 46 'Misuse of Market Power' in General

The CCA prohibits misuse of market power, which occurs when a corporation with substantial market power takes advantage of that power for a prohibited anti-competitive purpose.[77] The provision is of general application, and the recent Harper Review reinforced the principle that Australia's competition laws should have economy-wide application and not be directed towards the conduct of any specific sector.[78] Consistent with this approach, there are no 'safe harbours' or other presumptions in relation to the legality or otherwise of online platforms based on their nature or scope. There are also no formal (or informal) ACCC guidelines setting out likely treatment in relation to online platforms.[79]

Although there is currently no separate guidance for misuse of market power, it is clear that large online sales platforms will frequently feature firms with substantial market power, and there are some general principles that can be drawn from other cases to theorise how they might operate in relation to these platforms.

First, before conduct will contravene the provision, it is necessary to establish that the corporation holds 'substantial market power'. The process for making this assessment was set out above. Second, whether this conduct will be prohibited depends crucially on demonstration that the conduct was referable to the substantial

[75] See ss 46(3)–(3D) CCA.

[76] Harper Report, p. 317 referencing the Business Council of Australia's (BCA) draft report submission.

[77] As noted in Sect. 2.2.1, above, this test will change to a competition based test if Bill 2016 is passed.

[78] Harper Report, p. 307.

[79] The ACCC released *Platform Operators in the Sharing Economy: A guide for complying with the competition and consumer law in Australia* in 2016, available at https://www.accc.gov.au/publications/platform-operators-in-the-sharing-economy, '*Platform Operators in the Sharing Economy*'. However, this is a general guide covering competition and consumer issues and does not address the issue of misuse of market power directly.

market power (that it involved a 'taking advantage' of that power) and that the corporation had the purpose of '(a) eliminating or substantially damaging a competitor of the corporation or of a body corporate that is related to the corporation in that or any other market; (b) preventing the entry of a person into that or any other market; or (c) deterring or preventing a person from engaging in competitive conduct in that or any other market'.[80]

The take advantage element[81] has traditionally been the most problematic, and, although there have been no such cases, this would be equally true of cases involving online sales platforms. In particular, if a corporation lacking market power could engage in the conduct, or it would be commercially rational for them do so, then a firm with substantial market power will not be held to have 'taken advantage' of their market power, regardless of the competitive effect that might flow from the conduct. Types of conduct that could potentially fall within the scope of the provision include anti-competitive rebates, tying, bundling, exclusive dealing (or related sales distribution restrictions), predatory pricing[82] and price discrimination.[83]

### 2.4.1 Leveraging Market Power

For purposes of the misuse of market power provision, it is important to note that market power need not exist in the market in which the exclusion or other harm to competition is alleged to be taking place. Consequently, for example, a large supermarket with substantial market power in the retail grocery market can contravene the provision if it takes advantage (uses) that power for the purpose of harming competition or competitors in another market in which it lacks market power. This was the scenario in the *QWI* High Court case. BHP was found to have misused its market power by leveraging the substantial market power it held in the upstream market for steel products to reduce competition (and thereby aid its subsidiary) in the downstream market for rural fencing.[84] In this way, leveraging market power in one market to gain competitive advantage, either for itself or another entity (whether related or otherwise), in a market in which the corporation does not enjoy market power can be captured by the prohibition.

[80] Subsection 46(1) CCA.

[81] See generally Katharine Kemp, 'Taking Advantage' of Substantial Market Power, and Other Profit-Focused Tests for Unilateral Anticompetitive Conduct, (2015) 41(3) Monash University Law Review 655.

[82] Existing separate predatory pricing provision, based on market share and potentially problematic for two-sided platforms, is likely to be repealed.

[83] There was previously a separate price discrimination provision but it was repealed in 1195. Periodically there are calls to revive it but these have been repeatedly rejected, most recently by the Harper Panel (Harper Report, recommendation 31). Consequently, price discrimination is only unlawful if it satisfies the general conditions for misuse of market power.

[84] It did this by constructively refusing to supply the 'Y-Bar' steel product to downstream competitors of its wholly owned subsidiary, AWI, which prevented them making and supplying 'star picket fences' in competition with QWI's subsidiary.

## 2.4.2 Cases

There have been few section 46 cases, and none of those fully litigated have involved online sales platforms. However, there has been one case involving an online sales platform. In 2011, a consent decision was made in *Ticketek*,[85] in which Ticketek admitted that it had contravened the CCA. The nature of the consent decision, which involved parties agreeing to certain facts and conduct, means that it is not possible to evaluate the court's approach to online sales platforms. Ticketek agreed that it held a large share of the ticketing related service market; that there were barriers to entering into the market to provide 'full service' offerings, such as that provided by Ticketek to Venue Operators and Promoters[86]; that there was limited existing competitive constraint (with only one other large rival, Ticketmaster, operating at the time); and that, at the relevant time, Ticketek had a substantial degree of market power in the ticketing related service market. Ticketek also agreed that its conduct had been 'materially facilitated' by that market power and that therefore the 'take advantage' element had been satisfied and that the conduct had been engaged in for one of the prohibited purposes.

Despite the admissions resulting in reduced published competition analysis, the case does provide a useful example of a refusal to deal involving an online sales platform constituting a contravention of Australia's misuse of market power provision. Ticketek is an event ticketing company, claiming to host 'Australia's number one Entertainment Events website' and that it operates a 'market leading mobile platform' for sports and entertainment events.[87] In 2009, it refused requests by certain entertainment companies to implement in its ticketing system certain discounted prices to be published by a competitor, Lasttix Pty Ltd, for certain events. Lasttix, while promoting the sale of tickets, including publishing details of prices, did not have the capability or scale to provide full service in the way Ticketek did at the time.[88] The refusals were admitted by Ticketek and found to have been engaged in for the purpose of deterring or preventing Lasttix from engaging in competitive conduct in the 'Ticketing Related Service Market'.[89] Total penalties of AU$ 2.5 million were ordered against Ticketek, incorporating a substantial discount for their cooperation with the ACCC.

---

[85] *Australian Competition and Consumer Commission v Ticketek Pty Ltd* [2011] FCA 1489.

[86] *Australian Competition and Consumer Commission v Ticketek Pty Ltd* [2011] FCA 1489, para 70.

[87] Ticketek homepage (http://premier.ticketek.com.au/. Accessed 8 June 2017).

[88] Para 18. Lasttix's business was described in the Statement of Agreed Facts (para 24) as 'the business of supplying, or offering to supply, Ticketing Related Services in Australia to promote the sale of tickets. Lasttix's primary means of promoting the sale of tickets was through the provision of services to Promoters in relation to discount ticket offers for events through either the Lasttix or MyTickets businesses.' Those who chose tickets promoted by Lasttix would be re-directed to actually purchase the ticket elsewhere, such as Ticketek (para 26).

[89] *Australian Competition and Consumer Commission v Ticketek Pty Ltd* [2011] FCA 1489 (paras 1 and 2).

### 2.4.3 Review and Changes

**A Competition-Based Test**

The recent Harper Review considered whether or not the existing misuse of market power provisions should be amended to focus more directly on the effect of conduct rather than its purpose. The review panel concluded that the existing provision was not 'fit for purpose'[90] and recommended that it be repealed and replaced with a provision that would prohibit a corporation with substantial market power engaging in conduct having the purpose or effect of substantially lessening competition.[91] This recommendation was subsequently accepted by the government after further public consultation,[92] and the substance of the recommendation has been incorporated into Bill 2016. It will no longer be necessary to demonstrate a direct link between the market power held and the anti-competitive purpose or effect.

The ACCC will release guidelines to assist parties to determine whether or not their conduct is likely to contravene the Act. The ACCC released a draft *MMP Framework* in September 2016. The *MMP Framework* makes clear that the new provision will not alter the ACCC's approach to market definition or to assessing substantial market power and would not change its approach to analysing whether certain conduct substantially lessened competition.[93]

The *MMP Framework* identifies refusals to deal, predatory pricing, tying and bundling, and margin/price squeeze as types of conduct that may give rise to misuse of market power claims, and several examples of conduct that might constitute anti-competitive conduct of this nature are given; none specifically relate to online sales platforms. The *MMP Framework* also sets out conduct unlikely to raise concerns, including innovation, 'efficient conduct designed to drive down costs', price matching and 'responding efficiently to other forms of competition in the market such as product offering and terms of supply'.[94]

**Exemptions and Authorisation**

It is not currently possible for conduct that contravenes section 46 to be pre-authorised by the ACCC. The Harper Review recommended both that individual authorisation and block exemptions be available for section 46 conduct and other anti-competitive conduct. This would enable the ACCC to weigh public benefits, including efficiencies, against likely anti-competitive effects to determine whether proposed conduct should be authorised. Importantly, it is only possible to receive authorisation in advance of conduct taking place. Individual authorisation has been available for all other forms of conduct for decades but has not been available for the purpose-based misuse of market power provision. There are, therefore, a

[90] Harper Report, p. 347.

[91] Harper Report, recommendation 30.

[92] Treasury, Consultation on Competition Policy Review Final Report, 31 march 2015 and Treasury, Options to Strengthen the Misuse of Market Power Laws: Discussion Paper, 11 December 2015.

[93] MMP Framework (para 4.4).

[94] MMP Framework (para 4.7). None of these examples refer specifically to online platforms.

considerable number of successful authorisation applications that parties can look into to form a view about whether or not conduct is likely to be authorised.[95]

It has not, however, previously been possible to obtain 'block exemptions' for any categories of anti-competitive conduct under the CCA. If proposed changes are passed, it will be possible for the ACCC to create block exemptions for categories of conduct that are unlikely to substantially lessen competition or that are likely to produce public benefits (including through efficiencies) that would outweigh any anti-competitive detriment.[96] It is not clear whether, for example, the ACCC might consider that certain types of distribution arrangements by large firms might be considered to produce welfare-enhancing efficiencies such that they should benefit from block exemptions.

## 2.5 Integration

As the Deloitte Study pointed out, there is a growing trend of online sales platforms becoming vertically and horizontally integrated. This then 'raise[s] the prospect of any integrated platforms with market power using that market power to force or incentivise their suppliers and/or consumers to support the integrated business model, in order for the platform to maximise revenues'.[97]

### 2.5.1 Merger Law

Mergers, which include acquisitions of share or assets, are prohibited where they substantially lessen competition. There is no level of asset or share acquisition required in order to trigger the prohibition. As a consequence, non-controlling share or asset acquisition can contravene section 50 of CCA if they have the effect of substantially lessening competition.

Procedurally, there is no formal requirement to notify the ACCC of a proposed merger; however, in practice, parties proposing to merge typically notify the ACCC of the proposed merger, which is then informally reviewed by the ACCC to assess its likely impact on competition. The legality of mergers is rarely litigated, with merging parties generally withdrawing merger plans or modifying arrangements to satisfy the ACCC's concerns, if any.

When assessing whether the proposed acquisition is likely to substantially lessen competition, the ACCC compares the likely future competitive environment with the proposed acquisition to the likely future without the acquisition.[98] As noted

[95] The ACCC does not provide any guidance in its *draft Framework*, but indicates that guidance 'on the implementation of the revised authorisation test will be provided in the final s 46 guidelines' (para 5.1).

[96] Harper Report, recommendation 39.

[97] Deloitte Study, p. 22.

[98] Expedia/Wotif PCA, para 31 and Merger Guidelines, para 3.16.

above, the term 'substantial' has been interpreted as meaning 'real or of substance',[99] although the ACCC has noted that the 'precise threshold between a lessening of competition and a substantial lessening of competition is a matter of judgement and will always depend on the particular facts of the merger under investigation. Generally, the ACCC takes the view that a lessening of competition is substantial if it confers an increase in market power on the merged firm that is significant and sustainable. For example, a merger will substantially lessen competition if it results in the merged firm being able to significantly and sustainably increase prices.'[100]

In the context of mergers, online sales platforms have been considered as new and disruptive technologies with relatively low barriers to entry with the result that significant mergers have been permitted. One of the most prominent merger reviews involving online platforms took place in 2014, when the ACCC considered a proposed acquisition by Expedia of Wotif, both online travel agents (OTAs). Wotif was an Australian company[101] that derived the vast majority of its revenue from the supply of online accommodation booking services[102] and had, at one time, been the leading online travel agent in Australia.[103] Wotif had, however, 'lost its position' as the leading Australian OTA, with its shares declining, at the same time Booking.com experienced 'significant growth' to become Australia's largest OTA at the time.[104] Expedia was, and remains, a leading global OTA. Combined with Booking.com, they represented the top three OTAs in Australia, with smaller OTAs not generally considered a 'significant source of bookings' by accommodation providers.[105]

The ACCC undertook market inquiries and expressed the preliminary view that the acquisition may raise competition concerns in the 'market for the online distribution/booking of Australian competition'; in particular, the ACCC was concerned that the acquisition may increase the commission rates charged by Expedia to accommodation providers in Australia and reduce the amount of promotional opportunities offered by online travel agents to accommodation providers within Australia.[106] The ACCC also indicated, however that the merger was unlikely to raise competition concerns on the 'consumer side of the two-sided market for the online

[99] Trade Practices Legislation Amendment Bill 1992, explanatory memorandum, para 12, as cited in *Merger Guidelines*, para 3.5.

[100] *Merger Guidelines,* para 3.5.

[101] Wotif promotes the fact that it was 'founded in a Brisbane garage' and has 'heaps of local knowledge' (Wofit homepage, www.wotif.com, accessed 6 June 2017).

[102] It also supplied booking services for flights and other travel products.

[103] See, eg, Jamie Freed, Why the ACCC approved the Expedia purchase of Wofif, Australian Financial Review, 15 January 2015, http://www.afr.com/it-pro/why-the-accc-approved-the-expedia-purchase-of-wotif-20150114-12qneo (accessed 6 June 2017).

[104] Expedia/Wotif PCA, paras 64 and 65.

[105] Expedia/Wotif PCA, para 60.

[106] Expedia/Wotif PCA, para 28.

distribution/booking of Australian accommodation'[107] or the market for the online distribution of air travel or other travel products.[108]

After receiving further submissions in response to its initial concerns, the ACCC concluded that the acquisition was unlikely to substantially lessen competition.[109] Despite not challenging the merger, the ACCC released a 'Public Competition Assessment' setting out the reasons for its decision. As part of its assessment, the ACCC considered a number of markets, most significantly the market for the 'online distribution/booking of Australian accommodation', which was described by the ACCC as a 'two-sided market where positive network effects exist'.[110] It was, the ACCC concluded, the 'eyeballs' generated by the OTAs through their investment that were considered of value to accommodation providers, with the result that the ACCC focussed on the supplier rather than consumer side of the market when assessing competitive effects.

Applying the HMT and the SSNIP test, the ACCC concluded that brick-and-mortar stores were not in the same market as online channels because 'accommodation providers are unlikely to switch enough inventory from online channels to bricks and mortar travel agents to make a small but significant increase in online distribution costs [commission rates] unprofitable'.[111] This was largely because a significant portion of consumers expressed a 'preference for comparing a wide range of accommodation providers', assessing traveller reviews and the convenience of booking online and that they did not consider brick-and-mortar travel agents a close substitute for OTAs.[112] Conversely, customers who typically purchased from travel agencies valued the planning and advice services they offered and were unlikely to switch to online channels.

OTAs did, however, compete with hotels that could restrict rooms offered through OTAs and adopt strategies to channel customers directly to them to avoid the commission fee.[113] In addition, while 'metasearch sites' were not considered in the same market, the ACCC observed that they 'increasingly compete with OTAs for consumer eyeballs'[114] and were 'important to the competitive' market dynamic because they 'provide an expanding avenue for accommodation providers to bypass OTAs and transact directly with consumers'.[115]

---

[107] Expedia/Wotif PCA, para 29.

[108] Ibid.

[109] The acquisition, worth AU$703, subsequently took place (http://www.wotif.com/vc/media/corporate-news-and-innovation/expedia-inc-completes-acquisition-wotif-group-266 (accessed 8 June 2017)).

[110] Expedia/Wotif PCA, para 43.

[111] Expedia/Wotif PCA, para 49.

[112] Expedia/Wotif PCA, para 49.

[113] Expedia/Wotif PCA, para 54.

[114] Even where they do not 'currently provide a booking function in their own right', but rather 'connect consumers to an OTA or other site' (Expedia/Wotif PCA, para 56).

[115] Expedia/Wotif PCA, para 56.

In relation to its competition evaluation, the ACCC noted that, despite Wotif's decline in market share, many industry participants considered Wotif a 'vigorous and effective competitor'; in particular, it offered lower rates of commission compared with Expedia and Booking.com.[116] Wotif also enjoyed brand awareness, as the first major Australian OTA, and had more hotels in Australia listed than any other OTA.[117] Concern was expressed that Expedia and Booking.com would increase their commission rates post-acquisition when the competitive constraint imposed by Wotif was removed.[118]

Nevertheless, the ACCC noted that the industry was highly dynamic and that, in recent years, meta-search engines had emerged that imposed a 'significant competitive threat to OTAs',[119] with some, like TripAdvisor, incorporating features resembling the services of an OTA. The various 'innovative commercial responses to consumer demand for online booking facilities'[120] was considered likely to continue with the 'pace and breadth' of new methods for online distribution strongly suggesting 'that it is a dynamically competitive market'.[121] The proposed acquisition was considered unlikely to 'impede the degree of dynamic change in the market'.[122]

The ACCC observed that barriers for a new entrant to achieve sufficient scale to compete with Expedia, Wotif or Booking.com would be high and would include significant sunk costs in the form of advertising.[123] However, the ACCC observed that recent changes to the market, which included consideration of significant global players, like Amazon, that might have the ability to overcome those barriers, combined with developments in adjacent markets, such as meta-search platforms like TripAdvisor and Google, would ensure that the market remained dynamic and there would be significant competitive constraints on OTA incumbents.[124]

---

[116] Expedia/Wotif PCA, para 58.

[117] Expedia/Wotif PCA, para 61.

[118] Expedia/Wotif PCA, para 62.

[119] Expedia/Wotif PCA, para 83: meta-search websites help consumers bypass OTAs that increase 'the ability of accommodation providers to reduce their reliance on the major OTAs' and obtain a 'greater proportion of bookings directly' (para 81).

[120] Expedia/Wotif PCA, para 76.

[121] Expedia/Wotif PCA, para 77.

[122] Ibid.

[123] The ACCC concluded that 'a new OTA would be able to access a sufficient volume of hotel inventory to enter the market as accommodation providers generally have an incentive to distribute their inventory across a wide range of platforms to access as many potential consumers as possible' and this is 'facilitated by channel managers' – but, acknowledges that 'a new OTA would face significant costs in engaging a sufficient number of staff to approach, enter contracts and maintain relationships with these accommodation providers' (para 88) – there would be significant sunk costs through advertising (Expedia/Wotif PCA, para 89) and this may present a barrier to an OTA 'achieving a sufficient scale to constrain the incumbents' (Expedia/Wotif PCA, para 89). In current form ACCC accepted there may be significant barriers to entry or expansion to compete with Wotif, Expedia or Booking.com.

[124] Expedia/Wotif PCA, 41 PCA.

Although the ACCC conceded that there was potential for Expedia to 'raise commission rates to accommodation providers post-acquisition',[125] the ACCC also concluded that the dynamic nature of the market meant that accommodation providers would have opportunities to reduce reliance on OTAs, and this would restrict the ability of the OTAs to increase commissions.[126]

### 2.5.2 Bottleneck Issue: National Access Regime Law and Section 46

A law dealing with the essential facility doctrine could also be relevant to online sales platform. For instance, an online platform can act as an essential facility for suppliers because a duplicated online platform does not attract customers to the same extent as does the original, established platform with specific innovative features.[127] Thus, a specific online platform can behave as a monopolist (or, at least, an entity with significant market power).[128] However, as we explain below, the Australian specific law dealing with essential facilities, the national access regime law, will not apply to this example for a number of reasons, including the fact that duplication of an online platform is both possible and not 'uneconomical'.

Australia does not apply the essential facility doctrine in the same way as, for instance, the United States of America. In general, section 46 (misuse of market power) deals with situations where a natural monopolist and/or an owner of a bottleneck in a bottleneck industry misuses its market power, for example, in the form of a refusal to supply or provide access. This section has been used successfully in such situations in the past.[129]

Nevertheless, since the enactment of the *Competition Policy Reform Act 1995* (Cth), which amended the CCA, Australia has also made provision for the regulation of 'essential facilities' markets. This takes the form of both generic and industry-specific access regimes,[130] which provide a mechanism for entities operating in upstream or downstream 'dependent markets' to obtain access to essential facilities in some situations. In the context of online sales platforms, it will be difficult to obtain access via this regime.[131] The primary mechanism for obtaining such

[125] Expedia/Wotif PCA, 92 PCA.

[126] Expedia/Wotif PCA, 81 PCA.

[127] See, e.g., A Ezrachi and M. E. Stucke, *Virtual Competition – The Promise and Perils of the Algorithm Driven Economy*, Harvard University Press 2016; Martyn Taylor, Competition Law in High Technology Industries: Insights for Australia', Competition Law Conference, Sydney, 30 May 2015.

[128] For instance, Google search engine; Facebook, Amazon.

[129] *NT Power Generation Pty Ltd v Power and Water Authority* (2004) 219 CLR 90; *Queensland Wire Industries v Broken Hill Proprietary Co Ltd* (1989) 167 CLR 177.

[130] The industry-specific access regimes include a telecommunications access regime, contained in Pt XIC of the CCA and the *Telecommunications Act 1997* (Cth).

[131] Indeed, the generic access regime was drafted in the mid-1990s, well before the rapid development of the digital world and it has never been used in connection with the digital economy, in particular, online sales platforms.

access is to have a service 'declared', after which negotiation for access can take place. The first hurdle is to establish that there is a service. Although the definition of service in section 44B includes 'a communications service or similar service',[132] which could capture online sales platforms, the 'supply of goods',[133] 'the use of intellectual property'[134] and 'the use of a production process'[135] are expressly excluded from the definition of 'service' for the purposes of the access regime. As online sales platforms frequently involve the supply of goods, and this is excluded from the scope of the access regime, the circumstances in which the regime will apply are quite limited.

In addition, before a service can be declared, five criteria must be satisfied, including the following:

(a) that access… would promote a material increase in competition in at least one dependent market…;
(b) that it would be uneconomical for anyone to develop another facility to provide the service;
(c) that the 'facility is of national significance, having regard to: (i) the size…; or (ii) the importance… to trade or commerce; or (iii) the importance of the facility to the national economy;
(d) [that it is not already subject to a certified access regime (this may be the case if individual states have provided access to a facility) and]
(e) that access (or increased access) to the service would not be contrary to the public interest'.[136]

Of these, the second (that it would be uneconomical to duplicate) and the third (that it be of national significance) are likely to be the greatest hurdles in relation to online sales platforms. It will generally not be 'uneconomical' to duplicate online sales platforms.[137]

[132] Section 44B(c) CCA.

[133] Section 44B(d) CCA.

[134] Section 44B(e) CCA.

[135] Section 44B(f) CCA.

[136] Section 44H(4) CCA.

[137] Precisely what measure of 'uneconomical' is used for this purpose has been the subject of extensive litigation and several reviews. This criterion has been interpreted in different ways by the courts. The current interpretation is based on a 'private profitability test' where the word 'uneconomical' means 'unprofitable' and the criterion would be satisfied if it is not profitable for anyone including the owner of the existing facility to duplicate it: *The Pilbara Infrastructure Pty Ltd v Australian Competition Tribunal* [2012] HCA 36; *Pilbara Infrastructure Pty Ltd v Australian Competition Tribunal* [2011] FCAFC 58; *Re Fortescue Metals Group Limited* [2010] ACompT 2; *Re Duke Eastern Gas Pipeline Pty Ltd* [2001] ACompT 2; *Re Sydney International Airport* (2000) ATPR ¶ 41-754 at 40, 793. The Harper Review and Productivity Commission Review (Productive Commission 2013, *National Access Regime*, Inquiry Report No 66 (Canberra), p. 160) recommended that the test be refused to one of 'natural monopoly', which is reflected in the Bill 2017. If passed, the criterion will assess the facility 'used 'to provide the service could meet the total foreseeable demand in the market' over the declaration period 'at the least cost compared to any 2 or more facilities' (proposed s 44CA, Bill 2017).

It is also likely to be difficult to demonstrate that an online platform is of 'national significance', although there may be some instances in which the 'volume of commerce' associated with the platform may be sufficient to satisfy this criterion.

There are, as a result, likely to be limited circumstances in which a third party can obtain access to an online sales platform by way of Australia's generic access regime. However, it is important to recall that the general prohibition on misuse of market power may also be contravened where a corporation takes advantage of a bottleneck created by their online sales platform to prevent or deter competition. This was usefully demonstrated in the case of *ASX v Pont Data*,[138] discussed in the next section.

### 2.5.3 Exclusionary Conduct and Exclusive Dealing: Control over Digital Information

The competition law case of *ASX v Pont Data* was discussed in the Productivity Commission's research paper on 'Digital Disruption'[139] as an example of the recognition in Australia 'that commercial controls over the flow of computerised information can breach competition law'.[140] In this case, ASX's restrictive contractual conditions preventing Pont Data from reselling electronic information and imposing a new fee structure were held to have contravened section 46 (misuse of market power).[141]

This case is important for considering potential anti-competitive conduct in connection with online sales platforms for a number of reasons, including the following:

- It establishes that digital flow of information can constitute a relevant market.
- In that context, any ownership and trading with digitalised information is important for determining the relevant market and potentially market power.
- It also illustrates and proves the points of vertical integration and bottlenecks in online sales, as introduced and discussed above.

ASX is an Australian public company that operates the Australian Securities Exchange (at the time of the case known as the Australian Stock Exchange). At the relevant time, it had a legislated monopoly on share clearing in Australia. It also operates in another relevant market—'an "information market" – for the supply of

[138] *ASX Operations Pty Ltd v Pont Data Australia Pty Ltd (No 2)* (1990) 21 FCR 385, appealed (1991) 27 FCR 492; *ASX Operations Pty Ltd v Pont Data Australia Pty Ltd (No 1)* (1990) 27 FCR 26, (1990) 27 FCR 460 at 486.

[139] Australian Government Productivity Commission, Digital Disruption: What do government need to do?, Research Paper, June 2016, pp. 60–61, available at http://www.pc.gov.au/research/completed/digital-disruption ('Digital Disruption'). The Productivity Commission provides independent research and advice to the Australian Government.

[140] Digital Disruption, p. 61.

[141] *ASX Operations Pty Ltd v Pont Data Australia Pty Ltd (No 2)* (1991) 27 FCR 492 at 486.

information about activities on stock exchanges'.[142] In this case, the information market was divided into upstream wholesale market, where ASX had substantial market power, and downstream retail market, where ASX competed, via its subsidiary JECNET, with other retailers, including Pont Data. The upstream market was a bottleneck market, as the wholesale information was essential for operation in the dependent downstream market. In that regard, the Federal Court pointed out that '...wholesaling activities, actual or potential, are to be seen as an important feature or element in the information market as understood in this case'.[143] Thus, ASX was a vertically integrated entity operating in the dependent market via its subsidiary JECNET.

The facts presented in the court showed that JECNET had not been successful. In particular, it had lost money for several years and had been described in an internal report as 'poorly regarded'.[144] Pont Data, on the other hand, had been making a profit on the downstream market. ASX decided to address that situation by leveraging its power in the upstream market into the dependent downstream retail market for the sale of information. It did this by forcing Pont Data and others to sign a new contract that included a restriction on the resale of information and an increase of the wholesale price. Pont Data alleged that this conduct amounted to ASX subsidising its unsuccessful business, JECNET, and that this had an adverse impact on JECNET's competitors and contravened both section 46 (misuse of market power) and section 47 (exclusive dealing).[145] On appeal, the Full Federal Court upheld the decision at first instance that

> [ASX] took advantage of market power for the purpose of deterring the retail competitors of JECNET from engaging in competitive conduct, by imposition of the fee structure in the agreements, as well as by imposing other terms in the agreements and by requiring a tripartite form for the Dynamic Agreement.[146]

In reaching its decision, the court made clear that merely charging monopolistic prices is not anti-competitive[147]; Australia's misuse of market power provision is focussed on exclusionary and not exploitative conduct. However, in this case, ASX was a vertically integrated entity, and evidence demonstrated that the imposition of the higher fees was designed to prevent its competitors from competing, was not justified by any increase of cost and was not applied to JECNET, with the result that JECNET's competitors were discriminated against.[148]

As a result, ASX was held to have contravened both section 46 and section 47, the latter of which required demonstration that the conduct did, in fact, have the purpose or effect of substantially lessening competition. This implies that the same

[142] *ASX Operations Pty Ltd v Pont Data Australia Pty Ltd (No 2)* (1990) 21 FCR 385 at 412.
[143] *ASX Operations Pty Ltd v Pont Data Australia Pty Ltd (No 2)* (1990) 27 FCR 460, at 462.
[144] *ASX Operations Pty Ltd v Pont Data Australia Pty Ltd (No 2)* (1990) 27 FCR 460 (para 6).
[145] *ASX Operations Pty Ltd v Pont Data Australia Pty Ltd (No 2)* (1990) 21 FCR 385 at 409.
[146] *ASX Operations Pty Ltd v Pont Data Australia Pty Ltd (No 1)* (1990) 27 FCR 460 at 486.
[147] *ASX Operations Pty Ltd v Pont Data Australia Pty Ltd (No 2)* (1991) 27 FCR 492 at 502.
[148] *ASX Operations Pty Ltd v Pont Data Australia Pty Ltd (No 2)* (1990) 21 FCR 385 at 418.

situation could also contravene the proposed section 46, contained in Bill 2016, which applies the same competition test.

## 2.6 Bargaining Power

### 2.6.1 Section 46 'Misuse of Market Power' and Bargaining Power

A corporation with significant bargaining power can contravene section 46 by demanding a most-favoured-nation clause from suppliers. This was demonstrated in the case of *Safeway.*[149] Safeway was the largest supermarket chain and the largest bread retailer in Victoria (the second most populous state in Australia). The relevant market was the market 'for the sale and acquisition of bread by wholesale in Victoria'.[150] Safeway's conduct, which involved refusing to acquire bread from a supplier if the supplier sold bread for less to another buyer, was held to constitute a misuse of market power. In order to find a contravention, the court was required to find that Safeway held substantial market power and that it had taken advantage of that power for an anti-competitive purpose.

In relation to the first of these requirements, the Full Court of the Federal Court of Australia found that significant 'monopsony power' satisfies the requirement of significant market power and, in this case, could be determined by Safeway's ability to secure more favourable terms of purchase than competing buyers, including the best prices from its suppliers.[151] The court explained that despite the fact that Safeway was not always successful in forcing the best price policy upon its suppliers, it had substantial market power because it was able to reduce the quantity sold by the plant bakers concerned. Indeed, due to its bargaining power, it was able to effectively increase the pressure on plant bakers to comply with Safeway's price condition because there was not another retailer (or retailers) to whom they could supply all of their products.[152]

In relation to the second requirement, Safeway's refusal to buy if the supplier in question was selling for less to another retailer constituted taking advantage of Safeway's substantial power. Finally, it was done with the prohibited purpose of deterring or preventing a person from engaging in competitive conduct[153]; in particular, Safeway had the purpose of deterring or preventing its suppliers (plant bakers) and certain of the independent retailers to whom those plant bakers supplied from engaging in competitive conduct in the form of discounting.[154]

---

[149] *ACCC v Australian Safeway Stores Pty Ltd* (2003) 129 FCR 339.

[150] Ibid, at [297].

[151] Ibid, at [300].

[152] Ibid, at [314]–[315], [323].

[153] Section 46(1)(c).

[154] See ibid, at [335]–[346].

### 2.6.2 Collective Bargaining

Entities, most likely suppliers, dealing with an online sales platform that possesses (significant) bargaining power can utilise the provisions in the CCA allowing for collective bargaining notification[155] or authorisation.[156] These processes are designed to allow smaller vertical participants, with minimal bargaining power on the vertical chain, to negotiate their conditions collectively without infringing the cartel laws. In the case of notification, collective bargaining can take place on the condition that the small businesses involved notify the ACCC and that the ACCC does not object to that notification for the reason that any public benefit likely to result from the conduct would not outweigh the anti-competitive detriment associated with the notified conduct. Alternatively, a group of small suppliers or buyers can apply to the ACCC for the authorisation of their agreement to bargain collectively. Unlike notification, which will result in the conduct being allowed to take place unless the ACCC objects, collective bargaining authorisations require the ACCC to make a positive finding that the collective bargaining proposed would result in a benefit to the public and that that benefit would outweigh any lessening of competition likely to flow from the conduct.

The collective bargaining notification and authorisation provisions have been used in practice,[157] although typically in relation to traditional markets rather than online platforms.[158] A recent example including sales platforms that was not successful involved the 2016 application by five Australian banks for authorisation to enter into collective bargaining with Apple, regarding access to the Apple Pay platform and the Near-Field Communication (NFC) controller in Apple's iPhone devices.[159] The ACCC decided in March 2017 that the public benefit claimed by the banks, such as increased innovation and investment in digital wallets, increased consumer choice in digital wallets and mobile payments and increased adoption of mobile payment technology in Australia, did not outweigh the potential distortion in the competitive application of new technology by the banks. Granting authorisation, the ACCC concluded, could 'reduce the competitive tension between the banks for

[155] Part VII, Division 2, Subdivision B of division 2 CCA.

[156] Part VII, Division 1 CCA.

[157] The Harper Report notes that 'the provisions are not being used as frequently as they might', at p. 86.

[158] For example, in 2016 a group of dairy farmers notified the ACCC that it intended to collectively bargain in relation to terms and conditions of raw milk supply arrangements with Woolworths (a major supermarket) and Milk2Market Pty Ltd. The notification was allowed to stand, with the ACCC indicating that it considered the likely public benefit associated with the arrangement would outweigh any anti-competitive detriment. Manning Valley Dairy Farmers – Collective Bargaining Notifications – CB00326 and CB00327 (ACCC collective bargaining notifications register, http://registers.accc.gov.au/content/index.phtml/itemId/1194750/fromItemId/815577).

[159] Available at http://registers.accc.gov.au/content/index.phtml/itemId/1197444/fromItemId/401858.

the supply of different payment options to consumers and may distort competition between the mobile operating systems'.[160]

### 2.6.3 Bargaining Power and Consumer Law

The Australian Consumer Law (ACL)[161] compliments and sometimes overlaps with the Australian competition law. The ACL is particularly important in relation to online sales platforms. Although, historically, penalties have been much more limited for consumer rather than competition law breaches under the CCA, recent reviews of the ACL have recommended significant increases to these penalties.[162]

Broadly, the ACL prohibits misleading or deceptive conduct and false or misleading representation, unconscionable conduct and unfair contract terms. They also impose mandatory consumer guarantees on suppliers. The ACCC has developed Guidance for platform operators focussing predominantly on the consumer law in the CCA.[163]

**Unconscionable Conduct**

The unconscionable conduct prohibition in the ACL is the one most likely to overlap with the competition provisions of the CCA and, at times, appears to have been used as an alternative to a misuse of market power claim.[164] It prohibits a person that supplies or acquires goods or services from engaging in conduct that is, 'in all the circumstances, unconscionable'.[165] Factors that the court may have regard to when

[160] ACCC, ACCC denies authorisation for banks to collectively bargain with Apple and boycott Apple Pay'(media release, 31/3/2017), available at https://www.accc.gov.au/media-release/accc-denies-authorisation-for-banks-to-collectively-bargain-with-apple-and-boycott-apple-pay.

[161] The Australian Consumer Law is contained in Schedule 2 of the CCA. For constitutional reasons it operates federally and within Australian territories via the CCA and within Australian states via state enabling legislation.

[162] Commonwealth of Australia, Australian Consumer Law Review: Final Report, Consumer Affairs Australia and New Zealand (CAANZ), 19 April 2017) (recommending that the maximum penalties be aligned with breaches of the competition provisions (p 87)); Productivity Commission, Consumer Law Enforcement and Administration, Research Report, March 2017, available at http://www.pc.gov.au/inquiries/completed/consumer-law/report/consumer-law.pdf (agreeing with the CAANZ review that 'there is a strong case for increasing maximum financial penalties for breaches of the ACL' (p 11) and finding that '[m]aximum financial penalties available under the ACL are small relative to the benefits that a business can accrue by breaching the ACL' (finding 4.5, p 143)).

[163] *Platform Operators in the Sharing Economy.*

[164] See, eg, A. Merrett, ACCC signals strategic change in battle with supermarkets, The Conversation, 6 May 2014, https://theconversation.com/accc-signals-strategic-change-in-battle-with-supermarkets-26288, suggesting that the 'facts upon which the case is based could have been framed as a misuse of market power'.

[165] Section 21 ACL. Where section 21 does not apply the ACL also prohibits a person engaging in unconscionable conduct 'within the meaning of the unwritten law' (section 20). This is typically more difficult to demonstrate and is less relevant in the context of online sales platforms.

making this assessment include the relative bargaining power of the supplier and customer, whether 'undue influence or pressure was exerted on, or any unfair tactics were used against, the customer'; 'the extent to which the supplier was willing to negotiate terms'; the terms themselves and the conduct engaged in after the contract was entered into; and the extent to which the parties 'acted in good faith'.[166]

The most prominent case involving unconscionable conduct was decided in 2014, with the Federal Court declaring that Coles, one of Australia's two major supermarket chains, had engaged in unconscionable conduct in its dealings with certain suppliers. In the course of her judgment, Justice Gordon observed:

> Coles' misconduct was serious, deliberate and repeated. Coles misused its bargaining power. Its conduct was 'not done in good conscience'. It was contrary to conscience. Coles treated its suppliers in a manner not consistent with acceptable business and social standards which apply to commercial dealings. Coles demanded payments from suppliers to which it was not entitled by threatening harm to the suppliers that did not comply with the demand. Coles withheld money from suppliers it had no right to withhold.
>
> Coles' practices, demands and threats were deliberate, orchestrated and relentless.

Although the circumstances in which conduct will become unconscionable will always be open to debate, it is not difficult to imagine how the prohibition might operate in relation to online sales platforms, particularly when large and dominant platforms impose strict conditions on their much smaller suppliers. In those circumstances, the ACCC may prefer to bring an action under the broader unconscionable conduct law than the misuse of market power law.

**Misleading Conduct**

The ACL contains broad and strict prohibitions on misleading conduct[167] and false advertising.[168] Most significantly, section 18 of ACL, which is among the most litigated provision in Australia,[169] provides that '[a] person must not, in trade or commerce, engage in conduct that is misleading or deceptive or is likely to mislead or deceive'.

Any conduct, including formal advertising, as well as labelling, imagery, statements and even silence, can contravene the prohibition if it creates a false impression about the product or service. In relation to online platforms, this is likely to take the form of false advertising about the quality or price of the product or service

---

[166] Section 22 ACL. The same considerations apply if the party accused of unconscionable conduct is an acquirer of goods or services rather than a supplier: section 22(2).

[167] Section 18 ACL.

[168] Section 29 ACL.

[169] It is clearly the most litigated provision in the CCA: see, eg, S. Seah, Unfulfilled Promissory Contractual Terms and Section 52 of the Australian Trade Practices Act [2000] *MurUEJL* 33 (the Act was renamed the Competition and Consumer Act and the development of the Australian Consumer Law resulted in section 52 being repealed and replaced by s 12 of the Australian Consumer Law; the prohibition remains substantively the same and its reputation as most litigated has not changed).

being advertised. This might include false product reviews.[170] The provision cannot be excluded, and it is not possible to rely on small print or disclaimers to avoid the operation of the provision.

One area in which online platforms may risk contravening the law is in relation to 'drip pricing', in which various fees and charges are displayed only incrementally. This practice has been held to constitute misleading conduct under section 18 of ACL, most notably in relation to the airlines Jetstar and Virgin Australia.[171] In addition to possibly constituting misleading conduct, 'drip pricing' may also contravene the ACL if an online sales platform promotes a price that represents only part of the price, without also including the total price at least as prominently (known as 'component pricing').[172] The single price advertised must include, for example, any tax, duty, fee, levy or other charge. Consequently, for example, an online platform selling airfares must not advertise a fare that excludes airport taxes, and a car sales site must not advertise a price that excludes mandatory delivery costs, unless the total price is also displayed at least as prominently.

Importantly, although contained in the ACL, the prohibition on misleading conduct is not restricted to conduct that misleads consumers. Consequently, a business misled by the conduct of another business may bring a claim under the provision or, perhaps more commonly, rely on the provision as a defence to a breach of contract claim. Component pricing, on the other hand, applies only to the supply or promotion of goods or services 'ordinarily acquired for personal, domestic or household use or consumption'.[173] This would, however, apply to the majority of sales made through online sales platforms.

---

[170] See ACCC, Managing online reviews, https://www.accc.gov.au/business/advertising-promoting-your-business/managing-online-reviews. Accessed 8 June 2017) observing that it considers 'encouraging family and friends' to write favourable reviews without disclosing their personal connection, writing poor reviews on other websites which 'do not reflect a genuinely held opinion' and soliciting others to write reviews about your business, or another business, when they have not experienced the good or service, to constitute misleading conduct. Failure to remove reviews known to be fake may also be misleading. See also R. Walker and R. Healy, Triple A Rated? Regulating Online Information Disclosures (2017) 25 AJCCL 4 (pp 10–11).

[171] See ACCC, 'Court finds that Jetstar and Virgin Australia engaged in misleading 'drip pricing' practices' (Media Release, 17 November 2015, https://www.accc.gov.au/media-release/court-finds-that-jetstar-and-virgin-australia-engaged-in-misleading-drip-pricing-practices). See also J. Clarke and P. Clarke, Jetstar and Virgin caught out for overlooking mobile commerce, The Conversation, 20 November 2015, https://theconversation.com/jetstar-and-virgin-caught-out-for-overlooking-mobile-commerce-50907) and R. Walker and R. Healy, Triple A Rated? Regulating Online Information Disclosures (2017) 25 AJCCL 4 (pp 8–9).

[172] Section 48 ACL.

[173] Ibid.

**Unfair Terms**
Consumers and, more recently, small businesses[174] enjoy legislative protection from unfair terms in standard form contracts.[175] Where major platforms deal with multiple small businesses through standard form contracts, this is likely to be particularly relevant. The ACL renders a term of a consumer or small business contract void if it is 'unfair' and contained in a standard form contract. A term is considered unfair if '(a) it would cause a significant imbalance in the parties' rights and obligations arising under the contract; and (b) it is not reasonably necessary in order to protect the legitimate interests of the party who would be advantaged by the term; and (c) it would cause detriment (whether financial or otherwise) to a party if it were to be applied or relied on'.[176]

**Consumer Guarantees**
The ACL also imposes guarantees on suppliers in relation to goods or services supplied to consumers. They cannot be excluded and apply to anyone selling goods or services, including platform operators.[177] The key guarantees are that goods are of acceptable quality,[178] that they will be fit for any purpose made known to the supplier,[179] that they will match any description of the goods provided by the supplier[180] and, in relation to services, that they will be rendered with due care and skill.[181]

## 2.7 Vertical Restraints: RPM and Exclusive Dealings

The Deloitte Study on the sharing economy and the recent EU Study on online platforms both recognised that there are incentives for vertical restraints to be applied in connection with online platforms and the sharing economy. This includes situations where a particular online platform[182] does not have significant market power. For instance, the Deloitte Study identified two common ways of imposing vertical restraints taking the form of exclusive practices:

---

[174] Since 12 November 2016. To be a small business contract, at the time it was entered into at least one party must employ fewer than 20 people and either (a) the upfront price must not exceed $300,000 or (b) if the contract operates for more than 12 months, the upfront price payable does not exceed $1,000,000 (Australian Consumer Law, section 23).

[175] Australian Consumer Law section 23. Section 27 provides that a contract is presumed to be a standard form contract unless demonstrated otherwise.

[176] Section 24 ACL.

[177] Supplier is defined as the person who supplied the goods.

[178] Section 54 ACL.

[179] Section 55 ACL.

[180] Section 54 ACL.

[181] Section 61 ACL.

[182] For the purposes of this chapter, an online sales platform.

1. Exclusive practices are imposed by traditional businesses because of a lack of regulatory neutrality: because fewer regulations are applied to online sales platform than to traditional businesses, the traditional businesses can be motivated to 'engage in anti-competitive conduct [such as protecting their territories and exclusive distribution] in order to maintain market share'.[183]
2. Exclusive practices are imposed by online sales platforms: 'sharing platforms could impose exclusivity on users of the platform, especially suppliers'.[184]

Australian competition law treats vertical restraints as unilateral practices. This includes not only misuse of market power (section 46) involving the imposition of restrictions on the conduct of buyers or sellers but also restraints imposed by corporations that lack any significant market power, including resale price maintenance (section 48), which is prohibited *per se*, and exclusive dealing (47), which is prohibited when it has the purpose or effect of substantially lessening competition.[185]

In relation to horizontal concerns, it is possible that vertical distribution arrangements may be found to constitute cartel conduct where the parties involved are found to be competitors or potential competitors in a relevant market. Importantly, this might extend to principal/agent arrangements, common in relation to online sales platforms. In this respect, the High Court recently confirmed that, in appropriate circumstances, principals may be found to be 'in competition' with their agents for sales and that, as a result, agreements between them might fall within the scope of the cartel laws.[186] The issue of principal and agent is discussed further in Sect. 2.8, below.

### 2.7.1 RPM

Resale price maintenance (RPM) is *per se* illegal under section 48. Part VIII, sections 96 to 100, then sets specific rules on RPM.[187] Part VIII, section 96(3), defines RPM for purposes of the prohibition, making clear that it applies to minimum resale price maintenance, not maximum resale price maintenance. The use of genuine recommended resale prices is excluded from per se prohibition.[188] The cases of *Prestige Motors*[189] and *Commodore Business Machines*[190] have made clear that the prohibition captures preventing buyers from advertising below a certain price (or only at a certain price), even if they can sell below (and above) the 'recommended price'.

[183] Deloitte Study, p. iii.

[184] Deloitte Study, p. iv.

[185] Except for one form of exclusive dealing, third line forcing, which is prohibited per se under the current s 47 of the CCA; however, the Bill 2017, in its Schedule 7, proposes to change the per se rule in relation to third line forcing to the rule of substantial lessening of competition.

[186] *ACCC v Flight Centre Travel* [2016] HCA 49.

[187] Section 4, which defines terms used in the CCA, only refers to Part VIII.

[188] See ss 97, 99 and 96(3)(b).

[189] *TPC v Prestige Motors Pty Ltd* (1994) ATPR 41-359.

[190] *TPC v Commodore Business Machines Pty Ltd* (1990) 92 ALR 563.

Prohibited RPM is based on the unilateral conduct of the supplier, rather than multilateral/bilateral conduct. Although it covers any agreements with buyers, under section 96(3), the supplier is primarily liable; it is the supplier that is presumed to be forcing, or in other ways influence, its buyers to maintain prices or it stops supplying because of RPM. Subsection 96(3) also includes situations where three persons of a vertical chain are involved in RPM; thus, the supplier would contravene section 96(3) of CCA if it forced or influenced its buyer to sell a product to the third person (the second buyer in the vertical chain) only on the condition that the second buyer maintains and/or agrees to maintain its retail price.[191] Importantly, however, while primary liability under the provision resides with the supplier, a buyer that initiates or encourages a supplier to engage in RPM can be found guilty of aiding and abetting RPM conduct.[192]

There is currently only one defence to per se RPM liability, which arises when the supplier's product has been used as a 'loss leader'. The 'loss leader defence' is applicable when a supplier withholds goods from a retailer who has, within the preceding year, sold those goods at less than cost, for the purpose of promoting their business or otherwise attracting customers that are likely to purchase *other* goods.[193] Furthermore, since 1995, suppliers have been able to apply for authorisation of RPM on public benefit grounds. Although there has only been one such application, it was successful.[194]

**RPM and Digital Online Sales**

The Harper Report discussed RPM in connection with digital retailing, highlighting the change of doing business since the introduction of anti-RPM law.[195] It did not suggest changing the relevant provisions on RPM in the CCA but did recommend the introduction of the notification system for RPM. The Harper Report justified this recommendation by arguing that an exception for RPM via the notification process would be easier and faster than via the authorisation exemption process and thus is likely to be used more frequently than the authorisation process. The Harper Report also recommended including an exemption for RPM conduct between bodies corporate as currently the RPM prohibition can cover maintaining prices between subsidiaries and/or a parent company and its subsidiary.[196] Bill 2017 includes both recommendations and proposes to change the CCA accordingly.

---

[191] Subsection 96(3)(e); see also, s 96(3)(d)(ii).

[192] See, for example, *Australian Competition and Consumer Commission v OmniBlend Australia Pty Ltd* [2015] FCA 871.

[193] Section 98(2) of the CCA. See also, *TPC v Orlane Australia Pty Ltd* (1984) 1 FCR 157.

[194] On 5 December 2014, the ACCC granted authorisation no. A91433 to Tooltechnic to set minimum retail prices on Festool products. The authorisation was granted until the end of 2018. The ACCC has been monitoring the situation. The principal argument for granting the authorisation was the prevention of free riding. The recent Bill 2017 proposes the notification system for RPM.

[195] Harper Report, p. 378.

[196] Harper Report, pp. 378–380.

## 2.7.2 Exclusive Dealing: Non-price Vertical Restraints

Unlike the approach to RPM, where only suppliers are primarily liable, (most commonly) unilateral conduct by either a supplier or a buyer can form exclusive dealings that contravene section 47. Section 47 is descriptive. It includes, among other things, tying, exclusive distribution and territorial[197] and customer allocation. Except for third line forcing,[198] such practices are only prohibited if they have the purpose, effect or likely effect of substantially lessening competition.

Section 47 includes situations where third parties are involved. For instance, the prohibition on third line forcing applies where a supplier forces its customer to purchase another product or service from a third party, in order to obtain goods or services from the supplier at all, or on particular terms.[199] For example, it is third line forcing to offer discounted petrol on the condition that the purchaser acquires goods or services from another party (such as a supermarket). This conduct is currently *per se* illegal; however, if Bill 2017 amends the CCA as proposed, third line forcing will be prohibited only if, in a particular case, it substantially lessens competition in its purpose, effect or likely effect.[200] Third line forcing could be relevant for the online sales platforms if, for instance, the platform forces its customers to purchase or sell other services or products or only offers a discounted price for product (a) on the condition that the purchaser also purchases product (b).

Another example of a third-party role in an exclusive dealing case (where the third party was competing with the infringer) is the recent case of *Visa*.[201] Indeed, this case shows how a restriction on using a third party for a specific service, in this case a digital financial service,[202] can contravene section 47 (and potentially also section 46). The ACCC and Visa Inc made a joint submission, in which they agreed that this conduct contravened exclusive dealing in the form of section 47(2)(d); no admissions were made in relation to misuse of market power, and the ACCC did not pursue this claim.

This case involved the conduct of Visa and its modification of the Visa International Operating Regulations (VIOR) in order to prevent the expansion of providers of Dynamic Currency Conversion (DCC) services relevant for international transactions. In practice, if the DDC was involved in an international

[197] Australia does not have comparable cases to the EU cases on vertical geographical territorial restrictions (such as C-260/09 *Activision Blizzard Germany GmbH v European Commission* [2011] ECR 419; T-450/05 *Automobiles Peugeot SA, Peugeot Nederland NV v Commission* [2009] OJ C205/32) and thus it does not differentiate between active and passive sales.

[198] Subsections 47(6)–(7).

[199] The prohibited third line forcing always includes two contracts of purchase or sale. It does not apply if there is only one contract and the product or service is considered a 'bundle'. Consequently, in e.g., *Castlemaine Tooheys Ltd v Williams and Hodgson Transport Pty Ltd* [1986] HCA 72, the court held that 'packaged beer' was a single bundled product, and not two separate products, for purposes of the third line forcing provisions.

[200] 200 Despite the per-se prohibition, third line forcing can be and frequently is notified.

[201] *ACCC v Visa Inc* [2015] FCA 1020 ('*Visa*').

[202] This could apply to online sales platforms too.

transaction, such a transaction was submitted in the cardholder's currency, as opposed to the merchant's currency, amounting to a single currency transaction. In situations where such DCC international transactions occurred, Visa did not earn fees that it would have otherwise earned if the transactions had happened as multi-currency transactions without any involvement of the DCC, and in some circumstances Visa was not earning any foreign exchange revenue from the DCC single currency transactions either.[203]

The modified version of the VIOR from the 27th of April 2010, among other things, allowed only 'DCC providers and merchant outlets already actively offering DCC services as at 30 April 2010'[204] to re-register. Potential new entrants were not allowed to register DCC services.[205] It was alleged that 'the effect was to restrict the expansion of DCC services on the Visa payment card network in Australia'.[206]

An example of exclusive distribution where an online sales platform was involved is an unsuccessful notification under section 47 of eBay Inc ('eBay'). In April 2008, eBay lodged a notification to obtain immunity from conduct that could potentially breach section 47. Specifically, eBay was intending to enter into an exclusive dealing arrangement with PayPal proposing to 'mandate the use of PayPal for almost all transactions on the eBay site'.[207] The ACCC revoked the notification on the basis that this conduct could restrict competition substantially, among other things, due to the fact that eBay was Australia's leading online sales platform and the notified conduct would restrict the payment choice of buyers.[208]

**Selective Distribution System**

Selective distribution as a type of distribution where buyers (or sellers) are selected based on given, selective criteria, such as those prohibiting online sales or prohibiting sales to particular customers or customer groups, can contravene both section 47 and section 46. In certain circumstances, these arrangements might also contravene the general prohibition on anti-competitive agreements, section 45. There have not yet been any cases in Australia dealing with genuine selective distribution, in which platforms have prohibited online sales or sales via online platforms.

Section 47 is a descriptive provision that prohibits only specific forms of vertical restraints, collectively referred to as 'exclusive dealing'. Despite the reference to 'exclusive dealing', section 47 covers a much broader range of restrictive distribution arrangements than those that would typically be considered 'exclusive dealing'

[203] *Visa*, [6]–[46].

[204] *Visa*, [49].

[205] *Visa*, [49]–[50].

[206] *Visa*, [50].

[207] ACCC, ACCC proposes to revoke immunity for eBay's PayPal only policy, (media relies, 12 June 2008), available at https://www.accc.gov.au/media-release/accc-proposes-to-revoke-immunity-for-ebays-paypal-only-policy.

[208] See ACCC, ACCC proposes to revoke immunity for eBay's PayPal only policy (media relies, 12 June 2008), available at https://www.accc.gov.au/media-release/accc-proposes-to-revoke-immunity-for-ebays-paypal-only-policy.

in other jurisdictions such as the US and the EU. For example, it covers situations where a corporation restricts its buyers to selling[209] online or to resupplying online. For instance, section 47(2)(f) prohibits supplying or offering to supply goods or services (at all or at a particular price or on particular conditions) on the condition that those goods or services will not be resupplied to 'particular persons or classes of person' (which may include online sales platforms) or 'in particular places or classes of places' (such as online).

Refusal to supply for the reason that the buyer does not follow such a selective condition is also captured,[210] and the provision also captures equivalent acquisition restrictions[211]; thus, for example, if an online sales platform acquired goods on the condition[212] that the person from whom they acquired did not (or did not except to a limited extent) supply goods to particular people or in particular places (for example, via their own online distribution channels), then that would fall within the scope of the exclusive dealing provision.[213]

Importantly, all of these forms of exclusive dealing are prohibited only when the unilateral conduct has the purpose, effect or likely effect of substantially lessening competition.[214] This requires proof that the 'effect on competition… is real or of substance',[215] although it does not need to be 'large or weighty'.[216] Conduct is likely to be anti-competitive if, for example, it raises barriers to entry or reduces price competition.[217] Although not all refusals to supply will satisfy this test, refusal to supply a single buyer (or to acquire from a single supplier) in a competitive market can lead to substantial lessening of competition where such a buyer (or supplier) is a vigorous competitor, for example, if it involves refusal to supply an important discounter with the result that the refusal will lead to an increase in prices for consumers.[218]

Exclusive dealing, particularly where it involves refusal to supply, may also constitute a misuse of market power. However, the application of section 47 and section 46 has its limits. The potential overlap between the exclusive dealing and misuse of market power provisions and potential limits of both provisions centred around

[209] The term 'supply' is defined widely in s 4 of the CCA and includes not only sale but also 'exchange, lease, hire or hire-purchase; and …in relation to services—provide, grant or confer'.

[210] Subsection 47(3).

[211] Subsections 47(4)–(5).

[212] The connotation 'on the condition' has a very wide meaning. The condition can be direct or indirect. It can be deduced from specific conduct or other relevant circumstances. (See *Visy Paper v ACCC* [2003] HCA 59; 2003) 216 CLR 1, at [8].)

[213] It is unilateral conduct which is prohibited. For further information, see above.

[214] Subsections 47(10).

[215] Trade Practices Legislation Amendment Bill 1992, Explanatory Memorandum, p 4.

[216] Trade Practices Legislation Amendment Bill 1992, Explanatory Memorandum, p 4.

[217] *Outboard Marine Australia Pty Ltd v Hecar Investments (No 6) Pty Ltd* (1982) ¶ATPR40-327, at 43, 987.

[218] See *Mark Lyons Pty Ltd v Bursill Sportsgear Pty Ltd* (1987) ¶ATPR 40-809, [1987] FCA 282.

selective distribution were demonstrated in *TPC v CSR Ltd.*[219] In that case, the parties were in disagreement whether the conduct in question involved a form of exclusive dealing (single branding) or selective distribution. The competition authority argued that North Perth Plaster Works Pty Ltd (NPPW) habitually purchased all its plasterboard from CSR Ltd; however, once it started to acquire plasterboard from one of CSR's competitors, CSR ceased supply. CSR argued that it was not refusing supply because of the acquisition from competitor, but rather that it utilised a selective distribution system in which it chose to supply only to buyers that were interested in carrying a full range of its plasterboard, and this did not include NPPW. The court agreed with the competition authority that this conduct constituted refusal to supply contravening both sections 46 and 47.[220] If the court had agreed with CSR that this was a genuine implementation of a selective distribution system, it may not have found an anti-competitive purpose or a taking advantage of market power under section 46 or a contravention of section 47.

In order to contravene section 46, it must be demonstrated that the application of the selective distribution system amounts to a taking advantage of market power for an anti-competitive purpose. Where there is a clear business justification for the application of a particular distribution system, it may be difficult to demonstrate that its application is related to its market power or that it has the necessary anti-competitive purpose. This was illustrated in the High Court decision of *Melway*,[221] which included exclusive dealership and not selective distribution.

In this case, Melway published the 'Melway's Street Directory', a detailed street directory of the Greater Melbourne area and, at the time, enjoyed a market share of around 80–90% for Melbourne street directories. The case involved the application of an exclusive distribution arrangement; the supplier, *Melway*, appointed exclusive distributors for specific sectors of the retail market and refused to supply to other distributors. Robert Hicks Pty Ltd (t/a Auto Fashions) placed an order for between 30,000 and 50,000 Melways and was refused. Hicks alleged that the refusal constituted a taking advantage of market power for an unlawful purpose; Melway claimed that it was merely implementing its successful exclusive distribution system. The High Court agreed with Melway, finding that Melway was not trying to foreclose the market and that Hicks was free to obtain street directories from other wholesalers but that it was merely implementing its long-running distribution system and that this, while limiting intra-brand competition, could improve inter-brand competition. The court observed:

> There was no legal obligation upon Melway to have any wholesale distributors at all. If it had chosen to do so, it could have supplied retailers directly itself, or it could have supplied the retail market through a single wholesale distributor. Distributorship arrangements may restrict intrabrand competition but promote interbrand competition.[222]

[219] *TPC v CSR Ltd* (1991) ATPR ¶41-076.

[220] *TPC v CSR Ltd* (1991) ATPR ¶41-076, at 52,148.

[221] *Melway Publishing Pty Ltd v Robert Hicks Pty Ltd* (1998) FCA 1379, appealed (1999) FCA 664, appealed (2001) 205 CLR, at 21. However, the proposed provision 46 under Bill 2016 requiring proving substantial lessening of competition could cover such conduct.

[222] Ibid, at [19].

Importantly, the court held, this was not an exercise of market power because it could have refused to supply in the absence of market power, and its refusal in this case did not deny Melway any extra sales (it simply meant that the sales went to its preferred segment distributor instead of Hicks). The court held[223]:

> … there are cases in which it is dangerous to proceed too quickly from a finding about purpose to a conclusion about taking advantage. That is especially so when, in a context such as the present, the purpose as referred to in s 46 is relatively narrow. The purpose presently in question is that of deterring a person from engaging in competitive conduct in a market. If a manufacturer supplies to a single distributor, or a limited number of distributors, then, from one point of view, turning down an application from a person who wishes to become an additional distributor will have the effect of preventing that person from engaging in competitive conduct. Purpose, in this connection, involves intention to achieve a result. Where distributorship arrangements are concerned, an intent to give a particular distributor exclusivity may constitute a very insecure basis for concluding that there had been a taking advantage of market power.[224]

These quotes show, among other things, that the threshold for proving misuse of market power under section 46 is currently very high (although Bill 2016 lowers the threshold to focus on competitive effects) and that the court is willing to accept arguments that conduct that limits intra-brand competition may nevertheless be held not to be anti-competitive if offset by improvements in inter-brand competition, both in the context of misuse of market power claims and when applying the competition test in the context of exclusive dealing.

### 2.7.3 International Price Discrimination: Geo-blocking

In Australia, international price discrimination, including the use of geo-blocking measures via online sales platforms, was raised as a potential competition issue in the Harper Report and, prior to that, in the House of Representatives Standing Committee on Infrastructure and Communications in July 2013.[225] Discrimination based on market segmentation can, these studies found, lead to Australian customers paying up to 200% more for cosmetics and up to 60% more for clothing.[226] There are arguments for and against such a measure where the supporters of this

[223] By majority; in a strong dissent, Justice Kirby held that there was misuse of market power. His Honour considered that the conclusion that the refusal to supply was unrelated to the market power was 'unrealistic' (para 75) and observed that in Sydney, where Melway did not enjoy the same sort of market dominance (holding closer to 10% of that market), there was an 'understandable willingness to embrace a different distribution' (para 85), suggesting that in enforcing its closed distribution system in Melbourne, Melway was 'not pursuing some universal philosophy of efficient market distribution' but was taking advantage of its market power (para 85).

[224] *Melway Publishing Pty Ltd v Robert Hicks Pty Ltd* (2001) 205 CLR, at [31].

[225] Harper Report, p. 351; The House of Representative Standing Committee on Infrastructure and Communications, 'Inquiry into IT Pricing' in July 2013, available at http://www.aph.gov.au/Parliamentary_Business/Committees/House_of_Representatives_Committees?url=ic/itpricing/report.htm.

[226] Harper Report, p. 351, referring to CHOICE, submission, pp. 13–15.

form of price discrimination are local Australian entities protecting their business.[227] The Harper Report did not recommend changing legislation in order to address this issue. Instead, it recognised the existence of 'the growth of distribution channels, both physical and technological [that] can help consumers and businesses overcome price discrimination'.[228] Thus, the Harper Report recommended alternatives to legislative mechanisms to overcome geo-blocking, in particular 'market solutions that empower consumers'.[229]

International price discrimination can also be facilitated by restricting parallel imports, which can negatively impact, for instance, online sales platforms such as Amazon and local online retailers. Some Australian legislation, such as the *Trade Marks Act 1995* (Cth) and the *Copyright Act 1968* (Cth), restricts certain parallel imports. With regard to the *Copyright Act 1968* (Cth), the ACCC explains:

> Such restrictions effectively provide an import monopoly to the domestic distributor and protect owners of the local IP rights from competition. The restrictions may also enable copyright owners to practice international price discrimination to the detriment of Australian consumers.[230]

The Harper Report recommended removing such restrictions 'unless it can be shown that the benefits of the restrictions to the community as a whole outweigh the cost; and the objectives of the restrictions can only be achieved by restricting competition'.[231]

## 2.8 Enforcement and Liability

There are a range of mechanisms by which settlements or 'Consent Decrees' might operate in relation to competition law generally. There are no special rules in relation to e-commerce platforms.[232]

The ACCC does not have judicial powers to rule on conduct that has taken place but may submit agreed facts and propose agreed penalties to the court. The court is not bound to follow the agreed penalty or penalty range but typically does so provided it considers the penalty within an appropriate range for the conduct involved.[233]

---

[227] For instance, Foxtel submitted that 'any attempt to assist Australians to circumvent geo-blocks will have a real impact on the Australian businesses that invest in Australian content, create Australian jobs and pay tax in Australia'. Harper Report, p. 353, (quoting Foxtel, DR sub, pages 11–12).

[228] Harper Report, p. 352.

[229] Harper Report, p. 354.

[230] Harper Report, p. 166 (quoting submission by ACCC, sub 1, page 60).

[231] Harper Report, Recommendation 13, p. 178.

[232] This is separate to 'authorisation' which the ACCC can grant on public benefit grounds ahead of the conduct occurring.

[233] It remains for the court to determine whether the jointly submitted penalties are appropriate. However, as long as they are within an acceptable range courts typically approve the agreed penalty. Recent doubt about the legality of joint civil penalty submissions was resolved by the High

Parties are incentivised to agree facts by the ACCC's cooperation policy for enforcement matters.[234] An example is the Ticketek misuse of market power case, referred to above.[235] In that case, Justice Bennett accepted the agreed facts submitted by the parties and with the jointly proposed penalties. In relation to penalties, Justice Bennett observed:

> It is in the public interest for litigation … to be concluded in the shortest time frame that is consistent with justice being done between the parties, freeing the Court and the Commission to deal with other matters. To that end, the Court has looked with favour upon negotiated settlements, provided that their terms recognise that the ultimate responsibility forth terms and making of the orders that resolve the proceedings lies with the Court.[236]
>
> Provided that the Court is satisfied that the terms of the orders are appropriate, it is in the public interest for the Court to make orders in part IV litigation on the terms that have been agreed between parties, so as to encourage parties to assist the Commission in its investigations and achieved negotiated settlements. The Court has recognised that, in addition to savings in time and costs, there is a public benefit in imposing agreed pecuniary penalties where appropriate as parties would not be disposed to reach such agreements were there unpredictable risks involved …[237]

### 2.8.1 Enforceable Undertakings

The ACCC may receive from parties 'enforceable undertakings'.[238] These constitute commitments, enforceable in court, that the party will or will not engage in particular forms of conduct. They are frequently used as merger remedies; for example, the ACCC may indicate that it will not oppose a merger subject to an enforceable divestiture commitment. However, they may also be adopted by the ACCC instead of pursuing formal enforcement in the courts or as part of a formal court remedy. For example, in 2009, the Federal Court declared by consent that Skins Compression Garments Pty Ltd had engaged in RPM in contravention of the CCA and, with the consent of the ACCC and the defendant, ordered that Skins give a section 87B undertaking to the ACCC that it would undertake compliance training.[239] In other cases, the ACCC has sought undertakings as an alternative to bringing court action. All such undertakings are public, with the ACCC publishing them on its website.

---

Court (*Commonwealth of Australia v Director, Fair Work Building Industry Inspectorate; CFMEU v Director, Fair Work Building Industry Inspectorate (CFMEU)* [2015] HCA 46) which confirmed that joint submissions on penalty were acceptable.

[234] ACCC, *ACCC cooperation policy for enforcement matters* (31 July 2002) (https://www.accc.gov.au/publications/accc-cooperation-policy-for-enforcement-matters).

[235] *Australian Competition and Consumer Commission v Ticketek Pty Ltd* [2011] FCA 1489. See Sect. 2.4.2.

[236] *Australian Competition and Consumer Commission v Ticketek Pty Ltd* [2011] FCA 1489 para 30.

[237] *Australian Competition and Consumer Commission v Ticketek Pty Ltd* [2011] FCA 1489 para 31.

[238] Section 87B CCA. The ACCC maintains an undertakings register: http://registers.accc.gov.au/content/index.phtml/itemId/6029.

[239] See http://registers.accc.gov.au/content/index.phtml/itemId/875264.

These arrangements are not without controversy. For example, in 2013, rather than institute proceedings alleging anti-competitive conduct or exclusive dealing, the ACCC received undertakings from Coles and Woolworths, the two largest supermarket retailers in Australia, that each would not provide 'shopper docket' fuel discounts of greater value than 4 cents per litre.[240] In some cases, such discounts had reached up to 45 cents per litre prior to the undertaking.[241] In addition to concerns that this effectively facilitated an agreement between the two major supermarket competitors to cap their discounts, the 'settlement' meant that the ACCC did not publish findings of its investigation into potential anti-competitive effects of the discounts, and the matter was never litigated. A decision on the merits may have increased certainty about the legality of this form of conditional discounting in Australia.[242]

### 2.8.2 Informal Agreements

The ACCC has also at times accepted informal agreements from parties under investigation that have been sufficient to mitigate its competition concerns. For example, in September 2016, the ACCC announced that Expedia and Booking.com 'have each reached agreement to amend price and availability parity clauses in their contracts with Australian hotels and accommodation providers', which it claimed would 'remove barriers to price competition between major online travel sites for hotel bookings'.[243] Little detail of how the agreement was reached and whether there would be any monitoring of its implementation was provided. It does not appear to have been accompanied by any formal undertakings but nevertheless brought to an end an ACCC investigation into online travel sites.

### 2.8.3 Private Actions

Private actions may be brought for any contravention of the CCA. Remedies available include injunctions to prevent the conduct continuing,[244] damages[245] and such

[240] Coles: http://registers.accc.gov.au/content/index.phtml/itemId/1128691; Woolworths: http://registers.accc.gov.au/content/index.phtml/itemId/1128693.

[241] ACCC concerned about escalating shopper docket discounts ACCC Media Release, 29 July 2013.

[242] The ACCC does not have judicial powers to find a contravention of the competition laws; only the courts have this power and they must provide reasons for their decision.

[243] Expedia and Booking.com agree to reinvigorate price competition by amending contracts with Australian hotels, ACCC Media Release 158/16, 2 September 2016.

[244] An exception to the availability of injunctions relates to mergers; although the ACCC may seek an injunction to prevent a merger, a private litigant does not have this option: s 80(1A). However, a private party may complain to the ACCC who may, if appropriate, seek an injunction and may, if the merger proceeds, seek damages for contravention of the Act.

[245] Section 82.

other orders as the court thinks appropriate to compensate the claimant or prevent or reduce loss or damage.[246] Damages are compensatory in nature, with a claimant able to recover 'the amount of the loss or damage' suffered as a result of the conduct.[247] Punitive damages are not available.

Class actions for cartel or other anti-competitive conduct are relatively rare,[248] despite a mechanism for representative proceedings being introduced in 1992.[249] There are a number of reasons for this, but one significant challenge is the fact that, where public proceedings taken by the ACCC are resolved by consent orders,[250] facts admitted by parties are not able to be used in subsequent private litigation. This is because they are not considered 'findings of fact' by the court.[251] There has been significant criticism of this limitation, and the Harper Panel recommended[252] that it be removed so that facts agreed by the parties could be used in follow-on private proceedings. Bill 2017 includes this modification and may result in more private litigation in the future.[253]

The competition laws may also be used as a form of defence to a breach of contract claim, although there are limited examples and none involving online platforms.[254] The way in which this could arise is through a claim that the contract, or a provision within it, is 'illegal'. It will be illegal if the conduct involved (i.e., the terms of the provision) contravenes the CCA; consequently, a cartel provision could not be enforced by the courts, so any party litigating to enforce such a clause would have it struck down by the courts as illegal. It is less clear whether other provisions of a contract that includes an illegal clause, such as a cartel clause, would still be enforced. Provided the 'illegal' clause or clauses could be severed from the contract, the rest of the contract may still be able to be enforced.

---

[246] Section 87.

[247] Section 82.

[248] See B. Dellavedova and R. Gilsenan, Challenges in Cartel Class Actions, (2009) 32 *UNSWLR* 1001.

[249] *Federal Court of Australia Act 1976* (Cth).

[250] The parties may agree, for purposes of the proceedings, agree that certain conduct has taken place and that there have been contraventions of the Act. They may jointly submit facts and propose orders (consent orders) which they court may adopt.

[251] Section 83 allows findings of fact to constitute prima facie evidence of that fact in subsequent proceedings.

[252] Recommendation 41 provided that the CCA should be amended so that admissions of fact could be considered prima facie evidence of those facts in subsequent proceedings.

[253] Bill 2017, Schedule 10. See also C. Beaton-Wells, Private enforcement of competition law in Australia – inching forwards?, (2016) 39 Melbourne University Law Review 681.

[254] Contract claims are ubiquitous; there are no litigated claims of which the authors are aware. There may have been settlements reached as a result of the potential for an illegality claim to be made.

### 2.8.4 General Liability

One of the issues involved in online sales on online platforms is the specific relationship between the platform and the supplier or buyer. For instance, it is common that online sales platforms operate as agents for the suppliers. The liability provisions under the CCA are broad enough to hold an online sales platform operator liable for restrictions of competition.

Section 76 of CCA (and section 79 of CCA for criminal conduct that requires a 'knowingly concerned' person), together with section 75B, sets the liability for anti-competitive conduct under Part IV. Broadly, both persons directly involved in anti-competitive conduct, and persons who *assisted* or *attempted* to contravene Part IV of the CCA can be liable. In particular, in addition to persons found to directly contravene the CCA, the court can order penalties against a person who[255]

(b) has attempted to contravene such a provision; or
(c) has aided, abetted, counselled or procured a person to contravene such a provision; or
(d) has induced, or attempted to induce, a person, whether by threats or promises or otherwise, to contravene such a provision; or
(e) has been in any way, directly or indirectly, knowingly concerned in, or party to, the contravention by a person of such a provision; or
(f) has conspired with others to contravene such a provision.

This is a valuable tool for online sales by online platforms. For instance, if a platform or related computer software is set in such a way that it leads to collusion or other anti-competitive practices and the provider of the platform or the owner of the software is aware of it, he/she can also be held liable.

A more specific and common issue for online sales platforms is the agent–principal relationships. As mentioned above, vertical restraints are perceived as unilateral conduct, unlike in the US or the EU, which require proving an agreement. This eliminates one of potential hurdles when dealing with the conduct of suppliers via online platforms operating as an agent. However, in general, conduct between principals and their agents can be also covered by the ACCC where an 'agreement'[256] is required.

### 2.8.5 Agency Issues

Australia's competition laws raise some interesting issues regarding agency arrangements. Genuine agency arrangements[257] will not be captured within the ambit of the *per se* resale price maintenance laws because the prohibition requires two separate sales or supplies. However, agency arrangements, as they involve agreements

[255] Section 76 CCA.

[256] The CCA refers to a 'contract, arrangement or understanding'.

[257] In which a supplier contracts directly with the consumer, albeit facilitated by the agent.

between the principal and agent, can be considered under the general anti-competitive conduct prohibition in section 45 of the Act.

More controversially, agency arrangements will not necessarily prevent the agent and principal being held to operate in the same market, with the result that they may be considered competitors and subject to the strict cartel laws. Importantly, no 'agency defence' exists under Australian law. There are anti-overlap provisions in the CCA, which means that where the conduct involved also constitutes resale price maintenance or exclusive dealing, as may be the case, for example, if a principal carves out territorial restrictions with its agents, the conduct will not fall within the scope of the cartel laws. However, the anti-overlap exemptions apply only *in so far as* the conduct overlaps.[258] Consequently, if the conduct separately involves exclusive dealing and cartel conduct, both prohibitions will apply.

There have recently been two significant cases considering this issue. In the first, the ACCC alleged that ANZ, a major Australian bank, had required one of its brokers to agree to limit the refund that it would provide in relation to ANZ home loans it arranged to ensure that it did not exceed the loan establishment fee waivers offered by ANZ bank branches. The second involved allegations by the ACCC that Flight Centre (a travel agent) had attempted to induce airlines to lower their direct-to-public ticket sales to help facilitate its 'Lowest Airfare Guarantee'. In each case, the ACCC alleged that the conduct in question constituted price fixing, which required that they establish that ANZ and Flight Centre were in competition with the broker and the airlines respectively.[259]

At first instance, the ACCC succeeded in its case against Flight Centre but failed in its case against ANZ. Both matters were appealed and heard before the same three members of the Full Federal Court. The court upheld Flight Centre's appeal and rejected the ACCC's appeal in the ANZ case, finding in each case that the parties were not competitors in any relevant market.[260] Despite the similar agency issues raised in each, the ACCC elected to appeal only the Flight Centre decision, which was heard before the High Court in 2016. The primary issue on appeal was whether Flight Centre was *in competition* with the airlines when it engaged in the relevant conduct.

In December 2016, the High Court determined, by majority,[261] that Flight Centre competed with airlines for the supply of airline tickets and that, as a result, its attempts to induce the airlines to lower their ticket sales prices constituted unlawful

---

[258] Sections 44ZZRR (relating to resale price maintenance) and section 44ZZRS (relating to exclusive dealing). See, eg, *Norcast S.ár.L v Bradken Limited (No 2)* [2013] FCA 235.

[259] The conduct involved preceded the current cartel laws and were therefore considered pursuant to the price fixing prohibitions which operated at the time; the principles relating to competition and price fixing remain the same under the current cartel laws and they also include *attempts* to collude.

[260] *ACCC v Australia and New Zealand Banking Group Limited* [2013] FCA 1206.

[261] *ACCC v Flight Centre Travel* [2016] HCA 49. Then Chief Justice, Robert French, dissented.

price fixing.[262] Although the relationship between Flight Centre and the airlines was essentially one of principal and agent, with Flight Centre receiving commissions from the airlines for selling seats on their flights, the majority of the High Court held that the relevant market in this case was the 'market for the supply, to customers, of contractual rights to international air carriage', and the parties competed in this market 'notwithstanding that Flight Centre supplied in that market as agent for each airline'.[263]

In this respect, Justices Kiefel and Gageler observed that a contractual right is a service under the CCA, and conferring a contractual right constitutes supply under the CCA,[264] with the result that making a contract conferring the right to supply of a service (air travel) was a supply of a service. Their Honours further noted that it is not inconsistent with the CCA for 'an agent and a principal' to both be 'suppliers of contractual rights against the principal' or for them to supply such rights in competition.[265]

In relation to arguments that principals should not be considered in competition with their agents, Justice Gordon observed that 'agent' was an abused word and held that, in this case, the description of Flight Centre as agent

> masks the proper identification of the rivalrous behaviours that occur at the point at which Flight Centre is dealing with its own customers … without reference to any interests of any airline. At that point, the description of Flight Centre as "agent" is simply wrong. At that point, Flight Centre in its own right was competing against all sellers of tickets, which includes the airlines and other travel agents. Flight Centre was not acting as agent.[266]

Her Honour went on to observe that even if Flight Centre was a true agent of the airlines, this was irrelevant for purposes of the price-fixing provisions.[267] The other members of the majority considered that the relationship between the parties was an agency relationship but nevertheless concluded that the nature of the agency in this case, in particular the ticket pricing discretion enjoyed by Flight Centre, meant that despite that relationship, the parties did compete in this case. In contrast, Chief Justice French, dissenting, concluded that the agency relationship precluded that there be competition between the parties.[268]

---

[262] For more detail see Julie Clarke, 'Flight Centre: Australian High Court finds agent competed with principal and breached cartel laws' (Competition Policy Blog, 9 January 2017), Justin Oliver and Paul Schoff, 'Agency and Competition Law in Australia Following *ACCC v Flight Centre Travel Group* (2017) 8 *Journal of European Competition Law & Practice* 321, Brent Fisse, 'The High Court Decision in ACCC v Flight Centre – Crash Landings Ahead?' (2017) 45 ABLR 61 and Brent FIsse, 'Facilitating practices, vertical restraints and most favoured customers: Australian competition law is ill-equipped to meet the challenge' (2016) 44 ABLR 325.

[263] *ACCC v Flight Centre Travel* [2016] HCA 49, para 26.

[264] *ACCC v Flight Centre Travel* [2016] HCA 49, para 80.

[265] *ACCC v Flight Centre Travel* [2016] HCA 49, para 82.

[266] *ACCC v Flight Centre Travel* [2016] HCA 49, para 175.

[267] *ACCC v Flight Centre Travel* [2016] HCA 49, paras 152–253.

[268] *ACCC v Flight Centre Travel* [2016] HCA 49, para 21.

The decision removes any doubt that agents can be considered in competition with their principal, especially where they are free to set their own price or conditions. Principals are, therefore, now more likely to be found to be competing with their agents whenever they also supply the relevant goods or services directly to customers, a common scenario in the case of online sales platforms.

**Recommendations to Revise the Law**

Although the High Court decision post-dated the Harper Report, the issue was a live one at the time of the review, and the Harper Panel recommended that an exemption be added to the cartel laws for 'trading restrictions that are imposed by one firm on another in connection with the supply or acquisition of goods or services'.[269] The Panel considered that it was more appropriate for these arrangements to be considered under the general anti-competitive conduct provision, which would ensure that they were 'assessed under a substantial lessening of competition test rather than a per se prohibition'.[270] This would be broader than an 'agency' defence as it would capture all vertical supply arrangements.

The Australian Government accepted this recommendation, and it formed part of an Exposure Draft Bill released in September 2016. It does not, however, appear in Bill 2017, and the reasons for the omission are unclear. As a result, it is unlikely that any agency exemption or broader vertical trading exemption from the cartel laws will be introduced in the near future.

In relation to online platforms, dual distribution arrangements, in which the platform operator sells as agent for the retailer, which also sells direct to the public, may now risk per se cartel liability in a wide range of situations.[271] It is easy to imagine, for example, how this issue might arise in relation to online booking agencies that enter into price parity arrangements with their suppliers. The ACCC has yet to bring a cartel case involving online platforms, other than that involving Flight Centre, but may be emboldened by its success in Flight Centre to bring further actions. It is not clear, for example, whether or not Expedia and Booking.com might be considered in competition with accommodation providers and, if so, whether price parity and other arrangements might contravene the cartel laws. The ACCC's announcement that, following an investigation, Expedia and Booking.com had agreed to amend price and availability parity clauses pre-dated the High Court's decision in *Flight Centre*. The press release announcing the 'agreement' contains no discussion about whether or not the ACCC considered the parties in competition or any other detail about the specific competition concerns that the ACCC held regarding these clauses.[272]

[269] Recommendation 27. See discussion on pages 364–365 of the Harper Report.

[270] Harper Report page 365.

[271] See, eg, Brent Fisse, 'The High Court Decision in ACCC v Flight Centre – Crash Landings Ahead?' (2017) 45 ABLR 61, 66.

[272] See Expedia and Booking.com agree to reinvigorate price competition by amending contracts with Australian hotels, ACCC Media Release 158/16, 2 September 2016. See also B. Fisse, The High Court Decision in ACCC v Flight Centre – Crash Landings Ahead? (2017) 45 ABLR 61, 66–67.

## 2.9 IP Protection: Section 51(3) of the CCA

The treatment of, and the interplay between, competition law and IP protection can also be relevant to online sales platforms. This is because such platforms can involve IP protection, most notably copyright protection. However, subsection 51(3) of the CCA exempts intellectual property (IP), including copyright, licensing and trademark arrangements, from the application of competition law provisions in Part IV, other than misuse of market power (section 46) and resale price maintenance (section 48). Subsection 51(3) states:

> A contravention of a provision of [Part IV] other than section 46, 46A or 48 shall not be taken to have been committed by reason of:
>
> (a) the imposing of, or giving effect to, a condition of:
> (i) a licence granted by the proprietor, licensee or owner of a patent, of a registered design, of a copyright or of EL rights within the meaning of the *Circuit Layouts Act 1989*, or by a person who has applied for a patent or for the registration of a design; or
> (ii) an assignment of a patent, of a registered design, of a copyright or of such EL rights, or of the right to apply for a patent or for the registration of a design;
> to the extent that the condition relates to:
> (iii) the invention to which the patent or application for a patent relates or articles made by the use of that invention;
> (iv) goods in respect of which the design is, or is proposed to be, registered and to which it is applied;
> (v) the work or other subject matter in which the copyright subsists; or
> (vi) the eligible layout in which the EL rights subsist;
> (b) the inclusion in a contract, arrangement or understanding authorizing the use of a certification trade mark of a provision in accordance with rules applicable under Part XI of the *Trade Marks Act 1955*, or the giving effect to such a provision; or
> (c) the inclusion in a contract, arrangement or understanding between:
> (i) the registered proprietor of a trade mark other than a certification trade mark; and
> (ii) a person registered as a registered user of that trade mark under Part IX of the *Trade Marks Act 1955* or a person authorized by the contract to use the trade mark subject to his or her becoming registered as such a registered user;
> of a provision to the extent that it relates to the kinds, qualities or standards of goods bearing the mark that may be produced or supplied, or the giving effect to the provision to that extent.

Section 51(3) has been widely criticised, and its repeal has been proposed by many,[273] including the Harper Report. The exempted IP rights can lead to a substantial lessening of competition, which would be prohibited in the CCA if not for the exemption under section 51(3). In this respect, the Harper Panel noted that '[i]n fields in which there are multiple and competing IP rights, such as the

[273] See, e.g., ACCC, ACCC submission to the Productivity Commission Inquiry into Intellectual Property Arrangements in Australia, November 2015, p. 14. https://www.accc.gov.au/system/files/ACCC%20Submission%20-%20PC%20inquiry%20into%20IP%20arrangements%20in%20Australia%20-%2030%20November.pdf. Accessed 11 May 2016; Australian Law Reform Commission also recommended repealed of s 51(3) in its report on 'Copyright and the Digital Economy' (November 2013), pp. 71–74; also see Harper Report, p. 108.

pharmaceutical or communications industries, cross-licensing arrangements can be entered into to resolve disputes but which impose anti-competitive restrictions on each licensee'.[274]

In the event the exemption was removed, the authorisation and notification processes could effectively ensure that any potential public benefits outweigh the restriction of competition.[275] At present, however, the exemptions in section 51(3) lead to the overprotection of IP, and this can have a restrictive effect on the competitive process in the digital world. Despite this significant criticism, section 51(3) remains in the CCA, and the current Bills do not propose its repeal.

## 2.10 Conclusion

Despite the fact that Australian competition law can effectively deal with various anti-competitive practices related to the growth of online sales platforms, such as anti-competitive restrictions between a principal and its agents, it may not be effective at capturing all potential concerns. For instance, the access regime is not fit for the purposes of the online sales platforms, which can potentially operate in bottleneck markets. Australia could consider changing the access regime in order to capture potential bottleneck issues created by online sales platforms, or alternatively, the ACCC could utilise section 46 for such conduct; the scope for the ACCC to utilise section 46 in this way may be expanded in accordance with Bill 2016.

Australia also overprotects IP rights in section 51(3). This can have restrictive effects on the competitive process in the digital world. Finally, the effectiveness of the CCA in connection with genuine selective distribution systems and other forms of vertical restraints involving online platforms still needs to be tested.

[274] Harper Report, p. 109.

[275] See, eg, Harper Report, p. 110.

# Austria

# 3

Astrid Ablasser-Neuhuber and Gerhard Fussenegger

With regard to EU and Austrian competition law, the term 'online sales platforms' might be easily misunderstood. Based on competition law practice (as outlined below), the term 'online sales platforms' in general is interpreted narrowly. Following such narrow approach, these platforms are exclusively equated with 'third party online sales platforms' of providers like Amazon or eBay. However, for the purposes of this report, the concept of online sales platforms includes all new digital economy in general, irrespective of whether the provider exclusively offers online platform services or not. Therefore, in this national report, the term 'online sales platform' follows that broad concept, including new digital economy as such. If '*third party* online sales platforms' are specifically referred to, this report considers online sales platforms in the narrow sense.

The present Austrian report consists of two sections. While the first part provides an overview of the main legal background, the relevant authorities and courts and a summary of Austria's legal practice in relation to online sales platforms, the second part discusses possible (further) competition issues in relation to online sales platforms and the question of whether new competition law concepts are needed to overcome these problems or whether the existing toolbox is sufficient.

A. Ablasser-Neuhuber (✉) · G. Fussenegger
bpv Hügel Rechtsanwälte GmbH, Vienna, Austria
e-mail: Astrid.Ablasser@bpv-huegel.com; Gerhard.Fussenegger@bpv-huegel.com



B. Kilpatrick et al. (eds.), *Antitrust Analysis of Online Sales Platforms & Copyright Limitations and Exceptions*, LIDC Contributions on Antitrust Law, Intellectual Property and Unfair Competition,
https://doi.org/10.1007/978-3-319-71419-6_3

## 3.1 The Competition Law Context of Online Sales Platforms in Austria

### 3.1.1 Legal Background

In Austria, competition law issues concerning online sales platforms are governed by the general antitrust provisions, i.e. the Austrian Cartel Act 2005 ('Cartel Act')[1] and the Competition Act,[2] which complements the Cartel Act and contains rules on the Federal Competition Authority (*Bundeswettbewerbsbehörde*—'FCA'), its tasks and some procedural rules. Following the EU's Directive 2014/104 on antitrust damage actions, which the Member States needed to implement in their legal systems by 27 December 2016, new amendments of the Cartel Act and the Competition Act entered into force on 1 May 2017. The amendment primarily intended to implement the Directive and therefore to create legal certainty for the enforcement of claims for damages arising from infringements of competition law. However, the amendment is more far-reaching and also includes provisions that are not related to the Directive, for instance a new threshold in merger control based on the value of the transaction. Furthermore, the Cartel Supreme Court will be entitled to decide also on substance (at least to a limited extent).

EU competition law must be directly applied in Austria if the infringement affects trade between Member States and—in general—can be also applied in analogy on purely national facts.

Article 101 TFEU and § 1 Cartel Act prohibit all agreements, decisions of associations and concerted practices that have as their object or effect the prevention, restriction or distortion of competition (and—concerning EU law—affect trade between Member States). Both provisions include a non-exhaustive list of infringements, e.g. price fixing, market sharing or limitation of production.

Also in reference to abuse of market dominance, the general rules (§ 5 Cartel Act and Article 102 TFEU) apply to online sales platforms.[3] The Cartel Act hereby does not provide for any definition of the term 'abuse'. However, it generally prohibits any abuse and again provides an indicative (but not exhaustive) list of respective practices of abuse. Reference, for instance, is made to limiting production, disadvantaging of contractual partners and the sale of goods below cost price.

The FCA defines 'abuse of market power' on its website as follows: 'Abusive practices by dominant companies may lead to disadvantage for other companies and customers that would not naturally occur or be possible in a setting of effective

---

[1] Bundesgesetz vom 5.7.2005 gegen Kartelle und andere Wettbewerbsbeschränkungen (Kartellgesetz 2005), BGBl I Nr. 61/2005 idF BGBl I Nr. 56/2017.

[2] Bundesgesetz über die Einrichtung einer Bundeswettbewerbsbehörde (Wettbewerbsgesetz—WettbG), BGBI I Nr. 62/2002 idF BGBl. I Nr. 56/2017.

[3] With regard to the Austrian approach concerning abuse of market dominance in detail, see Chapter 2 Austria, by G. Fussenegger, F. Schuhmacher and R. Tahedl, in: Këllezi, Kilpatrick and Kobel (eds), Abuse of Dominant Position and Globalization & Protection and Disclosure of Trade Secrets and Know-How, Springer 2017.

competition. Abusive practices include: imposing unfair prices, restriction of sales, deprivation of certain contractors, and selling goods below cost.'[4]

In the last 6 years, there has been one decision of the Cartel Court, where the Court found that an undertaking had abused its market dominance.[5] In some further proceedings, applications by the authority or private claimants have been dismissed for various reasons. None of the proceedings, however, dealt with online sales platforms.

Besides the FCA, another competition authority in Austria is the Federal Cartel Prosecutor (Bundeskartellanwalt, 'FCP'). Neither the FCA nor the FCP is entitled to impose antitrust fines; they are exclusively entitled to initiate a fining proceeding before of the Cartel Court (*Oberlandesgericht Wien als Kartellgericht*). Only the Cartel Court can impose a fine for competition law infringements. However, the fine imposed by the Cartel Court may not be higher than requested by the FCA and FCP. On appeal, the Cartel Supreme Court (*Oberster Gerichtshof als Kartellobergericht*) decides on the Cartel Court's rulings.

The above-named competition authorities and courts in Austria are also the competent authorities for online sales platforms.

### 3.1.2 Voidness

Based on the respective competition law clauses of § 1 (3) Cartel Act and Article 101 (2) TFEU, but also as a consequence of basic contract law principles, cartel infringements result in voidness of the respective agreements and decisions. Voidness applies *ex tunc*: invalid clauses cannot be enforced in general. Furthermore, parties can rely on voidness, even if they knew from the beginning that the clause/contract was infringing competition law and was therefore invalid. Hence, in Austria, competition law can be used as a defence against allegations of breach of contract, regardless of whether the contract party was aware of the infringement or not.

Concerning contracts including cartel infringements, the CJEU ruled that only that part of the contract becomes invalid that violates competition law. The consequences for the rest of the contract have to be determined in accordance with national law. Following settled case law in Austria, the question whether an infringement results in voidness of the whole contract or only a part of it must be interpreted in the context of the protective purpose of the rule (*Schutzzweck der Norm*) and whether the remaining agreement can be reasonably separated from the invalid clauses.[6]

Regarding the consequences under civil law, the Cartel Supreme Court has held that for lack of a legal basis, in cartel proceedings. the contracts concluded between

[4] See Cartels and Abuse Control. https://www.en.bwb.gv.at/CartelsAbuseControl/Seiten/default.aspx. Accessed 10 July 2017.

[5] See Supreme Cartel Court, decision of 11 November 2012, 16 Ok 1/12.

[6] See Supreme Court, decision of 13 March 2012, 10 Ob 10/12m.

the defendant and third parties cannot be declared void by the Cartel Court (but only by the respective civil courts).

### 3.1.3 Private Enforcement

Aggrieved competitors, as well as harmed customers, may bring a tort claim. Private plaintiffs may also invoke contractual claims and concepts such as illicit gains. The Cartel Act contains a number of measures intended to strengthen private enforcement. Damage actions and other private motions claiming infringements of competition rules can be brought before the civil courts. So far, it has been commonly understood that the prohibition of cartels and the prohibition of abuses of market dominant positions are so-called protective rules within the meaning of Section 1311 of the Austrian General Civil Code primarily protecting customers (and not only competitors). As mentioned before, the amendment of the Cartel Act 2017 brought substantial improvements for private claimants, including an explicit right for damage compensation for violation of competition law. Additionally, the new rules, inter alia, include a revision of statutory limitation periods, which deviate from general Austrian tort law. Furthermore, the amendments refer to an introduction of a presumption of harm, joint and several liability and privileged status of immunity recipients.

Compensation for punitive damages cannot be awarded in Austria.

### 3.1.4 Relevant Market

So far, in Austrian court decisions, there had been no definition of relevant markets concerning online sales platforms. Based on the general approach of demand substitution,[7] one has to look at the range of products or services that are viewed as substitutes by the consumer/customer. So far, there had been some legal commentary[8] but no indications by Austrian authorities and courts that the market definition approach would be different with regard to new economy/online sales platforms. Based on the traditional approach, the Cartel Court recently defined a national market with regard to online gambling and online betting. The national scope of the market was reasoned by the existing, consistent offer throughout the whole country.[9]

---

[7] Cf., Commission Notice on the definition of relevant market for the purposes of Community competition law OJ 1997 C 372 p. 5, para 15.

[8] Cf., A. Hiersche and A. T. Mayer, Die Ermittlungen der Europäischen Kommission gegen Google: Auf der Suche nach dem Produktmarkt, Marktmacht und Missbrauch (Teil I und Teil II), ÖZK 2016, 203.

[9] Cartel Supreme Court, decision of 21 December 2016, 16 Ok 11/16b.

### 3.1.5 Case Law Concerning Online Sales Platforms

Concerning online sales platforms, so far, no specific legislation or guidance exists in Austria, except the ban on hotel booking portals to demand 'best price' clauses from accommodation establishments, which was recently incorporated into the Austrian Unfair Competition Act.[10] Embedded in the general legal system of Austrian competition law, no distinction is made with regard to the justification of restrictions of competition regarding online sales platforms. Therefore, the benchmark for special competition law issues (e.g., most-favoured-nation clauses) concerning online sale platforms is always based on general and traditional principles of competition law, at least in a first step. It might be, of course, that the undertakings concerned would rely on special economic circumstances of online sales platforms. However, so far, such approach has not been reflected in judgments in Austria.

Furthermore, the Austrian cartel courts have not specifically ruled on 'online sales platforms' or 'new economy' companies. In this report, the authors will provide an overview with regard to certain actual topics in Austrian and EU competition law, which, to a certain extent, can be connected with the subject of the report.

#### 3.1.5.1 Restrictions on Internet Sales

The FCA, in its recent cartel investigations, has generally focused on vertical infringements. Regarding cartel infringements (Article 101 TFEU and Section 1 Cartel Act), over the last 5 years, approximately forty proceedings were dealt with before the Cartel Supreme Court, whereas in approximately thirty of these cases a fine was imposed. Several of these cases addressed Internet sales issues. Mostly, producers tried to prohibit their distributors from selling products online or below a minimum price.

*Pioneer* was fined in the amount of EUR 350,000[11] for violating Article 101 TFEU, namely agreeing in vertical price restrictions; *Pioneer* was also fined for hindering distributors from selling electronic products online. Without referring to a 'restriction by object', the Cartel Court considered this concerted practice of being a—literally—'key infringement'. So far, the highest fine that also covered restrictions on online trading amounted to EUR 2.9 million and was imposed on *Philips* for coordination regarding retail prices of its distributors. The investigations of the FCA were based on complaints of online distributors.[12] Furthermore, *MediaSaturn* and its suppliers had participated in vertical pricing agreements, also with regard to restricting online sales concerning various electronic goods. *Saturn* was fined EUR 1.2 million.[13]

*Grundig* was found to have engaged in resale price maintenance online. Following the press, approximately 50 online retailers, which sold *Grundig* products to/in

[10] See Sect. 3.1.5.2 below.

[11] Cartel Court, decision of 25 March 2014, 27 Kt 20/14.

[12] Cartel Court, decision of 26 March 2013, 29 Kt 26/13-6.

[13] Cartel Court, decision of 23 April 2014, 26 Kt 19/14.

Austria, were contacted by *Grundig* and urged to either increase their online prices or take the products off their respective website. Retailers that did not follow the instructions were partly not supplied anymore or had to pay higher purchase prices. A fine of EUR 372,000 was imposed on *Grundig*.[14]

*Samsung* was also found to have been involved in several vertical concerted practices—partly following requests from its distributors to increase online sales prices relating to certain electronic goods such as TVs or tablets. A fine of EUR 1.05 million was imposed.[15] Last, *Hewlett Packard* engaged in online resale price maintenance and was therefore fined EUR 640,000.[16] Among other things, *Hewlett Packard* required online retailers to set their selling prices to a specified amount. Otherwise, *Hewlett Packard* threatened to withhold its supply. *De Longhi*, inter alia, urged its dealers not to use price search engines and was fined EUR 650,000 for participating in vertical pricing agreements.[17]

#### 3.1.5.2 Hotel Booking Platforms

In 2015, based on investigations of NCAs (among them the FCA), *Booking.com* and *Expedia* changed their general terms and conditions concerning hotel booking platforms and withdrew their parity price clauses as agreed upon with hotels in 2015. Following these changes, hotels were able to offer cheaper rates (and conditions) via all channels (telephone, fax, brochures, direct contact, also other booking platforms) except the hotels' own websites, in relation to which the booking platforms maintained their best-price clause exclusivity.

The FCA was one of the EU-NCAs to accept remedies. Apparently, it had been initially planned that the platforms concerned would have to submit a remedy package to the FCA in exchange for a 'comfort letter' stating that, on the basis of the facts known to the FCA at the relevant point in time, they do not see a reason to file an application with the Cartel Court or at least in exchange for a letter confirming that the proceedings would not be continued.

However, the 'remedies process' ultimately was not finalised due to the amendment of the Austrian Unfair Competition Act. The Unfair Competition Act prohibits price exclusivity clauses ('best price' clauses) for hotel booking platforms *per se*: those platforms are also not entitled to agree with hotels on exclusivity clauses regarding the hotel's own website anymore. The request of a booking platform to contractually oblige the hotel operator not to underprice is now considered as 'an aggressive business practice' (with regard to all possible sales channels; in the law, reference is also explicitly made to the hotel's own website). Such 'aggressive business practice', under any circumstances, infringes the Austrian Unfair Competition Act.[18]

---

[14] Cartel Court, decision of 21 May 2014, 24 Kt 17/14.

[15] Cartel Court, decision of 09 September 2015, 24 Kt 35/15.

[16] Cartel Court, decision of 01 December 2015, 29 Kt 34/15.

[17] Cartel Court, decision of 14 November 2016, 25 Kt 6/16v.

[18] See Austrian Unfair Competition Act, Annex, para 32 in conjunction with § 1a (4) Austrian Unfair Competition Act, according to which the unlawful agreement shall be null and void; see also § 7 Austrian Price Indication Act.

The change in law is currently being challenged by booking platforms before the Austrian Constitutional Court. It is argued that the general prohibition on best-price clauses amounts to an undue legal discrimination under the Austrian constitution. During the public consultation of the amendment of the Unfair Competition Act, the FCA confirmed that the commitments submitted by *Booking.com* and *Expedia* were sufficient.[19] One might indeed doubt why only and explicitly hotel booking platforms are prohibited from demanding best-price clauses and why they are considered to act unlawfully irrespective of whether they are dominant or not and regardless of the circumstances of the case.

#### 3.1.5.3 Online Sales Platforms

To the authors' knowledge, third-party online sales platforms in the narrower sense, i.e. software applications that allow online businesses to manage their sales and operations, have been only occasionally touched upon in cartel proceedings in Austria. To date, court decisions do not particularly refer to online sales platforms. As outlined above, in one recent decision of the Cartel Court,[20] 'price search engines' were mentioned in the summary of the facts but not in the legal findings (which focused on the prohibited ban on Internet sales).

However, as Austria is a member of the European Union, the currently ongoing preliminary ruling proceedings in *Coty*[21] before the CJEU, which also addresses sales restrictions on third-party online sales platforms, could have a major impact on Austria. Even in purely national cartel cases, national cartel courts might refer to case law of the CJEU.

Coty focuses on distributing perfume in Germany from luxury brands such as Calvin Klein or Jill Sanders. Coty uses a selective distribution system in which their retailers must comply with guidelines. These guidelines include a total ban of online sales via third-party online sales platforms, such as Amazon and eBay. According to Coty, this measure is intended to preserve the prestige character of the distributed brands. Parfümerie Akzente, one of Coty's retailers, used Amazon to sell the products. Coty initially applied for an injunction against Parfümerie Akzente's actions. However, the district court Frankfurt dismissed the complaint, stating that the clause in question, banning online sales on third-party platforms, violates § 1 GWB, as well as Article 101 TFEU. Coty then lodged an appeal to the higher regional court Frankfurt. In its appeal, Coty argued that its distribution concept does not request a general ban on online sales. However, a specific prohibition to sell via online sales platforms would be necessary in order to protect its luxury brands.

---

[19] Gesetzesnovelle UWG und Preisauszeichnungsgesetz; Stellungnahme der Bundeswettbewerbsbehörde, of 29 June 2016. https://www.parlament.gv.at/PAKT/VHG/XXV/SNME/SNME_07075/imfname_543571.pdf. Accessed on 11 July 2017.

[20] Cartel Court, decision of 14 November 2016, 25 Kt 6/16.

[21] CJEU, case C-230/16, Request for a preliminary ruling from the Oberlandesgericht Frankfurt am Main (Germany), *Coty Germany GmbH v Parfümerie Akzente GmbH*.

The Higher Regional Court Frankfurt sought guidance from the CJEU. In its preliminary reference, the following questions were being presented to the Court:

1. Do selective distribution systems that have as their aim the distribution of luxury goods and primarily serve to ensure a 'luxury image' for the goods constitute an aspect of competition that is compatible with Article 101(1) TFEU?
2. If the first question is answered in the affirmative:
   Does it constitute an aspect of competition that is compatible with Article 101(1) TFEU if the members of a selective distribution system operating at the retail level of trade are prohibited generally from engaging third-party undertakings discernible to the public to handle Internet sales, irrespective of whether the manufacturer's legitimate quality standards are contravened in the specific case?
3. Is Article 4(b) of Regulation (EU) No 330/2010 (1) to be interpreted as meaning that a prohibition of engaging third-party undertakings discernible to the public to handle Internet sales that is imposed on the members of a selective distribution system operating at the retail level of trade constitutes a restriction of the retailer's customer group 'by object'?
4. Is Article 4(c) of Regulation (EU) No 330/2010 to be interpreted as meaning that a prohibition of engaging third-party undertakings discernible to the public to handle Internet sales that is imposed on the members of a selective distribution system operating at the retail level of trade constitutes a restriction of passive sales to end users 'by object'?

So far, the CJEU did not rule on the questions submitted. In its opinion from 26 July 2017,[22] Advocate General Wahl stated that the contested provision according to which Coty Germany prohibits its authorised retailers from using third-party platforms for Internet sales of the contract goods is not necessarily caught by Article 101 (1) TFEU where (1) it is dependent on the nature of the product, (2) it is determined in a uniform fashion and applied without distinction and (3) it does not go beyond what is necessary.

GA Wahl hereby takes the position that selective distribution systems relating to the distribution of luxury products are not necessarily caught by Article 101 (1) TFEU. In the General Advocate's view, a prohibition to use third-party platforms is likely to improve the luxury image of the products concerned. Furthermore, such prohibition is also proportional as compliance with the qualitative requirements that may be lawfully imposed in relation to selective distribution systems can be effectively ensured only if the Internet sales environment is devised by authorised resellers.

Even in the event that the restriction at issue is found, in principle, to be caught by Article 101 (1) TFEU, Advocate General Wahl points out that, in his view, the contested prohibition does not constitute a serious restriction within the meaning of

[22] CJEU, case C-230/16, *Coty Germany GmbH v Parfümerie Akzente GmbH, Opinion of Advocate General Wahl, delivered on 26 July 2017.*

Regulation No 330/2010, so that it is not automatically excluded from the benefit of a block exemption.

In principle, it is generally accepted in EU competition law that a total ban of online sales is considered as a restriction of passive sales, which infringes Article 101 TFEU. In its judgment in Pierre Fabre,[23] the CJEU pointed out that, in the light of the freedoms of movement, it does not accept arguments relating to the need to provide individual advice to the customer and to ensure his protection against the incorrect use of products, put forward to justify a ban on Internet sales. Furthermore, it was ruled that the aim of maintaining a prestigious image is not a legitimate aim for restricting competition and cannot therefore justify a finding that a contractual clause pursuing such an aim does not fall within Article 101(1) TFEU.

However, it is also generally acknowledged that several restrictions may be allowed to ensure qualitative requirements in selective distribution systems. Therefore, the main question is whether EU competition law allows prohibiting the sale on third-party online platforms in order to justify selective distribution systems and in order to protect quality requirements. In its vertical guidelines, the EU Commission states that 'where the distributor's website is hosted by a third party platform, the supplier may require that customers do not visit the distributor's website through a site carrying the name or logo of the third party platform'.[24] Following legal commentary, the Commission hereby accepts a general ban of third-party online sales platforms.[25] In its Final Report on the e-commerce sector inquiry,[26] the European Commission confirms 'that marketplace bans do not generally amount to a de facto prohibition on selling online or restrict the effective use of the internet as a sales channel'.

Such general ban was also accepted by German courts.

In the 'Scouts' proceedings, *Scout* prohibited its distributors to sell Scout school bags on auction platforms such as eBay. The Berlin Court of Appeal ruled that, in general, a distributor can be prohibited from reselling the school bag on auction platforms such as eBay as part of a selective distribution system. However, following the court, such ban is only valid if it is applied unanimously. In this particular case, 'Scout', which claimed that its school bags' high-quality image would be impaired if they were sold on auction platforms like eBay, distributed Scout products through a discount chain. The Court therefore found that the prohibition on using online sales platforms was discriminatory and therefore invalid.

Recently, the Higher Regional Court Düsseldorf confirmed in the 'Asics' ruling that the general prohibition for distributors to use price comparison sites constitutes

[23] CJEU, case C-439/09, *Pierre Fabre Dermo-Cosmétique SAS v Président de l'Autorité de la Concurrence and Others*, ECLI:EU:C:2011:649.

[24] Guidelines on Vertical Restraints, OJ2010 C 130, p. 1, para 54.

[25] See, e.g., J. Schultze, St. Pautke and D. Wagener, Vertikal-GVO, Praxiskommentar, 3rd ed, Verlag Recht und Wirtschaft, para 773.: '*The manufacturer's granted choice to prohibit its distributors the sale via third party plattforms within the scope of the vertical Block Exemption Regulation 330/2010 is of substantial practical importance*'.

[26] European Commission (2017) Report from the Commission to the Council and the European Parliament, para 41; {SWD (2017) 154 final}; http://ec.europa.eu/competition/antitrust/sector_inquiry_final_report_en.pdf. Accessed 10 May 2017.

a restriction of competition.[27] Following the Court, the prohibition is also not justified by branding and advisory services as consumers would not necessarily need or want to be advised in the case of running shoes or would also be able to get information on the Internet. Interestingly, the question whether the former distribution system of Asics was also in breach of core antitrust rules because of Asics' prohibition on its distributors to use Google AdWords and third-party online marketplaces was left open. The German Federal Cartel Authority (*Bundeskartellamt*) had ruled in first instance, and later argued before the Higher Regional Court Düsseldorf, that such a general ban on sales on third-party online sales platforms is a hardcore infringement for its own.

#### 3.1.5.4 Commission's E-Commerce Sector Inquiry

On 6 May 2015, the European Commission—as part of its Digital Single Market Strategy and on the basis of Article 17 of Regulation 1/2003—launched the sector inquiry into e-commerce. The Commission requested information from a variety of stakeholders in e-commerce markets throughout the EU both in relation to the online sales of consumer goods (such as electronics, clothing, shoes and sports equipment) and in relation to the online distribution of digital content.

On 10 May 2017, the Commission adopted the abovementioned Final Report on the e-commerce sector inquiry[28] and published an accompanying Staff Working Document,[29] which set out the main findings of the e-commerce sector inquiry. The views and comments submitted by stakeholders during the public consultation were taken into account. The report itself focuses in its first section on e-commerce of consumer goods, while the second section refers to e-commerce of digital content.

The main findings are the following:

- More and more manufacturers use their own retail shops in order to sell their products directly to the consumer. As a consequence, manufacturers are increasingly in direct competition with their distributors.
- Manufacturers increasingly rely on selective distribution systems. Hence, manufacturers are able to better control their distribution networks (especially in terms of quality of distribution and also concerning the retail price);
- Manufacturers include restrictions in their distribution contracts in order to better control its distribution. Examples include, inter alia, pricing restrictions, marketplace (platform) bans, restrictions on the use of price comparison tools and exclusion of pure online players from distribution networks.

[27] Higher Regional Court Düsseldorf, Decision of 5 April 2017, VI Kart 13/15 [V].

[28] European Commission (2017) Report from the Commission to the Council and the European Parliament, {SWD (2017) 154 final}; http://ec.europa.eu/competition/antitrust/sector_inquiry_final_report_en.pdf. Accessed 10 May 2017.

[29] European Commission (2017), Commission Staff Working Document, Accompanying the document Report from the Commission to the Council and the European Parliament, Final report on the E-commerce Sector Inquiry {COM(2017) 229 final}; http://ec.europa.eu/competition/antitrust/sector_inquiry_swd_en.pdf. Accessed 10 May 2017.

The report also pointed out licensing practices, which, following the Commission, 'may' be in breach of competition law. The Commission hereby referred to the fact that such assessment of licensing practices must consider the characteristics of the content industry.

From an Austrian perspective, it is of special interest that the FCA published some comments in the Commission's public consultation phase.[30] In its opinion, the FCA points out that e-commerce distributors very often are small undertakings that are economically dependent on the manufacturers, especially in selective distribution systems. From the authors' practical experience, depending on the special circumstances of the case and the business segment concerned, it cannot be excluded upfront that there might be also dominant (or at least powerful) e-commerce distributors, which manufacturers must rely on in order to succeed. In the author's view, this is of especial importance for small or middle-sized suppliers (in Austria, 99.7% of the total business economy were SMEs[31]). However, also the FCA in its opinion does not exclude that this might be the case.

In the FCA's view, distributors might be hesitant in submitting claims to the respective competition authorities. Hence, in the FCA's view, it might be that competition restraints will not be disclosed in the course of sector inquiries but only based on investigations, particularly dawn raids.

In substance and based on non-disclosed evidence, the FCA refers to the fact that manufacturers are increasingly introducing selective distribution systems in order to exclude traders that compete on prices. Quality criteria are very broadly defined, which allows the manufacturer to decide on a wide margin of discretion whether price-aggressive distributors can be excluded from the distribution system. Often, the manufacturer's threat to exclude dealers already helps to stabilise the (high) price level.

The FCA therefore does not accept that a ban on distributors to sell via third-party online platforms (or to sell on online platforms in certain other EU Member States) is generally in line with competition law, especially if the manufacturer itself sells its products via such online platforms, e.g. via Amazon. Under such circumstances, such a blanket ban on selling via third-party online platforms is considered to be 'unsuitable' as a quality criterion in selective distribution systems. Therefore, following the FCA's approach, such blanket ban—depending on the circumstances—might be considered as being a restriction of competition (the FCA itself does not explicitly refer to legal consequences). The FCA also refers to the fact that Amazon itself might be a member of the respective selective distribution system. Furthermore, due to the often small size of the distributors concerned, third-party online sales

[30] Bundeswettbewerbsbehörde (2016), Stellungnahme der Bundeswettbewerbsbehörde zum Zwischenbericht der Europäischen Kommission über die Sektoruntersuchung zum elektronischen Handel; http://ec.europa.eu/competition/antitrust/e_commerce_files/bundeswettbewerbsbehorde_de.pdf. Accessed 16 September 2016.

[31] Bundesministerium für Wissenschaft, Forschung und Wirtschaft (2016), Mittelstandsbericht 2016, Bericht über die Situation der kleinen und mittleren Unternehmen der österreichischen Wirtschaft; https://www.en.bmwfw.gv.at/Enterprise/Documents/Mittelstandsbericht_barrierefrei_15.11_Version3.pdf. Accessed November 2016.

platforms are of essential importance to compete on the market, while own websites might be a too high burden with regard to both time and money constraints for distributors.

The FCA also doubts that online sale prohibitions for certain premium products can be justified to protect the image of the product or the 'offline' advice in brick-and-mortar shops. Often, in the FCA's view, such bans can be considered as measure to avoid too low retail prices in order to stabilise prices. Again, following this approach, such ban might be therefore considered as an infringement, especially if the producer itself sells its products via online sales platform such as Amazon or eBay.

As a consequence of its sector inquiry, the European Commission announced in February 2017 that it had opened three investigations concerning consumer electronics, video game publishers and tour operators/hotels.[32]

According to the press release, allegedly, online retailers of electronic goods had been restricted by the respective manufacturers (namely Asus, Denon & Marantz, Philips and Pioneer) to set their own prices. Following the European Commission's press release, the effect of these suspected price restrictions may be aggravated due to the use by many online retailers of pricing software that automatically adapts retail prices to those of leading competitors. As a result, the alleged behaviour may have had a broader impact on overall online prices for the respective consumer electronics products.

The investigation in the video game sector[33] focuses on geo-blocking practices, where companies prevent consumers from purchasing digital content, in this case PC video games,[34] because of the consumer's location or country of residence.

Lastly, following complaints from customers, the Commission is investigating agreements regarding hotel accommodation concluded between the largest European tour operators on the one hand (*Kuoni, REWE, Thomas Cook, TUI*) and hotels on the other hand (*Meliá Hotels*). Again, the agreements allegedly discriminate customers on the basis of their location. Based on their location, customers would not be able to see the full hotel availability or book hotel rooms at the best prices.

In June 2017, the Commission announced that it is investigating whether clothing company Guess's distribution agreements restrict authorised retailers from selling online to consumers or to retailers in other Member States.[35]

---

[32] European Commission (2017) Press release; Antitrust: Commission opens three investigations into suspected anticompetitive practices in e-commerce; http://europa.eu/rapid/press-release_IP-17-201_en.htm. Accessed 2 February 2017.

[33] European Commission (2017) Press release; Antitrust: Commission opens three investigations into suspected anticompetitive practices in e-commerce; http://europa.eu/rapid/press-release_IP-17-201_en.htm. Accessed 2 February 2017.

[34] The undertakings concerned are Valve Corporation, owner of the Steam game distribution platform, and five PC video game publishers, namely Bandai Namco, Capcom, Focus Home, Koch Media and ZeniMax.

[35] European Commission (2017) Press release, Antitrust: Commission opens formal investigation into distribution practices of clothing company Guess; http://europa.eu/rapid/press-release_IP-17-1549_en.htm. Accessed 6 June 2017.

## 3.2 Antitrust Issues Generated by the Growth of Online Sales Platforms

Generally speaking, online sales platforms may trigger competition concerns only under specific conditions. In broad terms, the areas where issues could arise relate on the one hand to market power and unilateral conduct, such as market power abuse, and on the other hand to questions of anticompetitive behaviour between different market players. It may be stressed at this point, however, that online sales platforms genuinely enhance competition and have led to various positive effects for consumers and retailers, as prices decreased and became more transparent.

However, with regard to market power, online sales platforms might have a self-reinforcing effect, meaning the more users are present and the more products are traded, the more attractive a platform becomes, which in turn attracts even more users. In this regard, online sales platforms are comparable to other platforms on which goods are being traded in particular exchanges or exchange platforms, which success depends on their liquidity. Again, such high liquidity, of course, generally also has positive effects and may foster competition, as well as additional ways of distribution, which is characterised by high transparency and competitive pricing.

However, online platforms may create a lock-in effect, in the sense that certain products may only be available through the platform to the exclusion of multi-homing. The combination of market power and lock-in effects may create specific competition concerns—in case of an abuse of market power, such as (unjustified) high fees for platform users, concentration of data (as a means of 'payment'), exclusivity contracts or possible manipulation by the owner of the platform, who may also sell on the platform himself. In essence, there is no difference to other potential abuse of dominance cases and online platforms should be treated like any other market participant in this context.

Ways to overcome this problem, however, very much depend on whether producers and users are enabled to make use of other online platforms either alternatively or in parallel. In case of lock-in effects, possible remedies may relate to a strict approach towards exclusionary practices apt to foster dependencies of producers or users to one single platform. *If 'payment' is made through personal data, which in turn might also result in an excessive data collection, the German* Federal Cartel Authority seems to categorise this by analogy with excessive pricing as an existing concept under the rules of market power abuse.[36] So both tools (prohibition of exclusionary contracts, excessive pricing) are recognised tools in existing antitrust practice—and there does not seem to be the need for new concepts or further legal tools.

Apart from market power scenarios, online sales platforms could raise other competition concerns by facilitating the monitoring of price recommendations, resale price maintenance or collusive practices. In particular, certain algorithm may facilitate price coordination, and the unsolved question remains to what extent the

[36] Presentation by Julia Topel at the Conference 'Towards a digital Single Market: Competition law has parts to play' of the Association of European Competition Law Judges in Vienna.

use of such algorithms constitutes an infringement under Article 101 TEUF, respectively §1 Cartel Act.

Due to online sales platforms, both manufacturers and retailers also became able to easily monitor online retail prices and nowadays sometimes use pricing software. Consequently, the detection of deviations, for instance, from price recommendations has been significantly facilitated. It did not only become easier for producers to retaliate in response to deviations from their expected price levels, but also the incentives for retailers not to consider maximum/minimum prices prescribed by manufacturers may have been limited. Increased price transparency may also have the effect of facilitating or strengthening collusion between retailers, without the need to exchange sensitive information. However, the increase of price transparency via online platforms is to be considered as pro-competitive, and only an abuse of advantageous effects may infringe competition rules.

Another specific competition restriction was the application of so-called 'best price clauses' in hotel booking platforms, which meanwhile has become irrelevant since the Austrian legislator amended the Austrian Unfair Competition Act by putting this practice on the blacklist of inadmissible aggressive business practices (see Sect. 3.1.5.2 above).

Finally, competition concerns may arise and have already vastly arisen through the avoidance of online sales platforms.

Issues in this regard, for example, relate to selective distribution schemes, by means of which producers could make use of strategies to maintain prices at a certain level. In order to restrain online sales to local areas, producers separate offline from online authorisation while refusing the latter, if the domain name differs from the offline shop name. The intention is to prevent passive online sales beyond the local sales area, which is particularly questionable with regard to hybrid retailers (selling on- and offline). The prohibition of passive (online) sales as such would, however, not be in compliance with competition rules.

In this context, one of the main criteria for (or against) an authorisation for online sales is the behaviour of the retailer, more specifically the retailer's pricing policy. Retailers known for regularly undercutting the market price level would be given an authorisation to sell online by themselves or via sales platforms. Producers can (mis)use online sales platforms to monitor pricing policies of their retailers and exclude from their distribution system those among them who conduct an aggressive pricing policy. Still, in many cases, exclusion will be based on objective and qualitative criteria justifying certain restrictions.

Increased price competition on sales platforms may lead some producers to more frequently require in their distribution agreements the operation of a 'brick and mortar shop' by retailers, thereby effectively excluding pure online retailers from the distribution. It may be stressed that Regulation 330/2010 in principle allows for requirements that are meant to promote distribution quality or proper technical advice.

As outlined above, another competition issue arises where producers prevent retailers from selling on online marketplaces altogether. The question on the extent to which such a restriction complies with competition rules is not clarified yet since a reference for a preliminary ruling on this very question is currently pending before the Court of Justice of the EU (see C-230/16, *Coty Germany*). For details, reference is made to Sect. 3.1.5 above.

Are there ways to address these concerns? There does not seem to be a panacea for the wide range of possible competition restrictions that might relate to online sales platforms. Competition issues triggered by online sales platforms in many cases will not constitute competition law infringements and may well be justified. Moreover, restrictions still would have to be assessed against the background of pro-competitive effects that online sales platforms as such bring with them. Again, there does not seem to be the need for further or more specific tools in antitrust legislation—but existing tools may need to adapt to the new digital environment.

# Belgium

# 4

Steffie De Cock

## 4.1 Introduction

This chapter examines the impact of the digital economy on competition law enforcement in Belgium. One of its main goals is to assess the major competition issues generated by the growth of online sales platforms and how they should be resolved from a Belgian perspective. Online sales platforms constitute one example of many different types of online platforms, such as online advertising platforms, search engines, social media and creative content outlets, application distribution platforms, communication services and payment systems.[1]

Over the last years, the Belgian Competition Authority (the 'BCA') has not dealt with many vertical competition cases. The case law on online sales platforms is therefore limited. However, this trend is changing, and the BCA has declared in its 2016 annual report that the distribution sector will be a priority in 2017 as contracts between distributors and suppliers could lead to anti-competitive restraints. For example, suppliers can limit the opportunities for distributors to offer products or services online.[2] Recently, the BCA has conducted investigations in cooking

[1] European Commission (2016) Communication on Online Platforms and the Digital Single Market: Opportunities and Challenges for Europe, 2. http://eur-lex.europa.eu/legal-content/EN/TXT/PDF/?uri=CELEX:52016DC0288&from=EN. Accessed 19 May 2017; European Commission, Staff working document on Online Platforms, 1. https://ec.europa.eu/digital-single-market/en/news/commission-staff-working-document-online-platforms. Accessed 19 May 2017.

[2] Belgian Competition Authority (2017) Year Report 2016. https://www.bma-abc.be/sites/default/files/content/download/files/2016_jaarverslag_bma_0.pdf. Accessed 19 May 2017.

S. De Cock (✉)
Altius, Brussels, Belgium
e-mail: steffie.de.cock@icloud.com





B. Kilpatrick et al. (eds.), *Antitrust Analysis of Online Sales Platforms & Copyright Limitations and Exceptions*, LIDC Contributions on Antitrust Law, Intellectual Property and Unfair Competition,
https://doi.org/10.1007/978-3-319-71419-6_4

utensils, wine accessories and water softeners markets.[3] It has issued a decision on vertical restraints in agreements between an undertaking selling fresh bakers' yeast and bakeries.[4]

This chapter will first describe recent developments at the European level regarding online sales platforms. Second, it will discuss the most important Belgian decision concerning online sales platforms. Third, the impact of online sales on mergers will be outlined. Fourth, it discusses online sales restrictions that are mostly in selective distribution systems. This chapter concludes with some future recommendations and an evaluation about whether different competition law criteria should be applied to the new digital economy.

## 4.2 Background: Assessment of Online Marketplaces at the EU Level

The European Commission attaches great value to the Internet as a sales channel for reaching a wide variety of customers in different countries.[5]

On 25 May 2016, the Commission issued a Communication on online platforms and the digital single market in which it recognised that online platforms play a key role in innovation and growth in the digital single market. It states that 'they have revolutionized access to information and have made many markets more efficient by better connecting buyers and sellers of services and goods'.[6] The Commission Staff Working Document accompanying the Communication identified the benefits of online platforms for consumers, for businesses and their general economic and social benefits.[7]

On 10 May 2017, the Commission published its report on e-commerce ('Final Report on the e-commerce sector inquiry'),[8] together with a staff working

[3] Belgian Competition Authority (2017) Press release n°9-2017, The Belgian Competition Authority confirms the inspection at a company active in the distribution and sale of cooking utensils and wine accessories. https://www.belgiancompetition.be/sites/default/files/content/download/files/20170508_press_release_9_bca.pdf. Accessed 19 May 2017; Belgian Competition Authority (2017) Press release n°8-2017, The Belgian Competition Authority confirms the inspection at an undertaking active in the distribution and sale of water softeners.https://www.belgiancompetition.be/sites/default/files/content/download/files/20170505_press_release_8_bca.pdf. Accessed 19 May 2017.

[4] BCA, Case MEDE-I/O-13/0001, *Algist Bruggeman N.V.*, 22 March 2017.

[5] European Commission, Guidelines on Vertical Restraints, OJ 2010 C 130, p. 1.

[6] European Commission (2016) Communication on Online Platforms and the Digital Single Market: Opportunities and Challenges for Europe, 15. http://eur-lex.europa.eu/legal-content/EN/TXT/PDF/?uri=CELEX:52016DC0288&from=EN. Accessed 19 May 2017.

[7] European Commission (2016) Staff working document on Online Platforms, 11–15. https://ec.europa.eu/digital-single-market/en/news/commission-staff-working-document-online-platforms. Accessed 19 May 2017.

[8] European Commission (2017) Final Report on the E-commerce Sector Inquiry. http://ec.europa.eu/competition/antitrust/sector_inquiry_final_report_en.pdf. Accessed 1 June 2017.

document[9] ('Staff Working Document on the e-commerce sector inquiry').[10] These reports will be further discussed in Sect. 4.4 below.

The treatment of competition issues arising in the context of online sales at the EU level is important for Belgium as it might be expected that the BCA and the Belgian courts will follow EU law in future cases.[11]

## 4.3 Belgian Legislation and Jurisprudence Related to Online Sales

### 4.3.1 Legislation

#### 4.3.1.1 Restrictive Competition Practices

In Belgium, competition legislation is enshrined in Book IV of the Belgian Code of Economic Law (the 'CEL').[12] The prohibition on agreements, decisions of associations of undertakings and concerted practices that have as their object or effect the restriction of competition and the prohibition on the abuse of dominant position are respectively laid down in Articles IV.1 and IV.2 of the CEL. The rules are similar to Articles 101 and 102 TFEU. According to Article IV.4 of the CEL, the prohibition laid down in Article IV.1 of the CEL does not apply to agreements that enjoy the exemption provided for in Regulation 330/2010.[13] There exist no specific Belgian guidelines or directives about vertical restraints. However, the BCA and the Belgian courts and tribunals tend to apply the guidelines on vertical restraints issued by the Commission ('Guidelines on Vertical Restraints').[14] As they date from 2010, they do not respond to new issues resulting from the digital economy and online sales platforms. However, most of the general rules still apply and are relevant for Internet-related enterprises, just as they are for any other undertaking.

#### 4.3.1.2 Mergers

The rules on mergers are embedded in Article IV.6 to IV.11 of the CEL. Concentrations must be notified in Belgium if the undertakings concerned, taken together, have a

[9] European Commission (2017) Staff working document on the E-commerce sector inquiry. http://ec.europa.eu/competition/antitrust/sector_inquiry_swd_en.pdf. Accessed 1 June 2017.

[10] Together referred to as the 'E-commerce sector inquiry report'.

[11] Cass. 9 juni 2000, *Brussels International Trade Mart/S.C. Barlow en Amadeus B.V.B.A.*, *Arr. Cass.* 2000, 1071, www.cass.be, *J.L.M.B.* 2000, 1284, *T.B.H.* 2000, 493.

[12] Code of Economic Law, *Belgian Official Journal* 29 March 2013, p. 19975 ('CEL').

[13] Commission Regulation 330/2010 of 20 April 2010 on the application of Article 101(3) of the Treaty on the Functioning of the European Union to categories of vertical agreements and concerted practices, OJ 2010 L 102, p. 1.

[14] European Commission, Guidelines on Vertical Restraints, OJ 2010, C 130, p. 1 ('Guidelines on Vertical Restraints'); Antwerpen 28 September 2009, *Handelspraktijken & Mededinging*, 979; Gent 7 maart 2016, *TBM* 2016, jg. 4, 403–408; BCA, Case MEDE-I/O-13/0001, *Algist Bruggeman N.V.*, 22 March 2017, 7, 20–22, 28.

total turnover of more than EUR 100 million in Belgium,[15] and if at least two of the undertakings concerned each have a turnover of at least EUR 40 million in Belgium, unless the concentration has a 'Community dimension'.[16,17] The relevant turnover is the consolidated sales turnover in Belgium during the preceding financial year. On the seller's side, only the Belgian turnover generated by the target company or companies should be taken into account.[18] The parties must obtain approval for the proposed concentration before it can be implemented.[19]

In 2006, the 'significant impediment to effective competition' test was introduced in Belgian competition law as the substantive test for clearance, aligning it with Regulation 139/2004.[20] A particular feature of the Belgian merger control system is that a transaction must be approved by the Competition College if the post-merger joint market share of the parties in any relevant horizontal or vertical market does not exceed 25%.[21]

#### 4.3.1.3 Private Enforcement

Private enforcement of the competition law is also possible in Belgium. First, victims of anti-competitive behaviour can claim damages. Directive 2014/104 of the European Parliament and the Council of 26 November 2014 on certain rules governing actions for damages under national law for infringements of the competition law provisions of the member states and the European Union ('Directive 2014/104') has been implemented in Belgium.[22] This law, to a large extent, follows the rules set out in Directive 2014/104. The new rules only apply to court actions initiated since 26 December 2014.[23] Court actions initiated before this date will be governed by the

[15] Article IV.7, Section 1 CEL.

[16] Article IV.11 CEL.

[17] C. Verdonck and S. De Cock, Belgium. In: Knable Gotts (ed), The Merger Control Review, Law Business Research 2016, p. 113.

[18] Article IV.8 CEL; C. Verdonck and S. De Cock, Belgium. In: Knable Gotts (ed), The Merger Control Review, Law Business Research 2016, p. 113.

[19] Article IV.10, Section 5 CEL; C. Verdonck and S. De Cock, Belgium. In: Knable Gotts (ed), The Merger Control Review, Law Business Research 2016, p. 113.

[20] C. Verdonck and S. De Cock, Belgium. In: Knable Gotts (ed), The Merger Control Review, Law Business Research 2016, p. 113.

[21] Article IV.61, Section 2, 2° CEL; C. Verdonck and S. De Cock, Belgium. In: Knable Gotts (ed), The Merger Control Review, Law Business Research 2016, p. 113.

[22] The Law of 6 June 2017 regarding the insertion of a Title 3 'Actions for damages for competition law infringements' in Book XVII of the Code of Economic Law, regarding the insertion of definitions set out in Book XVII, Title 3 and Book I and regarding different modifications to the Code of Economic Law, *Belgian Official Journal* 16 June 2017, p. 63596 ('Law implementing Directive 2017/104').

[23] Art. 45 of the Law implementing the Damages Directive.

general rules on extra-contractual liability.[24] The implementation of the Directive means that any person suffering from harm caused by any competition law infringement is able to obtain full compensation for that harm under the principles of general law.[25] In Belgium, according to general law, damages should provide for the full recovery of the damaged person (including direct and indirect damages, such as loss of profits, etc.).[26] However, awarding punitive damages is not generally accepted in Belgium.[27]

In this regard, it is also worth noting that consumer organisations and other authorised organisations may introduce collective damages actions on behalf of any group of consumers.[28] Following the implementation of Directive 2014/104, the rules on collective damages actions have also been reviewed.

Second, claimants alleging competition law breaches may also bring a cease-and-desist action on the basis of Article XVII.1 of the CEL before the competent President of the Commercial Court.[29]

Third, competition law is also occasionally used as defence against allegations of breach of contract by arguing that the breached provision contravenes competition rules. We are not aware of any precedent regarding online sales in this respect.

#### 4.3.1.4 The Belgian Competition Authority

The BCA is composed of an investigation and prosecution body, the BCA's Investigation and Prosecution Service, and a decision-making body, the Competition College.[30]

---

[24] Article 1382 of the Belgian Civil Code, *Code Napoléon* 3 September 1807; Rb. Kh. Brussel 24 november 2014, A.R.A/08/06816, *Commissie/Otis e.a., TBM* 2015, 37–46; Brussel 14 januari 2015, 2010/AR/3112, *NMBS/Electrabel, TBM* 2016, 33–47; Rb. Kh. Brussel 24 april 2015, A/12/02291 en A/12/02293, *Belgische Staat/Liftenproducenten, TBM* 2015, 212–227; D. Gerard, Belgium. In: K. Gotts (ed), The Private competition enforcement review, Law Business Research Ltd 2016, p. 62.

[25] Art. 15 of the Law implementing the Damages Directive.

[26] D. Gerard, Belgium. In: K. Gotts (ed), The Private competition enforcement review, Law Business Research Ltd 2016, p. 62.

[27] In article 49, §1, 1° of the Royal Decree of 14 January 2013 regarding the determination of the implementation rules of public procurement and of public works concessions, *Belgian Official Journal* 14 February 2013, err., *Belgian Official Journal* 26 March 2013, an example of punitive damages can be found.

[28] Art. XVII.35–69 CEL; E. De Baere, A. Maertens and K. Willems, Belgische class action. Tien pijnpunten, NJW 2015, pp. 522–535.

[29] Procedure laid down in Article XVII.1–34 of the CEL. It concerns summary proceedings and gives rise to a judgment on the merits. However, urgency does not have to be proved to initiate these proceedings.

[30] Article IV.16, §2, 2° and 4° of the CEL.

### 4.3.2 Case Law

#### 4.3.2.1 The *Immoweb* Decision

The most important decision in Belgium for online sales platforms is the *Immoweb* decision, which the BCA issued on 7 November 2016.[31]

On 15 January 2016, the BCA's Investigation and Prosecution Service opened an *ex officio* investigation against Immoweb. Immoweb SA is the company behind www.immoweb.be, Belgium's most important real estate platform, which offers a large overview of real estate properties to buy or rent all over Belgium. The platform works as a matching platform between sellers and lessors of real estate on the one hand and potential buyers and lessees on the other hand. It also is a two-side marketplace that produces network effects: the more visitors the website has, the more useful it is for sellers and lessors to place their offers on the website. The placement of an offer by real estate agencies and individuals costs a small amount of money. The real estate portals also gain money by selling advertising space to third parties that want to advertise their products and/or services on the platform.

In this decision, the BCA's Investigation and Prosecution Service stated that 'Most Favoured Customer clauses' ('MFC clauses') inserted in the contracts between Immoweb and developers of software for real estate agencies could be at odds with the prohibition laid down in Articles 101 and 102 TFEU and Articles IV.1 and IV.2 of the CEL. However, Immoweb offered commitments, and therefore the BCA did not definitively rule on the question of whether the MFC clauses in the contracts between Immoweb and the developers of real estate software infringed Articles 101 and 102 TFEU (and their Belgian equivalents, Articles IV.1 and IV.2 of the CEL).

In what follows, we will discuss the relevant market and then the possible competition law restrictions.

#### Market Definition and Market Position of Immoweb

The relevant product market included online platforms offering only real estate, as well as online platforms offering an important amount of real estate properties, as both these types of platforms displayed similar characteristics, user conditions and prices. Such platforms were held not to be substitutable with real estate agencies' own websites, advertising material, advertisements in journals[32] and street advertisement boards, for different reasons. First, the geographic scope of online platforms was wider than the geographic scope of own websites' offers from real estate agencies, advertisements in journals and street advertising. Second, even at the local level, an online platform had a clear added value in comparison with all other

[31] BCA, Case MEDE-I/0-15/0002, *Immoweb*, 7 November 2016.

[32] The German Bundeskartellamt and the Higher regional tribunal of Düsseldorf have already decided that online real estate platforms and real estate advertisements in journals constitute separate markets: Bundeskartellamt (2015) Clearance of Merger of Online Real Estate Platforms. http://www.bundeskartellamt.de/SharedDocs/Entscheidung/EN/Fallberichte/Fusionskontrolle/2015/B6-39-15.pdf?__blob=publicationFile&v=2. Accessed 5 June 2017.

channels as it offered a large amount of real estate properties targeted at the localities in which the buyer would be interested. Third, a swift reaction was very important when buying or renting a real estate property, and online real estate platforms were updated much more rapidly in comparison with the other channels. Fourth, the information provided on a real estate platform (with images) was not comparable to the information provided in most of the advertisements.

In its decision on the relevant product market, the BCA referenced a decision from the German Bundeskartellamt, *Immowelt/Immonet*.[33] Even if the German Bundeskartellamt had not definitively concluded on the relevant product market, it indicated a certain preference for a separate market for online real estate platforms. The Bundeskartellamt stated that the interplay between the two groups of users of such an online platform (the sellers and lessors on the one hand and the buyers and lessees on the other) did not have to be distinguished for the purpose of the market definition.

As regards the relevant geographic market, the BCA's Prosecutor stated in the preliminary analysis that the relevant geographic market should be national due to national regulation of online platforms, the location of properties and the fact that these platforms operated on a national basis.

The Prosecutor decided that Immoweb had a dominant position on the relevant market based on three considerations: the average number of daily visitors to the website was high; the number of available goods was, at the time of the Prosecutor's preliminary analysis, two times higher than the average number of offers on competing platforms; and the *sales conversion ratio* of the goods offered on Immoweb was higher than the *sales conversion ratio* of competing undertakings. This was also in line with the views expressed as a response to requests for information from the BCA by real estate agencies, real estate platforms and software developers. Immoweb contested the findings of the Prosecutor about its dominant position.

### Restrictive Competition Practices

The BCA decided that the MFC clauses inserted in the agreements between Immoweb and developers of software for real estate agencies could be anti-competitive and could infringe Article 101 TFEU (and its Belgian equivalent, Article IV.1 of the CEL), as well as Article 102 TFEU (and its Belgian equivalent, Article IV.2 of the CEL). The relationship between Immoweb and the developers of software for real estate agencies works as follows. Real estate software developers offer software to real estate agencies enabling them to put their portfolio online on one or more platforms (like Immoweb) included in the software developer's listing. This means that real estate platforms must conclude agreements with real estate software developers to be included in their listing of platforms that the developer's clients, the real estate agencies, can access. Real estate platforms, such as Immoweb, pay a fixed amount to the software developers per real estate offer that the developers transfer to the online real estate platform. The MFC clauses in the contracts between Immoweb and the software developers stipulated that the developers had to offer more advantageous

[33] BCA, Case MEDE-I/0-15/0002, *Immoweb*, 7 November 2016, §13–14.

financial conditions to Immoweb if they offered these more advantageous conditions to a competitor of Immoweb. Given the important position of Immoweb in the market, a software developer must have Immoweb in its portfolio; otherwise, no real estate agent would be willing to conclude an agreement with that software developer. The BCA concluded that the system, as described here, had the effect that the entry, maintenance or development costs on the market of the online real estate platforms had been kept artificially high. The MFC clauses had the effect that the software developers were not able to conclude an agreement with Immoweb's competitors at a price lower than the fee agreed upon with Immoweb.

To remedy these preliminary concerns, Immoweb decided to offer commitments. Immoweb committed itself to unilaterally put an end to the MFC clauses in the contracts with the software developers. In addition, Immoweb committed not to include MFC clauses in contracts with software developers for a period of 5 years. Consequently, the BCA closed the investigation.

**Comment on the *Immoweb* Decision**

In the *Immoweb* decision, the BCA used the term 'Most Favoured Customer' clause as a variation on the notion of 'Most Favoured Nation' clauses or 'MFN clauses' coming from international commercial law.[34] These clauses are also sometimes called 'price parity' clauses. MFN clauses come in different shapes. The Immoweb decision concerned clauses that oblige a seller of a product or service (real estate software developers) to offer more advantageous conditions to a buyer of a product, the customer Immoweb, if it offers these more advantageous conditions to any other customers. It could be considered as a wide MFN clause as the price offered to Immoweb is compared to the price offered to any other customer of the real estate software developers.

Unlike the clauses in the Commission's *E-books* case, the MFC clauses that Immoweb inserted in its agreement with the real estate software developers did not concern the retail level of trade. The Commission's *E-books* case concerned the resale prices to end consumers.[35] The situation in the BCA's *Immoweb* decision is comparable to the Commission's *Amazon* case, where it also investigated clauses inserted in the agreements between Amazon and e-book suppliers that came down to the fact that e-book suppliers should offer conditions to Amazon as favourable as the conditions offered to any other e-book retailer.[36] Similarly, in the Commission's *film studios* case, the pay-TV broadcasters agreed to pay the film studio at least a price as high as the price offered to competing film studios.[37] The latter case

[34] F. E. Gonzalez-Diaz, The law and economics of most-favoured nation clauses, Competition law and policy debate 2015(1), p. 26.

[35] Commission Case AT.39847, *Ebooks,* 25 July 2013.

[36] In this case, however, also some other clauses were under investigation that were related to the price offered by the e-book retailers (Amazon and its competitors) at the retail level; Commission Case COMP/AT.40.153, *E-books MFNs and related matters*, 13 January 2017.

[37] See Press release in Commission Case COMP/38427, *Pay Television Film Output Agreements*: Commission (2004) Press release Commission closes investigation into contracts of six Hollywood studios with European pay-TVs. http://europa.eu/rapid/press-release_IP-04-1314_en.htm?locale=en. Accessed 19 May 2017.

concerned the (favourable) conditions offered to the supplier of the product, while the *Immoweb* decision concerned the conditions offered to the customer of the real estate software developers. In the Commission's *film studios* case, the goal is for the supplier to receive a price as high as possible, while in the *Immoweb* decision the goal was for the customer to receive a price as low as possible.

The above examples and comparisons show that MFN clauses come in different variations and should therefore be examined on a case-by-case basis depending on the specific circumstances of the market.[38] It is difficult to draw any definitive conclusions about the treatment of MFN clauses under competition law in Belgium and at the EU level as all the cases were closed by commitments by the competition authorities.[39] However, it is clear that MFN clauses may give rise to competition concerns when (1) they are used by dominant undertakings or undertakings with significant market power, (2) they are used in concentrated markets characterised by barriers to entry, (3) they cover a high proportion of the market, (4) they may facilitate collusion by increasing transparency and/or decreasing the incentive to lower prices.[40] The Staff Working Document on the e-commerce sector inquiry has also stated that price parity clauses may reduce competition between marketplaces and make entry or expansion for competing marketplaces more difficult.[41]

Even if the BCA had not come to a definitive conclusion, as commitments were offered, the MFC clauses in the agreement between Immoweb and the developers of real estate software had as an effect that Immoweb's competitors could not conclude agreements with real estate software developers on more advantageous conditions than Immoweb. The BCA found that this situation has led to artificially high entry, maintenance and development costs on the market of the online real estate platforms as, in practice, all real estate software developers had to have Immoweb in their platform listing. Consequently, the MFC clauses probably were leading to the exclusion of Immoweb's competitors from the market for online real estate platforms. These practices could be at odds with not only Article 101 TFEU, but also with Article 102 TFEU, as Immoweb was found to have a dominant position on the Belgian market for real estate platforms. Immoweb's position certainly played an important role in the BCA's assessment as MFN clauses to the benefit of dominant companies or companies enjoying significant market power could give rise to strong foreclosure or softening of competition effects.[42]

---

[38] F. E. Gonzalez-Diaz, The law and economics of most-favoured nation clauses, Competition law and policy debate 2015(1), p. 42.

[39] Please note that in Commission Case *Pay Television Film Output Agreements*, the investigation against Universal and Paramount remained open, as they did not offer any commitments.

[40] F. E. Gonzalez-Diaz, The law and economics of most-favoured nation clauses, Competition law and policy debate 2015(1), p. 42.

[41] European Commission (2017) Staff Working Document to the Final Report on the E-commerce Sector Inquiry. http://ec.europa.eu/competition/antitrust/sector_inquiry_swd_en.pdf. Accessed 19 May 2017.

[42] F. E. Gonzalez-Diaz, The law and economics of most-favoured nation clauses, Competition law and policy debate 2015(1), p. 42.

#### 4.3.2.2 Merger Control

On 16 May 2017, the BCA has announced that the turnover thresholds for notification of mergers in Belgium might be reviewed in the future, following the Commission's public consultation on the reform of the Merger Regulation and the reforms in several member states, such as Germany and Austria.[43] The Commission is examining whether the merger thresholds are still adapted to current reality as for example, 'big data' might be a source of market power, even for an undertaking with limited turnover.[44] The insertion of a threshold criterion that is not (only) based on turnover is one of the issues submitted to public consultation. The e-commerce sector inquiry report has also noted that all marketplaces participating in the inquiry reported that they collect individual customer data.[45]

The Belgian thresholds are quiet high in comparison with other countries, and therefore the BCA does not find it necessary to increase the thresholds.[46] Furthermore, the BCA does not see any particular need to decrease the thresholds as a response to the digital economy and considers that if the thresholds are decreased, then it should only apply to specific sectors.[47]

Online sales and their effects on competition law have also been considered in Belgian merger control decisions.[48] One of the questions that frequently have come up in the assessment of mergers is whether online sales of a particular good or service belong to the same product market as the physical sales. Some cases will be discussed below in which the BCA has decided that online and offline sales form different markets[49] (section "Online and Offline Sales Belong to Separate Product Markets"), where online and offline sales were held to belong to the same product market (section "Online and Offline Sales Belong to the Same Product Market")

---

[43] BCA (2017) Evaluation des seuils de notification des concentrations en Belgique, p. 5. https://www.belgiancompetition.be/sites/default/files/content/download/files/20170516_evaluation_seuils.pdf. Accessed 31 May 2017.

[44] E.g. Commission case M.7217, *Facebook/Whatsapp,* 3 October 2014.

[45] European Commission (2017) Staff Working Document to the Final Report on the E-commerce Sector Inquiry, §635–636. http://ec.europa.eu/competition/antitrust/sector_inquiry_swd_en.pdf. Accessed 19 May 2017.

[46] BCA (2017) Evaluation des seuils de notification des concentrations en Belgique, p. 5. https://www.belgiancompetition.be/sites/default/files/content/download/files/20170516_evaluation_seuils.pdf. Accessed 31 May 2017.

[47] BCA (2017) Evaluation des seuils de notification des concentrations en Belgique, p. 5. https://www.belgiancompetition.be/sites/default/files/content/download/files/20170516_evaluation_seuils.pdf. Accessed 31 May 2017.

[48] This section does not give an exhaustive overview of all Belgian merger decisions in which online sales have been discussed. The research was focused on decisions from 2010 in the wholesale/retail sectors and the sector of media, telecommunication and ICT.

[49] In the BCA's *Nationale Loterij* case, it was also found that the physical and non-physical distribution of sports betting belonged to separate product markets. However, this case did not concern a merger, but a complaint of infringement of Articles 101 and 102 TFEU and their Belgian equivalents; BCA, Case MEDE-P/K-13/0012 and CONC-P/K-13/0013, *Stanleybet Belgium NV/Stanley International Betting Ltd en Sagevas S.A./World Football Association S.P.R.L./Samenwerkende Nevenmaatschappij Belgische PMU S.C.R.L. t. Nationale Loterij NV*, 22 September 2015.

and where the BCA did not reach a definitive conclusion on the question (section "Cases Where Market for Online and Offline Sales Left Open").

**Online and Offline Sales Belong to Separate Product Markets**

In the *Rexel Belgium SA/La Grange Beheer SA – Immo LG SPRL* case of 21 May 2012, the Prosecutor identified the following separate markets: the wholesale market for sales of electrical products comprising electrical installation materials, lighting, cables and networks, HVAC products, security and communication products; the wholesale market for sales of electrical appliances; and the market for direct sales from producers to professional installers.[50] As regards Internet sales by the wholesalers, the Prosecutor found that Internet sales were more of a complement than a substitute for physical sales by the wholesalers and that pure online players did not exercise any competitive pressure on the wholesalers that were physically present in Belgium.[51] The notifying party in this case did not agree with the Prosecutor's findings.

In the *Belgacom NV/Wireless Technologies BVBA* case,[52] the BCA also made some reflections on market evolutions with the rise of online sales. In 2011, the acquisition by Belgacom of The Phone House distribution network had been approved provided that Belgacom, amongst other things, (1) resold nearly half of the acquired The Phone House points of sale, (2) operated the points of sale of The Phone House as a multi-operator distribution network for 5 years and (3) operated a 'Chinese Wall' policy for the multi-operator points of sale.[53]

On 11 May 2015, Proximus filed a request to have the multi-operator commitment, including the obligation to operate a 'Chinese Wall' in the multi-operator points of sale, lifted. Proximus argued that consumer behaviour had changed since the imposition of the commitments on Proximus in the BCA's decision of 23 December 2011.[54] Operators had adapted to new consumer behaviour by developing an omni-channel strategy in which the client had the opportunity to choose when and where to buy (online, brick and mortars, call centres, etc.).[55] Furthermore, Proximus produced a study in which it became clear that customers made more online comparisons before purchasing goods or services.[56]

The Prosecutor discussed two relevant markets in this case: the upstream retail market for mobile phone services and the downstream market for the distribution of

---

[50] BCA, Case CONC-C/C-12/0004, *Rexel Belgium SA/La Grange Beheer SA – Immo LG SPRL*, 21 May 2012, §40–41.

[51] BCA, Case CONC-C/C-12/0004, *Rexel Belgium SA/La Grange Beheer SA – Immo LG SPRL*, 21 May 2012, §41.

[52] BCA, Case MEDE-C/C-11/0010, *Belgacom NV/Wireless Technologies BVBA*, 23 June 2015.

[53] BCA, Case MEDE-C/C-11/0010, *Belgacom NV/Wireless Technologies BVBA*, 23 December 2011; C. Verdonck and S. De Cock, Belgium. In: Knable Gotts (ed), The Merger Control Review, Law Business Research 2016, p. 107–108.

[54] BCA, Case MEDE-C/C-11/0010, *Belgacom NV/Wireless Technologies BVBA*, 23 June 2015.

[55] BCA, Case MEDE-C/C-11/0010, *Belgacom NV/Wireless Technologies BVBA*, 23 June 2015, §115.

[56] BCA, Case MEDE-C/C-11/0010, *Belgacom NV/Wireless Technologies BVBA*, 23 June 2015, §117.

electronic communication products and services. As regards the latter, the Prosecutor decided that online sales were not included in this market.[57] However, he also noted that he would take into account the competitive pressure from non-physical points of sale.[58] Moreover, the Prosecutor agreed with the removal of the multi-operator commitment, including the obligation to operate a 'Chinese Wall' in the multi-operator points of sale, but it found that the imposition of certain transitory commitments was necessary to limit potential competition concerns during the transformation phase of The Phone House's points of sale to Proximus's points of sale.[59] The Competition College agreed entirely with the Prosecutor's view and conditionally lifted the commitments imposed on Proximus NV (previously known as Belgacom NV) in the context of the *Belgacom/Wireless Technologies* acquisition,[60] under which Belgacom had acquired the 'The Phone House' distribution network.[61]

#### Online and Offline Sales Belong to the Same Product Market

In the merger between Delhaize NV and Koninklijke Ahold, some online sales issues were also discussed.[62] Delhaize had supermarkets in seven countries and also offered some online services, with which consumers could buy products online from the Delhaize supermarket.[63] Delhaize.be allowed consumers to order online and pick up their purchases in a Delhaize store. Caddy Home was another online service in which purchases were delivered at home, and, lastly, Delhaize Wineworld left the choice for customers to pick up their wine or to have it delivered at home.[64] Ahold is active in the field of online sales of non-food products in Belgium through the website Bol.com.[65]

[57] BCA, Case MEDE-C/C-11/0010, *Belgacom NV/Wireless Technologies BVBA*, 23 June 2015, §158.

[58] BCA, Case MEDE-C/C-11/0010, *Belgacom NV/Wireless Technologies BVBA*, 23 June 2015, §158.

[59] Proximus agreed into the following commitments: (i) to give competitors using The Phone House network the right to withdraw from the network without any repercussions and within a relatively short time frame; (ii) to inform consumers in a clear way about which competitors would still offer services through the respective The Phone House points of sale; (iii) to clearly inform customers when a respective point of sale would become an exclusive Proximus point of sale; and (iv) to appoint a Monitoring Trustee; C. Verdonck and S. De Cock, Belgium. In: Knable Gotts (ed), The Merger Control Review, Law Business Research 2016, p. 108.

[60] BCA, Case MEDE-C/C-11/0010, *Belgacom NV/Wireless Technologies BVBA*, 23 December 2011.

[61] BCA, Case MEDE-C/C-11/0010, *Belgacom NV/Wireless Technologies BVBA*, 23 June 2015, §280–284; C. Verdonck and S. De Cock, Belgium. In: Knable Gotts (ed), The Merger Control Review, Law Business Research 2016, p. 108.

[62] BCA, Case MEDE-C/C-10, *Delhaize NV/Koninklijke Ahold NV*, 15 March 2016.

[63] BCA, Case MEDE-C/C-10, *Delhaize NV/Koninklijke Ahold NV*, 15 March 2016, §16–18, §39.

[64] BCA, Case MEDE-C/C-10, *Delhaize NV/Koninklijke Ahold NV*, 15 March 2016, §18.

[65] BCA, Case MEDE-C/C-10, *Delhaize NV/Koninklijke Ahold NV*, 15 March 2016, §22 and §46.

The BCA's Prosecutor found that horizontal overlaps existed on the markets for sales and for the purchase of daily consumption goods and on the market for franchising services in the supermarket sector.[66] As Bol.com was an online non-food retailer and to the extent that Bol.com could be able to use the Delhaize stores as pick-up points, there was also a vertical relationship between Ahold and Delhaize.[67]

As regards the relevant market, the Prosecutor decided first that the online sales of consumption goods in which the consumer ordered the products online and consequently picked them up in a physical pick-up point, formed part of the market for the sale of daily consumption goods and did not constitute a separate market.[68] The Prosecutor left the question open for home delivery services as the development of that activity by Delhaize was still very limited.[69] Consequently, it is interesting to note that the Prosecutor distinguished between online sales in which the consumer had to pick up purchases in the store and online sales in which the purchases were delivered at home. Second, the Prosecutor stated that the market research did not permit drawing definitive conclusions on the market about the purchase of daily consumption goods. He took into account, on the one hand, a segment of the market for the purchase of daily consumption goods according to product categories and, on the other hand, a segment for branded products and private labels.[70] Third, the Prosecutor decided that it was not necessary for the purposes of this merger notification to decide whether there existed a separate market for the offer of franchising services.[71]

**Cases Where Market for Online and Offline Sales Left Open**

In a case concerning the acquisition of *Club NV and Club Luxemburg SA by ZuidNederlandse Uitgeverij NV and Standaard Boekhandel NV*, the Prosecutor left the question open about whether a different market should be retained for online and offline sales of books to consumers. The Prosecutor stated that online sales are only 0–5% of Standaard Boekhandel's sales.[72] Moreover, an economic study had shown that in the Dutch book market, online sales only constituted 9.5% of the market.[73]

However, different third parties expressed the view that segmentation was necessary according to whether sales were made online or offline as both channels were

[66] BCA, Case MEDE-C/C-10, *Delhaize NV/Koninklijke Ahold NV*, 15 March 2016, §47.

[67] BCA, Case MEDE-C/C-10, *Delhaize NV/Koninklijke Ahold NV*, 15 March 2016, §48–49.

[68] BCA, Case MEDE-C/C-10, *Delhaize NV/Koninklijke Ahold NV*, 15 March 2016, §104.

[69] BCA, Case MEDE-C/C-10, *Delhaize NV/Koninklijke Ahold NV*, 15 March 2016, §105.

[70] BCA, Case MEDE-C/C-10, *Delhaize NV/Koninklijke Ahold NV*, 15 March 2016, §136.

[71] BCA, Case MEDE-C/C-10, *Delhaize NV/Koninklijke Ahold NV*, 15 March 2016, §150.

[72] BCA, Case MEDE-C/C-14/0007, *Acquisition of Club NV and Club Luxemburg SA by ZuidNederlandse Uitgeverij NV and Standaard Boekhandel NV*, 10 June 2014, §64.

[73] BCA, Case MEDE-C/C-14/0007, *Acquisition of Club NV and Club Luxemburg SA by ZuidNederlandse Uitgeverij NV and Standaard Boekhandel NV*, 10 June 2014, §63.

characterised by different promotion dynamics, different velocity and different geographical reach.[74]

The Prosecutor stated that two scenarios were possible for defining the relevant markets. In the first scenario, there would be (1) a market for the sale of books in the Dutch part of Belgium, irrespective of language (but with the exception of French titles), and (2) a market for the sale of books in the French part of Belgium, irrespective of language (but with the exception of Dutch titles).[75] In the second scenario, the markets would be defined according to a geographical division: (1) all books sold to consumers in Wallonia and Brussels, irrespective of language, and (2) all books sold to consumers in Flanders, irrespective of language.[76]

The Prosecutor concluded that there was only a limited horizontal overlap on the market for sales of books to consumers in the Dutch part of Belgium.[77] Therefore, no real competition concerns arose in this case. To come to this conclusion, the Prosecutor considered that traditional book shops would experience more and more competitive pressure from online sales through, for example, bol.com, amazon.com, etc.[78] The Prosecutor found that Standaard Boekhandel would only achieve very limited market shares in the Internet segment during the following 3–5 years as some very big players were active in this segment.[79] Finally, the Prosecutor stated that Standaard Boekhandel's concept, in which it offered physical book shops as full service points almost in every city and/or village centre, encouraged competition between online and offline sales points *within the same product market*.[80]

As in the *Rexel Belgium SA/La Grange Beheer SA – Immo LG SPRL* case, the Prosecutor noted in case *Cebeo/Cheyns* that sales by pure online players should not be included in the wholesale market for the sale of electrical materials.[81] However, in the competition analysis, the Prosecutor took into account that wholesalers did not need a local branch as wholesalers' clients mostly placed their orders by phone or via a website and deliveries were often made on the whole national territory.

[74] BCA, Case MEDE-C/C-14/0007, *Acquisition of Club NV and Club Luxemburg SA by ZuidNederlandse Uitgeverij NV and Standaard Boekhandel NV*, 10 June 2014, §59 and 60.

[75] BCA, Case MEDE-C/C-14/0007, *Acquisition of Club NV and Club Luxemburg SA by ZuidNederlandse Uitgeverij NV and Standaard Boekhandel NV*, 10 June 2014, §69.

[76] BCA, Case MEDE-C/C-14/0007, *Acquisition of Club NV and Club Luxemburg SA by ZuidNederlandse Uitgeverij NV and Standaard Boekhandel NV*, 10 June 2014, §70.

[77] BCA, Case MEDE-C/C-14/0007, *Acquisition of Club NV and Club Luxemburg SA by ZuidNederlandse Uitgeverij NV and Standaard Boekhandel NV*, 10 June 2014, §131.

[78] BCA, Case MEDE-C/C-14/0007, *Acquisition of Club NV and Club Luxemburg SA by ZuidNederlandse Uitgeverij NV and Standaard Boekhandel NV*, 10 June 2014, §140.

[79] BCA, Case MEDE-C/C-14/0007, *Acquisition of Club NV and Club Luxemburg SA by ZuidNederlandse Uitgeverij NV and Standaard Boekhandel NV*, 10 June 2014, §141.

[80] BCA, Case MEDE-C/C-14/0007, *Acquisition of Club NV and Club Luxemburg SA by ZuidNederlandse Uitgeverij NV and Standaard Boekhandel NV*, 10 June 2014, §150.

[81] BCA, Case CONC-C/C-16/0035, *Cebeo NV/Group Cheyns NV and Cheyns NV*, 14 December 2016, §94.

Competitive pressure was exercised by specialist-wholesalers and by pure online players.[82]

The Competition College stated that it could be left open whether pure online sales could be excluded from the wholesale market for the sale of electrical material.[83] However, it considered that these pure online sales could be included in the relevant market for the reason stated by the notifying party and the development potential of online sales. The notifying party, Cebeo, had argued first that more and more manufacturers had their own website and offered their products in this way directly to the final customer, without any need to pass through a wholesaler.[84] Second, Cebeo asserted that online sales constituted a real alternative distribution channel to offline sales and that pure players in the sector proposed a large offer at very attractive prices for professional installers.[85]

## 4.4 Restrictions of Online Sales and Selective Distribution

The e-commerce sector inquiry report indicated that retailers in Belgium have rarely reported having marketplace restrictions.[86] The results of the sector inquiry also reported that restrictions to sell on marketplaces were mostly found in selective distribution agreements.[87] Even if suppliers in Belgium often use selective distribution systems to control the distribution of their products, we are not aware of any cases reported in Belgium that are related to systems of selective distribution and online sales platforms. Should any such case arise in Belgium, it is likely that the BCA or the Belgian courts would follow the guidance by the Court of Justice of the European Union and the Commission in its Guidelines on Vertical Restraints and its recently published e-commerce sector inquiry report on selective distribution and sales via online marketplaces.

Even if the BCA's decisional practice regarding mergers often treats online and offline sales as separate markets, the Guidelines on Vertical Restraints provide that a supplier may impose criteria on online sales made by its distributors that are equivalent to the criteria imposed offline in the context of selective distribution.[88] In the same vein, a supplier may require that its distributors use third-party platforms

[82] BCA, Case CONC-C/C-16/0035, *Cebeo NV/Group Cheyns NV and Cheyns NV*, 14 December 2016, §136–149.

[83] BCA, Case CONC-C/C-16/0035, *Cebeo NV/Group Cheyns NV and Cheyns NV*, 14 December 2016, §20.

[84] BCA, Case CONC-C/C-16/0035, *Cebeo NV/Group Cheyns NV and Cheyns NV*, 14 December 2016, §66.

[85] BCA, Case CONC-C/C-16/0035, *Cebeo NV/Group Cheyns NV and Cheyns NV*, 14 December 2016, §66.

[86] European Commission (2017) Staff working document on the E-commerce sector inquiry, §463. http://ec.europa.eu/competition/antitrust/sector_inquiry_swd_en.pdf. Accessed 31 May 2017.

[87] European Commission (2017) Staff working document on the E-commerce sector inquiry, §470. http://ec.europa.eu/competition/antitrust/sector_inquiry_swd_en.pdf. Accessed 31 May 2017.

[88] Guidelines on Vertical Restraints, §54.

to distribute the contract products only in accordance with the particular criteria agreed between the supplier and its distributors for the distributors' sales via the Internet. The Guidelines have clarified that when the distributor sells via a third-party platform, the supplier may require that customers do not visit the distributor's website through a site carrying the name or logo of the third-party platform.[89] Therefore, the supplier may require that the distributor display the logo and/or brand of the goods on the website.[90] In its Staff Working Document on the e-commerce sector inquiry, the Commission has stated that sales via online marketplaces may be *de facto* excluded by a supplier if the distributor is prohibited from selling via marketplaces that visibly have their logo.[91]

In the e-commerce sector inquiry report, the Commission has confirmed the approach laid down in paragraph 54 of the Guidelines and has not considered marketplace bans as hardcore restrictions of competition law. It has stated that the question about sales via third-party platforms concerns *how* the distributor can sell products over the Internet and does not have as its object the restriction upon *where or to whom* distributors can sell the products.[92] The Commission has stated that 'marketplace bans do not generally amount to a de facto prohibition on selling online or restrict the effective use of the internet as a sales channel irrespective of the markets concerned'.[93] Consequently, according to the findings of the e-commerce sector inquiry, (absolute) marketplace bans should not automatically be considered as hardcore restrictions within the meaning of Article 4 b) and 4 c) of Regulation 330/2010. The Commission has also made it clear that this does not mean that absolute marketplace bans never infringe the EU competition rules.[94] The Commission also has been applying the test introduced by the Court of Justice of the European Union in the *Pierre Fabre* case to online marketplaces. This would mean that a ban or restriction on the use of online marketplaces should only constitute a hardcore restriction if it *de facto* constitutes a complete ban on online sales.[95] The Court of Justice decided in *Pierre Fabre* that 'in the context of a selective distribution system, a contractual clause requiring sales of cosmetics and personal care products to be made in a physical space where a qualified pharmacist

[89] Guidelines on Restraints, §54.

[90] N. Petit and D. Henry, Vertical Restraints under EU Competition Law: conceptual foundations and practical framework. In: Gheur and Petit (Eds), Vertical restraints and distribution agreements under EU competition law, Bruylant 2011, pp. 123–168.

[91] European Commission (2017) Staff working document on the E-commerce sector inquiry, §467. http://ec.europa.eu/competition/antitrust/sector_inquiry_swd_en.pdf. Accessed 31 May 2017.

[92] European Commission (2017) Staff working document on the E-commerce sector inquiry, §509. http://ec.europa.eu/competition/antitrust/sector_inquiry_swd_en.pdf. Accessed 31 May 2017.

[93] European Commission (2017) Final Report on the E-commerce Sector Inquiry, §41. http://ec.europa.eu/competition/antitrust/sector_inquiry_final_report_en.pdf. Accessed 1 June 2017.

[94] European Commission (2017) Final Report on the E-commerce Sector Inquiry, §43. http://ec.europa.eu/competition/antitrust/sector_inquiry_final_report_en.pdf. Accessed 1 June 2017.

[95] European Commission (2017) Staff working document on the E-commerce sector inquiry, §502–503. http://ec.europa.eu/competition/antitrust/sector_inquiry_swd_en.pdf. Accessed 31 May 2017.

must be present, resulting in a ban on the use of the internet for those sales, amounts to a restriction by object within the meaning of that provision where, following an individual and specific examination of the content and objective of that contractual clause and the legal and economic context of which it forms a part, it is apparent that, having regard to the properties of the products at issue, that clause is not objectively justified'.[96] However, it should be noted that the Court of Justice's ruling in *Pierre Fabre* arose in the context of a selective distribution system, while the Commission's findings are also related to online sales platforms outside the context of selective distribution. Finally, the Court of Justice has ruled on the matter on 6 December 2017 in the *Coty* case.[97]

In general, sales through third-party Internet platforms in selective distribution systems are not very likely to restrict 'intra-brand' competition. However, freeriding may occur when consumers visit a brick-and-mortar shop and receive information and services on a high-end good, which justifies the recourse to selective distribution, and then buys the good in question via a third-party platform. It is recognised in the e-commerce sector inquiry report that sales via third-party platforms offer opportunities for small and medium-sized dealers as sales via online marketplaces do not require high initial investments.[98]

Finally, the e-commerce sector inquiry report has also stated that marketplaces offer more and more features to address quality requirements from well-known brands. In this sense, the report has stated that some marketplaces offer the ability to design their own seller shop within a special area of the marketplace or to have specific showrooms designed in line with the requirements of the brand.[99]

---

[96] CJUE, C-439/09, *Pierre Fabre Dermo-Cosmétique SAS v. Président de l'Autorité de la Concurrence*, ECR 2011 I-09419, pt 47.

[97] CJEU, C-230/16, *Coty Germany vs. Parfümerie Akzente GmbH, 6 December 2017*; The Advocate General's opinion has been published on 26 July 2017. Advocate General Wahl has followed the viewpoint of the Commission in its E-commerce sector inquiry report to the following extent. First, he states that restrictions of use of online sales platforms may constitute infringements of article 101§1 of the TFEU, but the effects of the restrictions on competition have to be examined. Restrictions on the use of online sales platforms do not have to be classified as restrictions by object. Second, the restriction on the use of online sales platforms at issue in this case does not amount to the hardcore restrictions of competition law under Article 4, b) and c) of Regulation 330/2010. The Court of Justice's ruling goes in the same direction. It decides that Article 101§1 of the TFEU must be interpreted as not precluding a contractual clause which prohibited authorized distributors in a selective distribution system for luxury goods designed to preserve the luxury image of those goods from using in a discernible manner third-party platforms for the internet sales of the contract goods, on the conditions (1) that the clause has the objective of preserving the luxury image of those goods, (2) that it is laid down uniformly and not applied in a discriminatory fashion and (3) that it is proportionate in the light of the objective pursued.

[98] European Commission (2017) Staff working document on the E-commerce sector inquiry, §442, §449–451, §456. http://ec.europa.eu/competition/antitrust/sector_inquiry_swd_en.pdf. Accessed 31 May 2017.

[99] European Commission (2017) Staff working document on the E-commerce sector inquiry, §490–492. http://ec.europa.eu/competition/antitrust/sector_inquiry_swd_en.pdf. Accessed 31 May 2017.

## 4.5 Conclusion and Recommendations for the Future

The main competition issues generated by the growth of online sales platforms that have been discussed in this report are, first, 'Most Favoured Nation' clauses; second, the question about whether the value of big data should be taken into account for the Belgian merger notification thresholds; third, the impact of online sales in the market definition of merger cases; fourth, restrictions on sales via online sales platforms, which are mostly in selective distribution systems. A fifth important competition issue, not discussed in detail in this report, is increased price transparency.[100] On the one hand, consumers are able to compare prices more easily online, which leads to increased price competition and can affect competition on other factors, such as quality.[101] On the other hand, companies, which are in a horizontal or vertical relationship with each other, are also able to monitor more easily each other's prices.[102] This new feature of the digital economy will certainly affect competition law assessments.

In spite of the competition issues that have arisen with the new digital economy and the growth of online sales platforms, it is submitted that, in my opinion, there is absolutely no need to modify the basic and substantial competition law principles or objectives in the context of the new economy. In this regard, it should also be taken into account that digital markets are evolving very fast. Therefore, the criteria applied to the new economy may not be too specific as they would probably be outdated rapidly and not adapted to the fast-evolving realities of the new economy.[103]

In contrast to the Guidelines on Vertical Restraints, the current version of Regulation 330/2010 does not contain any specific rules on online sales. An update of the Guidelines on Vertical Restraints to include clearer rules on features of the new digital economy, like online sales platforms, might be useful to enhance uniformity within Europe and legal certainty for undertakings. However, the Commission has announced—after its e-commerce sector inquiry—that it did not find it necessary to issue new Guidelines on Vertical Restraints before 2022.[104] On the other hand, the new geo-blocking regulation complements basic competition law principles.[105] This regulation enhances uniformity and legal certainty within Europe as it

[100] European Commission (2017) Final Report on the E-commerce Sector Inquiry, §13 and §56. http://ec.europa.eu/competition/antitrust/sector_inquiry_final_report_en.pdf. Accessed 1 June 2017; R. Eccles, Online sales and competition law controls, International Journal of Franchising Law 2015 (13), p. 7; T. Kramler, The European Commission's E-commerce sector inquiry, Journal of European Competition Law & Practice 2017, p. 81.

[101] European Commission (2017) Final Report on the E-commerce Sector Inquiry, §12. http://ec.europa.eu/competition/antitrust/sector_inquiry_final_report_en.pdf. Accessed 1 June 2017.

[102] European Commission (2017) Final Report on the E-commerce Sector Inquiry, §13. http://ec.europa.eu/competition/antitrust/sector_inquiry_final_report_en.pdf. Accessed 1 June 2017.

[103] One might think of artificial intelligence, robots, self-driving cars, smartphones integrated in the human body.

[104] The current Regulation 330/2010 expires on 31 May 2022.

[105] Regulation of the European Parliament and of the Council of 28 February 2018 on addressing unjustified geo-blocking and other forms of discrimination based on customers' nationality, place

seeks to prevent discrimination within the internal market. Its objectives include giving customers throughout the EU better access to goods and services in the single market by preventing direct and indirect discrimination by traders artificially segmenting the market based on customers' residence.

As regards the application of competition law in specific cases, we highly support the view that the courts and competition authorities take into account the features of the new digital economy when assessing specific cases. However, it is our opinion that this brings nothing new as it is required for any proper competition law assessment that the relevant market and economic context of the case is thoroughly examined. A thorough examination of the economic context in a specific case might require that competition authorities, courts and lawyers master new technologies and have the capacity to interpret data and algorithms for the competition law assessment. The increased price transparency will also have to be taken into account.

The diverging case law in different EU member states regarding MFN clauses (for example, in the hotel sector) shows, on the one hand, the need for uniformity and legal certainty for undertakings at the EU level and on, the other hand, the need to take into account the specific market characteristics for any proper competition law assessment. However, on 17 February 2017, the European Competition Network stated in its final report on the results of the monitoring exercise in the hotel sector that it was committed to ensuring consistency in future cases.[106] Belgium participated in the hotel monitoring exercise, together with the Czech Republic, France, Germany, Hungary, Ireland, Italy, the Netherlands, Sweden and the United Kingdom.

---

of residence or place of establishment within the internal market and amending Regulations (EC) No 2006/2004 and (EU) 2017/2394 and Directive 2009/22/EC ('Geo-blocking regulation').

[106] ECN (2017) Outcome of the meeting of ECN DG's on 17-02-2017. http://ec.europa.eu/competition/antitrust/ECN_meeting_outcome_17022017.pdf. Accessed 31 May 2017.

# Brazil

# 5

Pedro Paulo Salles Cristofaro and Luisa Shinzato de Pinho

The Brazilian competition legal framework does not provide a different set of rules for each specific market or designate different institutions to enforce competition regulations. Both traditional and innovative markets—the "old" and the "new" economies—are subject to the same set of rules. Moreover, there are no competition law guidelines particularly relevant to the new economy or pertaining specifically to online sales platforms in Brazil.

Nevertheless, it is undeniable that the application of the same rules may be affected differently according to the specific characteristics of the markets in which anticompetitive conduct is practiced or in which mergers are carried out. In Brazil, the law requires the examination of the actual and potential economic effects arising from a particular act on a relevant market both with regard to the analysis of conducts and the control of concentration acts (although, as will be seen later, in some cases, there are some discussions about the burden of proving such economic effects).

The Internet reduces distances and increases markets, creates new barriers and eliminates others, and, above all, accelerates innovation in such a way that results in uncertainty about the future shape of a market or the potential effects of a certain conduct, making the analysis of the antitrust authorities more complex.

Although it is not yet possible to anticipate how future major competition/antitrust issues entailed by the growth of online sales platforms will be analyzed, former decisions of the Brazilian Antitrust Authority (CADE) can bring some light and allow some provisional answers to this question.

---

P. P. S. Cristofaro (✉)
Chediak Lopes da Costa Cristofaro Menezes Cortes Advogados, Rio de Janeiro, Brazil
e-mail: pedro.sallescristofaro@clcmra.com.br

L. S. de Pinho
Novotny Advogados, Rio de Janeiro, Brazil
e-mail: luisa.shinzato@novotny.com.br



B. Kilpatrick et al. (eds.), *Antitrust Analysis of Online Sales Platforms & Copyright Limitations and Exceptions*, LIDC Contributions on Antitrust Law, Intellectual Property and Unfair Competition,
https://doi.org/10.1007/978-3-319-71419-6_5

## 5.1 The Brazilian Antitrust System

The Brazilian Antitrust System is structured by the "Brazilian Antitrust Act"[1] (Antitrust Act) and is grounded on the principles of free competition, freedom of initiative, consumer protection, and prevention of abuse of economic power. Those are the primary guidelines that steer all other legal provisions on the matter, as well as the performance of CADE.

CADE is an independent agency and is responsible for merger reviews and for imposing penalties upon infringement of Brazilian antitrust provisions. Its decisions are final in an administrative level and may only be challenged in judicial courts. In the performance of these roles, CADE must abide by the legal principles and assure that they are followed by all economic agents.

Violations to the economic order are listed in Article 36 of the Antitrust Act and include acts under any circumstance that have as object or that may have the effect of (1) limiting, restraining, or in any way injuring free competition or free initiative; (2) controlling the relevant market of goods or services; (3) arbitrarily increasing profits; and (4) abusively exercising a dominant position, regardless of the agent's fault. According to this rule, economic agents that practice such acts are subject to penalties, even if the mentioned effects are not produced. The third paragraph of Article 36, in its turn, serves as a guide for the interpreter of the law, indicating conducts that may be considered unlawful in certain circumstances, to the extent that they fall under the aforementioned situations.[2]

[1] Federal Law (*Lei Federal*) No. 12,529 of 30 November 2011.

[2] Those are the examples of conducts indicated in Article 36 of the Antitrust Act: "I – to agree, join, manipulate or adjust with competitors, in any way: a) the prices of goods or services individually offered; b) the production or sale of a restricted or limited amount of goods or the provision of a limited or restricted number, volume or frequency of services; c) the division of parts or segments of a potential or current market of goods or services by means of, among others, the distribution of customers, suppliers, regions or time periods; d) prices, conditions, privileges or refusal to participate in public bidding; II – to promote, obtain or influence the adoption of uniform or agreed business practices among competitors; III – to limit or prevent the access of new companies to the market; IV – to create difficulties for the establishment, operation or development of a competitor company or supplier, acquirer or financier of goods or services; V – to prevent the access of competitors to sources of input, raw material, equipment or technology, and distribution channels; VI – to require or grant exclusivity for the dissemination of advertisement in mass media; VII – to use deceitful means to cause oscillation of the prices for third parties; VIII – to regulate markets of goods or services by establishing agreements to limit or control the research and technological development, the production of goods or services, or to impair investments for the production of goods or services or their distribution; IX – to impose, on the trade of goods or services, to distributors, retailers and representatives, resale prices, discounts, payment terms, minimum or maximum quantities, profit margin or any other market conditions related to their business with third parties; X – to discriminate against purchasers or suppliers of goods or services by establishing price differentials or operating conditions for the sale or provision of services; XI – to refuse the sale of goods or provision of services for payment terms within normal business practice and custom; XII – to hinder or disrupt the continuity or development of business relationships of undetermined term, because the other party refuses to abide by unjustifiable or anticompetitive terms and conditions; XIII – to destroy, render useless or monopolize the raw materials, intermediate or finished products, as well as to destroy, disable or impair the operation of equipment to produce, distribute

On the other hand, whenever market power is conquered by the agent's own merits and efficiency, it will not constitute a violation to the economic order and will be deemed lawful.

CADE must impose penalties to the economic agents upon sufficient evidence of commitment of the practices described above. As a general rule, CADE applies the rule of reason to the interpretation of the antitrust law, which considers as unlawful acts that may have the possible effect of unreasonably restricting competition. However, recent decisions issued by CADE in specific cases—such as horizontal price fixing and bid rigging—have considered the practice of the act as "unlawful by object"—on the ground that these acts, due to their nature, would have a high potential of restricting competition. As such, CADE would not have the burden of proving any actual or likely anticompetitive effects on the market to consider the conduct illegal and, consequently, apply the penalties defined by law. Such approach is even stricter with respect to hardcore cartel cases, in which the mere evidence of the practice would be enough for conviction.

The theory of acts that are "unlawful by object" was also considered by CADE in a case of retail price maintenance. On that occasion, it was considered that the fixing of minimum resale prices by an agent with a dominant position on the market would constitute a *quasi per se illicit* act that would result in the reversal of the burden of proof to the defendant. The imposition of resale prices is one of the examples of acts that may be considered illegal, according to item IX of para 3 of Article 36.

However, it cannot be said at this time that there is a consensus about the characterization of some illicit acts as unlawful by object or about the burden of proof in some competition matters. There are not enough cases capable of affirming a clear trend in CADE's jurisprudence or sufficient judicial decisions that confirm the understanding on the subject.

In general, the thesis that the characterization of unlawful acts against competition depends on CADE's demonstration of the potential adverse effects on the market after due investigation prevails. The various examples listed in the third paragraph of Article 36, including exclusivity clauses in vertical agreements, discrimination between suppliers or purchasers, and refusal to deal, would be, like most conducts, subject to a rule of reason and to the demonstration of negative effects, and the burden of proof would be on CADE.

---

or transport them; XIV – to monopolize or prevent the exploitation of industrial or intellectual property rights or technology; XV – to sell goods or services unreasonably below the cost price; XVI – to retain goods for production or consumption, except to ensure recovery of production costs; XVII – to partially or totally cease the activities of the company without proven just cause; XVIII – to condition the sale of goods on the acquisition or use of another good or service, or to condition the provision of a service on the acquisition or use of another good or service, and XIX – to abusively exercise or exploit intellectual or industrial property rights, technology or trademark."

This same rule is applied in CADE's assessment of most-favoured-nation clauses (MFN). That was the case with *Procedimento Preparatorio*[3] No. 08700.005679/2016-13, under which agreements among three relevant players of the online tourism market were investigated. The antitrust authority sustained that such provisions would be considered a violation to the economic order upon appraisal of their harmful effects to competition. CADE preliminarily recognized that such MFNs could produce such effects and determined production of additional evidence to confirm its understanding.

All such provisions and understandings shall equally apply to Internet-related businesses. Strictly speaking, the characteristics of this type of business, subject to constant changes and innovations, make the adoption of presumptions about the possible negative effects of conduct less likely while making the examination of competitive issues in light of the rule of reason more likely, especially in relation to vertical restraints. Therefore, acts such as bans on sales through third-party Internet platforms—as well as any other Internet-related exclusivity agreement—will probably be considered in light of the rule of reason. Thus, they will only be considered exclusionary practices upon evidence of their potential negative effects.

On the other hand, it is difficult to anticipate if Internet-related retail price maintenance will be assessed by the "unlawful by object" rule or by a rule of reason approach.

Upon assessment of a practice with unlawful effects, the economic agents may be subject to the pecuniary and nonpecuniary penalties set forth in Article 37 of the Antitrust Act, such as (1) payment of a fine of one-tenth percent (0.1%) to twenty percent (20%) of the gross sales of the company, group, or conglomerate in the last fiscal year before the establishment of the administrative proceeding, in the field of the business activity[4] in which the violation occurred, which will never be less than the advantage obtained, when the estimation thereof is possible; (2) the ineligibility for official financing and for participation in public biddings; (3) the registration of the wrongdoer with the National Registry for Consumer Protection; and (4) the conviction's publication in newspapers.

The Antitrust Act also sets forth the possibility of execution of leniency agreements and cease-and-desist agreements.

Leniency agreements are set forth in Article 86 of the Antitrust Act and allow that an economic agent involved in an unlawful act admit such practice and present a first-hand report with details of its conduct and of the other agents involved in the

[3] Preparatory Proceeding. The Preparatory Proceeding precedes an Administrative Investigation and an Administrative Proceeding. The purpose of the Preparatory Proceeding, which must be performed within a maximum period of 30 days, is just to verify if certain facts potentially may be considered unlawful and require an investigation (Article 66 of the Antitrust Act).

[4] The concept of "field of the business activity" is not identical to the notion of relevant market. At the time the Brazilian Antitrust Act was published, the legislator deliberately substituted the term "relevant market" by "field of the business activity" as a basis for calculating penalties. The concept of field of the business activity, however, was entirely new, generating uncertainties as to its scope. On May 29, 2012, CADE issued Resolution n. 3 that lists 144 fields of business activities that will serve as the basis for the calculation of the penalty.

practice. They can only be entered into with the first company that qualifies for this purpose. Upon confession and compliance with the conditions set forth in Article 86, including the cooperation with the investigations and administrative proceedings resulting from such cooperation, CADE may terminate any punitive action against that specific agent or reduce one (1) to two thirds (2/3) of the applicable penalty. Leniency agreements also benefit the individuals involved in the violation (management and employees of the party executing the leniency agreement) with the same reductions in the administrative penalties and by preventing the offering of a criminal complaint provided that they enter into the leniency agreement jointly with the relevant company and respect the imposed conditions.

Agents may also benefit from CADE's Leniency Plus program, which consists of the reduction of the applicable penalty for an agent that does not qualify for a leniency agreement in connection with a practice in which it has participated but that provides information on a second anticompetitive conduct that CADE had no prior knowledge of.

Leniency agreements are appropriate in cases of anticompetitive agreements, especially cartel formation, but do not apply to unilateral conducts. This is because one of the essential conditions for the execution of leniency agreements is the presentation of evidence capable of leading to the conviction of the other parties that practiced the offense.

On the other hand, cease-and-desist agreements (called "TCC" in Brazil—an acronym for "Termo de Compromisso de Cessação") are available both in relation to cartels (when it is no longer possible to conclude a leniency agreement) and in relation to unilateral conduct.

The execution of cease-and-desist agreements interrupts the course of the administrative proceeding, and if all the conditions set forth in the agreement are met, the proceeding may be dismissed. Individuals who are already involved in criminal proceedings cannot benefit from TCCs but, under certain circumstances, are entitled to negotiate different agreements with the Federal Police or the Public Prosecution by collaborating with investigations of the collusion.

The admission of guilt and the payment of monetary contribution to a federal fund for the protection of diffuse rights (which will represent a percentage of the fine imposed to the parties that do not negotiate a TCC) are required in cartel cases but may be dismissed in cases of unilateral conduct.

When TCC obligations are observed, the proceeding is dismissed without a decision on the merits. Only in case of breach of such commitment will the proceeding return to its due course and entail the issuance of a decision with precedent value by CADE and application of penalties. It can therefore be stated that, in relation to unilateral conducts in the online sales market that CADE may consider to have potential anticompetitive effects, the negotiation of a TCC can be an effective way of reducing contingencies.

The Brazilian legal system also ensures the right of those who have suffered damages due to anticompetitive conduct to be indemnified. In fact, the Brazilian

Federal Constitution establishes as a fundamental right the access to a court of law,[5] and the Brazilian Civil Code establishes the general rule according to which any person that by an unlawful conduct causes damages to other persons shall indemnify the victim[6]). Therefore, if the anticompetitive practice caused harm to a person or entity, this entitles such person or entity to request indemnification before a Brazilian court. It is even possible that, whereas CADE in its assessment does not recognize such conduct as a violation to the economic order, the Brazilian courts rule that such act was illegal, thus entailing the right to indemnification to the damaged person. The right to receive compensation in principle is not affected by the existence of leniency agreements or TCC.

Collective damages caused by anticompetitive conduct, as well as moral and financial damages suffered by individuals, can be subject to compensation and pursued by class associations and the public prosecutors. Brazilian law does not provide for punitive damages. It is important to note, however, that in spite of being legally admitted, claims for damages arising from anticompetitive conducts are still rare in Brazil.

CADE's antitrust enforcement has been generally in line with international standards, with CADE being very active in the various international cooperation organizations in which it participates, notably the International Competition Network (ICN). In this sense, no conflict or gap between Brazilian practice and international practice regarding the application of antitrust rules in relation to the online sales platforms should be expected.

## 5.2 Internet and Antitrust Assessments

The principles and provisions outlined above shall equally apply to the new economy of Internet-related businesses and enterprises. This new facet of Brazilian economy has been growing fast, and the number of economic agents in the field is expanding rapidly.

So far in Brazil, CADE's merger reviews have presented interesting questions and acknowledged material differences to the Internet-related businesses. In order to understand such differentiation, it is important to, in the first instance, provide a brief overview of CADE's proceeding when analyzing mergers.

The Antitrust Act establishes a premerger control in transactions in which (1) two or more previously independent companies merge; (2) one or more companies acquire, directly or indirectly, by purchase or exchange of stocks, shares, bonds, or securities convertible into stocks or assets, whether tangible or intangible, by contract or by any other means, total or partial control of one or more companies; (3) one or more companies are merged into one or more other companies; or (4) two or more companies enter into associative, consortium, or joint venture agreements.

[5] According to Article 5, item XXXV of the Federal Constitution, no law is able to exclude any harm or threat to someone's right from the consideration of the Brazilian courts.

[6] According to Article 186 of the Civil Code.

CADE's aim in such assessment is to prevent transactions that could eliminate competition in a substantial portion of a relevant market, create or strengthen a dominant position, or result in the domination of a relevant market of goods or services. Such transactions shall only be approved by CADE if proved that they could increase productivity or competitiveness, improve the quality of goods or services, or encourage efficiency and technological or economic development, as well as transfer a relevant part of the resulting benefits to consumers, despite the apparently negative effects.

For this assessment, CADE normally divides its analysis into the following stages: (1) definition of the relevant market, (2) analysis of the level of market concentration, (3) examination of the possibility of using market power as a result of the merger, and (4) comparison between the negative effects and the efficiencies resulting from the concentration act.[7]

Although this type of analysis is not mandatory, and may vary in some cases depending on specific circumstances, these steps apply in principle to any and all assessments of this nature and in respect of all market businesses, including transactions involving companies from Internet-related businesses.

### 5.2.1 Relevant Market

As mentioned above, CADE first identifies the group of economic agents, consumers, and producers that may be affected by the transaction in a determined geographic area. According to the "hypothetical monopolist" test—one of the analytic tools used by CADE to define a relevant market—the relevant market is the smallest group of products/services in the smallest geographic area needed for a hypothetical monopolist to impose "a small but significant and non-transitory" increase in prices.

In order to identify the products/services that are part of a certain relevant market, CADE assesses, from a demand perspective, which goods and services are considered substitutable by the consumer for their characteristics, prices, and usage. In order to assess this substitutability, CADE examines the possibility of consumers shifting their demand to other products.

From the geographical point of view, CADE's Guide to Analysis of Horizontal Concentration Acts recognizes that certain relevant markets are based on the location of the consumer, others in the location of suppliers, and others in both locations (mixed markets).

In merger reviews involving Internet-related products and services, this pattern has been applied. At first, one could attribute a global reach to any and all Internet businesses since websites can be accessed from any computer in the planet.

[7] CADE is not required to follow this order of analysis. In addition, as it has made clear in the Guide to Analysis of Horizontal Concentration Acts published in 2016, CADE may, in certain cases, adopt alternative ways for antitrust analysis, such as counterfactual analysis and simulations of the transactions' effects that may depend or not on the prior definition of the relevant market.

However, as CADE has already decided in *Processo Administrativo*[8] No. 08012.003386/2001-73, this global outreach is usually restricted by some barriers, such as (1) the website's language, (2) regulatory barriers, (3) product/service taxation, and (4) delivery and payment options. Ergo, upon analyzing the relevant geographic area, the World Wide Web's potential is not considered but rather the real boundaries of that agent's performance, considering the items mentioned above, including the nature of the products/services it offers and the consumers that the agent aims to achieve, the language options in the website, and the areas where it is able to deliver its products/services.

Such aspects have been restated by CADE in more than one occasion, with the acknowledgment that high transaction costs to ship products outside of the Brazilian territory[9] and advertising clearly focused on a determined group of consumers that might be able to purchase and receive the products/services[10] represent barriers that restrict the business's geographic area.

The geographic definition in Internet-related businesses may also vary according to the nature of the product/service. As such, the offer of "electronic products" (e.g., an e-book) may have an international reach since it does not encompass high transaction costs. On the other hand, the sale of products that must be shipped overseas involves greater transaction costs that could hinder the delivery, depending on the distance and the costs involved—sometimes the agent might not even have the means to ship the product to other countries—which would certainly influence the definition of the affected geographic area.

Another matter CADE has dealt with in merger reviews pertains to the differentiation of e-commerce platforms and traditional retail stores. The agency has endorsed that, despite being related, these two businesses are not the same for consideration of the affected relevant market. According to the decision issued in *Processo Administrativo* No. 08012.007893/2005-18, e-commerce does not replace traditional stores but rather supplements them. It is of a different nature, in which consumers focus on convenience, saving time and not worrying about product transportation. Therefore, the definition of the relevant market should not include any kind of retail service, considering traditional retail and e-commerce as two different markets.

### 5.2.2 Market Concentration

The definition of the relevant market entails the assessment of the level of concentration of the market and the agent's market share, which is the first step to

[8] Administrative Proceeding. The Administrative Proceeding is initiated when CADE's General Superintendence consider that there are indictments of an unlawful conduct. It is an adversarial proceeding, aiming to guarantee to the accused party wide defense in regard to the conclusion of the investigation (Article 69 of the Antitrust Act).

[9] *Processo Administrativo* No. 08012.006253/1999-46.

[10] *Processo Administrativo* No. 08012.003921/00-13.

determine if the economic agent is able to exercise market power. According to Article 36, para 2, of the Antitrust Act, "[a] dominant position is assumed when a company or group of companies is able to unilaterally or jointly change market conditions or when it controls 20% (twenty percent) or more of the relevant market, provided that such percentage may be modified by CADE for specific sectors of the economy."

The presumption of dominance established by the law is, however, relative (*juris tantum*). That is, CADE may consider the existence of a dominant position even in cases where the market share is below the 20% level, as well as, in view of the actual circumstances, to understand that companies with more than 20% of the market have no dominant position.

For the definition of the level of market share, CADE examines, as appropriate, the structure of the offer on the market (in cases involving sales power) or the structure of demand (in cases related to purchasing power).

### 5.2.3 Exercise of Market Power

A merger resulting in a large combined market share does not necessarily entail the exercise of market power. Neither is a merger involving a small combined market share completely free from the possibility of exercise of market power. Some circumstances may undermine the exercise of market power in the former situation or lead to it in the latter.

One of those elements is the possibility of entry of new competitors in the relevant market. In such context, the so-called barriers to entry constitute any hurdles that a new player must overcome to start performing in that market and that may put it at a disadvantage compared to the players. Some of these barriers are (1) high fixed costs; (2) sunk costs; (3) legal or regulatory barriers (such as operation licenses); (4) advantages exclusively owned by the parties, such as exclusive access to an input; (5) the need for considerable economies of scale or scope; (6) level of integration of the production chain; (7) consumers' loyalty to the established players' brands; and (8) possible reaction by the established players. The greater are the barriers to entry, the harder it will be for a new player to start performing in that market sector and easier for the established players to exercise market power. Consequently, the agents involved in the analyzed transaction could argue that the relevant market has few barriers to entry and that therefore their exercise of market power would be deterred.

Another element is the possible rivalry between players. Such would occur whenever the established players start acting aggressively as an offset to the likely exercise of market power by the agents involved in the merger so as not to lose their market share in light of the new economic agent. A significant and nontransitory increase in prices by such agents could boost the proposal of new—and better—offers to consumers by the other players. It would then be possible to allege that effective rivalry between players would counterbalance the possibility of exercise of market power. The possibility of importing products is also able to influence and prevent the exercise of market power since it would increase the number of substitute products.

The abovementioned elements must also be taken into consideration in merger reviews pertaining to Internet-related businesses. In *Processo Administrativo* No. 08012.011238/2006-37, CADE analyzed the merger between two well-known e-commerce companies in Brazil that would hold more than 20% market share after the transaction. Such circumstance could in theory be sufficient to prove that the new company would exercise market power, but CADE acknowledged that the absence of barriers to entry and the rivalry among the different players in the market would neutralize it. First of all, regarding barriers to entry, CADE assessed that the Brazilian e-commerce business was rapidly expanding and creating enough space for new players, with a great deal of innovation. In addition, costs required to start an e-commerce platform are relatively low, which makes barriers to entry in the market insignificant.[11] CADE also considered the fierce competition in the market since many of the established players would be able to react to the merger reorganizing and innovating its commercial and marketing strategies. Besides, there are many websites that compare prices among the different e-commerce platforms with no additional costs to the consumers, which deepens even more the competition among players.

In other proceedings[12] involving mergers in the online advertising business, CADE ruled that the raise in market concentration (either horizontal or vertical) entailed by the transaction did not increase the involved companies' market power due to the great number of other players in such a fragmented business.

### 5.2.4 Economic Efficiencies

Lastly, a merger resulting in a greater probability of exercise of market power may still be approved by CADE if it also brings about economic efficiencies, or increments of welfare, to the business. By balancing these two effects, CADE may consider that the merger, despite causing market concentration and the possibility of exercise of market power, brings more benefits than harm to the economy and especially to consumers. Some of those benefits are economies of scale and scope, new technology increasing efficiency, positive externalities, and compensatory market power (when the exercise of market power of the involved agent neutralizes or reduces the exercise of market power by another agent, such as an input supplier).

CADE has already dealt with mergers between companies aiming to increase their economic efficiencies by means of business-to-business (B2B) platforms, or e-procurement, more than once. The agents involved in such transactions usually look for reduction of transaction costs and increase in efficiency by creating

[11] This was also stated in Proceeding No. 08012.007893/2005-18.

[12] Proceeding No. 08012.003921/2000-13 and No. 08012.010855/2008-87.

platforms in which suppliers of services, inputs, or MRO[13] advertise their products/services to the platform's users.

In *Processo Administrativo* No. 08012.006980/00-35, the agents involved alleged that such practice would provide uniformity and agility in the purchase of MROs, as well as a better cost perspective related to such products. The B2B platform was designed to rationalize their MRO purchase proceedings and is open to other companies that might have the same interest. This way, they would be able to acquire such products jointly, which would give them more bargaining power and represent a scale gain to all participants. In its assessment, CADE understood that the purchasers would not exercise market power over the suppliers and approved the transaction.

Likewise, CADE approved[14] the creation of a B2B platform with suppliers and consumers of products and services related to engineering and civil construction. This platform would also be open to any interested companies and suppliers. In this case, CADE acknowledged that B2B platforms increase economic efficiency by raising productivity and encouraging price reduction. However, their very nature could encourage anticompetitive practices, like exchange of information, joint selling and purchasing, and exclusionary practices, such as imposing difficulties to the entry of new agents in the platform.

Therefore, in order to avoid such practices, the agency approved the transaction with some restrictions, such as prohibiting the involved companies from requesting the execution of exclusivity agreements to new members of the platform and establishing that the companies should provide mechanisms to guarantee that no commercially sensitive information would be exchanged. The restrictions were imposed due to CADE's recognition that B2B platforms may increase chances of (1) collusion, (2) monopsony exercise, and (3) exclusionary practices against competitors that are not part of the platform. In relation to this last topic, it was also understood that B2B market is very recent and in full expansion. Therefore, despite not displaying signs of potential exclusionary practices, it is important that CADE keep monitoring these platforms.

## 5.3 Conclusion

The new economy breaks paradigms and is changing the way the law is applied not only in Brazil but also in the whole world. This is due to the Internet's potential to innovate and to the way it is changing human and business relations and adding new features to them. This change will certainly present challenges to the Brazilian antitrust authority, which must keep track of the developments in Internet-related businesses in order to ensure an effective protection of consumers and free competition.

---

[13] Materials, repairs and operations, which are not directly related to the company's main activity.

[14] Proceeding No. 08012.003386/2001-73.

Adapting to this new scenario does not depend on a change of laws or regulations. It relies on CADE's ability to understand the market's functioning and adapt as quickly as it changes and evolves. It will be responsible for applying the already existent rules considering that this new market is extremely fragmented due to its few barriers to entry, few capital requirements, and high levels of innovation.

Even though the current Guide to Analysis of Horizontal Concentration Acts[15] does not have specific rules regarding the "new economy," it provides CADE the flexibility to analyze the markets and the effects of mergers, taking into account different factors such as the degree of innovation and maturity of the markets, the barriers (or lack of barriers) to the entry of new competitors, and the differentiation of products or services.

Although such Guide refers specifically to horizontal concentration acts, some of its principles must also be taken into account by CADE for the analysis of anticompetitive behavior.

At the moment, it seems that CADE's tendency with respect to online sales platforms is not to issue specific norms or guides but to analyze the markets on a case-by-case basis with certain flexibility and recognizing the peculiar characteristics of any specific relevant market.

[15] "*Guia de Analise de Atos de Concentração Horizointal*" approved and published by the Plenary of CADE on July 2016.

# France

# 6

Linda Arcelin, Nizar Lajnef, Annabelle Lebaudy,
Lauren Mechri, Florence Ninane, Michaël Vaz d'Almeida,
and Pascal Wilhelm

## 6.1 Introduction

A definition of digital platforms was introduced in French law in 2015[1] and subsequently modified in 2016.[2] It reads as follows:

[1] Law 2015-990 of 6 August 2015 for growth, activity and equal economic opportunities (the 'Macron Law').

[2] Law no 2016-132 of 7 October 2016 for a digital Republic.

L. Arcelin
La Rochelle University, La Rochelle, France
e-mail: linda.arcelin@univ-lr.fr

N. Lajnef (✉)
UGGC Avocats, Paris, France
e-mail: n.lajnef@uggc.com

A. Lebaudy · L. Mechri
Cabinet Borrel, Paris, France
e-mail: al@cabinetborrel.com; lm@cabinetborrel.com

F. Ninane
Allen & Overy LLP, Paris, France
e-mail: Florence.Ninane@AllenOvery.com

M. V. d'Almeida
Orrick Rambaud Martel, Paris, France
e-mail: mvazdalmeida@orrick.com

P. Wilhelm
Wilhelm & Associés, Paris, France
e-mail: pwilhelm@wilhelmassocies.com



B. Kilpatrick et al. (eds.), *Antitrust Analysis of Online Sales Platforms & Copyright Limitations and Exceptions*, LIDC Contributions on Antitrust Law, Intellectual Property and Unfair Competition,
https://doi.org/10.1007/978-3-319-71419-6_6

> Is qualified as operator of on-line platform, any natural or legal entity offering, on a professional basis, whether against remuneration or not, an online service of communication to the public relying on:
>
> 1 ° The classification or the referencing, by means of computing algorithms, of contents, of goods or services offered or put online by third parties;
>
> 2 ° Or the connection between several parties with the aim of the sale of a good, the supply of a service or an exchange or a sharing of a content, a good or a service.[3]

Online sales platforms are distinct from so-called collaborative digital platforms. The following analysis is limited to the main competition law issues related to the activity of the websites devoted to the intermediation for the sale of products or services between a professional and a consumer (B2C) or between professionals (B2B). This category of online sales platform includes *market places* (Amazon, PriceMinister), platforms of hotel and tourism reservation (Booking.com, Hotels.com), or media platforms (Spotify, Netflix).

While the French courts have issued two important decisions regarding online sales platforms within the field of selective distribution,[4] the French Competition Authority (the 'Authority') has dealt with online sales platforms in many decisions involving anticompetitive practices[5] or merger control.[6]

---

[3] Article L. 111-7 of the Consumer Code.

[4] Paris Court of Appeal, Pole 3 Chamber 1, 2 February 2016, RG no 15/01542, eNova Santé v Caudalie; Paris Court of Appeal, Pole 5 Chamber 4, 25 May 2016, RG no 14/03918, France Télévisions v Valentina Colombo, Coty France and Marvale LLC.

[5] Competition Authority, Decision No 15-D-06 of 21 April 2015 concerning practices implemented in the online hotel reservation sector (Decision upon which relies Paris Court of Appeal, Pole 5 Chamber 7, 8 October 2015, RG no 2015/11953 Synhorcat, Fagiht v. Booking.com B.V., Booking.com France SAS and Booking.com Customer Service France SAS); Decision No 14-D-18 of 28 November 2014 regarding practices implemented in the event-driven online sales sector (Decision upon which relies Paris Court of Appeal, Pole 5 Chamber 7, 12 May 2016, RG no 2015/00301, Brandalley v Showroomprivé.com, Vente-Privée.com, Autorité de la concurrence, Ministre de l'économie, de l'industrie et du numérique); Decision No 14-D-11 of 2 October 2014 regarding practices implemented in the train ticket distribution sector; Decision No 14-D-04 of 25 February 2014 regarding practices implemented in the online horserace betting sector; Decision No 09-D-06 of 5 February 2009 regarding practices implemented by SNCF and Expedia Inc. in the online travel sales sector (Decision upon which relies Paris Court of Appeal, Pole 5 Chamber 7, 23 February 2010, RG no 2009/05544, Expedia Inc., Karavel v SNCF, Voyages-SNCF.com, l'Agence Voyages-SNCF.com, VFE Commerce, iDTGV and Lastminute); Decision No 07-D-07 of 8 March 2007 regarding practices implemented in the sector of cosmetics and personal hygiene products.

[6] Competition Authority, Decision No 16-DCC-111 of 27 July 2016 on the acquisition of sole control of Darty by Fnac; Decision No 11-DCC-87 of 10 June 2011 on the acquisition of sole control of Media Concorde SNC by High Tech Multicanal Group.

## 6.2 Implementation

### 6.2.1 Restriction of Online Sales

Bans on sales through third-party Internet platforms in selective distribution systems could be looked at on a case-by-case analysis focussing on the effects of the practice as hindering intra-brand competition, particularly at the expense of small and medium-sized enterprises (SMEs). In its Final Report of 10 May 2017 on e-commerce, the European Commission pointed out that marketplaces are more important as a sales channel for smaller and medium-sized retailers, while they are of lesser importance for larger retailers, and that Member States with the highest proportion of retailers experiencing marketplace restrictions are Germany (32%) and France (21%). Such a prohibition could be considered as creating a barrier to entry from the point of view of SMEs, which do not necessarily have the sufficient resources to develop mobile applications with secure payment systems.

In a case-by-case effects assessment, a prohibition to sell on marketplaces could also be considered as harming consumers' interests, in particular if it significantly increases their research costs (1) or if the product is not broadly available by other means through a wide selective distribution network (2) and if the product is subject to little inter-brand competition (3).

The position of the Competition Authority (Sect. 6.2.1.1) and of French courts (Sect. 6.2.1.2) has progressively evolved on this matter and currently remains fluctuant.

#### 6.2.1.1 Position of the French Competition Authority

In a decision of 2007 regarding the distribution of personal care and cosmetic products,[7] the Competition Council (former designation of the Competition Authority) considered that a producer could reasonably refuse to appoint online sales platforms in its selective distribution network since at the time of the facts this distribution channel still caused *serious issues*. The concerned platforms failed at the time to provide sufficient guarantees regarding the quality and identity of the sellers. According to the Competition Council, such lack of guarantee could facilitate illegal sales outside the selective distribution network or the sale of counterfeit goods, thereby harming the image of the network.

However, the Competition Council acknowledged that, subject to this limitation, platforms had the 'ability [...] to meet the products' qualitative criteria', for example with the creation of virtual shops dedicated to authorised sellers. The Competition Council thus did not validate clauses prohibiting all sales on e-marketplaces in general. It carried out a concrete analysis of the guarantees offered by the platforms and suggested, as early as in 2007, that its position could change on that matter, provided that marketplaces adapt in order to meet the selective distribution systems' qualitative criteria.

[7] Competition Council, Decision No 07-D-07, 8 March 2007 relative to practices implemented in the sector of cosmetic and personal hygiene products.

In 2011, the ECJ, in the Pierre Fabre[8] ruling on the broader matter of Internet sales ban to authorised distributors, considered that such a restriction would constitute a restriction by object if, following an individual and specific examination of the content and the objective and legal and economic context, it is apparent that, having regard to the properties of the products at issue, the clause is not objectively justified. The Court added that the aim of maintaining a prestigious image is not a legitimate aim for restricting competition and cannot therefore justify a finding that a contractual clause pursuing such an aim does not fall within Article 101(1) TFEU.

Some saw this judgment as the end of general clauses prohibiting sales on e-marketplaces.

In 2012, in its opinion about e-commerce,[9] the Competition Authority adopted a less rigid position, directed towards an analysis of potential restrictive effects of such a clause rather than an analysis by object. It held that, in selective distribution networks, the prohibition imposed by some manufacturers on their distributors to sell through third-party online platforms, as a condition to be approved in the distribution network, would need to be proportionate to the objective pursued, whether it is the maintenance of the brand's image or the prevention of the sale of counterfeit goods or illegal resale outside of the network, when it resulted in a restriction of competition on the relevant markets.

This issue has been brought again before the Competition Authority, with two decisions concerning requests for interim measures in the field of distribution of brown products (consumer electronic products, particularly televisions).[10] But the Authority did not rule on this issue, considering that the plaintiff company failed to provide evidence that the clause prohibiting sales on e-marketplaces caused the deterioration of its financial position or immediate damages to its interests, which constitutes a condition to grant interim measures.

On 30 September 2014, the European Commission indicated that it would take up a part of this case, in the context of an ongoing investigation about various commercial practices and contractual restrictions in the field of consumer electronics sales, including the question of clauses banning sales on e-marketplaces.[11]

In this context, the Competition Authority rejected the requests for interim measures, noticing that the plaintiff's economic situation (the company Concurrence) had deteriorated even though it was commercialising products on marketplaces,

[8] CJEU, case C-439/09, *Pierre Fabre Dermo-Cosmétique SAS v Président de l'Autorité and Ministre de l'Économie, de l'Industrie et de l'Emploi*, ECLI:EU:C:2011:649.

[9] Competition Authority, Opinion No 12-A-20 of 18 September 2012 regarding the competitive functioning of e-commerce.

[10] Competition Authority, Decision No 14-D-07 of 23 July 2014 relating to practices implemented in the sector of brown products distribution, in particular televisions; No 15-D-11 of 24 June 2015 relating to a request of interim measures concerning practices implemented in the sector of brown products distribution, in particular televisions.

[11] Competition Authority, Decision No 15-D-11 of 24 June 2015 relating to a request of interim measures concerning practices implemented in the sector of brown products distribution, in particular televisions, §8.

which suggested that the financial deterioration was not linked to the clause prohibiting the sale of the brand's products on e-marketplaces.

In a case involving similar practices carried out by the sports brand company Adidas, the Competition Authority indicated in a press release dated 18 November 2015 (the decision is not available) that it closed its investigation in exchange for Adidas' commitment to remove from its contracts all clauses forbidding distributors to sell through marketplaces, provided that such marketplaces met certain qualitative criteria allowing them to be approved by the manufacturer.

Therefore, to this day, the Competition Authority never had the opportunity to adopt a final decision, following a litigation process, regarding the validity of clauses that prohibit approved distributors from commercialising products on e-marketplaces.

#### 6.2.1.2 Position of French Courts

By contrast, French courts have adopted a stricter position, also in the specific context of evidence provided in emergency interim proceedings.

In a case involving the cosmetics brand Caudalie, the company eNova Santé created the platform 1001pharmacie.com, allowing pharmacists to sell their products on a marketplace. Caudalie, which distributed its products within a selective distribution network approved by the French Competition Authority in 2007,[12] prohibited its authorised distributors to sell their products on marketplaces. When it noticed that its products were on sale on 1001pharmacie.com, Caudalie filed a summons for urgent proceedings on the ground of Article L. 442-6-I-6° of the French Commercial Code, which forbids participating in the violation of a prohibition against sales outside the network by a distributor bound by a selective distribution agreement exempted under competition law.

The Paris Commercial Court, in an order of 31 December 2014,[13] granted Caudalie's requests and ordered eNova Santé to cease all commercialisation of Caudalie's products and to delete all mentions of these products on the website 1001pharmacie.com, along with all referencing and links from other websites redirecting to its server and making reference to Caudalie's brand product range.

The company eNova Santé appealed this decision, arguing that the general prohibition to sell on online selling platforms had become contrary to competition rules.

In a judgment of 2 February 2016,[14] the Paris Court of appeal annulled the order of the Paris Commercial Court on the ground of the evolution of law and case law, in particular (1) the Competition Authority's decisions regarding practices in the field of brown product distribution, particularly televisions (see Sect. 6.2.1.1 above):

[12] Competition Council, Decision No 07-D-07 of 8 March 2007 regarding practices implemented in the field of personal care and cosmetic products distribution.

[13] Paris Commercial Court, President, Ordinance of 31 December 2014, RG no 2014060579, Caudalie v. eNova Santé.

[14] Paris Court of Appeal, Pole 1 – Chamber 3, judgment of 2 February 2016, 1001Pharmacie v. Caudalie, RG n° 2014060579.

(2) the commitments taken by Adidas before the Competition Authority (see Sect. 6.2.1.1 above); (3) the Bundeskartellamt decisions (Adidas and Asics in 2014 and 2015); and (4) a law professor's legal opinion.

The Court of Appeal concluded that a general reselling prohibition on an online sales platform, notwithstanding its features, could constitute, unless an objective justification is provided, a hardcore competition restriction excluded from the benefit of the EU individual exemption referred to in Article L. 442-6-I-6° of the French Commercial Code.

This judgment was given on the sole ground of the required standard of proof that the Court had to apply for an interim measure request, i.e. the possibility for the judge, even in the presence of a serious dispute, to order precautionary and rehabilitation measures necessary to prevent an imminent harm or to stop an obviously illicit trouble.[15]

On 13 September 2017, the Court de Cassation (French Supreme Court) quashed this judgment. According to the Cour de cassation, the Court of Appeal failed to explain how the decisions and legal advice quoted in its judgment could lead to consider that the hindering of Caudalie's selective distribution network, which had been approved by the Competition Council in 2007, did not create an obviously illicit trouble.[16]

Furthermore, as mentioned above, to this day, (1) the Competition Authority's practice regarding this subject is limited to a commitment procedure and an opinion since it did not make a decision on this matter in the brown products cases of 2014 and 2015, anticipating an upcoming decision from the European Commission; (2) the Bundeskartellamt's practice is also limited to a commitment procedure since it did not make a decision either on this topic in the Asics case[17]; (3) the complaint filed by eNova Santé on the merits of the case is currently pending; the European Commission is currently investigating this matter[18]; (4) in its final report published on 10 May 2017 concerning a sector inquiry on e-commerce, the European Commission stated that *without prejudice to the pending preliminary reference, the findings of the sector inquiry indicate that (absolute) marketplace bans should not be considered as hardcore restrictions within the meaning of Article 4(b) and Article 4(c) of the Vertical Block Exemption Regulation. This does not mean that absolute marketplace bans are generally compatible with the EU competition rules. The Commission or a national competition authority may decide to withdraw the protection of the Vertical Block Exemption Regulation in particular cases when justified by the market situation*[19]; and (5) a preliminary ruling on this issue was also referred to

[15] Article 873 of the Code of Civil Procedure.

[16] Cour de cassation, Commercial Chamber, Caudalie/eNova Santé, no 16-15.067.

[17] Bundeskartellamt, Restriction of online sales of Asics running shoes, Press release of 28 August 2015.

[18] Competition Authority, Decision No 15-D-11 of 24 June 2015 relating to a request of interim measures concerning practices implemented in the sector of brown products distribution, in particular televisions, §8.

[19] EU Commission Final report on e-commerce sector inquiry, published on 10 May 2017, §42.

the Court of Justice in a case opposing Coty Germany GmbH to Parfümerie Akzente GmbH.[20]

### 6.2.2 Abuse of a Dominant Position

In addition to the anticompetitive practices resulting from the agreements referred to above, online sales platforms have been found to engage in abusive exclusionary practices by French competition authorities (Sect. 6.2.2.2). The relevant market should, beforehand, be assessed (Sect. 6.2.2.1).

#### 6.2.2.1 The Relevant Market

French competition authorities resort to various criteria in order to define the relevant market, which naturally depend on the nature of the relevant products or services involved. The cases mentioned below constitute recent illustrations of the competition authorities' position concerning the definition of relevant markets when online sales platforms are concerned.

In the Voyages-sncf.com case (2009), the Competition Council analysed the substitutability between the services provided by traditional and virtual travel agencies.[21]

In order to analyse demand-side substitutability, the Competition Council found that *travel agencies' customers are, above all, price-sensitive and use the Internet to find out about the different offers*.[22]

Similarly, to analyse supply-side substitutability, the Competition Council stated that *both traditional and online distribution channels offer the same products at the same price* and recalled that *traditional and online travel agencies exert competitive pressure on each other, in terms of price since the consumers are very price-sensitive and use the Internet to find out about the different offers*.[23] Moreover, the Competition Council noted the absence of barriers to entry into the online sales market (*the technological supports and internet access services used are accessible to any potential entrant*) since travel agencies generally adopt a multi-channel strategy.

The Competition Council concluded that the services provided by online travel agencies do not constitute a separate product market and identified the relevant market as the market for services provided by travel agencies for leisure trips, therefore including online sales. This analysis has not been contested in the subsequent decisions issued in this case.

---

[20] Request for a preliminary ruling from the Oberlandesgericht Frankfurt am Main (Germany), lodged on 25 April 2016, *Coty Germany GmbH v Parfümerie Akzente GmbH*, Case C-230/16.

[21] Competition Council, Decision No 09-D-06 of 5 February 2009 regarding practices used by SNCF and Expedia Inc. in the online travel sales sector, §95–98.

[22] Competition Council, Decision No 09-D-06 of 5 February 2009 regarding practices used by SNCF and Expedia Inc. in the online travel sales sector, §10.

[23] Competition Council, Decision No 09-D-06 of 5 February 2009 regarding practices used by SNCF and Expedia Inc. in the online travel sales sector, §10.

In 2009, Venteprivée.com case raised difficulties in the definition of the relevant market.[24] The case had been referred to the Authority by the company Brandalley for potential abuses of its dominant position by Venteprivée.com. The investigation services had identified a relevant market for event-driven online sales of which Venteprivée.com held more than 80% and therefore had a dominant position.

The Authority considered that the existence of an event-driven online sales market was not established. According to the Authority, the differentiating elements identified were not specific to the event-driven online sales since such differentiating elements were also present in other distribution channels of unsold products (price, confidentiality, high-end positioning, stocks), and others should be tempered (impulse buying). The Authority considered that 'it should be examined whether other distribution channels of destocking products [stores or factory warehouses, physical stores primarily selling seasonal products but having, on an ancillary basis, a destocking area, physical destocking networks, physical showrooms, e-commerce websites, website of mail-order selling operators] are likely to exercise competitive pressure on event-driven online sales'.[25] However, given the changing characteristics and specificities of the event-driven online sales since the date of the events (2005–2011), the Authority considered that it no longer made sense—at the time it made its decision—to analyse the demand side substitutability for the period at stake: 'Given the changing characteristics and specificities of event-driven online sales in the period at stake, notably with the development of e-commerce websites offering destocking products, the substitution possibilities on the demand side are likely to have changed. Therefore, it is not conceivable on this day to analyse the demand-side substitutability for the period covered by the statement of objections notified. As a matter of fact, the market players' contemporary representation of the possibilities of substitution which were offered to them or which they considered as such nearly a decade ago, could not be considered today as reliable enough.'[26]

Concerning the geographical market, the Authority found that, even if the sales are made via their website, the fact that event sales companies had established specific websites for each country pointed to the existence of a local market. The Authority also considered that language barriers and the consumption habits from one country to the other showed the existence of a national geographic market.

This analysis was subsequently confirmed by the Paris Court of Appeal in its judgment of 12 May 2016.[27] The judgment is, however, currently under review by the Cour de cassation.

---

[24] Competition Authority, Decision No 14-D-18 of 28 November 2014 regarding practices used event-driven online sales sector.

[25] Competition Authority, Decision No 14-D-18 of 28 November 2014 regarding practices used event-driven online sales sector, §113.

[26] Competition Authority, Decision No 14-D-18 of 28 November 2014 regarding practices used event-driven online sales sector, §115.

[27] Paris Court of Appeal, Pole 5 Chamber 7, 12 May 2016, RG 2015/00301, Brandalley v Showroomprivé.com, Vente-Privée.com, Autorité de la concurrence, Ministre de l'économie, de l'industrie et du numérique.

In its opinion on the competitive operation of electronic trade, the Authority found that 'Despite the increasing convergence between the channels, differences still remain between e-commerce websites and stores in terms of assortment and services provided to the clients' while admitting the competitive pressure exercised by online selling players on traditional distributors for some categories of products and for some consumers.[28]

In the Booking.com decision (2015), the Authority noted that the sale of hotel 'overnight stays' were distinct from tour packages that are composed of various products and that meta-search engines have a vertical relationship with online travel agencies (OTAs) since they only marginally competed with them in their relationship towards the hotels. The Authority has identified *the market for the supply of 'overnight stays only' reservation services by French hotels on OTAs (online hotel booking platforms and online travel agencies), with the exception of the hotels' direct channel and notably their website, meta search engines and search engines.*

After having taken into account the views of the hoteliers, who did not regard these different channels as substitutable to OTA channels, and to Booking.com, which argued that most hotels did not have the means to ensure their Internet visibility by registering directly with meta-search engines and search engines, the Authority concluded that 'In case of a small but permanent increase in OTAs' commission rates, the redirection of hoteliers' demand to these other channels would not be sufficient to make this price rise unprofitable for an hypothetical monopolist'. Thus, the Authority restricts the market definition to the supply of 'overnight stays only' reservation services by French hotels on OTAs, with the exception of the hotels' direct channel and notably their website, meta-search engines and search engines.[29] The market is therefore limited to online sales.

In the FNAC-Darty merger case (2016),[30] the Authority took into account the competitive pressure exercised by online sales operators, examining the demand redirections if FNAC or Darty increased their prices, whether this pressure comes from pure players (such as Amazon or Cdiscount) or from the websites of traditional retail stores that extend online their physical in-store selling. Then the Authority included for the first time online sales platforms in the retail market for brown products (consumer electronic products such as televisions, photographic cameras, audio products: MP3, DVD and Blu-ray players …) and grey products (consumer electronic products such as communication and multimedia: tablets, laptop computers, smartphones, etc.), which have been limited until now to traditional in-store distribution.

[28] Competition Authority, Opinion No 12-A-20 of 18 September 2012 on the competitive operation of electronic trade, §201.

[29] Competition Authority, Decision No 15-D-06 of 21 April 2015 regarding practices implemented by Booking.com B.V., Booking.com France SAS and Booking.com Customer Service France SAS in the online hotel reservation sector, §100.

[30] Competition Authority, Decision No of decision 16-DCC-111 regarding the acquisition of the Darty company by the Fnac group.

The Authority observed a standardisation of product lines and services available online, a standardisation of prices between both distribution channels and that most customers make their purchase decision by arbitrating between online and in-store products. This decision is currently under review by the Conseil d'Etat (Administrative Supreme Court).

#### 6.2.2.2 The Dominant Position

The National Digital Council (Conseil National du Numérique, CNNum) initiated a reflexion about the adaptation of the notion of dominant position beyond the market share criterion *in order to take into account more generally the power to exclude or to damage innovation: control of key resources, critical points of access, visibility, information, etc.*, advocating integration by the conceptual tools of regulation (*the fact that the platform sometimes constitutes itself a market*).[31] However, some important criteria in the digital sector (i.e., detention of databases[32]) are not specific to the digital market.

The decisions of the Competition Council, and then of the Competition Authority, show that the concepts and reasoning of competition law are adaptable to the digital sector.[33]

In the FNAC-Darty merger case,[34] the Competition Authority took into account for the first time online sales in assessing market power. The Authority chose a 50% market share threshold for brown and grey products—instead of the 40% market share threshold it traditionally used in its previous practice—to presume the existence of dominance, in order to identify the areas where the concentration was likely to affect competition.

The Authority stated that the consideration of a higher threshold was justified by the integration of online sales in the local competitive analysis. According to the Authority, *the increased use of internet, inasmuch as it makes the market far more transparent, in particular as regards prices and products, limits broadly the players' market power even when they have relatively high market shares in some local areas, by giving consumers an alternative for their purchases.* Moreover, *online sales account for an increasing share of the electronic products sales.*

#### 6.2.2.3 The Abuse

Some abuses are linked to the two-sided nature of the market in which the dominant undertaking operates. Thus, the position of platforms on the Internet has sometimes led them to develop an activity on a third side of the market placing them in a situation of competition. This is the case of Google, which has been condemned by the

[31] CNNum, Report on the neutrality of platforms, 2014, p. 28.

[32] Competition Authority, Decision No 14-D-06 of 8 July 2014 regarding practices implemented by Cegedim in medical database sector.

[33] Bruno Lasserre, Hearing by the Committee of reflection and proposals on the law and the liberties for the age of the digital technology, 7 July 2015.

[34] Competition Authority, Decision No of decision 16-DCC-111 regarding the acquisition of the Darty company by the Fnac group.

European Commission on 27 June 2017 for favouring its Google shopping service with its search engine.[35]

Other abuses may include denying access to data, which is anticompetitive if the data at stake constitutes an essential facility, a concept delimited by the European and French authorities.[36] In its decision Cegedim, the Competition Authority was very cautious in qualifying the database as essential facilities, considering that they were technically feasible by competitors, even if this was not easy because of the reference value of the tool in question and not essential to the point of rendering impossible any alternative solution.[37]

Nevertheless, even if a database is not characterised as an essential facility, denying access, even implicitly,[38] in a discriminatory manner by a dominant company may constitute an abuse of a dominant position since it significantly distorts competition.[39] The Authority may, therefore, order the holder of the database to make available consumer data, provided that said consumers do not object to such disclosure,[40] which shows the interactions between competition law and the protection of personal data.

Some contractual abuses include across-platform parity agreements (APPAs), which tend to organise the alignment of the offers of one party with that of a third party and the subsequent amendment of the contract. It obliges the debtor not to present better offers (in particular tariffs) than those offered by his partner. The practice was common in hotels, the reservation centres imposing hoteliers referenced not to offer on their own website services on more favourable terms and at lower prices than those displayed by the platform. In addition to the competition between platforms that is asphyxiated, suppliers are also deprived of any commercial autonomy, especially as far as pricing is concerned. The Authority considered that the parity clauses could lead to a reduction in competition between Booking.com and competing platforms and to squeeze out new entrants to the market. It has accepted the commitments offered by Booking aimed in particular at the abolition of tariff and room availability parity clauses.[41] Likewise, the tribunal de commerce

[35] European Commission, Press release 27 June 2017, IP/17/1784.

[36] Competition Authority and Bundeskartellamt, Competition law and data, 16 May 2016; AFEC, Report on digital economy, February 2016.

[37] Competition Authority, Decision No 14-D-06 of 8 July 2014 regarding practices implemented by Cegedim in the medical database sector. Questioned about this qualification of essential facilities, the Court of Appeal of Paris avoided the issue, acknowledging the inadmissibility of the request (Paris Court of Appeal, Pôle 5, Chamber 5–7, 24 September 2015, RG No 2014/17586); Cour de cassation, 21 June 2017, No 15-25941.

[38] Comm. CE, Guidance on the Commission's enforcement priorities in applying Article 82 of the EC Treaty to abusive exclusionary conduct by dominant undertakings, 24 February 2009.

[39] Competition Authority, Decision No 14-D-06, of 21 April 2015 regarding practices implemented by Booking.com B.V., Booking.com France SAS and Booking.com Customer Service France SAS in the online hotel reservation sector, §192 et seq.

[40] Competition Authority, Decision No 14-MC-02 of 9 Sept. 2014 regarding a request for interim measures submitted by Direct Energie in gas and electricity sectors.

[41] Competition Authority, Decision No 15-D-06 of 21 April 2015 regarding practices implemented

de Paris (Paris Commercial Court), ruling on the basis of Article L. 442-6 I 2° of the Commercial Code, which condemns significant imbalanced clauses in contracts concluded between commercial partners, considered that the tariff parity clause was null and void.[42]

The Law of 6 August 2015 for growth, activity and equal economic opportunities (known as the Macron Law) introduced in the Tourism Code an article prohibiting parity clauses in the hotel sector (Article L. 311-5-1). The result, however, is not very satisfactory, as shown in the 'Assessment of the effectiveness of commitments undertaken by Booking.com before the Authority' of 9 February 2017.

The conditions for referencing on a digital platform and in particular a search engine, an essential factor of visibility for any company, can also prove to be abusive. For example, Google's terms and conditions for its AdWords service have been examined in several cases. It has been considered that if Google is free *to define its AdWords content policy*, it is not exempt *from the obligation to implement this policy under objective, transparent and non-discriminatory conditions*,[43] which has sometimes been criticised.[44]

In the case Voyages-sncf.com in 2009, the Competition Authority considered that SNCF had abused its dominant position by (1) requiring online travel agencies to use a licence to access the essential facility at a very high cost (barrier to access to the market), (2) operating the voyages-sncf.com website while being exempted from using the charged essential facility (discriminatory practice), (3) preventing access to voyages-sncf.com's competitors to the 'Printed Ticket' feature, (4) setting discriminatory conditions for the distribution of 'Last Minute' tickets and iDTGV tickets (low-cost offer) and (5) applying discriminatory terms of remuneration through commissions paid for the supply of its train tickets.[45] SNCF did not challenge these accusations and proposed commitments[46] in order to remedy the competition concerns. The following legal actions taken in this case were not destined to challenge these competition concerns and remedies.[47]

---

by Booking.com B.V., Booking.com France SAS and Booking.com Customer Service France SAS in the online hotel reservation sector.

[42] Tribunal de commerce de Paris, 13e ch., 7 May 2015, RG No 2015/000040.

[43] Competition Authority, Decision No 13-D-07 of 28 February 2013, e-Kanopi, pt. 47.

[44] Competition Authority, Decision No 10-MC-01 of 30 June 2010 regarding a Request of interim measures from Navx; 10-D-30 of 28 October 2010 regarding practices implemented in online advertising sector.

[45] Competition Council, Decision No 09-D-06 of 5 February 2009 relating to practices implemented by SNCF and Expedia Inc. in the sector of online travel sales.

[46] SNCF committed to enable online travel agencies to distribute SNCF train tickets under the same technical conditions as the voyage-sncf.com website, to enable the function 'Ticket Printed' for online travel agencies, to allow the display of the iDTGV offers on the same web pages as other SNCF railway offers, and to no longer apply discriminatory conditions of remuneration.

[47] Paris Court of Appeal, 23 February 2010, RG No 2009/05544; Cour de cassation, 10 May 2011, No R 10-14.866 (withdrawal); Cour de cassation, 10 May 2011, No H 10-14.881 (requests for preliminary ruling of the CJEU); CJEU, 13 December 2012, case C-226/11; Cour de cassation, 16 April 2013, No H 10-14.881 (rejection); Cour de cassation, 11 June 2013, No H 10-14.881 (amendment).

In the case of the online horse race betting, in 2014, the Competition Authority considered that PMU had, through its online platform dedicated to horse race betting, implemented a practice known as betting pools[48] of its online and offline stakes. Such a practice could be characterised as abuse of a dominant position.[49] Indeed, the Authority admitted that this practice could have, on the competitive functioning of the online horse race betting market, an effect of capture of the demand, a hindering effect for new entrants and an eviction effect on alternative operators already present. Competitors that do not benefit from the resources of the offline monopoly are not in a position to offer such an attractive offer. PMU proposed commitments aimed in particular at separating online and offline bets.

## 6.3 Consent Decrees and Cease Agreements

French law offers two means of dispute resolution to undertakings subject to liability for anticompetitive practices: the settlement and commitment procedures. These negotiated procedures are applicable to all sectors, including e-commerce,[50] and may, in theory, be initiated whatever the infringements of competition at stake. The commitment procedures applied in the online platform sector are mentioned above. However, to our knowledge, no major decision of transaction has been issued by the Competition Authority in the online sales sector.

The settlement procedure enables undertakings to acknowledge their involvement in anticompetitive practices and their liability for it. The transaction proposed by the Authority sets the maximum and minimum amount of the incurred fine, which, in theory, limits its amount.[51]

The commitment procedure, provided for in Article L. 464-2 I of the Commercial Code, allows the Competition Authority to accept commitments proposed by undertakings, aiming at remedying the competition concerns identified. The commitments can be proposed in addition to a settlement procedure or autonomously. The commitment procedure normally applies to situations raising competition concerns that can easily be waived by a simple behavioural modification, such as unilateral or vertical practices of refusal or of insufficient competitive tendering. It does not apply in cases where the offence against the economic public order requires a financial penalty (for example, in case of cartels or abuse of dominant position causing an important damage to the economy). If the Authority considers that the commitments proposed solve the competitive concerns identified by the instruction,

[48] The practice of pooling consisted in, for PMU, to pool in a single mass for each bet and for each online bets made on Pmu.fr with those made under its monopoly 'offline'.

[49] Competition Authority, Decision No 14-D-04 of 25 February 2014 relating to practices implemented in the online horserace betting sector.

[50] Competition Authority, Decision No 09-D-06 of 5 February 2009 regarding practices implemented by SNCF and Expedia Inc. in the online travel sales sector.

[51] Article L. 464-2 III of the Commercial Code.

the Authority issues a decision making the commitments mandatory. This decision ends the administrative procedure.

There is also a possibility for the Authority to refuse commitments proposed by the concerned undertakings when the damage caused to the economy is too important. The exclusionary practices are viewed as particularly serious.[52] The commitment procedure is rarely implemented in this context.

For example, in a decision concerning the online sales of theatre show tickets, the Authority accepted a number of commitments, including the implementation of a compliance programme on competition rules in the e-commerce sector. The proposed commitments did not put an end to the instruction procedure but lowered the amount of the penalty by 10%.[53]

The decision by which the Competition Authority accepts and makes proposed commitments mandatory can be preceded by a negotiation phase. This decision does not rule on the undertaking's liability. Neither does it prevent victims of the anticompetitive practices at stake to take legal action in order to obtain compensation. Some authors believe that the commitment procedure weakens competition law as the level of evidence provided is not satisfactory, which affects legal predictability. Indeed, if the commitment decision solves the situation on the market, it does not clarify the competition questions at stake.[54] This analysis can, however, be tempered by the possibility to study the commitments accepted by the Authority in order to identify the behaviour required by the Competition Authority in similar cases.

The Competition Authority strictly controls the implementation of commitments taken by undertakings and may sanction their infringement by imposing a flat-rate financial penalty up to 5% of their average daily turnover for each day of infringement. In addition, the Macron Law[55] introduced the possibility for the Authority to order injunctions or prescriptions to undertakings that have not fulfilled their commitments in the time intended. These measures may replace or extend the unfulfilled obligations.[56]

The monitoring of the commitment compliance is carried out according to a simplified procedure, different from the classic competitive analysis led in anticompetitive practice instruction procedures. It is not necessary to prove the fraudulent

[52] *'when the notified charges involve exclusionary practices on the part of a dominant undertaking, these are generally viewed as serious since they are capable of having the effect of hindering the access and the development of competitors on the market by means which do not constitute competition on the merits'*, Competition Authority, Decision No 17-D-06 of 21 March 2017 regarding practices implemented in the sector of gas, electricity and energy services, §172.

[53] Competition Authority, Decision no 12-D-27 of 20 December 2012 regarding practices identified in the show ticketing sector.

[54] F. de Bure, « Engagez-vous, qu'ils disaient… » – Retour sur la politique d'engagements des autorités de concurrence, dix ans après », RLC, n°54, 1 October 2016.

[55] Law No 2015-990 of 6 August 2015 for growth, activity and equal economic opportunities ('Macron Law').

[56] Article L 430-8 IV 3° of the Commercial Code.

intent of the wrongdoer, the existence of an anticompetitive practice or the seriousness of the breach for the market concerned.[57]

## 6.4 Private Enforcement

French law includes provisions allowing the victim of an infringement of competition law to bring a private action against the offender in order to obtain damages.

Compensation for the damage suffered can be obtained in two situations. In the first case, the victim may bring a tort private action based on Articles 1240 and 1241 of the Civil Code. This action is brought either autonomously before the civil judge (stand-alone action) or following the public action of the Competition Authority (follow-on action).[58] In the second case, where the victim is a consumer, it may join a group litigation initiated by an approved consumer association as a result of the sanction of the infringement by the Competition Authority.[59]

These actions are brought before courts of the judicial order that are specialised in the implementation of competition law, provided that Articles L. 420-1 to L. 420-5 of the Commercial Code are invoked,[60] or before the administrative courts, where the offender or the victim of the competition violations is a public person.[61]

In view of the limited number of tort actions for damages implemented,[62] European Directive 2014/104/EU of 26 November 2014 introduced rules to encourage private actions by victims.[63] The transposition of this Directive into French law introduced new articles, L. 481-1 et seq. and R. 481-1 et seq., in the Commercial Code, which include rules relating to the communication and production of documents, the effect of the decision of the Competition Authority, the passing on of additional costs, and joint and several liability.[64]

---

[57] Competition Council, Decision No 08-D-24 of 22 October 2008 relating to the water leasing and distribution and purification in Saint-Jean-d'Angély.

[58] Paris Court of Appeal, 2 July 2015, No 13/22609, EDF/Nexans; Cour de cassation, Commercial Chamber, 3 June 2014, no 12-29482, for *follow-on actions*, also, Cour de cassation, Commercial Chamber, 13 January 2015, no 13-21886; Court of Appeal of Paris, 14 December 2011, No 09/20639, for *stand-alone actions*.

[59] Articles L. 623-1 to L. 623-32 of the Consumer Code, introduced by Law no 2014-344 of 17 March 2014 and its implementing Decree No 2014-1081 of 24 September 2014.

[60] Articles L. 420-7 of the Commercial Code, R.420-3, R.420-4 and R.420-5 of the Commercial Code for mainland France and R.914-1, R.924-1 and R.954-1 of the Commercial Code for the Overseas Collectivities; also, Cour de cassation, Commercial Chamber, 9 November 2010, no 10-10937.

[61] Cour de cassation, Civil Chamber No 1, 29 September 2004, no 02-18335, EDF c/SNIET.

[62] Circular of 23 March 2017, BOMJ No 2017-03 of 31 March 2017.

[63] Directive 2014/104/UE of the European Parliament and of the Council of 26 November 2014 on certain rules governing actions for damages under national law for infringements of the competition law provisions of the Member States and of the European Union.

[64] Ordinance No 2017-303 of 9 March 2017 and Decree No 2017-305 of 9 March 2017.

Article L. 481-2 of the Commercial Code introduces an irrefutable presumption of breach and liability when the existence of the anticompetitive practice and the attributability of the infringement have been established by a final decision of the Competition Authority. This includes decisions imposing penalties to undertakings, as well as decisions made in the context of a non-challenge or a settlement procedure.

However, decisions to accept commitments made by the undertaking concerned do not fall within the presumption since the decision does not characterise a competition law violation.[65] In such a case, as in the case of non-compliance with commitments or in a stand-alone action, the victim shall bear the burden to prove the existence of an infringement of competition law.

## 6.5 Conclusion

At first sight, the contentious practice of the French Competition Authority does not seem to reflect a specific sensitivity for the new economy as compared to other sectors. However, such sensitivity seems to be developing in the Authority's advisory function (advocacy). A few of the Authority's opinions are issued after a binding referral by the government prior to the enactment of an administrative or legal text involving competition[66] or price issues or by sectoral regulators.[67] But most of the opinions issued by the Authority are those resulting from a referral by the Minister of the Economy or resulting from self-referrals made by the Authority, which shows the particular attention of the French Authority. Since 2010, it has delivered two global opinions on the issue,[68] and a third one is underway.[69]

In addition, there are two studies on the sector, conducted jointly with two other European competition authorities[70]: (1) Study of 16 December 2014 on 'Economic analysis of open and closed systems', carried out with the Competition and Market

[65] Circular du 23 mars 2017, BOMJ No 2017-03 of 31 March 2017, Sheet No 4.

[66] Competition Authority, Opinion No 13-A-12 of 10 April 2013 regarding a project of order of Minister of Social Affairs and health concerning the best practice of dispensation of medicine by electronic way.

[67] Competition Authority, Opinion No 17-A-09 of 5 May 2017 regarding a request from the Authority of Regulation of the Electronic Communications and the Posts concerning the fifth cycle of analysis of the wholesale markets of the high-speed and very high-speed.

[68] Competition Authority, Opinion No 10-A-29 of 14 December 2010 regarding the competitive functioning of the on-line advertising (request from the Minister); Opinion No 12-A-20 of 18 September 2012 regarding the competitive functioning of the e-commerce sector; Decision No 11-SOA-02 of 1 July 2011 concerning a self-referral for an opinion on the e-commerce sector.

[69] Competition Authority, self-referral, Decision No 16-SOA-02 of 23 May 2016 concerning a self-referral for an opinion on the exploitation of data in the on-line advertising sector.

[70] Study of 16 December 2014 on "*The economics of open and closed systems*", with the Competition & Market Authority; Study of 10 May 2016 on "*Competition law and data*", with the Bundeskartellamt.

Authority, and (2) Study of 10 May 2016 on 'Competition law and data', carried out with the Bundeskartellamt.

This mode of regulation, intervening at an early stage and therefore before irreversible changes in the market occur, allows faster and more flexible assessments that are adapted to the sector. Nevertheless, questions can be raised as to the binding force of this *soft law* tool.

# Germany

7

Thomas Hoeren

## 7.1 Introduction

The development of the new economy sector raises new questions in all legal fields—antitrust law is no exception. Online sales are an omnipresent alternative to purchasing at brick-and-mortar shops. The advantages of these purchasing methods for competition are obvious: online sales make it possible for the end client to gather information on products and sellers without great effort. Above all, the possibility to compare prices strengthens the buyer's position. Online sales thus strengthen both inter- and intra-brand competition. The effects on inter-brand competition are even bigger on third-party platforms because the user is informed about alternative products and other sellers' offers. That of course motivates manufacturers and trademark proprietors to restrict the possibility of online sales in order to decrease inter- and intra-brand competition and thus strengthen their products' position on the market. Antitrust law has to give an answer to the question of how far these interests can justify a restriction on online sales.

A high percentage of online sales are conducted with the involvement of very few third-party platforms (e.g., Amazon or eBay). Consequently, the platform operators can influence the competition on the online sales market to a great extent. Antitrust law provides the legal framework for examining their actions.

This article aims at giving an overview on the national statutory and case law concerning the application of antitrust law to online sales platforms.

Firstly, this report presents the legal bases of German and European antitrust law. That includes providing information about how the law is enforced in both administrative procedures and civil law suits. Secondly, possibilities of prohibiting or

T. Hoeren (✉)
Westfälische Wilhelms-Universität, Münster, Germany
e-mail: hoeren@uni-muenster.de



B. Kilpatrick et al. (eds.), *Antitrust Analysis of Online Sales Platforms & Copyright Limitations and Exceptions*, LIDC Contributions on Antitrust Law, Intellectual Property and Unfair Competition,
https://doi.org/10.1007/978-3-319-71419-6_7

restricting online sales of goods by vertical agreements are examined. Emphasis is laid on the question as to whether bans on online sales via third-party platforms in selective distribution systems can be in line with antitrust law. Furthermore, latest case law concerning the possibility of most-favoured-nation conditions for online platforms will be discussed.

Less regard is given to merger control cases as these are not of high practical relevance in regard to online sales platforms.

## 7.2 German and European Antitrust Law

### 7.2.1 Governing Law

Two antitrust laws are applicable within the Federal Republic of Germany. The German national antitrust law is codified in the Act Against Restraints of Competition (hereinafter GWB).[1] Besides, Article 101 TFEU and Regulation 139/2004 on the control of concentrations between undertakings govern the European antitrust law. The application of the TFEU provisions is limited to cases that have an impact on the European Single Market.[2] If that is the case, the two legal regimes are generally of parallel application.[3]

Issues arise whenever the two antitrust regimes produce different legal results for the same case. As a general principle, EU law prevails if it is stricter.[4] If the national law is stricter, § 22 GWB and Article 3 of the Regulation 1/2003 solve the conflict. In regard to *restriction of competition*, the lawmaker pointed out in § 22 (2) GWB that national law may not prohibit behaviour that is allowed under European antitrust law. In cases dealing with an *abuse of dominant market power*, § 22 (3) GWB states that the application of stricter provisions of the GWB remains unaffected. If EU law is applicable in *merger control cases*, the national law's application is prohibited according to § 22 (4) GWB.

#### 7.2.1.1 Restriction of Competition

§ 1 GWB states that 'agreements between undertakings, decisions by associations of undertakings and concerted practices which have as their object or effect the prevention, restriction or distortion of competition shall be prohibited'. On the EU level, Article 101 (1) TFEU codifies the same. The criterion of restriction of competition is not legally defined.

---

[1] An official English translation can be found here: http://www.gesetze-im-internet.de/englisch_gwb/. Accessed 6 June 2017.

[2] H.-J. Bunte and F. Stancke, Kartellrecht, 3rd ed, C.H. Beck 2016, p. 55.

[3] H.-J. Bunte and F. Stancke, Kartellrecht, 3rd ed, C.H. Beck 2016, p. 58.

[4] H.-J. Bunte and F. Stancke, Kartellrecht, 3rd ed, C.H. Beck 2016, p. 59.

For the national law, it is generally acknowledged that the prohibition aims at protecting the economic freedom of action of all market players.[5] Consequently, the question if and in how far this freedom is limited is the starting point in order to examine if the criterion is fulfilled. Furthermore, the restriction has to be appreciable,[6] meaning that it has to be suitable to have effects on the relevant market.[7] Often, the question whether a behaviour meets these criteria has to be solved by referring to case law.[8] There are also certain cases in which a restriction of competition is not given although the afore-mentioned criteria are fulfilled. These cases have been developed by antitrust case law,[9] for instance with regard to vertical restraints in selective distribution systems.

As there is neither a consistent definition of competition on the EU level nor a clear line drawn by EU case law, it is harder to determine a restriction of competition within the meaning of Article 101 (1) TFEU.[10] However, the existing case law allows to conclude that a restriction of competition is given if the commercial freedom of action of the involved market players is limited.[11] Besides, the CJEU pointed out in some judgments that an agreement's impact on third parties[12] and its impact on the European Single Market[13] are important factors in examining whether a

[5] W. Berg and M. Mudrony. In: Berg and Mäsch (eds), Deutsches und Europäisches Kartellrecht, 2nd ed, Luchterhand 2015, § 1 GWB para. 46; K. Krauß. In: Langen and Bunte (eds), Kartellrecht Kommentar Band 1, 12th ed, Luchterhand 2014, § 1 GWB para. 121.

[6] Federal Court of Justice, Decision of 14 October 1976, Case No. KZR 36/75 – *Fertigbeton I*, NJW 1977, pp. 804–805; W. Berg and M. Mudrony. In: Berg and Mäsch (eds), Deutsches und Europäisches Kartellrecht, 2nd ed, Luchterhand 2015, Art. 101 AEUV para. 90 ff.; K. Krauß. In: Langen and Bunte (eds), Kartellrecht Kommentar Band 1, 12th ed, Luchterhand 2014, § 1 GWB para. 163.

[7] Federal Court of Justice, Decision of 9 March 1999, Case No. KVR 20/97 – *Lottospielgemeinschaft*, GRUR 199, pp. 771–775; K. Krauß. In: Langen and Bunte (eds), Kartellrecht Kommentar Band 1, 12th ed, Luchterhand 2014, § 1 GWB para. 167.

[8] D. Hengst. In: Langen and Bunte (eds), Kartellrecht Kommentar Band 2, 12th ed, Luchterhand 2014, Art. 101 AEUV para. 148.

[9] K. Krauß. In: Langen and Bunte (eds), Kartellrecht Kommentar Band 1, 12th ed, Luchterhand 2014, § 1 GWB para. 123.

[10] V. Emmerich. In: Immenga and Mestmäcker (eds), Wettbewerbsrecht Band 1, Art. 101 AEUV para. 107.

[11] ECJ, case C-306/96, *Javico v Yves Saint Laurent Parfums*, ECR 1998 I 1983: '*an agreement intended to deprive a reseller of his commercial freedom*'; CFI, case T-368/00, *General Motors Nederland and Opel Nederland v Commission*, ECR 2003 II 4491; V. Emmerich. In: Immenga and Mestmäcker (eds), Wettbewerbsrecht Band 1, Art. 101 AEUV para. 109; D. Hengst. In: Langen and Bunte (eds), Kartellrecht Kommentar Band 2, 12th ed, Luchterhand 2014, Art. 101 AEUV para. 147.

[12] E.g. CJEU, case C-279/06, *CEPSA Estaciones de Servicio SA v LV Tobar e Hijos SL*, ECR 2008 I 6681.

[13] E.g. CJEU, case 26/76, *Metro SB-Großmärkte GmbH & Co. KG v Commission of the European Communities*, ECR 1977 1875.

behaviour is a restriction of competition. Again, case law plays an important role.[14] And like in the national law, the restriction has to be appreciable.[15]

If the criteria are indeed met, the behaviour can, however, fall under an exception under both legal regimes. § 2 GWB is applicable to solely national cases. In its first sub-paragraph, the provision allows agreements between undertakings, decisions by associations of undertakings or concerted practices on the condition that they contribute to improving the production or distribution of goods or to promoting technical or economic progress while allowing consumers a fair share of the resulting benefit. An undertaking cannot rely on the exception if the afore-mentioned behaviour imposes concerned restrictions on undertakings that are not indispensable to the attainment of these objectives or if it affords such undertakings the possibility of eliminating competition in respect of a substantial part of the products in question. It is obvious that this exception is drawn very narrowly so that it is usually hard for a defendant to prove that the requirements are met in the case at hand. On the EU level, Article 101 (3) TFEU is applicable.

§ 2 (2) GWB stipulates that exceptions to § 1 GWB can also derive from the so-called block exemption regulations of the European Council and the parliament of the European Union. These regulations specify the blanket clause of § 2 (1) GWB[16] and thus bring legal certainty. The various regulations apply to different groups of agreements (e.g. vertical[17] and horizontal agreements) or to different industrial sectors (e.g. the insurance sector).[18] In EU law, no conjunction to the block exemption regulation is needed as they are directly applicable.[19]

With the Seventh Amendment to the Act Against Restraints of Competition, the German lawmaker aligned § 1 GWB to Article 101 (1) TFEU so that eventually the criteria became the same.[20] The same can be said of the exceptions to the prohibition of § 1 GWB, which are codified in § 2 GWB and are in line with Article 101 (3) TFEU.[21] This allows to make references to decisions of the European Commission, Guidelines of the European Commission and judgments dealing with a violation of

[14] C. Grave and J. Nyberg. In: Loewenheim, Meessen, Riesenkampff, Kersting and Meyer-Lindemann (eds), Kartellrecht, 3rd ed, C.H. Beck 2016, Art. 101 Abs. 1 AEUV para. 257.

[15] CJEU, case 22/71, *Béguelin Import/G.L. Import Export*, ECR 1971 949; V. Emmerich. In: Immenga and Mestmäcker (eds), Wettbewerbsrecht Band 1, Art. 101 AEUV para. 116.

[16] J. Nordemann. In: Loewenheim, Meessen, Riesenkampff, Kersting and Meyer-Lindemann (eds), Kartellrecht, 3rd ed, C.H. Beck 2016, § 2 GWB para. 28.

[17] See Sect. 7.3.1 for more details.

[18] J. Nordemann. In: Loewenheim, Meessen, Riesenkampff, Kersting and Meyer-Lindemann (eds), Kartellrecht, 3rd ed, C.H. Beck 2016, § 2 GWB para. 32 ff.

[19] Cf. J. Nordemann. In: Loewenheim, Meessen, Riesenkampff, Kersting and Meyer-Lindemann (eds), Kartellrecht, 3rd ed, C.H. Beck 2016, Art. 101 Abs. 3 AEUV para. 14.

[20] J. Nordemann. In: Loewenheim, Meessen, Riesenkampff, Kersting and Meyer-Lindemann (eds), Kartellrecht, 3rd ed, C.H. Beck 2016, § 1 GWB para. 10; H.-J. Bunte and F. Stancke, Kartellrecht, 3rd ed, C.H. Beck 2016, pp. 257 f.

[21] J. Nordemann. In: Loewenheim, Meessen, Riesenkampff, Kersting and Meyer-Lindemann (eds), Kartellrecht, 3rd ed, C.H. Beck 2016, § 2 GWB para. 7; H.-J. Bunte and F. Stancke, Kartellrecht, 3rd ed, C.H. Beck 2016, p. 258.

Article 101 (1) TFEU. To put it in a nutshell, there are no conflicts between national and European antitrust law with regard to the prohibition of restrictions of competition.

#### 7.2.1.2 Abuse of Dominant Position

§ 19 (1) GWB and Article 102 (1) TFEU prohibit the abuse of dominant market power by one or several undertakings. As distinct from § 19 GWB, Article 102 (1) TFEU can only be violated if the undertaking(s) has/have a dominant market power on the European Single Market or a substantial part of it. The two provisions are not congruent so that a legal gap between the systems exists. However, the EU law—if applicable—regularly comes to the same result as the national law because the underlying value judgments correspond.[22]

An undertaking has a *dominant position* within the meaning of Article 102 (1) TFEU on the market if it has 'a position of economic strength [...] which enables it to prevent effective competition being maintained on the relevant market by giving it the power to behave to an appreciable extent independently of its competitors, customers and ultimately of its consumers'.[23] Several undertakings can have a dominant market position if they operate as a collective entity on the relevant market.[24]

§ 18 GWB defines the criterion of dominant market power for the application of national law. To strengthen legal certainty, the national law provides for rebuttable presumptions[25] of a dominant market power in § 18 (4)–(6) GWB. For example, a single undertaking is presumed to have dominant market power if it has a market share of at least 40%; three or less undertakings are presumed to have dominant market power if their combined market share reaches 50%. According to § 18 (1) GWB, an undertaking has dominant market power as a supplier or purchaser of a certain type of goods or services on the relevant market when it either has no competitors or is not exposed to any substantial competition or has a paramount market position in relation to its competitors. § 18 (3) GWB then enumerates factors that have to be taken into account when assessing the market position of an undertaking.

Although these factors were developed for the traditional economic sectors, they are of relevance for the *new economy sector*, too. Besides, the list of factors is

---

[22] J. Nothdurft. In: Langen and Bunte (eds), Kartellrecht Kommentar Band 1, 12th ed, Luchterhand 2014, § 19 GWB para. 23; U. Loewenheim. In: Loewenheim, Meessen, Riesenkampff, Kersting and Meyer-Lindemann (eds), Kartellrecht, 3rd ed, C.H. Beck 2016, § 19 para. 4. See, as an example, Federal Court of Justice, Decision of 29 June 2010, Case No. KZR 31/08 – *GSM-Wandler*, MMR 2010, pp. 786–790; Federal Court of Justice, Decision of 4 March 2008, Case No. KVR 21/07 – *Soda-Club II*, WM 2008, pp. 893–900.

[23] CJEU, case 27/76, *United Brands Company and United Brands Continentaal BV v Commission of the European Communities*, ECR 1977 1875.

[24] CJEU, case C-395/96, *Compagnie maritime belge transports et al. v European Commission*, ECR 2000 I 1365.

[25] A. Bardong. In: Langen and Bunte (eds), Kartellrecht Kommentar Band 1, 12th ed, Luchterhand 2014, § 18 GWB paras. 204, 207.

non-exclusive[26] so that the characteristics of the new economy sector can be taken into account adequately.[27] However, with the development of the new economy sector, hitherto unknown questions in regard to the assessment of an undertaking's position in the market arise.

Within this sector, so-called *two-sided markets* are ubiquitous. Two-sided markets are networks in which one undertaking offers services in two directions.[28] Within these markets, so-called *indirect network effects* arise if the attractiveness to use the service for a customer on one side of the platform (e.g., advertiser on Google) depends on the size of the customer on the other side of the platform (e.g., search engine user).[29] These effects arise in regard to online sales platforms like Amazon or eBay, too[30]: the more that distributors make use of the platform, the more buyers will use the service and vice versa. The service provider regularly subsidises the group of customers that causes more indirect network effects at the other group's charge.[31] Consequently, the financial strength on one market is not a reliable factor for the assessment of the undertaking's market position.[32] The national lawmaker has recognised that problem and is willing to introduce a new sub-paragraph, (3a), to § 18 GWB that is in particular applicable to two- or more-sided markets.[33] According to that provision, inter alia, direct and indirect network effects (No. 1) have to be taken into account when accessing the undertaking's position on the market. Besides, the lawmaker plans to introduce further factors to face the challenges that result from the growth of the new economy sector, for instance the parallel use of services and the effort that the user has to make to switch to another system (No. 2) and the undertaking's access to data being relevant to competition (No. 4).

It is furthermore questionable if the presumptions of § 18 (4)–(6) GWB fit to the new economy sector as this sector is characterised by a high pressure for innovation. In the new economy sector, today's market shares may be vanished tomorrow and thus cannot be a reliable factor in order to assess an undertaking's market position.[34]

---

[26] A. Fuchs and W. Möschel. In: Immenga and Mestmäcker (eds), Wettbewerbsrecht Band 2, § 18 GWB para. 124.

[27] T. Körber, Analoges Kartellrecht für digitale Märkte?, WuW 2015, pp. 120–133.

[28] H. Bergmann and L. Fiedler. In: Loewenheim, Meessen, Riesenkampff, Kersting and Meyer-Lindemann (eds), Kartellrecht, 3rd ed, C.H. Beck 2016, Art. 102 AEUV para. 44; C. Ewald. In: Wiedemann (ed), Handbuch des Kartellrechts, 3rd ed, § 7 para. 71; T. Höppner and J. Grabenschröer, Marktabgrenzung bei mehrseitigen Märkten am Beispiel der Internetsuche, NZKart 2015, pp. 162–168.

[29] C. Ewald. In: Wiedemann (ed), Handbuch des Kartellrechts, 3rd ed, § 7 para. 71.

[30] T. Höppner and J. Grabenschröer, Marktabgrenzung bei mehrseitigen Märkten am Beispiel der Internetsuche, NZKart 2015, pp. 162–168.

[31] C. Ewald. In: Wiedemann (ed), Handbuch des Kartellrechts, 3rd ed, § 7 para. 72.

[32] C. Ewald. In: Wiedemann (ed), Handbuch des Kartellrechts, 3rd ed, § 7 para. 72.

[33] BT-Drs. 18/10207, p. 14.

[34] R. Podszun and U. Schwalbe, Digitale Plattformen und GWB-Novelle, Überzeugende Regelungen für die Internetökonomie?, NZKart 2017, pp. 98–106; T. Körber, Analoges Kartellrecht für digitale Märkte?, WuW 2015, pp. 120–133.

In the course of the Ninth Amendment to the GWB, the lawmaker will implement 'innovation-driven competitive pressure' as a relevant factor for the assessment of market power (§ 18 (3a) No. 5 GWB).[35] This will, however, leave the legal presumptions of market dominance untouched.

According to the case law of the Court of Justice of the European Union, an *abuse of dominant market power* is given if the undertaking's behaviour 'influence(s) the structure of a market where, as a result of the very presence of the undertaking in question, the degree of competition is weakened and which, through recourse to methods different from those which condition normal competition [...] on the basis of the transactions of commercial operators, has the effect of hindering the maintenance of the degree of competition still existing in the market or the growth of that competition'.[36] The adoption of that definition for the application of § 19 (1) GWB is largely acknowledged.[37] The question whether or not a behaviour fulfils these requirements has to be answered on a case-by-case basis taking into account the opposing interests of the affected undertakings and the lawmaker's intention to guarantee free competition and free market access.[38] That includes examining whether the behaviour results in efficiency advantages.[39] The burden of proof for these advantages rests with the dominant undertaking.[40] It is only met if the undertaking shows that (a) the behaviour is indispensable to reach the efficiency advantage, (b) likely negative effects on competition and on consumer welfare are compensated by the efficiency advantage and (c) the conduct does not eliminate effective competition.[41] As courts tend to interpret national law in the light of European law,[42] the defence should be accepted in the context of § 19 (1) GWB as well.

---

[35] BT-Drs. 18/10207, p. 14.

[36] ECJ, case 85/76, *Hoffmann-La Roche & Co. AG v Commission of the European Communities*, ECR 1979 461.

[37] A. Fuchs. In: Immenga and Mestmäcker (eds), Wettbewerbsrecht Band 2, § 19 GWB para. 82a; U. Loewenheim. In: Loewenheim, Meessen, Riesenkampff, Kersting and Meyer-Lindemann (eds), Kartellrecht, 3rd ed, C.H. Beck 2016, § 19 GWB para. 13; M. Wolf. In: Bornkamm, Montag and Säcker (eds), Münchener Kommentar zum Europäischen und Deutschen Wettbewerbsrecht Band 2, 2nd ed, C.H. Beck 2015, § 19 GWB para. 29.

[38] J. Busche. In: Busche and Röhling (eds), Kölner Kommentar zum Kartellrecht Band 1, 1st ed, Carl Heymanns Verlag 2017, § 19 GWB paras. 15 f.; M. Wolf. In: Bornkamm, Montag and Säcker (eds), Münchener Kommentar zum Europäischen und Deutschen Wettbewerbsrecht Band 2, 2nd ed, C.H. Beck 2015, § 19 GWB para. 34.

[39] ECJ, case C-95/04 P, *British Airways v European Commission*, ECR 2007 I 2331; CFI, case T-288/97, *Irish Sugar v Commission of the European Communities*, ECR 1999 II 2969.

[40] F. Bulst. In: Langen and Bunte (eds), Kartellrecht Kommentar Band 2, 12th ed, Luchterhand 2014, Art. 102 AEUV para. 143.

[41] European Commission, Guidance on the Commission's enforcement priorities in applying Article 82 of the EC Treaty to abusive exclusionary conduct by dominant undertakings, OJ 2009, C 45, p. 2, para. 30.

[42] Federal Court of Justice, Decision of 4 November 2003, Case No. KZR 2/02 – *Depotkosmetik im Internet*, GRUR 2004, pp. 351–352.

In order to strengthen legal certainty, both legislators provided for non-exhaustive examples for the abuse of dominant market power in § 19 (2) GWB and Article 102 (2) TFEU.[43] For example, § 19 (2) No. 1 GWB states that an abuse exists if a dominant undertaking directly or indirectly impedes another undertaking in an unfair manner or directly or indirectly treats another undertaking differently from other undertakings without any objective justification. These criteria can be met if a dominant player refuses to deal or to supply.

§ 20 (1) GWB widens the scope of application of § 19 (2) No. 1 GWB in regard to undertakings with relative market power. The provision applies to undertakings 'if small or medium-sized enterprises as suppliers or purchasers [...] depend on them in such a way that sufficient and reasonable possibilities of switching to other undertakings do not exist'. The examination of whether an undertaking is small or medium sized is generally governed by a horizontal comparison (size compared to other competitors).[44] The provision covers cases in which the small or medium-sized enterprise is dependant from a manufacturer of brand products because customers have the reasonable expectation that these products are part of a complete range of products.[45]

European antitrust law does not provide for a similar provision so that there is a distinct gap between the legal systems.[46] According to § 22 (3) GWB, stricter national law is even applicable in cases in which the behaviour is not covered by Article 102 (1) TFEU.

The afore-mentioned provisions are also applicable in the *new economy sector*. However, the specialities of that sector, in particular the specialities of *two-sided markets*, have to be taken into account adequately.[47] Whereas one can, for example, assume that a dominant undertaking misuses its position in traditional market sectors if it permanently offers its products or service for free, this is not the case in the new economy sector.[48] In this sector, the offer can in fact lead back to the economic decision to increase the financial burden for one side in favour of the other side of the market that causes more indirect network effects. Consequently, the question whether market power on one market is indeed abused cannot be answered without

[43] The provisions relevant to online sales platforms will be discussed later on; see Sects. 7.3 and 7.4.

[44] Federal Court of Justice, Decision of 24 September 2002, Case No. KVR 8/01 – *Konditionenanpassung*, NJW 2003, pp. 205–208; J. Nothdurft. In: Langen and Bunte (eds), Kartellrecht Kommentar Band 1, 12th ed, Luchterhand 2014, § 20 GWB para. 74.

[45] Federal Court of Justice, Decision of 9 May 2000, Case No. KZR 28/98 – *Designer Polstermöbel*, GRUR 2000, pp. 1108–1111; M. Lorenz. In: Berg and Mäsch (eds), Deutsches und Europäisches Kartellrecht, 2nd ed, Luchterhand 2015, § 20 GWB para. 13.

[46] J.-M. Schultze, S. Pautke and S. Wagener, Die Gruppenfreistellungsverordnung für vertikale Vereinbarungen – Praxiskommentar, 3rd ed, Verlag Recht und Wirtschaft 2011, para. 94.

[47] T. Körber, Konzeptionelle Erfassung digitaler Plattformen und adäquate Regulierungsstrategien, ZUM 2017, pp. 93–101.

[48] T. Körber, Konzeptionelle Erfassung digitaler Plattformen und adäquate Regulierungsstrategien, ZUM 2017, pp. 93–101.

considering the other market.[49] The lawmaker did not take the chance to implement new legal provisions in the course of the Ninth Amendment to the GWB and thus left it to the legal practice to solve problems arising from the new economy sector.

#### 7.2.1.3 Mergers

§§ 35 ff. GWB governs the national merger control. According to § 35 (1) GWB, the merger control provisions are applicable if the merging undertakings had a combined worldwide turnover of more than EUR 500,000,000 in the last business year or if the domestic turnover of one concerned undertaking was more than EUR 25,000,000 and that of another concerned undertaking was more than EUR 5,000,000. As a general rule, § 36 (1) GWB states that a merger has to be prohibited if it would significantly impede effective competition, in particular if a dominant position would be created or strengthened. The legal definition of § 18 (1) GWB (see Sect. 7.2.1.2 above) can be used in order to examine whether the merger creates or strengthens a dominant position.[50] The legal presumptions of § 18 (4) and (6) GWB are only applicable in cases of an alleged creation of a dominant position.[51] There are, however, exceptions to the prohibition according to § 36 (1) s. 2 GWB (improvements that outweigh the impediment; markets with an annual turnover of less than EUR 15,000,000; special terms for newspaper and magazine publishers).

On the EU level, Merger Regulation 139/2004 is the most important source of law. The application of the national law is not possible if the merger falls under the EC Merger Regulation, § 35 (3) GWB. According to Article 1 (1) and (2) Regulation 139/2004, that is the case if the combined aggregate worldwide turnover of all concerned undertakings is more than EUR 5,000,000,000 and the aggregate Community-wide turnover of one of them is more than EUR 250,000,000 unless each of the undertakings concerned achieves more than two thirds of its Community-wide turnover within one and the same Member State. Article 1 (3) EC Merger Regulation extends the scope of application. In these cases, the European Commission is exclusively competent to conduct merger control.

Article 2 (3) EC Merger Regulation states that a concentration that would significantly impede effective competition in the common market or in a substantial part of it, in particular as a result of the creation or strengthening of a dominant position, shall be declared incompatible with the common market. The definition of a dominant market position is the same as in Article 102 (1) TFEU (see Sect. 7.2.1.2 above).

The rise of the *new economy sector* raises the question whether the turnover parameter can still be the relevant factor to make a concentration subject to national

---

[49] T. Körber, Analoges Kartellrecht für digitale Märkte?, WuW 2015, pp. 120–133.

[50] H. Kahlenberg. In: Loewenheim, Meessen, Riesenkampff, Kersting and Meyer-Lindemann (eds), Kartellrecht, 3rd ed, C.H. Beck 2016, § 36 GWB paras. 13 ff.; M. v. Merveldt. In: Berg and Mäsch (eds), Deutsches und Europäisches Kartellrecht, 2nd ed, Luchterhand 2015, § 36 GWB para. 25.

[51] M. v. Merveldt. In: Berg and Mäsch (eds), Deutsches und Europäisches Kartellrecht, 2nd ed, Luchterhand 2015, § 36 GWB para. 30.

or EU merger control. In the new economy sector, services are often offered free of charge for the user so that the undertaking's turnover remains low. However, undertakings often have high market shares, and the transaction volumes are remarkable. A prime example for that problem is Facebook's takeover of WhatsApp (600,000,000 users), having a transaction volume of USD 19,000,000,000.[52] The German lawmaker recognised that problem and will react to it by implementing a new subparagraph, (1a), to § 35 GWB.[53] According to that provision, merger control shall be conducted in cases in which (a) the concerned undertakings had a combined worldwide turnover of more than EUR 500,000,000 in the last business year; (b) one of the concerned undertakings had a turnover of more than EUR 25,000,000, but no other undertaking concerned had a turnover of more than EUR 5,000,000 in the last business year; (c) the consideration is worth more than EUR 400,000,000; and (d) the acquired undertaking does considerable business on the national market.

### 7.2.2 Definition of the Relevant Market

The assessment of the relevant market is crucial when examining whether a behaviour restricts competition on the market or whether an involved undertaking has dominant market power. A broad definition of the market will make antitrust violations less likely and vice versa.[54] One has to consider that the timely basis of analysis in merger control cases is different from the other cases of antitrust violation as the core question with merger control is whether there *will be* a dominant position after the undertakings concentration.[55]

In both the national and the European systems, the relevant market is defined by the overlap of the product market and the geographic market. Furthermore, a temporal parameter may also be relevant in some cases, for instance where there is a temporary scarcity of the good.[56]

The examination of the relevant *product market* is demand-side oriented. Products are offered on the same market if the demander sees one product as an alternative to the other (substitutability).[57] Parameters like the good's or service's

---

[52] T. Körber, Analoges Kartellrecht für digitale Märkte?, WuW 2015, pp. 120–133.

[53] BT-Drs. 18/10207, p. 22 f.

[54] Cf. H.-J. Bunte and F. Stancke, Kartellrecht, 3rd ed, C.H. Beck 2016, p. 173.

[55] A. Bardong. In: Langen and Bunte (eds), Kartellrecht Kommentar Band 1, 12th ed, Luchterhand 2014, § 18 GWB para. 54.

[56] ECJ, case 77/77, *Benzine en Petroleum Handelsmaatschappij BV BV et al. v Commission of the European Communities*, ECR 1978 1513; Federal Court of Justice, Decision of 26 May 1987, Case No. KVR 4/86 – *Gekoppelter Kartenverkauf, UEFA-Cup*, NJW 1987, pp. 3007–3009; Cf. H.-J. Bunte and F. Stancke, Kartellrecht, 3rd ed, C.H. Beck 2016, p. 176.

[57] ECJ, case 31/80, *NV L'Oréal and SA L'Oréal v PVBA 'De Nieuwe AMCK'*, ECR 1980 3775; Federal Court of Justice, Decision of 24 October 1997, Case No. KVR 17/94 – *Backofenmarkt*, GRUR Int 1997, pp. 637–640; J. Busche. In: Busche/Röhling (eds), Kölner Kommentar zum Kartellrecht Band 3, 1st ed, Carl Heymanns Verlag 2016, Art. 102 AEUV para. 19.

quality, their prices and purpose are included in the examination.[58] Courts conduct the so-called SSNIP test[59]: two products belong to one market if customers would change to the other product in case of a small but significant increase (5–10%) of the price. The SSNIP test is, however, not suited for defining the product market in each and every case as customers are not always price-sensitive.[60]

The question whether online offers can be an alternative to offline offers and vice versa can only be answered on a (demand-side oriented) case-by-case basis. For example, online offers cannot be seen as an alternative if personal advice or physical examination of the product is necessary in order to reach a purchase decision.[61]

The *new economy sector* partially calls these principles into question. The SSNIP test often fails as services are offered free of charge.[62] The vast majority of legal scholars are, however, of the opinion that a market can exist even in that case.[63] One has to agree with this since the user at least 'pays' for the service by transmitting his personal data to the service provider.[64] Nonetheless, some courts took the opposite position.[65] The national legislator has recognised that problem and will clarify the legal situation by implementing a new sub-paragraph, (2a), in § 18 GWB in line with the majority opinion.[66]

The definition of the relevant market causes particular difficulties in regard to *two-sided markets* (see Sect. 7.2.1.2 above). Although the vast majority of legal scholars are of the opinion that each side is to be treated as one market,[67] practitioners were faced with legal uncertainty up to now. With the planned implementation

[58] H.-J. Bunte and F. Stancke, Kartellrecht, 3rd ed, C.H. Beck 2016, pp. 173 f.

[59] ECJ, case 27/76, *United Brands Company and United Brands Continentaal BV v Commission of the European Communities*, ECR 1977 1875.

[60] H.-J. Bunte and F. Stancke, Kartellrecht, 3rd ed, C.H. Beck 2016, pp. 174.

[61] K. Beckmann and U. Müller. In: Hoeren, Sieber and Holznagel, Handbuch Multimedia-Recht, 38. EL, C.H. Beck 2014, part 10 para. 45.

[62] H.-J. Bunte and F. Stancke, Kartellrecht, 3rd ed, C.H. Beck 2016, p. 174; T. Höppner and J. Grabenschröer, Marktabgrenzung bei mehrseitigen Märkten am Beispiel der Internetsuche, NZKart 2015, pp. 162–168.

[63] Regional Court Berlin, Decision of 19 February 2016, Case No. 92 O 5/14 Kart – *Google Presseausschnitt*, ZUM 2016, pp. 879–884; H. Bergmann and L. Fiedler. In: Loewenheim, Meessen, Riesenkampff, Kersting and Meyer-Lindemann (eds), Kartellrecht, 3rd ed, C.H. Beck 2016, Art. 102 AUEV para. 47; T. Höppner and J. Grabenschröer, Marktabgrenzung bei mehrseitigen Märkten am Beispiel der Internetsuche, NZKart 2015, pp. 162–168; B. Paal, Internet-Suchmaschinen im Kartellrecht, GRUR Int 2015, pp. 997–1005; R. Podszun and B. Franz, Was ist ein Markt? – Unentgeltliche Leistungsbeziehungen im Kartellrecht, NZKart 2015, pp. 121–127.

[64] T. Höppner and J. Grabenschröer, Marktabgrenzung bei mehrseitigen Märkten am Beispiel der Internetsuche, NZKart 2015, pp. 162–168; B. Paal, Internet-Suchmaschinen im Kartellrecht, GRUR Int 2015, pp. 997–1005.

[65] Higher Regional Court Düsseldorf, Decision of 9 January 2015, Case No. VI-Kart 1/14 (V) – *HRS-Bestpreisklauseln*, NZKart 2015, pp. 147–152.

[66] BT-Drs. 18/10207, p. 14.

[67] T. Höppner and J. Grabenschröer, Marktabgrenzung bei mehrseitigen Märkten am Beispiel der Internetsuche, NZKart 2015, pp. 162–168; T. Körber, Analoges Kartellrecht für digitale Märkte?, WuW 2015, pp. 120–133.

of § 18 (2a) GWB, however, the lawmaker makes clear that he prefers the majority opinion because both sides of the market are never free of charge.[68] In order to define the relevant market in two-sided markets, the assessment must, however, include the other side of the market as indirect network effects have to be taken into account.[69] The specialties of the new economy sector have to be taken into account when examining if the behaviour constitutes an antitrust violation (see Sects. 7.2.1.2 and 7.2.1.3 above).

The definition of the *geographic market* is demand-side oriented as well.[70] The geographically relevant market can be described as the area in which the conditions of competition in regard to the product market are sufficiently homogeneous.[71] It must be possible to distinguish the market from neighbouring areas.[72] For the national law, § 18 (2) GWB states that the relevant geographic market may be broader than the scope of the GWB. If the purchaser of the good or service is not willing to overcome physical distances to purchase the alternative good or enjoy the alternative service, they are not offered on the same geographic market.[73] It is thus possible that more than one geographic market exists within the territory of the European Union[74] or within the Federal Republic of Germany.[75]

Although offers on the Internet are accessible around the world, this does not lead to the conclusion that the whole world is the geographically relevant market.[76] As in every other market, factors like the web page's language, legal and cultural barriers, as well as the transportability of goods, have to be considered.[77]

---

[68] C. Kersting and S. Dworschak, Win-Win-Situation of mehrseitigen Märkten: Google muss nicht zahlen, ZUM 2016, pp. 840–846.

[69] H. Bergmann and L. Fiedler. In: Loewenheim, Meessen, Riesenkampff, Kersting and Meyer-Lindemann (eds), Kartellrecht, 3rd ed, C.H. Beck 2016, Art. 102 AEUV para. 48; R. Dewenter, J. Rösch and A. Terschüren, Abgrenzung zweiseitiger Märkte am Beispiel von Internetsuchmaschinen, NZKart 2014, pp. 387–394.

[70] H. Bergmann and L. Fiedler. In: Loewenheim, Meessen, Riesenkampff, Kersting and Meyer-Lindemann (eds), Kartellrecht, 3rd ed, C.H. Beck 2016, Art. 102 AEUV para. 106.

[71] ECJ, case 27/76, *United Brands Company and United Brands Continentaal BV v Commission of the European Communities*, ECR 1977 1875; J. Busche. In: Busche and Röhling (eds), Kölner Kommentar zum Kartellrecht Band 3, 1st ed, Carl Heymanns Verlag 2016, Art. 102 AEUV para. 33.

[72] ECJ, case 27/76, *United Brands Company and United Brands Continentaal BV v Commission of the European Communities*, ECR 1977 1875; J. Busche. In: Busche and Röhling (eds), Kölner Kommentar zum Kartellrecht Band 3, 1st ed, Carl Heymanns Verlag 2016, Art. 102 AEUV para. 33.

[73] Federal Court of Justice, Decision of 6 December 2011, Case No. KVR 95/10 – *Total/OMV*, WM 2012, pp. 2111–2119; J. Busche. In: Busche and Röhling (eds), Kölner Kommentar zum Kartellrecht Band 3, 1st ed, Carl Heymanns Verlag 2016, Art. 102 AEUV para. 36.

[74] J. Busche. In: Busche and Röhling (eds), Kölner Kommentar zum Kartellrecht Band 3, 1st ed, Carl Heymanns Verlag 2016, Art. 102 AEUV para. 32.

[75] E.g. Federal Court of Justice, Decision of 6 December 2011, Case No. KVR 95/10 – *Total/OMV*, WM 2012, pp. 2111–2119.

[76] K. Beckmann and U. Müller. In: Hoeren, Sieber and Holznagel, Handbuch Multimedia-Recht, 38. EL, C.H. Beck 2014, part 10 para. 59.

[77] K. Beckmann and U. Müller. In: Hoeren, Sieber and Holznagel, Handbuch Multimedia-Recht, 38. EL, C.H. Beck 2014, part 10 para. 59.

### 7.2.3 Enforcement of the Law

There are several possibilities for the enforcement of German and European antitrust law.

#### 7.2.3.1 Administrative Procedure

First of all, there is the possibility of an *administrative procedure* that is regularly conducted by the German Federal Cartel Office in Bonn. Besides, every federal state maintains an own cartel office. These authorities are only responsible for handling cartel cases if effects of an agreement between companies are limited to the territory of one federal state (§ 48 (2) GWB). According to § 54 (1) GWB, the competition authority institutes proceedings ex officio or upon application by outsiders. The administrational procedure and the authorities' far-reaching enforcement powers are laid down in §§ 54–62 GWB. The competition authorities are, inter alia, allowed to issue prohibition orders (§ 32 GWB) and to impose fines on companies and responsible natural persons for violating antitrust law (§ 81 GWB). As a legal remedy against the authorities' decisions, an appeal is possible according to § 63 (1) GWB, for which the higher regional courts are competent (§ 63 (4) GWB). §§ 63 ff. GWB set out special rules for the court procedure. Although the courts conduct an administrative procedure, § 73 GWB declares several important provisions of the German Courts Constitution Act and the German Code of Civil Procedure (hereinafter 'ZPO')[78] applicable in these cases. Decisions of higher regional courts are generally subject to judicial review by the Federal Court of Justice, § 74 (1) GWB.

According to § 50 (1) GWB and Article 5 of Regulation 1/2003, the German authorities are generally also competent to enforce Articles 101 and 102 TFEU. Article 5 Regulation 1/2003 enumerates the measures that can be chosen by the competent authority in order to enforce Articles 101 and 102 TFEU (prohibition orders, interim measures, imposition of fines). The national authorities' competence, however, leaves the European Commission's authority to enforce European antitrust law unaffected (Articles 4 and 5 Regulation 1/2003). The Commission may, inter alia, issue prohibition orders (Article 7 Regulation 1/2003) and may impose fines on undertakings (Article 23 Regulation 1/2003).

The administrative procedure regularly ends with the termination of the proceedings or an administrative deed purporting one of the afore-mentioned sanctions. However, proceedings can be settled during the administrative procedure in cases before the German cartel offices, as well as before the European Commission.[79]

The Federal Cartel Office has published a fact sheet on this possibility for proceedings involving the imposition of fines.[80] According to these guidelines,

[78] An official English translation can be found here: https://www.gesetze-im-internet.de/englisch_zpo/englisch_zpo.html. Accessed 6 June 2017.

[79] H.-J. Bunte and F. Stancke, Kartellrecht, 3rd ed, C.H. Beck 2016, pp. 244, 427.

[80] Federal Cartel Office, Fact Sheet on Settlements in proceedings involving the imposition of fines, February 2016: http://www.bundeskartellamt.de/SharedDocs/Publikation/DE/Merkbl%C3%A4tter/Merkblatt-Settlement.pdf?__blob=publicationFile&v=2. Accessed 6 June 2017.

a settlement can be entered into if the affected party formally accepts the alleged facts of the case and the suggested fine. The settlement agreement may not include a waiver in regard to legal remedies against the fine.[81] After a settlement agreement has been made, the administrative procedure is still closed by the imposition of a fine.[82] The cartel office grants the affected party a reduction in the amount of up to 10%.[83] The German authorities are, however, bound to the Basic Law of the Federal Republic of Germany (hereinafter GG). Article 3 (1) GG codifies the general principle of equal treatment by the state that is violated if different decisions are made in cases with equal facts. In the administrative antitrust practice, the cases will, however, regularly differ from each other substantially.[84]

In EU law, Article 10a of Regulation 773/2004 governs the settlement procedure. According to Article 10a of Regulation 773/2004, the proceeding still ends with an administrative decision in line with Article 7 or Article 23 Regulation 1/2003.

The possibility of settlements leads to the problem that courts are hindered to rule upon cases that might have precedent value. It is nevertheless an effective means to stop antitrust violations and makes economic sense for both the undertakings and the cartel offices.

#### 7.2.3.2 Civil Lawsuits

Antitrust law can also be enforced via *private lawsuits* before the regional courts. § 33 (1) GWB provides affected persons with the claim to demand rectification of infringements and to desist from further infringements in case of a violation of a provision of the GWB or Articles 101 and 102 TFEU. The group of affected persons is legally defined as 'competitors or other market participants impaired by the infringement'. Competitors are undertakings that are active on the same relevant market in both product-related and geographical dimensions, whereas other participants can be consumers or undertakings that are active on the relevant market as suppliers or customers of goods or services.[85] There is also the possibility to sue for certain associations, § 33 (2) GWB. § 33 (3) GWB provides for the right to demand compensation on the condition that the violation was made intentionally or negligently. Compensation can even be demanded if the plaintiff did not incur losses because he resold goods or services that were sold at an excessive price. Distinct from other legal systems, German antitrust law does not allow to claim punitive

[81] Federal Cartel Office, Fact Sheet on Settlements in proceedings involving the imposition of fines, February 2016, p. 2.

[82] Federal Cartel Office, Fact Sheet on Settlements in proceedings involving the imposition of fines, February 2016, p. 3.

[83] Federal Cartel Office, Fact Sheet on Settlements in proceedings involving the imposition of fines, February 2016, p. 3.

[84] H.-H. Schneider. In: Langen and Bunte (eds), Kartellrecht Kommentar Band 1, 12th ed, Luchterhand 2014, preface to §§ 54 ff. para. 20.

[85] V. Emmerich. In: Immenga and Mestmäcker (eds), Wettbewerbsrecht Band 2, § 33 GWB paras. 11 ff.; G. Mäsch. In: Berg and Mäsch (eds), Deutsches und Europäisches Kartellrecht, 2nd ed, Luchterhand 2015, § 33 GWB paras. 21 f.

damages.[86] This can be ascribed to the general principle in German tort law that compensation shall not lead to an enrichment of the wronged party.[87]

An antitrust violation can also be used as a *defence against allegations of breach of contract*.[88] According to § 1 GWB, in conjunction with § 134 of the German Civil Code (hereinafter 'BGB'), contractual agreements that unduly restrict competition are void.[89] A violation of Article 101 (1) TFEU has the same legal consequence according to Article 101 (2) TFEU. If an agreement is the result of a prohibited conduct of a dominant undertaking (§ 19 GWB) or of a prohibited conduct of an undertaking with relative or superior market power (§ 20 GWB) or violates Article 102 TFEU, the contractual provision is void according to § 134 BGB.[90]

The burden of proof rests with the defendant in all these cases.

Before filing a lawsuit, cease-and-desist orders with penalty clauses are also common in legal practice. If the addressee signs the declaration, the other party gets a contractual claim for payment of the penalty.[91] The standard of proof for that claim is lower than for the tort claim of § 33 GWB. The plaintiff only has to prove that the contracting party's behaviour contradicts the agreement.

After a lawsuit has been filed, it is possible that cases are closed not by a judgment but by court or out-of-court settlements, as in every other civil case. This derives from the principle of party disposition that dominates the civil procedure.[92] These possibilities are not explicitly laid down in the ZPO but accepted by customary law.[93] Settlements are civil contracts.[94] Consequently, every behaviour that contradicts the settlement entitles the other party to demand compensation according to § 280 (1) BGB. This contractual claim is independent from the tort claim codified in § 33 (3) GWB. It is of high relevance that the law presumes the responsibility of the

[86] J. Topel. In: Wiedemann (ed), Handbuch des Kartellrechts, 3rd ed, § 50 para. 90.

[87] J. Flume. In: Bamberger and Roth (eds), Beck'scher Online-Kommentar BGB; J. Topel, § 249 para. 48. In: Wiedemann (ed), Handbuch des Kartellrechts, 3rd ed, § 50 para. 90.

[88] See, for example, Regional Court Frankfurt a. M., Decision of 31 July 2014, Case No. 2-3 O 128/13 – *Logo-Klauseln*, NZKart 2015, pp. 243–244 in the case of a ban of sales on third-party platforms.

[89] W. Berg and M. Mudrony. In: Berg and Mäsch (eds), Deutsches und Europäisches Kartellrecht, 2nd ed, Luchterhand 2015, § 1 GWB para. 96; H.-J. Bunte and F. Stancke, Kartellrecht, 3rd ed, C.H. Beck 2016, p. 283.

[90] H.-J. Bunte and F. Stancke, Kartellrecht, 3rd ed, C.H. Beck 2016, pp. 195, 327, 342.

[91] Federal Court of Justice, Decision of 12 July 1995, Case No. I ZR 176/93, GRUR 1995, pp. 678–681; R. Schmidt. In: Heussen and Hamm (eds), Beck'sches Rechtsanwalts-Handbuch, 11th ed, C.H. Beck 2016, § 36 para. 34; A. Ottofülling, Die Unterlassungserklärung und ihre Folgen, DS 2015, pp. 13–15.

[92] H.-J. Musielak. In: Musielak and Voit (eds), Zivilprozessrecht, 14th ed, Vahlen 2017, Introduction para. 35.

[93] Cf. H. Wolfsteiner. In: Rauscher and Krüger (eds), Münchener Kommentar zur Zivilprozessordnung Band 2, C.H. Beck 2013, § 794 para. 8.

[94] M. Habersack. In: Säcker, Rixecker, Oetker and Limperg (eds), Münchener Kommentar zum Bürgerlichen Gesetzbuch Band 6, § 779 para. 33; cf. A. Staudinger. In: Schulze (ed), Bürgerliches Gesetzbuch, 9th ed, Nomos 2017, § 779 para. 7.

defendant in regard to the breach of contract. The burden of proof thus shifts to the defendant,[95] whereas in tort claims it is upon the plaintiff to prove fault.

§ 307 ZPO codifies that where a party acknowledges a claim, the court has to rule in accordance with this acknowledgment (consent decree). In that case, no decision on the merits is made.[96]

Although there are no statistics on the application of the afore-mentioned means in antitrust cases concerning e-commerce platforms, one has to assume that they are broadly used. This of course leads to the well-known problem that courts are hindered from ruling on potential precedent cases that would help to clarify the legal situation.

## 7.3 Vertical Restraints for the Online Sales Market

Attention has to be paid to vertical restraints of competition. Article 1 (1) a) of Regulation 330/2010 defines vertical agreements as 'an agreement or concerted practice entered into between two or more undertakings each of which operates, for the purposes of the agreement or the concerted practice, at a different level of the production or distribution chain, and relating to the conditions under which the parties may purchase, sell or resell certain goods or services'. This definition can also be used for solely national cases.

### 7.3.1 Governing Law

Vertical agreements can violate § 1 GWB (prohibition of agreements restricting competition) or, in interstate cases, Article 101 (1) TFEU. If the provision is indeed violated (see Sect. 7.2.3 above), the violation can still fall under an exception to the applicable provision. In interstate cases, Regulation 330/2010 provides for a number of exceptions. In conjunction with § 2 (2) GWB, Regulation 330/2010 is also applicable solely to national cases.[97]

Article 2 (1) Regulation 330/2010 points out that, as a general rule, Article 101 (1) TFEU does not apply to vertical agreements. Article 2 (2)–(4) Regulation 330/2010 sets more specific rules for special cases (vertical agreements between an association of undertakings and its members or between such an association and its suppliers, transfer of intellectual property rights, vertical agreements between competitors). If Article 2 Regulation 330/2010 is applicable, it is then necessary to examine whether Article 3, 4 or 5 Regulation 330/2010 contains an exception to the

[95] R. Schulze. In: Schulze (ed), Bürgerliches Gesetzbuch, 9th ed, Nomos 2017, § 280 para. 15.

[96] Federal Court of Justice, Decision of 17 March 1993, Case No. XII ZR 256/91, NJW 1993, pp. 1717–1719; H.-J. Musielak. In. Musielak and Voit (eds), Zivilprozessrecht, 14th ed, Vahlen 2017, § 307 para. 15.

[97] J. Nordemann. In: Loewenheim, Meessen, Riesenkampff, Kersting and Meyer-Lindemann (eds), Kartellrecht, 3rd ed, C.H. Beck 2016, § 2 GWB para. 21.

general rule that vertical agreements are not covered by Article 101 (1) TFEU. According to Article 3 (1) Regulation 330/2010, an agreement can only be excluded from the legal prohibition if neither the supplier's nor the buyer's market share exceeds 30% of the relevant market. Article 4 Regulation 330/2010 covers hardcore restrictions of competition. If a vertical agreement contains hardcore restrictions, the whole agreement does not fall under the block exemption, as codified in Article 2 Regulation 330/2010 (all-or-nothing principle).[98] Article 5 Regulation 330/2010 contains exceptions for non-compete clauses. In contrast to Article 4 Regulation 330/2010, only the single contractual clause falling under Article 5 Regulation 330/2010 is not covered by Article 2 of the said Regulation.[99]

Regulation 330/2010 is further specified by the European Commission's Guidelines on Vertical Restraints (hereinafter 'Guidelines on Vertical Restraints').[100] Although these guidelines are only binding for the European Commission itself, they are of high practical importance.[101] German courts tend to refer to the guidelines without discussing their legal significance in solely national, as well as in interstate, cases.[102]

If no exception of Regulation 330/2010 applies to the case at hand, there still is the possibility that the agreement falls under § 2 (1) GWB or under Article 101 (3) TFEU, which provides for individual exceptions. However, as the exceptions are narrowly formulated, it is usually hard for the defendant to prove that the requirements are met in the case at hand.

It is always upon the defendant to substantiate and prove that the criteria of the exemptions are met.[103] However, the burden of proof rests upon the plaintiff in regard to the question whether or not a hardcore restriction of competition (Article 4 Regulation 330/2010) is given.

---

[98] J.-M. Schultze, S. Pautke and S. Wagener, Die Gruppenfreistellungsverordnung für vertikale Vereinbarungen Praxiskommentar, 3rd ed, Verlag Recht und Wirtschaft 2011, para. 516.

[99] K. Beckmann and U. Müller. In: Hoeren, Sieber and Holznagel, Handbuch Multimedia-Recht, 38. EL, C.H. Beck 2014, part 10 para. 142; J.-M. Schultze, S. Pautke and S. Wagener, Die Gruppenfreistellungsverordnung für vertikale Vereinbarungen Praxiskommentar, 3rd ed, Verlag Recht und Wirtschaft 2011, para. 840.

[100] An English version can be found here: http://ec.europa.eu/competition/antitrust/legislation/guidelines_vertical_en.pdf. Accessed 22 May 2017.

[101] J. Nordemann. In: Loewenheim, Meessen, Riesenkampff, Kersting and Meyer-Lindemann (eds), Kartellrecht, 3rd ed, C.H. Beck 2016, Art. 101 Abs. 3 AEUV para. 19; J.-M. Schultze, S. Pautke and S. Wagener, Die Gruppenfreistellungsverordnung für vertikale Vereinbarungen Praxiskommentar, 3rd ed, Verlag Recht und Wirtschaft 2011, para. 29; J. Dreyer and N. Lemberg, Möglichkeiten und Grenzen der Beschränkung des Internetvertriebs, BB 2012, pp. 2004–2010.

[102] E.g. Federal Court of Justice, Decision of 4 November 2003, Case No. KZR 2/02 – *Depotkosmetik im Internet*, GRUR 2004, pp. 351–352; Higher Regional Court Frankfurt a.M., Decision of 22 December 2015, Case No. 11 U 84/14 (Kart) – *Funktionsrucksäcke*, MMR 2016, pp. 634–639.

[103] Cf. Art. 2 Implementation Regulation; J. Nordemann. In: Loewenheim, Meessen, Riesenkampff, Kersting and Meyer-Lindemann (eds), Kartellrecht, 3rd ed, C.H. Beck 2016, Art. 101 Abs. 3 AEUV para. 209; M. Schweda and J.-C. Rudowicz, Verkaufsverbote über Online-Handelsplattformen und Kartellrecht, WRP 2013, pp. 590–600.

Vertical restraints can also be prohibited by § 19 (1)–(2) No. 1 GWB, in conjunction with § 20 (1) GWB. § 2 (1) and (2) GWB are not applicable to such a violation.[104] Nonetheless, the exceptions of Regulation 330/2010 are relevant since agreements covered by the regulation cannot be 'unfair' within the meaning of § 19 (2) No. 1 GWB.[105]

### 7.3.2 Restriction of Online Sales via Web Shops

The Internet provides potential consumers with the possibility to gain more and more information about products and distributors and to compare them. This helps consumers to reach a well-considered purchase decision. The possibilities of the 'new economy' thus enormously strengthen inter- and intra-brand competition. Another crucial point for manufacturers is the so-called free rider problem that, above all, arises with the sale of high-quality branded goods[106]: distributors may concentrate exclusively on online sales and are thus able to offer goods for a relatively low price, whereas other distributors engage in stationary trade and are faced with higher costs (e.g., for specialised consulting services or rents), which hinder them from offering the goods at similar conditions. In that situation, consumers often tend to make use of the stationary trader's service and eventually buy online.

Consequently, the manufacturer's interest in banning online sales is obvious.

Agreements containing a *total ban of online sales* always constitute a restriction of competition and thus fall under the provisions of Article 101 (1) TFEU and § 1 GWB.[107] A manufacturer does not profit from the exception of Article 2 (1) Regulation 330/2010 when totally banning online sales because Article 4 lit. b) Regulation 330/2010 excludes, inter alia, restrictions of the customers to whom a buyer may sell the contract goods. The total contractual ban of online sales would hinder the buyer to reach the group of online shoppers and is thus a hardcore restriction within the meaning of Article 4 lit. b) Regulation 330/2010.[108]

The criteria of the 're-exception' to this hardcore restriction, as codified in Article 4 lit. b) i) Regulation 330/2010, could only be met if online sales via one's own websites would be considered as a means of 'active sales'. An 'active sale' requires

[104] J. Nordemann. In: Loewenheim, Meessen, Riesenkampff, Kersting and Meyer-Lindemann (eds), Kartellrecht, 3rd ed, C.H. Beck 2016, § 2 GWB para. 62.

[105] J.-M. Schultze, S. Pautke and S. Wagener, Die Gruppenfreistellungsverordnung für vertikale Vereinbarungen Praxiskommentar, 3rd ed, Verlag Recht und Wirtschaft 2011, para. 94.

[106] K. Beckmann and U. Müller. In: Hoeren, Sieber and Holznagel, Handbuch Multimedia-Recht, 38. EL, C.H. Beck 2014, part 10 para. 140.

[107] CJEU, case C-439/09, *Pierre Fabre Dermo-Cosmétique SAS v Président de l'Autorité de la concurrence*, ECR 2011 I 9419; Federal Court of Justice, Decision of 4 November 2003, Case No. KZR 2/02 – *Depotkosmetik im Internet*, GRUR 2004, pp. 351–352.

[108] Federal Court of Justice, Decision of 4 November 2003, Case No. KZR 2/02 – *Depotkosmetik im Internet*, GRUR 2004, pp. 351–352; M. Baron. In: Loewenheim, Meessen, Riesenkampff, Kersting and Meyer-Lindemann (eds), Kartellrecht, 3rd ed, C.H. Beck 2016, Art. 4 Vert-GVO para. 259.

that a distributor takes advertising actions to win single consumers to purchase the advertised goods.[109] Normally, the consumer will, however, search for online offers of the needed goods himself so that web shops generally have to be characterised as a means of 'passive sales'.[110]

In selective distribution systems (see Sect. 7.3.3.1 below), Article 4 lit. c) Regulation 330/2010 is applicable. The total ban of online sales constitutes a restriction of passive sales to end users and is thus prohibited.[111]

It is, however, possible for the seller to allow the buyer the online sale of the contract goods only on the condition that the buyer operates a stationary business at the same time.[112] In that case, the criteria of Article 4 lit. b) Regulation 330/2010 are not fulfilled as the Internet turnover of the buyer is not affected by this agreement.

*Dual pricing models* (different prices for online and offline distributors) in general are also considered as a hardcore restriction of competition within the meaning of Article 4 lit. b) Regulation 330/2010.[113] This also applies to cases in which dual-pricing models are realised by cash backflows.[114] The European Commission is of the opinion that such an agreement can be covered by the exception of Article 101 (3) TFEU in cases in which online sales lead to 'substantially higher costs for the manufacturer'.[115] The Commission exemplary refers to cases in which the manufacturer will be faced with more customer complaints or warranty claims. It further points out that agreements offering the distributor a fixed fee in order to support its online or offline activities withstands antitrust law. This statement is only in line with the foregoing observations if one furthermore requires that the fixed fee covers extra efforts and expenses.[116]

Manufacturers could furthermore have the idea to operate a *Retail Price Maintenance System* to protect stationary businesses. Article 4 lit. a) Regulation

[109] Para. 51 of the Guidelines on Vertical Restraints; E. Johannsen and A. Wegner. In: Busche and Röhling (eds), Kölner Kommentar zum Kartellrecht Band 3, 1st ed, Carl Heymanns Verlag 2016, Art. 4 Vertikal-GVO para. 82; I. Innerhofer, E-Commerce im Fokus des Wettbewerbsrechts, ZVertriebsR 2013, pp. 266–272.

[110] Para. 52 of the Guidelines on Vertical Restraints; Federal Court of Justice, Decision of 4 November 2003, Case No. KZR 2/02 – *Depotkosmetik im Internet*, GRUR 2004, pp. 351–352.

[111] Para. 56 of the Guidelines on Vertical Restraints; CJEU, case C-439/09, *Pierre Fabre Dermo-Cosmétique SAS v Président de l'Autorité de la concurrence*, ECR 2011 I 9419.

[112] Federal Court of Justice, Decision of 4 November 2003, Case No. KZR 2/02 – *Depotkosmetik im Internet*, GRUR 2004, pp. 351–352; M. Baron. In: Loewenheim, Meessen, Riesenkampff, Kersting and Meyer-Lindemann (eds), Kartellrecht, 3rd ed, C.H. Beck 2016, Art. 4 Vert-GVO para. 259; S. Simon, Die neue Kartellrechtsverordnung (EU) Nr. 330/2010 für Vertriebs- und Lieferverträge, EWS 2010, pp. 497–503.

[113] M. Baron. In: Loewenheim, Meessen, Riesenkampff, Kersting and Meyer-Lindemann (eds), Kartellrecht, 3rd ed, C.H. Beck 2016, Art. 4 Vert-GVO paras. 255 ff.

[114] Federal Cartel Office, Decision of 18 June 2010, Case No. B 5 – 100/09; K. Beckmann and U. Müller. In: Hoeren, Sieber and Holznagel, Handbuch Multimedia-Recht, 38. EL, C.H. Beck 2014, part 10 para. 152.

[115] Para. 64 of the Guidelines on Vertical Restraints.

[116] J.-M. Schultze, S. Pautke and S. Wagener, Die Gruppenfreistellungsverordnung für vertikale Vereinbarungen Praxiskommentar, 3rd ed, Verlag Recht und Wirtschaft 2011, para. 762.

330/2010 expressly prohibits such behaviour. There only is the possibility to recommend a sale price as long as that recommendation does not amount to a fixed or minimum sale price as a result of pressure from, or incentives offered by, any of the parties.

Another possibility to restrict online sales is to contractually agree upon *limits on quantity* of online sales. An agreement that obligates the distributor to sell a percentage of the contract goods offline is covered by Article 4 lit. b) Regulation 330/2010 and is consequently not in line with the national and European antitrust law as long as the criteria of § 2 (1) GWB or Article 101 (3) TFEU are not met.[117] According to para. 52 lit. c) of the Guidelines on Vertical Restraints, it is yet possible to demand that the distributor sells a certain absolute amount offline. The European Commission further states that this absolute amount can be the same for all contractors or individually determined for each contractor by objective criteria (e.g., buyer's size or geographic location). The law thus acknowledges the manufacturer's interest in maintaining an effective stationary trade of the contract goods.[118]

### 7.3.3 Ban on Distribution via Third-Party Platforms in Selective Distribution Systems

As a consequence, some manufacturers try to at least prohibit sales via third-party platforms like eBay or Amazon that enormously strengthen intra-brand competition.[119]

#### 7.3.3.1 Definition and Legal Specialities

According to Article 1 (1) lit. e) Regulation 330/2010, a selective distribution system is 'a distribution system where the supplier undertakes to sell the contract goods or services, either directly or indirectly, only to distributors selected on the basis of specified criteria and where these distributors undertake not to sell such goods or services to unauthorised distributors within the territory reserved by the supplier to operate that system'. This definition is also acknowledged by German courts for purely national situations.[120] Whereas selective distributions systems restrict intra-brand competition, inter-brand competition is strengthened.[121]

This justifies that not every agreement in selective distribution systems constitutes a restriction of competition within the meaning of § 1 GWB, respectively

[117] Para. 52 lit. c) of the Guidelines on Vertical Restraints; J.-M. Schultze, S. Pautke and S. Wagener, Die Gruppenfreistellungsverordnung für vertikale Vereinbarungen Praxiskommentar, 3rd ed, Verlag Recht und Wirtschaft 2011, para. 757.

[118] S. Simon, Die neue Kartellrechtsverordnung (EU) Nr. 330/2010 für Vertriebs- und Lieferverträge, EWS 2010, pp. 497–503.

[119] M. Schweda and J.-C. Rudowicz, Verkaufsverbote über Online-Handelsplattformen und Kartellrecht, WRP 2013, pp. 590–600.

[120] K. Krauß. In: Langen and Bunte (eds), Kartellrecht Kommentar Band 1, 12th ed, Luchterhand 2014, § 1 GWB para. 276.

[121] Higher Regional Court Berlin, Decision of 19 September 2013, Case No. 2 U 8/09 Kart – *Schulranzen und -rucksäcke*, MMR 2013, pp. 774–779.

Article 101 (1) TFEU. According to the CJEU's case law,[122] a restriction of competition is not given in selective distribution systems if (a) resellers are chosen on the basis of objective criteria of a qualitative nature, (b) the conditions are not applied in a discriminatory fashion, (c) the characteristics of the product in question necessitate the conditions in order to preserve its quality and ensure its proper use and (d) the condition's criteria do not go beyond what is necessary. Even though these criteria have been developed for Article 101 (1) TFEU, the same standard applies solely to national cases that are governed by § 1 GWB.[123]

#### 7.3.3.2 Restriction of Competition

Several German courts have dealt with these criteria in cases in which *sales via third-party platforms* were prohibited by contract and came to different results.

The Higher Regional Court Frankfurt ruled that an agreement that prohibits resellers to offer the contract goods (functional backpacks) on *Amazon* is in line with antitrust law.[124] In the opinion of the court, consumers need sound advice for the purchase decision so that the third requirement of the CJEU's test was met. Furthermore, the court acknowledged that a luxury product image can justify a ban of online sales on third-party platforms. The latter argument is highly questionable as the CJEU decided that the purpose of protecting a product's prestigious image cannot justify a restraint of competition.[125] The Frankfurt court argued in this regard that the CJEU's judgment concerned a total ban of Internet sales and that, consequently, the judgment cannot serve as precedent for a ban of sales via third-party platforms. It further held that the contractual requirements do not go beyond the necessary scope as the court doubts that sound advice can be assured on third-party platforms as opposed to a reseller's own website. Besides, in the court's opinion, it is not possible to satisfy high product quality standards on these platforms as every product is presented in the same manner.

It is obvious that the court did not sufficiently consider the afore-mentioned CJEU judgment that does not differentiate between total bans and restricted bans of online sales.[126] Furthermore, the judges failed to take into account the possibilities

---

[122] Settled case law since ECJ, case 26/76, *Metro SB-Großmärkte GmbH & Co. KG v Commission of the European Communities*, ECR 1977 1875; CJEU, case C-439/09, *Pierre Fabre Dermo-Cosmétique SAS v Président de l'Autorité de la concurrence*, ECR 2011 I 9419.

[123] Higher Regional Court Frankfurt a. M., Decision of 22 December 2015, Case No. 11 U 84/14 (Kart) – *Funktionsrucksäcke*, NZKart 2016, pp. 84–88; Higher Regional Court Berlin, Decision of 19 September 2013, Case No. 2 U 8/09 Kart – *Schulranzen und -rucksäcke*, NZKart 2014, pp. 72–75; K. Krauß. In: Langen and Bunte (eds), Kartellrecht Kommentar Band 1, 12th ed, Luchterhand 2014, § 1 GWB para. 277; D. Zimmer. In: Immenga and Mestmäcker (eds), Wettbewerbsrecht Band 2, § 1 GWB para. 327.

[124] Higher Regional Court Frankfurt a. M., Decision of 22 December 2015, Case No. 11 U 84/14 (Kart) – *Funktionsrucksäcke*, NZKart 2016, pp. 84–88.

[125] CJEU, case C-439/09, *Pierre Fabre Dermo-Cosmétique SAS v Président de l'Autorité de la concurrence*, ECR 2011 I 9419.

[126] Cf. the judgment of the previous instance: Regional Court Frankfurt a. M., Decision of 18 June 2014, Case No. 2-03 O 158/13 – *Funktionsrucksäcke*, MMR 2017, pp. 777–778; cf. M. Schweda

that Amazon provides to present products. In comparison to other third-party platforms (compare next passage dealing with eBay) Amazon's shop system[127] does not substantially differ from regular online shops run by the distributor.[128]

Ironically, the Higher Regional Court Frankfurt later moved forward to clarify the legal situation by referring the matter to the CJEU for preliminary ruling in another case raising similar questions.[129] The CJEU will have to, inter alia, rule on the question whether the aim of maintaining a luxury product image is acknowledged by European antitrust law. Furthermore, the court will have to decide whether the general ban of sales via third-party platforms, irrespective of a manufacturer's legitimate quality standard, can withstand the CJEU's four-prong test so that no restriction of competition is given. The CJEU's judgment in this case is awaited for the end of this year.[130]

The *eBay* platform has a special status among third-party platforms: The Higher Regional Court Karlsruhe decided that a provision banning the sale on eBay can withstand antitrust law.[131] In the decided case, the contracting parties agreed upon general requirements concerning the online presentation of the contract goods (school bags). It was explicitly agreed that an offer on eBay is not fulfilling these requirements at the moment. According to the court, the agreement was in line with the CJEU's criteria and thus did not constitute a restraint of competition. As the contract puts demands on the good's presentation, the chosen criteria were objective and of a qualitative nature. The court stated that the requirements that aimed at leading the customer to the distributor's stationary business were necessary to ensure the goods' proper use as orthopaedic considerations were of importance for the purchase decision. Eventually, the scope of the requirement was not objectionable. However, the court pointed out that its decision does not apply to cases in which an offer is made by using the eBay shop system because the contractual presentation requirements can be fulfilled in that case. The court furthermore denied a violation of §§ 19 (2) No. 1, 20 (1) GWB for the same reasons. Although the court acknowledged the reseller's interest in using eBay (low investment and maintenance costs compared to an own website), it held that the manufacturer's, respectively the trademark proprietor's, interests in adequately presenting its goods prevailed in case of the prohibition of single offers on eBay.

---

and J.-C. Rudowicz, Verkaufsverbote über Online-Handelsplattformen und Kartellrecht, WRP 2013, pp. 590–600.

[127] See these Amazon stores as an example: https://www.amazon.de/Marc-O-Polo/b?ie=UTF8&node=1695518031. Accessed 6 June 2017; https://www.amazon.de/b?node=8537844031 Accessed 6 June 2017.

[128] Cf. M. Schweda and J.-C. Rudowicz, Verkaufsverbote über Online-Handelsplattformen und Kartellrecht, WRP 2013, pp. 590–600.

[129] Higher Regional Court Frankfurt a. M., Decision of 19 April 2016, Case No. 11 U 96/14 Kart – *Depotkosmetik II*, NZKart 2016, pp. 236–239.

[130] CJEU, case C-230/16, *Coty*.

[131] Higher Regional Court Karlsruhe, Decision of 25 November 2009, Case No. 6 U 47/08, CR 2010, pp. 116–121.

As opposed to this, the Higher Regional Court Berlin ruled that even offers in eBay shops are likely to impair the product's image as consumers associate eBay with a 'flea market' that contradicts the manufacturer's interest in signalising the high quality of the contract good.[132] The court explicitly stated that this is not the case with every third-party platform.

The *Federal Cartel Office* dealt with bans on third-party platforms as well.

In the *Adidas case*, the authority prohibited the use of a contractual ban to sell Adidas products via third-party platforms in a selective distribution system on the basis of both Article 101 (1) TFEU and § 1 GWB.[133] The contractual ban was limited to so-called open marketplaces, being defined as platforms that allow either C2C trading or trading of used and damaged products or sale of the same good by more than one distributor. The cartel office applied the CJEU's four-prong test and came to the result that the agreement constituted a restriction of competition. In the authority's opinion, a total ban of sales via third-party platforms does not constitute an objective criterion of a qualitative nature being necessary to ensure a high quality standard. Furthermore, it pointed out that, as a less severe means, there regularly is the possibility to contractually agree upon specific rules for the (online) presentation of the contract goods. The Federal Cartel Office also found the restriction to be appreciable. The authority argued that online distribution via third-party platforms is an essential distribution channel and emphasised that third-party platforms allow small and medium-sized enterprises to enter into the online distribution market.

The *Asics case* was solved similarly by the Federal Cartel Office. The authority found that (a) a contractual agreement hindering a distributor from selling the contract goods online by making use of price search engines, as well as (b) a provision prohibiting the use of Asics' trademarks on any third-party web page and (c) a provision prohibiting the distribution via third-party platforms, violated Article 101 (1) TFEU and § 1 GWB.[134] The cartel office laid emphasis on the fact that the provisions would hinder authorised dealers from improving the traceability of their offers. It pointed out that the online distribution via third-party platforms has to be considered as an essential distribution channel. In the authority's opinion, the contractual agreements failed the CJEU's test because they were not purely objective and went beyond the necessary scope.

The *European Commission* seems to take a different view on this matter in its staff working document accompanying the final report on the e-commerce sector inquiry.[135] The Commission indicates that an agreement only constitutes a restriction of competition within the meaning of Article 101 (1) TFEU if a ban of sales via third-party platforms 'de facto amounts to a total ban of the use of the internet'.[136] However, these observations are not binding.

[132] Higher Regional Court Berlin, Decision of 19 September 2013, Case No. 2 U 8/09 Kart – *Schulranzen und -rucksäcke*, MMR 2013, pp. 774–779.

[133] Federal Cartel Office, Decision of 27 June 2014, Case No. B 3 – 137/12.

[134] Federal Cartel Office, Decision of 26 January 2016, Case No. B 2 – 98/11.

[135] http://ec.europa.eu/competition/antitrust/sector_inquiry_swd_en.pdf. Accessed 26 July 2017.

[136] Para. 502 f. Staff Working Document Final Report E-Commerce Sector Inquiry.

The latest German case law and the Federal Cartel Office's decision practice tend to classify the ban of online sales via third-party platforms as a restriction of competition. This opinion deserves to be endorsed as bans on sales via third-party platforms will at least fail the fourth prong of the CJEU's test.[137] Even if one would still accept the manufacturer's interest in protecting the product image after the CJEU's Pierre Fabre judgment, manufacturers could also design their contracts in a way that certain requirements are imposed on the online presentation of goods, instead of banning sales via third-party platforms. One has to acknowledge that sales via third-party platforms enormously strengthen intra-brand competition. Whereas a reseller's own home page is likely to be lost in the World Wide Web, the offer is easily detectible on these platforms[138] and the user is able to compare different offers without leaving the platform's website. For small and medium-sized enterprises, the possibility to offer their goods via such platforms often is the only way to launch the online market without being faced with high costs for the development and the maintenance of the website.[139] Consequently, bans of sales via third-party platforms negatively affect intra-brand competition. As manufacturers should be aware of the possibilities that some platforms offer for the presentation of goods, one could conclude that the paramount aim of general bans is to impede intra-brand competition. The manufacturer's or trademark proprietor's interest in an appropriate presentation of its goods is adequately acknowledged if resellers have to regard special rules in regard to the presentation. If the manufacturer is of the opinion that certain third-party platforms cannot meet these requirements, a contractual provision repeating that opinion and taking into account that the presentation possibilities may change in the future can help to clarify the contract. In that case, the CJEU's criteria are met so that no restriction of competition is given.

#### 7.3.3.3 Exemptions

If one regards bans of sales via third-party platforms as restrictions of competition, it has to be examined whether manufacturers can rely on exceptions to the prohibition (see Sect. 7.2.1.1 above).

General bans on sales via third-party platforms could constitute a hardcore restriction of competition within the meaning of Article 4 lit. b) or Article 4 lit. c) Regulation 330/2010. The first provision, inter alia, covers restrictions of the customers to whom a buyer may sell the contract goods. The latter provision concerns restrictions of active or passive sales to the end user by the agreement. It is highly controversial whether total bans on sales via third-party platforms fall under these provisions.

[137] M. Schweda and J.-C. Rudowicz, Verkaufsverbote über Online-Handelsplattformen und Kartellrecht, WRP 2013, pp. 590–600.

[138] M. Schweda and J.-C. Rudowicz, Verkaufsverbote über Online-Handelsplattformen und Kartellrecht, WRP 2013, pp. 590–600.

[139] M. Schweda and J.-C. Rudowicz, Verkaufsverbote über Online-Handelsplattformen und Kartellrecht, WRP 2013, pp. 590–600.

The vast majority of *German courts* ruled that a general ban of sales via Internet marketplaces constitutes a hardcore restriction within the meaning of Article 4 lit. b) Regulation 330/2010 and argued that the provision would already be fulfilled if the restriction makes it significantly more difficult to reach more or other consumers.[140] The judges stated that this was the case because consumers enjoyed the advantages of sales via Internet marketplaces (comparability, traceability). The Regional Court Kiel explicitly referred to paras. 52 and 50 of the Guidelines on Vertical Restraints.[141] In a similar case, the Higher Regional Court Munich ruled differently, arguing that Article 4 lit. b) Regulation 330/2010 could only be fulfilled if the restriction aims at a definable group of customers.[142] In the above-mentioned request for preliminary ruling,[143] the Higher Regional Court Frankfurt moved forward to clarify the legal situation by asking the CJEU whether Article 4 lit. b) Regulation 330/2010 is fulfilled in cases of total bans on sales via third-party platforms.[144]

In regard to Article 4 lit. c) Regulation 330/2010, the *Federal Cartel Office* indicated in its Adidas case that a general ban on using third-party platforms constitutes a hardcore restriction within the meaning of this provision.[145] In the Asics case, the cartel office repeated its opinion but pointed out that the legal situation is unclear.[146] The authority, however, argued that the ban would substantially restrict the possibilities for distributors to sell the contract goods online to end clients. Especially, small and medium-sized enterprises would be dependent on the possibility to make use of third-party platforms to enter into the online market. Equivalent measures could not have been taken in the stationary business. Furthermore, the cartel office pointed out that sales via third-party platforms do not per se cause negative effects on a product's presentation. Emphasis was laid on the advantages of the use of third-party platforms for the end client (less search effort, better comparability) and on the seller's possibility to require a specific presentation of the contract goods. The *Regional Court Frankfurt* ruled in the same way.[147]

---

[140] Higher Regional Court Berlin, Decision of 19 September 2013, Case No. 2 U 8/09 Kart – *Schulranzen und –rücksäcke*, MMR 2013, pp. 774–779; Higher Regional Court Schleswig, Decision of 5 June 2014, Case No. 16 U Kart 154/13 – *Partnervereinbarung*, NZKart 2014, pp. 364–366; Regional Court Kiel, Decision of 8 November 2013, Case No. 14 O 44/13 Kart – *Digitalkameras*, MMR 2014, pp. 183–184.

[141] Regional Court Kiel, Decision of 8 November 2013, Case No. 14 O 44/13 Kart – *Digitalkameras*, MMR 2014, pp. 183–184.

[142] Higher Regional Court Munich, Decision of 2 July 2009, Case No. U (K) 4842/08 – *Partnervereinbarung*, NZKart 2014, pp. 364–366.

[143] CJEU, case C-230/16, *Coty*.

[144] Higher Regional Court Frankfurt a. M., Decision of 19 April 2016, Case No. 11 U 96/14 Kart – *Depotkosmetik II*, NZKart 2016, pp. 236–239.

[145] Federal Cartel Office, Decision of 19 August 2014, Case No. B 3 – 137/12.

[146] Federal Cartel Office, Decision of 26 January 2016, Case No. B 2 – 98/11.

[147] Regional Court Frankfurt a. M., Decision of 31 July 2014, Case No. 2-3 O 128/13 – *Logo-Klauseln*, NZKart 2015, pp. 243–244.

The *European Commission* seems to take the opposite view. It argues that bans of sales via third-party platforms only regulate how but not to whom the contract goods can be sold and consequently cannot be considered a hardcore restriction within the meaning of Article 4 lit. c) Regulation 330/2010.[148] The Commission, however, points out that the CJEU might rule differently in the upcoming Coty judgment.[149]

Proponents of this view often refer to para. 54 of the Guidelines on Vertical Restraints. According to that provision, Article 4 Regulation 330/2010 does not hinder the manufacturer from requiring *that customers do not visit the distributor's website through a site carrying the name or logo of the third party platform.* However, this cannot serve as an argument for the opinion denying a hardcore restriction within the meaning of Article 4 lit. b) or c) Regulation 330/2010. The provision's purpose is to prevent consumers from thinking that they contract with the third-party platform.[150] This concern is baseless in regard to most third-party platforms. Users of eBay are well aware that not eBay itself offers products online but registered sellers. On the Amazon marketplace, the offer contains the notice that Amazon is not a contracting party. This gets even more obvious if the offer is made by using the eBay shop system[151] or a shop on Amazon. As the Commission points out the importance of online distribution as a distribution channel in other parts of the Guidelines on Vertical Restraints, one can conclude that para. 54 is formulated too broadly. The provision is at least outdated as the new possibilities that third-party platforms provide for presenting products could not be taken into account. Furthermore, the guidelines are not binding for courts (see Sect. 7.3.1 above).

According to para. 56 of the Guidelines on Vertical Restraints, agreements restraining online sales may only impose requirements that are equivalent to the requirements in the stationary business. A similar restriction for brick-and-mortar shops is not imaginable.[152]

The *Higher Regional Court Frankfurt*, being aware of the legal uncertainty, asked the CJEU whether total bans on sales via third-party platforms constitute a hardcore restriction to competition within the meaning of Article 4 lit. c) Regulation 330/2010.[153] The court made clear that it doubts that a general ban on sales via third-party platforms can be justified by a legitimate interest of the manufacturer.

---

[148] Para. 509 Staff Working Document Final Report E-Commerce Sector Inquiry.

[149] CJEU, case C-230/16, *Coty*.

[150] Regional Court Frankfurt a. M., Decision of 18 June 2014, Case No. 2-03 O 158/13 – *Funktionsrucksäcke*, MMR 2017, pp. 777–778; Regional Court Kiel, Decision of 8 November 2013, Case No. 14 O 44/13 Kart – *Digitalkameras*, MMR 2014, pp. 183–184.

[151] Regional Court Kiel, Decision of 8 November 2013, Case No. 14 O 44/13 Kart – *Digitalkameras*, MMR 2014, pp. 183–184.

[152] M. Schweda and J.-C. Rudowicz, Verkaufsverbote über Online-Handelsplattformen und Kartellrecht, WRP 2013, pp. 590–600.

[153] Higher Regional Court Frankfurt a. M., Decision of 19 April 2016, Case No. 11 U 96/14 Kart – *Depotkosmetik II*, NZKart 2016, pp. 236–239.

#### 7.3.3.4 Conclusion

The afore-mentioned cases show that it is highly controversial whether bans on sales via third-party platforms are in accordance with antitrust law. Practitioners are confronted with legal uncertainty.[154] However, the awaited judgment of the CJEU is likely to clear the legal situation. In conclusion, the total ban of sales via third-party platforms is seen very critical by German courts. Bans of sales via specific third-party platforms have to be examined carefully taking into account the platform's presentation possibilities and the manufacturer's interest in the ban.

### 7.3.4 Most-Favoured-Nation Conditions

Most-favoured-nation conditions (hereinafter 'MFNC') occur in the new economy sector, as in every other economic sector. In regard to online sales platforms, the most relevant case of application of MFNC involves contractual provisions that impose a contractual duty on sellers to guarantee that the product is not offered on another platform for a lower price. The specialty in these cases is that the party using the MFNC is not part of the supply chain but a third party.[155]

The Regional Court Munich had to decide on the accordance of such an agreement between Amazon and its sellers with antitrust law in an action for a preliminary injunction.[156] The MFNC used by Amazon included online sales via the seller's own website, as well as other third-party platforms. The court decided that such an agreement violates § 1 GWB. As the MFNC eventually dictates the price the seller demands on Amazon, his economic freedom of action is enormously restricted so that Amazon's behaviour constituted a restriction of competition within the meaning of Article 101 (1) TFEU and § 1 GWB.[157]

As Amazon most probably has a market share of more than 30%, the undertaking could not rely on Article 2 Regulation 1/2003 according to Article 3 (1) Regulation 1/2003. But even if that had not been the case, the MFNC would constitute a hardcore restriction of competition according to Article 4 lit. a) Regulation 1/2003.[158] This provision covers agreements that have 'as their object the restriction of the buyer's ability to determine its sale price without prejudice to the possibility of the supplier to suppose a maximum sale price [...]'. MFNC like the one used by Amazon are only covered by the provision's re-exception (maximum sale price) on the first view. If one considers the effects that the agreement has on other platforms,

[154] Cf. K. Beckmann and U. Müller. In: Hoeren, Sieber and Holznagel, Handbuch Multimedia-Recht, 38. EL, C.H. Beck 2014, part 10 para. 160.

[155] I. Bodenstein, "Marketplace"-Händler zur Preisparität verpflichtet? – Amazon-AGB auf dem kartellrechtlichen Prüfstand, GRUR-Prax 2010, pp. 260–263.

[156] Regional Court Munich I, Decision of 22 April 2010, Case No. 37 O 7636/10 (not published).

[157] I. Bodenstein, "Marketplace"-Händler zur Preisparität verpflichtet? – Amazon-AGB auf dem kartellrechtlichen Prüfstand, GRUR-Prax 2010, pp. 260–263.

[158] I. Bodenstein, "Marketplace"-Händler zur Preisparität verpflichtet? – Amazon-AGB auf dem kartellrechtlichen Prüfstand, GRUR-Prax 2010, pp. 260–263.

one recognises that indeed Amazon dictates a minimum price for these offers (higher than the price on Amazon).[159] In case of a dominant market share (see Sect. 7.2.1.2) of Amazon, § 19 GWB is violated as well.

In a case decided by the Higher Regional Court Düsseldorf, MFNC were used by a hotel booking portal (HRS).[160] The court ruled that the MFNC that prohibited the hotelier to make offers on other platforms for a lower price violated Article 101 (1) TFEU and § 1 GWB. The judges held that the agreement leads to a market foreclosure on the market for hotel portals. It would be impossible for new portals to enter into the market if their potential contracting parties (hoteliers) were hindered to offer their rooms for a lower price than on other platforms. In regard to the market for hotel rooms, the court pointed out that competition is enormously restricted as the hoteliers cannot react to a decreasing demand on one platform by reducing the price only on that platform. Consequently, the hotelier will most likely not reduce the price so that end clients cannot profit from a lower price that would otherwise be possible. The court did not take a stand on whether the agreement constitutes a vertical restraint. As the portal's market share was above 30%, the violation could not be justified by Regulation 330/2010 according to its Article 3 (1). It furthermore denied the exception of Article 101 (3) TFEU, respectively of § 2 (1) GWB.

## 7.4 Conclusion

In an overall assessment, German and EU antitrust law is ready to handle problems arising in the context of online sales platforms.

The legal provisions prohibiting behaviour that restricts competition are drafted broad enough to take the characteristics of the new economy sector into account adequately on a case-by-case basis. As German and EU antitrust law relies on both administrations and private entities to enforce antitrust law, violations can be eliminated effectively. The definition of the relevant market, however, is a difficult point as the criteria that were developed for traditional economic sectors do not always fit into the new economy sector. The German lawmaker recognised that problem and will introduce new legal provisions regarding the specialties of the new economic sector.

The restriction of online sales is a matter of high relevance in European and national law. A total ban of online sales, as well as the introduction of a price maintenance system, is never possible. Even restrictions of online sales by dual-pricing systems or limits on the quantity of the goods sold online are only possible in special cases as German and European antitrust law and the courts applying that law acknowledge the high importance of online sales and its positive effects on competition. Practitioners are, however, still faced with legal uncertainty in regard to the ban

[159] I. Bodenstein, "Marketplace"-Händler zur Preisparität verpflichtet? – Amazon-AGB auf dem kartellrechtlichen Prüfstand, GRUR-Prax 2010, pp. 260–263.

[160] E.g. Higher Regional Court Düsseldorf, Decision of 9 January 2015, Case No. VI-Kart 1/14 (V) – *Enge Bestpreisklauseln*, NZKart 2015, pp. 148–152.

of online sales via third-party platforms as the relevant case law is inconsistent. Following the new lines lately drawn by German courts and the Federal Cartel Office, total bans of sales via third-party platforms are not in line with antitrust law. Qualitative requirements for the online presentation of goods have to be examined on a case-by-case basis.

Most-favoured-nation conditions used by third-party platforms such as Amazon or hotel booking platforms violate antitrust law in the opinion of German courts.

# Hungary

# 8

Álmos Papp and András Horváth

## 8.1 The Competition Law Context of Online Sales

### 8.1.1 Competition Law Framework

The Competition Act[1] serves as a general code for the regulation of Hungarian competition law. The Competition Act regulates the entire scope of competition matters, such as unfair competition, unfair manipulation of business decisions, agreements on the restriction of competition (horizontal and vertical), abuse of dominant position, merger control proceedings, and private enforcement of claims. The Competition Act also sets forth basic organizational rules of the Hungarian Competition Authority (HCA) enforcing competition law in Hungary.

The Competition Act aims to create a competitive market environment that serves the economy and social progress. Pursuant to the Competition Act, this requires the introduction of competition laws to prohibit trading practices that disregard the requirements of fair competition or that have the capacity to restrict competition and prevent the concentration of undertakings that are detrimental to competition.

The members of the working group preparing the chapter were Gusztáv Bacher, Virág Balogh, Adrienn Dömők, Márton Horányi, Anikó Keller, Márton Kocsis, Ádám Liber, Márk Pánczél, Ákos Réger, István Szatmáry, Pál Szilágyi, Péter Virág and Péter Vörös.

[1] Act LVII of 1996 on the Prohibition of Unfair Trading Practices and Unfair Competition.

Á. Papp (✉)
Bán, S. Szabó & Partners, Budapest, Hungary
e-mail: apapp@bansszabo.hu

A. Horváth
Hegymegi-Barakonyi and Partner Baker & McKenzie, Budapest, Hungary
e-mail: andras.horvath@bakermckenzie.com



B. Kilpatrick et al. (eds.), *Antitrust Analysis of Online Sales Platforms & Copyright Limitations and Exceptions*, LIDC Contributions on Antitrust Law, Intellectual Property and Unfair Competition,
https://doi.org/10.1007/978-3-319-71419-6_8

The prohibitions identical with rules stipulated in Articles 101 and 102 TFEU are set forth in Section 11 and Section 21 of the Competition Act.[2]

[2] Section 11 of the Competition Act reads as follows:

(1) Agreements and concerted practices between companies, as well as the decisions of the organizations of companies established based on the right of association, their public bodies, associations and other similar (hereinafter referred to collectively as "association of companies") (hereinafter referred to collectively as "agreements"), which are aimed at the prevention, restriction or distortion of economic competition, or which may display or in fact displays such an effect, are prohibited. An agreement concluded between companies that are not unrelated shall not be construed as such.
(2) This prohibition shall, in particular, apply to the following:
a) fixing the purchase or sales prices, and defining other business conditions directly or indirectly;
b) restricting manufacture, distribution, technical development or investment or keeping them under control;
c) dividing the sources of supply and restricting the freedom of choosing from among them, as well as excluding specific trading parties from the purchase of certain goods;
d) dividing the market, excluding any party from selling, and restricting the choice of means of sales;
e) preventing any party from entering the market;
f) where, in respect of transactions of an identical value or of the same nature, certain partners are discriminated against, including the setting of prices, payment deadlines, discriminatory sales or purchase conditions or the employment of methods which cause disadvantage to certain business partners in the competition;
g) rendering the conclusion of a contract conditional upon undertaking any commitment which, due to its nature or with regard to the usual contractual practice, do not form part of the subject of the contract.

Section 21 of the Competition Acts reads as follows:

It is prohibited to abuse a dominant position, in particular:
a) to fix purchase or sales prices unfairly in business relations, including where general contract terms and conditions are applied, or to stipulate unjustified advantages by any other means, or to force the acceptance of detrimental terms and conditions on the other party;
b) b to restrict production, distribution or technical development to the detriment of final trading parties;
c) to refuse to establish or maintain business relations adequate for the nature of the transaction without any justification;
d) to influence the other party's business decisions for the purpose of gaining unjustified advantages;
e) to withdraw goods from general circulation or to withhold goods without justification prior to price increases or for the purpose of causing prices to rise, or by means otherwise capable of securing unjustified advantages or causing a disadvantage in competition;
f) to render the supply and acceptance of goods contingent upon the supply or acceptance of other goods, or to render the conclusion of a contract conditional upon undertaking any commitment which, due to its nature or with regard to the usual contractual practice, does not form part of the subject of the contract;
g) in connection with transactions of an identical value or of the same nature, to discriminate against certain business partners without due cause, including the setting of prices, payment deadlines, discriminatory sales or purchase conditions or the employment of methods which cause disadvantage to certain business partners in the competition;

Although the Competition Act contains several special procedural rules applicable to the proceedings of the HCA, the APA,[3] which contains the basic administrative procedural rules, is also applicable. From January 1, 2018, Act CL of 2016 on the General Rules of Public Administration Procedures has entered into force as the new act on administrative procedure. With its entry into force, competition supervision procedures will fall outside the scope of the APA, and it is likely that all procedural rules will be included in the Competition Act. This major overhaul is underway and is expected to enter into force early 2018.

In addition to the rules of the Competition Act on unfair manipulation of business decisions applicable to B2B relations, unfair commercial practices in B2C relations are regulated by the UCP Act.[4] The UCP Act aims to protect the interest of consumers, to foster fair market practices, and to improve the efficiency of combating unfair commercial practices, recognizing the weight of self-governance to eliminate unfair commercial practices and to foster the enforcement of codes of conduct established within the framework of self-governance. The UCP Act is enforced by the HCA if the commercial practice is capable of significantly affecting competition (e.g., nationwide practice). The UCP Act implements the Unfair Commercial Practices Directive.[5]

### 8.1.2 Sector-Specific Regulation

The Civil Code[6] contains the general rules for concluding contracts by electronic means. These include the provisions on the information to be provided by the service provider before the conclusion of the contract and the process of conclusion (electronic contractual declaration and confirmation). The same rules applicable to the provision of information society services are set forth in the E-Commerce Act.[7] Both the Civil Code and the E-Commerce Act implement the Directive on Electronic

h) to force competitors off the relevant market, or to use excessively low prices which are based not upon better efficiency in comparison to that of the competitors, so as to prevent competitors from entering the market;
i) to hinder competitors from entering the market in any other unjust manner; or
j) to create a market environment that is unreasonably disadvantageous for the competitors or to influence their business decisions for the purpose of gaining unjustified benefits.

[3] Act CXL of 2004 on the General Rules of Administrative Procedures and Services.

[4] Act XLVII of 2008 on the Prohibition of Unfair Business-to-Consumer Commercial Practices.

[5] Directive 2005/29 of the European Parliament and of the Council of 11 May 2005 concerning unfair business-to-consumer commercial practices in the internal market and amending Council Directive 84/450, Directives 97/7, 98/27 and 2002/65 of the European Parliament and of the Council and Regulation 2006/2004 of the European Parliament and of the Council ('Unfair Commercial Practices Directive'), OJ 2005 L 149, p. 22.

[6] Act V of 2013 on the Civil Code.

[7] Act CVIII of 2001 on Electronic Commerce and on Information Society Services.

Commerce.[8] With respect to these aspects of online sales, special rules apply to financial services marketed via means of distance communication. These are set forth in the Financial Distance Marketing Act,[9] which implements the Directive on Distance Marketing of Financial Services.[10] The B2C Contract Regulation[11] contains more general rules, applicable to all distance contracts between undertakings and consumers; however, some of its provisions may also apply to online sales.

### 8.1.3 National and Supranational Competition Law

As Hungary is a Member State of the European Union, both Hungarian competition law and EU competition law directly apply if a conduct is capable of (appreciably) affecting the trade between Member States.[12] In the context of competition law, there is no conflict or gap between the standards of the national system and the supranational legal system to which Hungary is subject, i.e. the laws of the European Union.

The relationship of Hungarian and EU competition laws is mainly regulated by way of Regulation 1/2003.[13] In the context of Regulation 1/2003,[14] national competition laws mean all those national laws that predominantly pursue the same objective as that pursued by Articles 101 and 102 TFEU.[15] Article 1 of Regulation 1/2003 establishes the direct applicability of Articles 101 and 102 TFEU, while Article 3 regulates the relationship between Articles 101 and 102 TFEU and national competition laws.

According to the procedural rule set forth in Article 3(1) of Regulation 1/2003, national competition authorities and national courts also apply Articles 101 and 102 TFEU, where they apply national competition law to agreements or practices that fall under Articles 101 and 102 TFEU. According to the rule of substance set forth in Article 3(2) of Regulation 1/2003, agreements and concerted practices that affect

---

[8] Directive 2000/31 of the European Parliament and of the Council of 8 June 2000 on certain legal aspects of information society services, in particular electronic commerce, in the Internal Market ('Directive on Electronic Commerce'), OJ 2000 L 178, p. 1.

[9] Act XXV of 2005 on the financial service contracts concluded as distance contracts.

[10] Directive 2002/65 of the European Parliament and of the Council of 23 September 2002 concerning the distance marketing of consumer financial services and amending Council Directive 90/619 and Directives 97/7 and 98/27, OJ 2002 L 271, p. 16.

[11] Government Regulation No 45/2014 (II. 26.) on the detailed rules of contracts between businesses and consumers.

[12] Commission Notice Guidelines on the effect on trade concept contained in Articles 81 and 82 of the Treaty, OJ 2004 C 101, p. 81.

[13] Council Regulation 1/2003 of 16 December 2002 on the implementation of the rules on competition laid down in Articles 81 and 82 of the Treaty, OJ 2003 L 1, p. 1.

[14] This interpretation is based on Recital 8 and 9, as well as Article 3(3) of Regulation 1/2003.

[15] The relationship of EU and national merger control is separately regulated by way of the EU Merger Regulation (Regulation 139/2004), while national laws on B2C unfair commercial practices were fully harmonized by way of the Unfair Commercial Practices Directive.

trade between Member States and that are not prohibited by Article 101 TFEU cannot be prohibited under national competition law. The situation is different with unilateral practices covered by Article 102 TFEU. Namely, Member States remain free to adopt and apply stricter national laws on their territories, i.e. Member States can prohibit unilateral practices that are not prohibited by Article 102 TFEU.

It must be noted that although there is no express obligation to harmonize EU competition law and national competition law, Hungarian competition law very much mirrors its EU counterpart.

### 8.1.4 Competition Case Law

Competition cases concerning online sales are listed in Table 8.1.

### 8.1.5 Guidelines on Vertical Restraints

The HUVBER[16] provides for guidance on vertical restraints. This mirrors Regulation 330/2010.[17] Therefore, when interpreting the HUVBER, the EU Guidelines on Vertical Restraints are most helpful since Hungarian guidelines to this topic do not exist. These rules are general and sector-neutral in their nature and are relevant to the vertical relationships of Internet-related and computer software enterprises as well.

### 8.1.6 Sector Inquiry

The market of online travel agencies (OTAs) was subject to sector inquiry in Hungary from 2013 to 2016. The HCA published the final report of the sector inquiry on June 8, 2016 ("Sector Inquiry Report").[18] The online hotel booking market in the tourism sector showed several traits, which drew the attention of European competition authorities, including the HCA, to the sector. There were concerns that the price-parity clauses (most-favored-nation or most-favored-customer clauses, in short MFN or MFC) may distort or restrict competition.

---

[16] Government Regulation No 205/2011 (X. 7.) on the exemption of certain categories of vertical agreements from the prohibition of restriction of competition.

[17] Commission Regulation 330/2010 of 20 April 2010 on the application of Article 101(3) of the Treaty on the Functioning of the European Union to categories of vertical agreements and concerted practices, OJ 2010 L 102, p. 1.

[18] The full version of the Hungarian language Sector Inquiry Report is available at: http://gvh.hu//data/cms1034253/Agazati_vizsgalat_online_szallashelyfoglalas_piacan_vegleges_jelentes_2016_06_08.pdf. The English language executive summary of the Sector Inquiry Report is available at: http://www.gvh.hu/data/cms1034473/Agazati_vizsgalat_online_szallashelyfoglalas_piacan_vegleges_jelentes_2016_06_08_a.pdf.

**Table 8.1** Competition cases concerning online sales

| Nr | Case number | Parties to the procedure | Type of procedure | Market definition | Decision of the HCA |
|---|---|---|---|---|---|
| 1 | VJ/55/2013 | Alcon Services AG Hungarian Branch<br>Novartis Hungária Kft.<br>Alcon Hungária Gyógyszer-kereskedelmi Kft. | Agreement on the restriction of competition | Contact lenses and contact care products | The HCA found that the undertakings concerned restricted competition by creating and operating a rebate system to the detriment of the online retailers of CIBA contact lenses and care products. The HCA imposed a fine on Alcon Services AG Hungarian Branch (HUF 51,356,000 ~ EUR 165,670) and Alcon Hungária Gyógyszerkereskedelmi Kft. (HUF 52,343,000 ~ EUR 168,850).[a] |
| 2 | VJ/113/2013 | Allegro Group HU Kft.<br>Hotel Outlet Internetes Utazásközvetítő Kft. | Unfair commercial practices | Offers related to accommodation | The HCA terminated the procedure. |
| 3 | VJ/70/2014 | Booking.com B.V. | Unfair commercial practice | Offers related to accommodation | The HCA terminated the procedure. |
| 4 | VJ/106/2015 | Portfolion Regionális Magántőke Alap<br>Szallas.hu Kft.<br>OTP Bank Nyrt.<br>Magyar Export-Import Bank Zrt. | Merger | Online accommodation search, comparison and booking services | The HCA approved the merger. |
| 5 | VJ/17/2017 | Booking.com Hungary Kft.<br>Booking.com International B.V.<br>Booking.com B.V. | Agreement on the restriction of competition | Online accommodation search, comparison and booking services | The HCA alleges that the undertakings concerned coordinated the prices of hotels and accommodation service providers. The case is still pending. |

[a]The decision of the HCA is currently under judicial review

#### 8.1.6.1 Focus of the Inquiry

As stated in the Sector Inquiry Report, there are three main fields in which the HCA received notes or remarks from market players.[19] These are the following:

(a) Remarks related to comparative advertising

It was noted in case of a certain OTA that its website unlawfully suggested that it did not charge any fee compared to other OTAs. This practice put the OTA in question in a favorable light compared to its competitors. Nevertheless, the comparative nature of the advertisements was not confirmed in these cases, and therefore no competition supervision procedure was commenced.

(b) Remarks regarding the "best price" expression

Other remarks related to the use of "best price" statement in different forms on OTA websites. The HCA concluded that the OTAs in question made package offers, which were formed uniquely. Therefore, it was possible that the offer in question was the best price offer in the market, and therefore no competition supervision procedure was commenced.

(c) Practices listed in the third group of remarks that were suitable for commencing competition supervision procedure

The HCA took into consideration whether basic prices indicated in OTA websites were actually applied and, consequently, whether the discounts compared to the basic prices indicated on OTA websites were actually real. The HCA also examined (1) whether the "best price guarantee" was suitable for indicating to the consumers that the relevant OTA offered the most favorable prices, (2) whether such statements were suitable for influencing consumers' decisions, and (3) whether such statements were actually true. The procedures were conducted not because of classic antitrust violations but rather for alleged breach of UCP rules.

#### 8.1.6.2 Agency Agreements

In the Sector Inquiry Report, the HCA also examined agreements between hotels and OTAs qualifying as agency relationships. In terms of agency relationships, competition law differentiates between genuine agency agreements and nongenuine agency agreements:

1. The genuine principal–agent relationship is a vertical relationship in which the parties in question constitute an economic unit from a competition law perspective, even though under Section 15 of the Competition Act they qualify as undertakings that are independent from each other. The agent in such relationship is not considered as an economically autonomous market player or as an independent undertaking. Therefore, if the two companies conclude a genuine agency contract, it may not qualify as a restrictive agreement under Section 11 of the Competition Act.
2. Nongenuine agency agreements also have the formal attributes of agency agreements. But in reality, the agents are independent market players from the

[19] See Sector Inquiry Report, p. 65.

principal. Therefore, nongenuine agency agreements fall under the prohibition on restrictive agreements.

3. Genuine and nongenuine agency agreements may be differentiated on the basis of the extent of the risks undertaken by the agent. Similarly to para. 16 of the Guidelines on Vertical Restraints,[20] Hungarian jurisprudence[21] also lists the factors that support that a contract does qualify as a genuine agency agreement (as the agent does not undertake risks associated with the market presence and the sale of goods in question) as follows:
    (a) the agent is not the owner of the contractual goods;
    (b) the agent does not contribute to the costs of distribution;
    (c) the agent does not take part in the promotions of the principal (and, especially, does not bear the costs of marketing);
    (d) the agent does not build up stocks at its own cost, whereas remaining products may be returned;
    (e) the agent does not provide additional services, such as repairs, at its own costs;
    (f) the agent does not make promotional investments at its own costs;
    (g) the agent does not bear liability for damages related to the products;
    (h) the agent does not bear liability for the breach of contract by customers.

#### 8.1.6.3 MFN Clauses

The HCA also examined the MFN clauses:

(a) MFN/MFC or antidiscrimination clauses also drew the attention of national competition authorities. Relating to online booking systems, rate (or room) parity agreements belong to the group of MFN clauses. MFN clauses qualify as vertical agreements, while MFN clauses within agreements between OTAs and hotels are considered as platform MFNs. This means that the agent (or platform) does not buy the product/service; it only creates the connection between the OTAs and the consumers, whereas the agent (platform) is paid a commission. Platform MFNs have four problematic effects: (1) platform MFN clauses may make it difficult for new competitors to enter the market of platforms (entry barriers), (2) they weaken the competition between platforms, (3) such clauses make collusion between platforms and sellers easier, and (4) they grant information on the operational costs of other platforms.

(b) MFN clauses qualify as vertical agreements but may be exempted from Article 101 TFEU and Section 11 of the Competition Act—in particular when the market share of the parties does not exceed 30% (block exemption). MFN clauses must always be subject to a case-by-case assessment. The anticompetitive impact of an MFN clause will depend mostly on the market situation surrounding

---

[20] Guidelines on Vertical Restraints, OJ 2010 C 130, p. 1.

[21] Kommentár a tisztességtelen piaci magatartás és a versenykorlátozás tilalmáról szóló 1996. évi LVII. törvényhez, Budapest, 2014, HVG-ORAC, p. 218.

the parties, the specificities of the market, and the monitoring of, and the sanctions attached to, a breach of the MFN by the parties.

(c) In general, in an MFN agreement, one party agrees to perform a certain activity in favor of the other party under "most favored" conditions. Within MFN clauses, platform MFN clauses require the seller not to sell its product cheaper via another platform. The indirect beneficiaries of such agreements are the OTAs or platforms, whereas the direct beneficiaries are the consumers or buyers.

(d) MFN clauses are typically rate-parity agreements, but there are clauses that relate to other conditions. In the case of rate parity, the seller (that is, the hotel) agrees not to offer more favorable prices to other buyers (OTAs), which means that the seller offers its best offer to the buyer with which it has concluded the MFN clause. The rate-parity clause is somewhat narrower in comparison to MFN clauses because rate parity concerns only prices, while MFN clauses can relate to other conditions too. A hotel may offer more favorable prices or conditions to its other contractual partners (other OTAs that the hotel has agreements with) if it also offers such favorable conditions to the OTA with which it has concluded the MFN clause.

(e) In the case of broad MFN clauses, the obligor (i.e., hotel) of the MFN clause agrees that it will not grant more favorable conditions (either by its own, direct sales system or through other sales channels) to any other OTAs than those granted to the obligee of the MFN clause. Meanwhile, in the case of narrow MFN clauses, the obligor is bound by such obligation only concerning its own sales system but not concerning the indirect sales system. This means that in the case of a narrow MFN clause relating to online sales, the obligor may offer more favorable conditions (via its offline sales channels and in case of direct sales) than the ones offered to the obligee of the MFN clause.

The HCA also published the comments of market players during the sector inquiry.[22] Szallas.hu, a major OTA in Hungary, stated that it switched to the practice of narrow parity. Meanwhile, Expedia disagreed with the assessment regarding the static level of commissions and the lack of innovation on the Hungarian market. Expedia also stated that the practice of OTAs to apply MFN clauses fell under the scope of block exemption (it shall be noted that Expedia also switched to the use of narrow parity). Expedia also made a note on the billboard effect of OTAs and the risk of the free riding of hotels on the investment of OTAs. It argued that parity clauses were introduced for investment protection reasons. Expedia also disagreed with the HCA's opinion that the agreements between OTAs and hotels were non-genuine agency agreements. Hotels also made remarks. They argued that narrow parity would not benefit them as it would not allow hotels to offer cheaper prices via their own sales channels than the ones offered via OTAs. They also stated that MFN

[22] The full version of the Hungarian language summary of comments is available at: http://www.gvh.hu//data/cms1034254/Agazati_vizsgalat_online_szallashelyfoglalas_piacan_eszrevetelek_2016_06_08.pdf.

clauses distorted competition and a high level of commissions drove up prices charged by hotels to customers. They concluded that the abolition of parity clauses would greatly benefit the market.

As a result of the sector inquiry, OTAs switched to the use of narrow-rate parity clauses. Therefore, OTAs in the future may only stipulate that a hotel may not give less favorable conditions to the OTA in question than what is indicated on the hotel's website. However, the parity clause will not concern other OTAs or other sales channels, such as phone, fax, or e-mail. This also means that hotels can provide discounts to consumers directly.

## 8.2 Market Analysis in Case of Online Sales

One of the cornerstones of the application of competition law is the determination of the relevant product and geographical market in which the relevant practice is applied. Also, certain practices are only prohibited in the possession of market power (e.g., abuse of dominance).

### 8.2.1 Market Definition in Case of Online Sales

The definition of the relevant market is regulated in Section 14 of the Competition Act,[23] similarly to the Relevant Market Notice.[24] This definition is applied also in case of online sales.

[23] Section 14 of the Competition Act reads as follows:

(1) The relevant market shall be defined with regard to the goods subject to the agreement and to the geographical territory.
(2) In addition to the goods for which the agreement is concluded, the goods considered as reasonable substitutes in terms of use, price, quality and the conditions of performance (substitution in demand) shall also be taken into account, as well as the factors involved in substitution in supply.
(3) A geographical territory is an area, outside of which:
a) a business partner is unable to purchase the goods, or is only able to purchase the goods under substantially less favorable conditions; or
b) the seller of the goods is unable to sell the goods, or is only able to sell the goods under substantially less favorable conditions.

[24] Commission Notice on the definition of relevant market for the purposes of Community competition law, OJ 1997 C 372, p. 5.

The HCA published an OECD Contribution in 2000 on electronic commerce and competition.[25] In the OECD Contribution, the HCA gave a general overview of the then relevant situation and the potential problems. The OECD Contribution indicated in 2000 that there were no indications of possible problems concerning e-commerce from an antitrust perspective. However, there were several procedures regarding web-based advertisements, which were investigated because of the breach of rules on unfair commercial practices.

In the OECD Contribution, the HCA laid down the principles for defining the relevant market. In the case of e-commerce, the relevant product is a special service that shows both the characteristics of Internet services and traditional trade services. In the case of the Internet services, the HCA distinguishes between access provision and content provision.

With respect to geographic markets, the OECD Contribution states that the criteria of considerably less favorable conditions must be assessed on case-by-case basis. Therefore, the geographical market would mean the geographical area where no additional costs, such as customs duties, tax, and transport costs, would emerge. Downloadable software or lightweight products (books, CDs) from the neighboring countries would meet the requirements of the above geographical area. However, the OECD Contribution noted that in case of certain products or services, it may be reasonable to define the market as the territory of Hungary.

In the Allegro case,[26] the relevant product was defined as offers related to accommodation. The sale of the accommodation was not of direct but rather indirect interest to Allegro as Allegro was paid commission based on the sales of Hotel Outlet. Only the communication related to the hotels were the subject matter of this proceeding. The HCA concluded that not the respective hotel offers were relevant from a competition law perspective but the name of the website introduced and used by Allegro, the message carried by it, the information included in the newsletters/website, and the slogan applied systematically by Hotel Outlet.

In the Alcon case,[27] the relevant market was the market of contact lenses and contact care products. As Alcon's framework contracts also applied to contact lenses and care products, and from the retailer's perspective it is not relevant which types of products are sold, the relevant market was the market of contact lenses and care products, whereas the geographical boundaries of the relevant market were those of Hungary.

[25] The full version of the Hungarian language contribution is available at: http://www.gvh.hu/data/cms1022123/hu_atev_oecdh_elker00_m.pdf. The full version of the English language contribution is available at: http://www.gvh.hu/data/cms1022135/us_atev_oecdh_elker00_a.pdf.

[26] VJ/113/2013.

[27] VJ/55/2013.

**Table 8.2** Hungarian and EU block exemption rules

| Market power | Hungary | European Union |
|---|---|---|
| 20% | Government Regulation No 202/2011 (X. 7) on the exemption of certain categories of specialisation agreements from the prohibition of restriction of competition | Commission Regulation 1218/2010 of 14 December 2010 on the application of Article 101(3) of the Treaty on the Functioning of the European Union to certain categories of specialisation agreements, OJ 2010 L 335, p. 43 |
| 25% | Government Regulation No 206/2011 (X. 7) on the exemption of certain categories of research and development agreements from the prohibition of restriction of competition | Commission Regulation 1217/2010 of 14 December 2010 on the application of Article 101(3) of the Treaty on the Functioning of the European Union to certain categories of research and development agreements, OJ 2010 L 335, p. 36 |
| 30% | HUVBER | Regulation 330/2010 |

### 8.2.2 Market Power in Case of Online Sales

The definition of dominance is regulated in Section 22 of the Competition Act,[28] similarly to the Abuse of Dominant Position Notice.[29] Market power can be interpreted as the level of market shares in case of which a restriction may fall under a block exemption. Hungarian competition law also contains the market level powers relative to block exemption regulations, similarly to EU competition law (see Table 8.2).

[28] Section 22 of the Competition Act reads as follows:

(1) A dominant position shall be deemed to be held on the relevant market (Section 14) by persons who are able to pursue their economic activities to a large extent independently of other market participants without the need to substantively take into account the market reactions of their suppliers, competitors, customers and other trading parties when deciding their market conduct.
(2) In assessing whether a dominant position exists, the following factors shall be considered in particular:
(a) the costs and risks of entry to and exit from the relevant market, and the technical, economic and legal conditions that have to be met;
(b) the assets, financial strength and profitability of the undertaking or the group of undertakings [Section 15(2)], and the trends in their development;
(c) the structure of the relevant market, the comparative market shares, the conduct of market participants and the economic influence of the undertaking or the group of undertakings on the development of the market.
(3) A dominant position may be held by a single undertaking, a group of undertakings, jointly by more than one undertaking, or jointly by more than one group of undertakings.

[29] Communication from the Commission – Guidance on the Commission's enforcement priorities in applying Article 82 of the EC Treaty to abusive exclusionary conduct by dominant undertakings, OJ 2009 C 45, p. 7.

Also, the *de minimis* rule regulated in Section 13 of the Competition Act,[30] similarly to the De Minimis Notice, could be interpreted suggesting that—in case the combined market share of the parties does not exceed 10%—there is no market power.

The above definitions are also applied in case of online sales.

The OECD Contribution stated that barriers to enter the market could lead to the evolution of a dominant position. In the case of a merger between OTAs, which is subject to prior authorization, the HCA may prevent the evolution of a dominant position.

## 8.3 Legal Analysis in Case of Online Sales

Before analyzing in detail the most relevant type of restrictions (those in case of selective distribution agreements), it is worth presenting the general framework of the legal analysis of restrictions with respect to online sales.

### 8.3.1 Types of Infringements

As mentioned above, Hungarian competition law prohibits restrictive agreements and abuses of dominances. Prohibited restrictive agreements can be horizontal and vertical. The prohibition extends to restrictions by object and restrictions by effect.

At present, there is limited case law for antitrust cases involving e-commerce and online sales platforms in Hungary. So far, only a few merger and vertical restraint decisions, and mostly decisions related to unfair commercial practices, have been published.

[30] Section 13 of the Competition Act reads as follows:

(1) Agreements of minor importance shall not be subject to prohibition.
(2) An agreement shall be construed of minor importance if the combined share of the parties to the agreement and of the companies that are not independent from such parties does not exceed ten per cent in the market in question. The requirement of a market share of ten per cent or less shall be satisfied during the term of the agreement or in each calendar year if the said term covers more than one year.
(3) Subsection (1) shall not apply to agreements between competitors or concerted practices which have as their object the restriction, prevention or distortion of competition, such as the fixing or coordination of purchase or selling prices or other trading conditions, the allocation of production or sales quotas, the sharing of markets, including bid-rigging, restrictions of imports or exports (hereinafter referred to as "cartel"), including any agreement aiming, directly or indirectly, for fixing purchase or sale prices, or concerted practices.
(4) The provisions of Subsections (1)-(3) notwithstanding, any agreement that is able to create an environment, in conjunction with other agreements of the like, whereby competition in the relevant market is substantially obstructed, restricted or distorted, shall be subject to prohibition. The Hungarian Competition Authority shall have powers to declare an agreement illegal, in which case no penalty shall be imposed.

## 8.3.2 Exclusionary Practices

### 8.3.2.1 Prohibition of Exclusionary Practices

Although the categorization of exclusionary practices does not explicitly appear in the Competition Act, both bilateral/multilateral and unilateral exclusionary practices are prohibited:

- Section 11 (2) b) (restriction of distribution), c) (exclusion from purchasing), d) (exclusion from selling) and f) (prevention of market entry) of the Competition Act all refer to exclusionary practices in the form of an agreement, concerted practice, or decision of an association of undertakings.
- Section 21 b) (restriction of distribution), c) (refusal to deal), i) (prevention of market entry) of the Competition Act all refer to exclusionary practices in the form of abuse of a dominant position.

In case law, exclusionary practices were assessed as a form of abuse of a dominant position. According to the case law, exclusionary practices are anticompetitive if they harm efficient competition. Competition law protects efficient competition leading to an outcome most beneficial for consumers rather than market players.[31] Furthermore, exclusionary practices are anticompetitive even if they are not successful in foreclosing competitors.[32] Otherwise, foreclosure effect was assessed as a theory of harm in case of other abusive practices.[33]

We are not aware of any abuse of dominant position cases in the area of online sales platforms in Hungary. Nevertheless, the above standards for assessing exclusionary practices are also applicable to all Internet-related business markets.

### 8.3.2.2 Structural Prerequisite for Exclusionary Practices

In case of exclusionary practices in the form of agreements, concerted practices, or decisions of an association of undertakings, there is no structural prerequisite for the prohibition to apply. However, safe harbors apply (see below Sect. 8.3.2.3), and market shares falling outside the safe harbor may be considered as a prerequisite for the prohibition.

In case of exclusionary practices in the form of abuse of a dominant position, the structural prerequisite is the dominant position of the undertaking carrying out the practice. Although there are no Hungarian guidelines on prerequisites (e.g., market share) for a dominant position, the HCA refers to the Abuse of Dominant Position Notice, which sets forth that in case of a market share below 40%, a dominant position is not likely.[34]

[31] VJ/10/2002, para 44.

[32] VJ/78/2003, para 43.

[33] In case of predatory pricing: VJ/10/1997, VJ/76/1999, VJ/39/2009 and VJ/32/2012.

[34] Abuse of Dominant Position Notice, para 14.

#### 8.3.2.3 "Safe Harbor" for Exclusionary Practices

In case of exclusionary practices in the form of agreements, concerted practices, or decisions of an association of undertakings, the HUVBER provides for a safe harbor. Pursuant to Section 3 of the HUVBER, it is the supplier's market share on the market where it sells the contract goods or services and the buyer's market share on the market where it purchases the contract goods or services that determine the applicability of the block exemption. In order for the block exemption to apply, the supplier's and the buyer's market share must be 30% or less on their relevant markets respectively.

In case of exclusionary practices in the form of abuse of a dominant position, the safe harbor is if the undertaking has no dominant position (see Sect. 8.3.2.2 above).

### 8.3.3 Use of Trademarks

Restrictions on online sales are sometimes due to the protection of trademarks. The reseller/distributor is in general entitled to use the manufacturer's trademarks; however, it shall use the trademarks only for advertising the products. The principle of exhaustion constitutes a limit of the trademark rights. We are not aware of any published Hungarian court decision on preventing the distributors to sell the product on third-party platform.

As the Trademark Act[35] is based on the Trademark Directive,[36] which provides full harmonization relating to the scope of the exclusivity rights arising from the trademark right, the case law of the Court of Justice of the European Union (CJEU) can provide for guidance.

Regarding the exhaustion of the rights, Article 7(1) of the Trademark Directive provides that "The trade mark shall not entitle the proprietor to prohibit its use in relation to goods which have been put on the market in the EEA under that trade mark by the proprietor or with his consent."

This rule means that if the retailer acquires the ownership of the goods, it can resell them. The purpose of the exhaustion principle is to facilitate the trade within the EU Member States and to promote competition (intra-brand competition). The CJEU established that in case of exhaustion, when trademarked goods have been put on the EU market by the trademark holder, a reseller is not only free to resell those goods, but it is also free to make use of the trademark for advertising to bring to the public's attention the further commercialization of those goods.

There is only one exception in Article 7(2) of the Trademark Directive, which provides that the exhaustion "shall not apply where there exist legitimate reasons for the proprietor to oppose further commercialization of the goods, especially where the condition of the goods is changed or impaired after they have been put on the market."

---

[35] Act XI of 1997 on the Protection of Trademarks and Geographical Indications.

[36] Directive 2008/95 of the European Parliament and of the Council of 22 October 2008 to approximate the laws of the Member States relating to trade marks, OJ 2008 L 299, p. 25.

In the Dior case,[37] the CJEU analyzed the dispute that Dior's luxury cosmetic products, which are distributed in a selective distribution system by selected retailers, were advertised in ad papers of Evora, which operates a chain of chemists' shops. Although they have not been appointed as distributors by Dior, the shops sell Dior products, which Evora obtained by means of parallel imports. The legality of reselling those products has not been challenged. The CJEU found that damage done to the reputation of a trademark may, in principle, be a legitimate reason to oppose the use of the trademark for further commercialization of goods. As regards prestige goods, the CJEU stated that the reseller must not act unfairly in relation to the legitimate interests of the trademark holder and must endeavor to prevent its advertising from affecting the value of the trademark by detracting from the prestigious image of the goods in question. However, the CJEU concluded that the trademark holder may not oppose the use of the trademark, in ways customary in the reseller's sector of trade (i.e., chemists' shops), for bringing to the public's attention the further commercialization of the trademarked goods, unless it is established that such use seriously damages the reputation of the trademark.

The CJEU has applied the exhaustion principle in the BMW case[38] started against the owner of a garage, concerning its advertisements for the sale of second-hand BMW cars and repairs of BMW cars. In view of the CJEU, BMW cannot prohibit the use of its trademark by another person for informing the public that it is a specialist in the sale of second-hand BMW cars, provided that the advertising concerns cars, which have been put on the EU market under that trademark by the proprietor or with its consent.

On the other hand, it may constitute a legitimate reason for opposing the use if the trademark is used in a reseller's advertising in such a way that it may give rise to the impression that there is a commercial connection between the reseller and the trademark holder and that the reseller's business is affiliated to the trademark holder's distribution network or that there is a special relationship between the two undertakings. Such advertising is contrary to the obligation to act fairly in relation to the legitimate interests of the trademark holder, and it affects the value of the trademark by taking unfair advantage of its distinctive character or reputation. It is also incompatible with the specific object of a trademark, which is to protect the trademark holder against competitors wishing to take advantage of the status and reputation of the trademark. If, on the other hand, there is no risk that the public will be led to believe that there is a commercial connection between the reseller and the trademark holder, the mere fact that the reseller derives an advantage from using the trademark in that advertisements for the sale of goods, which are in other respects honest and fair, and the use of the trademark lends an aura of quality to its own business does not constitute a legitimate reason within the meaning of Article 7(2) of the Trademark Directive.

---

[37] ECJ, case C-337/95, *Christian Dior SA v. Evora BV*, ECR 1997 I 1603.

[38] ECJ, case C-63/97, *Bayerische Motorenwerke AG (BMW) and BMW Nederland BV and Ronald Karel Deenik*, EU:C:1999:82.

In connection with that, a reseller that sells second-hand BMW cars cannot in practice communicate such information to its customers without using the BMW trademark. In consequence, such an informative use of the BMW trademark is necessary to guarantee the right of resale and does not take unfair advantage of the distinctive character or reputation of that trademark. Whether advertising creates the impression that there is a commercial connection between the reseller and the trademark holder is a question to be decided in the light of the circumstances of each case.

Considering the above case law, it can be concluded that if the trademark holder wants to prevent the sale of goods bearing his trademark by third-party retailers, it shall find out

- whether the goods are original or counterfeit products, and
- if original, what is the commercial source of the products, namely whether the manufacturer sold them first within the EU or outside.

The retailer does not infringe the trademark if it sells original products that had been placed on the EU market by or with the consent of the trademark holder. The retailer usually bears the burden of proof that the relevant goods are original and the products had been placed on the EU market by the trademark holder or with its consent and thus that trademark rights were exhausted. However, this allocation of burden of proof is unsuitable for cases in which the trademark holder has created a specific distribution system to prevent parallel imports, where an actual risk of market foreclosure exists if the retailer must disclose the dealers it supplies. In such a case, the trademark holder could influence, based on either contractual agreements or on the actual behavior, the distribution partner to stop supplying dealers, which were excluded from the distribution system.

If the goods are original and were placed on the market by the trademark holder, the supplier can prevent the reseller's advertising only if the website gives the impression that there is a commercial connection between the retailer and the trademark holder. Thus, the overall outlook of the retailer's website needs to be examined. The overall outlook is influenced by the following:

- the domain name,
- whether the website uses the manufacturer's logo or only the word format of the trademark without the logo,
- the use of graphic elements and colors, which may create confusion with the manufacturer's distribution network.

### 8.3.4 Efficiency

Since antirust cases concerning online sales platforms do not usually fall within the scope of restrictions by object (where assessment of anticompetitive effects are not necessary), efficiency is one of the key elements that the HCA takes into account. Efficiencies can tip the balance in such practices, and the restriction can be considered procompetitive (or at least not anticompetitive) despite certain anticompetitive elements of the investigated undertaking's business conduct. However, the criteria of the acceptance of efficiencies are strict. The company under investigation is required to show that the efficiencies meet the conditions set out in the relevant provisions of the Competition Act and the TFEU (elaborated in Sect. 8.4.2 below).

In the Sector Inquiry Report, the HCA evaluated the potential efficiencies of MFN clauses. The assessment of efficiencies is based on three distinct potential procompetitive features of price-parity clauses:

- avoidance of "free riding,"
- strengthening intra-brand competition,
- reducing potential price discrimination.

In the absence of price-parity clauses, hotels could free ride on comparison websites offering lower prices on their own websites: if consumers were aware of such practices, they may search for and select their accommodation on the OTAs, then look for smaller prices (bargains) on the hotel's own website. This may discourage OTAs from further investing in their services. The HCA included in its assessment that—according to a consumer survey done in the course of the sector inquiry—free riding is a genuine business threat in Hungary.[39]

Intra-brand competition can be strengthened by price-parity clauses because consumers only need to check a single OTA website in order to find the best valued accommodation. The Sector Inquiry Report points out that with the right level of price-parity clauses (i.e., narrow MFN clauses) even inter-brand competition is facilitated.[40]

Finally, price-parity clauses can hinder accommodation managers from applying different prices to different consumers (for example, for the same hotel room), but the HCA did not develop a complete theory of harm and so did not reach a conclusion on this basis.[41]

## 8.4 Online Sales in Selective Distribution Systems

### 8.4.1 The Definition of Selective Distribution

The definition of selective distribution system is stipulated in Section 1 para. 5 of HUVBER,[42] similarly to Regulation 330/2010.

[39] See Sector Inquiry Sector, p. 93.

[40] See Sector Inquiry Sector, p. 95.

[41] See Sector Inquiry Sector, p. 81 and p. 94.

[42] 'Selective distribution system' means a distribution system where the supplier undertakes to sell the contract goods or services, either directly or indirectly, only to distributors selected on the basis of specified criteria and where these distributors undertake not to sell such goods or services to unauthorized distributors within the territory reserved by the supplier to operate that system.

Selective distribution agreements restrict the number of authorized distributors on the one hand and the possibilities of resale on the other. The restriction of the number of dealers depends not on the number of territories but on selection criteria linked in the first place to the nature of the product. The restriction on resale is not a restriction on active selling to a territory but a restriction on any sales to nonauthorized distributors, leaving only appointed dealers and final customers as possible buyers. Selective distribution is almost always used to distribute branded final products.

As set forth in para. 175 of the Guidelines on Vertical Restraints, purely qualitative selective distribution and quantitative selective distribution can be distinguished. Purely qualitative selective distribution selects dealers only on the basis of objective criteria required by the nature of the product (e.g., training of sales personnel, the service provided at the point of sale, a certain range of the products being sold, etc.). This form of selective distribution is not anticompetitive if (1) the nature of the product necessitates a selective distribution system, to preserve its quality and ensure its proper use; (2) distributors are selected on the basis of objective criteria of a qualitative nature, laid down uniformly and made available to all potential distributors, and applied in a nondiscriminatory manner; and (3) the selection criteria is necessary and proportionate. The main difference between qualitative and quantitative systems is that in quantitative systems, the number of distributors is directly (e.g., fixing the number of distributors) or indirectly (e.g., minimum or maximum sales) limited.

### 8.4.2 Block Exemption and Individual Exemption of Selective Distribution

As all vertical agreements, qualitative and quantitative selective distribution is exempted by the HUVBER as long as the market share of both supplier and buyer each does not exceed 30% and hardcore/excluded restrictions are not present. Block exemption applies regardless of the nature of the product concerned and regardless of the nature of the selection criteria. The HUVBER, similarly to Regulation 330/2010, sets forth the hardcore restrictions, which removes the benefit of block exemption in respect of the entire agreement in question. In case of selective distribution, these are (1) RPM, (2) restriction of sales to authorized distributors, (3) restriction of sales to end users, and (4) restriction of cross-supplies. Excluded restriction (where only the specific clause is null and void, not the entire agreement) in case of selective distribution is when the supplier limits the possibility of the distributor to sell specific competing brands.

Selective distribution not falling under block exemption, but not containing hardcore or excluded restrictions, is subject to case-by-case analysis. This assessment may lead to the finding that the distribution system (1) is not anticompetitive, (2) breaches the prohibition of anticompetitive agreements, or (3) falls under individual exemption due to the efficiencies created.

The HCA would likely follow the Guidelines on Vertical Restraints with respect to whether limitations on online sales in a selective distribution system are anticompetitive or not. In particular, that quality standards set by the supplier regarding online sales of the distributor are not anticompetitive in themselves (para. 54 of the Guidelines on Vertical Restraints), but the imposition of criteria for online sales that are not equivalent to the criteria for offline sales is anticompetitive (para. 56 of the Guidelines on Vertical Restraints).

The criteria for individual exemption are set forth in Section 17 of the Competition Act,[43] similarly to Article 101(3) TFEU. In case of limitations imposed by the supplier on online sales, the supplier would need to present evidence that the criteria for individual exemption are met.

### 8.4.3 Restriction of the Use of Online Sales Platforms in a Selective Distribution System

There is no Hungarian case law related to restrictions of sales through third-party Internet platforms. Hungarian practice will likely follow the guidance that is to be laid down in the Coty case,[44] where the CJEU will rule on whether bans on sales through online marketplaces in selective distribution systems is a restriction of competition by object and whether the preservation of a "luxury image" is an aspect of competition that is compatible with Article 101(1) TFEU. According to the opinion of AG Wahl,[45] contractual clauses prohibiting the use of third-party online sales platforms is compatible with Article 101(1) TFEU as long as the criteria under which purely qualitative selective distribution is not anticompetitive are met. The AG found that such a prohibition does not qualify as a restriction of sales to end users or as a restriction of passive sales; therefore, it cannot be considered as a hardcore restriction. It remains to be seen whether the CJEU will follow AG Wahl's opinion. However, the European Commission came to the same conclusion in its E-commerce Sector Inquiry.[46]

---

[43] Section 17 of the Competition Act reads as follows:

The prohibition defined in Section 11 shall not apply to an agreement if:

a) it contains facilities to improve the efficiency of production or distribution, or to promote technical or economic development, or the improvement of means of environmental protection or competitiveness;
b) a fair part of the benefits arising from the agreement is conveyed to final trading parties;
c) the concomitant restriction or exclusion of economic competition does not exceed the extent required for attaining the economically justified common goals;
d) it does not contain facilities for the exclusion of competition in connection with a considerable part of the goods concerned.

[44] CJEU, case C-230/16, *Coty Germany vs. Parfümerie Akzente GmbH.*

[45] Opinion of Advocate General Wahl delivered on 26 July 2017 in Case C-230/16 *Coty Germany GmbH v Parfümerie Akzente GmbH*, EU:C:2017:603.

[46] See Report from the Commission to the Council and the European Parliament, Final report on the E-commerce Sector Inquiry, 10.5.2017 COM(2017) 229 final, para 42.

The HCA may also take into account the CJEU's judgment in the Pierre Fabre case.[47] Under this decision, a (contractual or *de facto*) ban on the use of the Internet as a method of marketing did qualify ("at the very least") as a restriction of passive sales; therefore, it was considered as a hardcore restriction. However, the European Commission in the E-commerce Sector Inquiry found that marketplace bans cannot be equated to a prohibition to sell via the Internet; therefore, the relevance of this decision in this context may be limited.[48] Furthermore, pursuant to para. 54 of the Guidelines on Vertical Restraints, where the distributor's website is hosted by a third-party platform, the supplier may require that the distributor's website be not linked from a site carrying the name or logo of the third-party platform.

Restrictions on sales through third-party Internet platforms, as opposed to total ban on Internet sales, are narrower forms of online resale restraints. In essence, total ban on Internet sales (be it in any distribution arrangements, including selective distribution systems) leads to a prohibition from using the Internet for any sales by the distributor. Yet restrictions on sales through third-party Internet platforms (often referred to as "distribution channel related restrictions" or "platform bans") forbid the sales via predefined online platforms while leaving the sales permitted through other online channels.

Total ban on Internet sales typically constitutes an infringement of competition law (see the judgment of the CJEU in the Pierre Fabre case). The compatibility of distribution-channel-related restrictions with competition law is debated. These restrictions usually prohibit the distributors from using the renowned "open sales platforms" or "marketplaces" that have the largest outreach among customers, such as eBay, Amazon, or Alibaba. For a distributor, selling through these open sales platforms is a cost-effective way to reach a high number of customers without the need to invest in separate websites. Manufacturers (particularly those of high-quality branded products), in turn, frequently try to distance themselves from these open sales platforms where their products are displayed among numerous similar (in some instances possibly counterfeit) products of questionable quality. For these reasons, manufacturers often prohibit the use of these open sales platforms for their distributors or require certain quality criteria that they fail to meet.

The resulting restrained online visibility affects small and medium-sized dealers more adversely as they usually have limited resources for creating, adequately maintaining, and promoting their own online stores than their large rivals. In that sense, these platform bans constitute significant barriers to enter the market as they raise the costs of sufficient online presence. Further, even if a small and medium-sized dealer invests in its own online store, its customer outreach will not be comparable to that of the worldwide active open sales platforms. The limited online presence reduces the competitive pressure they are able to exert on large online distribution networks and brick-and-mortar stores. As a consequence, the

[47] ECJ, case C-439/09, *Pierre Fabre Dermo-Cosmétique SAS*, EU:C:2011:649.

[48] See Commission Staff Working Document – Accompanying the document Report from the Commission to the Council and the European Parliament, Final report on the E-commerce Sector Inquiry, 10.5.2017, SWD(2017) 154 final, para (503).

distribution-channel-related restrictions ultimately may result in appreciable detrimental effects on both intra-brand and inter-brand competition.

In the Alcon case,[49] the HCA took a hard line against restrictions of online commerce, ruling that the operation of a rebate system in which online distributors must meet more onerous conditions to get discounts than brick-and-mortar shops is a restriction of competition by object. The HCA regarded this as an agreement that the distributor pays a higher price for products sold online than offline, which is a hardcore restriction following para. 52(d) of the Guidelines on Vertical Restraints. Therefore, the agreement could not benefit from a block exemption, and it was not exempted individually. However, this decision did not go into the issue of prohibiting retailers from selling via third-party Internet platforms.

The right of suppliers in a (lawful) selective distribution system to prevent authorized distributors from selling to unauthorized distributors follows from the HUVBER. An analogy could be drawn here with prohibiting retailers from selling via third-party Internet platforms. If such an approach were adopted, a marketplace ban could be block exempted under the relevant market share thresholds.

Note that there is no presumption under Hungarian law that it is lawful to restrict sales to third parties. In fact, nevertheless, outside of the (lawful) selective and exclusive distribution systems, the scope for such restrictions is extremely limited. However, to the extent that distributors sell through, rather than to, the third-party Internet platform, the ban may not constitute a restriction of the customers to whom the distributor may sell.

The European Commission's E-commerce Sector Inquiry has also found that marketplace bans do not have the object of segmenting markets in the internal market based on territory or customers because they concern the question of how the distributor can sell the products over the Internet and do not have the object of restricting where or to whom distributors can sell the products.

From an economic perspective, such restrictions or bans can have both pro- and anticompetitive effects, and hence they may serve or damage consumer interests. Whether pro- or anticompetitive effects dominate is dependent on the overall welfare effects of the particular case. These effects should be weighed against each other on a case-by-case basis.

Such restrictions are anticompetitive if—in the long term—they lead to higher prices, lower quality, or restrictions on product choices. In an OTA setup, this could typically materialize in the form of lessening competition across platforms or barriers to market entry. If authorized distributors are obliged to use certain platforms only, this could lead to both unilateral price increases (due to market power of these platforms) and price increases through coordination between platforms. An efficient platform entry may solve these problems, but barriers to entry are already in place in the form of these restrictions and bans.

However, restrictions can also have procompetitive effects, e.g., through eliminating the possibility of free riding. In the case of OTAs, there are significant upfront costs involved when the platform is set up. An OTA also must pay for regular

[49] VJ/55/2013.

software updates, IT personnel, etc. to make consumer experience better (consumers can efficiently find the most suitable accommodations). If restrictions were not allowed, OTAs may not invest in such quality-enhancing features. They would be worried that consumers just use their services and once the most suitable accommodation is found, they would look for a cheaper alternative to pay for that accommodation.

## 8.5 Cooperation with Authorities

In Hungarian competition law, settlement procedures[50] have to be distinguished from commitment decisions.[51] Under Hungarian competition law, commitment decisions and settlements can be applied both for restrictive agreements and unilateral practices.

To date, unfortunately there are no HCA decisions in connection with online sales platforms, but theoretically the HCA may adopt a commitment decision or apply a settlement procedure also in case of anticompetitive restrictions applicable to such platforms.

### 8.5.1 Commitment Decision

A commitment decision is reached when the HCA accepts the undertakings of a party to proceed in a specific way to bring its conduct in line with the provisions of the applicable laws. The HCA may only accept such commitments if it properly ensures the protection of the public interest.

Undertakings proposing commitments want to avoid an infringement decision by voluntarily bringing their conduct in line with competition rules. Thus, one of the main purposes of the commitment is to close the proceedings of the HCA without any declaration of the infringement. Commitments become binding upon the HCA's decision to accept the undertaking's commitment proposal. This means that the undertaking that proposes commitments is not obliged to acknowledge its liability or to assist the HCA in investigating its own or other parties' misconduct beyond the obligation to act in good faith in the course of the procedure and not to mislead the HCA. A proposal for commitment may be filed at any time before the proceedings terminate. However, if the proposal is filed at an early stage of the proceedings (in the investigation phase) and therefore the HCA's procedural costs are substantially decreased, then the HCA may consider this as a reason in favor of accepting the commitment. If the HCA accepts the undertaking's commitments, the HCA does not impose fines and does not even declare the undertaking's conduct illegal. Then

[50] Section 73/A of the Competition Act.

[51] Section 75 of the Competition Act.

the HCA adopts a decision to dismiss the proceedings and to compel the party in question to undertake that commitment.

When the HCA imposes commitments on a party, it may launch a so-called follow-up investigation in order to assess whether the party has complied with the undertakings in the commitment decision. The HCA may revoke the commitment decision and impose a fine if the original decision was based on misleading information from the party in question or if the party has failed to comply with the imposed commitments. The deadlines of the follow-up investigation are much shorter (3 months, which may be prolonged for a total of 9 months). The difference in this case from the normal procedure is that the HCA needs to prove the noncompliance or the misleading conduct of the relevant party.

### 8.5.2 Settlement Procedure

In settlement procedures, the HCA, after the investigation report of the case handlers (i.e., when the facts have already been established), invites the parties to admit their involvement in the infringement under investigation. The undertaking participating in a settlement procedure may receive a reduction of up to 30% from the fine.

Settlement is aimed at the swift termination of the competition proceedings. The settlement declaration has to contain an acknowledgement of the undertaking's participation in the infringement. This means that successful settlement does not involve more far-reaching conduct requirements being imposed on the undertaking in addition to what the HCA may otherwise impose. In other words, it is not a precondition of a successful settlement that the undertaking commits to correct its conduct or indemnify third parties, etc.

It is the competition council (the decision-making body of the HCA) that may propose to the undertaking to file a settlement declaration. The competition council may do this before the statement of objections is finalized, which also means that the undertaking that makes a settlement declaration is not obliged to assist the HCA in investigating its own or other parties' misconduct. If the competition council makes such a proposal, the undertaking must answer within the deadline set by the competition council, which cannot be more than 15 days.

If the undertaking makes a settlement declaration, it has to indicate to the HCA what it considers as the acceptable maximum amount of fines. If the HCA imposes fines in excess of this amount or if the statement of objections or the final decision significantly differs from the settlement declaration, the settlement declaration may be withdrawn. In such case, the undertaking's previous acknowledgement of the infringement cannot be used as evidence.

The Settlement Notice[52] deals with the question of noncompliance with settlement decisions. The party that participates in a settlement procedure may only revoke the written settlement statement in the following circumstances:

- the HCA decision differs on the merits from the settlement agreement between the party and the HCA;
- the fine imposed on the relevant party is higher than the maximum amount of fine set out in the settlement agreement between the party and the HCA.

If the party concerned unlawfully revokes the settlement statement or otherwise breaches its obligation to cooperate under the settlement rules (confidentiality requirement, waiving the right to apply for remedy against the final decision of the HCA, etc.), the HCA may decide to close the settlement procedure and proceed in the ordinary course. In that case, the HCA may use the documents obtained during the settlement procedure as evidence, and the party's breach of its obligation will be considered by the HCA as an aggravating circumstance in the setting of the fine. The HCA may also impose a procedural fine on the party in question. The difference in this case from the normal procedure is that the HCA needs to prove that the party to the settlement procedure breached its obligation listed above.

### 8.5.3 Effects of Commitment and Settlement

Commitment decisions help the clarification of law since this tool is normally used in cases where, for example, there is no crystallized case law and, therefore, undertakings may be uncertain how to act. By way of a commitment decision, the HCA can signal if a certain conduct is problematic and the commitments accepted can show the "way out."

As settlement decisions are supposed to be used if the unlawfulness of a conduct is crystal clear and the finding of an infringement is supported by evidence, this type of decision does not hinder the development of standards of analysis, although—clearly—it does not improve it either.

The commitment most likely to be accepted by the HCA is a compensation of affected consumers. Thus, a commitment decision leads directly to consumer remedies. However, a successful settlement procedure may also mean that victims of the infringement will be compensated sooner since the HCA's procedure terminates in a shorter time and there will not be any lengthy subsequent judicial review procedure.

The undertakings also must bear in mind that their acknowledgement of the infringement in the settlement declaration may put other undertakings, which still dispute the infringement, in a more difficult situation.

[52] Notice No. 3/2015 of the President and Vice-President of the HCA on settlement procedures, the Hungarian language Notice is available at http://www.gvh.hu//data/cms1035560/2015_3_egyezsegi_kiserlet_kozlemeny_egyseges_szerkezetben_20170115.pdf.

## 8.6 Private Enforcement in Case of Online Sales

### 8.6.1 General Considerations

In Hungary, private antitrust litigation and damage actions are possible, and they are based on the general rules of Hungarian law governing liability for damages caused in noncontractual situations and relationships. The applicable rules for damage actions are in line with the Antitrust Damages Directive,[53] which was implemented into the Competition Act in December 2016 and entered into force on January 15, 2017.

The Hungarian regime applies the full compensation system, which ensures that any natural or legal person that has suffered harm caused by an infringement of competition law is able to claim and to obtain full compensation for that harm. In order to avoid any overcompensation, it is expressly stated in the Competition Act that passing-on defense is available, so the defendant in an action for damages can invoke as a defense against a claim for damages the fact that the claimant passed on the whole or part of the overcharge resulting from the infringement of competition law.

The Competition Act also ensures that the final decision of the HCA is binding on the courts in the infringement part of the decision; therefore, only the quantification of harm shall be proved in the court proceedings. The burden of proof regarding the quantification is on the claimant; however, a very unique Hungarian rule can be invoked by the claimants in case of cartels. According to this rebuttable presumption, it is presumed that the antitrust infringement had a 10% effect on the prices. The defendants can rebut this presumption (e.g., if proven that claimants passed on the overcharge), but the claimants can also prove that they suffered more damages, i.e. the degree of the overcharge exceeded 10%.

### 8.6.2 Punitive Damages

No punitive damage claim is available in the Hungarian civil law regime. By virtue of the *non bis in idem* principle, no one can be held liable twice or more for the same conduct, i.e. the damage actions cannot aim to penalize the infringing party; the only objective can be to restore the situation that existed before the damage had been caused. The HCA may impose a fine on the infringing parties (which financial penalty is of a public law nature rather than a civil law consequence); however, the sole objective of the civil court proceedings is and can only be to compensate the entire loss suffered by the claimant by granting damages. The Hungarian full compensation doctrine also excludes overcompensation, by means of punitive or multiple damages.

[53] Directive 2014/104 of the European Parliament and of the Council of 26 November 2014 on certain rules governing actions for damages under national law for infringements of the competition law provisions of the Member States and of the European Union, OJ 2014 L 349, p. 1.

### 8.6.3 Use of Competition Law as Defense

The link between the civil law consequences of an unlawful agreement and an antitrust infringement is created by the Competition Act when declaring that for any agreement or other arrangement violating the prohibition of anticompetitive conducts (provided for by the Competition Act) the general civil law rules and consequences relating to unlawful contracts are equally applicable. Such contracts are null and void under Hungarian law, and the most important consequence of such nullity is the unenforceability of the agreement. If an agreement is unenforceable, none of the parties are entitled to enforce the performance of the other party at court. Note that the general rule relates to the partial nullity of contracts only; i.e., only the unlawful part of the agreement is null and void, unless the nullity relates to such a significant element of the agreement without which the parties would not have entered into the agreement. Having said that, agreements violating competition rules are—as a general rule—unlawful since such significant terms are affected by unlawfulness (such as pricing, territorial restrictions, etc.), which results in the complete nullity of the agreement.

As stated above, any of the parties can refuse to perform such an unlawful agreement by referring to nullity. If the other party disputes the nullity of the agreement, it in principle can take legal action against the nonperforming party to enforce performance (and by alleging that nonperformance was a breach of the agreement). In such a scenario, the party not intending to perform the agreement can refer to the nullity thereof based on its conflict with competition law. If such a defense is successful, the court will declare the agreement as null and void from the date of entering into the agreement by the parties, and as such no breach of the agreement can be established (null and void agreements cannot be breached). Consequently, the party successfully defending its position by reference to the unlawfulness due to competition law violations will be exempt from the liability for breach of contract (vis-à-vis the other contracting party). Nevertheless, vis-à-vis third parties, the liability of both parties still remains in place should it be the case that their competition law infringement has caused damages to third parties. Such noncontractual liability cannot be lawfully excluded and can only be mitigated—to a certain extent—by applying for leniency or entering into settlement.

Further, a successful civil law defense will not result in an exemption from any competition law consequences (fines) or criminal law consequences (in case of bid rigging) either. Such consequences can only be avoided if the relevant party seeks leniency under the rules of competition law (public administrative law) or potentially under criminal law. According to newly introduced Hungarian competition law rules, leniency is possible even in vertical relationships (in RPM cases). It is again noted that not even full immunity from fines granted in a leniency program will result in lifting the civil law liability for damages caused by competition law violations.

We are not aware of cases in the area of online sales platforms in Hungary where a contractual term was alleged to be unlawful due to competition law infringement and the party alleging such unlawfulness has defended its breach by referring to the nullity of the said term.

## 8.7 Applying Competition Law to the New Economy

In Hungary, there are no antitrust or competition law rules and case law that would suggest that changes in the substance of the competition rules are required in order to deal more sensibly with the "new economy" of "Internet-related" and "computer software" enterprises.

Competition laws have had to grapple with a range of problems that—though not unique to the new economy—are more prevalent, more important, or simply more complex when applied to the new economy. The general nature of the competition rules gives them an important advantage over most other legal rules because they apply to the factual circumstances of a particular case, no matter how quickly industries develop or change. This allows them to keep pace with technological developments, in a way that more specific regulatory frameworks cannot.

The competition rules stay the same, but the application of these rules is remarkably adaptable to changing circumstances. Thus, there is no need for new rules or new principles or a challenge to the fundamentals of competition enforcement. However, there is a need to understand the markets of new industries and how principles of competition law are applicable to those industries. This requires competition authorities to understand the underlying technology/business model and to closely follow market developments.

The Internet-related new economy may benefit consumers from several aspects:

- It can increase transparency, both in terms of the goods and services available and the price of those goods and services.
- It can reduce transaction costs, ultimately benefitting consumers.
- It can lead to growth in the size of markets and lowering barriers of entry: it allows companies to compete in wider geographic areas than would otherwise be possible. The availability of goods and services of the company on the Internet allows them to enter otherwise not reachable markets. Although consumer demand and regulatory considerations may moderate these benefits, these factors are changing in parallel with the development of the new economy: consumers are more ready to purchase online, and both product regulations and online regulations are becoming more and more harmonized.

The above benefits may require a shift in the analysis of restrictions connected to online sales. However, these benefits need to be assessed on a case-by-case basis. Also, a change in the assessment of restrictions by object in this field seems unlikely. Currently, the benefits of online sales cannot be categorized; thus, competition law regulation (e.g., adopting online-specific block exemption regulations) does not seem possible.

# Italy

# 9

Francesca La Rocca

## 9.1 Background

The Internet is at the centre of our daily life, and according to some recent surveys, 95% of Italians between the age of 25 and 44 use smartphones to surf online. Even more interestingly, there has been a steady growth in the use of e-commerce in recent years.[1] In 2016, this growth regarded the sector of luxury goods and finance investment in particular, where more and more consumers use apps to conclude their transactions.[2]

However, Italy still lags behind the main western markets (United Kingdom, France, Germany and USA), where the use of e-commerce has almost quadrupled.[3] Moreover, data show that only a small percentage of Italian enterprises trade online.[4]

[1] Google Consumer Barometer 2015 – Insight of Italy. https://storage.googleapis.com/think-v2-emea/docs/infographic/CB_wave_2_Italy_infographic_translated_FINAL_4.pdf. Accessed 13 June 2017.

[2] Think with Google, Ricerca di Mercato. Shopping, Finanza e Viaggi: il Ruolo dei Siti e delle App per Dispositivi Mobili nel Percorso verso l'Acquisto. https://www.thinkwithgoogle.com/intl/it-it/research-study/shopping-finanza-e-viaggi-il-ruolo-dei-siti-e-delle-app-per-dispositivi-mobili-nel-percorso-verso-lacquisto/. Accessed 13 June 2017.

[3] Eurostat, Digital Economy and Society Statistics – Households and Individuals. http://ec.europa.eu/eurostat/statistics-explained/index.php/Digital_economy_and_society_statistics_-_households_and_individuals. Accessed 13 June 2017.

[4] Eurostat, Digital Economy and Society statistics – Enterprises. http://ec.europa.eu/eurostat/statistics-explained/index.php/Digital_economy_and_society_statistics_-_enterprises. Accessed 13 June 2017.

F. La Rocca (✉)
Studio Legale Sena e Tarchini, Milan, Italy
e-mail: senatarchini@senatarchini.com





B. Kilpatrick et al. (eds.), *Antitrust Analysis of Online Sales Platforms & Copyright Limitations and Exceptions*, LIDC Contributions on Antitrust Law, Intellectual Property and Unfair Competition,
https://doi.org/10.1007/978-3-319-71419-6_9

In 2016, online sales B2C increased by 16–17% in Italy compared to the previous year, achieving a turnover of EUR 16 billion, while the annual growth for the B2B is approximately 20%, with a turnover of EUR 28.8 billion.[5]

From a legal standpoint, specifically regarding the definition of the relevant market, the main question is whether online distribution and e-commerce are a separate market from the traditional 'brick and mortar' one.

Furthermore, we should consider whether EU and national competition laws in force—in particular Regulation 330/2010 on vertical agreements—are adequate to solve all issues raised by e-commerce.

One of the main novelties of Regulation 330/2010 concerned online sales. The need to protect sales online derives from the fact that the advantages that this form of sale brings to the consumers are twofold. The first concerns the prices. Not only are online prices often lower, but they also constitute a competitive pressure on the prices practised by the physical shops. In addition, the possibility to shop online, enabling cross-border commerce, widens the range of the products from which consumers can choose.

However, online sales may have an adverse impact, for example, on luxury brands, due to the fact that an indiscriminate access to the sales network of virtual operators can disrupt the orders and the traditional dynamics, with undue forms of unfair competition against traditional 'brick and mortar' distributors.

A further cause for concern for producers and chains of traditional distribution drifts from the necessity to limit free riding. A typical example of free riding is when a buyer of a technological product that goes to a brick-and-mortar shop to benefit from pre-sale services and acquire all necessary information to decide whether to buy or not purchases online.

Lastly, geo-blocking, the practice by which e-commerce sites filter out users based on location, is relatively widespread in the EU[6] and in Italy, which gives rise to novel issues that the current law is unable to solve.

## 9.2 Substantive Law

The relevant competition rules in Italy are Article 101 TFEU and Article 2 of Law 287/1990 on restrictive agreements. Article 101 TFEU states that agreements for the purchase or sale of goods or services concluded between non-competing undertakings, between certain competitors or by certain associations of retailers of goods are generally considered unlawful, unless all conditions stated in its paragraph 3 are met. Therefore, a restrictive agreement is allowed if it contributes to improve the production or distribution of goods or to promote technical or economic progress, while allowing consumers a fair share of the resulting benefit, and one that does not

[5] Casaleggio Associati, E- Commerce in Italy 2016, 3 May 2017. https://www.casaleggio.it/focus/rapporto-e-commerce-in-italia-2017/. Accessed 10 June 2017.

[6] Commission Staff Working Document 18 March 2016, SWD (2016). http://ec.europa.eu/competition/antitrust/ecommerce_swd_en.pdf. Accessed 25 May 2017.

impose on the undertakings restrictions that are not indispensable to the attainment of these objectives and afford such undertakings the possibility of eliminating competition in respect of a substantial part of the products in question.

Article 101 TFEU corresponds to the Italian provision Article 2 of Law 287/1990 on antitrust, but considering that usually the restriction on online sales have an impact on intra-Community commerce, direct referral is made to the EU rule.

This is also because Article 1, paragraph 4, Law 287/1990 imposes an interpretation of the Italian antitrust norms that conform to the principles of the European antitrust and competition legislation; therefore, the application of Article 2 of Law 287/1990 would hardly bring different conclusions in comparison with the application of Article 101 TFEU.[7]

The prohibition of the restrictive agreements covers both horizontal and vertical agreements. The latter intervene among two or more working enterprises operating at a different level of the chain of production or distribution. The prohibition of restrictive vertical agreements deals in particular with online sales as a type of distribution channel.

The European Commission has adopted Regulation 330/2010, related to categories of vertical agreements and concerted practices, and the relative Guidelines on Vertical Restraints.[8]

The Regulation is binding for the Italian Competition Authority and for the Italian judges,[9] while the Guidelines on Vertical Restraints are not mandatory for the national authorities.

Regulation 330/2010 establishes the conditions by which categories of vertical agreements can be considered compatible with Article 101 TFEU and, therefore, are automatically exempted from the prohibition of Article 101 TFEU.

According to Article 4, let. b), of Regulation 330/2010, restriction of 'passive sales' is considered a hardcore restriction, while the restriction of territory regarding 'active sales', when it is limited to the clients or to the territories reserved to the supplier or attributed exclusively to another distributor, is allowed.

In any case, to be able to benefit from the automatic exemption of Regulation 330/2010, the market share of both parties to the agreement, supplier and buyer, must not exceed the threshold of 30%. The market share of the supplier is calculated on the basis of the data related to the value of the sales on the market where it sells the contract products to the buyer, while the market share of the buyer in based on the market where it purchases the contract products. For agreements between small and medium-sized undertakings, it is generally not necessary to calculate markets

[7] This is true also in consideration of Article 3 para 2 of Regulation 1/2003, under which national competition law may apply stricter laws on their own territory, but they can only do so to the extent that such laws do not impact upon the application of Article 101 TFEU (formerly Article 81 TCE) to those that affect trade between Member States.

[8] The Commission Regulation 330/2010 of 20 April 2010 has substituted the previous Commission Regulation 2790/99, of 22 December 1999 on the application of Article 81 para 3 of the Treaty to categories of vertical agreements and concerted practices.

[9] Only specialised courts have judicial competence on antitrust matters.

shares. The previous Regulation 2790/99 limited the evaluation only to the market share of the supplier.

Online sales are considered to be passive sales because it is a reasonable way to allow consumers to reach the distributor. Therefore, every distributor should be able to sell the products online.[10] Consequently, from the moment that the restriction of passive sales constitutes a hardcore restriction, any attempt to limit the use of the Internet by the producer does not enjoy any benefit of the exemption stated by the Regulation, and it is very unlikely that it can satisfy the conditions of exemption under Article 101 para 3 TFEU; however, not all sales made on the Internet should be qualified as a passive sale.

The Guidelines on Vertical Restraints recognise that there are some restrictions to the use of the Internet that are compatible with the Regulation because they are directed to prevent ways of promotion or sale that can qualify as active sales. The Guidelines on Vertical Restraints give a series of examples of online active and passive sales. They are useful examples, but they do not succeed in eliminating all the uncertainties regarding the application of the rules.

Indeed, the definition of 'passive sale' given by the Guidelines on Vertical Restraints is not entirely clear. It defines one determined advertising action as 'passive sale' because the underlying investment is interesting for the distributor if it does not reach territories or groups of clients assigned to other distributors.[11] The distinctive criterion is based therefore on an element of subjectivity, which can lead to conflicting conclusions. In practice, the uncertainty is not insignificant: it deals with establishing if a restriction is qualifiable as hardcore or not, and the conclusion may also have an impact on the validity of the whole distribution contract, making the parties liable to administrative fines by the Italian Competition Authority or the European Commission and damage action brought by third parties.

Only a few cases have been decided by the Italian Competition Authority and judges.

## 9.3 Restriction of Online sales

### 9.3.1 Restrictions Considered as Passive Sales

The Guidelines on Vertical Restraints give a few examples of passive sales; restrictions on passive sales in vertical agreements are hardcore restrictions and fall outside the Commission's block exemption regulation on vertical restraints.[12]

They clarify that if a customer chooses to be kept automatically informed by the distributor and this leads to a sale, then that is considered passive selling. Therefore, information disseminated through a newsletter requested by customers situated anywhere cannot be forbidden.

[10] Para. 52 of the Guidelines on Vertical Restraints.

[11] Para. 52 of the Guidelines on Vertical Restraints.

[12] Para. 51and 52 of the Guidelines on Vertical Restraints.

Also, the choice of language used on the website or for communications is considered a passive form of marketing. According to this, a distributor to which the producer has assigned the Italian territory will be able to insert on its own website special options that allow the consumer to enter the same contents in different languages.

These provisions raised some complexities also in light of the definition of passive sale. Indeed, it is not clear why an Italian distributor would consider it interesting to translate its site in another language, for example in Swedish, if it is not to sell in such country. Furthermore, it has been argued that the use of domain names and currencies different from the one used on the territory assigned to the distributor (for example, the 'xxx.se' domain name or the Swedish crown currency) shall be considered an active sale.[13]

Furthermore, it may be considered a hardcore restriction a clause that prohibits the distributor to allow consumers of another country to visit its website or that obliges the distributor to automatically redirect consumers to the site of the supplier or other exclusive distributors.[14] However, this does not exclude the possibility that the distributor's website may offer links to websites of other distributors or the supplier.

An agreement pursuant to which the exclusive distributor is obliged to terminate transactions over the Internet once the consumer's credit card data reveal an address that is not within the distributor's exclusive territory is also considered a hardcore restriction.[15]

Another restriction of passive selling consists in an agreement in which the distributor shall limit its proportion of sales made over the Internet.[16] On the other hand, it is possible for the supplier to impose that a certain percentage of sales is made offline, but it cannot be established a maximum threshold, in value or volume, of sales that can be made through the Internet channel.

Lastly, it is considered a hardcore restriction an agreement that the distributor shall pay a higher price for products intended to be resold online than products intended to be resold offline.[17] However, fixed fees (not a variable fee where the sum increases with the realised offline turnover as this amounts indirectly to dual pricing) aiming to sustain the efforts of offline or online sale of the buyer are allowed. However, it is not entirely clear in practice what modalities would be allowed. In effect, in case the producer establishes a fixed remuneration for the sales online, combined with a fixed quantity of products to sell, this would correspond to a system of dual pricing, which is exactly what the rule wants to avoid.

The Guidelines on Vertical Restraints state that an agreement that provides for dual pricing may profit from an individual exemption if the sales online substantially

[13] E. De Giorgi, Le Vendite On-line e la Normativa Antitrust. In: G.Cassano, G. Scorza and G. Vaciago (eds), Diritto dell'Internet, CEDAM 2013, p. 368.

[14] Para. 52, let. a) of the Guidelines on Vertical Restraints.

[15] Para. 52, let. b) of the Guidelines on Vertical Restraints.

[16] Para. 52, let. c) of the Guidelines on Vertical Restraints.

[17] Para. 52, let. d) of the Guidelines on Vertical Restraints.

leads to higher costs for the manufacturer than do offline sales. This may happen in the event the online selling provokes more complaints and warranty claims for the manufacturer.[18] This specific provision is inspired by a Dutch case in which the distributor sold online kitchens without providing instructions or an installation service, and the manufacturer had to supply this information and assistance.[19]

In 2013, the Italian Competition Authority started an inquiry[20] on the conditions of online sale imposed by Enervit, a manufacturer of integrators and alimentary products intended to satisfy the demand connected to specific sports nutrition activities, upon its own distributor, which foresaw the formulation of a minimum price of resale, in the form of an indication of a maximum percentage of discount applicable to the consumer, and the imposition of an obligation of sale of the product exclusively on the territory and through channels allocated exclusively to the distributor. In the course of the proceedings, Enervit offered a set of commitments that the Italian Competition Authority considered likely to overcome the antitrust concerns raised in the decision of opening the proceeding. More precisely, Enervit committed to not send any letter or communication to its distribution network providing for the application of an extra discount on the supply price in case of compliance with the minimum resale price suggested and to consider null and void the letter sent to only one pharmacy containing such a provision; to not influence in any manner, either directly or indirectly, its online and offline distributors in the definition of their resale pricing strategy; and to send its 'pure' online distributors and dealers a communication informing them that they are completely free to determine the sell-out prices and related discounts. These measures were considered likely to guarantee the effective freedom of distributors in determining their resale prices so as to eliminate any risk of intra-brand competition restriction to the benefit of final consumers.[21]

More recently, on 17 May 2017, the Italian Competition Authority started an investigation against Cadel, a manufacturer and supplier of pellet and wood burning stoves for alleged online sales restrictions, in breach of Article 101 TFEU.[22] The target of the Italian Competition Authority's investigation is the commercial policy that Cadel has adopted at least since 2006 for its online distribution channels with the apparent strategic aim to preserve a proper margin and prevent online dealers from selling Cadel trademarked products at absurdly low prices.

The relevant product market affected by under scrutiny business practices of Cadel is the market for the manufacture and commercialisation of pellet stoves and kitchens.

The Italian Competition Authority had concerns that some of the rules and terms included in the Cadel online commercial policy would constitute anti-competitive vertical restraints as they would limit to a relevant extent the marketing of the Cadel products via online channels.

---

[18] Para. 64 of the Guidelines on Vertical Restraints.

[19] District Court Zutphen, 8 August 2007, n. 79005/HA ZA 06-716.

[20] Italian Competition Authority, 20 November 2013, n. 24619.

[21] Italian Competition Authority, 9 July 2014 n. 25021, *Enervit -Distribution contracts.*

[22] Italian Competition Authority, 17 May 2017, n. 26616, *Restrizioni alle vendite online di stufe.*

More precisely, the Italian Competition Authority's attention was attracted by the terms in Cadel's commercial policy. Indeed, Cadel required online dealers to charge the minimum sale prices, which were the list prices and the maximum discounts indicated by Cadel. The Italian Competition Authority took the position that such arrangements would be an RPM, which is a competition restraint by object. The Italian Competition Authority also stressed that the alleged RPM concerns the online distribution channels that are considered by the European Commission as powerful tools to reach as many customers as possible.

Further restrictions on online sales imposed by Cadel included the following: an obligation to market the Cadel products only through Italian sites registered with the domain '.it', a prohibition on using languages other than Italian for online offers of Cadel products, delivery of Cadel products limited to the Italian territory, a stipulation that only the dealers admitted to the Cadel distribution network were allowed to offer and sell the Cadel products online.

The Italian Competition Authority had concerns that such terms and rules might give rise to anti-competitive territorial restriction to the online sales of Cadel's products.

### 9.3.2 Objective Justification for Online Sales Restrictions

Exceptionally, some hardcore restrictions stated in a vertical agreement may be objectively necessary, and therefore they do not fall within the prohibition laid down by Article 101 TFEU.

Even if no specific rule is provided regarding online sales, it can be maintained that a limitation of online selling of goods due to public prohibition of sale of dangerous substances to determined clients for health and security reasons is allowed. However, to invoke the security norms and the clause on dangerous products, there should be a specific law imposing those norms for the goods that are the subject of the agreement.

### 9.3.3 Restrictions Justified to Protect the Quality of the Distribution and to Prevent Free Riding

The Guidelines on Vertical Restraints admit the possibility of imposing a series of direct obligations to the distributor to safeguard the quality of the distribution (for instance, in terms of pre- and after-sale services) and to prevent the possibility that online distributors take advantage of investments made by those distributors that use physical stores.

Firstly, the supplier may require its distributors, as a condition for becoming a member of its distribution system, to have at least one brick-and-mortar shop.[23]

[23] Para. 54, of the Guidelines on Vertical Restraints.

More specifically, according to the Guidelines on Vertical Restraints, the producer may exclude purely virtual distributors from its own sales network. The fact that the supplier can also require the distributor to have 'one or more brick and mortar shops'[24] allows the supplier to avoid a situation whereby a distributor with a single physical shop with a limited proportion of sales (thus de facto an online distributor) may compete with distributors that have invested in physical shops. It is also possible for the producer to require that the distributor limit its store and deposit to an allocated territory or area.[25]

However, the final report of the EU commission on e-commerce[26] has recognised that even if the brick and mortar requirements are generally covered by Regulation 330/2010, certain requirements to operate at least one brick-and-mortar shop without any apparent link to distribution quality and other potential efficiencies may require further scrutiny in individual cases.

On the other hand, it is questionable if the producer may require from the distributor that the products sold online have to be collected in a brick-and-mortar shop. Probably the answer will vary according to the type of product.

Furthermore, the manufacturer may require, without limiting the online sales of the distributor, that the buyer sell at least a certain absolute amount (in value or volume) of products offline to ensure an efficient operation of its brick-and-mortar shop.[27] It is also specified that the absolute amount of required offline sales can be the same for all buyers or determined individually for each buyer on the basis of objective criteria, such as buyer's size in the network or its geographic location.

Another possibility for the manufacturer is to require that the distributor's website also offer a number of links to websites of other distributors or suppliers.[28] In this way, the consumer will be able to visit the website in its own language, and the quality of the distribution system is maximised.

Lastly, the manufacturer may require quality standards for the usage of the Internet website to resell its goods, just as the supplier may require for a shop or for selling by catalogue or for advertising activities.[29]

The standards that the manufacturer may require to be met may regard the quality and the characteristics of the website or the modalities of selling via the Internet.

For the time being, no decision has been made by the Italian Competition Authority or judges that clarify what kind of quality standards may be considered lawful.

However, the requests made by the manufacturer to the distributor to dedicate a special space on the website for the products and not to associate the products with

[24] Para. 54, of the Guidelines on Vertical Restraints.

[25] Para. 50, of the Guidelines on Vertical Restraints.

[26] Report from the Commission to the Council and the European Parliament, Final report on the E-commerce Sector Inquiry. http://ec.europa.eu/competition/antitrust/sector_inquiry_final_report_en.pdf. Accessed 29 May 2017.

[27] Para. 52, of the Guidelines on Vertical Restraints.

[28] Para. 52, of the Guidelines on Vertical Restraints.

[29] Para. 54, of the Guidelines on Vertical Restraints.

others that could diminish their image or value, to give information and specific suggestions on the products with the possibility for consumers to ask questions regarding the products and to ensure specific terms of delivery may all be considered compatible with Regulation 330/2010.[30]

The Guidelines on Vertical Restraints also envisage that a manufacturer may require that its distributors use third-party online platforms (such as marketplaces) to distribute its products only in accordance with the standards and conditions agreed between the manufacturer and its distributors. However, the quality standard should not discriminate the sales online to advantage the sales offline.[31]

There is no specific rule that states if a prohibition to use a specific form of online sales (such as auctions) or to use online marketplaces (such as Amazon or eBay), because deemed by the supplier to be harmful for the image of its product, should be considered a hardcore restriction or not. Nevertheless, it may be claimed that absolute marketplace bans do not generally amount to a de facto prohibition to sell online, but they concern the way the distributor sells its products online and do not have the object to restrict where and to whom distributors can sell.[32] This solution would be consistent with the case law of the European Court of Justice.[33]

## 9.4 Online Sales and Selective Distribution

The notion of selective distribution is contained in Article 1, let. 3), of Regulation 330/2010, according to which a system of selective distribution is when the supplier undertakes to sell the goods or services that are the object of the contract directly or indirectly to selected distributors on the basis of specific criteria and in which these distributors undertake not to sell such goods or services to unauthorised retailers in the territory that the supplier has reserved for such system.[34] Therefore, only designated retailers and end consumers can become buyers.

Selective distribution systems are an important distribution model for luxury and premium-branded goods. The use of quality criteria that retailers need to meet in order to become part of the distribution network allows manufacturers to have a

[30] A. Frignani and A. Sonnati, La Distribuzione via Internet nell'Unione Europea prima e dopo il Regolamento 330/2010: I Giudici Hanno Compreso l'Economia di Internet?, Diritto del commercio Internazionale, 2016, p. 627.

[31] Such principle had been stated by the European Court of Justice in two cases: ECJ, case C-26/76, *Metro SB-Großmärkte GmbH & Co. KG v Commission of the European Communities*, ECR 1977 1875; ECJ, case C-31/80, *NV L'Oréal and SA L'Oréal v PVBA De Nieuwe AMCK*, ECR 1980 3775.

[32] Preliminary report of E-commerce Sector Inquiry, para. 469. http://europa.eu/rapid/press-release_IP-16-3017_en.htm. Accessed 20 May 2017.

[33] CJEU, case C-439/09, *Pierre Fabre Dermo-Cosmétique SAS v. Président de l'Autorité de la Concurrence and Ministre de l'Économie, de l'Industrie et de l'Emploi*, ECR 2011 I 9419.

[34] Differently from exclusive distribution agreements in distribution agreements the restriction of the number of dealers depend on selection criteria linked to the nature of the product and not on the number of territories. Another difference is that restriction on resale is a restriction on any sales to non-authorised distributors and not a restriction on active selling to a territory.

better control of the distribution quality and to alleviate free riding by retailers that do not make adequate investments in providing a quality consumer experience.

Within selective distribution systems, two types are distinguished. The first category comprises systems of purely qualitative selective distribution, in which the retailers are entirely selected on the basis of objective criteria related to the nature of the product, the level of professional qualification of the personnel employed to the sales, the service provided by every authorised points of sale, the sale of one determined range of products. Purely qualitative selective distribution systems do not fall within the prohibition of Article 101 TFEU, provided that three conditions are met: the nature of the product in question must make a system of selective distribution necessary, in the sense that such system is necessary to preserve the qualities and to ensure a correct use of the product; the choice of the distributors must indiscriminately occur according to the objective criteria of a qualitative nature; and the criteria in question must not go beyond what is necessary.[35]

On the other hand, quantitative selective distribution limits in a more direct way the potential number of distributors, for example imposing a minimum or maximum level of purchases and fixing the number of distributors.

According to para. 56 of the Guidelines on Vertical Restraints, dealers in a selective distribution system should be free to sell, both actively and passively, to all end users, also with the help of the Internet. Therefore, it is a hardcore restriction for a supplier to impose any obligation that prevents the designated retailers from using the Internet to reach a greater number and a variety of customers, by imposing criteria for online sales that are not overall equivalent to those imposed for brick-and-mortar stores.

However, this does not mean that the criteria imposed for online sales must be identical to those imposed for offline sales but rather that they should pursue the same goals and achieve similar results, and any difference should be justified by the different nature of these two distribution modes. Indeed, the main point is to prevent measures that limit sales on the Internet.

Anyway, the producer may impose quality standards also regarding the website and require that the distributor have at least one brick-and-mortar shop and where it should be located.

In such regard, the Italian Chamber of Fashion held the distribution via brick-and-mortar shops to be of great importance for the fashion industry. Indeed, according to the Italian Chamber of Fashion, this requirement contributes towards enhancing consumers' experience, in particular given that fashion articles are designed to be tried on and worn by consumers and their quality to be judged in person. In addition, it stated that this approach minimises free riding by pure online sales players on the significant investments made by high-quality physical points of sale.[36]

[35] CJEU, case C-439/09, *Pierre Fabre Dermo-Cosmétique SAS v. Président de l'Autorité de la Concurrence and Ministre de l'Économie, de l'Industrie et de l'Emploi*, ECR 2011 I 9419, para 41.

[36] Camera Nazionale della Moda Italian, Contribution to the Public Consultation on the European Commission's Preliminary Report on the E-commerce Sector Inquiry, http://ec.europa.eu/competition/antitrust/sector_inquiries_e_commerce.html. Accessed 20 May 2017.

Lastly, according to the Guidelines on Vertical Restraints,[37] a supplier, in order to prevent sales to non-authorised dealers, can restrict its selected dealers from selling more than a given quantity of contract products to an individual end user.

## 9.5 MFN Clauses and the Definition of Relevant Market

In 2014, the Italian Competition Authority took action against the online travel agencies named Booking and Expedia in order to examine whether the 'Most Favoured Nation' (hereinafter 'MFN') clauses of the contracts concluded by the two online travel agencies (OTA) and their hotel partners in Italy may integrate a vertical restriction in violation of Article 101 TFEU.

In its contracts with hotels, Booking.com obliged them to always offer their best prices, maximum room capacity, and best cancellation and booking conditions in comparison with what they offered on other platforms and through their online and offline direct booking channels. Similar clauses exist with regard to other significant platforms, such as Expedia.

The Italian Competition Authority held that such conditions could infringe Article 101 TFEU because they could result in a restriction of competition between platforms since the level of commissions applied to hotels by platforms does not affect room rates applied to end users, which boost platforms to raise commission rates. Furthermore, an MFN clause creates entry barriers for new platforms and creates eviction risks.

During the legal proceedings, Booking and Expedia spontaneously undertook to modify the contracts by removing 'wide MFN clauses' and equivalent measures, consisting in price and non-price (e.g., availability) parity clauses, with respect to other OTAs and to the hotel's offline channels, which is expected to stimulate competition between platforms and restore hotels' abilities to differentiate prices between platforms. However, Booking.com would be allowed to continue using 'narrow MFN clauses' preventing hotels from offering lower prices through their own website. Hotels remain free to advertise discounts online without publishing the amount of such discounts and to grant the OTA different availability conditions than through their own sales channels. Therefore, the Authority dismissed the cases because the grounds for action no longer prevailed.

The Italian Competition Authority admitted that allowing narrow MFN clauses may be necessary to prevent hotels from free riding on the important investments made by platforms, such as the cost of marketing and maximum visibility through search engines allowing the hotel partner to offer better prices and conditions on its offline channels.

These decisions are also interesting because the Authority has expressly stated that the 'relevant market' to be considered in those cases was the Italian online market, distinguished from one of distribution through traditional physical stores. This is in consideration of the fact that every day consumers prefer to book their hotels

[37] Para. 56 of the Guidelines on Vertical Restraints.

online, the agency taxes and the services offered by the online agency are different from the ones offline; thanks to online travel agencies, hotels can reach a higher number of potential consumers.

However, this difference is not so explicit in all the markets.

In the market of consumer goods, for example, the buyer can have advantages, thanks to the complementarity of both channels. Indeed, the online experience provides important information on the characteristics and availability of the products, and consumers can read reviews on them. However, only offline can the consumer understand the quality of the goods and take better advantage of the pre- and after-sale services.

## 9.6 European Commission's E-Commerce Sector Inquiry

On 6 May 2015, the European Commission launched the sector inquiry into e-commerce as part of the Digital Single Market Strategy on the basis of European Union competition rules.

On 15 September 2016, the Commission published a Preliminary Report on the e-commerce sector inquiry setting out its initial findings.[38]

On 10 May 2017, the Commission adopted the Final Report on the e-commerce sector inquiry and published the accompanying Staff Working Document, which sets out the main findings of the e-commerce sector inquiry, taking into account the views and comments submitted by stakeholders during the public consultation. The Report is divided into two separate sections: the first section covers e-commerce of consumer goods, and the second focuses on e-commerce of digital content.[39]

The Report confirms that the growth of e-commerce over the last decade, and in particular increased online price transparency and price competition, had a significant impact on companies' distribution strategies and consumer behaviour.

In particular, a large proportion of manufacturers have decided over the last 10 years to sell their products directly to consumers through their own online retail shops, thereby competing increasingly with their distributors.

Furthermore, the Report shows that the use of selective distribution systems has increased, where products can only be sold by pre-selected authorised sellers, allowing manufacturers to better control their distribution networks, in particular in terms of the quality of distribution, as well as prices.

Consequently, the use of contractual restrictions to better control product distribution has also increased. Depending on the business model and strategy, such restrictions may take various forms, such as pricing restrictions, marketplace (platform) bans, restrictions on the use of price comparison tools and exclusion of pure online players from distribution networks.

---

[38] Preliminary report of E-commerce Sector Inquiry. http://europa.eu/rapid/press-release_IP-16-3017_en.htm. Accessed 30 May 2017.

[39] Report from the Commission to the Council and the European Parliament, Final report on the E-commerce Sector Inquiry. http://ec.europa.eu/competition/antitrust/sector_inquiry_final_report_en.pdf. Accessed 29 May 2017.

Some of these practices may be justified, for example in order to improve the quality of product distribution; others may unduly prevent consumers from benefiting from greater product choice and lower prices in e-commerce and therefore warrant Commission action to ensure compliance with EU competition rules.

With respect to digital content, the results of the sector inquiry confirm that the availability of licences from content copyright holders is essential for digital content providers and a key factor that determines the level of competition in the market.

The Report points to certain licensing practices that may make it more difficult for new online business models and services to emerge. Any assessment of such licensing practices under the EU competition rules has, however, to consider the characteristics of the content market.

One of the key findings of the sector inquiry is that almost 60% of digital content providers that participated in the inquiry have contractually agreed with right holders to 'geo-block'.

## 9.7 Geo-blocking

Geo-blocking is a practice used by online sellers where access to Internet content is restricted based upon the user's geographical location.

There might be justified reasons for traders not to sell cross-border, such as the need to register at the tax authority in the country of destination, higher shipping costs or costs arising from the application of foreign consumer law. While outside barriers create additional complications and extra costs for the trader, differences in the treatment of customers are based on objective criteria.

However, discrimination between EU customers based on the desire to segment markets along national borders, in order to increase profits to the detriment of foreign customers, is considered as unjustified geo-blocking.

Geo-blocking and other geographically based restrictions undermine online shopping and cross-border sales by limiting the possibility for consumers and businesses to benefit from the advantages of online commerce.

In 2015, a Commission survey found that only 37% of websites actually allowed cross-border customers to reach the final step before completing the purchase by entering payment details, while 38% of the respondent consumer goods retailers and 68% of respondent digital content providers geo-block consumers located in other EU Member States.

In May 2016, the Commission made a legislative proposal after assessing the responses from a public consultation held in 2015. This proposal prohibits the blocking of access to websites and other online interfaces and the rerouting of customers from one country to another. It furthermore prohibits discrimination against customers in specific cases of sale of goods and services and does not allow the circumventing of such a ban on discrimination in passive sales agreements. Therefore, online sellers will not be able to discriminate against consumers elsewhere in the EU in their general terms and conditions (including those relating to pricing) on the basis of their nationality, place of residence or even their temporary location. Both consumers and businesses as end users of goods or services are affected by such practices and should therefore benefit from the rules set out in this proposal. Transactions where goods or services are purchased by a business for resale should, however, be excluded in order to allow traders to set up their distribution systems in compliance with European competition law.

Some sectors remain, for the time being, outside the scope of the draft Regulation. These include audiovisual services (such as the broadcasting of sports events that are provided pursuant to exclusive territorial licences) and financial, transport, electronic communication or healthcare services.

On 25 April 2017, the European Parliament's Committee on Internal Market and Consumer Protection voted to approve amended draft legislation to ban unjustified geo-blocking in B2C relationships and now begin the negotiations with the Council and the Commission with the aim of reaching an agreement on the final legislation.

## 9.8 Conclusions

Over the past decade, the Web has quickly become a powerful channel for the distribution of goods. Its development has brought about significant changes in distributors' strategies. The expansion of the Internet has also created new economic players, including online-only sellers, such as eBay and Amazon.

More and more goods and services are traded over the Internet worldwide. However, the Commission's Digital Single Market Strategy has underlined that cross-border online sales within the EU are only growing slowly and have identified a number of regulatory barriers that hinder cross-border e-commerce and proposes different initiatives to address these.

There are also indications that businesses may themselves establish barriers to cross-border online trade, with a view to fragmenting the market along national borders and preventing competition. The Commission has therefore launched an inquiry to gather market information in order to better understand the nature, prevalence and effects of these barriers and to assess them in light of EU antitrust rules.

The preliminary results of the Commission's competition sector inquiry on e-commerce show that the use of these restrictions is widespread throughout the EU.

Under certain circumstances, these practices may make cross-border shopping or online shopping in general more difficult and ultimately harm consumers by preventing them from benefiting from greater choice and lower prices in e-commerce. Such behaviour may breach competition rules that prohibit anti-competitive agreements between undertakings.

In order to overcome this anti-competitive practice, it is important to harmonise the laws at least between EU countries, given that the Internet allows commerce worldwide. However, not everything can be predicted and disciplined by the law; therefore, national competition authorities and judges will have to assess on a case-by-case basis, having regard to the characteristics of a specific product and the geographic market, whether certain agreements may restrict competition and whether enforcement is necessary in order to ensure effective competition.

# Sweden

# 10

Robert Moldén, Henrik Nilsson, and Dagne Sabockis

## 10.1 Introduction

In 2017, almost 10% of all trade in Sweden was made online. According to the Swedish Retail and Wholesale Council, approximately 20% of all Swedish retail sales will be made online as early as 2020.[1] A recent report of the Swedish Competition Authority shows that while online trade constitutes a relatively small part of the overall trade in Sweden, nevertheless the general growth of online trade in the EU puts additional competitive pressure on the Swedish companies.[2] Moreover, the European Commission's Digital Single Market Strategy[3] currently

[1] Report of the Swedish Trade Council on the importance of trade ('Handelns betydelse. Då, nu och i framtiden'), 2017, pp. 29–30. The report can be accessed at handelsradet.se/ekonomiska-radet.

[2] Swedish Competition Authority's Report 2017:2 on competition and growth in the digital markets ('Konkurrens och tillväxt på digitala marknader'), March 2017, p. 148. The report can be accessed at www.konkurrensverket.se/globalassets/publikationer/rapporter/rapport_2017-2.pdf.

[3] Communication from the Commission to the European Parliament, the Council, the European Economic and Social Committee and the Committee of the Regions, 'A Digital Single Market Strategy for Europe', COM(2015) 192 final.

R. Moldén (✉)
Front Advokater, Gothenburg, Sweden

Stockholm School of Economics, Stockholm, Sweden
e-mail: Robert.Molden@front.law

H. Nilsson
Wesslau Söderqvist, Stockholm, Sweden
e-mail: Henrik.Nilsson@wsa.se

D. Sabockis
Stockholm School of Economics, Stockholm, Sweden

Wesslau Söderqvist, Stockholm, Sweden
e-mail: dagne.sabockis@phdstudent.hhs.se



B. Kilpatrick et al. (eds.), *Antitrust Analysis of Online Sales Platforms & Copyright Limitations and Exceptions*, LIDC Contributions on Antitrust Law, Intellectual Property and Unfair Competition,
https://doi.org/10.1007/978-3-319-71419-6_10

being implemented means that a package of new EU legislation in the area of online sales will directly affect the Swedish markets. It is likely that it will also have ripple effects on EU and Swedish competition law.

## 10.2 Positive Law

### 10.2.1 Swedish Competition Law in Overview

The Swedish Competition Act of 2008[4] contains provisions prohibiting anti-competitive agreements and abuse of a dominant position, which constitute copies of Articles 101 and 102 TFEU.[5] According to the *travaux préparatoires* behind the

---

[4] Konkurrenslagen (2008:579).

[5] The relevant provisions of the Swedish Competition Act prohibiting both horizontal and vertical anti-competitive cooperation between undertakings are the following:

> Chapter 2, Article 1: 'Agreements between undertakings shall be prohibited if they have as their object or effect, the prevention, restriction or distortion of competition in the market to an appreciable extent, if not otherwise regulated in this act.
>
> This shall apply, in particular, to agreements which:
>
> 1. directly or indirectly fix purchase or selling prices or any other trading conditions;
> 2. limit or control production, markets, technical development, or investment;
> 3. share markets or sources of supply;
> 4. apply dissimilar conditions to equivalent transactions with other trading parties, thereby placing them at a competitive disadvantage; or
> 5. make the conclusion of contracts subject to acceptance by the other parties of supplementary obligations, which by their nature or according to commercial usage have no connection with the subject of such contracts.'
>
> Chapter 2, Article 2: 'The prohibition in Article 1 does not apply to agreements which
>
> 1. contribute to improving the production or distribution or to promoting technical or economic progress;
> 2. allow consumers a fair share of the resulting benefit;
> 3. only impose on the undertakings concerned restrictions which are indispensable to the attainment of the objective referred to in paragraph 1, and
> 4. do not afford such undertakings the possibility of eliminating competition in respect of a substantial part of the utilities in question.'
>
> Chapter 2, Article 6: 'Any agreements or provisions included in agreements that are prohibited under Article 1 shall be void.'
>
> The relevant provision of the Swedish Competition Act prohibiting abuse of a dominant position is the following:
>
> Chapter 2, Article 7: 'Any abuse by one or more undertakings of a dominant position on the market shall be prohibited.
>
> Such abuse may, in particular, consist in
>
> 1. directly or indirectly imposing unfair purchase or selling prices or other unfair trading conditions,
> 2. limiting production, markets or technical development to the prejudice of consumers,

preceding Competition Act,[6] the fact that the substantive provisions of the Swedish Competition Act are in line with those of EU competition law means that the Commission's practice and jurisprudence of the Court of Justice of the European Union can serve as guidance when interpreting the Swedish Competition Act.[7]

The Swedish Supreme Court has, in a case concerning the existence of a dominant position,[8] concluded that the substantive provisions of Swedish competition law are in line with the corresponding provisions of EU competition law to the extent that it in effect does not matter for the outcome whether Swedish or EU competition law is applied.

Public enforcement of Swedish competition law is assigned to the Swedish Competition Authority[9] and its approximately 150 employees. In the majority of cases handled by the Swedish Competition Authority, the procedure is very similar to that of the Commission's DG Competition and to that of most other national competition authorities in the EU. The Swedish Competition Authority is entitled to take both final and interim injunction decisions on its own,[10] ordering an ongoing violation of Swedish or EU competition law to be terminated; such decisions can be combined with a penalty to be paid in case the antitrust offender does not comply with the injunction decision.[11] Moreover, the Swedish Competition Authority is entitled to take decisions making voluntary commitments mandatory, under threat of penalty payments.[12] The Authority is also entitled to issue non-mandatory fine orders.[13]

A peculiarity of Swedish procedural competition law consists of the fact that the Swedish Competition Authority may not take any mandatory decision on its own to impose fines for breaches of Swedish or EU competition law. In these cases, the Swedish Competition Authority has to sue the undertakings involved before the Swedish Patent and Market Court at Stockholm District Court.[14] It is thus the Swedish Patent and Market Court that may impose a fine, as a first instance court.

---

3. applying dissimilar conditions to equivalent transactions with other trading parties, thereby placing them at a competitive disadvantage, or
4. making the conclusion of contracts subject to acceptance by the other parties of supplementary obligations, which by their nature or according to commercial usage have no connection with the subject of such contracts.'

[6] The Swedish Competition Act of 1993, Konkurrenslagen (1993:20).

[7] See prop. 1992/93:56 p. 21.

[8] Judgment of the Swedish Supreme Court in case T 2808-05 of 19 February 2008, *The Ystad Harbour Case*.

[9] Konkurrensverket.

[10] Chapter 3, Articles 1 and 3 of the Swedish Competition Act.

[11] Chapter 3, Article 1 and Chapter 6, Article 1 of the Swedish Competition Act.

[12] Chapter 3, Article 4 and Chapter 6, Article 1 (2) of the Swedish Competition Act.

[13] Chapter 3, Article 17 of the Swedish Competition Act; if the undertaking to which the fine order is addressed does not consent to the order within the time specified, the Swedish Competition Authority may initiate court proceedings concerning fines instead.

[14] Patent- och marknadsdomstolen; see Chapter 7, Article 1 of the Swedish Competition Act. Patent- och marknadsdomstolen replaced the previous Marknadsdomstolen on the 1 September 2016.

The judgments of the Swedish Patent and Market Court can only be appealed to the Swedish Patent and Market Court of Appeal at Svea Court of Appeal.[15] The general rule is that a further appeal to the Swedish Supreme Court is not possible. The Swedish Act on Patent and Market Courts of 2016 does allow exceptions from this regulation, yet only when the Patent and Market Court of Appeal deems such an appeal to be needed. According to the preparatory works behind the Act on Patent and Market Courts of 2016,[16] an appeal to the Swedish Supreme Court could come into question only if there is a general need for a more overarching precedent where other areas of law come into play as well.[17] There are no known judgments that have been appealed to the Swedish Supreme Court under this regulation yet.

A 2016 government-commissioned report proposed expanding the powers of the Swedish Competition Authority to also include the issuing of fines without a prior ruling of the Patent and Market Court. The idea is to align the Competition Authority's powers with those of the European Commission, as well as make the enforcement of competition law more effective.[18] A draft bill based on the report was submitted to the Swedish Council of Legislation (Lagrådet) for further scrutiny in August 2017.[19] As of 1 January 2018, the Swedish Competition Act was modified, entitling the Swedish Competition Authority to take decisions to block mergers. However, the Swedish Competition Authority did not receive any additional rights to take decisions on its own in other areas of competition law.

Another peculiarity of Swedish competition procedural law is that private injunction claims to cease any ongoing infringement of Swedish or EU competition law may not be brought directly to court. First, a complaint has to be made to the Swedish Competition Authority. If the Swedish Competition Authority decides to investigate the matter, the Authority would take an injunction decision, which then could be appealed to the Swedish Market Court; in these proceedings, the complainant does not enjoy any standing as a party. If, however, the Swedish Competition Authority decides not to pursue the case, the complainant obtains a so-called subsidiary right of action. The complainant can then directly lodge her case at the Swedish Patent and Market Court, which may then take an injunction decision.[20]

---

[15] Patent- och marknadsöverdomstolen, www.patentochmarknadsoverdomstolen.se.

[16] Lag (2016:188) om patent- och marknadsdomstolar.

[17] See prop. 2015/16:57, p. 165.

[18] See Swedish Government Official Report SOU 2016:49 on expanding the decisive rights for the Swedish Competition Authority (En utökad beslutanderätt för Konkurrensverket).

[19] Lagrådsremiss Ändringar i konkurrenslagen of the 17 of August 2017 is available at www.regeringen.se/4a3c7a/contentassets/82fc8f5e617247779ae5d20151f59ee4/andringar-i-konkurrenslagen-slutlig-webb.pdf.

[20] Chapter 3, Article 2 of the Swedish Competition Act.

### 10.2.2 Definition of the Relevant Market

Swedish competition law is highly influenced by EU competition law and should be interpreted in the light of the Treaties of the EU.[21] Therefore, all competition cases of the CJEU, the regulations of the Council of the EU, as well as the notices, guidelines and other documents of the European Commission, are of relevance even in the Swedish jurisdiction. Thus, the main rules on market definition are to be found in the Commission's Notice on the relevant market.[22] The Notice on the relevant market is followed by the Swedish Competition Authority and the Swedish courts.[23] The relevant market is thus defined according to the EU competition law, according to which both a relevant product and a relevant geographic market need to be defined. The Commission's Notice on the relevant market stipulates as follows:

> A relevant product market comprises all those products and/or services which are regarded as interchangeable or substitutable by the consumer, by reason of the products' characteristics, their prices and their intended use.[24]
>
> The relevant geographic market comprises the area in which the undertakings concerned are involved in the supply and demand of products or services, in which the conditions of competition are sufficiently homogeneous and which can be distinguished from neighbouring areas because the conditions of competition are appreciably different in those area.[25]

Both product and geographical markets are tested by looking at the substitution of the product or the geographical area from the consumers' perspective. A hypothetical, *small but significant non-transitory increase in price* is used as a test to define the relevant market: the SSNIP test. If a 5–10% increase in price of a certain product would result in the consumers substituting the product with a different one, or if this would mean that the consumers choose a product from a different geographical area, the product market, or in the latter case the geographical market, should be considered as belonging to the same relevant market. An additional requirement is that the substitution leads to a decrease of profitability for the undertaking in question. The SSNIP test is then applied in greater geographical areas and with different products, until the increase in price does not result in demand substitution. Substitution on the supply side is taken into consideration in cases where the suppliers are able to switch their production quickly and without significant additional costs as a response to small and permanent changes in the prices. Potential competition is not taken into account at this stage.[26]

The report of the Swedish Competition Authority shows that Swedish companies are facing competition from other European countries online as a result of the

[21] See prop. 1992/93:56 p. 21.

[22] Commission Notice on the definition of relevant market for the purposes of Community competition law, OJ 1997 C 372, p. 5.

[23] See, *e.g.*, case NJA 2008 s 120 of the Swedish Supreme Court of 19 February, 2008.

[24] Notice on the relevant market, para. 7.

[25] Notice on the relevant market, para. 8.

[26] Notice on the relevant market, paras 14–24.

growth of online trade in the EU. In practice, this means that the relevant geographic market will in the future more often include not only different parts of Sweden but also other countries in the EU or EFTA.[27]

### 10.2.3 Cases Dealing with Internet-Related Markets

Swedish precedent on online sales platforms and other Internet-related markets is still fairly scarce. Guidance is currently mainly sought in the decisions of the Swedish Competition Authority. Relevant decisions are presented first in a chronological and then in a thematic order below.

**The *Reitan* Case of 2006**[28]
*Reitan Servicehandel AB* had obliged its franchisees *Pressbyrån* and *7-Eleven* convenience store chains to use a computer program to price *Reitan's* products, which constituted the major part of the franchise stores' inventory. The program made it difficult for the franchisees to individually set prices on such products. The Swedish Competition Authority also found that the franchisees in practice also followed the recommended prices provided in *Reitan's* system. The investigation was closed after *Reitan* made certain voluntary commitments making it easier for the franchisees to deviate from the recommended prices.

**The *Make Up Store* Decision of 2010**[29]
Similarly to the previous case, *Make Up Store* was put under investigation by the Swedish Competition Authority for the use of a certain cashier system. *Make Up Store* recommended its franchisees to use the same system; however, only *Make Up Store* could change the prices in the system. The investigation of *Make Up Store* was closed after the company offered voluntary commitments consisting of changing the cashier system so that the franchisees were enabled to set the prices themselves.

**The *Booking.com* Decision of 2015**[30]
An online travel agency, *Booking.com*, operated an online platform on which consumers could search for, compare and book hotel rooms. Customers could make bookings directly on *Booking.com*; however, the hotels connected to the platform were not allowed to offer lower prices on any other platforms, including their own websites. The Swedish Competition Authority initially viewed this as an

[27] Report of the Swedish Competition Authority on competition and growth in the digital markets, p. 148.

[28] Decision of the Swedish Competition Authority of 6 February 2006, file ref. 994/2004.

[29] Decision of the Swedish Competition Authority of 15 December 2010, file ref. 402/2010. Robert Moldén, one of the authors of this report worked at that time as a Senior Case Officer at the Swedish Competition Authority and served as senior advisor ('projektråd') to the case-team handling the Make Up Store case.

[30] Decision of the Swedish Competition Authority of 15 April 2015, file ref. 596/2013.

anti-competitive conduct, but the investigation was closed after *Booking.com* offered a set of voluntary commitments, including a commitment not to enter into or enforce obligations that require hotels to offer room prices on *Booking.com* that are equal to or lower than those offered on any other online travel agency.

### The *Expedia* Decision of 2015[31]

At the same time as the *Booking.com* case, the Swedish Competition Authority also investigated *Expedia*, one of *Booking.com's* competitors. *Expedia* applied the same type of price parity clause as *Booking.com* towards the hotels that were connected to its platform. Also in this case, a voluntary commitment by *Expedia* to discontinue the application of its narrow price parity clause in the agreements with the hotels was accepted by the Swedish Competition Authority, and the investigation was closed.

### The *Onlinepizza* Decision of 2016[32]

*Onlinepizza*, an online platform where consumers could order meals from restaurants connected to the platform, was investigated by the Swedish Competition Authority for possibly pressuring its clients not to cooperate with a competing online platform, *Pizzahero*. *Pizzahero* claimed that *Onlinepizza* applied an exclusivity clause in its agreements with the restaurants. The Authority concluded that the clause was not exclusive, either formally or in practice. Also in this case, the investigated company decided to make a voluntary clarification of the non-exclusivity of the clause, which the Competition Authority accepted, then it closed the investigation.

### The *Nasdaq OMX* Case (Ongoing)[33]

The Swedish Competition Authority filed a lawsuit against *Nasdaq OMX AB* for an abuse of its dominant position towards its competitor, *Burgundy*. The Swedish Competition Authority claimed that *Nasdaq* pressurised its server provider, *Verizon*, to deny *Nasdaq's* competitor, *Burgundy*, access to *Verizon's* servers. According to the Authority, the denial of access to *Verizon's* servers, where both *Nasdaq* and many strategically important clients were hosted, created a competitive disadvantage for *Burgundy*. The Court found that *Nasdaq* had a de facto decisive power of the part of the server hall that it rented from *Verizon*, based on the contract between the two. Hence, *Nasdaq* had the right to prohibit further connections to its servers, why no abuse was found.

---

[31] Decision of the Swedish Competition Authority of 5 October 2015, file ref. 595/2013.

[32] Decision of the Swedish Competition Authority of 4 April 2016, file ref. 658/2015.

[33] Judgment of the Swedish Patent and Market Court, ref. no. PMT 7000-15 of 15 January 2018, Swedish Competition Authority v Nasdaq.

**European Commission's *Google* Online Comparison Shopping Case**[34]

The Commission found that *Google* abused its dominance, among others, on the Swedish online search engine market by giving an illegal advantage to its own comparison shopping service in its search results. *Google's* own comparison shopping service was shown on the first page of the search results, whereas other comparison shopping services were displayed much lower in the following pages. This practice increased the online traffic for *Google's* services and limited the traffic to its competitors. The abuse was found in 13 European countries, and the total fine issued was EUR 2.42 billion.

#### 10.2.3.1 Cases on Retail Price Maintenance (RPM)

**The *Reitan* Case of 2006**[35]

According to the franchise agreements between *Reitan Servicehandel i Sverige AB* and its franchisees in the *Pressbyrån* and *7-Eleven* chains, the franchisees had to use a specific computer program for the pricing of their products, which was also used for calculating the franchise fee. Through the computer program, Reitan supplied its franchisees with recommended consumer prices. The Swedish Competition Authority found that the program made it practically difficult for the franchisees to set prices individually to consumers. Moreover, the Authority found that the franchisees to a large degree followed the recommended prices. *Reitan* offered to make a voluntary commitment that would make it easier for the franchisees to deviate from the recommended prices and apply individual retail prices. The Swedish Competition Authority accepted these commitments under the threat of fines amounting to SEK 3 million.[36] The Competition Authority did not mention the technical aspects of the price-setting arrangements. However, the reasoning of the Authority's decision does suggest that the way the technical system was set up constituted the reason behind the Competition Authority's investigation in the first place.

**The *Make Up Store* Decision of 2010**[37]

In this case, the Swedish Competition Authority started an investigation of *Make Up Store's* control of the prices set by its franchisees. *Make Up Store* used a certain cashier system, which it also recommended to its franchisees. This system provided fixed prices for all products, and only *Make Up Store* was enabled to change the prices in the system, thus making it technically impossible for franchisees to set their own prices. *Make Up Store* also provided the franchisees with

[34] Commission Decision in the Case number 39740. The main pints of the reasoning of the Commission can be found in the Commission's Press Release of the 27 of June 2017, IP/17/1784.

[35] Decision of the Swedish Competition Authority of 6 February 2006, file ref. 994/2004.

[36] Case Ä 3237-06 at the Stockholm District Court, 24 March 2006.

[37] Decision of the Swedish Competition Authority of 15 December 2010, file ref. 402/2010. Robert Moldén, one of the authors of this National Report worked at that time as a Senior Case Officer at the Swedish Competition Authority and served as senior advisor ('projektråd') to the case-team handling the Make Up Store case.

shelve-top product information labels with printed prices, as well as internal order lists with fixed prices. The Swedish Competition Authority's preliminary view was that this kind of resale price maintenance infringed Chapter 2, Article 1, of the Swedish Competition Act. The company offered voluntary commitments, which, in short, consisted of changing the cashier system so that the franchisees were able to change the prices themselves. In addition, the company changed the prices in the order lists from fixed to recommended, as well as the routines for the shelve-top product information. The Swedish Competition Authority accepted these commitments and closed the investigation. The decision of the Swedish Competition Authority does mention that there were technical barriers for the franchisees to choose their own prices for *Make Up Store's* products. Yet it does not state that the *Make Up Store's* cashier system required any special legal attention due to the technical nature of such a possible anti-competitive arrangement.

#### 10.2.3.2 Cases on Most Favoured Nation (MFN) Conditions

**The *Booking.com*[38] and *Expedia*[39] Decisions of 2015**

*Booking.com*, an online travel agency, operated an online platform on which consumers could search for, compare and book hotel rooms. The consumers could search and compare different hotels on the platform free of charge. Also, the hotels connected to *Booking.com* paid a commission fee only if a booking was made through the platform. However, the agreement between *Booking.com* and the hotels included a term that prohibited the connected hotels from offering a lower price in their own sales channels and on competing platforms. The Swedish Competition Authority's preliminary assessment was that the so-called most favoured nation clause or price parity clause could violate the prohibition of anti-competitive cooperation in Chapter 2, Article 1, of the Swedish Competition Act.

At the same time, the Swedish Competition Authority investigated *Expedia*, a competitor of *Booking.com*, for using the same type of price parity clause as the one applied by *Booking.com*. In addition, the agreement between *Expedia* and the hotels contained parity clauses regarding room availability, cancellation policy and breakfast.

In its decision in the *Booking.com* case, the Competition Authority stated that the price parity clause had effects on both horizontal and vertical relationships. Competition between *Booking.com* and its competitors was restricted since no competitor cooperating with the hotels connected to *Booking.com* could offer lower prices than the ones on *Booking.com*. Moreover, the clause could constitute a barrier to entry in regard to new and small platforms that are not able to compete with low commission fees. The vertical effects of the price parity clause were, however, not considered to be problematic from the competition law perspective. The Competition Authority found that hotels and *Booking.com* as such operated on different markets and that the vertical price parity was necessary for *Booking.com* to be able to

[38] Decision of the Swedish Competition Authority of 15 April 2015, file ref. 596/2013.

[39] Decision of the Swedish Competition Authority of 5 October 2015, file ref. 595/2013.

continue providing the search and comparison services to consumers free of charge. Without such a clause, the hotels would have an incitement to offer lower prices on their own channels, thus escaping the commission fees due to *Booking.com*. The Competition Authority came to the same conclusion in its *Expedia* decision, referring to the decision in the *Booking.com* case.

During the investigation, both companies offered voluntary commitments to discontinue the application of their narrow price parity clauses. The Swedish Competition Authority accepted the commitments, asked the Stockholm District Court to place the companies under threats of penalty payments and closed the investigations, stating that the conduct that was initially regarded as anti-competitive was no longer applied. In both cases, the price parity clauses requiring the hotels to refrain from offering lower room prices on hotels' own websites were not seen as restrictions of competition with the reasoning that the hotels and the online travel agencies did not compete on the same market. Therefore, the Authority concluded that such vertical price parity clauses did not pose any threat to competition.

#### 10.2.3.3 Cases on Exclusionary Behaviour

**The *Onlinepizza* Decision of 2016**[40]

The Swedish Competition Authority dealt with an online platform, *Onlinepizza*, through which consumers could order meals from restaurants that were connected to the platform. After a complaint from *Pizzahero*, a competitor of *Onlinepizza*, the Swedish Competition Authority decided to investigate *Onlinepizza's* alleged pressure towards its clients to either choose *Onlinepizza* or *Pizzahero's* platform by applying an exclusivity clause in its agreements with the restaurants. However, the Competition Authority found that the clause in the agreements between *Onlinepizza* and the restaurants did not constitute an exclusivity clause either formally or in practice. Therefore, the Authority dismissed the case. It should, however, be noted that *Onlinepizza* updated the relevant clause, making its non-exclusivity clearer on a voluntary basis during the investigation. The reasoning of the Competition Authority does not include any discussion regarding the fact that the object for the investigation was an online platform.[41]

**The Ongoing *Nasdaq OMX* Case**[42]

A case that has received a lot of media attention in Sweden is the ongoing *Nasdaq* case. The Swedish Competition Authority filed a lawsuit against the stock exchange company *Nasdaq OMX AB* for abusing its dominant position in the market for trading services for Swedish, Danish and Finnish shares. The Competition Authority

---

[40] Decision of the Swedish Competition Authority of 4 April 2016, file ref. 658/2015.

[41] This was the second time *Onlinepizza* was notified to the Swedish Competition Authority – for a more or less the same conduct. The first notification took place in 2013, by another competing online platform *Pizza24*. The Competition Authority did not proceed with the claim and *Pizza24* sued *Onlinepizza* in front of the Swedish Market Court. The Court stated that the relevant market could not be defined and dismissed the claim without discussing the competition rules further; see Judgment of the Swedish Market Court in case MD 2015:1 of 10 February 2015, Pizza24 Nordic.

[42] Judgment of the Swedish Patent and Market Court, ref. no. PMT 7000-15 of 15 January 2018, Swedish Competition Authority v Nasdaq.

claimed that *Nasdaq* raised a barrier to entry for *Burgundy AB*, a competing stock exchange market, by pressurising *Nasdaq's* server provider, *Verizon*, to deny *Burgundy* the possibility to use *Verizon's* services. Both *Nasdaq* and its clients had their servers placed in *Verizon's* premises, which reduced the costs and the speed of communication among them. The Competition Authority claimed that by having its servers placed in the same server hall as *Nasdaq* and its clients, *Burgundy* would have been able to reduce the costs and the speed of communication between its actual and potential clients. The Authority's investigation showed that the speed of the communication is one of the main competitive advantages for the stock exchange markets and that the server hall was hosting several of the most important clients in the market. After conducting a dawn raid in *Nasdaq* and *Verizon's* premises in 2011, the Competition Authority claimed to have found documents proving that *Nasdaq* threatened to move all its business out of *Verizon's* premises, as well as to make this affect the global relations between *Nasdaq* and *Verizon*, which made the latter to cancel all its negotiations with *Burgundy*. The Competition Authority asked the Swedish Patent and Market Court to issue a fine of SEK 31 million (around EUR 3 million) against *Nasdaq* for hindering *Burgundy* from competing on fair and equal terms by abusing its dominant position. This corresponds with the highest possible fine under the circumstances according to the Swedish competition legislation.[43]

The lawsuit of the Competition Authority contains a thorough description of the specifics of the stock exchange market, pointing to its high time and technology sensitivity. In the lawsuit, the Authority argues that a big part of all the stock exchange is based on algorithms that are set up in advance and allow the sale and purchase of the stocks to be executed automatically.

The Swedish Patent and Market Court found errors in the way the Competition Authority had defined the relevant market and stated that despite *Nasdaq's* high market shares, the presumption of dominance was not applicable in this case. The Court thus made an overall evaluation of the evidence, where factors such as earlier monopoly history, importance of liquidity, potential competition, barriers to entry, *Nasdaq's* pricing, countervailing buyer power, market shares and whether *Nasdaq* was a necessary trading partner were considered. The Court found that *Nasdaq* was dominant on the EU-wide market for trading services for Swedish, Danish and Finnish shares, but that it had not abused its position. The Court concluded that *Nasdaq* had a de facto decisive power of the part of the server hall that it rented from *Verizon*, which was based on its contract with *Verizon*. *Nasdaq's* contractual rights were thus attacked by *Verizon* and *Burgundy* collectively, in which case, the Court stated, *Nasdaq* must have had some freedom in its actions. The judgment is currently under appeal by the Swedish Competition Authority.

### European Commission's *Google* Online Comparison Shopping Case[44]

One of the most recent cases in which exclusionary anti-competitive behaviour on the Swedish online markets, among others, was punished is the European

[43] Chapter 3, Article 6 of the Swedish Competition Act.

[44] Commission Decision in the Case number 39740. The main pints of the reasoning of the

Commission's decision of 27 June 2017 fining *Google* for abusing its dominant position on the market for online search engines. The Commission opened the case on the European level in 2010 and, 7 years later, concluded the investigation by stating that *Google* showed its own comparison shopping service much higher in its search results than *Google's* competitors on the comparison shopping service market online. According to the Commission, this meant that *Google's* competitors received less visitors. Moreover, the abusive practice allowed *Google* to expand its own market shares significantly and to the prejudice of its competitors and the consumers.[45] *Google* and its parent company, *Alphabet*, were fined EUR 2.42 billion in total, a fine that will have to be paid if the companies do not stop the abusive practice within 90 days from the Commission's decision. The case is now pending in front of the General Court, after *Google's* appeal in September 2017.

### 10.2.4 Compensatory Damages Arising from Competition Law Infringements

The possibility of damages in case of competition law violations is regulated in the Swedish Competition Damage Act of 2016.[46] A company that intentionally or negligently causes damage by infringing Chapter 2, Article 1 or Article 7, of the Swedish Competition Act or Article 101 or Article 102 TFEU is liable for damages that arise from that infringement. The person harmed by the infringement has the right to full compensation for actual loss and for loss of profit, as well as the payment of interest. All companies taking part in an infringement are jointly and severally liable for the damages; however, the right to compensation expires by statute of limitations 5 years after the damage has ceased. It is interesting to note that in cartel cases, damage is presumed.

Punitive damages based on competition law infringements are not awarded under Swedish law. The general principle is that the damages awarded cannot be higher than the damages suffered. The principle was recently reiterated in the EU Damages Directive, which explicitly prohibits punitive damages.[47] The Directive was implemented in Sweden by the Swedish Competition Damages Act of 2016, mentioned above.[48]

A recent Swedish case where a company was sued for damages due to violations of Chapter 2, Article 2, of the Swedish Competition Law by another private

Commission can be found in the Commission's Press Release of the 27 of June 2017, IP/17/1784.

[45] According to the Commission, since the beginning of the abuse in each country, *Google's* comparison shopping service increased its traffic 45 times in the United Kingdom, 35 times in Germany, 29 times in the Netherlands, 17 times in Spain and 14 times in Italy. In Sweden, the exclusionary practice was implemented since 2013, but *Google's* increase in the Swedish market is not mentioned in the public documents yet. See the Commission's Fact Sheet on the case, 27 of June 2017, MEMO/17/1785.

[46] Konkurrensskadelagen (2016:964). The Act implements the EU Directive 2014/104 of the European Parliament and of the Council of 26 November 2014 on certain rules governing actions for damages under national law for infringements of the competition law provisions of the Member States and of the European Union, JOEU 2014 L 349, p. 1.

[47] Directive 2014/104, see Recital 3.

[48] Konkurrensskadelag (2016:964), see Chapter 3, Article 1.

undertaking shows that the burden of proof in private damages lawsuits appears to be difficult to meet—at least under the previous regulation of private damages in competition infringement cases.[49] It remains to be seen whether the new Swedish Competition Damage Act of 2016 will ease the burden in practice.

### 10.2.5 Competition Law as a Defence Against Breach of Contracts

Competition law can be used as a defence against allegations of breach of contract by arguing that the obligation breached is unlawful. One of the most interesting judgments in Sweden in this regard is the *SAS* v *Luftfartsverket* case. On 27 April 2001, the Göta Court of Appeal ruled that Luftfartsverket, the Swedish authority in charge of civil aviation, had abused its dominant position by discriminating against *SAS*, which had to pay higher fees than its competitors for using a specific terminal at the Stockholm Arlanda airport.[50] The case did not involve any damages. However, the Göta Court of Appeal found that the abuse by Luftfartsverket entailed nullity, which meant that as a result of the judgment *SAS* was reimbursed for payments of fees and was liberated from future fees to an overall amount of more than EUR 100 million. The judgment was appealed to the Swedish Supreme Court, which on 12 November 2002 decided not to grant leave of appeal.[51]

## 10.3 Competition Law in the Context of the New Economy

### 10.3.1 The Choice Between General or Specific Criteria in Competition Law

The above-mentioned cases show that exclusionary practices occur in Internet-related business markets in Sweden. However, there are no special criteria for determining whether a practice is exclusionary in Internet-related markets. The issue has not been discussed in the Swedish Competition Authority's decisions or the Swedish Patent and Market Court's judgments. The criteria are thus the same as under the general rules in the Swedish Competition Act.

The Swedish Retail and Wholesale Council's report of 2017 shows that almost 10% of all trade in Sweden is done online today and that more and more businesses are entering the online arena.[52] According to the Swedish Retail and Wholesale

[49] Judgment of the Swedish Market and Patent Court of the 29 of June 2017, ref. nr. T 2673-16, Yarps Network Services AB v Telia Company AB.

[50] Judgment of the Göta Court of Appeal in Case T 33-00 Staten genom Luftfartsverket v Scandinavian Airlines System.

[51] Decision of the Swedish Supreme Court in Case T 2137-01.

[52] The same conclusion is made by the Commission in the Report 'Final report on the E-commerce Sector Inquiry', SWD(2017) 154 final, as well as the Swedish Competition Authority in the report Competition and growth in digital markets.

Council, approximately 20% of all retail sales will take place online in Sweden by 2020–2025.[53] Thus, from the long-term perspective, it is questionable whether the criteria for exclusionary practices in Internet-related markets should be separated from the traditional markets.

The official report Swedish Competition Authority on e-commerce and the sharing economy in the Swedish markets issued in March 2017 should be mentioned in this context as well. In May 2016, the Swedish government instructed the Swedish Competition Authority to examine the effects of e-commerce and sharing economy on competition and to propose new actions that should be undertaken by the government if needed. The ensuing report concluded that even though online trade is constantly growing, new legislation is not required.

The report shows that consumer behaviour is mainly affected by two factors, namely prices and secure online payment methods.[54] Issues such as the need for more transparent pricing, the risk for price coordination, the companies' access to digital infrastructure and the importance of electronic identification systems are highlighted in the Authority's report.[55] However, no new regulation is proposed. Similarly, in the area of the sharing economy, the report mentions that the investigations of the Competition Authority in online markets are increasingly complex, but the Authority concludes that the fact that competition law infringements may take new shapes today does not require new competition rules. At the same, the Authority is of the opinion that the new economy, especially the sharing economy, requires that the investigation methods of the Competition Authority are updated in the same speed as the innovation on the markets.

In the area of mergers in the sharing economy, the Swedish Competition Authority mentions that other indicators apart from the current market thresholds might be needed to make a proper investigation. Apart from the current merger thresholds, the report suggests using the acquisition price of an online platform as an additional notification threshold.[56]

Thus, the Swedish Competition Authority's view does not appear as completely definite. The above-discussed *Nasdaq* case currently before the Swedish Patent and Market Court of Appeal will hopefully provide more clarity on the application of competition rules in the context of online sales platforms and possibly on whether the law should become more sensible with regard to companies operating in Internet-related markets.

---

[53] Report of the Swedish Trade Council on the importance of trade ('Handelns betydelse. Då, nu och i framtiden'), 2017, pp. 29–30. The report can be accessed at handelsradet.se/ekonomiska-radet.

[54] Report of the Swedish Competition Authority on competition and growth in the digital markets, p. 149.

[55] Report of the Swedish Competition Authority on competition and growth in the digital markets, p. 46 and 149.

[56] See Report of the Swedish Competition Authority on competition and growth in the digital markets, pp. 155–156.

### 10.3.2 Efficiency as a Defence in Antitrust Cases

In cartel cases, there is room for arguing that a degree of cooperation increases efficiency of the defendant in order to escape the prohibition in Chapter 2, Article 1, of the Swedish Competition Act. However, all four requirements listed in the exception in Chapter 2, Article 2, of the same Act (which mirrors Article 101(3) TFEU) must be met. Thus, the cooperation must

1. contribute to improving the production or distribution of goods or to promoting technological or economic progress;
2. allow consumers a reasonable share of the resulting benefits;
3. only impose, on the undertakings concerned, restrictions that are indispensable to the attainment of the objective referred to in subsection 1; and
4. do not afford the undertakings concerned the possibility of eliminating competition in respect of a substantial proportion of the products in question.[57]

Generally, once an anti-competitive object or effect of an agreement has been established, it is difficult to argue that efficiency gains should make an agreement or concerted practice escape the prohibition in Chapter 2, Article 1, of the Swedish Competition Act. To the knowledge of the authors of the report, there are no Swedish cases related to online sales where an anti-competitive horizontal agreement was allowed because of arguments of efficiency. However, it is more likely that the exemption in Chapter 2, Article 2, is applicable in vertical agreements than in horizontal ones.

In general, it is possible for a company in a dominant position to justify a behaviour that would otherwise constitute an abuse by demonstrating that the behaviour can be outweighed or at least counterbalanced by efficiencies arising from that behaviour. However, this is only possible as long as the efficiencies also benefit consumers. Thus, Chapter 2, Article 2, of the Swedish Competition emphasises the effect of the behaviour on the consumers in the same way as Article 102 TFEU. In the legal doctrine, it has been argued that the possibility to justify a behaviour of a dominant undertaking under Article 102 TFEU through the efficiencies that the behaviour creates corresponds to the exemption rule in Article 101(3) TFEU, which is applicable in cartel cases.[58]

## 10.4 The Structures of the Markets

### 10.4.1 Vertical Restraints in Online Markets

All six Swedish cases discussed above deal with vertical relationships. The conclusion can therefore be drawn that competition rules on vertical agreements are often relevant when online sales platforms come into question. However, in the

[57] Chapter 2, Article 3, Swedish Competition Act of 2008.

[58] J. Karlsson and M. Östman, Konkurrensrätten – En handbok, 5th ed., Karnov Group Sweden AB 2014, Stockholm, p. 668, n. 115 with the reference to L. Henriksson, Konkurrensrättsöverträdelser – Ekonomisk analys i den juridiska processen, Norstedts Juridik 2013, Stockholm.

*Booking.com* and *Expedia* decisions, the Swedish Competition Authority found that only horizontal effects of the most favoured nation clauses applied by the travel agencies constituted infringements of competition law.[59] Vertical effects were not considered as problematic. This is in line with the general idea behind Swedish and EU competition law that vertical agreements do not raise the same competition concerns as horizontal agreements.[60]

In principle, all vertical practices are block exempted by Regulation 330/2010[61] if the market share threshold of 30% is not exceeded, with the exception of restrictions that remove the benefit of the block exemption, namely hardcore restrictions and excluded restrictions.[62] As long as the market shares of the companies engaged in a vertical cooperation arrangement do not exceed the thresholds mentioned above, the net effect of vertical agreements is presumed not to harm consumers and is therefore considered to fall within a safe harbour, although this presumption can be withdrawn by the Swedish courts if appreciable anti-competitive effects occur.[63]

There is no *lex specialis* regulating the special case of online sale platforms in Swedish competition law. The rules described above are applied in all relevant competition cases, including the ones relating to online sales platforms. The Commission's Guidelines on Vertical Restraints are, however, more thorough when it comes to online sales.[64] Paragraph 52 of the Guidelines states:

> The internet is a powerful tool to reach more and different customers than will be reached when only more traditional sales methods are used and this is why certain restrictions on the use of the internet are dealt with as (re)sales restrictions. In principle, every distributor must be allowed to use the internet to sell products.

The hardcore restrictions in Article 4 Regulation 330/2010 are also relevant for companies operating in online environments. Hardcore restrictions are very likely to have negative effects on competition even when companies are within the 30% market share threshold mentioned above and are therefore excluded from the scope of the exemption in Regulation 330/2010.[65] The Commission's Vertical Restraints Guidelines give further guidance on the interpretation of Article 4 Regulation 330/2010 when it comes to online sales.[66]

---

[59] See the Decisions of the Swedish Competition Authority in *Booking.com*, p. 6 and *Expedia*, p. 3.

[60] J. Karlsson and M. Östman, Konkurrensrätten – En handbok, 5th ed., Karnov Group Sweden AB 2014, Stockholm, p. 285. See also CJEU, case C-32/11 *Allianz Hungária Biztosító & Others*, ECLI:EU:C:2013:160. For an in-depth analysis of Swedish competition law related to vertical constraints, see L. Henriksson, Distributionsavtal – vertikala avtal och konkurrensrättsliga aspekter, Norstedts Juridik 2012, Stockholm.

[61] Commission Regulation 330/2010 of 20 April 2010 on the application of Article 101(3) of the Treaty on the Functioning of the European Union to categories of vertical agreements and concerted practices, OJ 2010 L 102, p. 1, Article 4.

[62] Articles 4 and 5 of the Regulation 330/2010.

[63] Commission Guidelines on Vertical Restraints, OJ 2010 C 130, p. 1, para. 176.

[64] Commission Guidelines on Vertical Restraints, OJ 2010 C 130, p. 1.

[65] See Regulation 330/2010, Recital 10.

[66] See Commission's Guidelines on Vertical Restraints, paras. 47–64.

Regulation 330/2010 expires in 2022, but the Commission has recently stated that it does not see it necessary to review it earlier than what is planned.[67] Having in mind that the online trade is steadily growing, it is possible that a greater emphasis will be put on the new economy when Regulation 330/2010 is reviewed. For the time period prior to the review, one should expect to see more Commission investigations in the e-commerce sectors in order to 'contribute to a consistent application of the EU competition'.[68]

### 10.4.2 Agreements of Minor Importance

As a complement to the Swedish Competition Act of 2008,[69] the Swedish Competition Authority has provided guidelines on how to interpret Swedish competition law. In 2017, the Competition Authority published its present Guidelines on agreements of minor importance.[70]

These provisions are in most aspects identical with those provided by the EU Notice on agreements of minor importance,[71] which quantifies what is not an appreciable restriction of competition under Article 101 of the TFEU. The main principle of the EU Notice is the same, i.e. that an agreement that would otherwise be caught by Article 101 of TFEU, respectively Chapter 2, Article 1, of the Swedish Competition Act, falls outside the scope of the above-mentioned articles as long as the aggregate market share held by the parties to the agreement does not exceed 10% in case of horizontal agreements and 15% in case of vertical agreements.[72]

The Swedish Guidelines do, however, differ from the EU Notice in one important aspect. The Swedish Guidelines contain provisions that are more generous as regards the possibility of SMEs to enter into non-hardcore horizontal agreements. Pursuant to Article 7 of the Swedish Guidelines, cooperation between enterprises does not fall under the prohibition of Chapter 2, Article 1, of the Swedish Competition Act as long as the annual net turnover of each of the contracting parties does not exceed SEK 30 million and their joint market share is less than 15%, compared to the 10% market share threshold applicable to horizontal cooperation agreements under the EU Notice.

[67] Report from the Commission to the Council and the European Parliament, 'Final report on the E-commerce Sector Inquiry', SWD(2017) 154 final, para 74.

[68] Report from the Commission to the Council and the European Parliament, 'Final report on the E-commerce Sector Inquiry', SWD(2017) 154 final, para 75.

[69] Konkurrenslagen (2008:579).

[70] General Guidelines of the Swedish Competition Authority on agreements of minor importance, KKVFS 2017:3 (Konkurrensverkets allmänna råd om avtal av mindre betydelse (bagatellavtal) som inte omfattas av förbudet i 2 kap. 1 § Konkurrenslagen).

[71] Commission Notice on agreements of minor importance which do not appreciably restrict competition under Article 101(1) of the Treaty on the Functioning of the European Union (de minimis), OJ 2014 C 291, p. 1.

[72] The Swedish Guidelines now refer to the current EU Notice on agreements of minor importance.

### 10.4.3 Market Power in the Area of Online Sales Platforms

The criterion for market power is not regulated by the Swedish legislator, but market power is recognised as a relevant factor in competition cases. For example, in the *Onlinepizza* decision of 2016, the Swedish Competition Authority explicitly stated that the level of market power affects the extent of an anti-competitive behaviour.[73] It did not discuss the definition of market power further. According to the Commission, market power is

> ...the ability to maintain prices above competitive levels or to maintain output in terms of product quantities, product quality and variety or innovation below competitive levels for a not insignificant period of time. The degree of market power normally required for a finding of an infringement under Article 101(1) is less than the degree of market power required for a finding of dominance under Article 102.[74]

Market power was also discussed in the Swedish Competition Authority's recent report on competition and growth in the digital markets. The report states that a large number of users and access to large amounts of data can give a platform significant market power even if it does not have a high turnover. High market value and large number of users are given as two examples of market power in markets where online platforms are used. The report concludes that there is a risk of mergers between platforms with low turnover but strong market power falling outside of the current merger reporting thresholds, even though the merger may de facto significantly impede competition on the market. The Competition Authority suggests to also pay attention to the acquisition price of the target undertaking.[75]

## 10.5 Voluntary Commitments and Their Effects on the Development of the Law

Chapter 3, Article 4, of the Swedish Competition Act allows companies to make voluntary commitments in cases where a possible competition law infringement has been identified. If the Swedish Competition Authority agreed to the commitments, it may end its investigation. Moreover, the Competition Authority may ask the Patent and Market Court to couple the decision of the Competition Authority with penalty fines in case the company does not comply with the commitment.

Among the cases described above, the ending of an investigation by voluntary commitments appears to be common in the area of Internet-related markets. When this is the case, the Competition Authority does not take a final decision on whether the investigated company committed a competition law offence or not. It does provide certain reasoning behind such decisions, but the precedent effect of such decisions cannot be compared to rulings of the court.

[73] Decision of the Swedish Competition Authority of 4 April 2016, file ref. 658/2015, p. 4.

[74] Commission Guidelines on Vertical Restraints, OJ 2010 C 130, para 97.

[75] Report of the Swedish Competition Authority on competition and growth in the digital markets, p. 155.

However, this does not necessarily mean that such voluntary commitments go unnoticed. It may be unlikely that a higher court would refer to the reasoning of such decisions, but the Swedish legislator is not prevented from taking decisions of this type into consideration. In fact, the Swedish Government Official Report on increasing the Swedish Competition Authority's powers—a type of pre-legislative report that later serves as a basis for the adoption and even the interpretation of the legislation—includes the above-mentioned *Booking.com* and *Expedia* decisions of the Swedish Competition Authority.[76]

### 10.5.1 Burden of Proof

The standard of proof is in practice not entirely the same in cases of non-compliance with voluntary commitments and in cases of competition law violations. Antitrust violations require that it is fully proved that all the relevant criteria in the Swedish Competition Act are fulfilled for the Swedish Patent and Market Court to be able to find that an infringement exists. Neither fines nor damages can be ordered before an infringement is found.

Moreover, the Swedish Market Court's precedence clearly states that administrative fines in competition cases are of a criminal nature.[77] The result of such a finding is that the European Convention on Human Rights must be taken into consideration where competition law is violated as well. This means that principles such as *ne bis in idem* or the presumption of innocence—as well as the relevant precedent of the European Court of Human Rights—are fully applicable in competition cases where fines are imposed.[78]

However, it should be pointed out that in the case of non-compliance with a voluntary commitment where high penalty fines are coupled with the company's voluntary commitment, it is enough that such a commitment is breached for the company to be forced to pay the penalty fine.[79] Legally, such penalty fines are not classified as fines for breaching competition law, and no aspects of criminal

[76] Swedish Government Official Report SOU 2016:49 on expanding the decisive rights for the Swedish Competition Authority (En utökad beslutanderätt för Konkurrensverket), p. 159.

[77] See Decision of the Swedish Market Court in case MD 2015:4 of 17 April 2015, Swedavia, para. 25. The Market Court based its decision on the Judgment of the European Court of Human Rights in the case *A. Menarini Diagnostics S.R.L. v. Italy*, no. 43509/08 and the case C-501/11 P, *Schindler Holding Ltd and others v Commission*, ECLI:EU:C:2013:522, paras 30–38.

[78] Other Swedish cases where the European Convention on Human Rights was also relevant were Judgment of the Swedish Market Court in case MD 2009:11 of 18 May 2009, NCC AB and others v Swedish Competition Authority, Judgment of the Swedish Market Court in case MD 2013:5 of 12 April 2013, TeliaSonera AB and others v Swedish Competition Authority and Judgment of the Swedish Patent and Market Court of Appeals, ref. nr. PMT 7497/16 of 28 April 2017, Aleris Diagnostik and others v Swedish Competition Authority.

[79] See Chapter 6 of the Swedish Competition Act.

procedure can be applied in these cases.[80] Therefore, the burden of proof is not necessarily borne by the competition authority when voluntary commitments, coupled with penalty fines, are breached. Yet, from the perspective of the companies, the effects of the penalty fines, especially when the sum is high, may be similar to those of fines for breaches of competition law.

[80] See Decision of the Swedish Market Court in case MD 2015:4 of 17 April 2015, Swedavia, paras 44–59.

# Switzerland

# 11

Annemarie Streuli

## 11.1 Introduction

With the development of the digital market, market conditions and consumers' behaviour have changed drastically over the past decade. The use of the Internet as a decisive medium before making any purchase decision is increasing.[1]

Pursuant to a 2016 market survey on online and distance trading in Switzerland, e-commerce represented, in 2016, 6.9% of Swiss retail trade, which amounted to CHF 7.8 billion, i.e. an increase of 8.3% compared to 2015.[2] The evolution of e-commerce in Switzerland is most noticeable in the fields of fashion and household electronics. Pursuant to this market study, by 2019, at least 20% of the non-food retail products will be sold through e-commerce. The online business is also expected to increase and transform itself over the next years. According to some experts, chat-based forms are expected to supplement forms or interactions used via browser and mobile applications. Experts also foresee the use of fully automated purchase processes and digital assistants.[3]

The author would like to thank Mr Aaron Feldman for his help in proofreading the present contribution.

[1] DPC 2011/3, Behinderung des Online-Handels, p. 373 para 12 citing S. Van Baal and K. Hudetz, Das Multi-Channel-Verhalten der Konsumenten, Institut für Handelsforschung an der Universität zu Köln, 2008.

[2] Market Study 'Marché Suisse du Commerce en Ligne et à distance 2016' made by VSV, GFK Switzerland and Media Focus Schweiz GmbH, available at https://www.vsv-versandhandel.ch/fr/facts/la-suisse-en-chiffres/. Accessed on 4 July 2017.

[3] R. Wölfle and U. Leimstoll, E-Commerce Report Schweiz 2017, Management summary p. 1.

A. Streuli (✉)
Python, Geneva, Switzerland
e-mail: astreuli@pplex.ch



B. Kilpatrick et al. (eds.), *Antitrust Analysis of Online Sales Platforms & Copyright Limitations and Exceptions*, LIDC Contributions on Antitrust Law, Intellectual Property and Unfair Competition,
https://doi.org/10.1007/978-3-319-71419-6_11

The growing importance of the Internet in the current retail market has strong advantages: it facilitates the gathering of information, provides consumers with greater choice, improves the quality of services and thus increases intra-brand and inter-brand competition. For distributors, the use of the Internet increases their geographical reach. Direct trading also enables lower distribution costs and allows distributors to develop new business models.[4]

Furthermore, Switzerland currently faces the challenge of cross-border consumerism caused by the specifics of the Swiss market, often referred to as the *Swiss price island*. It is no secret that prices in Switzerland are far higher than those found in its neighbouring countries. In recent years, consumers increasingly sought to purchase either food or retail products from abroad. There is also a tendency for consumers to gather information on retail prices from the Internet and to proceed with a comparison with those in the neighbouring countries such as France, Italy or Germany prior to making a purchase. According to the e-commerce market study, since 2012, online shopping tourism has greatly increased. In 2016 alone, cross-border consumerism increased by 18%. This online shopping tourism has direct consequences, not only on Swiss brick-and-mortar shops but also on Swiss online platforms. With the increased presence of foreign firms and the online presence of brands, Swiss domestic companies are put under pressure. In September 2016, an alliance of politicians, entrepreneurs, small and medium enterprises, and consumer organisations launched a popular initiative[5] to combat unfair-pricing practices regarding imported products.[6] According to the initiative committee, multinational companies arbitrarily increase the price of imports into Switzerland. This initiative aims at guaranteeing the non-discriminatory procurement of goods and services from abroad and at preventing the distortion of competition caused by the unilateral conduct of companies with significant market power.[7] The initiative committee currently has 18 months to collect at least 100,000 signatures for this initiative to be submitted to a popular national vote. If accepted by the Swiss voters, the Swiss Federal Constitution, as well as the cartel law and regulations, shall be amended accordingly.

Considering the effect that e-commerce and online shopping tourism can have on the domestic market, Swiss manufacturers may have an interest in protecting their investments by limiting online sales. This report aims to review the general Swiss antitrust rules before focusing further on their application and limitations in the field of e-commerce in Switzerland.

[4] DPC/RPW 2017/1 Annual Report 2016 of the Competition Commission, p. 70.

[5] The popular initiative system enables, in Switzerland, citizens to seek a decision on an amendment to the Constitution.

[6] S. Hirsbrunner, Mit kartellrechtlichen Mitteln faire Preise erzwingen, SJZ 113/2017 p. 329.

[7] Federal popular initiative available at https://www.admin.ch/ch/f/pore/vi/vis469.html, see also DPC/RPW 2017/1 Annual Report 2016 of the Competition Commission, p. 69.

## 11.2 Legal Framework

### 11.2.1 The Cartel Act

The legislation governing cartels in Switzerland is the Federal Law on Cartels and Other Restraints of Competition of 6 October 1995, lastly amended in 2014 ('Cartel Act').[8] Its clear objective[9] is to 'prevent the harmful economic or social effects of cartels and other restraints of competition and, by doing so, to promote competition in the interests of a liberal market economy'. The purposes of the Cartel Act include not only consumer welfare[10] and general social welfare[11] but also the contribution to the creation of a single Swiss market, open to the outside world and, more specifically, to the European market.[12] Such purposes must serve as a background for the interpretation of each provision of the Cartel Act.[13]

The Cartel Act is focused on three competition aspects: (1) anti-competitive agreements,[14] (2) abuse of a dominant position,[15] as well as (3) merger control.[16] This report is limited to anti-competitive agreements and abuse of a dominant position, to the exclusion of merger control.

### 11.2.2 The General Notices of the Competition Commission

The Cartel Act is complemented by various federal ordinances. In addition, the Swiss Competition Commission has drafted various notices[17] including but not limited to (1) the Notice on the Treatment of Vertical Restraints dated 28 June 2010, which is further detailed in an explanatory statement, (2) the Notice on the Treatment of Vertical Restraints in the motor vehicle sector and (3) the Notice on SMEs.

Swiss law and the Competition Commission's notices are strongly influenced by the law of the European Union as the Swiss Competition Commission aims at ensuring that Switzerland applies the same rules as in its neighbouring countries and thus

---

[8] RS 251.4 available on the website www.admin.ch.

[9] Article 1 of the Cartel Act.

[10] V. Martenet and P. Tercier, in Commentaire Romand, droit de la concurrence, (ed. V. Martenet, C. Bovet and P. Tercier) 2nd edition, 2013, ad. Article 1 Cartel Act N 16, citing DPC 2010/3, France Telecom/Sunrise, p. 493 para 43, 359 and 412.

[11] V. Martenet and A. Heinemann, Droit de la Concurrence, Quid iuris ? Band/Nr. 6, 2012, p. 37.

[12] V. Martenet and P. Tercier, in Commentaire Romand, droit de la concurrence, (ed. V. Martenet, C. Bovet and P. Tercier) 2nd edition, 2013, ad. Article 1 Cartel Act para 22.

[13] Martenet and P. Tercier, in Commentaire Romand, droit de la concurrence, (ed. V. Martenet, C. Bovet and P. Tercier) 2nd edition, 2013, ad. Article 1 Cartel Act para 13.

[14] Article 5 Cartel Act.

[15] Article 7 Cartel Act.

[16] Articles 9 and 10 Cartel Act.

[17] Article 6 Cartel Act.

mitigating the risk of isolating the Swiss market.[18] That being said, even if Swiss law is significantly influenced by European rules and case law, Swiss competition law is independent from EU law and must be interpreted autonomously.[19] The EU rules may only be used as a means of interpretation of Swiss law in cases where the Swiss legislator intended to align Swiss law with European law.[20]

While the notices are most certainly applied by the Swiss Competition Commission, they, however, do not bind the Swiss civil and appeal courts, which nevertheless often refer to them, as means of interpretation. These notices are also from time to time amended in accordance with the latest case law. In its 2017 explanatory statement, the Competition Commission provided some useful insight on how selective distribution systems and restrictions on e-commerce are treated from an antitrust perspective.

## 11.3 Restrictions to Competition

### 11.3.1 The General Rules of the Cartel Act

The Cartel Act prohibits unlawful 'binding or non-binding agreements as well as concerted practices between undertakings operating at the same or at different levels of production which significantly limit competition as their object or effect in a market for specific goods or services'.[21]

The simple existence of an anti-competitive agreement is not always in itself unlawful. The Cartel Act only considers agreements illegal if they eliminate effective competition or restrict competition without being justified on grounds of economic efficiency.

Certain agreements[22] and concerted practices, the so-called hardcore cartels, are presumed to eliminate effective competition and are directly sanctioned by fines. On the one hand, in horizontal relationships, agreements that aim at directly or indirectly fixing prices; limiting the quantities of goods or services to be produced, purchased or supplied; or allocating markets geographically are considered as hardcore restrictions to competition.[23] On the other hand, in vertical relationships, agreements that set fixed or minimum resale prices as well and/or provide for absolute territorial protections are considered as hardcore restrictions to competition.[24]

[18] Notice on the treatment of Vertical Restraints dated 28 June 2010, available in French and German at https://www.weko.admin.ch/weko/fr/home/documentation/communications---notes-explicatives.html.

[19] Swiss Federal Case law ATF 137 II 199, JdT 2011 I. p. 157, 166 pt 4.3.1.

[20] Swiss Federal Case law ATF 137 II 199, JdT 2011 I. p. 157, 166 pt 4.3.1.

[21] Articles 4 and 5 para 1 Cartel Act.

[22] Articles 5 paras. 3 and 4 Cartel Act.

[23] Article 5 para 3 Cartel Act.

[24] Article 5 para 4 Cartel Act and Article 10 of the Notice on the Treatment of Vertical Restraints.

Pursuant to recent case law, such hardcore restrictions are considered as illegal, regardless of the intensity or scope of the impact on competition.[25]

For other restraints on competition, the competition authorities review the objects and the effects of the agreements on competition on a case-by-case basis. Due to the large amount of possible restrictions on competition, Swiss law does not provide for a fixed definition of competition restrictions. The broad definition of illegal restraints enables the competent authorities to address the constant evolution of the market and therefore the new challenges generated by the growth of e-commerce. The principal criterion to determine if an agreement is illegal is the intensity of its antitrust effects.[26] On this basis, the Competition Commission elaborated on certain rules on the qualitative and quantitative effects of agreements and listed the agreements that it considers as significant impediments to competition.[27]

With regard to agreements that are not listed as being significant impediments to competition, the Competition Commission takes into account the market share to determine the impact of a specific agreement. Such agreements are usually considered as non-significant restrictions, provided that the market shares of the parties to the agreement do not have an aggregate market share of 15%.[28] In case several vertical agreements lead to a cumulative effect, the market share threshold drops to 5%. The Notice on SMEs also provides that horizontal agreements are usually not considered as causing a significant restriction on competition if the entities have an aggregate market share of 10%.[29]

The defendant(s) in an antitrust legal proceeding may still justify the use of such an agreement that significantly restricts competition on the ground of economic efficiency.[30]

Pursuant to the Cartel Act,[31] agreements affecting competition are deemed to be justified on grounds of economic efficiency if they are necessary to reduce production or distribution costs, improve products or production processes, promote research into or dissemination of technical or professional know-how, or exploit resources more rationally and if they will under no circumstances enable the parties

---

[25] Swiss Federal Case law 2C_180/2014 dated 28 June 2016, Gaba/WEKO. In this ruling, the Federal Tribunal considered that the vertical agreements on territories are considered as hardcore cartels that presumably lead to the elimination as well as significant restriction of effective competition.

[26] M. Amstutz, B. Carron and M. Reinert, in Commentaire Romand, droit de la concurrence, (ed. V. Martenet, C. Bovet and P. Tercier) 2nd edition, 2013, ad. Article 5 Cartel Act para 2.

[27] Articles 10 and 12 of the Notice on the Treatment of Vertical Restraints.

[28] Article 13 of the Notice on the Treatment of Vertical Restraints. F. Hoffet, M. Dietrich and M. Thomann, Vertical Agreements, in Getting the Deal through, available on: https://gettingthedealthrough.com/area/41/jurisdiction/29/vertical-agreements-switzerland/. Accessed July 18, 2017.

[29] Notice on SME's, section 3 para. 1 let. a and b.

[30] Article 5 para 1 and 2 Cartel Act; Swiss Federal Case law 2C_180/2014 dated June 28, 2016, Gaba/WEKO, see also Article 16 of the Notice on the Treatment of Vertical Restraints.

[31] Article 5 para 2 Cartel Act.

involved to eliminate effective competition. The list of purely economic[32] criteria set by the Cartel Act[33] is limited. Further justifications, whether based on political, cultural or other considerations, are therefore not taken into account. The Swiss Federal Council may, however, in exceptional cases and at the request of the undertaking(s) involved, authorise agreements affecting competition if they are necessary for compelling public interest reasons.[34]

The Competition Commission provided further details regarding its approach to the ground of economic efficiency in its Notice on the Treatment of Vertical Restraints.[35] First, as a general rule, the agreement is considered as justified on grounds of economic efficiency, without any further investigation, if the supplier's market share on the relevant market on which it sells its products and services is below 30% and if the market share of the purchaser on the relevant market on which it purchases the products and services is below 30%. It should, however, be noted that this rule is not applicable if (1) the agreement is presumed to be unlawful,[36] (2) if the agreement is considered as a significant impediment to competition[37] or if (3) the agreement has a cumulative effect, together with other agreements on the relevant market.

Second, the Competition Commission shall review the justifications on a case-by-case basis. Companies may notably invoke, as justification on grounds of economic efficiency, (1) the protection, for a limited period of time, of investments that aim to open up new products and/or geographical markets; (2) the necessity to insure the uniformity and quality of products; (3) the protection of investments linked to a contractual relationship (the hold-up issue); and the (4) free riding by third entities.[38]

### 11.3.2 Applicable Rules to Online Sales

The Swiss Competition Commission views online sales as positive for competition. It first considers that it is a well-known fact that the Internet increases transparency for consumers. With a few computer mouse clicks, the consumer can, in a short time frame, obtain a general overview of the market structure and the products for sale and compare their prices.[39] Moreover, the Swiss Competition Commission considers that online sales may have somewhat of a disciplinary effect on the prices set by

---

[32] M. Amstutz, B. Carron and M. Reinert, in Commentaire Romand, droit de la concurrence, (ed. V. Martenet, C. Bovet and P. Tercier) 2nd edition, 2013, ad. Article 5 para 255.

[33] Article 5 para 2 Cartel Act.

[34] Article 8 Cartel Act.

[35] V. Martenet and A. Heinemann, Droit de la concurrence, quid iuris? Band/Nr. 6, 2012, p. 95.

[36] Article 10 of the Notice on the Treatment of Vertical Restraints.

[37] Article 12 para 2 of the Notice on the Treatment of Vertical Restraints.

[38] Article 16 para 4 of the Notice on the Treatment of Vertical Restraints.

[39] DPC/RPW 2011/3 Behinderung des Online-Handels, p. 374 paras 16 ff.

brick-and-mortar shops, and it therefore puts pressure on the manufacturer's margins and prices.[40]

#### 11.3.2.1 Online Sales Restrictions

The Swiss Cartel Act does not provide for any specific rules on online sales. It prohibits unlawful restraints on competition on both vertical and horizontal restraints *on the relevant market*. The Competition Commission distinguishes two cases: (1) the restriction of passive sales and (2) the general restrictions of online sales.

Internet sales are considered as passive sales under Swiss law,[41] unless the distributor makes specific efforts to reach clients established outside the attributed territory.[42]

The restriction of passive sale to certain clients is not considered as hardcore restriction to competition[43] as hardcore restrictions apply only in relation to a grant of a specific territory or the setting of fixed resale prices.[44] Such bans are, however, still considered as unlawful by the competition authorities, who shall review them on a case-by-case analysis,[45] but are not subject to fines.[46] Consequently, the prohibition or restriction of Internet sales fall outside the scope of hardcore restrictions to competition, unless there are other exceptional circumstances leading to the conclusion of an unlawful hardcore cartel, on prices or on absolute territorial protection, which are subject to fines.[47]

In this context, the explanatory statement of the Competition Commission recently developed new guidance on the restriction of online sales and on the exceptional circumstances that could lead the authorities to consider that the prohibition or restriction of sales over the Internet are considered as hardcore agreement, subject to fines.[48] Those circumstances are reviewed on a case-by-case basis. For vertical agreement on prices, qualified circumstances include (1) the direct or indirect influence from the manufacturer in the determination of the resale prices, such as an influence of the rebate policy of the retailer, and (2) other measures taken by the manufacturer such as threats, intimidation, sanctions, delivery delays or

---

[40] DPC/RPW 2011/3 Behinderung des Online-Handels, p. 386 para 111.

[41] Article 3 of the Notice of Notice on the Treatment of Vertical Restraints.

[42] Article 2 of the Notice on the Treatment of Vertical Restraints, see also the Explanatory Statement on the Notice on the Treatment of Vertical Restraints, para 21.

[43] Article 5 para 4 Cartel Act.

[44] M. Amstutz, B. Carron and M. Reinert, in Commentaire Romand, droit de la concurrence, (ed. V. Martenet, C. Bovet and P. Tercier) 2nd edition, 2013, ad. Article 5 para 626.

[45] Article 5 para 1 Cartel Act.

[46] DPC/PRW2011/3 Behinderung des Online-Handels, p. 382 paras 76 ff.

[47] Explanatory Statement on the Notice on the Treatment of Vertical Restraints, para 9 bullet point 4. Available on https://www.weko.admin.ch/weko/fr/home/documentation/communications--notes-explicatives.html.

[48] Explanatory Statement on the Notice on the Treatment of Vertical Restraints, paras 18 ff, citing DPC/RPW 2011/3, Behinderung des Online-Handels, 381, p. 381 para 69 and DPC 2014/1 Kosmetikprodukte (Dermalogica) 195, p. 198 para 140.

suspensions, or even termination of the distribution agreement in case the prices set by the manufacturer are not respected.[49]

The *geo-blocking practices* are also considered as qualified circumstances. In this case, according to the Competition Commission, territorial agreements are considered to be qualified circumstances if they provide that (1) a distributor will prevent final consumers in Switzerland to have access to its website and/or will reroute the client automatically towards the web page of the manufacturer and/or of the Swiss distributors or that (2) the distributor will stop the transaction if the client's credit card reveals that the client is not from the attributed territory.[50]

#### 11.3.2.2 Most Favoured Nation Clauses

In its 2015 decision, the Competition Commission reviewed the most favoured nation clause ('MFN' clause) applied by the online travel booking platforms Booking.com, Expedia and HRS until 2015. Those online platforms had barred hotels from fixing lower prices, from offering more room capacities and/or from offering better conditions, such as cancellation policies, to other distribution channels. The MFN clause applied to most of the distribution channels, including competing online platforms.[51] The Competition Commission considered that the broad MFN clauses applied by these online-booking platforms were unlawful as they eliminated competition.

Following investigations in France, Italy and Sweden, the online platforms adapted their MFN clauses in 2015 by removing their wide parity clauses. The online platforms, however, kept their 'narrow MFN clauses' barring hotels from offering lower prices on their own website. With the new narrow MFN clauses, the hotels are, however, entitled to offer lower prices on their direct distribution channels if those prices are not public and to determine freely their prices, room capacities and other better conditions on competing online platforms.[52] The Swiss Competition Commission mentioned that those new narrow MFN clauses appeared to be less restrictive but considered that their effect on the market still had to be reviewed in the future. Based on this lack of meaningful empirical data on the effects of the narrow MFN clauses on the relevant market, the Competition

[49] Explanatory Statement on the Notice on the Treatment of Vertical Restraints, para 19, citing DPC/RPW 2011/3, Behinderung des Online-Handels, p. 381, para 71 and DPC/RPW 2014/1 Kosmetikprodukte (Dermalogica) p. 198, para 140, see also DPC 2014/2, Jura, p. 413, paras 62 ff.

[50] Explanatory Statement on the Notice on the Treatment of Vertical Restraints para 20, citing DPC/RPW 2011/3, Behinderung des Online-Handels, p. 381, para 74 and DPC 2014/1 Kosmetikprodukte (Dermalogica) p. 198 para 142, see also DPC 2014/2, Jura, p. 413, para 62.

[51] J. Xoudis, Chroniques, jurisprudences européennes et étrangères, Concurrences N°2-2016 p. 235.

[52] J. Xoudis, Chroniques, jurisprudences européennes et étrangères, Concurrences N°2-2016 p. 235.

Commission refused to settle amicably on those narrow MFN clauses and is currently monitoring related cartel and political developments in Switzerland and abroad.[53]

### 11.3.2.3 Online Sales and Selective Distribution

#### Definition of Selective Distribution

Selective distribution agreements are agreements in which the supplier undertakes to sell its products only to authorised dealers, selected on specific qualitative and quantitative criteria and in which those dealers undertake not to sell the products to unauthorised distributors.[54]

The Competition Commission applies specific rules to purely qualitative selective distribution agreements, which are defined as agreements that consist in authorising dealers only on the basis of objective criteria of a qualitative nature, required by the nature of the product or service, such as staff training, services provided and/or the range of products sold.[55] The Competition Commission considers that said agreements are admissible under three conditions.

First, the nature of the product in question necessitates a selective distribution to preserve the nature, quality or good use of the product. The qualitative selective distribution system is vastly used in various sectors such as motor vehicles, technology, luxury and premium-branded products.[56] Ordinary products that are not luxury goods or technical products do not justify the development of purely qualitative selective distribution systems.[57] The limitation of the sale of its product to an authorised seller is justified by the intrinsic qualities of the product and by the fact that the distribution must be operated in accordance with the modalities set by the manufacturer. Such modalities include an obligation to have qualified staff to counsel the consumer, to respect the corporate identity and/or to provide after-sale services.

Second, the resellers must be chosen on the basis of objective criteria of a qualitative nature, which are laid down uniformly and which are made known to all potential dealers and applied in a non-discriminatory manner.

Third, the criteria applied by the manufacturer must not go beyond what is necessary.[58]

The agreements that fulfil the three conditions are lawful, regardless of the importance of the market shares of the concerned undertakings as they are not considered as significant impediment to competition.[59]

---

[53] DPC/RPW 2017/1 Annual Report 2016 of the Competition Commission, p. 62.

[54] Article 4 para 1 and Article 12 para b (iii) of the Notice on the Treatment of Vertical Restraints.

[55] Article 4 para 2 of the Notice on the Treatment of Vertical Restraints.

[56] V. Jäggi, La distribution sélective et le développement du réseau, liberté de contracter ou obligation d'agrément, SJ 2013 II p. 1.

[57] V. Jäggi, La distribution sélective et le développement du réseau, liberté de contracter ou obligation d'agrément, SJ 2013 II p. 4, see also DPC/RPW 2010/1, Gaba, p. 84 para 147.

[58] Article 14 of the Notice on the Treatment of Vertical Restraints.

[59] Explanatory Statement on the Notice on the Treatment of Vertical Restraints para 16.

### Unlawful Online Sales Restrictions in Selective Distribution Systems

The Notice on the Treatment of Vertical Restraints and its explanatory statement provide for specific rules regarding online sales in the field of selective distribution systems.

As mentioned above, agreements that contain a restriction or prohibition of online passive sales to distributors and/or end users are considered as unlawful cartels. This rule is particularly relevant for selective distribution systems as the prohibition of online passive sales not only bars the distributors from selling to end customers but also bars passive sales between authorised distributors and/or retailers.

Consequently, in a selective distribution system are considered as significant impediment to competition any obligation that aims at deterring the authorised dealers to use the Internet to reach the largest possible numbers and variety of clients by imposing to such dealers online sales condition that are not equivalent to those applicable to the offline sales.[60] Authorised dealers must be able to sell, both actively and passively, to end users, through online sales.[61] The Competition Commission specifies that this does not mean that the condition of online sales must be exactly the same as those of the offline sales. However, those conditions must follow the same objective and achieve comparable results. Any difference must moreover be justified by the different nature of those two modes of distribution.[62]

In 2014, the Competition Commission also clarified that, in a selective system, unlawful restrictions are those aiming at deterring the *authorised* dealers to use the Internet. Consequently, a manufacturer's refusal to provide repair services covered by a warranty for machines sold over the Internet does not breach the Swiss Cartel Act as long as this refusal is limited to the sale by undertakings that were not part of the manufacturer's selective distribution system.[63]

### Free Riding as Justification on Grounds of Economic Efficiency

Free riding is defined as the situation where a manufacturer, a distributor and/or a reseller takes advantage of the promotional efforts of another manufacturer, distributor or reseller.[64]

In its 2011 decision regarding household appliances, the Competition Commission specifically analysed the question of free riding as a justification of the ban of online sales. It considered that the issue of free riding of online sellers at the

---

[60] Competition Commission Explanatory statements, para 23.

[61] Explanatory Statement on the Notice on the Treatment of Vertical Restraints, para 23. Cf. also the Guidelines on Vertical restraints, para 56 applicable by analogy in Switzerland available at http://eur-lex.europa.eu/legal-content/FR/TXT/?uri=celex:52010SC0411.

[62] Explanatory Statement on the Notice on the Treatment of Vertical Restraints para 23. Cf. also the Guidelines on Vertical restraints para 56, applicable by analogy in Switzerland available at http://eur-lex.europa.eu/legal-content/FR/TXT/?uri=celex:52010SC0411.

[63] C. Bovet and A. Alberini, recent developments in Swiss Competition law, SZW 2015 S 42, para 6, citing DPC/RPW 2014/2, Jura, p. 416 para 86.

[64] M. Amstutz, B. Carron and M. Reinert, in Commentaire Romand, droit de la concurrence (ed. V. Martenet, C. Bovet and P. Tercier) 2nd edition, 2013, ad. Article 5 Cartel Act N 303.

expense of brick-and-mortar shops was not a decisive justification. First, part of the consumers of household appliances are professional buyers that do not need any specific advice or presentation of the product before making a purchase.[65] Second, some of the end consumers, such as tenants, never have access to the information and advice from the seller. Third, consumers have access to the supplier's showroom to obtain information from the manufacturer. The Competition Commission also noted that the free riding issue was bi-directional as 23% of the consumers gathered information online before purchasing their products from a brick and mortar point of sale.[66] The Competition Commission further noted interdependency between online and brick-and-mortar shops, which were viewed as complementary by some of the consumers. Based on those facts, the Competition Commission considered that the restriction of online sales was not the appropriate tool to limit free riding. It rather suggested, for instance, to compensate brick-and-mortar shops for their additional expenses.[67]

#### Admissible Restraints of Online Sales in a Selective Distribution System

In its 2011 decision,[68] the Competition Commission acknowledged that manufacturers may impose certain criteria on a website in order to ensure that the online sale activities of an authorised dealer are coherent with the distribution model of the manufacturer. While this applies to all sales on the Internet, for the Competition Commission, the right to set various criteria for online sales is particularly relevant in the selective distribution systems.[69]

That being said, those standards and points-of-sale requirements must be exclusively related to the contractual product. Other standards within the selective distribution system, in particular in relation to other brands, are prohibited.[70]

For instance, the manufacturer may request specific quality standards and the existence of a physical point of sale as conditions for all members of the selective distribution system.[71]

The manufacturer may also require from the authorised dealers that sell products via the Internet to make sure that the identity of the dealer, as well as its physical point of sale(s), is clearly mentioned and visible on its website.[72] With regard to online sales, the dealers are entitled to use domain names that are different from their trade or business names, provided that their domain name is not objectively

[65] DPC/RPW 2011/3 Behinderung des Online-Handels, p. 391 para 150.

[66] DPC/RPW 2011/3 Behinderung des Online-Handels, p. 392 para 153.

[67] DPC/RPW 2011/3 Behinderung des Online-Handels, p. 393 para 162.

[68] DPC/RPW 2011/3, Behinderung des Online-Handels, p. 395 para 189, see also the Explanatory Statement on the Notice on the Treatment of Vertical Restraints para 24.

[69] Explanatory Statement on the Notice on the Treatment of Vertical Restraints, para 24.

[70] DPC/RPW 2011/3 Behinderung des Online-Handels, p. 395 para 189.

[71] Explanatory Statement on the Notice on the Treatment of Vertical Restraints para 24, citing DPC/RPW 2011/3, Behinderung des Online-Handels, p. 395 para 189.

[72] DPC/RPW 2011/33, Behinderung der Online-Handels, p. 395 para 189.

disadvantageous to the brand.[73] According to various authors, the manufacturer may also impose certain quality standards regarding the website and its presentation and may, in a selective distribution system, prohibit the sales of products, by its authorised dealers, on third-party platforms, such as 'eBay'.[74] Neither the Competition Commission nor the courts have issued any ruling on the ban to use third-party platforms.

## 11.4 Abuse of Dominant Position

### 11.4.1 The General Rules

According to the Cartel Act, a dominant position is exercised on a market when a single undertaking or several undertakings enable suppliers or consumers to behave to an appreciable extent independently from other participants in the market. The dominance of a company (or companies) is determined on a case-by-case basis, which depends not only on the market share but also on the market shares of its competitors, the entry barriers, as well as the general structure of the market and its evolution. According to case law and the leading authors, a dominant position does not depend per se on a high market share. That being said, a market share of over 50% can be used as an indication of the presence of a dominant position.[75]

Swiss law does not prohibit the existence of dominant undertakings but only prohibits the abuse of said dominant position in the market, by either hindering other companies from starting or continuing to compete or by disadvantaging trading partners. The Cartel Act[76] lists the behaviour that are in particular considered unlawful: (1) the refusal to deal; (2) the discrimination between trading partners in relation to prices or other conditions of trade; (3) the setting of unfair prices or other unfair conditions of trade; (4) the undercutting of prices or other conditions directed against a specific competitor; (5) the limitation of production, supply or technical development; and/or (6) the conclusion of contracts on the condition that the other contracting party agrees to accept or deliver additional goods or services. The company with a dominant position may, however, justify its behaviour on legitimate business grounds.[77]

[73] DPC/RPW 2011/33, Behinderung der Online-Handels, p. 395 para 189.

[74] M. Amstutz, B. Carron and M. Reinert, in Commentaire romand, droit de la concurrence (ed. V. Martenet, C. Bovet and P. Tercier) 2nd edition, 2013,ad. Article 5 Cartel Act para 636.

[75] DPC/RPW 2016/1 Online-Buchungsplattformen für Hotels, p. 121 para 419.

[76] Article 7 para 2 Cartel Act.

[77] E. Clerc, in Commentaire Romand, droit de la concurrence (ed. V. Martenet, C. Bovet and P. Tercier), 2nd edition, 2013, ad. Article 7 I para 99.

### 11.4.2 Specific Rules Applicable to Third Party Online Platforms

With regard to e-commerce, in particular with regard to two-sided markets, such as third-party online platforms, a particular characteristic of said platforms is the 'indirect network effect', which may create a dominant position. This effect occurs when the use of the platform of one group of users depends directly on the participation of the second group of users. For instance, for hotel online-booking platforms, the more hotels and end consumers use the platform, the more attractive the platform becomes for both group of users.[78] This indirect network effect may create a high market concentration with only a few dominant undertakings sharing the market.[79]

Swiss case law on the dominant position of e-companies is scarce. To this day, the Swiss Competition Commission only investigated one case. In its 2016 decision, the Competition Commission reviewed the market position of the hotel online-booking platform Booking.com, either alone or with two other undertakings, Expedia and HRS. It determined that there existed strong signs that showed Booking.com benefitted from a dominant position in the online-platform market. Those signs included Booking.com's strong market share of 70–80% in 2013 and the absence of a correcting effect of a potential competition or a counter-power of hotels.[80] The Competition Commission, however, failed to establish a link between the unlawful parity clauses applied by Booking.com (see Sect. 11.3.2.2 above) and Booking.com's dominant position and thus to prove that Booking.com's behaviour on the relevant market and the restrictions imposed to its commercial partners constituted an abuse of its market position.[81]

## 11.5 The Definition of the Relevant Market

### 11.5.1 In General

Both the analysis of the restrictions to competition and the abuse of dominant market power require an analysis on the 'relevant market'. The market is defined by three criteria: the product market, the geographical market and, on some occasions, the temporal market.[82]

According to the Swiss Ordinance on the Control of Concentrations,[83] which applies to the other fields of the Cartel Act, the product market 'comprises all those goods or services that are regarded as interchangeable by consumers on the one

[78] DPC/RPW 2016/1 Online-Buchungsplattformen für Hotels, p. 92 para 188.

[79] M. Blatter, Digitalisierung – Herausforderung für die Wettbewerbspolitik, Sic ! 2016 p. 380.

[80] J. Xoudis, Chroniques, jurisprudences européennes et étrangères, Concurrences N°2-2016 p. 235.

[81] DPC/RPW 2016/1 Online-Buchungsplattformen für Hotels, p. 120 paras 412 ff.

[82] Article 11 para 3 of the Ordinance on the Control of Concentrations, also applicable to the restrictions to competition and to the abuse of dominant position.

[83] Article 11 para 3 of the Swiss Ordinance on the Control of Concentrations RS 251.4.

hand and by suppliers on the other hand with regard to their characteristics and intended use'. In cartel agreements, the Competition Commission analyses the interchangeability of a product principally from the demand-side perspective.[84] The notion of product market depends notably on the objective characteristics of a product (price,[85] use and properties) but remains highly subjective as it takes into account the preferences in the market and depends on complex economic appreciations.[86]

The geographic market 'comprises the area in which on the one hand consumers purchase and on the other hand suppliers sell the goods or services that constitute the product market'. The temporal criterion of the 'relevant market' is rarely used but can apply when the consumer cannot substitute products that are available in different time periods that the seller cannot offer continuously.[87]

### 11.5.2 The Relevant Market in E-Commerce

According to the Competition Commission, the integration of Internet-related structures or sales in the definition of the relevant market must be determined on a case-by-case basis and depends exclusively on the circumstances of the relevant market field.[88]

For instance, in its 2011 decision regarding kitchen and laundry appliances, the Competition Commission considered that products sold both online and offline were part of the same market. The relevant retail market for kitchen and laundry appliances included the online sales as such sales were considered passive sales.[89] The Competition Commission noted that those online sales not only favoured the price transparency as they reduced costs and saved time for the end user to find a competitive retailer but also led to an increase in competitive pressure.[90]

In a 2013 case, the Competition Commission analysed the market of books written in French and had to determine whether e-books and online sales were interchangeable with printed books. Despite the growth of the e-books market in Europe,

---

[84] Decision of the Competition Commission of 27 May 2013: marché du livre écrit en français, p. 103 para 464 and and p. 115 para 520.

[85] Decision of the Competition Commission of 27 May 2013: marché du livre écrit en français, p. 110 para 493.

[86] Decision of the Competition Commission of 27 May 2013: marché du livre écrit en français, p. 99 para 445.

[87] E. Clerc and P. Këllezi, in Commentaire Romand, droit de la concurrence (ed. V. Martenet, C. Bovet and P. Tercier) 2nd edition, 2013, ad. Article 4 para 2 Cartel Act, N 108.

[88] Decision of the Competition Commission 27.05.2013, marché du livre écrit en français, p. 118 para 533.

[89] DPC 2011/3, Behinderung des Online-Handels, p. 387 paras. 114 and ff.

[90] DPC 2011/33, Behinderung der Online-Handels, p. 379 para 55 ff, see also DPC 2014/1 Kosmetikprodukte (Dermalogica) p. 195 para 113.

e-book commerce was considered as marginal and was therefore excluded from the notion of the 'relevant retail market'.[91] As for printed books sold online, the Competition Commission acknowledged that the online market of printed books was growing, but at the time of the investigation, between 2005 and 2011, it considered it as limited as it progressed only to attain 10% of the total book purchases. In its analysis, the Competition Commission considered that the strong Swiss currency played a determining role in the market penetration of the online sellers. Consequently, the fact that the demand did not shift to online sellers is a strong indicator that the online market and the brick and mortar retail market were at the time not interchangeable. The Competition Commission, however, decided to leave this question unanswered.[92]

The notion of the relevant market must be carefully reviewed in regard to third-party online platforms that are two-sided markets, active on both the demand and the sale sides. According to the Competition Commission, when the platform does not participate in any transaction between the buyer and seller or when such transaction is not observable, it can make sense to distinguish two separate markets.[93] On the contrary, in case a transaction takes place on the online platform, the Competition Commission encompasses, in one single market, both the demand and the supply sides.[94] In its 2015 decision, the Competition Commission considered that the online-booking platforms constituted the relevant market[95] and that such online-booking platforms could not be substituted with other distribution channels, such as travel agencies or the direct reservation channel, whether through phone, email and/or hotel home pages.[96]

## 11.6 Procedure and Sanctions

Under Swiss law, two independent[97] proceedings are available in case of violation of the Cartel Act: the civil and the administrative procedures. The existence of one procedure does not bar the filing of a claim in the other procedures.

[91] Decision of the Competition Commission 27.05.2013, marché du livre écrit en français, p. 105 para 476.

[92] Decision of the Competition Commission 27.05.2013, marché du livre écrit en français, p. 119 para 536.

[93] DPC/RPW 2016/1, Online-Buchungsplattformen für Hotels, p. 93 Para. 194.

[94] M. Blatter, Digitalisierung – Herausforderung für die Wettbewerbspolitik, Sic ! 2016 p. 380.

[95] DPC/RPW 2016/1, Online-Buchungsplattformen für Hotels, p. 100 para 253.

[96] A. Wijesundera and D. Mamane, Competition and antitrust in the digital age, 30 March 2017, Ilo on Demand, Competition & Antitrust – Switzerland.

[97] J-M. Reymond in Commentaire Romand, droit de la concurrence (ed. V. Martenet, C. Bovet and P. Tercier) 2nd edition, 2013,ad. Rem. Article 12ss Cartel Act N 38.

### 11.6.1 Civil Procedure

A person hindered by an unlawful restraint of competition may file a civil claim before the cantonal civil courts.[98] In its claim, the claimant may request the elimination of or desistance from the hindrance, damages or the surrender of unlawfully earned profits. If the legality of a restraint of competition is questioned in the course of the civil proceedings, the civil courts shall refer the case to the Competition Commission for an expert report.[99] The civil courts are not bound by the expert report of the Competition Commission but must motivate their decision if they choose not to follow the expert report.

Civil claims are very rare in Switzerland. The important costs of civil proceedings and the high burden of proof have a strong deterrent effect on such filing. Moreover, the administrative procedure is a very attractive alternative as it enables a hindered company to simply notify the Competition Commission of the existence of an unlawful behaviour.[100]

### 11.6.2 Administrative Procedure

The administrative procedure of the Competition Commission is by far the most developed and the most used procedure. This procedure is a very attractive alternative as it enables a hindered company to simply notify the competition authorities of the suspected existence of an unlawful behaviour.[101]

The Competition Commission's Secretariat may initiate preliminary investigations on its own initiative or following information or a denunciation of third parties. If the Competition Commission's Secretariat considers that there are indications that the concerned undertakings have violated the Cartel Act, it may open a formal investigation. The investigation may lead to a formal decision in which the competition authorities state that the behaviour of the concerned undertakings is unlawful and order specific measures to restore competition.

The Competition Commission may hand down a direct sanction—a fine—to undertakings that participate in hardcore cartels or abuse a dominant position.[102] Other restrictive practices will not lead to direct sanctions. The direct sanctions, considered as criminal penalties under Article 6 of the European Convention on Human Rights, can amount to 10 per cent (10%) of the turnover that the company

[98] Article 12 Cartel Act.

[99] Article 15 para 1 Cartel Act.

[100] R. Jacobs and J. A. Bürgi, G. Giger, Should private enforcement of antitrust law be encouraged, and if so, by what measures? National Report Switzerland, 2006 available at http://www.asas-concurrence.ch/pub/asas_04_016a.pub.pdf.

[101] R. Jacobs, J. A. Bürgi and G. Giger, Should private enforcement of antitrust law be encouraged, and if so, by what measures? National Report Switzerland, available at http://www.asas-concurrence.ch/pub/asas_04_016a.pub.pdf.

[102] Article 49a Cartel Act.

achieved in Switzerland during the previous 3 financial years. The amount of the fine depends on the duration and severity of the unlawful behaviour, as well as the likely profit that resulted from such behaviour. According to the ordinance on sanctions (the 'Ordinance') applicable to unlawful restraints in competition,[103] the competition authorities may also take into account both aggravating circumstances, such as multiple recurrences, particularly high profits, a leading role in the restraint, non-cooperation or obstruction of investigations, and mitigating circumstances, such as a passive role in the restraint and cooperation in the investigation.[104]

Furthermore, in case of an amicable settlement, the Cartel Act[105] provides that a breach of the settlement, of a non-appealable ruling or of a decision to the advantage of the undertaking shall be fined. In principle, the fine shall depend on the likely profit that resulted from the unlawful behaviour.[106]

### 11.6.3 Settlement Agreements

The Competition Commission's Secretariat is entitled to propose settlement agreements[107] to the concerned undertakings if it deems that the behaviour in question is illegal. If the proposal is approved by the concerned undertakings, it has to be submitted for approval by the Competition Commission. The Commission's decision approving the amicable settlement may not leave open the question of the infringement of the Cartel Act. The competition authorities must therefore, in their settlement agreement, first review the conditions of the Cartel Act to determine the illegality of the defendant's behaviour before settling the consequences and sanctions of such behaviour.[108] The sanction of this behaviour is determined by the Competition Commission and cannot be settled amicably with the infringing undertakings. The competition authorities, however, do take into account the cooperation of the concerned companies in determining the fine. In such settlement agreements, the companies, moreover, undertake to refrain from committing any unlawful behaviour in the future.[109] As complete decisions on the illegality of a specific behaviour, the settlement agreements help with the development of analysis standards and have precedential value. Settlement agreements under Swiss law are frequent as they enable a fast and efficient resolution of a dispute.

---

[103] RS 251.5.

[104] Articles 5 and 6 of the Ordinance.

[105] Article 50 Cartel Act.

[106] L. Moreillon, Commentaire Romand, Droit de la concurrence, ad. Article 50 Cartel Act N9.

[107] Article 29 Cartel Act.

[108] P. Këllezi, Les accords amiables conclus avec les autorités de la concurrence et leurs implications pour les entreprises in Développement récents en droit commercial III, 2014, p. 107.

[109] M. Strebel, C. Pétermann and R. Bucher, Overview of the law and enforcement regime relating to Cartels in Global Legal Insights – Cartels, 5th ed. 2017, London.

In recent years, the Competition Commission has approved settlement agreements in the field of online distribution. In the case of Electrolux AG and V-Zug AG, two market leaders in the field of kitchen and laundry appliances, the Competition Commission considered that the general ban of online sales on the own website of the distributor and the strict restrictions of online sales, leading to a de facto prohibition, were unlawful. The infringing undertakings and the Competition Commission found a settlement agreement in which the undertakings undertook to allow their selective distributor to sell their products on their own websites. The Competition Commission, however, acknowledged that the supplier can require quality standards for the use of the Internet, the existence of a physical point of sale, as well as the clear indication of the identity of the distributor and the location of the point(s) of sale on the distributor's website.[110] According to the settlement agreement, the distributor may also be authorised to use a domain name of an online business that differs from the distributor's company name, provided that there are no reasons indicating that the chosen domain name is objectively disadvantageous for the supplier's brand and that the website clearly indicates the distributor's company name at first sight. In case of doubt, the supplier may examine the domain name and give the distributor a notice of its decision within a month.[111]

## 11.7 Conclusion

Digitalisation is transforming the economy. It has enabled the development of new business models and has stimulated competition in many fields of commerce. The new opportunities brought by digitalisation are, however, accompanied by new challenges for the undertakings, as well as for the competition authorities.

While Swiss competition law was drafted for traditional brick-and-mortar shops, its broadly drafted provisions are adaptable to the markets' evolution and to new distribution models.

That being said, on the Competition Commission's own admission, the competition law assessment of the development of e-commerce is complicated and requires 'certain empirical values which the competition authorities are gathering during the ongoing investigations'.[112]

Considering that the competition authorities review the legality of a behaviour, based on empirical data and on a case-by-case analysis, caution is advised to companies that intend to create new business models, restrict and/or impose conditions to online sales. While we salute the Competition Commission's new explanatory statements on the e-commerce conditions, with the ever-evolving e-market, the criteria applicable to online sales remain unclear and difficult to predict.

[110] DPC/RPW 2011/3 Behinderung des Online-Handels, p. 396 para 189 (B) (1).

[111] DPC/RPW 2011/3 Behinderung des Online-Handels, p. 396 para 189 (B) (3).

[112] DPC/RPW 2017/1 Annual Report 2016 of the Competition Commission, p. 69.

Last but not least, companies present in the EU and in Switzerland would be well advised to review the rules set by Swiss law before implementing conditions for online sales in Switzerland. While Swiss law is very similar to European law in many ways, both laws are not entirely harmonised.

On the basis of the above, the issues generated by the growth and evolution of the e-commerce must be resolved on a global level. As e-commerce has an international reach, harmonised e-competition rules would be welcome to enable companies to have a better grasp on the allowed practices on the Internet.

# United Kingdom

# 12

Vineet Budhiraja

## 12.1 The Structure of UK Competition Law Regime

### 12.1.1 The Competition Act 1998 and Other Competition Statutes in the UK

The Competition Act 1998 is a statute exclusively concerned with competition law, which takes effect across the entirety of the United Kingdom. It is not the only statute that concerns competition law—the other major piece of primary legislation is the Enterprise Act 2002, which contains the UK's merger control rules, rules on market studies and investigations, as well as rules on the investigation and enforcement of certain consumer law matters, and creates a criminal 'cartel offence'. The Consumer Rights Act 2015, which came into force on 1 October 2015, reformed the UK's regime for private actions in competition law and expands the jurisdiction of the Competition Appeal Tribunal to hear stand-alone actions for damages.

The Competition Act 1998 contains two core prohibitions: the Chapter I prohibition regulates anti-competitive agreements, decisions of undertakings or concerted practices in similar terms to Article 101 of the Treaty on the Functioning of the European Union (TFEU)—extending only to trade within the UK, not between the EU Member States. The Chapter II prohibition regulates the abuse of a dominant position within the UK in similar terms to Article 102 of the TFEU, again with emphasis on the UK. The Chapter II prohibition contains a non-exhaustive list of

The author is grateful to the Competition Law Association's working group on Question A on 13 June 2017 for its valuable comments and input. Any errors remain the author's own.

V. Budhiraja (✉)
Watson Farley & Williams LLP, London, UK
e-mail: vbudhiraja@wfw.com



B. Kilpatrick et al. (eds.), *Antitrust Analysis of Online Sales Platforms & Copyright Limitations and Exceptions*, LIDC Contributions on Antitrust Law, Intellectual Property and Unfair Competition,
https://doi.org/10.1007/978-3-319-71419-6_12

conduct that may amount to abuse; in principle, the scope of the prohibition can expand to include other conduct.

### 12.1.2 Enforcement, Concurrency and Consequences of Breach

In the UK, the Competition and Markets Authority (CMA) is the primary body enforcing competition law.[1] It combines the functions of the former Competition Commission and the Office of Fair Trading, which have since been abolished.[2] In addition, various sector regulators may also apply UK competition law, concurrently with the CMA. These bodies are[3] the Office of Communications ('Ofcom'),[4] the Gas and Electricity Markets Authority (GEMA, often referred to as 'Ofgem'), the Water Services Regulatory Authority (WSRA, often referred to as 'Ofwat'), the Office of Rail Regulation (ORR), the Northern Ireland Authority for Utility Regulation (often referred to as 'Ofreg'), the Civil Aviation Authority (CAA, in relation to designated airports and air traffic control), the Payment Systems Regulator (PSR, part of the Financial Conduct Authority), the Financial Conduct Authority (FCA) itself[5] and Monitor, the health service regulator.[6]

The competition authorities have issued a substantial body of guidance on the application of competition law to regulated industries. These include the following: *Regulated Industries Guidance on concurrent application of competition law to regulated industries*,[7] *The Application of the Competition Act in the telecommunications sector*,[8] *Application in the energy sector*,[9] *Application to services relating to railways*[10] and *Guidance on the application of the Competition Act 1998 in the water and sewerage sectors*.[11] In addition, there are several Memoranda of Understanding between the CMA and specific regulators on the exercise of

[1] The CMA describes itself as an independent non-ministerial department: https://www.gov.uk/government/organisations/competition-and-markets-authority/about. Accessed 25 October 2017.

[2] Enterprise and Regulatory Reform Act 2013, with effect from 1 April 2014, section 26(1) and (2).

[3] Competition Act 1998, section 54.

[4] Ofcom is the successor to five separate communications regulators including the Director General of Telecommunications, which is referred to below and which previously had concurrent competition powers.

[5] In this paper, I refer to the CMA to represent the UK authorities generally, but in relation to specific cases I use the name of the actual regulator that took the decision.

[6] Health and Social Care Act 2012, section 72.

[7] CMA10 (March 2014).

[8] OFT 417 (February 2000).

[9] OFT 428 (January 2005).

[10] OFT 430 (October 2005).

[11] OFT 422 (March 2010).

concurrent powers,[12] guidelines on the use of enforcement powers[13] and prioritisation principles.[14]

Decisions of the CMA may be appealed in the first instance to the Competition Appeal Tribunal. The CMA may hear follow-on damages cases, and under the Consumer Rights Act 2015, stand-alone damages and injunctions cases. The Chancery Division of the High Court retains its jurisdiction to hear stand-alone actions.[15]

Contravention of competition rules can lead to (a) guilty firms being fined up to 10% of their group worldwide turnover, (b) actions for damages from customers and/or competitors that may have suffered harm by the guilty firm's anti-competitive activities, (c) individuals being disqualified from being a company director and (d) individuals involved in cartels, in certain circumstances, being imprisoned for up to 5 years and/or imposed unlimited fines.

### 12.1.3 Relationship with EU Law

The interplay between EU competition law and UK competition law is mainly governed by what is often referred to as the Modernisation Regulation, which came into force on 1 May 2004.[16] Article 3 of the Modernisation Regulation requires the national competition authorities of the EU Member States, when applying their national competition rules to an agreement or conduct that may appreciably affect trade between EU Member States, to apply Article 101 and/or Article 102 of the TFEU at the same time and to not prohibit such an agreement and/or conduct under its national rules if it would be permitted under the corresponding EU rules.

For instance, the CMA's guidelines on agreements and concerted practices[17] state that the application of Article 101 of TFEU to an agreement in question will depend on its assessment of whether that agreement may have an effect on trade between EU Member States. The CMA will have regard to the guidance set out in the

---

[12] See, for example, those between the CMA and: the Northern Ireland Authority for Utility Regulation (May 2014); the Financial Conduct Authority (June 2014); the Civil Aviation Authority (June 2014), the Water Services Regulation Authority (June 2014) and with Ofcom (June 2014).

[13] For example, *Ofgem, Enforcement guidelines on complaints and investigations* (June 2012); *Ofcom Enforcement Guidelines: Ofcom's guidelines for the handling on competition complaints and complaints concerning regulatory rules* (July 2012); and *Monitor Enforcement Guidance* (28 March 2013).

[14] For example, *Ofwat, Prioritisation Principles: application to the Competition Act 1998* (September 2010).

[15] See the Competition Law Practice Direction, stated to be up to date to 10 September 2013 but not reflecting Treaty of Lisbon numbering changes or recent UK competition reform legislation: http://www.justice.gov.uk/courts/procedure-rules/civil/rules/competitionlaw_pd. Accessed 25 October 2017.

[16] Council Regulation 1/2003 of 16 December 2002 on the implementation of the rules on competition laid down in Articles 82 and 82 of the Treaty, OJ 2003, L 1, p. 1.

[17] See OFT 401, Agreements and concerted practices: Understating competition law at para 4.3.

European Commission's notice[18] when making its assessment. This means that, in practice, the CMA may choose to apply one or both of UK competition rules and EU competition rules. The CMA's guidance on penalties for the infringement of competition rules, however, makes it clear that in cases where an undertaking has infringed both the EU prohibition and the corresponding UK prohibition, the undertaking will not be penalised twice for the same anti-competitive effects.[19]

However, the national competition authorities cannot, under the Modernisation Regulation, decide that that there has been no breach of EU competition rules. In 2011, the Court of Justice of the European Union (CJEU), following a preliminary reference from the Polish Supreme Court, ruled that allowing national competition authorities of the EU Member States to decide that there has been no breach of Article 102 of TFEU would call into question the system of co-operation established by the Modernisation Regulation and would also undermine the powers of the European Commission. According to the CJEU, a negative decision on the merits of the case by a national competition authority could undermine the uniform application of EU competition rules as it might prevent the European Commission from finding subsequently that the practice in question amounted to breach of EU competition rules.[20]

Moreover, the UK courts and the relevant competition authorities are required by section 60 of the Competition Act 1998 to ensure that there is consistency between the principles applied and decisions reached by each of them and 'the principles laid down by the TFEU and the European Court, and any relevant decisions of that Court'.

### 12.1.4 Relevant Market

Defining the relevant market is central in determining the direction of a competition assessment of the agreement or conduct in question. The CMA notes in its guidance, '[m]arket definition is not an end in itself but a key step in identifying the competitive constraints acting on a supplier of a given product or service. Market definition provides a framework for competition analysis…[and] is usually the first step in the assessment of market power.'[21] The CMA's guidance largely reflects the European Commission's Notice on market definition.[22]

Article 81 of TFEU/Chapter I prohibition applies only to agreements that have as their object or effect an *appreciable* prevention, restriction or distortion of

[18] See Commission Notice — Guidelines on the effect on trade concept contained in Articles 81 and 82 of the Treaty, OJ 2004, C 101, p. 81.

[19] See OFT 423, OFT's guidance as to the appropriate amount of a penalty at para 1.17.

[20] CJEU, case C-375/09 – *Prezes Urzędu Ochrony Konkurencji i Konsumentów v Tele2 Polska sp. zoo, now Netia SA w Warszawie*, ECR 2011 I 3055.

[21] See OFT 401, Market definition: Understanding competition law at para 2.1.

[22] European Commission Notice on the definition of the relevant market for the purposes of Community competition law, OJ C 372, p. 5.

competition. In order to test appreciability, it is generally necessary to define a relevant market and then demonstrate the appreciable effect of the agreement on competition on that relevant market.[23] Similarly, Article 82 of TFEU/Chapter II prohibition only regulates the conduct of dominant undertakings. Both the CMA and the European Commission would consider an undertaking to be dominant only if the relevant undertaking had substantial market power, which in turn requires the competition authority to define the relevant market.

In defining the relevant market, both authorities use what is known as the 'hypothetical monopolist' or SSNIP (small but significant non-transitory increase in price) test. The essence of the test is to determine the narrowest product group and geographic area over which a hypothetical monopolist controlling those products in that area could profitably maintain 'supra competitive' prices, i.e. prices that are at least a small but significant amount above competitive levels. This narrowest product group and geographic area is generally considered to be relevant market.

A relevant market typically involves a relevant product market and relevant geographic market. However, in certain circumstances, it might be necessary to consider temporal markets as well. For instance, in certain situations, it would be impossible for customers to substitute between time periods. This is usually the case in transport markets, where peak-hour customers would not consider peak and off-peak tickets as substitute products. In practice, first the relevant product market is defined, and thereafter, the relevant geographic market.

However, the SSNIP test is not completely helpful in two-sided markets such as e-commerce for goods and services, or the online search engine market, as a firm active on a two-sided market sells two products or services to two different sets of consumers and demand from one type of consumer depends on the demand from the other set of consumers and vice versa. One side of the market may be subsidised or funded by the other side of the market; for instance, advertisers pay search engines for the attention of users, but the users do not pay the search engine for the searches made by them.

### 12.1.5 Market Power

The Chapter II prohibition/Article 102 TFEU deals with abuse of a dominant position by a dominant undertaking. To determine whether an undertaking holds a dominant position involves two steps: (a) defining the relevant market as per above and (b) assessing the degree of market power or economic strength of the undertaking in question.

There are usually three key factors to consider when assessing the degree of market power of an undertaking: first, *the market position of the undertaking itself*

[23] However, if an agreement has as its object the prevention, restriction or distortion of competition then it is not necessary for the European Commission or the national competition authority to define the relevant market prior to finding an infringement of competition. See ECJ, case T-62/98 *Volkswagen AG v Commission*, ECR 2000 II 2707, at pts 230 to 232.

*and its competitors.* Generally, market shares of an undertaking and its competitors are good first indicators of market power/dominance. In most circumstances, a large market share equates to a dominant position. This is because '[a]n undertaking which has a very large market share and holds it for some time, by means of the volume of production and the scale of the supply which it stands for – without those having much smaller market shares being able to meet rapidly the demand from those who would like to break away from the undertaking which has the largest market share – is by virtue of that share in a position of strength which makes it an unavoidable trading partner and which, already because of this secures for it, at the very least during relatively long periods, that freedom of action which is the special feature of a dominant position'.[24] As a rule of thumb, market shares significantly and consistently above 50% are likely to be strong indicators of dominance. Market shares above 40% may be relevant and significant for the purposes of finding dominance, depending upon changes in level over time, the market share of competitors, etc. Market shares between 30% and 40% indicate that it is unlikely, but possible, based on other factors for there to be dominance.[25] Market shares below 30% are unlikely to raise dominance concerns in normal circumstances. However, in many cases, it would also be necessary to consider other factors such as the nature of the market and the competitiveness of the other participants on that market.

Second factor is *barriers to entry and expansion.* This essentially means difficulties or barriers faced by competing undertakings in entering a market. These difficulties may be due to lack of technical resources/capability, intellectual property rights, etc. For instance, a dominant undertaking may benefit from economies of scale where they can lower their average costs with a higher level of production.[26] Similarly, if fixed costs such as R&D or marketing constitute a high proportion of total costs incurred by the dominant undertaking, then this is likely to be a barrier to market entry. Sometimes barriers to entry may be technical in nature. These could be patent rights or industry standards that may not be readily accessible to a potential entrant.[27]

Third is *countervailing market power.* This entails consideration of relative market power of competing firms and whether there are significant actual or potential competitors that may exert effective competitive constraints on the dominant undertaking. Moreover, it is possible for customers of an undertaking to constrain the behaviour of an undertaking in question due to their strong bargaining position. This is referred to as 'countervailing buyer power'. However, for buyer power to exist, it

[24] ECJ, case 85/76 *Hoffmann-La Roche v Commission,* ECR 1979 461 at pt 41.

[25] The European Commission's view is that a market share below 40% is unlikely to amount to dominance. See Article 102 Enforcement Priorities Guidance, OJ 2009 C 45, p. 7: Vol II, App C14.

[26] In case T-336/07 *Telefónica de España v Commission* judgment of 29 March 2012, the General Court agreed with the European Commission's decision that Telefónica de España's dominant position in the regional wholesale market in part was possible because of economies of scale and scope of magnitude not available to other operators.

[27] EGC, case T-321/05 *AstraZeneca v Commission*, ECR 2010 II 2805.

is necessary that there be credible alternative suppliers on whom the customers could call upon or that it be possible for customers to sponsor a new entrant.[28]

Market shares are, however, not always indicative of market power in the digital market because of the relatively young and fast-growing nature of the market. For instance, the European Commission noted in its decision to clear the WhatsApp/Facebook merger 'that the consumer communications sector is a recent and fast-growing sector which is characterised by frequent market entry and short innovation cycles in which large market shares may turn out to be ephemeral. In such a dynamic context, the Commission takes the view that in this market high marker shares are not necessarily indicative of market power....'[29] This perhaps explains why there has not been many abuse of dominance cases in the online sales platforms sector both at the EU and the UK levels, and the competition authorities focus on the prohibition of anti-competitive agreements in regulating the online sales market.

## 12.2 Online Sales: A New Challenge?

### 12.2.1 Introduction

In recent years, e-commerce, i.e. sales via online channels—supplier's/retailer's own website, as well as third-party marketplaces like Amazon—has experienced exponential growth around the globe. In the EU, the average annual growth rate in the online sales of goods was approximately 22% between 2000 and 2014.[30] In 2015, according to the European Commission's estimates, more than 50% of the EU population shopped online. However, only 16% of online purchasers shopped from a seller based in another EU Member State.[31]

Online sales generally involve vertical agreements between a brand manufacturer and its distributors/retailers. Generally, vertical agreements are considered to be less likely to be harmful from a competition law perspective than horizontal agreements between competitors.[32] This is because of the typically complementary

[28] See case COMP/38113 *Prokent-Tomra,* [2009] 4 CMLR 101. Available at: http://ec.europa.eu/competition/antitrust/cases/dec_docs/38113/38113_250_8.pdf. In this case the products supplied by Tomra were not part of its customers' core activities and it was unlikely for customers to place strategic orders to subsidise and actively build up competing suppliers to whom they could then divert their orders. Therefore, the European Commission found there was no countervailing buyer power to affect Tomra's dominance.

[29] See case No. COMP/M.7217, *Facebook/WhatsApp,* para 99. Available at: http://ec.europa.eu/competition/mergers/cases/decisions/m7217_20141003_20310_3962132_EN.pdf.

[30] Commission Staff Working Document, *Geo-blocking practices in e-commerce: Issues paper presenting initial findings of the e-commerce sector inquiry conducted by the Directorate-General for Competition,* SWD (2016) 70 final.

[31] See Eurostat, *Digital Single Market: promoting e-commerce for individuals.* Available at: http://ec.europa.eu/eurostat/data/database?node_code=isoc_bdek_smi.

[32] See Commission Notice: Guidelines on Vertical Restraints, OJ 2010, C 130, p. 1, para 98.

relationship between the parties in a vertical agreement, where exercise of market power by one party would normally demand for sales by the other. Vertical agreements could contain a number of vertical restraints in the form of exclusive distribution agreements, selective distribution agreements, exclusive purchase obligations, franchising, etc. In many circumstances, vertical restraints can lead to better investment, more efficient sales and economies of scale. They also have the potential to address 'problems that arise when a manufacturer seeks to incentivise investment by the retailer in marketing the supplier's goods or in providing additional services to end-users (the 'free rider' problem) or either the supplier of the buyer has made client-specific in order to market the goods (the 'hold up' problem)'.[33] However, such restraints may also result in negative effects on competition, namely (a) anti-competitive foreclosure of access to the market, i.e. making it difficult for a new entrant to enter the market or for an existing market player to improve its market position; (b) softening competition between a supplier and its competitor and/or facilitating collusion between suppliers; (c) softening competition between a buyer and its competitor and/or facilitating collusion between buyers, etc.[34]

On 21 April 2010, the European Commission adopted Regulation 330/2010 block exempting agreements between manufacturers and distributors for the sale of products and services.[35] Regulation 330/2010 introduced a broad approach to exemption of vertical restraints based in part on the terms of the vertical agreement in question and in part on market power of the parties. Essentially, Regulation 330/2010 will apply if the market share of both the seller on the selling market and the buyer on the buying market does not exceed 30% and the agreement in question does not contain 'hardcore' restrictions, such as imposition of a fixed or minimum resale price, certain territorial restrictions etc.[36]

While Regulation 330/2010 applies to all sectors of the economy, and applies equally to both traditional sales channels and the rapidly growing online sales channels, it does contain certain specific rules on online sales. For instance, Article 4(b) of Regulation 330/2010 provides that any restriction of the territory into which, or of customers to whom, a buyer may sell the contract goods is a hardcore restriction. One of the exceptions to this is that a seller is permitted to prevent a distributor from *actively* selling into a territory or to a customer group that has been exclusively allocated to a different distributor or to the supplier itself.[37] The Vertical Guidelines state that, as a general rule, online sales should be

[33] Bellamy & Child, European Union Law of Competition, 7th ed, Oxford University Press 2013.

[34] See footnote 32 above, para 100.

[35] Commission Regulation 330/2010 of 20 April 2010 on the application of Article 101(3) of the Treaty on the Functioning of the European Union to categories of vertical agreements and concerted practices, OJ 2010, L 244, p. 35 ('Regulation 330/2010'). Regulation 330/2010 came into force on 1 June 2010 and it applies until 31 May 2022.

[36] Where an agreement includes a hardcore restriction, the European Commission presumes that the agreement falls within Article 101(1) of the TFEU and not to fulfil the exemption criteria of Article 101(3) of the TFEU.

[37] The European Commission distinguishes between active sales and passive sales. Active sales mean actively seeking customers, for example by direct mail or media advertisement targeted at a

considered to be passive sales so that restriction on online sales may amount to a hardcore restriction. It identifies a number of examples of such hardcore restrictions, such as restricting access to a website by customers based in another exclusive territory or a requirement that a distributor must decline transactions over the Internet if the payment details of a customer indicate that the customer is located outside the exclusive territory of the distributor. Conversely, it is possible for a distributor to restrict active selling into exclusive territories or to customer groups over the Internet. For example, ban on sending unsolicited e-mails to individual customers or paying a search engine to display advertisements specifically to users in another territory is permissible under Regulation 330/2010.

### 12.2.2 E-Commerce Sector Inquiry

In its Work Programme 2015 (adopted on 16 December 2014), the European Commission made the completion of a digital single market a priority. Its subsequent communication (in May 2015) on the Digital Single Market Strategy sets out various actions to achieve a digital single market.[38] The European Commission's Digital Single Market Strategy is directed at achieving three main objectives: (a) better online access to goods and services, (b) creating an environment where digital networks and services can prosper and (c) maximising the growth potential of the digital economy. Similarly, the UK government's strategic priorities for the CMA has identified that the CMA should focus on 'developments in new emerging markets, such as online digital market places and use of data…[and]…develop expertise in the impact new emerging markets are having on competition, innovation and consumer choice'.[39]

To support its Digital Single Market Strategy, the European Commission launched an inquiry into the e-commerce sector in May 2015 as it was concerned that businesses were restricting online sales to limit price competition and cross-border sales. The prime focus of the inquiry was on consumer goods, such as clothing, shoes, household appliances, toys, sports equipment, etc., as well as on digital content such as audiovisual and music products. The final report of the European

---

specific territory or customer group or establishing a branch in a territory that is exclusively allocated to another distributor. Passive sales mean responding to unsolicited customer requests from customers located in a territory exclusively allocated to another distributor. See Vertical Guidelines at p. 13.

[38] Communication from the Commission to the European Parliament, the Council, the European Economic and Social Committee and the Committee of the Regions 'A Digital Single Market Strategy for Europe', COM (2015) 192, final.

[39] See Government's response to the Consultation on the Strategic Steer to the Competition and Markets Authority (December 2015). Available at: https://www.gov.uk/government/uploads/system/uploads/attachment_data/file/481040/BIS-15-659-government-response-governments-strategic-steer-to-the-competition-and-markets-authority.pdf. Accessed 25 October 2017.

Commission found 'that the growth of e-commerce over the last decade had a significant impact on companies' distribution strategies and customer behaviour'.[40]

The European Commission further found that in relation to consumer goods, (a) price transparency has increased with online trade, such that customers are now able to instantaneously obtain and compare product and price information online and switch between offline and online sales channels with ease[41]; (b) price competition for both offline and online sales has increased as customers now have the ability to compare prices across several online retailers; however, this may affect quality, brand and/or innovation on the markets; (c) increased price transparency enables sellers to monitor their prices more easily[42]; and (d) third-party online marketplaces give retailers, especially small retailers, easier access to customers. But this could potentially clash with distribution policy of manufacturers.

According to the European Commission, these market trends have led to an (a) increase in competition between brand manufacturers and their own distributors as 64% of manufacturers that responded to the Commission's survey confirmed that they own online retail shops; (b) increase in the set-up of *selective distribution systems* as around 20% of manufacturers that responded to the Commission's survey reported that they have set up new selective distribution network, and nearly 40% introduced new criteria relating to online sales; and (c) increase in vertical restraints, such as pricing restrictions, online marketplace bans or restrictions on the use of price comparison tools that allow for a greater control over the distribution of products.

Regarding online sales of audiovisual and music products, the European Commission found that the key determinant for competition in digital content markets is the availability of the relevant rights. To transmit copyright-protected digital content, sellers are required to acquire rights to be able to lawfully market the content. These rights would typically include right to transmit via the Internet, broadband or cable technologies and to allow streaming or downloading of the content. Moreover, these rights can be licences, either on an exclusive or a non-exclusive basis, for a certain territory and/or for certain transmission, reception and usage technologies.

The European Commission concluded that rights used in licensing agreements for digital content tend to involve three main elements: (a) *technologies and usage rights*—technologies that a digital content provider is able to use lawfully to

---

[40] See Final report on the E-commerce Sector Inquiry, COM(2017) 229 final. Available at: http://ec.europa.eu/competition/antitrust/sector_inquiry_final_report_en.pdf. Accessed 25 October 2017.

[41] According to the European Commission, while this allows customers to find the best deal, it could also result in *free-riding* behaviour, i.e. use of pre-sale services offered by brick and mortar shops before making an online purchase, or search and compare products online before purchasing in brick and mortar shops.

[42] The European Commission found that two-thirds of the retailers used automatic software programmes that adjust their own prices based on competitors' prices. Moreover, pricing software makes it easier for brand manufacturers to police deviations from *recommended* retail prices and influence retailers' pricing policies.

transmit the content and allow the user to receive it; (b) *release and duration rights*—i.e., the period during which a digital content provider is lawfully entitled to offer the products, commonly referred to as 'release window or windows'; and (c) *geographic rights*—i.e., geographic area or areas in which a digital content provider may lawfully offer the digital content. The European Commission noted that licensing agreements do not give unrestricted use of licensed rights but include explicit terms and conditions—'contractual restrictions in licensing agreements are therefore not the exception but the norm in digital content markets'.[43]

The main competition concerns in relation to online sales that the CMA and/or the European Commission have identified in the last decade or so are as follows.

#### 12.2.2.1 Resale Price Maintenance (RPM)

RPM means the practice where an upstream supplier limits the freedom of downstream resellers, such as retailers or distributors, to set their resale prices, for example by requiring the retailer/distributor to sell at a particular price or only above a minimum price. This is presumed to restrict competition and to infringe the Chapter I prohibition and/or Article 101 of TFEU.

In May 2016, the CMA found Ultra Finishing Group Limited ('Ultra') to have been guilty of RPM in the online market for bathroom fittings.[44] In reaching its conclusion, the CMA stated that

> [t]he internet is a growing sales channel for the retail sale of bathroom fittings. The internet is an important driver of price competition between sales made through both online and offline channels due to: the increased transparency of prices on the internet; and the ability of resellers using the online sales channel to sell at lower prices.[45]

The CMA found that Ultra's online trading guidelines prevented resellers from selling or advertising Ultra branded products online below the recommended online price.[46] Therefore, it concluded that Ultra's RPM agreements would 'reduce price competition from online sales of bathroom fittings products; reduce downward pressure on the retail price of bathroom fittings products; and thereby potentially result in higher prices to consumers'.[47] The CMA imposed a fine of GBP 826,000 on Ultra after applying a 20% settlement discount for Ultra's admission of RPM and co-operation with the CMA's investigation.

---

[43] See footnote 40 above, p. 7.

[44] Case CE/9857-14, Online resale price maintenance in the bathroom fittings sector (10 May 2016). Available at: https://assets.publishing.service.gov.uk/media/573b150740f0b6155b00000a/bathroom-fittings-sector-non-conf-decision.pdf.

[45] See footnote 44 above, at p. 7.

[46] The CMA noted that Ultra implemented its trading guidelines through a copyright licence for the use of Ultra's images, which ensured that resellers signed up and adhered to its trading guidelines. Moreover, Ultra regularly monitored resellers' websites to check they were abiding by the trading guidelines, and threatened or took enforcement actions against non-compliant resellers, such as offering unfavourable terms of supply, ceasing or refusing to supply, or withdrawing the reseller's right to use its licensed images.

[47] See footnote 44 above, at p. 7.

In another case, on 24 May 2016, the CMA fined ITW Ltd ('ITW'), a UK-based manufacturer and supplier of commercial refrigeration products, GBP 2.2 million for restricting its dealers' ability to offer online discounts.[48] Foster Refrigerator UK ('Foster'), a business division of ITW, had issued a discounting policy to its entire network of resellers, whereby the resellers were prohibited from advertising any Foster products below a minimum advertised price both online and offline—the so-called MAP policy. The aim of the MAP policy was to improve the margins of resellers and to reduce the competitive pressure that Foster's traditional brick-and-mortar dealers faced from lower prices available online. The CMA found that Foster regularly monitored resellers' websites to check if resellers were abiding by the MAP policy and even asked its resellers to report instances of violation of its MAP policy by other resellers. Furthermore, Foster regularly took enforcement action to compel resellers to follow the MAP policy, which included threats to reduce terms of supply if the MAP policy is not followed or temporary or permanent closure of a dealer's account. The CMA took the same approach as in the Ultra case and concluded that

> …Foster's prohibition on advertising prices below the MAP genuinely restricted in practice the ability of resellers to determine their online sales prices at a price below MAP and, as such, amounted to resale price maintenance (RPM) in respect of online sales of Foster products.[49]

#### 12.2.2.2 Most Favoured Nation (MFN)

MFN or 'price parity' clauses are another way by which suppliers may control resale pricing, and in recent years, like a number of major competition authorities, the CMA has looked into the use of such clauses on online markets very closely. MFNs typically refer to an understanding between a supplier and its buyer where the supplier agrees that the buyer would favourably benefit from a lower price and/or discount that the supplier would offer.[50] The CMA's and other competition authorities' main concern is that such clauses could potentially restrict competition among various distribution channels—the supplier is obliged to price match with other sales channels or, at least, its own sales channel, and this could restrict the supplier's pricing freedom, soften price competition and deter market entry and/or expansions.

In September 2010, the Office of Fair Trading (OFT) launched an investigation into the suspected breaches of competition law by vertical agreement between

[48] Case CE/9856/14, Online resale price maintenance in the commercial refrigeration sector (24 May 2016). The CMA reduced ITW's fine by 30% for its admission and co-operating with the CMA under a settlement agreement, and agreement to set up a comprehensive competition compliance programme.

[49] See footnote 48 above, at p. 6.

[50] MFNs tend to be divided into two types: First, *Wide MFNs*, where the supplier is obliged to provide the buyer with identical or better prices and terms existing through any sales channel; and second, *Narrow MFNs*, where the supplier is obliged to provide the buyer with identical rates and terms as provided on supplier's own sales channels.

online travel agents (OTAs) and hotels. The OFT subsequently issued a statement of objections to Booking.com ('Booking'), Expedia Inc. ('Expedia') and InterContinental Hotels Group plc (IHG) in July 2012.[51] The main focus of the OFT's investigation was on the restriction on OTAs' ability to discount the rate at which room-only hotel accommodation bookings were offered to consumers. The OFT considered that such restrictions were 'by their very nature' anti-competitive because they eliminated price competition between OTAs. In July 2013, the parties involved offered commitments to the OFT, which were accepted in January 2014. While MFNs were not the focus of the investigations, the commitments offered by the parties did address MFN clauses, and OTAs committed to refrain from entering or enforcing any MFN clauses or similar provisions.[52]

The OFT's decision to accept commitments was later quashed by the Competition Appeal Tribunal on appeal by Skyscanner, the operator of a *meta-search* site that displays prices offered by third parties to assist consumers to compare prices.[53] Skyscanner's appeal was primarily against the OTAs' commitment to not publicise a specific level of discounts as it argued that this restricted the disclosure of pricing information and would negatively impact on price transparency in the meta-search and comparison market. Consequently, the case was remitted back to the CMA, who had by then taken over the role of the OFT.

In September 2015, the CMA decided to close the case on the basis of administrative priorities. Thereafter, in July 2016, the CMA launched a monitoring project in the hotel online booking sector in partnership with the European Commission and nine other national competition authorities of the EU Member States. The CMA noted:

> The questionnaires [which were sent to hotels across the UK as part of the project], which use a common approach across the 10 countries, will collect information to assess how that change [i.e. commitments from Expedia and Booking to drop MFN clauses], alongside other recent developments – including several investigations across Europe into a range of pricing practices in the online booking sector – have affected the market.[54]

However, on 6 April 2017, the CMA announced that in light of the findings of the European Competition Network report on the results of the monitoring project in the hotel online booking sector, it would not be prioritising further investigation into pricing practices in this sector at this stage. The CMA noted that the monitoring group's analysis shows a shift from wide to narrow MFNs in the UK and elsewhere

---

[51] See the press release dated 31 July 2012 issued by the Office of Fair Trading at http://webarchive.nationalarchives.gov.uk/20140402142426/http://www.oft.gov.uk/news-and-updates/press/2012/65-12. Accessed 25 October 2017. Both Booking and Expedia had entered into separate agreements with IHG.

[52] Case CE9320/10, Hotel Online Booking (2014), Annex 1 at para 21. Available at: http://webarchive.nationalarchives.gov.uk/20140402182554/http://www.oft.gov.uk/shared_oft/ca-and-cartels/hob-annexe1.pdf. Accessed 25 October 2017.

[53] *Skyscanner Limited v Competition and Markets Authority,* [2014] CAT 16.

[54] See press release issued by the CMA on 13 July 2016. Available at https://www.gov.uk/government/news/monitoring-project-launched-in-online-hotel-booking-sector. Accessed 25 October 2017.

coincides with a discernible increase in the levels of price differentiation between different OTAs in the last few years. According to the CMA, this suggests that *hotels are increasingly taking advantage of the ability to set different prices between different OTAs and are able to do so in response to differences in the competitive offers of these OTAs*. However, the CMA did conclude that *it is too early to reach any conclusions on whether so called 'narrow' parity clauses...should separately be regarded as giving rise to competition concerns and therefore warrant investigation by the CMA.*[55]

Separately, in November 2013, the OFT closed an investigation into price parity requirements imposed by Amazon in its agreements with third-party sellers whereby they were restricted from offering lower prices on other online sales channels after Amazon agreed to drop its policy on its UK marketplace, as well as across the UK. The OFT closed its investigation on the basis of administrative priority, without reaching a decision whether there had been an infringement of competition law.[56]

The CMA has also looked at MFNs in the context of private motor insurance (PMI) market in the UK. In September 2012, the OFT made a market investigation reference under the Enterprise Act 2002 to the then Competition Commission in relation to the supply or acquisition of PMI and related goods or services. The CMA's final report, published in September 2014, concluded that wide MFN clauses are likely to have an anti-competitive effect as (a) such clauses softened price competition between price comparison websites in relation to PMI because such websites did not face a possibility that a retail customer would find a same PMI policy at a cheaper price on a competing website and (b) there was little incentive for a price comparison website to compete with a competitor with a wide MFN clause to seek better PMI prices for their retail consumers from the insurers. Any such better price was also passed on to the competitor. Therefore, there was little reward for commission fee reductions and less disincentive against raising fees. Furthermore, according to the CMA, the softening of price competition between the price comparison websites regarding their services to PMI providers likely led to less entry, less innovation and higher commission fees, which in turn resulted in higher premiums. In contrast, the CMA concluded that the narrow MFN clauses were a legitimate tool used by price comparison websites to engender customer trust in their service offering, and absence of such clauses could seriously undermine their distribution channel.[57]

---

[55] See the CMA Update dated 6 April 2017, *Online travel agents: monitoring of pricing practices results*. Available at: https://assets.publishing.service.gov.uk/media/58e61bd5e5274a06b00000e8/update-6-april-2017.pdf. Accessed 25 October 2017. Also, see *Private motor insurance market investigation,* Final Report (24 September 2014) at para 60, where the Competition Commission, predecessor to the CMA, found that narrow MFN clauses would not raise the same concerns of softening price competition compared with wide MFN clauses.

[56] Case CE/9692/12, *Amazon online retailer: investigation into anti-competitive practices.* Available at: https://www.gov.uk/cma-cases/amazon-online-retailer-investigation-into-anti-competitive-practices. Accessed 25 October 2017.

[57] See Final Report, *Private motor insurance market investigation,* 24 September 2015 at paras 8.32 to 8.8.54. Available at: https://assets.publishing.service.gov.uk/media/5421c2ade5274a1314000001/Final_report.pdf. Accessed 25 October 2017.

### 12.2.2.3 Restriction on Online Sales

Online retailers are today increasingly competing with the traditional 'bricks-and-mortar' shops, and they potentially offer real competing choice to the consumers. For instance, increasingly, consumers can search for a product or service online, compare prices and order the product or service without stepping into a physical shop. Therefore, typically, now consumers have wider choices, and they are not restricted to shops in their local area or city like they were just a few years ago. This greater competitive choice usually equates to greater competitive pressures on price, quality, efficiency and innovation. Furthermore, as online selling does not require upfront investment in a store and many pre-sale services, they tend to exert downward pressure on and spur efficiency. However, on the other side of the coin, as noted above in Sect. 12.2.2, this may give rise to the 'free-riding' problem, which in the long term may make physical stores unsustainable and lead to their closure. Ultimately, consumer choice and quality of the retail experience may suffer as customers may not be able to walk into a store to look and feel a product and obtain advice from a shop assistant.

Currently, under the EU and the UK competition rules, generally provisions in vertical agreements between a seller and distributor/retailer that discriminate against online selling are considered as hardcore restrictions and are therefore prohibited. These restrictions include obligations on resellers to prevent customers in other territories viewing their website, terminate Internet transactions once credit card data show addresses outside the distributor's exclusive territory, make no online sales, limit the proportions of the sales that they make online and pay to the upstream supplier a higher price for products being resold online than for products being resold in bricks and mortar.[58]

However, it is permissible for a supplier to limit a reseller/distributor from online advertising that is specifically addressed to customers in other distributors' exclusive territories, oblige a reseller to sell a minimum absolute amount—by value or volume—in brick-and-mortar stores, oblige a reseller to observe certain quality standards for resale over the Internet—for example, that the reseller must have one or more brick-and-mortar shops or showrooms as a condition for being a member of a selective distribution system.[59]

The CMA generally distinguishes between instances on blanket bans on online sales, i.e. provisions that prevent resellers from selling online at all, and ban on online platforms, i.e. provisions that prevent resellers from selling through specific third-party platforms such as Amazon or eBay. The former are strictly prohibited and are seen as by 'object' restrictions of competition. On the other hand, the latter are seen as *a restriction on how a product is sold, but without closing off an outlet – and therefore as not being an "object" restriction, but rather one to be assessed case by case according to its effects.*[60]

---

[58] See footnote 32 above, at para 52.

[59] See footnote 32 above, at paras 52 to 54.

[60] Speech by Michael Grenfell, CMA Executive Director – Enforcement, 'Antitrust in the digital age', Competition Law Forum, 15 November 2016. Available at: https://www.gov.uk/government/speeches/michael-grenfell-on-antitrust-in-the-digital-age. Accessed 25 October 2017.

In June 2016, the CMA issued a statement of objections to Ping Europe Limited ('Ping') for an alleged breach of competition rules by operating an online sales ban, which prevents retailers selling Ping golf clubs online. The CMA stated: '[t]he internet is an increasingly important distribution channel and retailers' ability to supply via this channel should not be unduly restricted…Bans on internet trading can be a problem if they seek to prevent retailers reaching a significant proportion of customers…[the CMA will] consider any justifications put forward by Ping for the alleged conduct.'[61]

Interestingly, the CJEU is currently considering a request of the Higher Regional Court of Frankfurt for its guidance on the legality of online platform bans imposed by perfume and cosmetic maker Coty, Inc. ('Coty') on one of its authorised distributors.[62] The case arose from Coty's claim against its distributor that it had breached the conditions of their selective distribution system by selling perfume products on Amazon.de. In an earlier case, the German competition authority, Bundeskartellamt, had held such an online platform ban as likely to be an 'object' restriction.[63]

#### 12.2.2.4 Licensing Rights of Digital Content

As noted above in Sect. 12.2.2, the European Commission identified contractual restrictions in licensing agreements for digital content, such as movies, music, etc., as the main competition concern in the online market for digital content.

The European Commission found widespread use of geo-blocking measures by digital content providers.[64] Sixty-eight percent of digital content providers participating in the European Commission's inquiry reported to have restricted their online digital content services from other EU Member States, and 59% of them did so pursuant to contractual restrictions in their agreements with the rights holder.[65]

The Technology Transfer Block Exemption Regulation (TTBER) adopted by the European Commission applies to licensing agreements, referred to as technology transfer agreements, where a licensor permits the licensee(s) to use the licensed technology for the production of goods or services.[66] The TTBER applies to tech-

[61] See the CMA's press release dated 9 June 2016. Available at: https://www.gov.uk/government/news/cma-alleges-breach-of-competition-law-by-ping. Accessed 25 October 2017.

[62] CJEU, case C-230/16, *Request for a preliminary ruling from Oberlandesgericht Frankfurt am main (Germany) lodged on 25 April 2016 – Coty Germany GmbH v Parfümerie Akzente GmbH* (not yet published).

[63] See ASICS running shoes: Unlawful restrictions of online sales of ASICS running shoes, Bundeskartellamt (Germany), August 2015.

[64] Geo-blocking refers to commercial practices by which online providers prevent users from accessing and/or purchasing goods or digital content offered on their website based on the user's location or country of residence. Geo-blocking, however, differs from geo-filtering, which involves online providers allowing users to access and purchase goods cross-border, but on different terms and conditions based on the location of the user.

[65] See footnote 30 above, at para 66. The current TTBER came into force on 1 May 2014 and they replaced Commission Regulation 772/2004, the old TTBER.

[66] Commission Regulation 316/2014 of 21 March 2014 on the application of Article 101(3) of the Treaty on the Functioning of the European Union to categories of technology transfer agreements, OJ 2014, L.93, p. 17.

nology transfer agreements involving licences of patents, know-how and/or software copyright.[67] It does not apply to licensing of trademarks, copyright and other intellectual property rights, unless such licensing is not the primary object of the agreement and is directly related to the production of the contract products.

Under Article 4(2) of TTBER, a restriction in an agreement between two non-competing undertakings whereby the licensee is prohibited from passively selling into a territory or to certain customer groups falls outside the exemption provided by the TTBER. There are, however, a number of exceptions to this, including the restriction of passive sales into an exclusive territory reserved for the licensor, which is permissible. The accompanying guidelines to the TTBER further states that in exceptional circumstances, it may be possible to impose restrictions on passive sales by licensees into an exclusive territory or customer group allocated to another licensee *where substantial investments by the licensee are necessary to start up and develop a new market, restrictions of passive sales by other licensees into such a territory fall outside Article 101(1) for the period necessary for the licensee to recoup those investments.*[68]

Absolute territorial protection of intellectual property rights outside the scope of TTBER are also generally considered as a by object restriction of competition law under the EU rules. In *Consten & Grundig*, a case involving trademarks, the CJEU held that *undertakings must refrain from using rights under national trade mark law in order to set an obstacle in the way of parallel imports.*[69] This case involved an agreement between Consten and Grundig whereby Grundig agreed to appoint Consten as its exclusive distributor for the metropolitan territory of France, the Saar and Corsica of various electronic goods manufactured by Grundig, and carrying the GINT trademark. Grundig obtained the necessary trademarks from Consten and registered the same in France. As per the agreement, Consten was granted absolute territorial protection, i.e. ban on both active and passive sales into its territory. According to the ECJ, the Commission was right in its decision to prohibit Consten from using the GINT trademark to prevent parallel imports.

Similarly, in *Nungesser*, the European Court of Justice considered the use of intellectual property rights to protect an exclusive jurisdiction system and reconfirmed that absolute protection granted to a licensee to restrict parallel imports leads to artificial division of national markets in the EU, in contravention of the EU rules.[70]

---

[67] TTBER would only apply to technology transfer agreements where the prescribed market share thresholds are met – the combined market share of competing undertakings must not exceed 20% on the affected relevant technology and product market, or the individual market shares of non-competitors must not exceed 30% on the affected relevant technology and product markets.

[68] Communication from the Commission, Guidelines on the application of Article 101 of the Treaty on the Functioning of the European Union to technology transfer agreements, OJ 2014, C 89, p. 3, para 126. The guidelines further state that a period of two years would usually be enough for the licensee to recoup such investment.

[69] ECJ, cases 56&58/64 *Consten and Grundig v Commission* ECR 1966 299, pt 345.

[70] ECJ case 258/78 *Nungesser and Eisele v Commission* ECR 1983 2015, pt 61.

Then in *Football Association Premier League Ltd/Murphy*,[71] the European Court of Justice was asked by the English High Court, *inter alia*, to consider contractual restrictions imposed by the FA Premier League on broadcast licensees that were designed to preclude any members of the public receiving those licensees' broadcasts outside of the territory for which they held the licence. FA Premier League had earlier brought actions in the English High Court in relation to pubs that had sourced decoding equipment from abroad to enable them to screen live coverage of Premier League football matches at a lower cost than had they purchased the equipment from the UK broadcast licensee.[72] The defendants in the UK courts argued that the terms of FA Premier League broadcasting licence infringed Article 101 of TFEU. The European Court of Justice held that contractual prohibitions on the sale of and use of decoder equipment for viewing football matches were restrictions of competition by object. According to the court:

> …where a licence agreement is designed to prohibit or limit the cross-border provision of broadcasting services, it is deemed to have as its object the restriction of competition, unless other circumstances falling within its economic and legal context justify the finding that such an agreement is not liable to impair competition.[73]

It further stated:

> Such clauses prohibit the broadcasters from effecting any cross-border provision of services that relates to those matches, which enables each broadcaster to be granted absolute territorial exclusivity in the area covered by its licence and, thus, all competition between broadcasters in the field of those services to be eliminated.[74]

In July 2015, the European Commission issued a statement of objections to six major Hollywood film studios—Paramount, Disney, NBCUniversal, Sony, 20th Century Fox and Warner Bros—and Sky UK alleging that each of the studios and Sky UK had bilaterally agreed geo-blocking restrictions in breach of EU competition rules.[75] The restrictions in the agreements prevented Sky UK from making film content available through its online and satellite pay-TV services to consumers in other EU countries outside of the UK and Ireland, i.e. its licensed territories, and required the film studios to ensure that other broadcasters were prevented from making their pay-TV services available to consumers in the UK and Ireland in competition with Sky UK.

---

[71] CJEU, joined cases C-403/08 and C-429/08 *Football Association Premier League Ltd and others v QC Leisure and others and Derek Owen and Karen Murphy v Media Protection Services Ltd*, [2012] 1 CMLR 769.

[72] Case C-403/08 involved the suppliers of equipment that was sourced from Greece and the licensees of four pubs who had showed the coverage of Premier League matches from an Arab broadcaster. Case C-429/08 related to an appeal by a pub landlady, Karen Murphy, who had shown Premier League matches using Greek decoding equipment.

[73] See footnote 72 above, para 140.

[74] See footnote 72 above, para 142.

[75] See case AT.40023 – *Cross-border access to pay-TV*, case file. Available at: http://ec.europa.eu/competition/elojade/isef/case_details.cfm?proc_code=1_40023. Accessed 25 October 2017.

Paramount offered commitments to the European Commission in April 2016, which were later accepted by the Commission in July 2016. Accordingly, Paramount has agreed that its film broadcasting licences with broadcasters in the European Economic Area will not include contractual obligations to prevent or limit a broadcaster from responding to unsolicited requests from consumers within the EEA but outside of the broadcaster's licensed territory and require it to prohibit or limit broadcasters located outside the licensed territory from responding to unsolicited requests from consumers within the licensed territory.[76] The European Commission's investigation into contracts between Sky UK and other studios is still ongoing.

Furthermore, on 2 February 2017, the European Commission launched two separate investigations into geo-blocking practices in online sales of video games and hotel accommodation. First inquiry involves the largest PC game distribution platform, Steam, and its agreements with multiple video game publishers. The alleged geo-blocking in this case relates to game activation keys released by Steam in order to unlock games electronically. In this case, the activation keys are themselves geo-blocked, which means that a game purchased through Steam in one EU Member State could only grant access to users in that country. The second relates to geo-blocking and price discrimination allegedly designed to hinder cross-border trade. For example, the European Commission is investigating agreements between Meliá Hotels and the largest European tour operators, which allegedly discriminate between customers based on their location.[77]

On 6 February 2018, the European Parliament formally adopted at first reading the Europan Commission's proposed regulation addressing geo-blocking.[78]

## 12.3 Other Issues

### 12.3.1 Market Definition

As noted above in Sect. 12.1.4, market definition is central to a competition analysis whether under Article 101 TFEU/Chapter I prohibition or Article 102 TFEU/ Chapter II prohibition or merger control.

The growth of online sales platforms and digital services has also had a significant effect on how a relevant market is defined. *Are online services in the same*

[76] See case AT.40023 – *Cross-border access to pay-TV: Paramount, Commitments*. Available at: http://ec.europa.eu/competition/antitrust/cases/dec_docs/40023/40023_5274_2.pdf. Accessed 25 October 2017.

[77] See press release dated 2 February 2017 issued by the European Commission. Available at: http://europa.eu/rapid/press-release_IP-17-201_en.htm. Accessed 25 October 2017.

[78] See European Parliament legislative resolution of 6 February 2018 on the proposal for a Regulation of the European Parliament and of the Council on addressing geo-blocking and other forms of discrimination based on customers' nationality, place of residence or place of establishment within the internal market and amending Regulation (EC) No 2006/2004 and Directive 2009/22/EC. Available at: http://www.europarl.europa.eu/sides/getDoc.do?pubRef=-//EP//TEXT+TA+P8-TA-2018-0023+0+DOC+XML+V0//EN&language=EN. Accessed 11 May 2018.

*markets as traditional services? Should we regard online services as competitive constraints on more traditional services?*[79] Therefore, the advent of online sales platform means that the relevant market today for the sale of many goods or services would be broader than local or regional or national markets in the past.

### 12.3.2 Facilitating Collusion

While the main competition concerns, as noted in Sect. 12.2 above, revolve around businesses seeking to frustrate the use of new technologies, for instance by restricting access to online sales channel, or third-party online platforms, in some instances concerns may arise where businesses use digital technology to facilitate anti-competitive conduct. In August 2016, the CMA issued an infringement decision against Trod Ltd and GB eye Ltd for colluding on the market for online sales of posters and frames. In this case, both companies agreed not to undercut each other's prices for posters and frames sold on Amazon Marketplace in the UK. The agreement in question was put in place using an automated repricing software that adjusted each manufacturer's prices automatically to ensure they did not undercut each other.

Andrea Coscelli, CMA Acting Chief Executive, noted:

> As competition authorities, we need to stay alive to the potential for such software to be used in ways which seek covertly to distort markets, particularly in an age of increasingly 'intelligent', 'self-learning' technologies and algorithms. As the then US Assistant Attorney General Bill Baer recently commented following an investigation by our counterparts at the Department of Justice into the anti-competitive use of algorithmic software: 'We will not tolerate anti-competitive conduct, whether it occurs in a smoke-filled room or over the internet using complex pricing algorithms.[80]

---

[79] See footnote 60 above.

[80] Speech by Andrea Coscelli, CMA Acting Chief Executive, 'Staying ahead in digital marketplace', 9 September 2016. Available at: https://www.gov.uk/government/speeches/andrea-coscelli-staying-ahead-in-a-digital-marketplace. Accessed 25 October 2017.

# Part II

# Copyright Limitations and Exceptions

# International Report

# 13

Benoit Michaux

## 13.1 Introduction

This international report examines the increasingly complex balance between the interests of copyright owners, on one hand, and the interests of users of their work, on the other. In particular, it considers how the current laws and the court decisions of those countries that have prepared national reports strike that balance. In this regard, it reflects the critical comments that have been expressed by the national rapporteurs vis-à-vis the current system, identifies issues where there is scope for progress and seeks to open up new avenues to manage diverging interests.[1]

## 13.2 Background

### 13.2.1 The Key Challenges Related to the Question

In the field of intellectual property, copyright is probably one of the areas that call for the closest attention to the exceptions and limitations to the owner's rights. There are a number of reasons for this.

[1] The author is very grateful for the national reports which have been submitted from the following jurisdictions: *Austria* (Valerie Eder); *Belgium* (Manon Knockaert); *Brazil* (Felipe Barros Oquendo); *Czech Republic* (Radka MacGregor Pelikánová); *France* (Martina Isola and Guillaume Couet); *Germany* (Thomas Hoeren); *Hungary* (Zsófia Lendvai); *Italy* (Marco Francetti); *Poland* (Maria Obara-Piszewska and Filina Sztandera); *Romania* (Paul-George Buta); *Switzerland* (Sevan Antreasyan); *UK* (Eleonora Rosati).

B. Michaux (✉)
Hoyng Rokh Monegier, Brussels, Belgium

Université de Namur, Namur, Belgium
e-mail: benoit.michaux@hoyngrokh.com



B. Kilpatrick et al. (eds.), *Antitrust Analysis of Online Sales Platforms & Copyright Limitations and Exceptions*, LIDC Contributions on Antitrust Law, Intellectual Property and Unfair Competition,
https://doi.org/10.1007/978-3-319-71419-6_13

One such reason is the fact that the scope of copyright is extremely broad, both in terms of eligible subject matter and in terms of exclusivity in favour of the owner. Another reason is the fact that a constantly increasing number of activities implies the use of protected works, while those who conduct these activities might invoke legitimate rights and interests that deserve respect too.

Especially in the digital environment (even if the non-digital environment is also relevant), permitted use of copyright protected works is increasingly considered as a 'must-have', as a consequence of the development of new techniques or new business models (such as format shifting, distance learning, mobile applications for cultural institutions and big data).

Admittedly, in light of this, it is tempting to say that copyright laws should permit more uses without the copyright owner's consent. However, great care is required because the situation in each case may vary significantly and the respective interests of the owner and the user do not always deserve the same level of respect.

Indeed, the activities and the interests of the users of copyright works may be very different. They range from the non-commercial use by private individuals (e.g., private copy) to the commercial use by profit-making entities. The nature of the activities, the objectives pursued and the fact that the activity is conducted by a private individual or by a not-for-profit entity rather than by a profit-making entity can be decisive when considering the respective interests of the copyright owner and those of the user of the work.

To give an example, when it comes to digitisation, i.e. converting a work into data that can be read by a computer and transferred to other computers, the situations will vary depending on whether the digitisation is made by a private individual for his personal use, by a cultural not-for-profit entity officially organised by the authorities for archiving purposes, or by a profit-making organisation acting on a large scale for commercial purposes.

In this context, it is reasonable to state that the copyright protection system needs to consider solutions that strike a true balance between the legitimate interests of all parties involved, namely the copyright owners on the one hand and the users of copyright works on the other hand. Exceptions and limitations to copyright play a key role to this end. Indeed, they are supposed to ensure the balance required. The way the exceptions and limitations are worded and the fact that they generate or do not generate compensation in favour of the copyright owner are key when assessing if they are appropriate.

However, a growing number of questions arise as to whether the exceptions and limitations that are currently provided by the various legal instruments are sufficient to tackle this huge challenge. Are they readily understandable? Are they appropriate to the current and the future needs? Are they flexible enough? Are they proportionate? Is there any risk that they might constitute barriers to legitimate trade? Do they imply financial compensation that could negatively impact the balance? Do we need new exceptions? Must the list of exceptions and limitations be an open-ended list rather than a closed list, a non-exhaustive rather than an exhaustive one? Must the exceptions and limitations be mandatory, and if so, should all of them be mandatory? Should the law provide for a broad and flexible concept like 'fair use' or any other comparable concept rather than for a list of rigid and well-detailed exceptions and limitations?

### 13.2.2 Legal Background

The international agreements to be taken into consideration when dealing with the question include, *inter alia*, the following main instruments:

- Berne Convention for the Protection of Literary and Artistic Works of 9 September 1886, lastly amended on 28 September 1979;
- Agreement on Trade-Related Aspects of Intellectual Property Rights, adopted in Marrakesh on 15 April 1994;
- WIPO Copyright Treaty, adopted in Geneva on 20 December 1996.

Even though they are not truly indispensable to discuss the question, the following instruments may also be mentioned: the Beijing Treaty on Audiovisual Performances, which was adopted on 24 June 2012; the Marrakesh Treaty to Facilitate Access to Published Works for Persons Who Are Blind, Visually Impaired or Otherwise Print Disabled, adopted on 27 June 2013.

Moreover, as far as the European Union is concerned, attention has to be paid to Directive 2001/29/EC of the European Parliament and of the Council of 22 May 2001 on the harmonisation of certain aspects of copyright and related rights in the information society. Also to be mentioned is the proposal of Directive of 14 September 2016 in the framework of the copyright reform package, in particular concerning the exceptions related to research, education, libraries and big data.[2]

### 13.2.3 Preliminary Remarks About the Wording of the Question

The question, as adopted by the Executive Committee of ILCL, reads as follows: *To what extent do current exclusions and limitations to copyright strike a fair balance between the rights of owners and fair use by private individuals and others?*

The wording above gives rise to some questions. Therefore, it seems appropriate to give clarifications and, where necessary, to suggest alternative wording.

In particular, the following terms or expressions deserve explanations:

- 'exclusions' [to copyright]: this term may be read as synonymous with 'exceptions' [to copyright];
- 'Fair use' [by private individuals]: this expression has a broad meaning so that it cannot be limited to the specific meaning that it has in a legal system like the

[2] COM(2016) 593 final. Available at https://ec.europa.eu/transparency/regdoc/rep/1/2016/EN/1-2016-593-EN-F1-1.PDF. Accessed 29 October 2017.

United States; 'fair' refers to a use that is made in accordance with the legitimate interests and rights of the user and proportionate to these interests and rights;
- 'by (...) and others': this expression refers to other persons than 'private individuals', *inter alia*, individuals acting for profit, not-for-profit organisations, public entities, profit-making organisations (including business entities).

### 13.2.4 Preliminary Remarks About the Scope of the Question

The scope of the question is deliberately large. Actually, it seeks to cover any kind of restriction on copyright that results in a permitted use of the work without the consent of the copyright owner. The question uses the term 'exclusions', which is probably less usual in this context. This term may be understood as being synonymous with 'exceptions' even if, admittedly, it also refers to situations where the legislature has 'excluded' some content (such as political speeches or news of the day) from the benefit of copyright protection. The questionnaire below mostly uses the term 'exceptions' rather than 'exclusions'. Moreover, the term 'exceptions' used below is intended to cover 'limitations' as well.

Furthermore, the question does not distinguish between the various mechanisms implementing the restrictions on copyright, such as 'pure' exceptions (i.e., exceptions without any compensation for the copyright owner), exceptions with compensation for the copyright owner or compulsory licences.

## 13.3 Discussion of the Various Issues Related to the Question

### 13.3.1 Role and Importance of the Three-Step Test

Before getting into a detailed examination of the various exceptions and limitations to copyright, it seems critical to emphasise the role and the importance of the so-called three-step test in this context.

According to the terms of this test, as provided in the TRIPS Agreement and the WIPO Copyright Treaty, States shall confine limitations or exceptions to exclusive rights to certain special cases that do not conflict with a normal exploitation of the work and do not unreasonably prejudice the legitimate interests of the right holder.[3] To some extent, this test is provided in the Berne Convention as well.[4] The EU legislation contains a similar provision.[5]

[3]Article 13 of the TRIPs Agreement, see above; Article 10 of the WIPO Copyright Treaty, see above.

[4]See in particular Article 9 with respect to the right of reproduction.

[5]Article 5, para 5, of the Directive 2001/29 reads as follows: 'The exceptions and limitations provided for in paragraphs 1, 2, 3 and 4 shall only be applied in certain special cases which do not conflict with a normal exploitation of the work or other subject-matter and do not unreasonably prejudice the legitimate interests of the rightholder.'

As a consequence of this rule, States appear limited in their freedom to foresee exceptions and limitations. In particular, they need to make sure that the exceptions and limitations shall not be contrary to a normal exploitation of the work or cause unreasonable harm to the legitimate interests of the copyright owner. And, first of all, they may adopt exceptions and limitations only in special cases. In other words, the three-step test is a guarantee in favour of the copyright owner that his interests shall be safeguarded, at least to a certain extent.

In contrast, this rule does not *directly* provide for any specific and explicit guarantee for the benefit of the user of the work. Implicitly, the mere fact that a State foresees an exception or a limitation is deemed a sufficient way to meet the user's needs. There is no further indication in this rule about the fact that the exception should preserve the user's interests and ensure a proper balance between his interest and the interest of the copyright owner.

Having said that, it remains unclear how far this guarantee for the copyright owner is reaching. In particular, it is disputed whether it is a rule for the State legislature only or also for the State judicial authorities. In the second option, the courts would be to verify whether the exceptions and limitations comply with the test in concrete cases, while they would not in the first option. This is to say that the official position of each State in this respect is important to assess the effectiveness and the level of requirement of the three-step test.

The results that appear from the national reports on this subject can be summarised as follows.

In the majority of the EU Member States—with some exceptions that include the UK—the three-step test has been implemented into national legislation, due to the fact that the test is explicitly mentioned in Directive 2001/29.

Moreover, it seems that in most EU Member States—also in the UK—the three-step test serves as general guidance for the national courts when they apply national exceptions and limitations in specific cases. In this regard, the Austrian rapporteur emphasises that even when the three-step test is not implemented into national law (as is the case in Austria), the national exceptions and limitations must be interpreted in conformity with the three-step test as adopted in Directive 2001/29. As the Czech report indicates, the three-step test constitutes a universal interpretation rule for all free uses and compulsory licences. Admittedly, in many situations, the literal wording of the exceptions themselves already includes a language that aims to reduce the potential impact on the exploitation of the work and the legitimate interests of the copyright owner. But beyond this internal reduction, the three-step test may be viewed as an additional external tool to ensure that the exception or limitation at stake effectively stays within boundaries that are acceptable from the right owners' perspective.

It is worth referring to certain specific parts of the national reports in this respect. For example, in France, it appears that the courts may rely on the conditions of the (external) three-step test in order to deny the user the benefit of an exception even when the specific (internal) conditions for the exception are met. In Italy as well, it seems that the three-step test constitutes a general interpretative standard for the judges. The same applies in Belgium. Even though the three-step test was not implemented into national law in this country, the explanatory memorandum provides that courts can use the test as a guideline.

At the same time, it seems that in many countries, the number of cases where the judges rely on the three-step test remains rather modest. In Italy, for instance, the national rapporteur mentions that the judicial practical application of the test is not particularly widespread outside the scope of private copying disputes. In Hungary as well, it seems that the courts focus on the specific conditions required for the relevant exception rather than analysing the merits and the application of the three-step test. In the UK, the rapporteur explains that lack of a specific provision outlining the three-step test according to national law, together with the idea that the three-step test would be akin to the UK concept of 'fair dealing', is the principal reason as to why '[th]ere has been very little judicial consideration' of the three-step test in UK case law. That being said, in some countries, the reference to the three-step test is effective. In Romania, e.g., the courts have tended to verify the meeting of the special conditions first and, where satisfied, go on to verify whether the general conditions are also cumulatively met.

Actually, different factors may explain why only few decisions refer to the three-step test. This may have to do with the fact that the national law is considered to implement the test (e.g., in the UK the notion of 'fair dealing' is deemed equivalent to the three steps) or with the fact that in many cases, the internal test is unsuccessful so that there is no need to assess the compliance with the three-step test (see, e.g., the report for Poland).

Furthermore, when the court decisions rely on the three-step test—which does not occur frequently—in most cases they conclude that the application of the exception is not contrary to the test. In Germany, for example, the national rapporteur notes that the number of cases in which courts denied to apply an exception on the account of the three-step test is very low.

In non-EU countries, where the support for the three-step test is to be found only in the international instruments (Berne Convention, TRIPS, WIPO treaties), a similar trend is very clear. In the report for Brazil, the decisions referred to, in particular those handed down by the Superior Court of Justice, generally find that the exceptions at stake do comply with the three-step test. In Switzerland, the rapporteur has no national decision to mention where the court would have rejected the application of a national exception for the reason that it is contrary to a normal exploitation of the work or it unreasonably prejudices the legitimate interests of the copyright owner.

The reason why the exception is found to be contrary to the three-step test only in a few cases might have to do with the interpretation of the terms of the test. In Germany, for instance, the Federal Court of Justice decided that the normal exploitation is only endangered when the allegedly infringing use is in direct competition with the normal exploitation. For example, a textbook that was not only created for university use is not in direct competition with a document using parts of the textbook for university use.

In this regard, the Belgian national rapporteur suggests that the compliance with the three-step test is likely to be assessed in two different ways, namely an abstract way and a concrete way, whereby the latter is preferred in Belgium.

In the abstract way, the judge simply verifies whether the legal basis for the exception or limitation is designed in such a manner that it meets the general conditions of the three-step test.

In contrast, in the concrete way, the judge goes beyond the mere analysis of the legal provision. He seeks to find whether in the specific situation referred to him the application of the legal provision reveals inconsistencies with the three-step test.

The concrete approach, while it is deemed appropriate in many countries, is a source of repeating discussions. In particular, questions arise as to what has to be considered a 'normal' exploitation of the work and what has to be understood an 'unreasonable' prejudice to the legitimate interests of the copyright owner.

The *Tixdaq* case in the UK gives an illustration of these discussions. *Tixdaq* was a case concerning the unauthorised reproduction and making available of short extracts of television broadcasts of cricket matches. The court denied the defendant from benefiting from the exception for the purpose of reporting current events because the application of this exception would violate the three-step test. In particular, the court noted that 'conflict with a normal exploitation of the work or other subject-matter' refers to exploitation of the work by the copyright owner, whether directly or through licensees, while attention must be paid not only to current exploitations but also to potential exploitations in the future. Considering the third step (that the exception at hand must not 'unreasonably prejudice the legitimate interests of the rightholder'), the court found a balance to be struck between the copyright owners' legitimate interests and the countervailing interests served by the exception.

The German report mentions a recent case about the exception that allows making works available to the public for purposes of instruction and research. In that case, a distance university made available 91 of 476 pages of a textbook for psychology students. One of the questions was whether the university's use of the work conflicted with the normal exploitation of the work as there was no need for the students to purchase the book. The German Federal Court of Justice pointed out that the triple test is decisive for the application of exceptions to copyright. The federal judges decided that the normal exploitation is only endangered when the usage is in direct competition with it. As the textbook was not only created for university use, this was not the case.

It could be said that the more detailed is the analysis of each individual step of the three-step test, the more chances that a real balance can be found between the interests of the copyright owner and the interests of the users.

In contrast, some national reports tend to indicate that their national courts can be less detailed when they apply the three-step test. For example, the report for the Czech Republic mentions a decision of the Czech Supreme Court, which used one part of the three-step test (namely the prejudice to the legitimate interests of the copyright owner) in a general way. In the case concerned, the court rejected the free use defence in a situation where the work was made available between members of one and the same association. The court found that no licence was obtained to permit using the copyrighted work by others than the purchaser of the work and that an opposite interpretation would lead to an unjustified breach of the legitimate interests of authors.

All that being said, before taking a closer look at each individual step of the three-step test, the first exercise for the judge is to assess whether the use under criticism falls within the scope of the national exception or limitation. The reports for France and Poland put emphasis on this priority.

### 13.3.2 Closed vs Open-Ended List of Exceptions and Limitations

Generally speaking, the list of exceptions and limitations to copyright is an exhaustive list in all the countries covered by the national reports.

As a result of the harmonisation through Directive 2001/29, in all the EU Member States the system of exceptions and limitations is a closed one (see below). But the solution is not different in the non-EU countries that submitted a report (Brazil and Switzerland).

The Swiss rapporteur mentions in this regard that although not explicitly stated in the national law, the exceptions set forth in that law are exhaustive. As a consequence, any use that falls outside the list shall in principle not be permitted without authorisation from the copyright owner. Moreover, according to the Swiss Supreme Federal Court, the fundamental rights other than copyright shall not serve as a basis to extend or create a new exception to copyright, even though they should be taken into consideration when interpreting a copyright exception.

In Brazil, too, the number of exceptions is a closed number. That being said, the Brazilian rapporteur stresses that some exceptions have been written in such a way that they do not seek to define a specific situation but embrace several hypotheses. This applies, e.g., to the exception permitting the reproduction, in any works, of small stretches of pre-existing works, of any nature, or of integral works, in the case of plastic arts, when reproduction itself is not the main objective of the new work and does not prejudice the exploitation or cause unjustified prejudice to the legitimate interests of the authors.

In Romania as well, the list of exceptions provided by law is a closed one, meaning that in order for any exception to apply, the use must fall within the ones on the list, any other use being subject to the authorisation of the author and/or right holder.

Although the list of exceptions is clearly exhaustive in all the EU countries, a number of nuances and clarifications deserve to be mentioned.

First, it has been observed by several rapporteurs that the national numbers of exceptions have increased constantly, and more and more rapidly over recent times.

Second, some uses may be permitted by the courts even though they were not authorised by the copyright owner or specifically covered by an explicit exception or limitation. The French rapporteur refers in this respect to court decisions that have found that the uses at stake constituted non-infringing ‘accessory reproductions’ or ‘accidental inclusions’, i.e. uses that do not fall within the scope of the exclusive rights; said uses concern, for instance, cases where the work is not reproduced for itself but only in an accessory manner to the main subject (e.g., reproduction of a work in a documentary).

In the same way, the Austrian report emphasises that uses not falling within the scope of the exclusive rights can be viewed as limitations to the copyright—in a broad sense. Such uses include, according to the Austrian rapporteur, the mere consumption of the work and also—probably subject to some conditions—the exhibition of a published work.

Third, as the Austrian rapporteur indicates, national copyright law can provide for exceptions beyond the closed list if covered by the so-called grandfather clause, i.e. exceptions that were already provided by national law before the implementation of Directive 2001/29 and relate to non-digital uses.

Fourth, according to the Austrian rapporteur, limitations to copyright also arise from other areas like the principle of exhaustion, other rules and regulations outside of the Copyright Act (including, e.g., antitrust law) and enforcement of other fundamental rights. In contrast, the report for Poland mentions that there is no purpose in trying to devise any new forms of permissible use on the basis of any laws or regulations other than the Copyright Act. Likewise, according to the French rapporteur, since only the exhaustive list of exception allows uses without the consent of the author, there is no general situation in which other fundamental rights permit the use without the consent of the author (i.e., a 'general' situation outside copyright law itself). This is to say that the exceptions themselves are already thought and provided in order to balance fundamental rights other than copyright such as freedom of expression, right to private life, right to education and the right of the copyright owner. The formulation of those exceptions is already the result of this balance. The use must therefore comply with the conditions required for the application of the relevant exception. However, it always remains possible for the judge to see an 'abuse' of copyright because the copyright, even in its prerogatives under the moral right, is not discretionary. Similarly, the copyright cannot confer any immunity in light of the violations of the rights of third parties, whether these are focused on personality rights or simply the right of property. However, the reasoning might be different for rights that were not taken into account in the balance of the exceptions, such as competition or consumer law. Hence, those considerations, can eventually, in certain circumstances, limit the exercise of the copyright owner.

Fifth (and noting the Austrian report in this regard), in a still broader sense, copyright exceptions or limitations could be considered as addressing subject matters that are excluded from copyright protection, like law and decrees.

### 13.3.3 Missing Exceptions?

Since the list is a closed one in all the countries covered by the national reports, the question arises as to whether it disregards some users' fundamental rights that could justify exceptions or limitations that are not included.

To address this question properly, it seems necessary first to identify the different users' interests that have been taken into account in the current various pieces of legislation, as well as the extent to which they have been taken into consideration.

The national laws generally address all of the following users' fundamental rights and offer corresponding useful exceptions in this regard: education, research, access to culture and knowledge, freedom of expression and right to receive and disseminate information, privacy and private use, needs of people with disability, preservation of cultural heritage, public security, freedom of panorama.

No national reporter seems to suggest that his national list would be missing exceptions in relation to specific users' rights. On the contrary, the Czech report indicates that according to the general Czech opinion, the national list does not appear to overlook or unduly minimise any users' fundamental right.

### 13.3.4 Restrictive Interpretation Versus Flexible Interpretation

National rapporteurs often emphasise that the exceptions and limitations are generally subject to a strict interpretation. However, this does not necessarily exclude some nuances and even some reservations. Actually, there might be some differences between the national traditions in this respect.

The Italian rapporteur is particularly explicit about the principle of restrictive interpretation. He emphasises that due to their nature of special rules, the provisions relating to exceptions and limitations cannot give rise to analogous and extensive interpretations and must only be applied to cases expressly provided for. These rules, given that they are of an exceptional nature and, in particular, derogations from the general principle that reserves the right to use the work of the author, should be taken to be strictly interpretive and must therefore be excluded from the possibility of giving the words a meaning other than the literal meaning. Likewise, the Polish rapporteur indicates that as permissible use provisions impose limitations on the author's monopoly, they must always be interpreted restrictively, and any doubts must be resolved in favour of the right holder. In Romania, too, the courts have indicated that the exceptions and limitations must be interpreted narrowly and applied restrictively due, first and foremost, to their qualifications as exceptional situations carved out of the scope of the generally applicable copyright protection. The Hungarian rapporteur notes that there is very little or even no flexibility for the court, and he even refers to a rigidity of the rules. In contrast, the Austrian rapporteur seems to take the view that there is no reason to exclude the analogous application of the provisions concerning the exceptions. Moreover, there is apparently a tradition of higher flexibility in favour of parodies.

According to the Swiss rapporteur, as a matter of principle under Swiss law, exceptions provided in an act shall be interpreted restrictively. In addition, according to a general principle of interpretation under Swiss copyright law, in case of doubt, a statute shall be interpreted in favour of the author/copyright owner (*in dubio pro auctore*). But at the same time, there is a tendency not to apply those general principles in an overly systematic way.

The Belgian rapporteur notes that, on the one hand, the exceptions receive a strict interpretation, and, on the other hand, according to the jurisprudence of the Court of Justice, the effectiveness of the exceptions must be preserved, provided that the three-step test is satisfied.

A restrictive interpretation does not mean that there is no room for any flexibility. The Swiss rapporteur notes in this regard that some exceptions provide more flexibility than others, which are more specific. In the same way, the Brazilian rapporteur finds that there is some flexibility and scope for a wider interpretation of some exceptions. At a minimum, paragraph VIII of Article 46, by providing conditions for a use to be an exception rather than describing a specific hypothesis, already gives an opening to the adaptation of the rules for new situations.

Most national rapporteurs find that depending on their nature and/or purpose, certain exceptions or limitations may be or may not be subject to narrow conditions in terms of beneficiaries and commercial or non-commercial uses.

The following examples are illustrative in this respect:

- the requirement that the use must be *non-commercial* for the archival and backup exceptions in favour of the museums (Swiss Report), for the private copy of extracts (Brazilian Report), for the private representation within the family circle (French Report), for the freedom of panorama (Romanian Report), while such a requirement is *not applicable* to freedom of expression, parody or quotation (Brazilian Report);
- the requirement that the use must be reserved *for individuals* for the private copy *sensu stricto* (Swiss Report), while such a requirement is not applicable to the exception of the demonstration of the product for sale or the freedom to reproduce excerpts from newspapers (Brazilian Report);
- the requirement that the works concerned must correspond to a very precise category of works for orphan works or commercially unavailable works (Polish Report).

The UK rapporteur mentions that, generally speaking, some UK copyright exceptions are limited to certain beneficiaries and/or subject matter, while other exceptions are subject to a number of conditions and are limited to certain specified purposes (at times restrictively interpreted by courts, e.g. in the case of criticism or review).

### 13.3.5 Obligatory Versus Optional; Unwaivable Versus Waivable

Naturally, there could be some ambiguity regarding the discussion relating to the mandatory character of the exceptions, in particular those listed in Directive 2001/29/EC. This raises two questions. The first question is whether States are obliged to implement all the exceptions listed therein into their national law. The second question, which is more delicate, is whether the contractual override of exceptions that are adopted by national law is admissible or not.

The national reports concentrated on the second question (see below).

Before getting into the comments about that second question, it is worth addressing the first one. A brief comment may suffice to this end. With respect to the exceptions listed in Directive 2001/29, it is unanimously admitted that they all—but one—are optional in that the States are free to implement them or not. There is just one exception that is mandatory, namely the exception with respect to the temporary copies. This specific exception must be adopted by the EU Member States. All the other exceptions may be or may not be adopted by them, at their entire discretion.

The second question, as to whether the exceptions may be overridden by contract, is more delicate. Clearly, the countries concerned have opposing views in this regard.

First, a number of countries are in favour of the unwaivable character of the exceptions.

Within the EU, the Belgian rapporteur notes that under his national law, as a consequence of an express provision, all the exceptions are mandatory. Consequently, there is no possibility of derogation by contract. The imperative nature of the exceptions provides an answer to a major concern. Indeed, Directive 2001/29/EC encourages the use of contracts in the information society. The fear was therefore that copyright owners would abuse this possibility to prohibit, by contract, uses that are permitted by the law. The Belgian legislator wished to avoid such practices. Likewise, the Hungarian rapporteur indicates that, as the provisions of the Copyright Act are typically mandatory, the exceptions have to be regarded as mandatory as well, unless otherwise specified. Also in the UK, the initial position of the government appeared to be in favour of a broad prohibition of a contractual override of exceptions. But in the end, this prohibition seems to be less broad.

In non-EU States, there are positions that point in the same direction. The Swiss rapporteur takes the view that, although there is a debate on this subject, all the exceptions under his national law shall be considered—in principle—to be mandatory and, therefore, that they cannot be overruled by contract. The Romanian rapporteur notes that all the exceptions provided in his law are mandatory and similarly cannot be overruled by contract. He considers that this position has been confirmed by the jurisprudence.

At the other end of the spectrum we find States that are in favour of the contractual override of the exceptions, to a greater or lesser extent.

The Italian rapporteur notes that, generally speaking, contractual waiver can apply to exceptions. However, contractual override is excluded in certain cases where the nature of the exceptions is mandatory. The latter cases concern, for example, the freedom of parody, the quotation for criticism and discussion or use in the exercise of the right of chronicle, or uses for public security purposes or during a judicial, administrative or parliamentary proceeding. The French report mentions that, under French law, a contract can modulate the scope of the statutory exceptions or even paralyse them. In the same direction, the Polish rapporteur notes that the unwaivable character of permissible uses is not clearly stated in the law. However, it has been firmly established that the exceptions generally are not mandatory rules so that permissible use may be modified by contract. This is said to be justified by the need to respect one of the fundamental principles of civil law, i.e. freedom of contract, and by the fact that the law does not clearly prohibit the option of permissible use provisions being contractually limited or ruled out.

Between the two opposing views in favour of and against the contractual override of the exceptions, there are countries where the solutions are more confused. For example, the situation under German law is unclear. The German rapporteur notes that some exceptions are expressly declared mandatory, which does not necessarily mean that other exceptions are not. Moreover attention has to be paid to civil law rules that are applicable to this subject. As a consequence, it seems that the question as to whether specific exceptions are waivable must be considered on a case-by-case basis. According to the Austrian report, free uses can theoretically—in the absence of an express provision stating otherwise—be ruled out by contract, provided this is possible according to general civil law, which is, however, only rarely the case.

### 13.3.6 The Nature of the Rights Derogated: Reproduction and Communication Distinguished or Not

In some countries, situations can occur where, according to the terms of the law, reproduction is permitted while communication to the public is not. Such a failure could create a serious inconvenience in practice. Therefore, the question arises as to whether the national law makes a distinction between the kinds of use in terms of exceptions and whether case law provides for solutions in case of failures.

Many countries set forth that the question whether the law allows either a free reproduction or a free communication of the public, or both, may vary upon the use contemplated by the exception. Some exempted uses speak for themselves. For instance, private use will lead to a free reproduction only since no communication to the public is involved.

Some countries do not appear very specific in this respect. For example, the Brazilian rapporteur mentions that his law makes no distinction between reproduction and communication to the public, except in certain situations. Likewise, the Hungarian rapporteur notes that the free use exceptions are not defined along the lines of certain economic rights. Certain uses by certain persons in certain cases are allowed. The provisions on the exceptions do not make any distinction according to reproduction right or right of communication to the public. Other rapporteurs, like the Austrian rapporteur, emphasise that the national law can be extremely detailed concerning the nature of the rights that are derogated.

However, there are indeed situations where both rights are concerned, namely reproduction *and* communication to the public, while only one of them is specifically addressed by the legal exception. This is, e.g., the case, notes the French rapporteur, for quotation. This exception justifies a free communication to the public, even though the law only mentions a free reproduction. In such a situation, case law tends apparently to admit that even the right that is not specifically addressed by the legal terms may be derogated.

The Polish rapporteur mentions in this regard that a lot will depend on the purpose of the exception. For instance, the purpose of private use is to satisfy personal needs, i.e. not only a private reproduction but also the lending of a work to a friend. He distinguishes this situation from the situation where digital files are exchanged through peer-to-peer networks. This last situation involves complete strangers and thus a communication to the public. In the same direction, the Romanian rapporteur also notes that the purpose of the exception has to be taken into consideration. For example, the exempted making of a derivative of a work implies the use of the derivative thus made, without which the exception would miss its objective.

### 13.3.7 The Interaction Between Exceptions and Moral Rights

Some national reports (including France, Italy, Austria and Belgium) first emphasise that the exceptions derogate economic rights only and therefore not moral rights. The Polish report observes in this regard that even when the preservation of a specific moral right is not mentioned in the law, in particular the right of integrity, it must be respected.

That being said, the vast majority of the national rapporteurs, including the foregoing, expressly note that *de facto* the exceptions have an impact on moral rights. For instance, parody has an impact on the moral right of integrity, as emphasised by a number of national reports (Switzerland, UK). The Swiss rapporteur takes the view in this respect that the moral right cannot be opposed as such to the beneficiary of the exception of parody, failing which the exception would lose its raison d'être. The Brazilian rapporteur notes for his part that his law puts some limits in that the parodist may not cause discredit to the author.

Reciprocally, moral rights have forced legislators to provide for some kind of safeguards in their favour when regulating the exceptions. For example, the moral right of paternity is taken into consideration in the context of the exception of quotation, where the law requires that the source must be mentioned, as noted in certain national reports (Brazil, Switzerland and Austria). This requirement may be implicit according to the jurisprudence, says the Brazilian rapporteur about the freedom of panorama. The Italian rapporteur insists on the need to preserve the moral right of paternity. He recalls that the paternity right is always protected by the so-called mention of use: in any case, the title of the work and the name of the author always have to be mentioned. At the same time, he notes that the legislator himself recognises that in certain cases, the mention of the source may appear impossible. The Austrian rapporteur indicates that the way the source is to be mentioned may vary upon the circumstances and the good practices. Also, the Czech rapporteur notes that the mention of the source depends on what is feasible and customary. Common sense and the rule of reason also play a role in this regard, as suggested by the Polish report. As an example, the Polish rapporteur mentions a case where photos were shown in news feed for a time no longer than 2 s. The court decided in that case that the source did not need to be mentioned.

The French rapporteur adds that the quotation may not be prejudicial to the author. The Polish report indicates, in the same sense, that the quotation could be contrary to the right of integrity in case of a biased choice of quotation, which could generate a false impression.

In several national reports, special attention is paid to parody. Particularly, the limits aiming at preserving the moral rights of the author are delicate for this kind of use. The French rapporteur notes in this regard that the parodist must respect the 'rules of the genre' and may not cause an excessive denaturation of the work. In the same direction, the Brazilian rapporteur mentions that the parody may not cause discredit. The UK and Belgian rapporteurs both refer to the jurisprudence of the Court of Justice in the *Deckmyn* case,[6] where the court has found that even in the context of a parody, the copyright owners keep a legitimate interest in having their work not associated to racist or discriminatory messages. The developments of the UK law are quite specific and complex in relation to parody. The UK rapporteur observes that when he (quite recently) adopted the exception of parody, the legislature decided to include a reference to the need for a fair dealing with the original work so as to minimise the potential harm to relevant copyright owners. This seems to mean that the user may only make use of a limited, moderate amount of the initial work. Moreover, the parody involves a treatment of an earlier work, whereby such treatment might be prejudicial to the honour or reputation of the author of the original work.

A number of national rapporteurs (Switzerland, Austria, France and Belgium) conclude that a fair balance has to be struck between the uses covered by the exceptions and the respect of the moral rights of the author. On one side, to the benefit of the user of the exception, there is, for example, the fact that by their very nature, certain exceptions necessarily affect the moral rights, in particular the integrity, of the work and the fact that the source is sometimes hard to mention. On the other side, to the benefit of the author, there is the fact that the permitted use may not cause an excessive denaturation of the work and the fact that the mention of the source must happen in compliance with good practices. The Belgian rapporteur refers to EU law, which confirms the need to maintain a fair balance between the rights and interests of, respectively, the copyright owners and the users.

### 13.3.8 The Interaction Between Exceptions and Technological Measures

Obviously, technological measures aiming at the protection of the work (TPMs) could have a negative impact on the benefit of the exceptions. Actually, TPMs are likely to paralyse the exceptions. Therefore, it is worth investigating if and to what extent the national copyright laws permit TPMs to block the exceptions or, on the contrary, whether they help the users in benefiting from the exceptions.

---

[6] CJEU, case C-201/13, *Johan Deckmyn et Vrijheidsfonds VZW contre Helena Vandersteen e.a.*, ECLI:EU:C:2014:2132.

The interaction between TPMs and exceptions is regulated in Directive 2001/29/EC, so that the laws of the Member States have to be interpreted and applied in conformity with said Directive.

The French rapporteur emphasises that under his author-centric law, the users do not have a right to the exceptions. This means that, in practice, TPMs can prevent a user from benefiting the exceptions. In such a situation, the user has no choice but to negotiate an agreement with the copyright owner. That being said, if no agreement is found, the high authority HADOPI may help in finding a balanced solution.

As noted by the Austrian rapporteur, it is only in the event that voluntary measures are not taken by right holders (e.g., through an agreement with the user) that there is some obligation for the national legislature to allow for enforcement of the exceptions in favour of the user. But in a number of EU countries, including Austria, Belgium and Romania, that obligation upon the legislature does not apply when the objective is to enforce the private copy exception. Actually, as observed by the German rapporteur, only a (too) short list of exceptions is concerned by that obligation upon the right owners to guarantee an effective benefit of the exceptions. In addition, the legislature has no obligation to facilitate the benefit of the exceptions with regard to works that are the subject of an on-demand exploitation. Specifically, in Belgium for example, the users have standing to apply for a judicial injunction to obtain an actual benefit of the exception. A similar solution seems to be envisaged under Hungarian law, but at this stage, the procedure does not appear to have been put into place yet. In the UK, the user may issue a notice of complaint to the Secretary of State.

Moreover, as observed by the Belgian rapporteur, the user is exposed to criminal sanctions if he circumvents TPMs or commercialises tools or services that are aimed at circumventing TPMs. The Austrian rapporteur emphasises that those sanctions are applicable even when the ultimate use of the work—although not authorised by the copyright owner—is permitted by law. As the German rapporteur says, beneficiaries are not allowed to crack the protection themselves with the aim of benefitting from an exception.

In this respect, the Polish rapporteur takes the view that additional legislation work is welcome to make clear in the future that users may remove or circumvent TPMs, without being exposed to criminal sanctions, when the objective is to benefit from uses that are permitted by law.

In non-EU countries, sanctions are provided in case of activities aiming at the circumvention of TPMs. But there is apparently very little or even no legal basis for remedies in favour of users who seek to obtain an actual benefit of the exceptions and who are prevented from such a benefit due to TPMs. In this regard, the Swiss rapporteur notes that there is no obligation for the copyright owner to provide the means of benefitting from an exception to users, which may impede the effectiveness of exceptions. Likewise, the Brazilian rapporteur observes that his law is not concerned with determining that the author/right holder allows such exceptions to be fully exploited, nor does it evidence what the remedies would be in the case of a technological barrier against reproduction or one that prevents the full enjoyment of a legal exception.

### 13.3.9 Catch-All Exception

Unsurprisingly, all the national rapporteurs for the EU Member States confirm that their national law does not provide for a catch-all exception, such as a fair-use exception. Actually, the absence of such a catch-all provision results logically from the fact that the list of exceptions in Directive 2001/29/EC is a closed one (see above). The EU legislature has deliberately put into place an exhaustive list that details very precisely all the conditions governing each and every exception. Furthermore, the first step of the three-step test, namely the requirement that the exception must address a special case, disfavours the adoption of a catch-all exception.

Hence, the national laws of the EU Member States make use of narrowly defined exceptions. Moreover, due to their exceptional nature, the provisions are subject to a restrictive interpretation (see above). In other words, says the Italian rapporteur, while US law limits the subject matter of copyright in a pragmatic way by applying open and flexible evaluation criteria for the judicial definition of unauthorised uses, EU national copyright laws, like the Italian law, strictly define and limit the extent of free uses.

However, in some special cases, a broader interpretation of written exceptions can be necessary to ensure conformity with the Directive and/or higher internal rules (e.g., in Germany, Basic Law for the Federal Republic of Germany). Flexibility can also be explained by the purpose of the exception. The Czech rapporteur notes in this respect that under his national law, the free use for the personal needs of a natural person deserves a broad interpretation, i.e. it extends to each and any form of 'copying', i.e. not only to make a reproduction. This broad interpretation, i.e. extension of the 'fair use' for each and any form of 'copying' for personal or internal needs, is justified by a teleological approach, i.e. by the true intent of the legislature.

But apart from the foregoing, the EU national systems, generally speaking, show rigidity rather than flexibility. The Polish rapporteur observes in this respect that his national law does not allow for developing any new 'hybrid' kinds of permissible use. For example, you cannot take different permissible use regulations and pick up selected use requirements from them to form a 'combination' creating a new use category that would also be permissible.

As far as non-EU countries are concerned, the Swiss rapporteur confirms that his national law does not provide for a catch-all exception.

In contrast, the Brazilian rapporteur indicates that it intends to bring a closed list of exceptions; the Brazilian Copyright Act ends up creating a 'catch all' exception with item VIII of Article 46. This provision, in short, permits the free reproduction in any work of short extracts from existing works, regardless of their nature, or of the whole work in the case of a work of three-dimensional art, on the condition that the reproduction is not in itself the main subject matter of the new work. This exception allows, for example, the sample in music, the use of short extracts of audiovisual works in documentaries or even in works of fiction, amongst other uses of previous works. The Brazilian rapporteur takes the view that, even though the exact scope remains quite uncertain, it is consistent with the three-step step test.

### 13.3.10 Impact of Fundamental Rights Other Than Copyright

At first sight, a number of factors tend to indicate that there is little room for accepting that other fundamental rights could limit or even paralyse the exclusive rights of the author: the other fundamental rights have already been taken into consideration to design the exceptions within the copyright law, the list of the exceptions in the copyright law is a closed one, the conditions governing the exceptions in the copyright law have been precisely designed so that they may not be carved out by external rules.

However, as may be reflected by the developments of EU law, including the jurisprudence of the Court of Justice, it becomes increasingly clear that copyright may no longer be conceived as an intangible right, which is immune from other fundamental rights.

But not all the EU countries are already prepared to admit the interference of other fundamental rights.

For instance, the French rapporteur observes that under his national law, there is no general situation in which other fundamental rights permit the use without the consent of the author (i.e., a 'general' situation outside copyright law itself). This is to say that the exceptions themselves are already thought and provided in order to balance fundamental rights other than copyright such as freedom of expression, right to private life, right to education and the right of the copyright owner. The formulation of those exceptions is already the result of this balance. The use must therefore comply with the conditions required for the application of the relevant exception. However, it always remains possible for the judge to see an 'abuse' of copyright because copyright, even in its prerogatives under the moral right, is not discretionary. Similarly, copyright cannot confer any immunity in light of the violations of the rights of third parties, whether focused on personality rights or simply the right of property. The French rapporteur admits, however, that the reasoning might be different for rights that were not taken into account in the balance of the exceptions, such as competition law or consumer law. Hence, those considerations can possibly, under certain circumstances, limit the exercise of the copyright owner.

In the same direction, the Polish rapporteur seems to indicate that even though free uses are often supported by external (constitutional) values—such as privacy or access to culture—they are only permissible if they stay within the strict limits of the legal terms provided by the copyright law. Likewise, according to the Romanian rapporteur, in providing for the exceptions to copyright so as to also balance the exclusivity inherent to copyright protection with other fundamental rights (e.g., freedom of expression, right to information, right to education), the Romanian Copyright Law has excluded to a very large extent the situations where, outside the gambit of the exceptions so provided, a balancing exercise between copyright and other fundamental rights ought to be performed. Courts therefore seem to prefer giving voice to other fundamental rights within the scope of the existing exceptions and not against such. In the same sense, the Italian rapporteur concludes that it can be said that the Italian legal system is not inclined to extend the copyright exceptions for the purposes of fundamental rights since the latter are the foundations of the exceptions and limitations that can be found in the Italian Copyright Act. Basically, the Brazilian rapporteur shares the same views. He observes that the exceptions contained in the copyright law are considered as the fair and prior agreement between the fundamental rights of the author of the work and those protected under the exceptions. This, however, he notes, is a view constantly challenged by more progressive scholars, who understand that the list of exceptions contained in the law cannot encompass all situations in which, for the protection of a fundamental right, copyright should be limited.

Some national rapporteurs, while they maintain that the exceptions in the copyright law are already the result of a balance between copyright and other fundamental rights, are open for taking into account external higher rules, like constitutional rules. The Swiss rapporteur, for instance, notes that the fundamental rights protected by the Constitution should be taken into account when interpreting a copyright exception, even though they shall nevertheless not serve as a basis to extend or create a new exception to copyright. Also, the Hungarian rapporteur observes in the same sense that a new provision—forcing the courts to take into account the Hungarian Fundamental Law—could open the door to the possibility of giving effect to other fundamental rights and interests as incorporated by the Constitution in cases concerning copyright law. The same rapporteur takes the view, however, that, in practice, that provision should have little impact since the principle of strict interpretation is expressly confirmed in the copyright law and should ultimately prevail.

Other rapporteurs indicate that their systems could show more openness to interference by other fundamental rights. The Austrian rapporteur notes that the Austrian Supreme Court repeatedly recognised that the fundamental right of the freedom of expression protected by Article 10 of ECHR can restrict the copyrights in the individual case, even though only in extreme cases. The Belgian rapporteur explains the reasons why the Belgian authorities are particularly willing to take other fundamental rights in consideration when addressing copyright claims. Belgian courts have referred a number of cases to the Court of Justice in this respect. As a result, the CJEU has developed jurisprudence that made it clear that national authorities are under the obligation to strike a balance between the protection of copyright and the preservation of other fundamental rights such as freedom of expression, freedom to conduct business and respect of privacy (see CJEU judgments in *Scarlet*,[7] *Sabam*[8]

[7] CJEU, case C-70/10, *Scarlet Extended SA v Société belge des auteurs, compositeurs et éditeurs SCRL (SABAM)*, ECLI:EU:C:2011:771.

[8] CJEU, case C-360/10, *Belgische Vereniging van Auteurs, Componisten en Uitgevers CVBA (SABAM) v Netlog NV*, ECLI:EU:C:2012:85.

and *Deckmyn*[9]). Furthermore, to justify the need to strike a balance with other fundamental rights and other rules, the Belgian rapporteur also refers to the jurisprudence of the European Court of Human Rights and to the rules relating to competition law. The UK rapporteur also refers to the need to balance copyright with other fundamental rights, including in light of the jurisprudence of the CJEU.

### 13.3.11 Right to Compensation

Questions arise as to whether, having regard to the limitation or even the setting aside of the copyright, the author has a right to compensation.

There are significant differences between the various national systems—even within the EU.

For instance, the UK rapporteur mentions that his national law does not provide compensation in favour of the copyright owner. The solution is identical in Brazil. The Brazilian rapporteur notes that exceptions are absolute and do not give the copyright holder the right to be paid.

In contrast, in the vast majority of the countries, there is compensation in favour of the right owner for certain uses, while for other uses, there is no remuneration. This hybrid system applies to Germany, Switzerland, Austria, Italy, France, Poland, Czechia, Romania, Belgium and Hungary.

Even though the principle of a hybrid system is the same for all these countries, there are differences from country to country with regard to the exceptions that give right to compensation and those that do not.

The first category includes private use (Germany, Switzerland, France, Czechia, Romania, Belgium, Hungary), educational use (Switzerland, France, Belgium), use for scientific research (Belgium), use by people with disabilities (Switzerland), use by social institutions for the benefit of their members (Italy).

Even though some of them contain developments in this respect, most national reports abstain from detailing the various aspects of the compensation, in terms of calculation, and mechanisms aimed at preventing overcompensation.

### 13.3.12 The Making of Temporary Copies

In the digital environment, temporary copies are extremely frequent. Also, in many cases, they are necessary to enable a lawful use. A lot of activities and business models are likely to be confronted with them. Therefore, the exception permitting their making is of utmost importance. This exception is included in Directive 2001/29/EC. But questions arise as to whether the wording of this exception—both in EU and non-EU countries, if applicable—is sufficiently effective to allow the development of most of legitimate online activities and new business models.

[9] CJEU, case C-201/13, *Johan Deckmyn et Vrijheidsfonds VZW contre Helena Vandersteen e.a.*, ECLI:EU:C:2014:2132.

The exception at stake is expressed in Article 5, para 1, of Directive 2001/29, which reads as follows:

> 1. Temporary acts of reproduction referred to in Article 2, which are transient or incidental [and] an integral and essential part of a technological process and whose sole purpose is to enable:
>
> (a) a transmission in a network between third parties by an intermediary, or
>
> (b) a lawful use of a work or other subject-matter to be made, and which have no independent economic significance, shall be exempted from the reproduction right provided for in Article 2.

As far as non-EU countries are concerned, both the Brazilian and Swiss laws contain a similar provision.

The Swiss rapporteur states that the Swiss provision is modelled on the corresponding provision in the EU Directive. Actually, there is no divergence.

In contrast, the Brazilian provision shows certain differences. It reads as follows:

> The exclusive right of reproduction shall not be applicable where the reproduction is temporary and done for the sole purposes of making the work, phonogram or performance perceptible by means of an electronic medium, or where it is transitory or incidental, provided that it is done in the course of the use of the work that has been duly authorized by the owner.

The respective national reports contain the following comments in this respect.

As observed by the Polish rapporteur, the exception plays a useful role to permit the following uses: (1) reproduction in a computer's RAM when a CD is being played, (2) making copies during Internet browsing, (3) storage in cache memories, proxy servers or Internet routers. The Romanian rapporteur adds that under his national jurisprudence, this exception has been successfully used to permit the reproduction of musical works on a computer/server for the purpose of enabling subsequent streaming. He concludes that the current interpretation of the limitation, under his national jurisprudence, seems permissive enough to allow most legitimate online activities, possibly even those activities based on a model of p2p distribution. The UK rapporteur mentions that the exception is also applicable to temporary copies generated by an Internet end user. The Hungarian rapporteur mentions still another possible successful application of the exception, with regard to IPTV services, that is, the provision of television 'broadcasting' services based on broadband Internet protocols in a digital (encrypted) format. According to the Hungarian Council of Copyright Experts, the reproduction of such works by the IPTV service provider by utilising its own facilities was deemed to fulfil the requirements of the exception because it was necessary for facilitating subscribers' lawful use. It was therefore stressed that such interim reproduction of licensed works had not carried any independent economic significance.

However, beyond those permitted activities, there are undoubtedly a series of activities that clearly do not satisfy the conditions of this exception. In particular, the exception proves inapplicable to some streaming activities, to VCR online services and to Google news activities.

This inapplicability may not surprise since the conditions of the exception set quite high standards. In this respect, the Swiss rapporteur makes a useful in-depth analysis. He first emphasises that four conditions need to be cumulatively met. Then he comments on each of the four conditions. It appears that said conditions are particularly demanding requirements. In a nutshell, by way of illustration, the following copies may be problematic: (1) a copy that is stored for several days (because it is not transient), unless it only facilitates another use's process (in the latter case, it is incidental); (2) a copy that is not deleted automatically (because it is not part of an integral and essential part of a technological process); (3) a copy that does not enable a use that is either authorised by the copyright owner or permitted by law; and (4) a copy that can be substituted for a permanent copy (because it could generate revenues in that case, and therefore it would have an independent economic significance). Despite the demanding character of the exception, according to the Swiss rapporteur, it strikes the right balance between the interests at stake and is effective in enabling the development of legitimate online activities/new business models.

The German rapporteur made a detailed analysis on the technical side in relation to streaming platforms and portals. This analysis reveals, amongst other things, that streaming activities may not benefit from the exception, in particular, when they are related to sources that are evidently illegal. In the same sense, the UK rapporteur confirms that conclusion, stressing that the CJEU has excluded that the exception within Article 5 para 1 of the InfoSoc Directive would apply to viewers of unlawful streams (*Filmspeler*).[10]

Commenting on a judicial decision, the French rapporteur observes that the exception of transitional copy cannot be invoked in the hypothesis of a 'VCR online' service, which offers to its subscribers the possibility to record television programmes and to access their request of records, after decryption of those, since the copy made by the operator will be able, once decoded, to be retained in a definitive manner by its user. The court found in that case that the copy had an 'own economic value', considering the advertising revenues directly related to the number of users of the service and the volume of copies made for the account of these users.

The Belgian rapporteur mentions that under her national case law, the exception was found inapplicable to the Google News service. In short, the facts were as follows. The Google News service offers a selection of information from press articles. The mechanism is as follows: Google exploits the web servers of news organisations, copies and/or automatically summarise them in order to establish an information portal. This portal contains articles of the day or articles that correspond to the user's request in the search bar of the Google News service. Google News only provides a few lines and the title of the article but then refers to the agency's own website through hyperlinks. One important point is that the mechanism set up by Google also allows access to press articles that are no longer online on the agency's own website. All those actions are done without any prior authorisation from the copyright holders. In appeal, the court found that Google was unable to demonstrate

[10] CJEU, case C-527/15, *Stichting Brein v Jack Frederik Wullems*, ECLI:EU:C:2017:300.

the technical necessity to ensure an effective transmission of the copy made by the company. Consequently, the third condition according to which reproduction must constitute an integral and essential part of a technological process was not met. In addition, the court observed that the copy was not transitory or accessory in the present case. The cached copy was not limited to what is technically necessary to ensure the proper functioning of the service because, in reality, the copy remained as long as the press article itself was accessible on the original site, and beyond.

### 13.3.13 Exceptions Allowing the Freedom of Expression

The national reports mention a number of exceptions listed in their respective national laws that are rooted within freedom of expression. These exceptions include mainly review or criticism, quotation, news reporting/reporting of current events, freedom of panorama and parody.

Commenting on parody, the UK rapporteur emphasises that under his national law, this exception is subject to fair dealing conditions, which means that the parodist may only make a moderated, limited use of the initial work. She considers that, at first sight, the UK exception in this regard is less broad than the corresponding exception under French law.

Many national reports refer to the exception relating to 'current events'. Different issues may arise in this respect.

According to the Swiss case law, a press article does not form in itself a 'current event', so that the exception of reporting of current events cannot be used to reproduce it in its entirety.

However, it may be the case that under certain laws, works may be freely disseminated in their entirety for information purposes, in the context of 'reporting over current events'. The French rapporteur mentions in this respect an exception permitting the free dissemination of public speeches in their entirety. A number of significant limits have been set, though. In particular, the work must consist of a speech intended for the public, and the dissemination must occur via the press or broadcasting. But in the first place, the dissemination must pursue an objective of reporting over current news. As a consequence, the exception does not permit to publish a book of non-recent speeches. In contrast with that speech-related exception, under the general quotation-related exception, it is an absolute requirement that the quotation must be short. On another note, apart from the length of the copy, also the news-related character appears decisive. The French report refers in this regard to the press review exception, which is confined to topics of current concern, as opposed to non-ephemeral topics.

In relation to 'reporting over current events', the Belgian rapporteur explains that this exception is justified only under circumstances where the user has no time to obtain the copyright holder's consent. As a consequence, Google News has been denied the benefit of that exception because it used the works (press articles) for a period of 30 days, while during such a period, it was perfectly possible to obtain the right owners' authorisation.

The Swiss report reveals that under Swiss national jurisprudence, a quotation must be limited to a short extract so that it does not permit the reproduction of an entire press article. The Italian rapporteur emphasises that the quotation may not be for commercial purpose and that it may never compete with the original work.

The Polish report details the various issues that may arise concerning the quotation-exception. One of those relate to the purpose of the quotation. The rapporteur emphasises that the quotation must be 'necessary' in that it must illustrate the views of the individual who makes the quotation. The Belgian rapporteur also emphasises the importance of the objective pursued by the quotation, namely criticism, controversy or review. Hence, the Google News service has been denied the benefit of the exception because it used the work (press articles) without pursuing any objective of criticism, controversy or review.

A significant number of national reports reveal that under free-speech-related exceptions, no remuneration is due to the author. For example, the Brazilian rapporteur notes, in relation to parody and freedom of panorama, that these exceptions are mandatory and do not give rise to compensation. Likewise, the Austrian rapporteur indicates, in relation to the quotation-exception that the right holder is not entitled to remuneration. The same observation is made in the Polish report.

### 13.3.14 Subject Matter Excluded from the Benefit of Copyright Protection

In many countries, copyright protection is denied to certain subject matters, like political speeches, official documents, news of the day or mere items of press information. The question arises as to whether the national lists of unprotected material is sufficiently comprehensive.

In this regard, the Swiss rapporteur mentions that his national list does not exclude daily news and mere items of press information. He notes, however, that these types of 'works' may not be considered original enough to be protected by the copyright law. Likewise, the Austrian rapporteur observes that mere items of press information that simply report mere facts and statements without further commentary are not considered to be 'works' due to their simple nature and therefore do not enjoy copyright protection. In order for a press section to be considered a work, it has to reflect an individual intellectual activity. In the same direction, in relation to 'simple press news', the Polish rapporteur notes that it includes primarily factual press items without any analysis or commentary by the author, such as exchange rate quotations, stock exchange quotations, weather reports, TV or radio listings, movies or theatre schedules. Importantly, this category can include also more 'complicated' or 'sizeable' news items provided that their only and core benefit is to give information that some fact(s) occurred (news of natural catastrophes, poll results, sports results, staff changes in law firms, etc.).

The Romanian rapporteur takes the view that the list containing the ineligible subject matters is a closed one. But, at the same time, he considers that this is not really embarrassing because the courts use that list simply as a complement to the basic criteria for copyright protection.

It seems to result from the national reports that, generally speaking, there is no concern about the fact that a national list would omit a subject matter that evidently does not deserve copyright protection. In most cases of this kind, the general standards for eligibility may perfectly serve to exclude that kind of subject matters. In particular, the originality test or the notion of creation will be helpful to conclude that the subject matter at stake does not match the criteria. This being said, situations may occur where the subject matter, although consisting of an original creation, should be ineligible for copyright protection. That is, for instance, the case for public speeches in public court hearings. In this last case, it is worth permitting the free use of the speeches, but only to the extent it is required for public information purposes.

### 13.3.15 Education Exceptions

Because, more than ever, education is key, especially in the information society, it is worth verifying whether the national systems are performing adequately in this respect, in particular in the field of distance education.

Evidently, most countries realise that progress has to be made on this subject. According to the UK rapporteur, UK copyright law has recently broadened its education exceptions, which also cover distance learning.

It appears that in some countries, at this stage, the education exceptions remain quite limited. For example, for Brazil, the rapporteur refers to low-level exceptions, like the permission for the student to make a transcript of the class.

But even in countries that tend to be more favourable for free education uses, generally speaking, these uses come up against a number of major difficulties that could paralyse some learning activities, in particular distance learning. These difficulties frequently result from the demanding wording of the conditions that the uses are subject to. These conditions may vary from country to country, even though a number of them are common. The following obstacles may be mentioned in this respect: free use is limited to small parts of the work; not every kind of work is eligible for free use; free use may only be made by official, not-for-profit institutions; free use may only be made for illustration of teaching, so that other education activities like preparation or follow-up are not covered; communication through computers must take place on the premises of the institution; communication must take place through a secure if not a closed network; and remuneration is due to the author.

Some extracts of certain national reports deserve special attention to illustrate how these conditions apply.

The Swiss rapporteur notes that under his system, the education exception typically applies at all levels (kindergarten, primary school, middle and high school and universities), whether public or private. While it is apparently debated, the Swiss rapporteur takes the view that this exception should apply to distance learning to the extent that access controls to the lectures and teaching materials (i.e., providing access only to the teacher and the students) are properly implemented as this would in principle satisfy the 'triple test'. The Swiss law does not explicitly distinguish according to whether the classes are held within a non-profit organisation or in a commercial environment. However, some scholars are of the view that the educational exception should not apply in the context of continuous education especially, when it is organised by a for-profit organisation.

The German rapporteur notes that under his law, it is permissible to make available small parts of works for illustration in teaching. Distance learning institutions are also beneficiaries of that exception, even though they have to make use of technical protection measures (e.g., passwords for online platforms) in order to make sure that the work is only made accessible to the participants of the instructed group. A number of additional limits are set. Beneficiaries must be not-for-profit institutions. Only small parts of the work may be made available. The purpose must be to illustrate teaching. But the government considers amending the system in order to broaden the exception. In the future, the exception should also apply to preparation and follow-up learning activities, beyond the teaching itself. In addition, the law will clarify the notion of 'small' parts of the work.

The French rapporteur mentions limits that are common in many countries, like the kind of works that may be used, the amount of the work that may be freely used (in terms of 'extract') and the exclusion of other activities than the teaching in the strict sense. Also, he comments on the remuneration that is due to the author.

The Austrian rapporteur notes that the exception is not applicable to works that, according to their nature and design, are intended to be used in schools and/or teaching purposes. He regrets that distance learning is not favoured. In this respect, he observes that profit-making institutions may not benefit from the exception. Furthermore, wording like 'to the extent that this is justified by the respective purpose' leads to considerable legal uncertainty.

The Polish rapporteur considers that under his law, the education exception is much broader than in many other countries. He emphasises in this regard that it expressly covers distance learning as well, provided that the students have been identified by the institution. In contrast, it does not permit organising open mass participation online courses (MOOCs), online courses being open to an unlimited number of participants who are not known even to the educational institution that is organising the course. Under Polish law, no remuneration is due to the author.

Interestingly, the Belgian rapporteur mentions that the Belgian legislature has put in place a specific exception in order to promote distance learning, which permits free communication subject to a number of conditions. First, the beneficiary must be an institution recognised or officially organised by the public authorities. Second, the communication must take place through a secure communication with appropriate measures. Third, the communication must be within the normal activities of the institution. Then the classical conditions for teaching exceptions are also required for distance learning. The communication must be done only for the purpose of illustration of the teaching, without seeking a profit and without undermining the normal exploitation of the work. Finally, the source and name of the author must be indicated unless this is impossible.

Commenting on distance learning, the Hungarian rapporteur notes that communication of the works for education purposes may only take place through computers terminals, if those devices are operated on the premises of educational institutions. He concludes that therefore, in its present form, the Hungarian copyright act precludes the possibility of providing copyright material for students at remote locations under the free use regime.

### 13.3.16 Big-Data-Related Activities

Big data are clearly strategic for the economy. Therefore, it seems indispensable to check whether big-data-related activities—which imply text and data mining—are facilitated through effective exceptions by the national laws, in their current version or in a version to be adopted in the near future.

In essence, text and data mining is an electronic process for machines to explore and analyse very large quantities of data (texts, images or any other kind), including copyright protected works, in order to extract relevant information. This exploration process makes it necessary to make copies of the data, which means that when the data consist of protected works, said works are reproduced. Because the copies concern huge amount of works and they are made in recording time, it is hardly conceivable to obtain the consent of the author. As a consequence, an exception seems indispensable.

The Belgian rapporteur explains that the exception of temporary reproductions (see above) might be inapplicable in this regard, including because it is not established that the copies are temporary and they have no independent economic significance.

As the German reporter indicates, the critical point in relation to big data is that to gain evaluable data sets it may be necessary to reproduce works in huge quantities by automatic means. Hence, an exception to this end appears appropriate. However, the conditions under which the works should be freely reproduced need a close attention. Different aspects have to be taken into consideration in this regard, in particular the purpose of the use and the profile of the beneficiaries.

In the EU proposal of Directive of September 2016, the exception relating to text and data mining is mandatory and should serve both for non-commercial and commercial purposes. At the same time, its benefit is limited to research organisations.

The UK rapporteur emphasises that the UK law is different from the EU proposal at least in two respects. First, it is limited to non-commercial use. Second, it is open for any lawful user, while the EU exception may be used by research organisations only, namely universities, research institutes, not-for-profit or public interest research-intensive organisations. France has also adopted a text and data mining exception for non-commercial purpose only that allows the reproduction of works without limitation in terms of volume or format.

At this point, the German law does not provide for an exception. But the government prepared a draft bill. According to this draft, an exception will allow text and data mining for science and research purpose. As a result, it will be permissible to make works available to a limited circle of persons for joint scientific projects and to third parties in order to make it possible for them to verify the scientific quality. The exceptions will only apply if the user pursues non-commercial purposes. Likewise, a pre-draft has been prepared in Switzerland to permit text and data mining.

Austrian copyright law does not yet provide for a text and data mining exception. Neither does the copyright law in Romania, Belgium and Hungary. This leads the Hungarian rapporteur to conclude that with regard to the interest of furthering scientific advancement, it would be wise to reconsider the scope and applicability of free use exceptions to accommodate the needs of technology based on big data analytics.

### 13.3.17 Exhaustion of Copyright

The notion of exhaustion of intellectual property rights is fundamental under EU law since it is directly related to the essential freedom of free movement of goods. Moreover, it has been expressly included in the Community legislation, and as a consequence, it has been interpreted as a community notion. The *UsedSoft* jurisprudence (hereinafter 'UsedSoft')[11] of the Court of Justice has made it clear that, to some extent, exhaustion may be applicable with respect to intangible copies. In particular, the court decided that when a copy of certain software has been authorised for download and for subsequent use for an indefinite period of time and when the value for that consent is the same as the economic value of the copy, this operation constitutes a purchase agreement; as a consequence, the copy may be further distributed, the copyright owner not being longer in a position to oppose such a distribution.

The question arises as to how that jurisprudence is applied in the Member States, also in relation to non-software works. Another question is whether a similar jurisprudence is applicable in non-EU countries.

In this last respect, as far as Switzerland is concerned, it seems that the *UsedSoft* solution is basically applicable. However, it ceases to apply in situations where the work has been licensed for a limited amount of time, which occurs, e.g., in the field of entertainment with respect to licences granted to consumers.

The Brazilian rapporteur notes that the Brazilian copyright law follows the exhaustion of rights upon first sale. But he does not report any specific solution with regard to digital works.

The German report is probably the most emblematic for EU Member States countries. The German rapporteur provides for interesting comments regarding the *UsedSoft* solution. He notes that although the exhaustion principle refers to tangible goods, and therefore does not directly apply to online distribution of works, the (controversial) question is whether it can be applied by analogy to cases dealing with digital works (online exhaustion). German courts and some legal scholars are

[11] CJEU, case C-128/11, *UsedSoft GmbH v Oracle International Corp.*, ECLI:EU:C:2012:407.

of the opinion that this is not the case. They point out, a.o., that the CJEU's *UsedSoft* judgment cannot be transposed to other digital works than software because the legislation is not the same (two different directives). Additionally, recital 29 of the InfoSoc Directive explicitly states that 'the question of exhaustion does not arise in the case of services and on-line services in particular'. Finally, they emphasise that from an economic point of view, tangible copies and digital works are not comparable: whereas traditional storage devices like CDs are subject to deterioration, this is not true for files so that works on the primary and secondary markets directly compete with each other without qualitative differences. Furthermore, files could be reproduced without loss and any number of times. However, the arguments above can be rebutted. First of all, recitals of directives are not binding, and in addition recital 29 of Directive 2001/29 appears outdated. Second, the EU *UsedSoft* teaching may be a valid model for digital works. In economic terms, it is not understandable why the traditional book buyer should be able to resell the book, whereas e-book buyers do not have that possibility. Any other result would provide copyright proprietors with the possibility to circumvent the principle of exhaustion by only relying on online distribution. At the same time, it is the copyright proprietor's very own risk that digital works do not deteriorate when he decides to open up to the online-distribution market. Additionally, the possibility of numerous reproductions is irrelevant for the right of distribution and the question of exhaustion. The right of reproduction never exhausts so that each and every reproduction has to be covered by another exception to copyright. Finally, any other result would eliminate a functioning digital single market within the European Union. This being said, as long as the legal discussion goes on and judgments of the highest courts do not clarify the legal situation, one cannot say that the current copyright law sufficiently acknowledges the challenges of the digital society. The lawmaker is consequently asked to explicitly extend the principle of exhaustion to cases of online distribution.

And indeed, in many other EU Member States, there is uncertainty about the discussion as to whether exhaustion is available as a general principle applicable to any work under any format (including non-software work in digital format), or rather it only applies to digital copies of computer programs. This uncertainty is reported by the national rapporteurs for UK, Austria and Belgium. The Polish rapporteur also notes the same uncertainty, even though he seems inclined to mention a slight preference in favour of a liberal construal allowing for online exhaustion in general.

Having said that, the French rapporteur refers to a decision of the French Supreme Court that seems to extend the position by the CJEU in the *UsedSoft* judgment, at least with regard to music files distributed online. In contrast, the Italian rapporteur seems to maintain that with reference to copies originated by downloading the work in digital format, instead, the rights to public communication and reproduction must be taken into account. In this case, circulation of the copies made by transferring the work in digital format to a storage media is subject to the right holder's authorisation because their transmission through digital channels does not exhaust the distribution right. In the same sense, the Romanian and the Hungarian rapporteurs recall that their laws expressly exclude exhaustion in respect of the making available right, which would apply to online situations where the work has been made available in a digital format.

### 13.3.18 Panorama Exception

Many countries provide for an exception ensuring the freedom of panorama with respect to works permanently situated in public places, such as buildings or sculptures. As a result, said works may be freely used, to a certain extent.

Also here, detailed conditions seem appropriate to limit the permitted use, as to the format, the purpose and the profile of the users. But the specific conditions in this respect tend to vary from country to country.

With regard to the format, the concern is that the permitted use should be prevented from competing with the initial format. The UK law provides in this respect that the use shall consist of the making of a graphic representation, a photograph, a film or an image. The Swiss law refers to a depiction, whereby the depiction may not serve the same purpose as the original work. Many countries provide for similar limitations (to a greater or lesser extent) with respect to the format, e.g. Brazil, Austria and Poland.

The French law provides that the use must be made by an individual and may not pursue a commercial purpose. Also, the Romanian law does not permit commercial uses. In contrast, commercial uses are permitted in other countries, including Austria and Poland.

In certain countries, such a Belgium, the limitations are more far-reaching in that the permitted use may not have as purpose the work itself.

The Italian law does not provide for a panorama exception. However, there are provisions in specific laws concerning cultural goods and public domain goods that facilitate the making of photographs.

### 13.3.19 Reprography, Private Copying and Other Private Uses

The national reports all comment on exceptions related to reprography, private copying and other private uses. The terminology may be shortly clarified in this respect. Reprography refers to the reproductions on paper or any similar medium, effected by the use of any kind of photographic technique or by some other process having similar effects. Private copying refers to reproductions on any medium made by a natural person for private use and for ends that are neither directly or indirectly commercial. Other private uses refer, for example, to a communication in a family circle.

Although these topics are at first sight distinct subject matters, they prove interrelated. For instance, the *HP vs Reprobel* judgment of the Court of Justice made it clear that although the provision of Directive 2001/29 does not make that distinction, with regard to the exception of reprography, a distinction has to be made according to whether the reproduction is made by any user or by a natural person for private use.

These topics have given rise to immensely complex debates. Some of the main questions raised about reprography and private copying are as follows: Do they also cover counterfeit copies made from unlawful source? Can the national law provide that the fair compensation in favour of the authors will be allocated (at least in part) to the publishers? How should the fair compensation be calculated?

The CJEU has answered these questions as follows, in summary. With regard to the unlawful source, the exceptions relating to reprography and private copying may not apply to counterfeit reproductions made from unlawful source. With regard to the allocation of a part of the remuneration in favour of the publishers, the Belgian system as submitted to the CJEU is not valid in that it does not guarantee that the publishers are under the obligation to ensure a direct or indirect benefit to the authors. With regard to the calculation of the fair compensation, within certain limits, Member States are allowed to set up a system providing for two forms of remuneration, namely a lump sum and a proportional remuneration.

The objective of the current report is not to comment on each and every piece of national legislation in the various countries concerning these topics. Rather, it seems appropriate to make some general findings.

Private use in general extends beyond private copy to include other forms of private uses like the lending of copies to close friends.

Private copies may be made outside the family circle, by a third-party service provider, even though they must be for the personal use of the commissioner (as noted in the report for Poland and Switzerland). The French rapporteur notes that under the current law, the maker of the copy and the user must be one and the same person. However, he mentions that a shift is expected; i.e., in the future, it will be admitted that the copy may be made by a third party if ordered by the final user. The German rapporteur mentions that reproductions made by others are covered as long as no payment is received therefore or the reproductions are on paper or a similar medium and have been made by the use of any kind of photomechanical technique or by some other process having similar effects. Yet the exception applies to reproductions of individual contributions released in newspapers and periodicals and small parts of a released work made by public libraries that are transmitted by post or facsimile as long as it is for the commissioner's personal use. For the reproduction and transmission of works in other electronic form, further criteria have to be fulfilled.

In certain countries, private copies are permitted regardless of the size of the work copied; i.e., the whole work may be copied and not just extracts (Poland), while in other countries, the copy is only permitted to the extent that it is limited to short extracts (Brazil).

In certain countries, there is no remuneration for the author of the work copied (Brazil), while in other countries, there is such a remuneration (Switzerland and EU Member States; see, amongst others, the reports for France, Italy, Austria, Poland, Czechia and Hungary), either indirect (Switzerland and Poland) or direct or both

(Belgium). It shall be noted on this last point that the CJEU admitted the principle of a twofold remuneration, subject to some limitations (*HP vs Reprobel*).[12]

Private copies made from unlawful source deserve special attention. According to the jurisprudence of the CJEU (*ACI Adam*),[13] they are not covered by the exception, and therefore they do not give rise to payment in the framework of the system of fair compensation, which applies to permitted private copies. That being said, some EU national laws seem to provide that the person that makes the reproduction from unlawful source is only deprived of the benefit of the private copy exception if the source used is obviously unlawful (Germany and Austria).

Apart from the general findings above, it is worth noting that the exception for personal copies was quashed in the UK for the reason that the exception, as formulated in the law, did not provide for a fair compensation.

### 13.3.20 Global Assessment of the Balance Between Copyright Owners' Rights and Users' Rights

In the global assessment of the balance of rights—namely the rights of the right owners, on the one hand, and the rights of the users, on the other hand—a distinction should be made between EU countries and non-EU countries. The former countries are expected to stick to the general policy of the EU legislature and the CJEU in managing the balance pursued. The latter countries are supposed to have a higher degree of freedom of action. With respect to that distinction, the UK takes a specific place, as a result of the Brexit and also as a result of its tradition of common law.

Specifically, the UK rapporteur envisages opportunities in a scenario of a 'hard' Brexit. Possibly, she notes, the UK might decide to inject some additional flexibility into its own system of copyright exceptions. This might be so by means of (1) an open-ended clause, in addition to existing exceptions that would encompass uses that could not fall within the scope of the other exceptions and employ the language of the three-step test, or (2) even introducing a system of fair use similar to that in place in jurisdictions like the US.

In the same direction, the Swiss rapporteur shows that there can be a temptation to adopt a catch-all exception. The upside hereof would be more flexibility, while the downside would be less certainty. Therefore, the rapporteur leaves the door open for new exceptions to consider for addition to the list, namely with regard to transformative use (user-generated content), research and distance learning.

One of the main conclusions of the Brazilian rapporteur is that his national copyright law reveals a need for an urgent update. In particular, the legislature should adopt appropriate provisions with regard to online uses of works and, more generally, uses of works under digital format. Concerning the list of exceptions, one of the necessary additions should be the insertion of a special provision to favour the

[12] CJEU, case C-572/13, *Hewlett-Packard Belgium SPRL v Reprobel SCRL*, ECLI:EU:C:2015:750.

[13] CJEU, case C-435/12, *ACI Adam BV and Others v Stichting de Thuiskopie and Stichting Onderhandelingen Thuiskopie vergoeding*, ECLI:EU:C:2014:254.

mass digitisation of works for the benefit of libraries. Further modifications should seek to improve the legal certainty of the existing exceptions.

Turning to the EU Member States, the conclusions take another form.

Obviously, the EU authorities put a lot of effort into forcing a real balance of interests between right owners and users. But at the same time, they are dependent on the closed character of the list of exceptions.

EU Member States are supposed to find a strong guidance in the judgments of the CJEU. However, it seems that the teachings of these judgments take a lot of time before they find their way to an efficient translation into national laws. Moreover, directives are by definition quite general, and therefore it should be up to the Member States to bring some specifications where convenient.

A significant number of EU rapporteurs complain that their national provisions are either too vague or too narrow. Some examples are worth highlighting.

For instance, the Polish rapporteur regrets that his national law failed to specify or supplement EU law provisions in relation to orphan works, such as the obligation to make a prior 'diligent search' or the determination of the 'fair compensation' or the extension of the categories of orphan works. The same rapporteur seems to suggest that the jurisprudence of the CJEU concerning private copying and unlawful source should be supplemented under national law, by providing that the exception will apply in each case where the user has an at least reasonable belief that the work he is using was made available in a lawful manner.

The Belgian rapporteur (herein followed by the Hungarian rapporteur) also concludes that rigidity is one of the main weaknesses of the EU system of exceptions. She therefore pleads for a more flexible approach at national level. The solution she refers to tends to rely on categories of exceptions (i.e., teaching, culture access, freedom of expression). When this categorisation is established, all the uses made in order to achieve the purpose would be, in principle, valid. This has the advantage to permit a dynamic interpretation by the judge and the preservation of the effectiveness of the exceptions. As a legal safeguard, the three-step test could be a precious guide for the judge in order to decide if an act of reproduction or communication to the public is legitimate *in concreto*.

The Romanian rapporteur is concerned about the uncertainty of the rules, which is particularly prejudicial to the interests of the users. He proposes to facilitate declaratory judgments for the benefit of the users, even though it could be more preferable to bring more clarity in the legal texts themselves.

Whatever is the direction for further developments, one thing is crucial for both the Polish and the Hungarian rapporteurs: there is a clear need for a permanent debate between the stakeholders, which, according to the Polish rapporteur, could even justify the creation of a platform to enable exchanges of views.

## 13.4 Conclusions and Resolutions

The national reports delivered a rich analysis on a significant number of exceptions, even though not all the exceptions were discussed.

The reports all reflect the need to fully respect copyright as a fundamental right, whereby the principles of the three-step test and a strict interpretation of the exceptions play a key role. At the same time, they realise that a balance has to be struck between the protection of copyright and the protection of other fundamental rights, whereby the exceptions and limitations to copyright are crucial.

The reports all point at critical concerns regarding this balance. These concerns often relate to (1) the closed nature of the list of exceptions, (2) the rigidity of the limits and conditions that apply to the exceptions and (3) the uncertainty about the scope, the limits or the conditions of the exceptions. One of the challenges in this respect results from the fact that, to some extent, these concerns appear to conflict with each other. For instance, on the one hand, there is a need to clarify certain exceptions, while on the other hand, there is a risk that an excessive clarification would increase the rigidity of the system.

The objective of the current report should not be to detail the margin of potential progress in relation to each and every legitimate interest of, respectively, the right owners and the users. Moreover, these interests are currently discussed at appropriate levels, namely the WIPO and the EU levels, in the context of specific exceptions such as education, research or big data.

Rather, the report should seek to find a general consensus about how to treat the balance between the rights of the right owners and the rights of the users and how to tackle the concerns mentioned above.

Therefore, the conclusions and the proposals of recommendations here below are quite modest in that they focus on a general approach. Furthermore, they should be designed in such a way that they remain compatible with the different national traditions.

### 13.4.1 Conclusion 1

All the national reports reflect the importance of the three-step test. That principle is not only enshrined in the leading instruments on international and EU levels, but also in practice it should really serve as a one of the most solid guidance for adopting and applying exceptions to the copyright. The greater is the attention to other rights than copyright, the more relevant the three-step test becomes.

Admittedly, there is some vagueness concerning the question as to whether the test has to be applied in abstract or in a concrete way. In the latter case, the test is a tool for the judge to assess whether in the specific case referred to him each of the conditions is met. This is a reason to clarify that the test is not only a prescription for the national legislature when it adopts an exception but also an obligation for the courts when they assess the admissibility of a defence in a specific matter. To this end, it is necessary to ensure an appropriate implementation of the three-step test into national legislation.

In light of the reasons above, the first resolution adopted at the LIDC's Rio Congress 2017 therefore reads as follows:

> LIDC stresses the crucial importance of the three-step test when exceptions must be interpreted and applied. It recognizes that the test has to be concretely applied by the courts when they assess if in the specific matter referred to them the users of the works are entitled to benefit from the exception they claim. National law should provide for such an obligation upon the courts.

### 13.4.2 Conclusion 2

There is a consensus about the fact that the balance between the rights and the interests of the right owners and those of the users of works is an essential principle. It appears that this main concept should serve as guidance not only for the legislature when they adopt an exception but also for the courts when they assess the merits of a claim or a defence in a specific matter. Admittedly, the national judges and the citizens are expected to know this leading rule. However, such a general principle might gain in transparency, and also it could obtain a greater symbolic value if it were to be enshrined in national law.

Therefore, the LIDC adopted the following second resolution at the Rio Congress 2017:

> LIDC emphasizes the particular importance of the balance to be struck between the rights and interests of both the copyright owners and the users of works. It recognizes that the balance has to be concretely struck by the courts when they assess if in a specific matter referred to them the right owners or the users of the works should succeed in their claim or their defence. National law should provide for such an obligation upon the courts.

### 13.4.3 Conclusion 3

Overall, there is a significant demand for a system providing for a clear identification of the cases that justify the application of exceptions and limitations. Such a demand fits in with the requirement made by the first condition of the three-step test that exceptions and limitations shall only apply in certain special cases. Furthermore, it tends to ensure a solid framework that favours predictability and transparency for the benefit of both the right owners and the users.

The discussion as to whether it is preferable to opt for a closed list of exceptions and limitations rather than an open-ended list is far from easy.

On the one hand, as it may appear from the experience within the EU, if the preference goes for the open-ended list, the risk is that the divergences between the countries will increase. This could have a major negative impact not only on the single market at EU level but also, at a higher level, on the digital uses in general since said uses take place in a cross-border environment.

On the other hand, the national reports confirm that in light of the ever-increasing technological developments, the rigidity of a closed system constitutes a major concern.

As a consequence, it may be wise to maintain a system based upon a closed list, while at the same time a special attention has to be paid to solutions that seek to ensure some flexibility. At this point, it does not appear that there is a clear-cut solution on the table concerning a flexible model that could achieve a consensus. But at least, the willingness to reach this consensus should be expressed at the level of LIDC.

Therefore, the LIDC adopted the following third resolution at the Rio Congress 2017:

> LIDC notes that there is a significant demand for a solution ensuring a clear identification of the cases which justify the application of exceptions and limitations. Therefore it recommends a system which provides for a clear list of exceptions and limitations. While acknowledging the benefits of a closed list, LIDC is concerned about an excessive rigidity in this respect. Therefore, it recommends a system which is based on a closed list of exceptions, and it calls for a further reflection upon solutions which can provide for flexibility.

### 13.4.4 Conclusion 4

In line with the foregoing, many national rapporteurs point at the need to define in a precise and clear manner the scope of the exceptions, as well as the conditions subject to which they will apply.

A number of examples in this respect are mentioned in the reports. For instance, several rapporteurs emphasised that a clarification is needed as to whether the exhaustion principle also applies to intangible copies of non-software works. Also, various national reports indicate that the users deserve more certainty with regard to private copying when the copy at stake originates from an unlawful source. This request for a higher certainty should be taken into consideration. Also, preference should be given to harmonisation.

In light of the above, the following fourth resolution has been adopted at the LIDC's Rio Congress 2017:

> LIDC notes that there is a significant demand for a solution ensuring a clear identification of the scope, the limits and the conditions relating to the application of exceptions and limitations. For instance, questions such as whether the private copying exception may apply even when the source is unlawful or whether exhaustion applies to intangible copies are still insufficiently settled. Therefore LIDC recommends that legal provisions should define said scope, limits and conditions in a clear and preferably harmonized manner.

### 13.4.5 Conclusion 5

The national reports note that where supranational instruments present the list of exceptions and limitations as an optional list, with the consequence that each country is free to adopt the exceptions or not, in whole or in part, the risk is that the divergences between the countries will further increase. Many reports indicate that such a risk may have negative effects on cross-border uses, in particular in a digital environment.

Therefore, the following fifth resolution was adopted at the LIDC's Rio Congress 2017:

> LIDC recognizes that, where international instruments set out exceptions and limitations as being optional, that may have negative effects on cross-border uses, in particular in a digital environment.

### 13.4.6 Conclusion 6

Many reports give special attention to the fact that the exceptions and limitation may be undermined in practice. They note in particular that contractual arrangements and the use of TPMs may hinder or impair the effective benefit of the exceptions and limitations. This is a matter of concern that should be addressed by legislation and international instruments of harmonisation.

Therefore, the LIDC adopted the following sixth resolution at the Rio Congress 2017:

> LIDC notes that exceptions and limitations are weakened if they can be overridden by contracts or bypassed by TPMs. Therefore, LIDC recommends that this issue should be expressly addressed by legislation and international instruments of harmonization.

# Austria 14

Valerie Eder

## 14.1 Overview of the Austrian System

Exceptions to copyright law are only permissible in Austria if encompassed by a specific provision providing for this exception. The Austrian Copyright Act[1] does not include a catch-all clause comparable to the "fair-use" regime known from the Anglo-American area.

The exceptions in the Austrian Copyright Act can be categorized into so-called *free uses*, *legal licenses*, and *compulsory licenses*. While free uses (freie Werknutzungen) have to be tolerated by the rights holder without remuneration (see Sections 41ff Austrian Copyright Act), other uses, so-called legal licenses, do entitle the rights holder to remuneration. The Austrian Copyright Act further provides for compulsory licenses, granting the user an enforceable claim to conclude a license with the rights holder where the law does not already provide for the right to use the work without the consent of the right holder, also entitling the rights holder to remuneration.

*Remuneration* claims can usually only be asserted by the competent collecting society for the respective type of works for and in the name of the copyright holder. The compensation is regulated in a highly differentiated manner. In most cases, tariffs are negotiated by the collecting societies with the relevant user representatives, providing for a balance of interests. Where such negotiations fail, an arbitration committee can be called upon.

[1] Bundesgesetz über das Urheberrecht an Werken der Literatur und der Kunst und über verwandte Schutzrechte (Urheberrechtsgesetz).

V. Eder (✉)
Gassauer-Fleissner Rechtsanwälte GmbH, Vienna, Austria
e-mail: v.eder@gassauer.com



B. Kilpatrick et al. (eds.), *Antitrust Analysis of Online Sales Platforms & Copyright Limitations and Exceptions*, LIDC Contributions on Antitrust Law, Intellectual Property and Unfair Competition,
https://doi.org/10.1007/978-3-319-71419-6_14

Some of these exceptions *apply uniformly to all categories of works* (literature, music, fine arts), e.g. free uses for official use, own or private use, persons with disabilities, or reporting of daily events and *uses*, including the reproduction, dissemination, or making available to the public. Other exceptions distinguish in a very detailed manner in both regards:

- For example, pursuant to Section 41 of the Austrian Copyright Act, entitled "free uses in the interest of justice and administration," works protected by copyright may be used without the consent of the copyrights holder for the purposes of public security or to ensure the proper conduct of administrative, parliamentary, or court proceedings. The scope of this provision covers, in principle, all types of works and extends to all types of use, including the availability on the Internet. Also, courts, authorities, and legislative bodies may use (for example, copy or publish) copyright-protected works without regard for possible limitations provided by the Copyright Act and without consent of the rights holder, if and as long as this is necessary in the course of their activity.
- As another example, Section 42d Austrian Copyright Act, entitled "persons with disabilities," permits the noncommercial use of a published work without the consent of the copyright holder for reproduction and dissemination, as well as making available to the public, for persons with disabilities in a form suitable for them, to the extent that their access to the works is considerably impeded or made impossible. As apparent from the wording of the provision, the permitted uses according to this exemption are the reproduction, the dissemination, and the making available to the public for persons with disabilities.

The Austrian system of free uses, legal licenses, and compulsory licenses therefore provides for a very detailed and differentiating system of exceptions to copyright. The list of exceptions of the Austrian Copyright Act is a closed list; however, limitations to copyright also arise from other areas:

- Some works are *expressly excluded* from copyright protection by Section 7 Austrian Copyright Act, entitled "free works," which reads in English translation as follows: "Laws, orders, official decrees, public notices and decisions, or official works produced exclusively or mainly for official use of the kind specified in Section 2 items 1 [works of language of any kind, including computer programs] or 3 [works of a scientific or didactic nature which consist of pictorial representations in two or three dimensions, unless they constitute works of art], shall not enjoy copyright protection."
- As the exclusive exploitation rights of the copyrights holder in Sections 14 ff of the Austrian Copyright Act are also worded as a closed list, *uses outside of this list* also constitute limitations of the copyright holder's right, if the term limitation is understood in a broad manner. Uses that are not reserved for the copyrights holder include most importantly the mere consumption of the work and also the exhibition of a published work and other uses.
- A further limitation of the copyright owner's right is the principle of *exhaustion* restricting the author's distribution right. According to Section 16 para 3 Austrian

Copyright Act, works that have been put into circulation by transfer of ownership in a Member State of the EU or the EEA with the consent of the rights holder are not subject to the exclusive right of distribution of the rights holder.

- Lastly, limitations of copyright can arise from *antitrust laws*. In exceptional circumstances, the use of the exploitation rights exclusively reserved for the rights holder or the refusal to grant authorizations for use may constitute an abuse of a dominant position according to Section 5 para 1 of the Austrian Cartels Act[2] or Section 102 of TFEU.[3] As a consequence, the rights holder in such cases could not rely on his/her right of exclusion but would be obliged to conclude a contract for the use of the work in return for an appropriate remuneration.[4]

## 14.2 Moral Rights

Moral rights are generally not affected by the exceptions to copyright. The relationship between the author's moral rights and free uses is regulated by Section 57 Austrian Copyright Act. According to this provision, reductions, additions and other changes to the work itself, to the title of the work, or to the author's designation must be assessed in line with the provision safeguarding moral rights, i.e. Section 21 Austrian Copyright Act, even if the user can rely on an exception. The meaning and essential nature of the work must not be distorted in any event.

Section 57 of the Austrian Copyrights Act regulates the moral rights very precisely for certain exceptions, e.g. stipulating that the source of the quoted work must always be stated clearly in the use of works for churches and schools, for recording, for inclusion in a program, for quoting parts of a work, or for use in the context of the panorama exception. In these cases, the source and the title of the work to be used must be indicated in accordance with Section 21 para 1 Austrian Copyright Act. In other cases, which are not expressly regulated, the general rule of Section 57 para 4 applies, according to which the source of the goods is to be determined according to bona fide and the established practices of the trade customs.

Moral rights conferred by the Austrian Copyright Act are set out in Sections 19–21 and include the protection of authorship (*Schutz der Urheberschaft*), the right of affirmation (*Schutz der Urheberbezeichnung*), and the right to the protection of works (*Werkschutz*). Moral rights of the author are not transferable.

The right to claim authorship pursuant to Section 19 Austrian Copyright Act is indispensable. Other rights can be excluded by contract within certain limits. However, the disclosure of authorship is not mandatory, and it can therefore be agreed upon in a contract that the authorship will not be affixed (e.g., with ghostwriters).[5]

---

[2] Bundesgesetz vom 22. November 1972, mit dem Bestimmungen über Kartelle und Vorschriften zur Erhaltung der Wettbewerbsfreiheit erlassen werden (Kartellgesetz).

[3] See, i.a., ECJ, case C-241/91 and C-242/91, *RTE and ITP v Commission*, ECR 1995 I 743; CFI, case T-201/04, *Microsoft v Commission*, ECR 2007 II 3601.

[4] See i.a. OGH [Austrian Supreme Court] 09 April 2002, 4 Ob 17/02g, "*EDV-Firmenbuch.*"

[5] Walter, Österreichisches Urheberrecht. Handbuch. I. Teil, 893.

The protection of works pursuant to Section 21 safeguards the integrity of the work by restricting the possibility to alter the work after it is no longer in the right holder's control. According to para 1 of this provision, where a work is used in a manner that makes it available to the public or where it is reproduced for the purpose of dissemination, no abridgements, additions, or other alterations to the work itself, its title, or the designation of author may be made, even by a person entitled to such use, unless the author consents thereto or unless the law permits such alteration. Such alterations, in particular, are permissible if necessitated by the manner or purpose of the authorized use of the work.

The provisions of para 1 apply to the originals of works even where such originals are not used in a manner that makes the work available to the public.

According to para 3 of the said provision, the fact of having given his/her consent to alterations that are not specifically designated does not prevent the author from opposing distortions, mutilations, or other alterations of the work that seriously violate his/her moral interests in the work.

In summary, as mentioned above, according to Section 57 Austrian Copyright Act, moral rights are to be observed also in the case of exceptions to copyright. In the absence of any special regulation in Section 57 Austrian Copyright Act, whether or not the designation of origin can be omitted is governed according to bona fide and the established practices of the trade customs. In the absence of a contractual agreement or a two-way trade agreement, this will have to be examined very carefully by any user and will be at the discretion of the courts. In connection with official use (Section 41 Austrian Copyright Act, as discussed above under Sect. 14.1), the author's name must be provided, if not for insuperable difficulties.

The Austrian Copyright Act therefore carries out a balance of interests between the author's moral rights and the practical requirements for exceptions, whereby the former is granted adequate protection without unduly restricting the practice.

## 14.3 Objectives

The exceptions in the Austrian Copyright Act (free uses, legal licenses, and compulsory licenses) are the result of a balancing of interests of the rights holder and those of the general public. The InfoSoc Directive contains no obligation for Member States to integrate these exceptions in their national legislation other than the exception for temporary acts of reproduction, which is mandatory. Therefore, EU law does not contain a final balance of interest binding the EU Member States, leaving this to the national level. The Austrian Copyright Act as a result of this balance of interests includes exceptions taking into account several fundamental rights and objectives, including education, research and access to culture and knowledge, freedom of expression and right to receive and disseminate information, privacy and private use, needs of people with a disability, preservation of cultural heritage, public security, and freedom of panorama.

## 14.4 Fundamental Rights

Other that having been taken into account by the Austrian legislator and in that regard leading to the exceptions explicitly listed in the Austrian Copyright Act, fundamental rights in themselves can in certain circumstances prevail above copyright so that ultimately the use of a work is permitted without the consent of the copyright owner. The Austrian Supreme Court repeatedly recognized that the fundamental right of freedom of expression protected by Article 10 of ECHR can restrict copyrights in an individual case, rejecting applications for an injunction according to the Copyright Act based on this fundamental right.[6] Restrictions could also be based on other fundamental rights, e.g. the freedom of science or the right to artistic freedom. The Supreme Court, however, emphasizes that restrictions of the rights of the copyrights holder based on fundamental rights may only be applied in extreme cases.

Whether the fundamental right is given priority over copyright is to be decided on the basis of a balance of interests. The right of the author to decide how and if his/her work is used and to demand remuneration for such uses is weighed against the interest of the person who through the use of the work wishes to communicate facts or express opinions. The basic prerequisite for any justification for an interference with copyright by the fundamental right of freedom of expression is that the economic interests of the author are not affected and the fundamental right cannot be exercised without interference with the copyright or the right to protection of rights.[7]

In this respect, the restrictions on exclusive copyrights must be limited to certain special cases that do not affect the normal exploitation of the work or unduly violate the legitimate interests of the author or copyrights holder. The right to freedom of expression is intended to restrict the copyright only where use of the protected text would otherwise be impossible or only inadequately possible and would not prejudice the author's interest in the use or a "normal" exploitation of the work of the use.

## 14.5 The "Triple Test"

In international conventions like the Berne Convention,[8] the triple test is generally designed as a directive and a limitation for the national legislator. However, it also has an indirect effect on national law since works, whose country of origin is a country other than Austria that is party to the Berne Convention, can rely directly on the minimum protection rights conferred therein, one of it being the triple test. In this context, the Austrian Supreme court held that the (meanwhile amended) private use exception in the Austrian Copyright Act regarding sheet music was not in line

[6] OGH 12 June 2001, 4 Ob 127/01g "*Medienprofessor*", OGH 12 September 2001 4 Ob 194/01k "*WienerLandtagswahlkampf*", OGH 02 July 2002, 4 Ob 135/02k "*Soziales Netz*", OGH 14 March2005, 4 Ob 266/04b "*Afrikadorf*", OGH 11 August 2005, 4 Ob 146/05g "*Smith Freunde*", OGH 21 November 2006, 4 Ob 195/06i "*unsachliche Berichterstattung*".

[7] OGH 24 June 2003, 4 Ob 105/03z – "*Foto des Mordopfers*".

[8] Berne Convention for the Protection of Literary and Artistic Works (1886).

with Article 9 para 2 Berne Convention prior to the introduction of the remuneration for reprographic reproductions (regulated in Section 42b Austrian Copyright Act and discussed in more detail below under Sect. 14.6.3).[9]

The TRIPs Agreement extended the triple test to all objects and exploitation rights (Article 13), which also has been adopted by the WIPO Copyright Treaty (Article 10) and applies to the performance rights regulated by the WIPO Performances and Phonograms Treaty as well (Article 16).

Under EU law, exceptions to copyright are mainly regulated in Article 5 of the InfoSoc Directive. The exceptions listed therein are mostly facultative and therefore give EU Member States the possibility, but not the obligation, to transpose such exceptions in national legislation. All exceptions therein are subject to the triple-step test. As some of the exceptions provided in Article 5 InfoSoc Directive are worded in a very general manner while others are set out in great detail, the triple test serves not only as a limitation for national legislators but also as a general guideline.

The Austrian Copyright Act does not provide for a specific provision implementing the triple test, which led to some criticism. In addition to the above-described indirect effect on national law, limitations to copyright will have to comply with the triple test as the provisions of the Austrian Copyright Act have to be interpreted in conformity with Article 5 of the InfoSoc Directive.

## 14.6 Exceptions in the Austrian Copyright Act

As mentioned above, the Austrian Copyright Act, *inter alia*, includes exceptions for uses for education, research, access to culture and knowledge, freedom of expression, the right to receive and disseminate information, privacy and private use, needs of persons with disabilities, preservation of cultural heritage, public security, and freedom of panorama. Some of the exceptions in the Austrian Copyright Act are discussed below in more detail.

### 14.6.1 Exceptions for Temporary Acts of Reproduction

The Austrian Copyright Act provides for an exception allowing temporary acts of reproduction that are necessary to enable a lawful use. The exception was introduced in the Austrian Copyright Act with the Amendment Act 2003 based on the almost identical provision in Section 5 para 1 of the InfoSoc Directive. It is the only mandatory exception of this Directive and has no equivalent in international conventions. The provision is tailored for the online context, but not limited thereto, and also applies to all services of the information society, e.g. the mobile network UMTS. The exception can be found in Section 41a Austrian Copyright Act and reads as follows:

[9] OGH 31 January 1995, 4 Ob 143/94, "*ludus tonalis*".

Temporary reproduction is permissible,

1. if it is transient or incidental, and
2. if it is an integral and essential part of a technological process, and
3. if its whose sole purpose is to enable a transmission in a network between third parties by an intermediary, or a lawful use and
4. if it has no independent economic significance.

### 14.6.2 Exceptions for Specific Content

The Austrian Copyright Act does not provide for a list of exceptions for specific contents. Some exceptions do, however, relate to a specific content. These exceptions can be found in different parts of the Austrian Copyright Act. One example is the exception for political speeches according to Section 43 Austrian Copyright Act, which reads in para 1 as follows:

> Speeches made in an assembly responsible for the conduct of public affairs, or in the course of proceedings before a court of law or other public agency, as well as political speeches given in public, may be reproduced, disseminated, publicly delivered and broadcast for the purpose of reporting.

Where a speech of such nature has been reproduced on an audio medium, such medium may, however, only be distributed with the consent of the author. The reproduction and distribution of such speeches in compilations are reserved to the author.

The rights holder cannot prohibit the free uses described in para 1 and is not entitled to remuneration. If the speech is used, the source and the name of the author, the title, and the time and date of the speech have to be cited.

The Austrian Copyright Act also provides for an exception for news of the day. Individual sections contained in a newspaper or periodical concerning current economic, political, or religious issues may be reproduced and disseminated in other newspapers and periodicals. This does not apply where reproduction is expressly prohibited. A statement reserving the rights accompanying the section or in the heading of the newspaper or periodical is sufficient in this regard.

Mere items of press information that simply report mere facts and statements without further commentary are not considered to be "works" due to their simple nature and therefore do not enjoy copyright protection. In order for a press section to be considered a work, it has to reflect an "individual intellectual performance," e.g. by using several different sources for the drafting of the article.

However, even though such mere items of press information are excluded from copyright protection, some protection is conferred by Section 79 Austrian Copyright Act (entitled "Protection of News"—Nachrichtenschutz), protecting such sections for 12 h from the time of publication.

As mentioned above, some works are expressly excluded from copyright protection by Section 6 Austrian Copyright Act due to their content and nature. Paragraph 1 of the provision in its English translation reads as follows:

> Laws, orders, official decrees, public notices and decisions, or official works produced exclusively or mainly for official use of the kind specified in Section 2 items 1 [works of language of any kind, including computer programs] or 3 [works of a scientific or didactic nature which consist of pictorial representations in two or three dimensions, unless they constitute works of art], shall not enjoy copyright protection.

Cartographic works produced or adapted by the Federal Standards and Survey Office and intended for distribution are excluded from the scope of this exception.

### 14.6.3 Exceptions for Private Copies

Article 42 Austrian Copyright Act titled "Reproduction for own and private use" provides for exceptions for the reproduction of individual copies of a work for private use, i.e. noncommercial use, or a person's own use.

According to Article 42 para 5 Austrian Copyright Act, the exception for a person's own or private use is not applicable if the original used was obviously produced or made available to the public illegally. This wording was introduced by the amendment of the Copyright Act of 2015. The terms "obviously illegally" and "made available to the public" are not specified any further in the statutory provisions and, so far, have also not been defined any further by case law.

There is no further guidance in the provision regarding the term "individual copies" that is used in several paragraphs. The meaning of this term has to be determined according to the circumstances of each specific case. The Austrian Supreme Court in a case from 1998 allowed for 19 copies of a magazine dummy to be made in preparation for an editorial meeting. In contrast, German case law suggests a maximum of seven pieces to satisfy the requirement of making only "individual copies."

The provision, *inter alia*, encompasses the following exceptions:

- *Reproduction on paper or similar material for a person's own use* (para 1): every person, i.e. natural and legal persons, may make individual copies and paper or similar material for his/her own use. It is not limited to private use; individual copies on paper or similar material can therefore also be made for commercial uses, as long as the copies are not made available to the public.
- *Reproduction on other material for a person's own use for research* (para 2): individual copies on material other than paper or similar materials can be made by every person for the purposes of research to the extent that this is justified for the purpose of pursuing noncommercial purposes. For the purpose of noncommercial use for research (only), individual copies can therefore be made on digital storage media as well.
- *Media monitoring* (para 3): every person may produce individual copies of works published in the context of the reporting of daily events for their own use, provided that the use is only analogous. Paragraph 3 does not use the wording "on paper or similar material." The exact meaning of this differentiation is unclear.
- *Reproduction on other material for a natural person's private use* (para 4): any natural person may produce individual copies on a medium other than paper or

similar materials for private use if it does not directly or indirectly serve commercial purposes.

The requirements and the scope of the exceptions are therefore different regarding the reproduction on paper or similar material compared to reproduction on other, e.g. digital or electronic, materials. The provision also differentiates between a person's own use and private use and provides for a number of special rules, e.g. for research purposes, schools and universities, and media monitoring, as well as exceptions, e.g., for entire books, sheet music, or the construction of a building according to a plan.

The provision used to have a broader scope, allowing the current exception for reproduction on paper or similar materials for reproduction on all materials, but was restricted with the amendment of the Copyright Act of 2003 to be in line with Article 5 para 2 lits a and b of the InfoSoc Directive.

The private use exception is therefore restricted in some areas, especially regarding digital copies, which is, however, at least partly due to the legislative limitations conferred by the InfoSoc Directive. Due to this issue and the generally highly complex structure, the provision is unclear and leads to legal uncertainty.

**Compensation for a Person's Own or Private Use (Section 42b Austrian Copyright Act)**
The copyright owner is entitled to reasonable remuneration if it is to be expected that a work that is broadcast by radio, made available to the public or stored on a storage medium manufactured for commercial purposes, will be duplicated for a person's own or private use according to Article 42 paras 2–7 Austrian Copyright Act, when storage media of any kind suitable for such duplications are commercially marketed in Austria (storage media remuneration).

If a work of its kind is to be expected to be duplicated by means of reprographic or similar procedures for a person's own use, the copyright owner is entitled to an appropriate remuneration (reprographic remuneration) (1) if a device intended for the purpose of performing such reproductions is commercially marketed (remuneration for equipment) in Austria or (2) if a reproduction device is operated in schools, colleges, facilities for vocational training or other education and training, research facilities, public libraries, or facilities that provide reproducing equipment for remuneration (operator remuneration).

Both the storage media remuneration and the reprographic remuneration cannot be claimed by the copyright owners themselves but can be claimed only by collecting societies (Verwertungsgesellschaften). Tariffs for the reprography are set by agreements between the competent collecting societies and the competent bodies of the chamber of commerce.

### 14.6.4 Exceptions for Education

Section 42 para 6 Austrian Copyright Act provides for an exception for schools and other educational institutions for educational purposes that is broader than the general own and private use exception regulated in Section 42. According to this provision, schools, universities, and other educational establishments may, for the purpose of education or teaching, reproduce and disseminate copies of a work to the extent necessary for a particular class or course; this also applies to sheet notes. On materials other than paper or similar materials, this is, however, only permissible for noncommercial purposes. This right does not apply to works that, according to their nature and design, are intended to be used in schools and/or teaching purposes.

In general, the copyright owner is entitled to reasonable remuneration if it is to be expected that his work will be broadcast, made available to the public or stored on a storage medium manufactured for commercial purposes, or duplicated for a person's own or private use according to this exception, when storage media of any kind suitable for such duplications are commercially marketed in Austria (storage media remuneration).

Further, schools, universities, and other educational institutions may, for the purpose of education or teaching, reproduce and make available to the public published works for the purpose of illustration in the classroom for a clearly defined circle of subjects or course participants, to the extent that this is justified by the respective purpose and for pursuing noncommercial purposes (Section 42g Austrian Copyright Act). As this exception is only applicable if the works are reproduced or made available for a clearly defined circle of subjects, publication on online platforms requires access restrictions. Although this exception applies to all uses, it does not apply to works that, according to their nature and design, are intended for school or teaching purposes. As a further exception from the rule, cinematographic works may only be used if at least 2 years have elapsed since the first performance of the film work in Austria, in German or in a language of a national group recognized in Austria. The copyrights holder is entitled to remuneration, which can be claimed by collecting societies.

The Austrian Copyright Act also provides for a specific exception for the public rendition of cinematographic works and connected musical works (Article 56c Austrian Copyright Act), allowing this use to an extent justified by the purpose of education. The copyrights holder is again entitled to reasonable remuneration, which can be claimed by collecting societies.

These provisions do not cover all aspects of distance learning, although the scope of the provision was extended considerably in regard to this purpose with the Amendment of the Copyright Act in 2015. As the exceptions, as far as reproduction on materials other than paper or similar materials is concerned, only applies to educational establishments that pursue noncommercial purposes, it excludes other educational establishments and makes it more difficult to provide high-quality distance learning. Further, wording like "to the extent that this is justified by the respective purpose" leads to considerable legal uncertainty for teachers. It is not sufficiently clear how this wording is to be interpreted—a narrow interpretation would lead to a situation where additional reading material that should help to understand the material and provide further and deeper insight in a subject, but is not discussed in the lecture itself, might not be covered by the exception. This results in a situation where teachers are very restrictive in providing such materials to avoid liability. Another factor deterring teachers from providing these materials to students is the complexity of the whole provision and the differentiation between many—very similar—situations, adding to the legal uncertainty.

### 14.6.5 Exceptions for Research

Section 42 para 2 Austrian Copyright Act provides for a broader exception for the purpose of research compared to the general own and private use exemption regulated in Section 42. Pursuant to this regulation, everyone may produce individual copies of the work, including on materials other than paper for purposes of research, to the extent that this is justified for pursuing noncommercial purposes.

As discussed in more detail below under Sect. 14.6.3, there is no further guidance in the Austrian Copyright Act regarding the term "individual copies." How many copies still can be considered as "individual copies" therefore has to be determined in each individual case according to the specific circumstances.

As mentioned above, the copyright owner is entitled to reasonable remuneration if it is to be expected that his/her work will be broadcast, made available to the public or stored on a storage medium manufactured for commercial purposes, or duplicated for a person's own or private use according to this exception, when storage media of any kind suitable for such duplications are commercially marketed in Austria (storage media remuneration).

There is a further exception in Section 42a Austrian Copyright Act, which generally provides for the possibility to produce individual copies for another person's own use free of charge or—under very restricted circumstances—for a fee, most importantly when the reproduction is carried out by means of reprographic or similar procedures. Paragraph 2 of this provision allows public facilities that collect workpieces to produce individual copies on request free of charge for a school's own use or for a person's own or private use for the purpose of research on all materials (and therefore not only by using reprographic or similar procedures but also by scanning the work).

A further exception for own and private use allows publicly accessible facilities that collect workpieces to make a reproduction for the inclusion in their own archive, if and to the extent that the reproduction is justified by this purpose. This is only permissible on materials other than paper (or similar materials) if the user does neither directly nor indirectly pursue a commercial purpose (Section 42 para 7 Austrian Copyright Act). Based on this exception, such facilities are allowed to digitalize their whole collection.

The Austrian Copyright Act currently does not contain a data mining exception.

### 14.6.6 Exceptions for the Freedom of Expression

The exception for quotations of Section 42f Austrian Copyright Act is one of the most important exceptions allowing for freedom of expression.[10]

Accordingly, all published works can be produced, disseminated, broadcast, made available to the public, and used for public lectures, performances, and screenings for the purpose of quotation, provided that its use is justified in its scope by this purpose. The provision in para 1 lists a number of examples where such use would be justified. The rights holder is not entitled to remuneration for uses based on this exception.

Further, the exception for the reporting of current events in Section 42c Austrian Copyright Act safeguards the freedom of expression as well, permitting that works that become perceivable to the public during the reporting of current events to be reproduced, disseminated, broadcast, or used for public lectures, performances, or presentations to the extent justified by the purpose of information.

To a certain extent, the exceptions for education and research, discussed in detail below, contribute to the protection of the freedom of expression as well.

### 14.6.7 The Panorama Exception

The Austrian Copyright Act provides for an especially broad panorama exception in Section 54 para 5.[11]

---

[10] Section 42f Austrian Copyright Act reads in English translation as follows:

(1) A published work may be reproduced, disseminated, broadcast, made available to the public and used for public lectures, performances and screenings for the purpose of the quotation, provided that its use is justified in its scope by this special purpose. This is particularly permissible if:

1. individual works, after their publication, are included in a scientific work which forms the principal object; A work of the kind referred to in Section 2 item 3 [works of a scientific or didactic nature which consist of pictorial representations in two or three dimensions, unless they constitute works of art] or a work of the visual arts may only be included for the purpose of explaining the content;
2. published works of the visual arts in a scientific or instructional lecture, which form the principal object, are merely publicly presented for the purpose of explaining the contents, and the duplicating pieces required for this purpose are produced;
3. individual points of a published work of literature in a self-sufficient new work;
4. the individual passages of a published work of music are given in a work of literature;
5. the individual parts of a published work are listed in a separate, new work.

(2) For the purposes of this provision, a work which has been made available to the public in a manner which is accessible to the general public is to be regarded as equivalent to a published work.

[11] It reads as follows:

(1) It shall be permissible […]

(5) to reproduce, disseminate, present in public by means of optical devices and broadcast and make available to the public works of architecture after their construction or other works of

The panorama exception according to Section 54 para 5 Austrian Copyright Act covers many uses, i.e. to reproduce the works, e.g. by photographing, drawing, or sketching; to disseminate the works; to present in public "by means of optical devices," e.g. by projecting images of the exterior of a building in public; to broadcast them; and to make them available to the public. The reconstruction of works of architecture, the reproduction of a work of painting or the graphic arts for a permanent installation in a public place, as well as the reproduction of works of the plastic, are not exempt.

The panorama exception according to Section 54 para 4 Austrian Copyright Act is also referred to as "freedom of the image of the road and landscape" (Freiheit des Straßen- und Landschaftsbildes), which gives the impression that only the exterior of a building would be covered by this exception. As the term "works of architecture" is considered to cover the interior architecture of a building as well, the exception actually covers the interior of a building as well, such as stairwells, courtyards, a porch, individual halls, rooms, portals, and doors. What is required, however, is that they are reproduced, disseminated, etc in connection with the structure because their connection with a certain space makes them an integral part of a "work of architecture." If these objects are reproduced on their own, without a recognizable connection with others, or with the space surrounding them, the described uses are not covered by the exception.

The purpose of the reproduction is irrelevant; commercial purposes can therefore be pursued as well. The exception therefore allows the use, for example, for marketing postcards, calendars, posters, etc.

The free use of the work according to Section 54 para 4 Austrian Copyright Act is neither dependent on the consent of the author or the right holder, nor is it remunerated.

## 14.6.8 Exceptions for the Preservation of Cultural Heritage

The central exception for the preservation of cultural heritage in the Austrian Copyright Act is the exception for orphaned works in Section 56e Austrian Copyright Act, which implemented Directive 2012/28/EU.[12] Pursuant to this provision, publicly accessible facilities that collect workpieces may, under certain circumstances, produce works and make them available to the public if after a diligent search to find its copyright holder(s), the identity or location of the copyright holder(s) is still unknown (orphan works).

---

Article permanently located in a public place; this provision shall not extend to the replication of a work of architecture and the reproduction of a painting or a graphic work for the purpose of placing such reproduction permanently in a place of such kind, or to the three-dimensional reproduction of a three-dimensional work.

[12] Directive 2012/28 of the European Parliament and of the Council of 25 October 2012 on certain permitted uses of orphan works, OJ 2012, L 299, p. 5 (in the following: "Orphan Works Directive").

Further, Section 53 Austrian Copyright Act provides for the possibility to publicly perform works of music under certain circumstances, including a special provision for folk music.

The use of the work is permitted without the consent of the rights holder where the performance is given by a band composed of nonprofessional musicians or by a choir that pursues the goal to maintain folk customs as attested to by the competent provincial government and whose members do not participate for profit and where such performance consists, at least to a clearly preponderant extent, of folk music or of music or adaptations of music in the public domain. The provision is difficult to use in practice as it is very complex and quite narrow.

### 14.6.9 Exceptions for Public Security

Section 41 Austrian Copyright Act, titled "free uses in the interests of the administration of justice and public administration," provides for an exception for works when used as evidence in proceedings before courts or other authorities or for the purposes of administration of criminal justice and public safety.

### 14.6.10 Exceptions for Persons with a Disability

Section 42d Austrian Copyright Act provides for an exception to copyright for the noncommercial use of a published work. The provision allows for the reproduction and the dissemination, as well as making available to the public, for persons with disabilities in a form suitable for them without the consent of the right holder, if and as far as their access to the works is considerably impeded or made impossible.

## 14.7 Technological Protection Measures

According to Section 90b Austrian Copyright Act, the holder of exclusion rights on a computer program based on the Copyright Act that is using technical mechanisms for the protection of a program can claim injunctive relief and removal when means intended to eliminate or circumvent the technical protection mechanisms are placed on the market or possessed for commercial purposes.

Section 90c Austrian Copyright Act on the other hand relates to technical protection measures for works other than computer programs, stipulating that the holder of an exclusion right based on the Copyright Act using effective technical measures to prevent or limit infringement of this right can claim injunctive relief and removal:

1. if the person circumventing these measures knows, or has reasonable grounds to know, that he or she is pursuing that objective;
2. if the means are manufactured, imported, distributed, sold, rented, and used for commercial purposes;

3. if the means are advertised for sale or rent; or
4. if services to circumvent the means are rendered.

It is evident from the wording of the provisions that Section 90b relates only to computer programs, whereas Section 90c relates to all (other) categories of works. The provisions are worded differently as they are based on different directives, namely Directive 2009/24[13] (hereinafter Software Directive) and the InfoSoc Directive.

*Section 90c* Austrian Copyright Act implements Section 6 of the InfoSoc Directive, granting rights holders using technological protection measures to prevent infringements of his/her rights under specified circumstances a claim to injunctive relief and removal. The provision protects against the infringement of the right itself, as well as against preparatory measures.

Section 90c of the Austrian Copyright Act relates to the prevention of uses that infringe the exclusive rights of the copyright holder, while Article 6 para 3 InfoSoc Directive relates to all uses without the consent of the right holder. The Austrian provision therefore has a narrower scope than Article 6 of the InfoSoc Directive; for example, it would be permitted to make a copy of a work for private use based on the exception of Section 42 Austrian Copyright Act; however, the copy would be made without the consent of the right holder. In practice, the provision will have to be interpreted in accordance with the Directive. If Section 90c is to be interpreted in accordance with the Directive, such a private copy made by circumventing technical protection measures would be unlawful.

According to Section 6 para 4 InfoSoc Directive, Member States shall, in the absence of voluntary measures taken by right holders, including agreements between rights holders and other parties concerned, take appropriate measures to ensure that rights holders make available to the beneficiary of an exception provided for by national law in accordance with rights conferred by the Directive the means of benefiting from that exception, to the extent necessary to benefit from that exception and where that beneficiary has legal access to the protected work or subject matter concerned.

It is therefore only in the event that such voluntary measures are not taken by rights holders that there is some obligation for the national legislature to allow for enforcement. However, the exception for private use (excluding the reproduction on paper) is not covered by this obligation. Member States may, but are not obligated to, regulate the enforcement of reproductions for private use against technological protection measures. Unlike the German legislator (see Section 96b of the German Copyright Act), the Austrian legislator has not yet dealt with any remedial measures in the Austrian Copyright Act. The explanatory remarks to the Amendment Act 2003 state that the intention was to wait for the technological development, its practical implementation, and the reaction of the rights holders.[14]

[13] Directive 2009/24 of the European Parliament and of the Council of 23 April 2009 on the legal protection of computer programs, OJ 2009 L 111, p. 16.

[14] Explanatory remarks to the Amendment Act 2003 in *Walter*, Austrian Copyrights Act Nov 2003, §90c, 163 with commentary Walter, 167, Dillenz/Gutman, Urheberrechtsgesetz &VerwGesG, Section 90c para 63ff.

Technological protection measures are further strengthened by the 4th sentence of Section 6 para 4 InfoSoc Directive: in case of works or other subject matter that is made available to the public on agreed contractual terms in such a way that members of the public may access them from a place and at a time individually chosen by them, the national legislator is prohibited to introduce provisions restricting technological protection measures. This does not include services that are not on demand, such as streaming technologies and pay-per-view services.

It follows that if the copyrights holder offers works online (Section 18a Austrian Copyright Act), he/she may circumvent the exceptions to his/her copyright as provided in the Austrian Copyright Act by requiring users to conclude a contract before accessing the work. Therefore, the national legislator can permit the copying of a work of music purchased on CD for private use even if technological protection measures are circumvented but not if the work was legally downloaded from the Internet. Since this rule is mandatory, these provisions are binding on the national legislator.

The protection conferred by Section 90b is in comparison quite narrow; it is (only) directed to the placing on the market and commercial possession of preparatory instruments that facilitate a practical circumvention of technical protection measures. As a result, technical protection measures for computer programs enjoy a more limited legal protection than all other categories of works. The actual use of the computer program would, however, infringe exclusive exploitation rights of the copyrights holder (if not protected by a free use or other exception) and therefore also allow injunctive relief and removal.

## 14.8 The Principle of Exhaustion

As mentioned above under Sect. 14.1, the principle of exhaustion further limits the exploitation rights of the rights holder. According to Section 16 para 1 Austrian Copyright Act, the rights owner has the exclusive right to disseminate "workpieces," excluding others to market them or place them onto the market in a manner that makes the work accessible to the public without his/her consent. According to para 3 of this provision, this exclusive right of dissemination does not extend to works that have already been placed onto the market by transfer of ownership with the consent of the copyrights holder in a Member State of the European Community or in a Contracting State of the European Economic Area.

This rule does not apply to leasing and lending according to the provisions of Section 16a; although the copyright owner cannot prohibit noncommercial leasing and lending of his/her work, he/she is entitled to a financial remuneration. This remuneration can only be claimed by collecting societies.

Following a request for a preliminary ruling by the German Federal Supreme Court (BGH), the CJEU has permitted the sale of "second hand software" in its landmark decision *UsedSoft*[15] (affirming the possibility of digital exhaustion under the Software Directive) in relation to computer programs downloaded from the Internet.

In more detail, the CJEU has ruled that the principle of exhaustion, as laid down in Article 4 para 2 Software Directive, applies equally to tangible and intangible copies of software programs as the wording of the Software Directive does not differentiate in this regard. Accordingly, software distribution by download triggers exhaustion of the distribution right in regard to the downloaded copy. The CJEU argues that online transmission is the "functional equivalent" of the supply of a tangible medium and further states that the effect of exhaustion also extends to updates and patches provided by the copyrights holder after the download, e.g., on the basis of a maintenance contract. Based on this decision, reselling "used" software programs originally disseminated via download does not infringe the copyright holder's distribution right, provided that the originally downloaded copy is deleted or rendered unusable.

The CJEU confirmed the general principle of *UsedSoft* in its recent decision, C-166/15 *Microsoft*.[16] However, it remains unclear whether and to what extent this conclusion can be extended to works other than computer programs and that fall under the scope of the InfoSoc Directive.

## 14.9 Flexibility of the Austrian System

As already mentioned, the exceptions to copyright are regulated in a very detailed and differentiating manner and are limited to a number of very specific cases that are described in detail in the relevant provisions.

A lot of provisions differentiate with regard to the *categories of works* and with regard to the *purpose of the use* of the work (e.g., commercial or noncommercial purposes, research purposes, etc), as well as with regard to the person of the user, providing different scopes of exception for natural and legal persons and also for specific institutions. For example, as shown above, the exception for own and private use pursuant to Section 42 has a very different scope for individuals (natural persons) and legal persons and also has a much broader scope for schools, universities, and other educational institutions.

There is little room for flexibility as the list of exceptions in the Austrian Copyright Act is a closed list and additionally is not to be interpreted in an extensive manner.[17] Exceptions restricting the exclusive rights of the copyright owner are—as exceptions to a general rule—to be interpreted closely following the purpose of the specific exception. However, this does not necessarily mean that exceptions have to

[15] CJEU, case C-128/11, *UsedSoft GmbH v Oracle International Corp.*, ECLI:EU:C:2012:407.

[16] CJEU, case C-166/15, *Microsoft*, ECLI:EU:C:2016:762.

[17] Dillenz, Gutman, UrhG & VerwGesG, vor §§ 41 Rz 2 mwN bzw OGH vom 28.11.1978 "Betriebsmusik", ÖBl 1979, 51.

be interpreted in a strict manner; the analogous application of these provisions is, for example, not excluded.[18]

However, a somehow more generous approach was taken in regard to parodies in the Supreme Court case *Lieblingshauptfrau*,[19] effectively leading to a free use of a work, although the decision did not relate to a specific exception as the Austrian Copyrights Act does not provide for an exception for parodies or caricatures. In order to be permissible, the parody or caricature has to qualify as a "free adaption" of the parodied work. According to Section 5 para 2 of the Austrian Copyright Act, use made of a work in creating another work shall not make that other work an adaptation requiring the consent of the rights holder of the original if such work constitutes an independent new work in relation to the work used. This requirement was interpreted very generously by the Supreme Court in the case *Lieblingshauptfrau*, accepting that in case of parodies, a (significantly) lower threshold can be applied for the requirements that have to be met in order to qualify a work as an independent new work, i.e. a free adaption.

Free uses can theoretically—in the absence of an express provision stating otherwise—be ruled out by contract, provided this is possible according to general civil law, which is, however, only rarely the case.

## 14.10 Conclusion

The Austrian Copyright Law is determined in a relatively large amount by EU legislation and is a complex system of provisions balancing the rights of the copyright owner and the general public. The system is complex not least because of the lack of a catch-all clause; the Austrian Copyright Act—as described above—establishes very detailed exceptions that try to strike a fair balance in specific and sometimes also quite similar situations, resulting in complicated provisions and inconsistencies. Some of these issues are rooted in EU legislation, while others are due to the historic development of Austrian and EU Copyright Law.

As a result, the Austrian Copyright Act is in part quite complicated, leading to some amount of legal uncertainty for the user. This is especially true for the use in online situations, compounded by the fact that there remain some unanswered questions with regard to EU legislation in this area. A consolidation and simplification of the exceptions listed in the Austrian Copyright Act would be desirable, where possible within the framework of EU law.

[18] OGH 19 November 2002, 4 Ob 230/02f "*meischi.at*".

[19] OGH 13 July 2010, 4 Ob 66/10z "*Lieblingshauptfrau*".

# Belgium

# 15

Manon Knockaert

## 15.1 Introduction

Copyright law protects literary and artistic works that reflect the personality of the creator for 70 years beyond his or her death.

Copyright law offers a monopoly to the copyright owner. Nevertheless, over the years, exceptions to this exclusive right increased in order to meet the general interest and respect fundamental rights. At the same time, the exceptions have become more complex. The information society and the Internet challenge the intellectual property law that oscillates between always more protection and the desire to grab these new tools to encourage creation.

In this report, we will try to bring some clarity. We will focus on the main exceptions to copyright and briefly address exceptions to the law of databases and computer programs.

As a first step, we will give a brief overview of the history of exceptions in Belgian law before presenting preliminary and general considerations of the exception regime. A specific section concerns the triple test. Then we will outline the various exceptions available under Belgian law. Finally, we will tackle technical protection measures and the exhaustion rule. We conclude with an explanation of counterbalance between fundamental rights and the exclusive rights enjoyed by the copyright owner.

M. Knockaert (✉)
Research Centre in Information, Law and Society (CRIDS/NADI), University of Namur, Namur, Belgium
e-mail: manon.knockaert@unamur.be



B. Kilpatrick et al. (eds.), *Antitrust Analysis of Online Sales Platforms & Copyright Limitations and Exceptions*, LIDC Contributions on Antitrust Law, Intellectual Property and Unfair Competition,
https://doi.org/10.1007/978-3-319-71419-6_15

## 15.2 Historical Development of Exceptions in Belgian Law

In Belgium, the first national law on copyright appears in 1886. Exceptions from quotations for the purpose of criticism, polemics or teaching, as well as the reproduction in a newspaper of an article taken from another publication, emerged. The following laws enriched the list of exceptions: the laws of 1958[1] and 1994[2] and the transposition law of the Directive on the legal protection of databases.[3] With the transposition of another Directive, Directive 2001/29[4] on the harmonisation of certain aspects of copyright and related rights in the information society, nine exceptions are added.[5] European Directive 2001/29 lays down a list of exceptions for the Member States. National legislators are free to transpose into their national law all exceptions or some of them. Only one single exception is obligatory for all Member States: the exception for temporary acts of reproduction. If the Member States have the choice of the exceptions proposed by the European Union, they may not go beyond the scope of the list in Article 5 of Directive 2001/29.

The Belgian provisions on intellectual property are contained in the Code de droit économique (Code of Economic Law, hereafter referred to as 'CDE'). It is important to note that recent amendments have been made by the Law of 22 December 2016.[6]

Belgian law expressly excludes from copyright protection speeches made in deliberative assemblies, public court hearings or political meetings and the official acts of the authority (legal texts and decisions of courts and tribunals).[7]

---

[1] Insertion of the exception for reproduction and communication to the public for news reporting purposes.

[2] Insertion of exceptions of execution in the family circle, reprography, private copying, parody and execution of works during a public examination.

[3] Directive 96/9 of the European Parliament and of the Council of 11 March 1996 on the legal protection of databases, JO 1996 L 77, p. 20.

[4] Directive 2001/29 of the European Parliament and of the Council of 22 May 2011 on the harmonization of certain aspects of copyright and related rights in the information society, JO 2001 L 167, p. 10.

[5] Insertion of exceptions for provisional copies, performance in the context of school activities, the communication of works for the purpose of illustrating teaching, reproduction for preservation purposes by the listed institutions, and the consultation in These same establishments, ephemeral recordings made by broadcasting organisations, exceptions for the disabled, reproduction and communication intended to announce public exhibitions and sales of artistic works as well as the exception of reproduction in favour of hospitals, penitentiary establishments and establishments for assistance to young people; S. Dusollier et M. Lambrecht, Les exceptions ont 20 ans: âge de raison ou de refondation?. In Cabay, Delforge, Fossoul, Lambrecht, 20 ans de nouveau droit d'auteur, Anthémis 2015.

[6] Law modifying some provisions from the Code de droit économique, M.B. 2016, n° 2016011538, p. 91843.

[7] Article XI. 172, 6 1 para 2 and § 2 of the Code de droit économique.

In addition, the Berne Convention states: 'The protection of this Convention shall not apply to news of the day or to miscellaneous facts having the character of mere items of press information.'[8]

The enumeration is not exhaustive. Belgian copyright law protects only literary and artistic works that are originals. The expression literary and artistic work excludes technical inventions, purely technical operations, sports performances, ideas, principles, theories, styles, themes and methods.[9]

## 15.3 General Considerations Relating to Exceptions

### 15.3.1 Lawful Publication Condition

In Belgium, all the exceptions to the reproduction right and communication to the public rights are subject to a first condition: the lawful publication. It concerns the application of the moral right of disclosure of the author. It is up to the author to decide if his or her work is finished and may be revealed.[10]

### 15.3.2 Type of Exceptions

In Belgian law, a distinction between two types of exceptions can be made. First, some of the exceptions contained in the list provided by the Code de droit économique are strict exceptions, while others are legal licences.

For this first category, the legislator, making a balance between different imperatives, considered that the monopoly of the copyright owner could not have the effect of preventing uses considered as legitimate by the legislator. The second category provides for compensation in favour of the copyright owner. The right to financial compensation supersedes the exclusive rights conferred upon the copyright owner.[11]

### 15.3.3 Closed and Mandatory List

The Code de droit économique provides for a closed list of exceptions. Any other use outside the list requires the express authorisation from the owner.[12] The exceptions are subject to strict interpretation. However, the Court of Justice of the

[8] Article 2.8 Bern Convention.

[9] Article 9 (2) of the TRIPs Agreement; S. Dusollier and A. De Francquen, Manuels de droits intellectuels, Anthémis, 2015, p. 60 and p. 66.

[10] Doc 54 2122/001, p. 7.

[11] S. Dusollier and A. De Francquen, Manuels de droits intellectuels, Anthémis, 2015, p. 102.

[12] Consequently, Belgium do not have a "catch all" exception such as fair use.

European Union insists on the preservation of the effectiveness of the exceptions while remaining within the limits of the triple test.[13]

Furthermore, Belgian law has the particularity of expressly providing that all the exceptions are mandatory provisions. Consequently, there is no possibility of derogation by contract. The imperative nature of the exceptions is a major issue. Indeed, Directive 2001/29 encourages the use of contracts in the information society. The fear was therefore that copyright owners would abuse this possibility to prohibit, by contract, uses authorised by copyright. The Belgian legislator wished to avoid such practices.[14]

There is one restriction to this principle for computer programs. The Code de droit économique contains specific rules regarding the protection of computer programs. The Belgian law transposing Directive 2001/29 stipulates that exceptions for safeguarding, testing the program and decompiling are mandatory. On the other hand, the exception for normal use of computer programs is not imperative. According to Article XI. 299 § 1 CDE, the permanent or temporary reproduction of a computer program and the translation, adaptation, arrangement and any other alteration of a computer program shall not require an authorisation of the right holder where they are necessary for the use of the computer program by the lawful acquirer in accordance with its intended purpose, including for error correction. The same provision provides that this is only in the absence of specific contractual provisions.[15] Consequently, it is possible for the author to conclude a contract in which his or her authorisation is required for the accomplishment of acts necessary for the normal use of the computer program.

The Code de droit économique explicitly mentions that this list concerns exceptions to the economic rights of the author. As an example, some exceptions require a reference to the source and name of the author. This reflects the concern of the legislator to respect the paternity right of the author. The same is true in the precondition to the applicability of any exception to the lawful disclosure of the work.

The copyright owner retains the right to object to any modification of his or her work and to object to any distortion or modification of his/her work that would undermine his/her honour or reputation. While copyright permits the reproduction and/or communication of a work in some cases without having to obtain the authorisation of the right holder, the latter retains the right to claim his or her right to respect the integrity of his/her work. Directive 2001/29 calls for the maintenance of a fair balance of rights and interests between copyright owners and users.[16] In a

[13] S. Dusollier et M. Lambrecht, Les exceptions ont 20 ans: âge de raison ou de refondation?. In Cabay, Delforge, Fossoul, Lambrecht, 20 ans de nouveau droit d'auteur, Anthémis 2015, pp. 204–205.

[14] M.-C. Janssens, Les exceptions et restrictions au doit d'auteur en Belgique (Limitations and Exceptions to Copyright in Belgium) (1999). In The Boundaries of Copyright – Les Frontières du Droit d'Auteur, ALAI – Australian Copyright Council, 1999, p. 176. Available at SSRN: https://ssrn.com/abstract=2302525. Accessed 9 September 2017.

[15] S. Dusollier, Droit d'auteur et protection des œuvres dans l'univers numérique, Larcier 2005, p. 504.

[16] Recital 31; see CJEU, case C-467/08, *Padawan SL v Sociedad General de Autores y Editores de España (SGAE)*, ECR 2010 I 10055; CJEU, case C-201/13, *Deckmyn*, ECLI:EU:C:2014:2132. See

dispute concerning the parody exception, the European Court of Justice had the opportunity to point out that copyright owners have a legitimate interest in having their work not associated to racist or discriminatory messages,[17] despite the fact that all the conditions of the parody exception are satisfied in this case.

However, in order to avoid the undue invocation of the moral rights by the author to block the exception, there are some corrective mechanisms. This is of particular relevance as certain exceptions necessarily involve changes in the work, affecting the right to respect for the work of the author.

These mechanisms are the abuse of rights and the balance between various legitimate interests involved.[18]

For example, in a decision of 29 May 2008 of the Court of Appeal of Brussels, the exercise of the moral right of disclosure by the author (allowing him/her to decide sovereignly when his/her work is completed and can be known to the public) was found to be abusive. The Court of Appeal noted that the exercise of moral rights was, in this case, merely a means of negotiation with a view to obtaining more favourable contractual conditions.[19]

## 15.4 Triple Test

Directive 2001/29 reaffirms the triple test included in the Berne Convention for the Protection of Literary and Artistic Works of 1886. According to Article 5 (5), 'The exceptions and limitations provided for in paragraphs 1, 2, 3 and 4 shall only be applied in certain special cases which do not conflict with a normal exploitation of the work or other subject-matter and do not unreasonably prejudice the legitimate interests of the rightholder'.

The Belgian legislator did not take the opportunity of a transposition law to implement the triple test in the set of copyright rules contained in the Law of 30 June 1994. The reason provided was that the triple test is a well-known disposition. The triple test is so notorious that it is part of the domestic legal order.[20]

Furthermore, during the discussion, one of the ministers refused to insert the triple test because it could be an open door to legal uncertainty with the belief that exceptions could be incompatible with disposition 5 § 5 of the Directive.[21]

If the triple test is mainly a tool for the legislator in order to decide to implement one of more exceptions from the list established by Directive 2001/29 regarding the national situation, the explanatory memorandum shed light on the relationship

also B. Michaux, L'impression 3D: un défi supplémentaire pour le droit d'auteur. In B Michaux, L'impression 3D: défis et opportunités pour la propriété intellectuelle, Larcier, pp. 104–105.

[17] CJEU, case C-201/13, *Deckmyn*, ECLI:EU:C:2014:2132, pt 31.

[18] M.-Chr. Janssens, Le droit moral en Belgique, Les cahiers de propriété intellectuelle 2013 (25), p. 106–107.

[19] Brussels, 29 May 2008, *A&M*, 2009.

[20] Exposé des motifs, Doc. Parl., Ch. Rep., sess. 2003–2004, n° 51-1137/1, comments on Art. 4.

[21] DOC 51 1137/013, p. 15.

between the triple test and the judge. It provides that courts and tribunals can use the triple test as a guideline.[22]

Nevertheless, it is controversial if the judge, using the triple test as a guideline, has to appreciate the exception raised by one of the parties, in *abstracto* or in *concreto*. If we are in favour of an *in concreto* approach, the judge shall decide if an exception established by Belgian law respects effectively the conditions of the triple test in the specific situation referred to him or her.[23]

The *in abstracto* approach affords the judge to use the triple test to determine if the exception could apply in certain cases. It would be particularly useful in the context of new technologies in which an exception could be in conflict with the normal exploitation of the work or causes an unreasonable prejudice to the legitimate interest of the right holder.[24]

It appears that the possibility for the judge of an appreciation *in concreto* receives a favourable opinion of the majority of the doctrine. We may found a beginning of solution in the Explanatory Memorandum of the Proposal: 'The triple test will serve as an important guideline for the definition *and application* of limitations'.[25]

## 15.5 Exceptions

The Belgian legislator implemented into national law 18 exceptions from the list established by the Directive. Classically, exceptions are divided into two categories. First, there are exceptions that are concerned with balancing fundamental freedoms such as the right to information, freedom of the press and respect for privacy. Second, certain exceptions take into account the general interest.[26]

### 15.5.1 Exception for Temporary Acts of Reproduction

This is the only exception made compulsory for all Member States, provided in Article 5.1 of Directive 2001/29.

[22] Exposé des motifs, Doc. Parl., Ch. Rep., sess. 2003–2004, n° 51-1137/1, comments on art. 4, p. 15; F. Brison et B. Michaux, La nouvelle loi du 22 mai 2005 adapte le droit d'auteur au numérique, A&M 2005, p. 216.

[23] S. Dusollier, Droit d'auteur et protection des œuvres dans l'univers numérique, Larcier 2005, pp. 438–439.

[24] S. Dusollier, L'encadrement des exceptions au droit d'auteur par le test des trois étapes, IRDI 2005, p. 216.

[25] We underline. On this topic, see L. Guibault, Pre-emption issues in the digital environment: can copyright limitations be overriden by contractual agreements under European law? https://pdfs.semanticscholar.org/0a58/e9793a91061ea49607519732a10cfaefda51.pdf?_ga=2.104309568.1980474753.1495201101-1174523319.1495195011. Accessed 16 May 2017.

[26] S. Dusollier, Les exceptions au droit d'auteur dans l'environnement numérique: évolutions dangereuses, Communication commerce électronique 2001(9).

According to Article XI. 189 § 3: 'the author may not prohibit temporary acts of reproduction which are transitory or accessory and constitute an integral and essential part of a technical process and whose sole purpose is to enable transmission in a network between third parties by an intermediary or a lawful use of a protected work, and which have no independent economic significance'.

A particular illustration of this exception is the Belgian case of *Google c. Copiepresse.*

In 2003, the American company Google set up Google News. This service offers a selection of information from press articles. The mechanism is as follows: Google exploits the web servers of news organisations, copies and/or automatically summarises them in order to establish an information portal. This portal contains articles of the day or articles that correspond to the user's request in the search bar of the Google News service.

Google News only provides a few lines and the title of the article but then refers to the agency's own website through hyperlinks.

One important point is that the mechanism set up by Google also allows access to press articles that are no longer online on the agency's own website.[27] All those actions are done without any prior authorisation from the copyright holders.[28]

The collecting society, Copiepresse, intended to put an end to these acts.

In 2006, the President of the Tribunal of First Instance in Brussels did not retain any copyright exception and condemned Google.[29] The latter appealed against the decision by invoking, among other things, the exception of a provisional copy.

In 2011, the Court of Appeal of Brussels confirmed the infringement of copyright law.[30] Preliminarily, the judge noted that the Belgian law was applicable in this case.[31]

The judge considered the fact that Google takes portions of press articles from other sources, it constitutes an act of reproduction and communication to the public. The next step was to consider whether an exception to copyright applied in the present case. According to Google, the exception of temporary acts of reproduction applied. This argument did not convince the judge. He noted that Google was unable to demonstrate the technical necessity to ensure an effective transmission of the copy made by the company. Consequently, the third condition according to which reproduction must constitute an integral and essential part of a technological process was not met.[32]

---

[27] The functionality of the cache allows the link to be stored in a cache memory, which makes it possible to consult this copy at any time. You can see the appearance of an archive.

[28] Google's position to consider that nothing infringes copyright until the copyright holders are opposed cannot be followed. Copyright is conceived on the granting of a prior authorisation of the holders; Bruxelles (9e ch.), 5 mai 2011, *R.D.T.I.*, 44/2011, § 49.

[29] Pres. civ. Brussels, 13 February 2007, *A&M*, 2007/1–2, pp. 107 and seq.

[30] Brussels (9e ch.), 5 May 2011, *R.D.T.I.*, 44/2011.

[31] The judge based his decision on Article 5 (3) (a) of the Bern Convention and et Regulation 864/2007 of the European Parliament and of the Council of 11 July 2007 on the law applicable to non-contractual obligations (Rome II).

[32] Brussels (9e ch.), 5 May 2011, *R.D.T.I.*, 44/2011, § 25.

In addition, the judge noted that the copy was not transitory or accessory in the present case.[33] The cached copy was not limited to what is technically necessary to ensure the proper functioning of the service because, in reality, the copy remained as long as the press article itself was accessible on the original site, and beyond.[34]

### 15.5.2 Social Institutions

The Belgian law authorises the reproduction of TV programmes for hospitals, prisons and youth care establishments or assistance for persons with disabilities. The exception requires the fulfilment of two cumulative conditions. These institutions may not pursue profit-making purposes, and the reproduction must be reserved for the exclusive use of the natural persons residing there.[35] The communication of the works is unauthorised.

There is no provision for fair compensation for authors.

### 15.5.3 People with Disabilities

This exception appeared in Belgian law in the context of implementation of Directive 2001/29.[36] The legislator authorises the reproduction and communication to the public of works for the benefit of persons with disabilities. The exception is highly circumscribed and subject to several cumulative conditions. Firstly, the reproduction and communication of these works cannot be of a commercial nature. Secondly, such acts must also be limited to the extent required by the disability. Finally, the legislator ensures that concepts of the triple test are included. The acts of reproduction and communication cannot prejudice the normal exploitation of the work or cause undue prejudice to the legitimate interests of the author.[37]

### 15.5.4 Libraries, Museums and Archives

Belgian law permits the limited reproduction of works, in order to preserve cultural and scientific heritage, by libraries accessible to the public, museums or archives. Again, the exception requires four cumulative conditions.

---

[33] Brussels (9e ch.), 5 May 2011, *R.D.T.I.*, 44/2011, § 26.

[34] Google has also advanced the exception of fair use (which does not exist in Belgian law and in Directive 2001/29), as well as exceptions for quotation and reporting of current events. Google also considered that, in fact, it did not commit any act of communication to the public. The Court of Appeal dismissed all of his arguments.

[35] Article XI. 190, 17° CDE.

[36] Article 5.3 b) Directive 2001/29.

[37] Article XI. 190, 15° CDE.

Firstly, the number of authorised copies is limited to the purpose of heritage preservation. This excludes the reproduction of all works held by libraries, museums or archives. Secondly, such acts of reproduction shall not pursue any direct or indirect commercial advantage. Thirdly, reproduction shall not interfere with the normal exploitation of the work and, finally, may not cause unreasonable prejudice to the legitimate interests of the authors.[38]

This exception is included in the list established by Directive 2001/29.[39] However, the Belgian transposition is not identical to the provision contained in the Directive. Indeed, the scope of the exception does not extend to educational institutions. The Belgian legislator considered that the exceptions for illustrating education were sufficient to allow the exploitation of the work necessary for the activity of these establishments.[40]

A second exception concerns acts of communication. Libraries, educational establishments and scientists, museums and archives may allow the visitors to consult online works of their collection not offered for sale or subject to the respect of licences. The exception pursues a specific objective: for the purpose of research or private study. The consultation may only occur through dedicated terminals in the premises of establishments.[41]

### 15.5.5 Education and Research Purposes

The Belgian legislator is sensitive to permit, in different cases, the utilisation of a protected work in order to spread the culture in educational establishments and during school activities.

The use of works in the framework of teaching or scientific research entails the payment of compensation. The legislator instructs the King to fix this remuneration, taking into account the objectives of promoting educational activities.[42]

Four exceptions permit the reproduction of works. This is the exception of quotation, anthology, reprography and copy. Two exceptions allow the communication of works. This is the exception of execution in the context of school activities and e-learning.

#### 15.5.5.1 Exception of Quotation

Belgian law does not require authorisation from the author for quotations for teaching purposes or scientific research. Quotations shall, however, be made in

[38] Article XI. 190, 12° CDE.

[39] See Article 5.2, c) Directive 2001/29.

[40] S. Dussolier, Queen mary intellectual property research institute, p. 124. http://ec.europa.eu/internal_market/copyright/docs/studies/infosoc-study-annex_en.pdf.

[41] Article XI. 190, 13° CDE.

[42] It is regrettable that the legislator does not provide a more precise explanation of "the objectives of promoting educational activities".

accordance with honest practices and to the extent justified by the objective.[43] In the context of education, contrary to the general exception, the quotation shall be made in accordance with honest practices, and the legislator does not refer to the honest practices according to the profession. The exception of quotation for education or scientific purposes may occur outside a professional context.[44]

#### 15.5.5.2 Confection of an Anthology

An anthology is a collection of selected pieces of works. The making of an anthology involves acts of reproduction. However, the making of an anthology for teaching purposes will not imply the need to obtain authorisation from the copyright holders upon the death of the author.[45]

Conversely, during the life of the author, obtaining his or her prior agreement is obligatory.

In order to benefit from the exception, the users may not pursue direct or indirect commercial or economic advantage. In addition, the choice of the extract reproduced in the anthology, the presentation and the place of it must respect the moral rights of the author. The legislator imposes the payment of an equitable remuneration.[46]

#### 15.5.5.3 Exception of Reproduction

Belgian law does not allow the author of a literary or artistic work to oppose the reproduction made for the purpose of illustration of teaching or scientific research. Reproduction shall not be for profit, and the use shall not prejudice the normal exploitation of the work.[47]

The wording of the Belgian provision, like the European provision, contains an ambiguity. Indeed, it is not clear whether the condition of illustration, which must accompany the reproduction, is valid only for teaching or also for scientific research. In the first case, the exception applies only to acts of reproduction carried out for purposes of illustration of teaching and not for the purpose of illustration of scientific research.[48] The debate seems to be clarified with the explanatory memorandum

---

[43] Article XI. 191/1, 1° CDE.

[44] Doc 54 2122/001, p. 11.

[45] The copyright protection extends to the copyright holders for 70 years beyond the death of the author.

[46] Article XI. 191/1, 5° CDE.

[47] Article XI. 191/1, 3° CDE.

[48] Before the entry into force of the Law of 22 December 2016 amending the Code of Economic Law, the reproduction exception for purposes of illustration of teaching and scientific research was somewhat different: The fragmentary or integral reproduction of articles, works of plastic or graphic art, or that of short fragments of other works where such reproduction is effected on paper or on a similar medium by means of any photographic technique or any other method which produces a similar result, for the purpose of illustration of teaching or scientific research, to the extent justified by the non-profit-making aim pursued and which does not prejudice the normal exploitation of the work, provided that, unless this is not possible, the source, including the name of the author, is indicated. (Article XI. 190, 6° CDE).

of the Law of 22 December 2016. The exception concerns the illustration of teaching and illustration of scientific research.[49]

Therefore, copyright holders may not oppose such acts of reproduction but are entitled to obtain a fair compensation.

The user shall respect three conditions: first, the purpose of illustration[50] of teaching. This first condition introduces a first limitation to the use of the works by the professors. One can see there the concern to respect the exceptional nature of these provisions and to avoid that the use of literary and artistic works is the rule in education.

The reproduced work must be a useful and relevant support for the students. In other words, the reproduced work must serve as an accompaniment to teaching.[51]

Second, the reproduction shall be made to the extent justified by the non-profit-making purpose pursued.

The preparatory work for the law provides an important clarification. The activity must be non-profit. The organisational structure and the means of financing of the institution are not decisive factors.[52]

The non-profit does not necessarily mean that no price may be required. Indeed, a price may be imposed in order to cover the costs eventually generated provided it does not result in the realisation of a profit.

Third, the reproduction shall not prejudice the normal exploitation of the work.

For example, the reproduction of textbooks could impair the normal exploitation of the work more rapidly because the primary public is composed of teachers and students.[53]

The reproduction covers also the distribution. For example, it is possible for a teacher to distribute copies to the students. If the institution charges a fee for the copies, it might not be a way to receive profits.[54]

#### 15.5.5.4 School Activities

The authors may not object to the cost-free execution in the course of school activities, which may take place both within and outside the educational institution.[55]

This exception is not included in the list of exceptions set out in Directive 2001/29. However, it may be justified by the application of Article 5 (3) of the Directive. It allows national legislators to permit uses of minor importance where exceptions or limitations already exist under national law, if they only concern

[49] Article 34 of Explanatory Memorandum.

[50] This term refers to the Bern Convention (Article 10, § 2) and the Directive 2001/29/EC (Article 5, §3 a).

[51] Ph. Laurent, Les nouvelles exceptions au droit d'auteur en faveur de l'enseignement: l'ère de l'e-learning, A&M 2008(3), p. 184.

[52] Doc. parl., Chambre, sess 2003–2004, n° 1137/001, p. 11.

[53] Ph. Laurent, Les nouvelles exceptions au droit d'auteur en faveur de l'enseignement: l'ère de l'e-learning, A&M 2008(3), pp. 182–186.

[54] Doc 54 2122/001, p. 12.

[55] Article XI. 191/1, 2° CDE.

analogue uses and do not affect the free circulation of goods and services within the Community, without prejudice to the other exceptions and limitations contained in this provision.[56]

Two notions are important to understand properly the scope of the exception: the terms 'execution' and 'school activities'.

First, it seems that, by using the term 'execution', the legislator sought to depart from the notion of communication to the public. In Directive 2001/29, the communication to the public must be understood as 'all communication to the public not present at the place where the communication originates. This right should cover any such transmission or retransmission of a work to the public by wire or wireless means. This right should not cover any other acts.'[57]

Therefore, the Directive only deals with communication to an audience not present at the place of origin of the communication.[58] By opposition, the term execution would then refer to a communication to the public present at the place of origin of the communication.[59]

In order to ensure proportionality in the scope of the exception, the legislator wished to limit it to a sharing specified by a physical place and a time period.[60,61]

For example, the exception authorises the projection of works, live or recorded, as well as the presentation of PowerPoint,[62] the projection of a film or the broadcasting of music during the break.[63]

#### 15.5.5.5 E-Learning

The Belgian legislator has put in place an exception in order to promote distance learning.[64]

---

[56] Ph. Laurent, Les nouvelles exceptions au droit d'auteur en faveur de l'enseignement: l'ère de l'e-learning, A&M 2008(3), p. 188; F. Brison and B. Michaux, La nouvelle loi du 22 mai 2005 adapte le droit d'auteur au numérique, A&M 2005(3), p. 125.

[57] Article 3 Directive 2001/29.

[58] Recital 23.

[59] B. Michaux, Etendue des droits: jurisprudence choisie de la Cour de cassation, A&M 2004(5), p. 475.

[60] Ph. Laurent, Les nouvelles exceptions au droit d'auteur en faveur de l'enseignement: l'ère de l'e-learning, A&M 2008(3), pp. 187–188.

[61] However, some authors are of the contrary opinion. According to them, the term execution is a synonym for communication: H. Vanhees, Het 'publieke' karakter van een mededeling opnieuw het voorwerp van rechtspraak van het Hof van Cassatie, A&M 2006(2), p. 184. However, we disagree with regard to the definition of communication to the public at European level. Terms "in such a way that members of the public may access them from a place and at a time individually chosen by them", seem to be in contradiction with the requirement of a local communication.

[62] Ph. Laurent, Les nouvelles exceptions au droit d'auteur en faveur de l'enseignement: l'ère de l'e-learning, A&M 2008(3), p. 187.

[63] S. Dusollier, Queen Mary Intellectual Property Research Institute, p. 125. http://ec.europa.eu/internal_market/copyright/docs/studies/infosoc-study-annex_en.pdf.

[64] Article XI. 191/1, 4° CDE.

The exercise of the exception requires the respect of several conditions. First, the exception for the communication benefits the institutions recognised or officially organised by the public authorities. Second, communication can only take place through a secure communication with appropriate measures. Before the modification by Law of 22/12/2016, the legislator imposed that the communication takes place through a closed transmission network.[65]

Third, the communication must be within the normal activities of the institution.

Then the classical conditions for teaching exceptions are also required for distance learning. The communication of works can be done only for the purpose of illustration of the teaching, without seeking a profit and without undermining the normal exploitation of the work.[66] Finally, the source and name of the author must be indicated unless this is impossible.[67]

If the exception applies only to establishments recognised by the Belgian authorities, this would pose certain difficulties with regard to the free movement of services and the single European market. Indeed, it is uncertain if institutions established in Belgium but subsidised or recognised by other states could benefit from the exception. The same interrogation applies to the training offered to Belgian students and researchers from other countries.[68]

#### 15.5.5.6 Public Examination

Belgian law makes it possible to void the prior authorisation of the author for the execution of works in the framework of a public examination. This execution can take place inside the educational institution or outside.[69]

### 15.5.6 Current Events

This exception intends to achieve a balance between the exclusive right of copyright owners and freedom of expression and freedom of the press.

Aware of the needs and interests of the press to react and comment quickly on news, the legislator grants them a specific exception. Hence, journalists do not have to await the reception of the authorisation from the copyright owner. Belgian law authorises the reproduction and communication to the public of short fragments of

---

[65] For example: a network with which the teacher and students must have a password in order to benefit from the teaching; Doc. parl., Chambre, sess. 2°°3-2004, n° 1137/013, p. 34.

[66] The companies organising training for online teaching or any other institution other than pure educational or research establishment cannot benefit from this exception. On this topic, S. Dussolier, Queen mary intellectual property reseach institute, p. 127. http://ec.europa.eu/internal_market/copyright/docs/studies/infosoc-study-annex_en.pdf.

[67] Article XI. 191/1, 4° CDE.

[68] Ph. Laurent, Les nouvelles exceptions au droit d'auteur en faveur de l'enseignement: l'ère de l'e-learning, A&M 2008(3), pp. 190–191.

[69] Article XI. 191/1, 2° CDE.

works or plastic or graphic work for the purposes of news reporting. The reproduction and the communication have to be justified by the information purpose. However, the exception does not exempt from mentioning the source, including the author's name, unless it turns out to be impossible.[70]

The legislator makes a distinction between two types of works. Works of plastic or graphic art can be reproduced in their entirety, unlike all other works. Moreover, no compensation is due to the copyright owner.

In the case *Google v. Copiepresse* mentioned previously, Google tried to justify its service Google News on this exception. The Brussels Court of Appeal rejected this argument. The Court observes that the reason to the exception is that the information media may not require authorisation from the copyright owner because of the need for prompt information. The judge also recalled the principle of strict interpretation concerning exceptions.

According to the judge, Google may not invoke the impossibility to obtain authorisation from the holder because the company referenced the articles during 30 days. Indeed, it would be enough for the American company to conclude general contracts authorising the reproduction of fragments of articles in Google News.[71]

### 15.5.7 Quotation

Belgian law allows quotations made for the purpose of criticism, controversy or review without the need to obtain the prior permission of the copyright owner.[72] However, this exception requires several conditions. Firstly, the person must pursue one of the purposes enumerated. Secondly, the quotation must be in accordance with the honest practices of the profession and to the extent justified by the aim pursued. Finally, the source and name of the author must be mentioned unless this is impossible.[73]

Again, in the case of *Google c. Copiepresse*, the judge rejected the application of this exception. Google's 'quotes' do not pursue a goal of criticism, controversy or review. The articles arranged by Google in an automated way are not there as a quote in order to support a statement or defend an opinion. Google News is only an information portal. In addition, the citation must be in accordance with the honest practices of the profession. The judge was sensitive to the need for advertising revenue for journalists and news organisations. Google News takes the main part of the information contained in the various articles and saves for Internet users to have to go on the web page of the article.[74]

[70] Article XI. 190, 1° CDE.

[71] Pt 37.

[72] In another legal provision, the legislator also authorizes quotation for teaching and scientific research purposes.

[73] Article XI. 189, §1 CDE.

[74] Pts 31–35 of the decision.

### 15.5.8 Parody

According to Article XI. 190, 10° CDE, the author may not prohibit caricature, parody or pastiche, taking into account honest practices. The terms are general, and it is not easy to determine the scope of this exception. For this reason, the Brussels Court of Appeal, hearing a case concerning the racist parody of a work, referred a question to the Court of Justice of the European Union.

In the *Deckmyn* decision,[75] the Court of Luxemburg gave a definition to the notion of parody. The Court considers parody as an autonomous concept of European Union law. Thus, it requires a uniform interpretation within the various Member States. The Court also observes that, in the absence of a legal definition, reference should be made to common sense, taking into account the context in which it is used and the objectives pursued by the rules.[76] As consequence, the definition of parody is as follows: 'the essential characteristics of parody, are, first, to evoke an existing work, while being noticeably different from it, and secondly, to constitute an expression of humour or mockery'.[77]

The Court of Justice rejects the other conditions set out in the Belgian case law, namely that the parody should have an original character on its own, other than that of showing noticeable differences with respect to the original parodied work; could reasonably be attributed to a person other than the author of the original work itself; should relate to the original work itself or mention the source of the parodied work.[78] At present, only the two conditions are applicable to the exception of parody: the evocation of an existing work and the noticeable difference between the parody and the original work.

### 15.5.9 Privacy Purpose

#### 15.5.9.1 Exception to Copyright Law

Belgian law[79] enables reproduction and execution in the family circle and reserved for it. However, the legislator excludes partitions from the scope of the exception.[80]

The notion of family circle is understood as a limited number of persons united by an intimate social relationship.[81] Consequently, it goes beyond the strict family

---

[75] CJEU, case C-201/13, *Deckmyn,* ECLI:EU:C:2014:2132.

[76] Pt 19.

[77] Pt 20.

[78] Pt 21.

[79] Article XI. 190, 3° and 5° of the Code de droit économique.

[80] Prior to the entry into force of the Law of 22 December 2016, there was a distinction between works reproduced on paper or on a similar medium (known as the reprographic exception) and reproduction on any other medium than paper (private copying exception).

[81] During the discussion concerning the law of 22 December 2016 that amends the Code de droit économique, the Belgian legislator decided to maintain the use of "family circle" instead of the

context. For example, friends at a free-cost party reserved only to a small group fall within the notion of family circle.[82,83]

The Law of 22 December 2016 amends the Code de droit économique by amending the previous reprographic exception. Copyright shall not preclude the fragmentary or integral reproduction of articles, works of plastic or graphic art or that of short fragments of works fixed on paper or on any other similar medium where such reproduction is made on paper or on a similar medium. This exception applies to legal or natural persons for internal use in the course of their professional activities. Reproduction shall not prejudice the normal exploitation of the work.[84] This exception covers acts of reproduction and not communication to the public.

#### 15.5.9.2 The Compensation

**Before the Hewlett-Packard Belgium SPRL v Reprobel Decision**

In order to minimise the financial prejudice for copyright owners, European Directive 2001/29 requires Member States to provide for a system of compensation in favour of right holders. We might see the influence of the triple test that prohibits exceptions from undue prejudice to copyright holders. Equitable compensation is an autonomous concept of EU law and receives the same interpretation throughout the European Union.[85] On the other hand, the form, methods of financing and level of compensation are at the discretion of the Member States.[86,87]

Equitable compensation in Belgium has been subject to a number of decisions handed down by the national courts. We will explain some of them below.

The system set up to ensure fair compensation to authors and publishers in Belgium was as follows. It was a dual compensation system. Manufacturers, importers or intra-community acquirers[88] of devices enabling the copy of the protected work paid a fixed remuneration.

---

European Union concept. The European definition is reproductions on paper or any similar medium, effected by the use of any kind of photographic technique or by some other process having similar effects (Article 5.2 b). The two main reasons were that the change could lead to a legal insecurity and that the concept of family circle has to be interpreted in accordance with the Directive. Doc 54 2122/001, p. 10.

82 Cass., 26 January 2006, C.05.0219.N.

83 Cass. (1 Ch.), 18 February 2000, *R.W.*, 2000, p. 908; Cass. (1 Ch.), 21 November 2003, *A&M*, 2004, p. 35; Cass. (1 Ch.), 26 January 2006, *NjW*, 2006, p. 168; S. Dusollier and A. De Francquen, Manuels de droits intellectuels, Anthémis, 2015, p. 105.

84 New Article XI. 190, 5° CDE.

85 CJEU, case C-467/08, *Padawan,* ECR 2010 I 10055 and CJEU, case C-435/12, *ACI ADAM,* ECLI:EU:C:2014:254.

86 CJEU, case C-467/08, *Padawan*, ECLI:EU:C:2010:620, pt 37.

87 A. Cruquenaire, F. Delnooz, S. Hallemans, C. Ker and B. Michaux, Chronique de jurisprudence, RDTI 2015, p. 52.

88 The High Court of Belgium, Cour de Cassation, set aside a judgment from the Court of Appeal of Brussels. The Court of Appel decided that an occasional seller on DVD on eBay is not an intra-community acquire. Consequently, the Cour de Cassation has a broad interpretation of this notion

In addition, proportional remuneration was due by natural or legal persons that make copies of works. The legislator authorised, however, that the natural or legal persons that held a reproduction device at the disposal of others pay the sums. This proportional remuneration was determined according to the number of copies made. The legislator divided the remuneration equally between publishers and authors.[89]

In dealing with several cases, the Belgian courts and tribunals detailed the system.

On 18 April 2013, the Tribunal of First Instance of Liège had to settle a dispute between Auvibel and Amazon. Amazon complained that the Belgian system did not mention an explicit exemption for devices used exclusively for professional purpose. The judge, however, did not follow Amazon, pointing out that the Member States had a margin of appreciation.[90] The Court does not object to a system of financing that does not make any distinction between appliances put into circulation on a commercial or private basis. However, the system had to put in place a payback mechanism. The Court even allows Member States to establish a rebuttable presumption for private use.[91]

For the calculation of the compensation, Belgian law does not take into consideration any licence granted by the right holder. The Tribunal of First Instance of Brussels[92] did not find this incompatible with European law. The judge decided that, even if the author distributes his or her work under a free licence, he or she is entitled to receive fair compensation. Indeed, this distribution does not prevent the existence of an exception, in this case private copying. Consequently, users remain entitled to perform such acts, thereby prejudicing the interests of right holders. Fair compensation remains due, and the existence of a licence may not be taken into account when calculating the compensation.[93]

More fundamentally, a case between the Belgian collective management company Reprobel and Hewlett-Packard had a major impact in Belgium. An important decision from the Court of Justice invalidated several aspects of the Belgian system.

At stake was the proportion of the amount received as fair compensation that the author could pay to his or her publisher. Hewlett-Packard refused to pay the amounts due for reprography to the publisher. According to the company, only the author is the beneficiary of the fair compensation. The Tribunal of First Instance of Brussels[94]

and omit the fact that the Court of Justice limited the perception of a remuneration to merchants; A. Cruquenaire, F. Delnooz, S. Hallemans, C. Ker and B. Michaux, Chronique de jurisprudence, RDTI 2015, p. 56.

[89] See former Article XI. 235 ff CDE.

[90] Civ. Liège (7ème Ch.), 18 April 2013, *Auvibel c. Tecteo,* A&M, 2013/5, p. 387.

[91] See CJEU, case C-521/11, *Amazon c. Austro-Mechana,* ECLI:EU:C:2013:515, pts 24, 31–32; A. Cruquenaire, F. Delnooz, S. Hallemans, C. Ker et B. Michaux, Chronique de jurisprudence, RDTI 2015, p. 54.

[92] Civ. Bruxelles (réf.), 25 November 2013, *Auvibel c. Amazon.*

[93] CJEU, case C-457/11, *VG Wort*, ECLI:EU:C:2013:426, pt 37.

[94] Civ. Bruxelles, (16° ch.), 6 November 2012, J.L.M.B, 2013, p. 702.

upheld Hewlett-Packard's claim and decided that the national legal provision reserves half of the remuneration to publishers for works fixed on a graphic or similar support. On appeal, the Brussels Court of Appeal of Brussels decided to ask preliminary questions to the Court of Justice of the European Union.[95]

The Court of Justice delivered its judgment on 12 November 2015 and invalidated several aspects of the Belgian legislation.[96]

#### The Case Hewlett-Packard Belgium SPRL v Reprobel

The Court of Justice of the European Union begins by recalling a general rule. The level of prejudice for the authors is the core element for the determination of a fair compensation.[97]

Article 2 of the Directive does not identify publishers as the reproduction right holders. For this reason, they may not receive fair compensation under the exceptions of reprography and private copying. The Court based its decision on the factual circumstances of the case. In the situation, the compensation dedicated to publishers resulted in depriving right holders of reproduction rights of all or part of the fair compensation to which they are entitled. Moreover, there was no obligation for the publishers to ensure a direct or indirect benefit to the authors.[98]

Next, the Court rejects a compensation system that does not differentiate reproductions made from licit sources from those produced from illicit sources. Indeed, the Court excludes reproductions made from illicit sources from the scope of the exception. There is therefore no right to compensation for this second category.[99]

Finally, one of the questions asked was to determine the validity of a system combining two forms of remuneration. The first is a lump-sum payment upstream, calculated according to the maximum speed at which an apparatus performs reproductions. Next comes a proportional remuneration downstream varying according to the cooperation or not of the debtor of the compensation.

The Court of Justice, which is sensitive to the freedom left to Member States in determining the methods of financing and the collection of compensation, does not preclude a system of compensation upstream and downstream.[100] However, this system requires the respect of certain rules, with which Belgium does not comply. The Court specifies that upstream remuneration may be introduced only where it is not practicable to identify the users and therefore to assess the actual harm suffered by the holders of law. Upstream remuneration is therefore only an alternative. The

---

[95] Bruxelles (9° ch.), 23 October 2013, JLMB, 2014/10, p. 475.

[96] CJEU, case C-572/13, *Hewlett-Packard Belgium SPRL v Reprobel*, ECLI:EU:C:2015:750.

[97] The Court refers to recitals 35 and 38 of the Directive 2001/29.

[98] Pt 44.

[99] Pt 64.

[100] While it is in principle the persons who made the copies who are required to compensate the actual damage suffered by the right holders, the Court of Justice did not object to the fact that the costs for fair compensation are provided by persons with reproductive devices and supports. These can then pass on the cost of the user fee. The Court adopts this position with a view to efficiency and effectiveness.

Court condemns the upstream remuneration based on the reproduction speed of the apparatus. The reason is that the lump-sum right pays consideration to differences between users. Indeed, not all have the same needs, and not all exploit the devices to the same extent. The criterion employed, namely the maximum speed of the apparatus for producing the reproductions, does not take into account such a situation.[101]

Moreover, the Court condemns Belgium when it makes a distinction between the cooperation or not of the debtor, when determining the proportionate remuneration downstream. The Court points out that this does not change the level of the damage suffered and that, since the compensation was introduced with the precise objective of mitigating that damage, such a criterion is not valid.[102]

Finally, the law has to provide a mechanism of restitution in order to avoid and correct any situation of overcompensation.[103]

The Law of 22 December 2016 amended certain provisions of the Code of Economic Law in order to comply with the judgment of the Court of Justice. The Belgian legislator has decided to maintain the flat-rate remuneration for all private reproductions carried out in the family circle, whatever the medium is. This compensation shall be paid by the intra-community acquirer, manufacturer or importer of devices clearly used for reproduction.

Concerning the exception of reprography, the legislator retains only the proportional remuneration based on the number of reproductions actually made.

The Belgian legislator also points out that the Court of Justice condemns the payment of remuneration to publishers when the latter is deducted from the amount of the compensation due to the authors. According to the legislator, the Court does not condemn all types of remuneration for publishers. This right to remuneration shall be payable only for reproductions of works in paper or similar form to a paper or similar medium.[104] This compensation is in addition to the remuneration of the authors for the same acts of reproduction, without affecting it. This right in favour of publishers does not apply to digital reproductions.[105]

### 15.5.10 Panorama Exception

Belgian law has an exception for the reproduction and communication to the public of the work exhibited in a place accessible to the public, where the purpose of the reproduction or communication to the public is not the work itself.[106]

---

[101] Pts 65–88.

[102] Pt 79.

[103] Pt 85.

[104] Consequently, the remuneration to publishers does not apply for the exception of private copy. The Belgian legislator feared that it could be an infringement to the free movement of goods. See Doc 54 2122/001, p. 16.

[105] Articles XI. 229 CDE and following and Doc 54 2122/001, p. 4.

[106] Article XI. 190, 2° CDE.

## 15.6 Special Issues

### 15.6.1 Data Mining

Text and data mining is a mechanism for machines to read and analyse large quantities of digital content (texts or images). The aim is to analyse them in order to extract information. The usefulness of these tools is to allow analysing large amounts of data and in record time, thus exceeding human capacities.

In the field of copyright, this practice necessarily involves acts of reproduction of protected works because during their exploration, the computer tools make copies in order to be able to analyse the protected works adequately.

At present, there are no specific provisions in Belgian law concerning text and data mining. Therefore, it is necessary to consider what space of freedom the currently prevailing exceptions leave to the practices of text and data mining.

First is the exception for temporary acts of reproduction. As already discussed, Belgian law, following Directive 2001/29, allows temporary acts of reproduction that are transitory or accessory and constitute an integral and essential part of a technical process and whose sole purpose is to enable transmission in a network between third parties by an intermediary or a lawful use of a protected work and that have no independent economic significance. If nothing precludes the applicability of this exception to text and data mining, the need for vigilance remains. Indeed, in certain circumstances, the applicability of this exception seems uncertain. Depending on the technique used, the copies may be permanent.

Furthermore, it is not certain that the copy is free of any independent economic significance. Indeed, the copies made are inherent in the discovery of a new knowledge that could be exploited economically.

If the copy made during the exploration is a complete copy of the work in question, the exception of quotation could not be invoked either. The exception of illustration for scientific research is also inadequate. Indeed, text and data mining requires acts of reproduction to accomplish a research and not for its illustration.[107]

The European Union has put in place a directive on the intellectual protection of databases.[108,109] Databases may receive two protections through copyright and *sui generis* rights.

First, copyright protects databases, which, due to the selection or arrangement of their contents, constitute the author's own intellectual creation.

In addition, there is protection for databases, which have required a substantial investment in obtaining, verifying and/or presenting the data. Protection shall apply only to databases of which the producer is a national of a Member State of the

[107] C. Bernaut, Le cas particulier du text and data mining. In: C. Bernault (ed), Open access et droit d'auteur, Larcier 2016, pp. 180–186.

[108] Directive 96/9 of the European Parliament and of the Council of 11 March 1996 on the legal protection of databases, JO 1996 L 77, p. 20.

[109] Loi du 31 août 1998 transposant la directive 96/9 du 11 mars 1996 sur la protection juridique des bases de données, *M.B*, 14 November 1998, p. 36913.

European Union or has his or her habitual residence in the territory of the European Union.

Protection by the *sui generis* right allows the right holder[110] to oppose the extraction and/or reuse of quantitatively or qualitatively substantial parts of the database. It also makes it possible to oppose acts of extraction and reuse of non-substantial but repeated and systematic parts.

Text and data mining by copying and analysing the data contained in different databases could be considered as an unlawful extraction.[111]

The European Union is committed to amending Directive 2001/29. On this occasion, there is a clear desire to allow text and data mining. Indeed, in its proposal for revision, the European Commission intends to introduce a new mandatory exception for all Member States. This would allow public interest research organisations to apply text and data mining techniques to content that is legally available to them for scientific research purposes.[112]

Nevertheless, we can ask ourselves if this is the best solution. Indeed, there are some technical acts of reproduction. However, what is the most relevant in text and data mining is the information contained in the database and not the work itself.[113]

### 15.6.2 Big Data

Belgian law does not provide for an exception for big data activities. The *sui generis* right granted to the person taking the initiatives and bearing the risk of the investments authorises the latter to oppose any extraction and reuse of substantial parts[114] from the database. The law also prohibits the extraction or reuse of non-substantial but repeated and systematic parts. Those prohibitions in case of protected databases may hamper big data activities.

---

[110] The producer of database, the person who supports the investment.

[111] C. Bernaut, Le cas particulier du text and data mining. In: C. Bernault (ed), Open access et droit d'auteur, Larcier 2016, p. 173.

[112] Communication from the Commission to the European Parliament, the Council, the European Economic and Social Commitee and the Committee of the Regions, "Towards a modern, more European copyright framework", COM(2015) 626 final.

[113] S. Dusollier et M. Lambrecht, Les exceptions ont 20 ans: âge de raison ou de refondation?. In Cabay, Delforge, Fossoul, Lambrecht, 20 ans de nouveau droit d'auteur, Anthémis 2015, p. 209.

[114] Database right prohibits the extraction and reuse of substantial part, evaluated quantitatively or qualitatively. The expression "substantial part, evaluated quantitatively" refers to the volume of data extracted from the database and/or re-utilized, and must be assessed in relation to the volume of the contents of the whole of that database.

The expression "substantial part, evaluated qualitatively" refers to the scale of the investment in the obtaining, verification or presentation of the contents of the subject of the act of extraction and/or re-utilisation. A quantitatively negligible part of the contents of a database may in fact represent, in terms of obtaining, verification or presentation, significant human, technical or financial investment; CJEU, case C-203/02, *The British Horseracing Board Ltd and Others v William Hill Organization Ltd*, ECLI:EU:C:2004:695, pts 70–71.

## 15.7 Technical Protection Measures

Technical protection measures allow copyright owners to put in place computer tools to prevent users from performing certain acts that infringe their rights.[115]

Article 11 of the WIPO Treaty, Article 6 of European Directive 2001/29 and Belgian law provide legal protection for these technical measures.[116] Both the acts of circumvention of these measures and the manufacture, import, distribution, sale, rental, advertisement for sale or rental, or possession for commercial purposes of devices, products or components or the provision of services in order to circumvent any effective technological measure are subject to criminal prosecution.

The WIPO Treaty defines the concept of technical protection measures by referring to any technique used by the copyright owner to prevent users from performing acts that he or she would not have authorised. The risk was then that the licensees would use this opportunity to prevent the performance of acts in principle subject to exceptions to the monopoly of the right holder.

This is the reason why Article 6.4 of Directive 2001/29 provides that, in the absence of voluntary measures taken by right holders, the Member States shall respond appropriately to ensure that right holders make available to the beneficiary of an exception or limitation provided for in national law the means of benefiting from that exception or limitation provided that the beneficiary has legal access to the protected work.

Belgian law has transposed this possibility.[117] However, at both European and national levels, there is an important exception for private copy. In other words, Member States must allow individuals with lawful access to the work to be able to perform acts authorised by national law, in accordance with European provisions, except for private copy.[118]

Belgian law set up a judicial remedy before the President of the Tribunal of Commerce or Tribunal of First Instance when technical protection measures prevent the benefit of an exception. This action is open to the beneficiaries of the exceptions, the Minister for Economic Affairs, professional associations and consumer associations.

However, this solution is limited, first, because it does not apply to private copy and, second, because it does not apply either to works made available to the public upon request in accordance with the contractual arrangements agreed between the

---

[115] Cryptographic mechanisms, anti-copy measures, for examples.

[116] Articles XI. 291 and following CDE.

[117] Article 291, § 2 CDE.

[118] Voluntary measures must therefore be taken for exceptions to the making of an anthology, reprography whether for educational purposes or for private purposes, a digital copy for illustration purposes only, E-learning, heritage preservation, ephemeral recordings by broadcasters, exceptions for disabled people, exceptions for social institutions.

parties in such a way that members of the public may access them from a place and at a time individually chosen by them.[119]

Under Belgian law, there is also the fact that technical protection measures shall not prevent the legitimate purchasers of works from using them in accordance with their normal purpose. Here, too, the same remedy is available to the President of the Tribunal of Commerce or the President of the Tribunal of First Instance. As opposed to the precedent, this applies to both offline and online works.[120]

## 15.8 Exhaustion of Copyright

Only the author has the right to authorise the distribution to the public of the original or a copy of his or her work.[121] This is the right of distribution. The Court of Justice of the European Union had the opportunity to specify that the right of distribution implies a transfer of ownership of the object distributed.[122]

The rule of exhaustion counterbalances the right of distribution in favour of the author. The first sale in the European community of the original of a work or copies thereof by the right holder or with his or her consent exhausts the right to control the resale of that object within the European community. However, this right is limited to the territory of the European Union.[123]

The rule of exhaustion limits the right of distribution owned by the author, but the rule of exhaustion is also limited: the copyright owner must always authorise online services. Consequently, exhaustion applies only to tangible goods and not to goods made available online.[124]

However, there is an exception to this virtual territorial limitation for computer programs. Directive 2009/24 on the legal protection of computer programs expressly provides for the applicability of the exhaustion rule.[125] The Court of Justice ruled on the licensing of computer programs.[126] The case before the Court involved Oracle, which develops and distributes computer programs and Usedsoft. Usedsoft acquires licences from Oracle's clients and sells them back, on CD-ROMs or on the Internet. However, Oracle's licence agreements specified that the right to use the programs was non-transferable. Against the practices of Usedsoft, Oracle invoked its right of reproduction. The Court of Justice therefore analyses whether the exhaustion rule applies to the present case. Several conditions apply. There must be a first sale

[119] Articles XI. 336 and XI. 291, §3 CDE; F. Brison et B. Michaux, La nouvelle loi du 22 mai 2005 adapte le droit d'auteur au numérique, *A&M* 2005, pp. 218–221.

[120] Article XI. 291 § 4 CDE.

[121] Article XI. 165, al. 5 CDE.

[122] ECJ, case C-456/06, *Cassina,* ECR 2008 I 2731.

[123] Article XI. 165, al. 6 CDE.

[124] See pts 7 and 60 of CJEU, case C-128/11, *Usedsoft,* ECLI:EU:C:2012:407.

[125] Article 4.2 of the Directive 2009/24/EC and XI. 298 c) CDE.

[126] CJEU, case C-128/11, *Usedsoft,* ECLI:EU:C:2012:407.

within the European Union and with the agreement of the copyright owner. According to the Court, all the conditions were fulfilled in this case. In order for the relationship between Oracle and its customers to qualify as a sale, there must be a transfer of ownership. The Court considers that the concept of sale encompasses 'all forms of product marketing characterized by the grant of a right to use a copy of a computer program, for an unlimited period, in return for payment of a fee designed to enable the copyright holder to obtain a remuneration corresponding to the economic value of the copy of the work'.[127] The distinction according to the medium, namely a sale by downloading on a website or by the transmission of a physical medium, is not relevant in the present case. As a result, the rule of exhaustion is applicable, thus preventing the copyright owner from objecting to the resale of copies of its programs.[128]

It is now necessary to remain vigilant to any questions that might be put to the Court of Justice concerning the right of exhaustion for digital goods other than computer programs and which would not comply with a particular directive.

## 15.9 Intellectual Property and Fundamental Rights

It is mainly the right to freedom of expression that challenges copyright the most. This right is enshrined in Article 10 of the European Convention on Human Rights and in Article 11 of the Charter of Fundamental Rights.

The right to freedom of expression extends to the right to receive and to have access to information.[129]

However, this right is not in itself absolute. Paragraph 2 of Article 10 of the European Convention on Human Rights states:

> The exercise of these freedoms, since it carries with it duties and responsibilities, may be subject to such formalities, conditions, restrictions or penalties as are prescribed by law and are necessary in a democratic society, in the interests of national security, territorial integrity or public safety, for the prevention of disorder or crime, for the protection of health or morals, for the protection of the reputation or rights of others, for preventing the disclosure of information received in confidence, or for maintaining the authority and impartiality of the judiciary.

Even if the Directive imposes to provide for a high level of protection of intellectual property, the Member States (including national courts) must balance different fundamental rights and different legitimate interests.[130]

---

127 Paragraph 49.

128 Nevertheless, the reseller has to destroy his own copy; CJEU, case C-128/11, *Usedsoft*, ECLI:EU:C:2012:407.

129 D. Voorhoof, Copyright and the right to freedom of expression and information. In: Cabay, Delforge, Fossoul, Lambrecht, 20 ans de nouveau droit d'auteur, Anthémis 2015 p. 226.

130 CJEU, case C-360/10, *Sabam v Netlog*, ECLI:EU:C:2012:85,and Recital 4 Directive 2001/29.

In 2011 and 2012, two Belgian cases[131] were brought before the Court of Justice of the European Union in that respect. In the two cases, the Belgian collecting societies, which represented authors, wanted to impose upon an Internet service provider and upon an online social networking platform a system for filtering. This filtering measure was intended to prevent any infringement of copyright, exclusively at the expense of the ISP or social platform and for an unlimited period. In its decision, the Court ruled that intellectual property rights are not absolute rights. On the contrary, they must be counterbalanced with other fundamental rights, such as freedom of business and respect for privacy and freedom to receive information. Consequently, the application and enforcement of copyright rules may not have the effect of imposing complicated and costly measures. Furthermore, the injunction would involve a collection and identification of users' IP addresses,[132] and the system might not distinguish between unlawful and lawful content.[133]

In 2014, another Belgian case allowed the Court of Justice to recall the need for respect for fundamental freedoms. The Court rejected all Belgian conditions in order to admit the parody exception. The underlying objective is to make this notion as broad as possible in order to promote freedom of expression, to the detriment of the author's monopoly.[134]

In a recent case, the promotion of the public interest and the dissemination of knowledge prevailed over the exclusive right of the copyright owner. The pre-existence of an exception permitting the communication or making available of works in their collection for the purpose of research or private study to private individuals by means of specialised terminals was decisive.[135]

The European Court of Human Rights also admits[136] that copyright law may restrict freedom of expression. Such a restriction can only be justified if it is provided by law, has a legitimate aim and is necessary in a democratic society. The national authorities have a margin of appreciation in that respect. However, Member States have a reduced margin of appreciation for political expression and opinions expressed in a satirical or ironic way.[137]

---

[131] CJEU, case C-70/10, *Scarlet Extended v Sabam*, ECR 2011 I 11959 and case C-360/10, *Sabam v Netlog*, ECLI:EU:C:2012:85.

[132] For a case in which the Court of Justice decided that copyright correctly balanced with personal data protection: CJEU, case C-461/10, *Bonnier Audio AB e.a. v Perfect Communication Sweden AB, ECLI:EU:C:2012:219.*

[133] See CJEU, case C-314/12, *UPC Telekabel*, § 47.

[134] CJEU, case C-201/13, *Deckmyn*, ECLI:EU:C:2014:2132.

[135] CJEU, case C-117/13, *Technische Universität Darmstadt v Eugen Ulmer KG*, ECLI:EU:C:2014:2196. For a case where freedom of expression prevails: CJEU, case C-201/11, *UEFA v European Commission,* ECLI:EU:C:2013:519.

[136] ECtHR, *Ashby c. Donald et Neij Sunde c. Suède, 10 jan 2013, n° 367/69/08*; Bruxelles, 27 juin 1997, *I.R.D.I*, 1997, p. 270.

[137] D. Voorhoof, Copyright and the right to freedom of expression and information. In: Cabay, Delforge, Fossoul, Lambrecht, 20 ans de nouveau droit d'auteur, Anthémis 2015.

Competition law also permits, in certain situations, to rectify the position of the copyright owner through the abuse of dominant position. Depending on the position of the right owner, competition law may prohibit the improper exercise of his or her exclusive intellectual property right in certain circumstances.[138] The Court of Justice formulates three cumulative conditions. First, the refusal prevented the emergence of a new product for which there was a potential consumer demand. The second condition is the non-justification by objective considerations. Third, the refusal is likely to exclude all competition in the secondary market.[139]

## 15.10 Conclusion

The reason for the existence of intellectual property law is to stimulate creativity and to grant an appropriate remuneration for the authors.[140]

The exceptions to the exclusive rights of the authors exist in order to assure a social acceptability by the recognition of fundamental rights and general interest consideration. Nevertheless, the law is more and more complex with the negative consequence that exceptions create misunderstanding for citizens.[141]

The Europeanisation of the exceptions has the advantage of harmonisation between the various Member States. Nevertheless, the requirement of high level of protection for authors accompanied by a principle of strict interpretation for the exceptions of copyright law and the important decisions from the Court of Justice reduce the margin of appreciation for the Member States. This may lead to a disadvantage that limitations and exceptions do not coincide with the purpose and needs of a Member State. It seems that the complexity and rigidity of the system is the major challenge of copyright law. It has the consequence that a use may be a legitimate utilisation of the protected works but is rejected in order to respect the strict interpretation principle.[142]

Some authors of doctrine plead for reviewing the system. The idea is to abandon the system of a very detailed list of exceptions in order to adopt a categorisation of exceptions. Following this perspective, the European legislator would use categories of permitted use in order to counterbalance the monopoly of the authors with fundamental rights, such as teaching, culture access, freedom of expression, etc. When this categorisation is established, all the uses made in order to accomplish the purpose would be, in principle, valid. This has the advantage of permitting a

[138] ECJ, case C-238/87, *Volvo,* ECR 1998 6211; ECJ, case C-241/91, *Magill,* ECR 1995 I 743; ECJ, case C-418/01, *IMS,* ECR 2004 I 5039.

[139] B. Michaux, Le droit des bases de données, Kluwer 2005, pp. 69–82.

[140] See S. Dusollier and A. De Francquen, Manuels de droits intellectuels, Anthémis, 2015, p. 56ff.

[141] See S. Dusollier and M. Lambrecht, Les exceptions ont 20 ans: âge de raison ou de refondation?. In Cabay, Delforge, Fossoul, Lambrecht, 20 ans de nouveau droit d'auteur, Anthémis 2015, p. 219.

[142] S. Dusollier et M. Lambrecht, Les exceptions ont 20 ans: âge de raison ou de refondation?. In Cabay, Delforge, Fossoul, Lambrecht, 20 ans de nouveau droit d'auteur, Anthémis 2015, pp. 204–208.

dynamic interpretation by the judge and the preservation of the effectiveness of the exceptions. As a legal safeguard, the triple test could be a precious guide for the judge in order to decide if an act of reproduction or communication to the public is legitimate *in concreto*.[143] Perhaps this perspective is reflected in the recent reform of the Belgian law with the simplification of the reproduction exception for illustrating teaching and private copy by including all acts of reproduction on any medium.

[143] S. Dusollier et M. Lambrecht, Les exceptions ont 20 ans: âge de raison ou de refondation?. In Cabay, Delforge, Fossoul, Lambrecht, 20 ans de nouveau droit d'auteur, Anthémis 2015, pp. 213–219.

# Brazil

# 16

Felipe Barros Oquendo

## 16.1 Introduction: Protection of Copyrights and Exceptions in Brazil

Brazil is a signatory to the TRIPS Agreement, which establishes in Article 13 the so-called triple test to determine whether a use of a work is violating the copyright of a third party. This agreement was internalized in Brazilian law by Federal Decree No. 1,355 of 1994 and, therefore, since that date is enforced as federal law in the country.

However, even before signing the TRIPS agreement, Brazil had already internalized its three-step test when it signed the Berne Convention in 1967 during the Stockholm review.[1] In effect, Article 9, item 2, of the Convention states:

> It shall be a matter for legislation in the countries of the Union, and for special agreements existing or to be concluded between them, to permit the utilization, to the extent justified by the purpose, of literary or artistic works by way of illustration in publications, broadcasts or sound or visual recordings for teaching, provided such utilization is compatible with fair practice.

Notwithstanding international treaties, Brazil has enacted a federal law that regulates copyright—Federal Act No. 9.610 of 1998 (hereinafter "Copyright Act"). This law brings in its Article 46 a series of exceptions to the exercise of copyright that are more restrictive than the treaties. More particularly, however, attention is drawn to section VIII of this article of law, transcribed below:

The rapporteur would like to thank his associate, Ms. Daniela Camara Colla, for the inestimable aid with research and responding to the questions.

[1] Internalized into Brazilian law by Federal Decree No 75,699, of May 6, 1975.

F. Barros Oquendo (✉)
Di Blasi, Parente & Associates, Rio de Janeiro, Brazil
e-mail: felipe.oquendo@diblasi.com.br





B. Kilpatrick et al. (eds.), *Antitrust Analysis of Online Sales Platforms & Copyright Limitations and Exceptions*, LIDC Contributions on Antitrust Law, Intellectual Property and Unfair Competition,
https://doi.org/10.1007/978-3-319-71419-6_16

> VIII – the reproduction, in any works, of small stretches of pre-existing works, of any nature, or of integral works, in the case of plastic arts, when reproduction itself is not the main objective of the new work and does not prejudice the exploitation, reproduction nor cause unjustified prejudice to the legitimate interests of the authors.

This section brings some generic criteria to identify when a use of part of works or, in the case of the works of plastic arts, of the integral work can be treated as an exception or, on the contrary, should be considered copyright infringement.

The first criterion is that the reproduction of a small part of any work or of the entire work, in the case of creations of the plastic arts, is not the main objective of the new work. This criterion is construed as determining that the new work has to have different objectives from the work reproduced (in its entirety or in parts) and that it is substantially different from the work reproduced.

The second criterion is that reproduction does not prejudice the normal exploitation of the reproduced work. This criterion is construed in the sense that the new work cannot compete with the original and reproduced work, that is, the new work cannot be composed in a way that replaces the work reproduced.

Of course, this criterion is to be construed in a reasonable way, that is, if the person accessing the new work is satisfied with the partial or complete reproduction of the previous work, thus no longer longing to access the previous work, this effect cannot be directly and automatically attributed to the author of the new work, unless the structure of the new work is intended precisely to achieve this effect. For example, if one is satisfied with a short chapter from a novel reproduced in a book that brings together excerpts from several novels, it must be reasonably inferred that the person had no interest in reading the partially reproduced work and that this disinterest was not caused by the book. The same is true for the person who loses interest in accessing an original work of plastic art because he has seen a reproduction thereof in a magazine or a book: one should reasonably presume that this person would not have an interest in accessing the work in its original form, regardless of the content of the new work.

Ultimately, the third criterion is that reproduction in the new work does not cause unjustified harm to the authors of the earlier work. The criterion of no harm must be construed as having the purpose of preventing reproduction, which aims at substituting access to the original work. For example, an electronic site that, without the authorization of the right holder, reproduces the central chapters of a non-fiction book, i.e. those that bear the essence of the thesis purveyed in the work, can effectively undermine the normal exploitation of the work and cause harm (by diminishing sales of the work) to the author, albeit not reproducing the entirety of the work. On the other hand, if the same book is the object of a scathing criticism that sums up the thesis and quotes some essential passages from the book for its comprehension, and this criticism provokes in the reading public an aversion for the book criticized, this effect cannot be understood as unjustified harm because what leads the reader to stop acquiring the work is not the fact that he has already essentially read it, as in the first example, but because he relies on the opinion expressed by the critic, who persuades him, in a legal manner and using excerpts from previous work, not to access such work.

The use of these three criteria, in section VIII of Article 46 of the Copyright Law, has brought the triple-test mark provided for in TRIPS and the Berne Convention.

Nevertheless, the triple test provided for in TRIPS and the Berne Convention, as it has the force of federal law in Brazil, should also apply to all exceptions provided for in Article 46 of the Brazilian Copyright Act, some of which will be seen in detail along this chapter.

There is in Brazil a series of judicial cases that, in different contexts, apply the rule of the three-step test to exclude the legitimate rights of author. Some of these cases are highlighted below.

From the Superior Court of Justice:

> I. Law No. 9.610/98, regulating the matter in an extensive and strict manner, abolished the direct or indirect profit for the exhibition of the work as a criterion of the duty to pay author's remuneration, erecting as a taxable event only the circumstance of having promoted the public exhibition of the artistic work, in a place of collective frequency. II. Concerning musical performances, these do not depend on the author's authorization when performed in the family circle or for exclusively educational purposes in educational establishments, provided that there is no intention of profit. III. A "family circle" is understood not only as the enclosure of the home, in a strictly physical sense. The action that is allowed is the one performed within the limits of the family circle and with "family purpose". In this way, the execution that takes place in a venue where the family is not residing, but is momentarily intending to generate a family environment, should not suffer the incidence of copyright charges. IV. According to the Rule of 3 Steps, it is permissible to limit the author's exclusive right when: (i) he is faced with certain special cases; (ii) the use does not impair the normal exploitation of the work and (iii) the use does not cause unwarranted harm to the legitimate interests of the author. V. Special appeal heard and upheld.[2]

> I. Controversy over the possibility of collecting the copyrights of a religious entity for the performance of musical performances and environmental sounding in school, opening the Vocational Year, religious event, non-profit and with free admission. II. The need for systematic and teleological construction of the normative statement of art. 46 of Federal Act No. 9,610/98 in the light of the exceptions established by the special law itself, ensuring the protection of fundamental rights and constitutional principles in collision with the rights of the author, such as privacy, culture, education and religion. III. The effective scope of protection of the author's right to property (Article 5, XXVII, of the CF) arises only after considering the restrictions and limitations that oppose it, and must be considered, as such, those resulting from the exemplary role extracted from the statements of articles 46, 47 and 48 of Federal Act No. 9,610/98, construed and applied in accordance with fundamental rights. III. Use, as a criterion for the identification of restrictions and exceptions, of the three step test rule, which is governed by the Berne Convention and the WTO/TRIPS Agreement. IV. Acknowledgement, in the present case, under international conventions, that limiting the incidence of copyright "does not conflict with normal commercial use of works" and "does not unreasonably harms the interests of the author."[3]

[2] Superior Court of Justice. Special appeal N ° 1,320,007 – SE (2012/0082234-4) Rapporteur Justice Nancy Andrighi, Decision issued on September 9, 2013. Free translation of the abstract by the author.

[3] Superior Court of Justice. Special appeal N ° Special Appeal N ° 964404 – ES. Rapporteur Justice Paulo de Tarso Sanseverino. Decision issued on May 23, 2011. Free translation of the abstract by the author.

From the State Court of Appeals of Rio de Janeiro:

The main argument of the appellant is that it would be religious institution, without profits, and entrance to its events is free. The allegations were untruthful. In spite of the events having religious traces, the purpose thereof is the meeting of businessmen. Consideration of the annual fee collection to members beyond the various possible categories of corporate membership. Possibility of affiliation that if anything confirms the concept of association, as any other of the same nature. However, there is no way to define it as an exclusively religious entity, a characteristic that reflects in its events. The Berne convention, of which Brazil is a signatory, the great treaty on international protection of copyrights, produces a three step test, imposing limitations arising out of the right of author, running in the current phrase "the three-step test sets limits to limitations on author's rights". From this perspective, it is of great value the quotation of the three limits to the copyright, which are: (a) in certain special cases; (b) do not conflict with the normal commercial exploitation of the work; (c) do not unjustly harm the legitimate interests of the author. The association does not exceed the three step test rule, but it does not comply with any of the hypotheses referred to in articles 46, 47 and 48 of law 9.610/98, being therefore legitimate to be charged as a consideration of the use of copyrights. Appeal denied.[4]

Application of article viii of art. 46 of federal act No. 9610/98. Employment of small arts of "BACKSTAGE" and "HUMBLE PEOPLE" music, in the documentary "ALÔ, ALÔ TEREZINHA!". Ruling reversed. There is no doubt about the importance of the communicator to the national artistic context, as well as the great value of the documentary itself, which, like all works of this kind, is committed to portraying faithfully the subject matter. It is noted that, *in casu*, item VIII of art. 46 of Law 9.9610/98 perfectly conforms to the situation described, notably because of the reproduction of the small parts of the songs, in the documentary, aiming to accurately portray the programs presented by the great Abelardo Barbosa, one of the most important hosts of television shows between the 50s and 80s, and his important collaboration for television and popular culture in the Country.[5]

## 16.2 Exceptions to Copyrights Under Brazilian Law: An Overview

Chapter IV of the Brazilian Copyright Act, entitled "On Limitations to Copyright," brings a closed number of copyright exceptions. However, some exceptions have been written in such a way that they do not seek to define a specific situation but embrace several hypotheses. This is the case of the exception brought in section VIII of Article 46, cited and analyzed in the previous item.

Chapter IV of the Brazilian Copyright Law establishes a series of exceptions to copyright based on several fundamental rights.

The right to information bases the exception contained in subsection I, letter "a," of Article 46, which allows the transcription of newspaper news, granted that its authorship and source are mentioned. The same is true for the exception contained

[4]Appeal Court of Rio de Janeiro. Rapporteur Judge Antonio Saldanha Palheiro. Appeal No. 0225705-28.2011.8.19.0001. Decision issued on December 04, 2012. Free translation of the abstract by the author.

[5]Appeal Court of Rio de Janeiro. Rapporteur Judge Fernando Fernandy Fernandes. Appeal No. 0352238-03.2009.8.19.0001. Decision issued on March 8, 2011. Summary and free translation by the author.

in subsection I, letter "b," of the same Article, which allows newspapers to transcribe public speeches. However, these exceptions apply only to printed press and do not benefit online press.[6]

The purpose of letter "d" of this section is to safeguard the rights of the visually impaired to access information since it allows the reproduction of works in Braille or any other support appropriate to the visually impaired, provided it is not for profit. This exception has been widened to encompass any person with disabilities, as per the Accessibility Law (Federal Law No. 13,146, of July 6, 2015).[7]

Section II of Article 46 allows for private, non-profit copying. However, it restricts this right to the reproduction of excerpts, provided it is made for the copyist's own use. Thus, the impossibility of reproducing a work in its entirety for educational or research purposes directly affects students and researchers, who, to the fullest extent of the law, will have to acquire them.[8]

Section III is based on the right to freedom of expression, education, and access to information and culture by allowing the reproduction of excerpts from works for the purpose of study, criticism, or controversy, provided that reproduction is made to the extent appropriate to the purposes.[9]

---

[6]Article 46 of the Brazilian Copyright Act reads: The following shall not constitute violation of copyright:

I. the reproduction:
(a) in the daily or periodical press of news or informative articles, from newspapers or magazines, with a mention of the name of the author, if they are signed, and of the publication from which they have been taken;
(b) in newspapers or magazines of speeches given at public meetings of any kind;
(c) of portraits or other forms of representation of a likeness, produced on commission, where the reproduction is done by the owner of the commissioned subject matter and the person represented or his heirs have no objection to it;
(d) of literary, artistic or scientific works for the exclusive use of the visually handicapped, provided that the reproduction is done without gainful intent, either in Braille or by means of another process using a medium designed for such users;

[7]Article 42 of the Accessibility Law reads: A person with a disability has the right to culture, sport, tourism and leisure on an equal basis with other persons, and is guaranteed access to:

> I – cultural goods in an accessible format; II – television, film, theater and other cultural and sporting activities in an accessible format; and III – monuments and places of cultural importance and spaces that offer services or cultural and sporting events. Paragraph 1 – The refusal to offer intellectual work in a format accessible to the disabled person is prohibited, under any argument, *including under the claim of protection of intellectual property rights.* (emphasis added)

[8]Article 46, section II of the Brazilian Copyright Act reads: the reproduction in one copy of short extracts from a work for the private use of the copier, provided that it is done by him and without gainful intent.

[9]Article 46, section III of the Brazilian Copyright Act reads. the quotation in books, newspapers, magazines or any other medium of communication of passages from a work for the purposes of study, criticism or debate, to the extent justified by the purpose, provided that the author is named and the source of the quotation is given

The right to education and information is also protected under section IV, which allows the transcription of classes by students for their use in study, prohibiting, however, their publication without the permission of the teacher or speaker.[10]

The freedom of trade and the right of the consumer inspire the exception contained in section V, which allows the reproduction of musical, phonographic, and audiovisual works in devices that are being offered for sale, so as to demonstrate to consumers their operation.[11]

Educational law and privacy are protected under section VI, which allows the reproduction of dramaturgical and musical works in the family recess or, for didactic purposes, in schools, provided they are not for profit. One should note that audiovisual works are not covered by this exception, even if the reproduction or use is made without gainful intent.[12]

Section VII allows the reproduction of works protected by copyright in judicial and administrative proceedings based on the right of access to justice and due process of law.[13]

Section VIII seeks to cover all the cases not mentioned in the previous sections, provided they meet the three requirements addressed in the introduction.

Article 47 allows paraphrase and parody, provided the new work is not essentially a reproduction of the original work. However, this article brings a controversial addendum that excludes the paraphrase and the parody that generate discredit to the original work.[14]

The Brazilian courts have already applied such an exception to advertisements:

> Use of musical compositions in advertising campaign, without prior authorization; insertion with the purpose of making parody using the songs as a background; reproduction of short excerpts and for a few seconds that does not characterize copyright infringement. Law no. 9.610/98. The use of musical compositions was not for a long period, soon followed by information about the product for sale, a fact that authorizes the application of the provisions of Article 46, VIII, of the Law No. 9,610/98, to exclude the right to compensation, because there was no copyright infringement. I assume from the probative set that the small parts of the musical compositions were used as a background and with the intention of making a parody, in the carnival period. The reproduction of the musical compositions was not

[10] Article 46, section IV of the Brazilian Copyright Act reads: notes taken in the course of lessons given in teaching establishments by the persons for whom they are intended, provided that their complete or partial publication is prohibited without the express prior authorization of the person who gave the lessons.

[11] Article 46, section V of the Brazilian Copyright Act reads. The use of literary, artistic or scientific works, phonograms and radio and television broadcasts in commercial establishments for the sole purpose of demonstration to customers, provided that the said establishments market the materials or equipment that make such use possible.

[12] Article 46, section VI f the Brazilian Copyright Act reads: stage and musical performance, where carried out in the family circle or for exclusively teaching purposes in educational establishments, and where devoid of any profit-making purpose.

[13] Article 46, section VII f the Brazilian Copyright Act reads: the use of literary, artistic or scientific works as proof in judicial or administrative proceedings.

[14] Article 47 of the Brazilian Copyright Act reads: Paraphrases and parodies shall be free where they are not actual reproductions of the original work and are not in any way derogatory to it.

> the objective of the commercial, did not hinder its normal exploitation and did not even cause prejudice to the author.[15]

Finally, Article 48 provides an exception that protects freedom of panorama.[16]

In our view, the list is insufficient, especially if we consider such exceptions as a closed list.

As already said, to except paraphrase and parody from copyright, while conditioning this exception to the fact that the new work does not create discredit for the paraphrased or parodied, is to place in the hands of the titleholder and the judges an excessive power that ultimately curbs such artistic manifestations. Brazil counts several cases in which a parody had to be removed from circulation because it did not meet the condition of "not generating discredit."

This interpretation was put to the test in the conflict between famous Brazilian singer Roberto Carlos and a comedian who was running for congress called Tiririca. Tiririca employed in his political propaganda a parody of a famous music from Roberto Carlos, who then brought the case to justice. The District Court judge found infringement on the ground that the changed lyrics were not in fact parody as they were not employed on a comedy show but with the sole purpose of attracting votes.

The freedom to perform musical or dramaturgical pieces in the family recess and/or at school, for didactic purposes, demands an update. On the one hand, the exception resents the absence of audiovisual works and the reproduction of works of plastic arts, which are increasingly instrumental in education. On the other hand, it is not uncommon, for example, that such an execution be filmed and uploaded on video platforms such as Vimeo and YouTube and, for a variety of reasons, generate a huge repercussion (i.e., goes viral), including economic repercussion. In such cases, where does the family recess end and the public access begin? This is a matter unanswered by legislation and has not yet been judicially addressed.

Finally, there is much criticism voiced over the fact that there is no specific exception for orphan works or for works that have not been edited for a long time because of lack of interest or difficulties imposed by the authors' heirs. There are those who, in the name of access to culture and the duty of the State to protect public memory, have even defended a compulsory license of such works, to avoid their forgetfulness and to promote their diffusion.

In our view, there is some flexibility and scope for a wider interpretation of some exceptions. At a minimum, paragraph VIII of Article 46, by providing conditions for a use to be an exception, rather than describing a specific hypothesis, already gives an opening to the adaptation of the rules for new situations.

Several of the legal provisions determine that the exception only applies when the use is not for commercial purposes—the exception of reproduction for the visually impaired, the private copy of extracts, the execution of plays and musical pieces in the family recess and at school, for didactic purposes. Other cases, such as

---

[15] TJSP, Appeal No. 480.378-4/0, 9th Chamber of Private Law, Judge Rapporteur Carlos Stroppa, issued on June 10, 2008.

[16] Article 48 of the Brazilian Copyright Act reads: Works permanently located in public places may be freely represented by painting, drawing, photography and audiovisual processes.

freedom of opinion and parody and paraphrasing, as well as the quotation of newspaper news or works for didactic or critical and controversial purposes, are limited not by commercial use but rather by the reasonableness in the use. In fact, it would be unfeasible to prohibit the commercial purpose of a textbook that wanted to cite several literary works.

Some legal exceptions apply only to individuals: the transcription of classes, the private copy of excerpts, the execution of works in family recess. Others are exclusive to organizations or companies: the exception of the demonstration of the product for sale, the freedom to reproduce excerpts in newspapers, books, and magazines.

In our view, the list of exceptions is mandatory, but it is a controversial issue, some experts understanding that exceptions to copyright could be negotiated by the parties in an agreement. Since there is a character of subjectivity in some of the legal dispositions, such as what are considered as *excerpts*, some points become susceptible of different interpretations. It is worth noting that under the terms of Article 4, "the agreements involving copyright are strictly construed":

> "Any other means of communication" can be interpreted as Internet, for example, Article 46, section III, of the Brazilian Copyright Act. In any event, under section IV of Article 46, the musical execution could be done through the internet via streaming.

It is possible to infer from the text of the exceptions that they are intended to confer a right to reproduction and a right of communication to the public. For example, the right of private copying is based on the right to reproduction, whereas the exception that allows the reproduction of news and public speech seems to be much more related to the right to communicate such content to the public.

Concerning the right of communication to the public, this is not explicitly mentioned in Article 46. However, as public execution is a species of the genus communication to the public, one could say that it is protected under Article 46, sections V and VI.

## 16.3 Exceptions to Copyrights and Moral Rights of the Author

Brazilian law establishes the following moral rights of the author.[17]

---

[17] Chapter II of the Brazilian Copyright Act reads:

> Moral Rights of the Author. 24. The moral rights of the author are understood to be the right: I. to claim authorship of the work at any time; II. to cause his name, pseudonym or conventional sign to appear or be announced as that of the author when the work is used; III. to keep the work unpublished; IV. to ensure the integrity of the work by objecting to any modification or any act liable in any way to have an adverse affect on the work or to be prejudicial to his reputation or honor as author; V. to amend the work either before or after it has been used; VI. to withdraw the work from circulation or to suspend any kind of use that has already been authorized where the circulation or the use of the work are liable to have an adverse affect on the reputation or image of the author; VII. to have access to the sole or a rare copy of the work that is lawfully in a third party's possession with a view to

In all the exceptions, the right to authorship, that is, to mention the author's name or pseudonym, is guaranteed: sometimes explicitly, as occurs in the text of Article 46, item I, letter "a" and subsection III, and sometimes implicitly, as is done with letter "b" of the same device or with Article 48, which guarantees freedom of panorama.

The right to mention of authorship is regularly applied by the Brazilian courts:

> In the present case, the appealed decision appears to be contrary to the evidence in the case, since the plaintiff has provided elements of minimum evidence to demonstrate compliance with the legal requirements for the grant of injunctive relief. Indeed, there is likelihood in plaintiff's allegations, given that the fact that a chapter of his book was published in Leandro Karnal's book was widely noticed and disseminated in specialized media, as is inferred from the reports of various magazines and newspapers. In addition, the fact was acknowledged by one of the editors and by the publisher, as it can be drawn from the exchanges of e-mails attached to the records. On the other hand, danger in waiting is patent given that every day that passes the copyrights of the plaintiff are being violated in a very serious way, with the insertion of a piece of work of his authorship in a book by someone else, without any mention or quotation to the true author of the chapter "Gothic pains, private pleasures." However, copyright is the set of legal rules which aim to regulate relations arising from the creation and use of intellectual works (artistic, literary or scientific) – these being understood as the creations of the spirit, in any form externalized – being disciplined at National and international level and including copyright and related rights. The rules of copyright impose on all members of society respect for these creations of the human spirit, while granting its creators the exercise of exclusive prerogatives. In this step, it is evident that with the continued sale of Leandro Karnal's books, with the chapter authored by Fernando Muniz, the readers themselves will be harmed, as they will buy a defective, incomplete and infringing copyrighted work. Appeal granted.[18]

On the other hand, the right to prevent any modification in the work (Article 24, section IV) is mitigated by the exception that allows the paraphrase and, especially, the parody, which almost always implies in the alteration of the original work. The limit for this exception, as already mentioned, is that the parody or paraphrase cannot cause discredit to the work or its author.

As already said, there is always a risk that this limitation to parody and paraphrase be transformed into a mechanism for the owner of the parodied or paraphrased work to unfairly oppose a use of the work by a third party.

Another issue is the attribution of authorship (Article 24, section II) when executing the freedom of panorama: although the authorship of a work in a public place is often not evident, there are precedents in Brazil in which it was considered that, after authorship is claimed, the person using the work cannot omit the author's name in credits.

An issue that, as far as we know, has not become a practical problem in Brazil is whether a work altered by the author or even removed from circulation by the will of the author (who has therefore retracted it) must be removed from future editions

---

preserving the memory thereof by means of a photographic or similar or an audiovisual process, in such a way that the least possible inconvenience is caused to its possessor who shall in any event be indemnified for any damage or prejudice suffered.

[18] Appeal Court of Rio de Janeiro. Rapporteur Renata Cotta. Appeal No. 0035473-23.2015.8.19.0000. Decision issued on August 20, 2015.

of collections and didactic works or works of literary criticism. In fact, this moral right aims to safeguard the author's right not to see his person and his public image linked to a work that he published under different circumstances. In this respect, not being able to extract the excerpts from this work of books and magazines of a didactic or critical character would be to empty the purpose of the norm. On the other hand, culture and collective memory can suffer greatly from the enforcement of this right in such circumstances.

## 16.4 Exceptions and Technical Devices

Although the Brazilian Copyright Act brings a list of exceptions, it is not concerned with determining that the author/holder allows third parties to fully exploit such exceptions, nor does it evidence what the remedies would be in the case of a technological protection against reproduction or one that prevents the full enjoyment of a legal exception.

On the other hand, the Brazilian Copyright Act deems as unlawful the disablement, alteration, or removal of technological barriers inserted into works.[19]

We do not know of any judicial case that discusses the use of technological protection in view of the right of the public to enjoy legal exceptions to copyrights.

However, it is possible to imagine some examples of conflicts, such as putting in place a dispositive motion that blocks copy of small portions of a music or audiovisual work, which prevents the exercise of the exception contained in item VIII of Article 46 of the Copyright Law.

Another example is audiovisual or musical works made available exclusively by streaming whose access is limited (for example, one can only listen to it a certain number of times per week or needs to make a new payment for its availability). In these cases, this limitation may in fact prevent the full enjoyment of the educational exception (Article 46, section VI of the Brazilian Copyright Act), whenever a special and facilitated access to educational institutions is not available.

Even if the law does not provide its own remedy, we understand that the recalcitrant owner can be sued by the one who has the right to enjoy the exception, in order to mitigate or remove his technological barriers to access the work. However, this is our opinion, and, to the best of our knowledge, the Brazilian judiciary has not had occasion to face this issue.

[19] Article 107 of the Brazilian Copyright Act reads. Without regard to the seizure of the equipment used, any person shall be liable to damages in an amount not less than that resulting from application of the provisions of Article 103 and its sole paragraph who: I. alters, removes, modifies or in any way disables technical devices that have been incorporated in copies of protected works and productions to prevent or restrict reproduction; II. alters, removes or in any way spoils the encrypted signals intended to restrict the communication to the public of protected works, productions or broadcasts or to prevent the copying thereof; III. without authorization removes or alters any rights management information.

## 16.5 Three-Step Rule in the Brazilian Copyright Act

Although it intends to bring a closed list of exceptions, the Brazilian Copyright Act ends up creating a "catch all" exception with item VIII of Article 46, mentioned below:

> The following shall not constitute violation of copyright:
>
> VIII. the reproduction in any work of short extracts from existing works, regardless of their nature, or of the whole work in the case of a work of three-dimensional art, on condition that the reproduction is not in itself the main subject matter of the new work and does not jeopardize the normal exploitation of the work reproduced or unjustifiably prejudice the author's legitimate interests.

This exception allows, for example, the sample in music, the use of short extracts of audiovisual works in documentaries or even in works of fiction, among other uses of previous works.

However, there is no public guide or test set by the courts for the correct application of this exception. This creates great insecurity on the part of both the holders and those interested in exploring this exception for reproduction of small stretches of works or full reproduction of works of fine arts.

The exception at hand reaches full reproduction (works of plastic arts) or excerpts (other works), provided that such use is not the purpose of the work itself, that it does not prejudice the regular exploitation of the preexisting work, or that it does not generate illegitimate damages to their holders.

Brazil is a civil law jurisdiction. Hence, the exceptions contained in the Copyright Act are considered as the fair and prior agreement between the fundamental rights of the author of the work and those protected under the exceptions.

This, however, is a view constantly challenged by more progressive scholars, who understand that the list of exceptions contained in the Act cannot encompass all situations in which, for the protection of a fundamental right, copyright should be limited.

The most controversial debate in this respect is that of orphan works or those that, although they have a well-known authorship, have been withdrawn from circulation by disinterested or overly demanding heirs who raise very high barriers to their reproduction/execution.

In one of the attempts to reform Brazilian copyright law, a provision was included for the compulsory licensing of rights in situations such as those mentioned above, but such legal dispositive was discarded by the Brazilian Congress.

## 16.6 Overview on Specific Exceptions

### 16.6.1 Temporary Acts of Reproduction

As per Article 30, paragraph (1), of the Brazilian Copyright Act:

30. In the exercise of the right of reproduction, the owner of copyright may make the work available to the public in whatever form and place and for whatever time that he considers appropriate, either for a consideration or free of charge.

(1) The exclusive right of reproduction shall not be applicable where the reproduction is temporary and done for the sole purposes of making the work, phonogram or performance perceptible by means of an electronic medium, or where it is transitory or incidental, provided that it is done in the course of the use of the work that has been duly authorized by the owner.
(2) Regardless of the manner of reproduction, the number of copies made shall be notified and checked, the person who reproduces the work being responsible for the keeping of such registers as will permit the author to verify the economic profits derived from exploitation.

There is no compensation to the copyright holder, and the exception is deemed as mandatory.

### 16.6.2 Freedom of Speech

The exceptions related to freedom of speech are contained in Articles 47 and 48 of the Brazilian Copyright Act. There is no compensation to the copyright owner, and they are mandatory.[20]

These exceptions have been enforced by the Brazilian courts:

> In order to analyze, in a few words, the subordination of the use of Victor Brecheret's work to the prior and express authorization of appellant Sandra [*reference omitted*]. Honorable Judge Luiz Sérgio de Mello Pinto rightly dismissed the necessity of prior and express authorization of the appellant, since what the book contemplates is the insertion of photographs that portray public works that certainly the author [Victor Brecheret] made to order [*reference omitted*].[21]

### 16.6.3 Public Speeches

In Brazil, there is no list of works that, although original, are not protected under copyright law. The list embedded in the Copyright Act (Article 8) only covers examples of works that are intrinsically lacking in originality and, consequently, do not deserve protection under the Act.[22]

---

[20] 47. Paraphrases and parodies shall be free where they are not actual reproductions of the original work and are not in any way derogatory to it. 48. Works permanently located in public places may be freely represented by painting, drawing, photography and audiovisual processes.

[21] São Paulo Appeals Court, Appeal No. 0119159-30.2006.8.26.0000, 9th Chamber of Private Law of the Court of Justice of São Paulo, Des. Piva Rodrigues, Decision issued on May 31, 2011.

[22] 8. The following shall be excluded from copyright protection within the meaning of this Law: I. ideas, normative procedures, systems, methods or mathematical projects or concepts as such; II. diagrams, plans or rules for performing mental acts, playing games or conducting business; III. blank forms intended for completion with all kinds of scientific or other information, and the instructions appearing thereon; IV. the texts of treaties or conventions, laws, decrees, regulations,

However, Article 46, section I, in its subheadings “a” and “b,” exempts copyright on news and public speeches in a way that allows them to be reproduced in newspapers, an exception already enlarged—at least in practical terms—for blogs and social media. The legal text of the exception also requires that the quoted text is not altered and the authorship and source are mentioned.

In any case, however, no payment is due to the authors or copyright holders of works reproduced under a legal exception.

### 16.6.4 Educational Environment

There are two mentions of exceptions related to studies that are embedded in law. The first is contained in item VI of Article 46 of the Copyright Law and allows the execution of a musical or dramaturgical work in school context for didactic, nonprofit purposes. If these requirements are met, there is no compensation expected for the author or owner of the work reproduced.

This exception is mandatory, that is, it cannot be removed by contract. In our view, the exception is broad enough to cover distance education, but there is no judicial discussion on the subject.

Another exception related to student life is the one that allows the transcription of class and/or content exposed in a lecture by the students for their use, being forbidden to divulge or commercialize their content without the permission of the teachers or lecturers (Article 46, section IV).

Other exceptions that may apply to an educational environment are the right of private copy of excerpts (Article 46, section II) and the exception for quotation of previous works (Article 46, section III).

### 16.6.5 Freedom of Panorama

Article 48 of the Brazilian Copyright Act provides for the freedom of panorama exception, which is mandatory, does not entail payment to the copyright owner, and allows use for profit.[23]

### 16.6.6 Research and Development

There is no specific exception for R&D under Brazilian law. However, Article 46, section VIII, should be applicable, and the user should always take care not to

judicial decisions and other official enactments; V. information in common use such as that contained in calendars, diaries, registers or legends; VI. names and titles in isolation; VII. the industrial or commercial exploitation of the ideas embodied in works.

[23] Article 48 of the Brazilian Copyright Act reads: Works permanently located in public places may be freely represented by painting, drawing, photography and audiovisual processes.

interfere with the normal exploitation of the reproduced work or to cause unjustified damage to the legitimate interests of its author.

### 16.6.7 Private Copy

The Copyright Act allows for copy of excerpts of a work, for private, non-profit, use. The owner of the copied work is not entitled to receive any compensation. The exception is mandatory.[24]

## 16.7 Exhaustion of Copyrights

As a rule, Brazil follows the exhaustion of rights upon first sale. However, Brazilian Federal Copyright Act establishes exceptions to exhaustion of rights in the so-called *droit de suite*. Article 38 of the Brazilian Copyright Act states that "the author has the irrevocable and inalienable right to collect a minimum of five per cent of any gain in value that may be achieved in each resale of an original work of art of manuscript that he has disposed of."

Also, the Berne Convention, which is incorporated into law in Brazil, establishes in its Article 14 *ter* that "the author, or after his death the persons or institutions authorized by national legislation, shall, with respect to original works of art and original manuscripts of writers and composers, enjoy the inalienable right to an interest in any sale of the work subsequent to the first transfer by the author of the work."

Besides these articles, Brazilian law does not establish any other exception to first-sale exhaustion. It is our belief, however, that copyright owners may build exceptions into agreements, as long as it is not a standardized or an end-consumer agreement.

## 16.8 Conclusions

Chapter IV of the Brazilian Copyright Act is one of the few sections of the legal document that has not yet been modified by subsequent laws, even though it was enacted in 1998.

The Act needs an update in general and exceptions in particular. There are a lot of issues arising from a legal text that has become dated, as pointed out in this report.

---

[24] Article 46 of the Brazilian Copyright Act reads: The following shall not constitute violation of copyright:

> (…); II. the reproduction in one copy of short extracts from a work for the private use of the copier, provided that it is done by him and without gainful intent.

For example, one cannot find in the Act a single mention to "internet" or "online" or any other related word. In a civil law country, this means that the legal regulation of use of copyrighted works on the Internet must be construed through systematic interpretation of the Act, always subject to different positions. This is a major source of risks to both right holders and exception users.

Another criticism that must be made is to the fact that the Act does not include audiovisuals in the exceptions for use in schools without any gainful intent, reflecting a dated view on didactic activities.

The exception that allows newspapers to freely use news pieces granted that authorship and source are mentioned should be expressly enlarged to encompass the Internet, as well as independent reporters and individuals.

The fact that lawful reproduction of previous works is limited to small excerpts is also a source of risks to all parties involved because there is no definition of "small excerpts," nor are there public guides or tests set up by courts to ascertain whether the excerpt of the work reproduced was "small" for the purposes of the Copyright Act.

Ultimately, the fact that a copy or digitization of a work can only be done in small excerpts and by the owner of a copy of the work impedes that libraries digitize copyrighted works to safeguard them from destruction, corruption, or loss. This restriction stands contrary to the current trends in other countries.

The Act should also be clearer as to whether the exceptions are mandatory, to what extent they may be restricted under agreement, and whether to expand the exceptions by setting up post-use compensation to right holders.

Brazilian copyright law is still far from being adequate for current times, and this inadequacy gets worse each passing day. Perhaps its excessive and outdated restrictions and legal framework are one of the causes of Brazil always appearing on lists of countries involved with counterfeiting and copyright violation. Hence, any step towards updating the Act might be a step towards removing Brazil from such dishonourable lists.

# Czech Republic 17

Radka MacGregor Pelikánová

The copyright regulation that is valid and applicable in the territory of the Czech Republic has sources from three legal systems—international, EU, and national.[1] The fundamental international sources of the Czech copyright include six international treaties regarding copyright, including the Berne Convention, and sixteen concerning intellectual property. The principal EU sources include especially EU Directives, including Directive 2001/29 on the harmonization of certain aspects of copyright and related rights in the information society ("InfoSoc Directive"). The principal national sources, i.e. the internal Czech sources, of the Czech copyright legal regime are the Czech copyright *lex specialis*, Act No. 121/2000 Coll., on Copyright and Rights Related to Copyright ("Copyright Act"), along with the Czech Constitution, Bill of Fundamental Rights and Freedoms, Civil Code, Antitrust Act, Administrative Order, and Criminal Code.

The author is grateful to the Czech Grant Agency, GA CR, which provided the support for this contribution via grant GA ČR No. 17-11867S "Comparison of the interaction between the law against unfair competition and intellectual property law, and its consequences in the central European context."

[1] R. MacGregor Pelikánová, History of the Czech Copyright Regulation, Journal on European History of Law, 2011, 2(2): 201–205.

R. MacGregor Pelikánová (✉)
Metropolitan University Prague, Strašnice, Czech Republic



B. Kilpatrick et al. (eds.), *Antitrust Analysis of Online Sales Platforms & Copyright Limitations and Exceptions*, LIDC Contributions on Antitrust Law, Intellectual Property and Unfair Competition,
https://doi.org/10.1007/978-3-319-71419-6_17

## 17.1 The Czech Copyright Act and the Author's Work Protected by Copyright

The Czech Copyright Act emanates out of the general principles of civil law and of special maxims that reflect its particularity and its subject matter (e.g., the maxim about the truthfulness of the authorship). Simultaneously, any binding international and European regulations are taken into account. Therefore, the current regulation continues to some extent the previous status and at the same time mirrors the obligations of the Czech Republic implied by its accession to two absolutely fundamental multinational treaties—from Rome and from Geneva, as well as its membership in the European Union, since 2004.

Regarding its nature, although the current Czech Copyright Act is predominantly perceived as a statute from the civil law area, which is distinctively reflected by the facultative trait of its provisions, it still embodies numerous public law strands of a mandatory nature. Therefore, its framework is rather strict and is firmly based on two critical elements, the author as a subject and the work as an object, and thus their definition is absolutely fundamental and at the same time inherently complex.[2] With some simplification, it can be summarized that the subjects are natural persons whose creative activity resulted in a unique and materially depicted outcome, and a copyrighted work can be a creation of one or more physical persons, which are known or unknown (a so-called anonymous work). This understanding and definition represent a continuation of the continental (European) regulations created back in 1886 by the international Berne Convention.[3]

Concerning its scope, the current Copyright Act includes pure copyright (right to literate, musical, artistic, photographic, and audiovisual work) and the hex of rights related to the copyright (the right of the performing artist; of the audio producer; of the audio-video producer, broadcaster, and TV emitter; of the promulgator of as yet unpublished works; and of the publisher) similar to its predecessors.[4]

Fundamentally, it is based on the continental (European) understanding of copyright linked to the traditional German and French conceptions and dualistically distinguishing personal (moral) rights and property (economic) rights. Furthermore, it includes a quantity of practical changes with an undeniable practical impact. In no particular order, it can be made as a reference to the extension of the length of the property copyright from the original 50 years to the new 70-year period since the decease of the author, the enlargement of the circle of beneficiaries and duty-owing persons, the increase in the amount of fines, the unified understanding of the license

[2] K. Schelle, J. Tauchen, J. Hejda, and R. MacGregor Pelikánová, Základy občanského práva. Kapitola 9: Autorské právo [Fundaments of the Civil law. Chapter 9: Copyright], 2nd ed, Ostrava: B.I.B.S., Key Publishing s.r.o. 2010, p. 217.

[3] H. Chaloupková and P. Holý, Autorský zákon – Komentář [Copyright Act – Commentaries], 4th Ed, Prague: C. H. Beck 2012, p. 3.

[4] R. MacGregor Pelikánová, History of the Czech Copyright Regulation, Journal on European History of Law, 2011, 2(2): 201–205.

agreement as principally a contract based upon payment, and the clear definition of the exclusive and nonexclusive license.[5]

As stated above, the subject matter of copyright is the protected author's work. An explicit and broad definition is included by Article 2 of the Copyright Act.[6]

The author must be a natural person who created the work (Article 5); the right to the author's work arises at the moment the work is expressed in any objectively perceivable form (Article 9), and it includes exclusive personal (moral) and exclusive property (economic) rights of the author to his or her work (Article 10). Exclusive personal (moral) rights include the right to decide about making the author's work public, the right to claim authorship, the right to the inviolability of the author's work, in particular, the right to grant consent to any alteration of, or other intervention in, his or her work (Article 11). The property (economic) rights of an author include the right to use work, which means, among others, to reproduce and distribute the original or copies, as well as the right to communicate the work to the public (Article 12). A special form of the right to communicate a work to the public is the right to make the work accessible, including electronic accessibility; see InfoSoc Directive.[7]

[5] R. MacGregor Pelikánová, History of the Czech Copyright Regulation, Journal on European History of Law, 2011, 2(2): 201–205.

[6] Article 2 Author's work

(1) The subject matter of copyright shall be a literary work or any other work of art or a scientific work, which is a unique outcome of the creative activity of the author and is expressed in any objectively perceivable manner including electronic form, permanent or temporary, irrespective of its scope, purpose or significance (hereinafter referred to as "work"). A work shall be especially a literary work expressed by speech or in writing, a musical work, a dramatic work or musical-dramatic work, a choreographic work and pantomimic work, a photographic work and a work produced by a process similar to photography, an audio-visual work such as a cinematographic work, a work of fine arts such as a painting, graphic or sculptural work, an work of architecture including an urban design work, a work of applied art, and a cartographic work.

(2) A computer program shall also be considered a work if it is original in the sense that it is the author's own intellectual creation. A database which by the way of the selection or arrangement of its content is the author's own intellectual creation, and in which the individual parts are arranged in a systematic or methodical way and are individually accessible by electronic or other means, is a collection of works. No other criteria shall be applied to determine their eligibility for that protection. A photograph or a work produced by a process similar to photography, which are original in the sense of the first sentence, shall be protected as a photographic work…

(6) The author's work pursuant to this Act are not especially the theme of a work as such, the news of the day and any other fact as such, an idea, procedure, principle, method, discovery, scientific theory, mathematical and similar formula, statistical diagram and similar item as such.

[7] M. Bartoň, Internetový odkaz jako užití díla [Internet link as a use of work] Revue pro právo a technologie, 2016, 14, 151.

## 17.2 The Delimitations, Exceptions, and Restrictions of the Protection by the Czech Copyright Act

Regarding the delimitation, exceptions, and restrictions of the protected, the Czech Copyright Act proceeds hierarchically.

Firstly, by Article 2, only a work that is a unique (possibly original) outcome of the creative activity of a human being and that is objectively expressed can be an author's work protected by copyright. If any of these criteria are not met, the copyright protection is excluded.

Secondly, by Article 2, certain outcomes are not the author's work, and consequently they can never ever benefit through the copyright regime and obtain copyright protection even if they *prima facia* satisfy the above-indicated criteria. These *ex lege* exclusions from the author's work definition cover the subject of the work, daily news, any fact by itself, an idea, proceeding, principle, method, discovery, scientific theory, a mathematical or similar formula, statistical graph, or similar subject as such.

Thirdly, by Article 3, it completely excludes from the protection two types of an author's works and justifies this as "exceptions from copyright protection in the public interest." These two types of works without copyright protection, and thus free for use, are official works, such as legal regulation documents, decisions, parliamentary publications, etc., and creations of traditional folk cultures. Naturally, these works satisfy the criteria to be considered an author's work, and their authors are still alive; nevertheless, by the operation of the law, they are, due to the public interest, free.

Fourthly, Article 14[8] strictly distinguishes between methods of diffusion to public, i.e. between the reproduction and distribution (dissemination) of a work in a tangible form and communication to the public of a work in an intangible form, i.e. the copyright exhaustion for the European Economic Area is provided only for works in the tangible form with a first sale in the EEA.

Fifthly, exceptions and restrictions of copyright are covered by Section 4 of the Czech Copyright Act and need to be interpreted according to Article 29; i.e., a restrictive application of the Berne triple test occurs. There follows an exhaustive list that does not look too systematic and uses various forms (free use, law license, delimitation, exception, restriction, etc.) with basically the same result—the free

[8] Article 14 Distribution

(1) The distribution of the original or a copy of a work is understood as making accessible to the public of work in the tangible form or other ownership title transfer to the original or a copy of the work, including their offering for this purpose.

(2) By the first sale or another first transfer of the ownership right to the original or to the copy of the work in the tangible form, which was done by the author or with his or her consent in the territory of any EU member states or a state belonging to the European Economic Area, exhausts the copyright of the author regarding the distribution in the EU and in the EEA. However, the right on the rent (for commercial profit) and on the loan (for non-commercial purposes) remains intact.

use of copyrighted work without any need to obtain a consent or license from the authors who benefit from the copyright.

## 17.3 The Czech UK Three-Step Test

The Czech Copyright Act includes Section 4, called Exceptions and Restrictions of Copyright, and its first provision is Article 29,[9] which explicitly provides for the so-called triple test. In general, the triple test is recognized as the interpretation rule, i.e. the guidelines for the interpretation of Copyright Act provisions dealing with various types of copyright restrictions, especially regarding the interpretation of Article 30 ff.

This triple requirement is taken into account seriously by courts in individual cases and is heavily mentioned by national scholars. Indeed, scholars underline that this is a universal interpretation rule for all free uses and law licenses.[10] The case law fully reflects this trend.

For example, the Czech Supreme Court in 30 Cdo 3474/2010 of November 30, 2011, decided that making accessible CDs owned by some members of an association without juridical personality to other members of this association cannot be qualified as an allowable free use (restriction on copyright), according to Article 30 of the Czech Copyright Act, because this activity has rather the features of a rental. By purchasing a CD, no license was obtained to permit using the copyrighted work (music recording) by others. An opposite interpretation would lead to an unjustified breach of the legitimate interests of authors. In other words, the Czech Supreme Court in this case confirmed the triple-test interpretation rule, interpreted Article 30 of the Czech Copyright Act accordingly, and, because of its third-step requirement (unreasonable prejudices to the legitimate interests of the author), rejected recognizing the copyright restriction. This judgment is fully in compliance with the judgment of the Czech Supreme Court in 30 Cdo 329/2008 from November 12, 2009, and the deliberation of the Czech Constitutional Court II. ÚS 423/10 from April 1, 2010, and even refers to them. Further, it needs to be pointed out that the Czech Supreme Court in 30 Cdo 3474/2010 from November 30, 2010 repeated the Explanatory Note to Article 29 of the Czech Copyright Act, according to which "Article 29 regulates a general principle, which is included in the Berne Convention and TRIPS Agreement, regarding restrictions on the exclusive copyright."

[9] Section 4 Exceptions and restrictions of copyright

Subsection 1 General provision
Artiww9

(1) Exceptions and restrictions of Copyright can be applied only in special cases provided for by this Act and only if such a use of copyrighted work does neither conflict with a regular use of the work nor disproportionally affect the legitimate interests of the author.

[10] H. Chaloupková and P. Holý. Autorský zákon – Komentář [Copyright Act – Commentaries], 4th Ed, Prague: C. H. Beck 2012, p. 53.

## 17.4 Specific Aspects of Czech Exceptions and Restrictions

Article 29 of the Czech Copyright Act explicitly and expressly states that restrictions can be applied exclusively to special cases mentioned by the Czech Copyright Act, i.e. Articles 30–Article 39 of the Czech Copyright Act. Hence, the first requirement from the triple test, the special cases clause, is strictly observed by the Czech national law, and these special cases must be set by the Copyright Act. (No other legislation can set them up!)

This legislative wording is fully respected and well confirmed by scholarly writings, as well as case law. There has not been any real successful attempt to indirectly expand this exhaustive list. For example, the Czech Supreme Court in 30 Cdo 3056/2012 from January 31, 2013, confirmed that this legislative provision needs to be interpreted in a restrictive manner, again referred to the triple test as to the general principle, and referred to the Berne Convention and TRIPS Agreement. In the given case, the Czech Supreme Court stated that the restriction on copyright granted to health care providers does not extend to a spa, namely to the Bertiny Spa Třeboň. Identically, the Czech Supreme Court in 30 Cdo 3093/2012 from March 28, 2013, reconfirmed that the list is exhaustive and cases included cannot be interpreted broadly; i.e., even the Lázně Aurora Spa Třeboň could not rely on the health care restriction on copyright in general. If a spa wants to use it, it has to distinguish between patients really obtaining necessary rehabilitation health from other (wellness) patients, and only the first group allows for relying on the restriction on copyright. Thus, the second group can enjoy copyrighted works via listening to the radio or watching TV, only based on a paid license.

### 17.4.1 Exhaustive List of Exceptions and Restrictions

Exceptions and restrictions of copyright are covered by Section 4 of the Czech Copyright Act and need to be interpreted according to Article 29, i.e. a restrictive application of the triple test. There follows an exhaustive list that does not look too systematic and uses various forms (free use, law license, delimitation, exception, restriction, etc.) with basically the same result—the free use of copyrighted work without any need to obtain a consent or explicit license from the authors of the copyright beneficiary. The exhaustive list from Articles 30 to Article 39 includes as follows:

- Article 30: not "use" under the Copyright Act and thus free—personal use without direct or indirect economic profit;
- Article 30a: no breach of copyright—making copies on paper for personal or internal use;
- Article 30b: no breach of copyright—use of work for repairing a device of a customer;
- Article 31: no breach of copyright—quotations/citations;

- Article 32: no breach of copyright—propagation of exhibition or sale of artworks;
- Article 33: no breach of copyright—use of works located in public places (panorama exception);
- Article 34: no breach of copyright—official and reporting license—use of works for public security, for court or administrative proceedings, in periodical press, public speeches, etc.
- Article 35: no breach of copyright—use of works for civic or religious ceremonies or of schoolworks;
- Article 36: no breach of copyright—restriction of copyright to a collection;
- Article 37: no breach of copyright—library license—libraries and schools making copies and making them available to third parties (in certain situations, fees to authors need to be paid);
- Article 37a: no breach of copyright—copying and making available "orphaned" works;
- Article 38: no breach of copyright—license for handicapped people;
- Article 38a: no breach of copyright—license for temporary copies;
- Article 38b: no breach of copyright—license for photos;
- Article 38c: no breach if insignificant auxiliary use of works;
- Article 38d: no breach of copyright—license to use works of fine art or architectonic works;
- Article 38e: no breach of copyright—license for social establishments, i.e. social care and health providers that are established not for profit;
- Article 38f: no breach of copyright—allowing antenna reception for TV or radio broadcasting for units in a building;
- Article 38g: no breach of copyright—if use of a work for caricature or parody purposes;
- Article 39: no breach—exhibiting original or copy of beaux art, photographic, or other works.

An overview of this rather fragmented list demonstrates that several fundamental rights and objectives, as well as public order interests and concerns, are reflected. Some special cases deal with reproduction (see Article 30, Article 30a, Article 33, Article 34, Article 37, Article 37a, Article 38, Article 38a, Article 38b, and Article 38e) while others with communication to the public (see Article 31, Article 32, Article 33, Article 34, Article 35, Article 37, Article 37a, Article 38d, Article 38f, and Article 39). Education and research is at least partially covered by Article 31, Article 35, and Article 37; access to culture and knowledge is at least partially covered by Article 3, Article 32, Article 33 Article 35, Article 37, Article 37a, Article 38a, Article 38d, and Article 39; freedom of expression and right to receive and disseminate information are at least partially covered by Article 1, Article 3, Article 34, and Article 37; privacy and private use are covered by Article 30; the needs of people with disability are covered by Article 38. Public security is at least partially covered by Article 34, and freedom of panorama is included in Article 3. The preservation of cultural heritage is not included between these special cases because already Article 3 takes care of it.

The above mentioned cases about South Bohemian spas, 30 Cdo 3056/2012 and 30 Cdo 3093/2012, which were rejected from the benefit of the special case for health care providers (because only some clients are true patients seeking medical and rehabilitation treatment, and other clients are rather wellness seekers), demonstrate the rigidity of the Czech understanding, interpretation, and application of the first requirement of the triple test.

The distinction between uses for commercial purposes and uses for noncommercial purposes and uses by individuals and uses by others (e.g., companies, organizations) is done on a general as well as a special basis.

### 17.4.2 Selected Exceptions and Restrictions from the Exhaustive List

The exhaustive list provided by the Czech Copyright Act has an impact on both the moral (personal) rights and the property (economic) rights of authors.

Regarding moral (personal) rights, in the majority provisions dealing with special cases belonging to the list, there is a direct requirement that the author of the work has to be indicated as long as this is feasible or customary; see, e.g., Article 31 quotations/citations, Article 32 propagation of exhibition or sale of artworks, etc. As a matter of fact, Article 31 is basically the only unique universal exception allowing to communicate to the public a work, protected by the copyright, of someone else without his or her consent.[11] This exception covers as well the "upload on the Internet" and has three levels—(1) citing extracts from published works in a justifiable extent, (2) citing extracts from works for review or criticism purposes, and (3) citing entire works for illustration or education purposes.

In addition, there are provisions dealing with special cases that directly affect the moral (personal) rights of the author in a restrictive manner. Namely, Article 38c deals with an insignificant auxiliary use of work and states that there is not any breach of copyright if someone randomly uses a work in relation to the planned main use of another work. Further, Article 39d provides for a license to use works of fine art or architectural works and allows changes in a completed building which is an expression of a copyrighted work in the necessary extent and while maintaining the value of the copyrighted work. In such a case, the author of the primary copyrighted work is only informed about it; his or her consent is not needed.

Regarding property (economic) rights, it can be stated that basically all provisions making the exhaustive list deal with it. Already the first of them, Article 30,[12]

---

[11] L. Jansa L et al. Internetové právo [Internet law].1st ed, Prague: Albatros Media a.s., 2016.

[12] Article 30 Free use

(1) The use of the work pursuant to this Act shall not mean its use for the personal need of a natural person, if the purpose is not to reach directly or indirectly economic or commercial profit, unless this Act provides otherwise.

clearly provides for free use in the case of the personal needs of a natural person, provided this does not have, directly or indirectly, a commercial purpose. In other words, according to Article 30, using or reproducing a copyrighted work for the personal needs of a natural person with a purpose, neither directly nor indirectly, to generate commercial profit is not considered to be use under Copyright Act, and thus it is freely available. This "free use" does not apply to computer programs and electronic databases. Also, pursuant to Article 30a,[13] it is not a breach of copyright if a natural person for his or her personal needs or a legal entity or a natural person conducting business for their internal use makes a reproduction of work on paper.

Interestingly, according to the commentaries to the Czech Copyright Act, Article 30 should be interpreted broadly; i.e., the free use for the personal needs of a natural person extends to each and every form of "copying," i.e. not just making a reproduction.[14] This broad interpretation, i.e. extension of the "fair use" for each and any form of "copying" for personal or internal needs, is justified by the teleological approach, i.e. by the true intent of the legislature.

Another discussion has developed around the extent of the group of beneficiaries for the clause "personal needs" and of the quantitative aspect of this benefit, namely how far Article 30 goes vis-à-vis beneficiaries of such a free use (needs of the individual or his or her family members or even of other more or less close persons?) and what is the quantitative extent (how many copies can be made?).

The Czech Supreme Court decided in 5 Tdo 234/2009 of March 25, 2009, regarding an individual having in his or her home 236 pieces of copies of CDs and DVDs, that this amount per se does not exclude the possibility of the "free use" restriction, i.e. that having 236 copies can still qualify for the free-use regime under Article 30. The Czech Supreme Court in this case reversed the judgments of the lower courts, which wrongly interpreted the Czech Copyright Act, particularly Article 30, as allowing only one single copy for personal needs. These lower courts followed strictly the literate interpretation approach and implied from the wording "making a record or a copy" that the grammatical singular means only one copy is allowed.

---

(2) Further, the Copyright shall not be infringed by someone who, for his or her personal use, makes a record, copy or imitation of a work.

(3) Unless this Act states otherwise, the use under this Act is the use of a computer program or electronic database even for personal needs of a natural person or own internal needs of a legal entity or business conduction natural person, including making copies of such work even for such needs.

[13] Article 30a Making copies on paper or similar medium

(1) The Copyright shall not be infringed if

a) a natural person for his or her personal need,
b) a legal entity or business making natural person for its own internal need,
c) someone based on an order from a natural person for his or her personal need,
d) someone based on an order from a legal entity or business making natural person makes a print copy of work on a paper or on a similar medium by photographic techniques or another method with a similar effect, except note transcript.

[14] H. Chaloupková and P. Holý, Autorský zákon – Komentář [Copyright Act – Commentaries], 4th Ed, Prague: C. H. Beck 2012, p. 56.

However, according to the Czech Supreme Court, the legislature's language uses the singular without excluding the meaning of the plural, and it is necessary to proceed always with a consideration of circumstances and embrace the purposive, or even the teleological, approach. Further, the Supreme Court referred to the triple test (three-step test) as implied by the decision of the WTO in the proceeding EC v. USA Act Nr. WTO WT/DS160/R(2000). Further, regarding the triple test, the Court stated that the 1st requirement is rather formal (specific cases), while the 2nd and 3rd requirements (no conflicts with normal exploration and no unreasonable prejudice) are rather material.

Thus, both case law and academia concluded that "personal needs" means the needs of family members but not of friends or colleagues; the copy must be made by the person with the need (such a person cannot ask someone else to do it for him or her), and a copy made based on the "exception" of Article 30 (free use) cannot later be used for internal needs of a legal entity or of a natural person doing business.[15]

Regarding downloading works from the Internet, the "exception" of Article 30 (free use) applies only to situations when a downloading person downloads for his or her personal needs and at the same time believes that the downloaded work was not placed on the Internet in breach of copyright.[16]

Another well-known special case is the use of a work located in a public area, i.e. the so-called panorama exception, which is explicitly included in Article 33.[17]

The Czech courts fully recognize the "panorama exception" and this even if the use leads to an indirect incorporation into another intellectual property asset. Namely, the Municipal Court in Prague confirmed in 8A 112/2010 and 9A 105/2010—involving Sedlčanská mouka (flour from Sedlčany)—that a third person can make a picture of a mill located in the town of Sedlčany without any permission from the owner of the mill or its architect, use this picture to label its product (flour and products made of flour), and even incorporate this picture into its logo and file a trademark application for the registration of such a logo.

---

[15] L. Jansa L et al., Internetové právo [Internet law].1st ed, Prague: Albatros Media a.s., 2016.

[16] L. Jansa L et al., Internetové právo [Internet law].1st ed, Prague: Albatros Media a.s., 2016.

[17] Article 33 Utilization of a work located in a public area

(1) Copyright shall not be infringed by whoever records or expresses by drawing, painting, graphic art, photography or film a work located on a square, in a street, in a park, on a public route or in any other public place; even more, copyright shall not be infringed by whoever further uses such an expressed, captured, or recorded work. If possible, it is necessary to indicate the name of the author, or the name of the person under which name the work is presented to the public, and the name of the work and its location.

(2) The provisions of paragraph (1) shall not apply to making a copy or an imitation of an architectural work or to the reproduction and distribution of the work by means of a three-dimensional reproduction.

While daily news is out of the reach of copyright by the operation of the author's work criteria (see Article 2), other public reporting may benefit by the special case called "official and reporting license," which is explicitly included in Article 34.[18]

The use of work for various ceremonies and school purposes is reflected by a heterogeneous and a little bit of a "catch all" special case included in Article 35.[19]

In sum, the Czech Copyright offers a number of special-case scenarios dealing with educational purposes. Firstly, Article 35(2) allows the use of a work for non-commercial purposes during school shows. Secondly, Article 35(3) allows a school or other education establishments to use a work created by a student for a noncommercial purpose during lectures or for its own internal needs. Thirdly, Article 37(1) allows, via the so-called library license, the school or educational establishment to (1) make a reproduction of a work for noncommercial purposes but for archive or conservation needs or to (2) make accessible to the public a work, the use of which is not covered by sales or license conditions, provided it is done exclusively for research and private study purposes or to (3) loan originals or copies of bachelor, master, Ph.D., Ph.Dr., and habilitation theses for research or private study purposes. Article 37(2) and Article 37 (5) specify that in the case of such loans, this person (e.g., educational establishment) has to present annual summary reports to a relevant collective administrator (collecting society) and has to pay them or directly the authors compensation as set out by Annex 1 to the Copyright Act.

However, the Czech Copyright Act does not include any special provision dealing explicitly with research, and thus research per se and as such is not a special case (1st Berne Convention requirement). Nevertheless, the research is (in)directly covered by other exceptions and restrictions of the Czech Copyright Act. Namely,

---

[18] Article 34 Official reporting license

There is no breach of copyright if someone uses

a) in a legitimate extent, a work based on the law for public securities, court or administrative proceedings purposes or for other official purposes or for Parliament proceedings and for making a recording about them;
b) work in the relation to news reporting relating current events, and this in the extent reflecting information purpose;
c) in the reflecting manner the work in periodical press, TV or broadcasting … to communicate news reporting about current political, economic, religious matters ….
d) political speech or extracts from public speeches or similar works in the extent reflecting the information purpose…

[19] Article 35 Utilization of the work as a part of civil and religious ceremonies, as a part of school performances and the utilisation of a school work

(1) Copyright shall not be infringed by whoever utilizes a work for non-commercial purposes during civil and religious ceremonies.
(2) Copyright shall not be infringed by whoever utilizes a work for non-commercial purposes during school performances performed exclusively by the pupils, students or teachers of the school or of the school or educational establishment.
(3) Copyright shall also not be infringed by the school or school or educational establishment if they use for non-commercial purposes for their own internal needs a work created by a pupil or student as a part of their school or educational assignments ensuing from their legal relationship with the school or school or educational establishment (school work).

researchers can possibly rely on Article 30 "free use" and research institutions on Article 37 "library license." Making copies can, in certain situations, at least theoretically, lead to a need to pay compensation stated by Annex 1 to the Copyright Act. The Czech law, namely the Czech Copyright Act, does not have any special provision dealing with big data and even does not mention this term or its equivalents.

Article 38a of the Czech Copyright Act is labeled "license for temporary reproductions" and provides that there is not a breach of a copyright if someone makes temporary reproductions, which are ephemeral, auxiliary, and without value per se and at the same time are an integral part of a technological process, and their purpose is to allow the transmission of a work or the legitimate use of a work. Otherwise, there are not any special regulations provided in order to address the (alleged) risk that technological protection measures could reduce or impair the enjoyment of restrictions, licenses, or exceptions to copyright. There is not any strong call for it. However, the Czech Republic closely follows the EU discussion about the 2nd copyright package and, in general, about the modernization of the EU copyright rules.

Although the Czech law is not inclined to expand or to add other special cases to the list provided by Article 29 et seq. of the Czech Copyright Act, there are still cases showing that judges can be more flexible, especially if provisions from constitutional law can be applied or are to be applied (e.g., from the Charter of Fundamental Rights and Freedoms). For example, the Czech Supreme Court in 30 Cdo 154/2011 of March 14, 2012, confirmed judgments of lower courts in this case and rejected the claim of the wife of ex-prime minister Petra Paroubková. She sued the publisher Ringier Axel Springer because it published, in its journal Reflex, comics "Green Raul," part 739, in which her sexual caricature was published. The courts balanced constitutional rights and freedoms, namely the right for the protection of privacy and freedom of speech, of belief, and of artistic activities. The lower judges, as well as the Supreme Court, reached the conclusion that, in the given case, the caricature concerned a politically exposed person, was founded upon a real basis, and did not breach the proportionality principle. In general, the caricature, entertaining imitation, and pastiche seem to be acceptable under the Czech law, especially if politicians and celebrities are involved and at least partially the truth is observed. Nevertheless, 30 Cdo 154/2011 and its aftermath generated a lot of discussions and contributed to the legislative change, which explicitly, expressly, and directly included the "pastiche" in the Czech Copyright Act. Hence, until 2017, the Czech Copyright Act did not include any copyright exception or restriction regarding the parody or caricature; i.e., processing another work or distributing a work for parody purposes did not constitute a special case (1st requirement of the Berne triple test) pursuant to the Czech law (Prchal, 2016).[20] However, Act No. 102/2017 Coll., amending the Copyright Act, finally introduced, commencing April 2017, this new "exception," i.e. a special case regarding caricature and parody. Thus, currently, the Czech Copyright Act makes absolutely clear that this is acceptable and breaches

[20] P. Prchal, Obhajoba výjimky pro účely parodie, karikatury, parafráze, koláže [Defense of the exception for parody, caricature, paraphrases, collages] Acta MUP, 2016, 1, 74.

neither copyright law nor (if other requirements are met) the Constitution; see Article 38g.[21]

### 17.4.3 Compensation in Favor of the Copyright Owner

The Czech Copyright Act neither provides a systematic remuneration system nor includes in every special case belonging to the list an appropriate model or formula for a compensation calculation. For some special cases, a clear remuneration calculation model is established, while for others not. The special cases with a preset partially clear remuneration model are, for instance, Article 30 on free use and Article 30a on making copies on paper or a similar medium, complemented by Article 25,[22] to which both Article 30 and Article 30a refer.

According to this Annex 1[23] to the Copyright Act, the one-time compensation to be paid is generally 3% from the sales price of the reproduction devices, while in the case of broadcasting and TV devices allowing recording it is 1.5% from the sales price of such devices. The compensation for each print reproduction of a work is

---

[21] Article 38g Licence for caricature and parody

There is not a breach of a copyright if someone uses a work for caricature or parody purposes.

[22] Article 25 Right to remuneration in connection with the reproduction of the work for personal needs or own internal need

(1) For published works, which can be reproduced for
a) personal needs of a natural person or internal needs of a legal entity (§30 and §30a) on a paper.
b) personal needs of a natural person based on an audio, audio-video or other recording … the author has right on a compensation.
(2) The person obliged to pay the compensation to the collective administrator (collecting society) is
a) a producer of device for making reproduction of recordings,
b) a producer of devices making print reproductions,
c) a producer of unrecorded carriers for recording,
e) provider of paid reproduction services for print copies (Article 30a).
(4) The compensation to be paid based on 2b) depends upon the probable number of device designed to make print reproduction pursuant to Article 30a …The probable number of these device is set as 20%. The compensation is calculated based on the average price of the device without added value tax.
(7) The Ministry of Culture sets in its Decree types of devices for making print reproduction and types of unrecorded carriers for recording and the fixed compensation. Further the amount of the compensation is set in Annex 1 to this Act.

[23] Annex 1 of the Copyright

3. One-time payment for on first sale of the devices for making record copies is 3% of its sale price. For broadcasting and TV receivers allowing to make audio, video or audio-video recording is 1.5% of the sale price of such receivers.
6. Remuneration for making one print copy of a work is
a) black and white – CZK 0.20 per page
b) colour – CZK 0.40 per page

CZK 0.20 in the case of a black-and-white copy and CZK 0.40 in the case of a colored copy. The probable number of the print reproduction is 70% for libraries and 20% for state offices and archives. The compensation for rental is CZK 0.50.

## 17.5 Assessment of the Czech System of Copyright Protection

Pursuant to the Czech law, delimitations, copyright exceptions, and restrictions are set in an explicit and rigid manner, and their interpretation is restrictive. There has not been any strong discussion or exchange of fundamental opinions about the extent of the list of exceptions, restrictions, and licenses; about the restrictive interpretation of special cases; and about the application of the triple test. Hence, it seems that according to the general Czech opinion, the fundamental rights or objectives appear not be prima facie overlooked or unduly minimized by the current list and its interpretation. The only potential real issue, the absence of the "caricature and parody" special case, has been already explicitly resolved.

So far, there are not any clear and prevailing opinion streams about a general dramatic imbalance or about a dramatic imbalance vis-à-vis particular issues or aspects. Copyright cases linked to the "fair use" are rather sporadic, and the case law is not fully developed in this respect. Basically, the only heavily objected to deficiency (objections voiced by academia, as well as the general public), namely the lack of the parody exception, was cured by the legislature a few months ago.

Overcompensation is a hot topic in the Czech Republic, but this is due exclusively to the rather aggressive practices of the collective administrators (collecting societies), i.e. entities compulsorily (by the law) administrating the copyright of authors. There are six, and especially one of them, the OSA—a civic association protecting copyright for musical works—has the reputation of going (too aggresively) after end users and challenging their use of exceptions and restrictions; i.e., the application of the fair-use doctrine/Berne triple test is under the close scrutiny of these collective administrators (collecting societies), and when there is (allegedly) an indication of an (allegedly) too broad application, they do not hesitate to step in and sue, i.e. start court proceedings.

## 17.6 Conclusion

The Copyright Act, as well as the entire Czech body of law covering copyrights, belongs in the twenty-first century and in a rather welcoming manner accommodates the challenges of our postmodern and high-tech society. Firstly, the current Copyright Act is not any reconstituted socialist act; instead, it is a relatively new law act prepared and drafted in accordance with correct, valid, and up-to-date society matching concepts. Secondly, the Czech Republic is, for over one decade, a full member of the EU and respects the *acquis communautaire*, as well as the new body of EU law, and implements it in a rather satisfactory manner. Thirdly, the Czech legislation has historically good continental roots, which did not get totally destroyed during the unpleasant communist era. Fourthly, the Czech Republic and its predecessors have always belonged to certain and stable parties of big international treaties and conventions dealing with intellectual property, including copyrights.[24]

The court system is much more efficient and effective than during the socialist Czechoslovakia era and the early years of the current Czech Republic; nevertheless, until today, it is challenging to bring, prove, and win a copyright case and manage to materialize the orders and instructions indicated in the judgment. The blame does not lie predominantly with judges; rather, it is on the entire society, which, until today, still underestimates and undervalues creative works and their authors, has a rather lower awareness of the true extent of copyright, and has a weaker drive to bring cases to court in order to establish a strong and consistent case law, especially on copyright exceptions and restrictions. This can be contrasted with overzealous collective administrators (collective societies) eagerly suing, and thus the majority of cases dealing with special cases are based on actions filed by these collective administrators (sometimes aggressively) trying to reduce the application of exceptions and restrictions and which, ultimately, were decided in a rather fair manner by judges.

[24] R. MacGregor Pelikánová, History of the Czech Copyright Regulation. Journal on European History of Law, 2011, 2(2): 201–205.

# France

# 18

Martina Isola and Guillaume Couet

## 18.1 Introduction

The French copyright regime has always been deeply rooted in natural law principles and has always been more favorable to the rights of authors compared to those of users.

As Mr. Desbois highlights, "in accordance with the French tradition [imbued with individualism], the French lawmaker rejected the view that works of the mind should be timely protected to stimulate literary and artistic activity,"[1] and as expressed in a study of 2003, "a single country appeared to be an exception to the recognition of the balance of interests [between authors' rights of those of users] which is paramount to copyright legislation: France. French Copyright Law, which is based on the respect of authors' works of the mind is focused on the latter."[2]

Indeed, if it has always been accepted that the law shall preserve a balance between the interests of authors and those of users, French legislation never provided for a "catch-all" exception—*i.e.*, a general exception that can be applied in various cases significantly different from each other—but set an exhaustive list of exclusions or limitations to authors' rights.

[1] H. Desbois, Le droit d'auteur en France, Dalloz, 3rd ed, 1978, No. 449–450, p. 538.

[2] A. Lepage, Overview of exceptions and limitations to copyright in the digital environment, e-Copyright Bulletin, January–March 2003 UNESCO.

M. Isola (✉)
Association Française d'Etude de la concurrence (AFEC), Paris, France

G. Couet
Association Française d'Etude de la concurrence (AFEC/AFEC Jeunes), Paris, France





B. Kilpatrick et al. (eds.), *Antitrust Analysis of Online Sales Platforms & Copyright Limitations and Exceptions*, LIDC Contributions on Antitrust Law, Intellectual Property and Unfair Competition,
https://doi.org/10.1007/978-3-319-71419-6_18

Moreover, until 1994, the only provision dealing with the exceptions to copyright was Article 41 of the Law on Copyright of 1957,[3] which recognized only four limitations to authors' rights, based on the safeguard of fundamental rights and freedoms of users (users' freedom of expression and right to privacy and the need to promote the dissemination of knowledge and culture).[4]

This article was codified under Article L. 112-5 of the French Intellectual Property Code (hereinafter "the IPC") by Law No. 92-597 of July 1, 1992.[5]

With the transposition into French law of the provisions of Directive 2001/29 of May 22, 2001,[6] by Law No. 2006-961 of August 1, 2006[7] (hereinafter "the Law of 2006"), the economic-based approach of copyright was incorporated under French law and the number of the exceptions to copyright substantially increased. These exceptions are currently listed under Article L. 122-5 of the IPC.[8]

---

[3] Law No. 57-298 of 11 March 1957 "*sur la propriété littéraire et artistique*".

[4] Article 41 of the Law on Copyright of 1957 used to provide that:

> Once a work has been disclosed, the author may not prohibit:
>
> 1°. Private and gratuitous performances carried out exclusively within the family circle;
>
> 2°. Copies or reproductions reserved strictly for the private use of the copier and not intended for collective use, with the exception of copies of works of art to be used for purposes identical with those for which the original work was created;
>
> 3°. On condition that the name of the author and the source are clearly stated:
>
> Analyses and short quotations justified by the critical, polemic, educational, scientific or informatory nature of the work in which they are incorporated;
>
> Press reviews;
>
> Dissemination, even in their entirety, through the press or by broadcasting, as current news, of speeches intended for the public made in political, administrative, judicial or academic gatherings, as well as in public meetings of a political nature and at official ceremonies;
>
> 4°. Parody, pastiche and caricature, observing the rules of the genre.

[5] Law No. 92-597 of 1 July 1992 "*relative au code de la propriété intellectuelle*".

[6] Directive 2001/29 of the European Parliament and of the Council of 22 May 2001 on the harmonisation of certain aspects of copyright and related rights in the information society, OJ 2001 L 167, p. 10.

[7] Law No. 2006-961 of 1 August 2006 "*relative au droit d'auteur et aux droits voisins dans la société de l'information*".

[8] According to Article L. 122-5 of the IPC:

> Once a work has been disclosed, the author may not prohibit:
>
> 1°. Private and gratuitous performances carried out exclusively within the family circle;
>
> 2°. Copies or reproductions reserved strictly for the private use of the copier and not intended for collective use, with the exception of copies of works of art to be used for purposes identical with those for which the original work was created and copies of software other than backup copies made in accordance with paragraph II of Article L. 122-6-1, as well as copies or reproductions of an electronic database;
>
> 3°. On condition that the name of the author and the source are clearly stated:
>
> a) Analyses and short quotations justified by the critical, polemic, educational, scientific or informatory nature of the work in which they are incorporated;

Besides, French law does not "officially recognize that copyright entails a *quid pro quo* in favour of society"[9] and excludes that the abovementioned exceptions can grant rights to their beneficiaries.[10]

---

b) Press reviews;

c) Dissemination, even in their entirety, through the press or by broadcasting, as current news, of speeches intended for the public made in political, administrative, judicial or academic gatherings, as well as in public meetings of a political nature and at official ceremonies;

d) Complete or partial reproductions of works of graphic or three-dimensional art intended to appear in the catalogue of a judicial sale held in France, in the form of the copies of the said catalogue made available to the public prior to the sale for the sole purpose of describing the works of art offered for sale.

e) The representation or the reproduction of excerpts of works, subject that the works are designed for educational purposes and partitions of music, for the exclusive purposes of illustration in the framework of teaching and research, including for the development and dissemination of examination subjects or of competitions organized in the extension of the lessons to the exclusion of any activity playful or recreational, when this representation or this reproduction is intended, in particular by means of a digital work space, to a public composed predominantly of pupils, students, teachers or researchers directly concerned by teaching, training or research activity requiring this representation or reproduction, that it is not the subject of any publication or dissemination to a third party to the public thus constituted, that the use of this representation or this reproduction does not give rise to any commercial exploitation and that it is offset by a negotiated remuneration on a lump sum basis without prejudice of the assignment of the right of reprographic reproduction referred to in Article L. 122-10;

4°. Parody, pastiche and caricature, observing the rules of the genre.

5°. Acts necessary to access the contents of an electronic database for the purposes of and within the limits of the use provided by contract.

6° The temporary reproduction presenting a transitional or accessory character, when it is an integral and essential part of a technical process and that it is for the sole purpose of enabling the lawful use of the work or its transmission between third parties by way of a network involving an intermediary; however, this temporary reproduction that can only bear on works other than software and databases must not have economic value of own;

7°The reproduction and the representation by legal persons and by the establishments open to the public, such as libraries, archives, documentation centers and cultural spaces multimedia, with a view to a strictly personal consultation of the work by persons with one or more impairments of motor functions, physical, sensory, mental, cognitive or psychic and prevented, the fact of these deficiencies, access to the work in the form in which the author makes it available to the public;

8° The reproduction of a work and its representation made for conservation purposes or intended to preserve the conditions of its consultation for the purposes of research or private study by individuals, in the premises of the establishment and on dedicated terminals by libraries accessible to the public by museums, or by archive services, subject that they seek no economic or commercial benefit;

9° The reproduction or representation, complete or partial, of a graphic, plastic or architectural art work, by way of written, audio-visual or online press, in an exclusive purpose of immediate information and in direct relationship with the latter, subject to indicate clearly the name of the author.

The first paragraph of this 9° does not apply to works, including photographic or illustration, which aim themselves to account for the information;

Software exceptions set forth in Directive 91/250 of May 14, 1991,[11] were transposed into Articles L. 122-6 and L. 122-6-1 of the IPC[12] by Law No. 94-361 of May 10, 1994.[13]

---

10° The copies or digital reproductions made from a lawful source, in view of the exploration of texts and data included in or associated with the scientific literature to the needs of the public research, to the exclusion of any commercial purpose. A decree lays down the conditions in which the exploration of texts and data is implemented, as well as the modalities of conservation and of communication of the files products in term of research activities for which they have been produced; these files are data from the research;

11° The reproductions and representations of architectural works and sculptures, placed permanently on the public road, carried out by natural persons, to the exclusion of any use of a commercial nature

The reproductions or representations which, inter alia by their number or their format, would not be in strict proportion with the exclusive purpose of immediate information or who would not be in direct relationship with the latter give rise to remuneration of authors based on the agreements or the tariffs in force in the professional sectors concerned.

The exceptions listed in this Article shall not affect the normal exploitation of the work or unreasonably prejudice the legitimate interests of the author.

The modalities for the application of this Article, in particular the characteristics and conditions of the distribution of the documents referred to in d) of 3°, are specified by a decree of the Council of State.

[9] A. Lepage, Overview of exceptions and limitations to copyright in the digital environment, e-Copyright Bulletin, January–March 2003 UNESCO.

[10] A. Lucas, Fasc. 1248, Droits des auteurs. Exceptions au droit exclusif, 14 April 2010.

[11] Council Directive 91/250 of 14 May 1991 on the legal protection of computer programs, OJ 1991 L 122, p. 42–46.

[12] According to Article L. 122-6 of the IPC:

Subject to the provisions of Article L122-6-1, the exploitation right belonging to the author of the software shall include the right to do or to authorize:

1°. The permanent or temporary reproduction of software by any means and in any form, in part or in whole. Insofar as loading, displaying, running, transmission or storage of the software necessitate such reproduction, such acts shall be possible only with the authorization of the author;

2°. The translation, adaptation, arrangement or any other alteration of software and the reproduction of the results thereof;

3°. The placing on the market for consideration or gratuitously, including rental, of the software or of copies thereof by any process. However, the first sale of a copy of software on the territory of a Member State of the European Community or of a State party to the agreement on the European Economic Area by the author or with his consent shall exhaust the right of placing on the market of that copy in all Member States, with the exception of the right to authorize further rental of a copy.

According to Article L. 122-6-1 of the IPC:

I. The acts referred to in items 1 and 2 of Article L122-6 shall not require authorization by the author where they are necessary for the use of the software by the person entitled to use it in accordance with its intended purpose, including for error correction. However, an author may by contract reserve the right to correct errors and stipulate any special conditions to which shall be subject the acts referred to in items 1 and 2 of Article L122-6, necessary to enable the entitled person to use the software in accordance with its intended purpose.

## 18.2 The Protection Granted by Copyright to the Authors of Works of the Mind

### 18.2.1 Works of the Mind Protected

Pursuant to Article L. 112-1 of the IPC, "rights of authors in all works of the mind [shall be protected], whatever their kind, form of expression, merit or purpose."

Articles L. 112-2 ff of the IPC[14] provide a nonlimitative list of examples of works of the mind protected by copyright.

---

II. A person having the right to use the software may make a backup copy where such is necessary to ensure use of the software.

III. A person having the right to use the software shall be entitled, without the authorization of the author, to observe, study or test the functioning of the software in order to determine the ideas and principles which underlie any element of the software if he does so while performing any of the acts of loading, displaying, running, transmitting or storing the software which he is entitled to do.

IV. Reproduction of the code of the software or translation of the form of that code shall not require the authorization of the author where reproduction or translation within the meaning of item 1 or 2 of Article L. 122-6 is indispensable for obtaining the information necessary to achieve the interoperability of independently created software with other software, providing that the following conditions are met:

1°. These acts are performed by a person entitled to use a copy of the software or on his behalf by a person authorized to do so;

2°. The information necessary to achieve interoperability has not previously been readily available to the persons referred to in item 1, above;

3°.and these acts are confined to the parts of the original software which are necessary to achieve interoperability.

The information thus obtained may not:

1°. Be used for goals other than to achieve the interoperability of the independently created software;

2°. Be given to others, except where necessary for the interoperability of the independently created software;

3°. Or be used for the development, production or marketing of software substantially similar in its expression, or for any other act which infringes copyright.

V. This Article may not be interpreted in such a way as to prejudice the normal exploitation of the software or to cause unreasonable prejudice to the author's legitimate interests.

Any stipulation contrary to the provisions of paragraphs II, III and IV of this Article shall be null and void.

[13] Law No. 94-361 of 10 May 1994 "*portant mise en oeuvre de la directive (C. E. E.) n° 91-250 du Conseil des communautés européennes en date du 14 mai 1991 concernant la protection juridique des programmes d'ordinateur et modifiant le code de la propriété intellectuelle*".

[14] According to Article L. 112-2 of the IPC:

Shall be considered works of the mind (…):

1° Books, pamphlets and other literary, artistic and scientific writings;

2° Lectures, addresses, sermons, pleadings and other works of such nature;

3° Dramatic or dramatico-musical works;

Article L. 112-3 of the IPC further provides that "[t]he authors of translations, adaptations, transformations or arrangements of works of the mind shall enjoy the protection afforded by this Code, without prejudice to the rights of the author of the original work. The same shall apply to the authors of anthologies or collections of miscellaneous works or data, such as databases, which, by reason of the selection or the arrangement of their contents, constitute intellectual creations. Database means a collection of independent works, data or other materials, arranged in a systematic or methodical way, and capable of being individually assessed by electronic or any other means."

Finally, Article L. 112-4 of the IPC states that "[t]he title of a work of the mind shall be protected in the same way as the work itself where it is original in character. Such title may not be used, even if the work is no longer protected under Articles L123-1 to L123-3, to distinguish a work of the same kind if such use is liable to create confusion."

### 18.2.2 Rights Conferred to the Authors

According to Article L. 111-1 of the IPC, "[t]he author of a work of the mind shall enjoy in that work, by the mere fact of its creation, an exclusive incorporeal property right which shall be enforceable against all persons."

This "exclusive incorporeal property right" includes both attributes of an intellectual and moral nature, the "moral right," and attributes of an economic nature, the "exclusive rights," whose benefit and scope depend on the nature of the work of the mind and the number of the authors who participated in its creation.

Article L. 113-2 of the IPC distinguishes four kinds of works of the mind and two kinds of authors:

---

4° Choreographic works, circus acts and feats and dumb-show works, the acting form of which is set down in writing or in other manner;

5° Musical compositions with or without words;

6° Cinematographic works and other works consisting of sequences of moving images, with or without sound, together referred to as audio-visual works;

7° Works of drawing, painting, architecture, sculpture, engraving and lithography;

8° Graphical and typographical works;

9° Photographic works and works produced by techniques analogous to photography;

10° Works of applied art;

11° Illustrations, geographical maps;

12° Plans, sketches and three-dimensional works relative to geography, topography, architecture and science;

13° Software, including the preparatory design material;

14° Creations of the seasonal industries of dress and articles of fashion. Industries which, by reason of the demands of fashion, frequently renew the form of their products, particularly the making of dresses, furs, underwear, embroidery, fashion, shoes, gloves, leather goods, the manufacture of fabrics of striking novelty or of special use in high fashion dressmaking, the products of manufacturers of articles of fashion and of footwear and the manufacture of fabrics for upholstery shall be deemed to be seasonal industries.

- individual work, created by a single author;
- work of collaboration, *i.e.* a "work in the creation of which more than one natural person has participated";
- composite work, *i.e.* a "new work in which a pre-existing work is incorporated without the collaboration of the author of the latter work";
- collective work, *i.e.* a "work created at the initiative of a natural or legal person who edits it, publishes it and discloses it under his direction and name and in which the personal contributions of the various authors who participated in its production are merged in the overall work for which they were conceived, without it being possible to attribute to each author a separate right in the work as created."

Concerning individual work, Article L. 113-1 of the IPC states that "[a]uthorship shall belong, unless proved otherwise, to the person or persons under whose name the work has been disclosed."

Pursuant to Article L. 113-3 of the IPC, joint authors of a work of collaboration share identical rights and can only use them by mutual agreement. When the contribution of the authors is of a different kind, and unless otherwise agreed between parties, each of the author may separately exploit his/her own personal contribution, without prejudice to the exploitation of the collaborative work.

Pursuant to Article L. 113-4 of the IPC, a composite work is the property of its author, subject to the rights of the author of the preexisting work.

Pursuant to Article L. 113-5 of the IPC, a collective work is the property of the natural or legal person under whose name it has been disclosed, and the author's rights shall vest in such person, unless provided otherwise.

#### 18.2.2.1 Moral Right

Pursuant to Articles L. 121-1 et seq. of the IPC, moral right grants authors the right to the integrity of their name, authorship, and work. This right cannot be undermined, whether a user benefits from copyright exception set forth in Article L. 122-5 of the IPC.

Attached to the person of the author, moral right, which is perpetual, inalienable, and imprescriptible, can be transmitted to authors' heir(s).

#### 18.2.2.2 Exclusive Rights

Pursuant to Articles L. 122-1 et seq. of the IPC, exclusive rights confer to authors the rights of reproduction, the right of communication to the public, and the right of distribution.

Exclusive rights, which may be transferred or licensed, lasts for the lifetime of authors, plus 70 years after their death. Copyrighted works of the mind can be used without authors' authorization or consent only under the limitative list of exceptions set forth in Article L. 122-5 of the IPC.

- Communication to the Public
  The right of communication to the public, or the right of representation/performance, grants authors the right to communicate their works of the mind to the

public by any mean, namely by public recitation, dramatic performance, public representation, public screening and transmission of the broadcast work in a public space, and broadcasting.

- Reproduction Right
  On the one hand, the right of reproduction grants authors of work of the mind the right to physically fix them by any process enabling their communication to the public, even indirectly.
  Indeed, according to Article L. 122-3 of the IPC:

> Reproduction shall consist in the physical fixation of a work by any process permitting it to be communicated to the public in an indirect way.
>
> It may be carried out, in particular, by printing, drawing, engraving, photography, casting and all processes of the graphical and plastic arts, mechanical, cinematographic or magnetic recording.
>
> In the case of works of architecture, reproduction shall also consist in the repeated execution of a plan or of a standard project.

On the other hand, the right of reproduction grants authors of works of the mind the right to prevent any unauthorized reproduction of their work since, according to Article L. 122-4 of the IPC, "[a]ny complete or partial performance or reproduction made without the consent of the author or of his successors in title or assigns shall be unlawful."

The same solution applies to translation, adaptation or transformation, arrangement or reproduction by any technique or process whatsoever.

Examples of copyright infringements are especially provided for in the IPC, such as reproduction, performance, dissemination, translation, adaptation, transformation, or arrangement, by any means whatsoever, of a work of the mind without the consent of its author. Trafficking, exporting, or importing infringing works also constitute copyright infringement.[15]

According to Article L. 335-2 of the IPC, "[a]ny edition of writings, musical compositions, drawings, paintings or other printed or engraved production made in whole or in part regardless of the laws and regulations governing the ownership of authors constitute an infringement or an offence."

Infringement in France of works of the mind published in France or abroad shall be liable to 3-year imprisonment and a maximum fine of EUR 300,000. The sale, exportation, and importation of infringing works are subject to the same sentence.

Where offences are committed in organized group, the sentence may be increased to 5-year imprisonment and a maximum fine of EUR 500,000.

Article L. 335-2 of the IPC further provides that any reproduction, performance, or dissemination of a work of the mind, by any means whatsoever, in violation of the author's rights, as defined and regulated by law, shall also constitute an infringement.

[15] See: INTERNET LAW – Basics of Copyrights Laws in France, IBLS Editorial Department.

The violation of any of the rights of an author of software, as defined in Article L. 122-6 of the IPC, and any total or partial uptake of a cinematographic or audiovisual work in movie theaters also constitute an infringement.

Article L. 335-2-1 of the IPC provides a 3-year imprisonment and a maximum EUR 300,000 fine for editing, making available to the public, or communicating to the public, knowingly and in whatever form, software clearly destined to the public of unauthorized works or of protected objects, and encouraging knowingly, including through an advertisement, the use of such software.

According to Article L. 335-4 of the IPC, any fixation, reproduction, communication, or making available to the public, on payment or free of charge, or any televisual broadcasting of a performance, a phonogram, a videogram, or a program made without authorization of the performer, that of the phonogram or videogram producer, or that of the audiovisual communication enterprise, where such authorization is required, shall be liable to 3-year imprisonment and a maximum fine of EUR 300,000.

Importation or exportation of phonograms or videograms made without the authorization of the producer or the performer, where such authorization is required, shall be subject to the same penalties.

Where the offenses provided for under this article are committed by an organized criminal group, the penalties will be increased to 5-year imprisonment and a maximum fine of EUR 500,000.

Failure to respect the author's moral rights can also constitute an infringement or an offense. Civil and criminal actions may be brought before courts either by the author or its licensee.

- Distribution

Under French law, the legal status of the right of distribution was complex until the transposition of the provisions of Directive 2001/29.

Indeed, except for software for which Article L. 122-6 of the IPC expressly recognizes a right of distribution, and the correlating principle of exhaustion, there was no express legal basis for the distribution right of other works of the mind.

To compensate for this lack of legal basis, French courts recognize the right of reproduction and Article L. 131-3 of the IPC, by extension, grants authors the right of destination over their works of the mind, which entitles them to authorize or prohibit any use of the reproductions of the works and, consequently, the right to oppose the distribution of tangible copies of copyrighted works of the mind.[16]

Regarding the distribution of copies of works of the mind subject to exhaustion, the provisions of Article 4 of Directive 2001/29 were transposed under Article L. 122-3-1 of the IPC.

According to this article, the first sale in a given country of the EU or the European Economic Area of a copy of a work of the mind by the author or the rights holder exhausts the distribution right within the whole EU and EEA. The copyright

[16] Court of Cassation, 1st Civil Chamber, 22 March 1988.

exhaustion is exclusively applicable to tangible copies of a work and affects only the distribution right.

For the exhaustion of copyright to be recognized, two conditions shall be fulfilled:

- a first marketing of the work of the mind in the territory of the European Economic Area;
- the consent of the author of the work of the mind to this circulation/marketing.[17]

The exhaustion of copyright is limited to the *material copies* of the work of the mind and has no effect on authors' moral right.[18]

Likewise, the rental and lending of copies of works of the mind are subject to the authorization of authors.[19]

Concerning software, the exhaustion of copyright is set forth in Article L. 122-6 of the IPC, which imposes the same conditions as Article L. 122-3-1 of the IPC.

Article L. 122-6 of the IPC was applied for the first time by the Creteil Commercial Court[20] on November 12, 1996, which ruled that the author cannot, after the first marketing of the work of the mind, impose conditions for the marketing based on copyright, except for the implementation of contractual agreements.[21]

However, the exhaustion of rights is excluded in respect of a license to use software.[22]

For example, in the case of a sale of software with a license explaining the terms of use, the principle of exhaustion is applicable, but the resale shall be accompanied by the restrictions resulting from the license of use.[23]

In any case, case law limits the exhaustion of rights to the sale of the "support" of the software and not the software itself.

In its decision *UsedSoft/Oracle*,[24] the Court of Justice of the European Union extended the exhaustion of rights to software marketed in an *intangible form*.

[17] See for further analysis the LIDC French report of 2014 on the exhaustion of rights, Turin Congress. http://www.ligue.org/uploads/documents/2014RapportBfrancais.pdf.

[18] See for further analysis the LIDC French report of 2014, Turin Congress. http://www.ligue.org/uploads/documents/2014RapportBfrancais.pdf.

[19] Court of Cassation, Commercial Chamber, 27 April 2004, No. 99/18464, *Pen c/ Nintendo*.

[20] Créteil Commercial Court, 12 November 1996.

[21] See for further analysis the LIDC French report of 2014, Turin Congress. http://www.ligue.org/uploads/documents/2014RapportBfrancais.pdf.

[22] Paris Court of Appeal, 23 September 1997, No. 93/491, 93/636, 93/13558, 93/2562; See for further analysis the LIDC French report of 2014 on the exhaustion of rights, Turin Congress. http://www.ligue.org/uploads/documents/2014RapportBfrancais.pdf.

[23] Douai Court of Appeal, 26 January 2009, No. 07/02368.

[24] CJEU, 3 July 2012, case C-128/11, *UsedSoft GmbH v Oracle International Corp*, ECLI:EU:C:2012:407.

This ruling was implicitly applied by the First Civil Chamber of Court of Cassation in a case on musical works. The latter considered that the qualification of the phonogram was independent of whether a tangible support exists and, based on this fact, ruled that the permissions given to performers included the disposal by downloading.

Hence, the Court of Cassation seems to extend the position adopted by the Court of Justice of the European Union, at least regarding music files distributed online.[25] This solution was confirmed by the decision of the Court of Justice of the European Union of January 22, 2015, according to which:

> Article 4(2) of Directive 2001/29/EC of the European Parliament and of the Council of 22 May 2001 on the harmonization of certain aspects of copyright and related rights in the information society must be interpreted as meaning that the rule of exhaustion of the distribution right set out in Article 4(2) of Directive 2001/29 does not apply in a situation where a reproduction of a protected work, after having been marketed in the European Union with the copyright holder's consent, has undergone an alteration of its medium, such as the transfer of that reproduction from a paper poster onto a canvas, and is placed on the market again in its new form.[26]

## 18.3 Exclusions and Limitations to Copyright Under French Law

### 18.3.1 Nature and Scope of the Exceptions to Copyright

Since the provisions set forth in the IPC already balance authors' right with users' fundamental rights—such as freedom of expression, privacy, the right to education—there is no fundamental rights under French law allowing the use of works of the mind without the author's consent.[27]

However, author's discretionary use of copyright can be deemed to be abusive, and copyright cannot grant immunity to authors from violations of users' rights.[28] Even economic rights, *i.e.* competition or consumer law, which are not considered in balancing the exceptions, can under specific circumstances limit the exercise of the rights by authors.[29]

---

[25] Court of Cassation, 1st Civil Chamber, 11 September 2013, No. 12/17794; See for further analysis the LIDC French report of 2014, Turin Congress. http://www.ligue.org/uploads/documents/2014RapportBfrancais.pdf.

[26] CJEU, case C-419/13, *Art & Allposters International BV v Stichting Pictoright*, ECLI:EU:C:2015:27.

[27] For an application, the Court of Appeal judged that there is no general enforceability of Article 10 of the ECHR to the author, because the right that it recognizes is already taken into account in the limits and exceptions provided by the law, Paris Court of Appeal, 30 May 2001.

[28] C. Caron, Abus de droit et droit d'auteur: Publications de l'IRPI, vol. 17, Litec, 1998, n° 21 to 62.

[29] A. Lucas, Fasc. 1248, Droits des auteurs. Exceptions au droit exclusif, 14 Avril 2010.

Parties can by mutual agreement modulate the scope of the exceptions or put them aside.[30] However, this solution cannot be applied to software since, according to Article L. 122-6-1 of the IPC, it shall be considered null and void any stipulation contrary to the provisions concerning backup copy, analysis, and decompilation.

## 18.3.2 General Principles

Regarding the granting of the exceptions, the following must be noted:

- The list of exceptions to copyright set forth in Article L. 122-5 of the IPC is exhaustive.
- All conditions laid down by the IPC shall be met, in an approach in *favorem auctoris*, meaning that those are of strict interpretation.
- The exceptions shall pass the "triple test."

### 18.3.2.1 The Exhaustive List of Copyright Exceptions Set Forth in Article L. 122-5 of the IPC

Despite the list of the exceptions sets forth in Article L. 122-5 of the IPC being substantially increased with the transposition into French law of the provisions of Directive 2001/29, this list remains closed, and any unauthorized use of works of the mind falling outside the scope of the exceptions is counterfeiting.

However, French courts exceptionally circumvent this principle by relying on the "accessory reproductions" theory.[31]

"Accessory reproductions" are works of the mind representing another work of the mind, such as photographs representing an architectural work. Since the object of the work of the mind it's the principal attractiveness, it is not an infringement of the copyrighted work, and as such its reproduction and representation are not subject to the exclusive rights of its author, who cannot oppose its copyright.

Moreover, French courts recognized in 2011 the "accidental inclusion" exception, ruling that the legislator took into account this exception when transposing Directive 2001/29, even if it ultimately did not expressly codify it.

The Court of Cassation held that a representation of a work in a documentary was never represented for itself but only in an accessory manner to the main subject, and that it should have been therefore regarded as an *accidental inclusion*, and underlined that the "accidental inclusion" exception, representing a limitation to the monopoly of the right of the author, is foreseen by Directive 2001/29 and that this

[30] See, to that effect, P.-Y. Gautier, Propriété littéraire et artistique; C. Alleaume, La contractualisation des exceptions, in Droit d'auteur et numérique: Propr. intell. 2007, p. 436–442, spéc. p. 438; Paris Court of First instance, 1st Civil Chamber, 30 April 1997.

[31] Nanterre Court of First Instance, 12 November 1997; Lyon Court of First Instance, 4 April 2001; Lyon Court of First Instance, 20 March 2003; Court of Cassation, 1st Civil Chamber, 12 June 2001; Paris Court of First Instance, 12 July 1990; Court of Cassation, 1st Civil Chamber, 15 March 2005; Bordeaux Court of First Instance, 13 June 2006.

provision was considered by the legislator in its preparatory works, even if not literally codified in the IPC.[32]

#### 18.3.2.2 The Strict Interpretation of the Exceptions

The exceptions shall be strictly interpreted.[33] Consequently, French courts only grant the exceptions specifically provided by the law but also assess their conditions of application in an "author favourable manner."[34]

Drawing on the case law of the Court of Justice of the European Union,[35] certain scholars underline that the hypothesis in which the exclusive right of authors is paralyzed shall be strictly interpreted.[36]

However, this principle does not imply that the exceptions shall be confine to their narrowest limits but implies that they shall be applied according to their "reason being."[37] According to the Court of Justice of the European Union, the rule of strict interpretation must not prevent to respect the "useful effect" of the exception and to respect its purpose.[38]

#### 18.3.2.3 The Transposition of the "Triple Test" into French Law

According to Article 5.5 of Directive 2001/29, "[t]he exceptions and limitations provided (…) shall only be applied in certain special cases which do not conflict with a normal exploitation of the work or other subject-matter and do not unreasonably prejudiced the legitimate interests of the right holder."

Hence, to be granted, all the exceptions shall:

- only be applied in certain special cases and shall not result in a general open-ended exemption from the obligation to protect the right concerned;
- not conflict with a normal exploitation of the work of other subject matter;
- not unreasonably prejudice the legitimate interests of the right holder; the principle of reasonable proportionality should prevail.[39]

The French Legislator introduced the "triple test" into French law in a way that this test became a "double test" since according to Article L. 122-5 of the IPC, "[t]he exceptions listed in this Article shall not affect the normal exploitation of the work or unreasonably prejudice the legitimate interests of the author."

Consequently, to be granted, the exceptions shall not conflict with a normal exploitation of the work of the mind and unreasonably prejudice the legitimate

---

[32] Court of Cassation, 1st Civil Chamber, 12 May 2011.

[33] Court of Cassation, 1st Civil Chamber, 3 March 1992.

[34] Paris Correctional Court, 24 January 1984; Paris Court of Appeal, 25 March 1982.

[35] CJEU, Case C-5/08, *Infopaq International A/S c/ Danske Dagblades Forening*.

[36] A. Lucas, Fasc. 1248, Droits des auteurs. Exceptions au droit exclusif, 14 April 2010.

[37] *Idem.*

[38] CJEU, Case C-403/08, *Football Association Premier League et a. c/ QC Leisure*.

[39] For further analysis, see WIPO Guide and Glossary, pp. 59–60; Senftleben, pp. 210–243; Ficsor, pp. 9–10.

interests of the author. French courts can refuse the user of a work of the mind the benefit of an exception even though the "internal" conditions are met.

The transposition of the "triple test" into French law received a mitigated reception from the doctrine.

Firstly, it was stressed out that the "triple test" was not a substantive rule to be transposed into national law but rather a methodological indication framing the application of the exceptions, which transposition was not imposed by Directive 2001/29.[40]

For other scholars, unlike international treaties, Directive 2001/29 does not expressly oblige Member States to transpose the exceptions but merely states that the latter are applicable under national law provided the conditions of the triple test are met.[41] Thus, the question is whether the "triple test" is intended to Member States or national courts. In the first hypothesis, the provisions of Directive 2001/29 should not be transposed, as it was the case in Germany, Belgium, Denmark, Italy, and the Netherlands. In the second hypothesis, the provisions of Directive 2001/29, harmonizing national legislation, shall be transposed and applied by national courts.[42]

Secondly, it was highlighted that the "triple test" has become, under French law, a "double test" since Article L. 122-5 of the IPC did not transpose the condition according to which the balance between authors' and users' rights shall only be assessed in specific cases, even if it is the first condition to be met under the "triple test," as provided for in international and European texts.

Thirdly, scholars are also critical of the fact that the notions of "normal exploitation" and "undue prejudice" are blurry and therefore do not frame the power of the judge but give him, on the contrary, more power on the interpretation of the exceptions.[43]

Fourthly, the practical application of the test remains open. Traditionally, the triple test is considered as a tool against the exceptions to the single service of the right holder; meanwhile, a part of the doctrine has proposed intermediate interpretations of the triple test, which lead to a reversal of its application in favor of the beneficiaries of exceptions.[44] The criteria of the triple test renew in any case the economic approach of exceptions in French law.

As an example of the case law, it has been held that the private copy exception cannot be an obstacle to the insertion, in the support reproducing a protected work, of technical measures intending to protect the work from copying when it would

---

[40] P. Gaudrat, « Propriété littéraire et artistique », Dalloz. 3rd Edition, January 2016.

[41] A. Lucas, Fasc. 1248, Droits des auteurs. Exceptions au droit exclusif, 14 April 2010.

[42] T. C. Vinje, Should We Begin Digging Copyright's Grave, p. 553; M. SENFTLEBEN, Copyright, Limitations and the Three-Step Test, p. 280.

[43] See among others: Ph. Gaudrat, "Propriété littéraire et artistique", Dalloz; Ph. GAUDRAT, "Le droit d'auteur au lendemain de la transposition: titre 1er de la loi no 2006-691 du 1er août 2006, V. droit commun", RTD com. 2007. 107.

[44] Minutes of the meeting of 15 May 2013 of the Commission on intellectual property of the Bar of Paris, directed by V. Téchené, Editor in Chief of Lexbase Hebdo – private edition.

have the "effect of impairing the normal exploitation of the work," which must be assessed considering the economic impact that such a copy may have in the context of the digital environment.[45] However, this judgment has been criticized heavily by some scholars as it blurs and does not provide an appropriately framed application of the test.[46]

### 18.3.3 The Specific Regime and Logic Behind Each Exception

Since the exceptions to copyright are an "autonomous notion which regime and scope shall be similarly applied in all Member States,"[47] national courts shall interpret the regime and the scope of the exceptions provided for in their national law in the light of the provision of Directive 2001/29 and the case law of the Court of Justice of the European Union.

A distinction is drawn between commercial and noncommercial uses of works of the mind. Article L. 122-5 of the IPC indicates for each exception whether the ban of noncommercial purposes is a requirement to benefit from that exception.

French copyright law provides for exceptions relating both to the "reproduction right" and to the "right of communication to the public."[48]

Specific exceptions to reproduction rights are those provided by L. 122-5, 6° IPC, with the exclusion of software and databases:

> Once a work has been disclosed, the author may not prohibit (…) [t]he temporary reproduction presenting a transitional or accessory character, when it is an integral and essential part of a technical process and that it is for the sole purpose of enabling the lawful use of the work or its transmission between third parties by way of a network involving an intermediary; however, this temporary reproduction that can only bear on works other than software and databases must not have economic value of own.

Specific exceptions to the right of representation are provided for representation in the family circle, for private representation, and for private copy, as set forth in Article L. 122-5, 1° and 2°, of the IPC:

> Once a work has been disclosed, the author may not prohibit:
>
> 1°. Private and gratuitous performances carried out exclusively within the family circle;
>
> 2°. Copies or reproductions reserved strictly for the private use of the copier and not intended for collective use, with the exception of copies of works of art to be used for purposes identical with those for which the original work was created and copies of software other than backup copies made in accordance with paragraph II of Article L. 122-6-1, as well as copies or reproductions of an electronic database.

---

[45] Court of Cassation, 1st Civil chamber, 28 February 2006, *Mulholland Drive*.

[46] Ph. Gaudrat, « Propriété littéraire et artistique », Dalloz.

[47] CJEU, case C-145/10, *Eva-Maria Painer v Standard VerlagsGmbH and Others*, ECR 2011 I 12533 and case C-201/13, *Johan Deckmyn and Vrijheidsfonds VZW v Helena* Vandersteen.

[48] A. Lucas, Fasc. 1248, Droits des auteurs. Exceptions au droit exclusif, 14 April 2010.

A set of common exceptions to the rights of reproduction and representation is set forth in Article L. 122-5, 3°, of the IPC:

> Once a work has been disclosed, the author may not prohibit (…) on condition that the name of the author and the source are clearly stated:
>
> a) Analyses and short quotations justified by the critical, polemic, educational, scientific or informatory nature of the work in which they are incorporated;
>
> b) Press reviews;
>
> c) Dissemination, even in their entirety, through the press or by broadcasting, as current news, of speeches intended for the public made in political, administrative, judicial or academic gatherings, as well as in public meetings of a political nature and at official ceremonies;
>
> d) Complete or partial reproductions of works of graphic or three-dimensional art intended to appear in the catalogue of a judicial sale held in France, in the form of the copies of the said catalogue made available to the public prior to the sale for the sole purpose of describing the works of art offered for sale.
>
> e) The representation or the reproduction of excerpts of works, subject that the works are designed for educational purposes and partitions of music, for the exclusive purposes of illustration in the framework of teaching and research, including for the development and dissemination of examination subjects or of competitions organized in the extension of the lessons to the exclusion of any activity playful or recreational, when this representation or this reproduction is intended, in particular by means of a digital work space, to a public composed predominantly of pupils, students, teachers or researchers directly concerned by teaching, training or research activity requiring this representation or reproduction, that it is not the subject of any publication or dissemination to a third party to the public thus constituted, that the use of this representation or this reproduction does not give rise to any commercial exploitation and that it is offset by a negotiated remuneration on a lump sum basis without prejudice of the assignment of the right of reprographic reproduction referred to in article L. 122-10.

Although this exception was initially thought in contemplation of the right of reproduction, it also covers the right of representation since the Court of Cassation rules that "the integral representation of a work (…) cannot be analysed as a short quotation"[49] and the Paris Court of Appeal states that "it is true that the right of quotation applies both to the right of reproduction and to the right of representation."[50]

Finally, among the exceptions, some allow full reproduction of the work, whereas others only allow partial one. Some allow complete borrowing of the work, while others require an additional personal contribution of the "borrower."

Usually, the exceptions do not provide for compensation in favor of the copyright owner, except for the exception regarding private copies and for the so-called "pedagogic exception."

---

[49] Court of Cassation, 1st Civil Chamber, 4 July 1995.

[50] Paris Court of Appeal, 4th Chamber, 30 May 2001.

#### 18.3.3.1 Representation Within the Family Circle

According to Article L. 122-5, 1°, of the IPC, "[o]nce a work has been disclosed, the author may not prohibit (…) private and gratuitous performances carried out exclusively within the family circle."

For this exception to be granted, the representations of the work of the mind shall be

- undertaken exclusively within the "family circle," which encompasses only relatives, close friends, and intimates;
- free and without any direct or indirect commercial purpose (no-entry fee, entertainment expenses, participation, *etc.*).[51]

These two conditions are cumulative.

Consequently, customers of kindergarten cannot be considered as falling into the scope of the "family circle."[52] Similarly, the projection of cinematographic works without the consent of the author, in a private place, on a periodic basis, and with third parties is deemed to be counterfeiting even if no financial contribution is sought.[53]

The noncommercial purpose condition is deemed fulfilled when the members of the "family circle" are not called upon to contribute to the representation costs.

Thus, the event-oriented character of an event organized by a famous fashion house for the anniversary of its creation does not fall under the scope of the "family circle," and tending indirectly to profit making does not respond to the requirement of noncommercial proposes.[54] The free nature of the representation is not a sufficient, but rather a necessary, condition to benefit from the exception.[55]

#### 18.3.3.2 Private Copying

According to Article L. 122-5, 2°, of the IPC:

> Once a work has been disclosed, the author may not prohibit (…) copies or reproductions reserved strictly for the private use of the copier and not intended for collective use, with the exception of copies of works of art to be used for purposes identical with those for which the original work was created and copies of software other than backup copies made in accordance with paragraph II of Article L. 122-6-1, as well as copies or reproductions of an electronic database.

Except for software or electronic databases, private copies or reproductions of works of the mind shall be made without the consent of authors only for private use.

Thus, a professional use of copies or reproduction of works of the mind is not considered as a private one and requires the consent of the author.[56] Likewise,

---

[51] Duala Court of First Instance, 3 March 1967; Paris Correctional Court, 24 January 1984.

[52] Grenoble Court of First Instance, 28 February 1968.

[53] Paris Correctional Court, 24 January 1984.

[54] Paris Court of Appeal, Pole 5, 1st Chamber, 8 February 2012, No. 10/13304.

[55] Rennes Court of Appeal, 20 June 1932.

[56] Court of Cassation, 1st Civil Chamber, 20 January 1969.

disclosure and distribution on the Internet of works of the mind without the author's consent are forbidden.[57]

When assessing this exception, the main issue lies in the identification of the copyist.

If French courts used to base their analysis on an economic-material approach, defining as a copyist any person holding a material copy of the work of the mind,[58] a shift towards an intellectual approach, defining as a copyist the person who chooses the work of the mind to be copied, was made under French law.

This approach, recognized by the case law of the Court of Justice of the European Union,[59] was indeed enacted into French law with Law No. 2011-1898 of December 20, 2011,[60] and applied by both the Criminal Chamber of the Court of Cassation[61] and the Council of State.[62]

Concerning copies of works of art, an additional condition is required: a different purpose between the copy and the original work of the mind, assessed according to the use that will be made of the copy, shall be established.

However, to date, French courts have not had the opportunity to apply this provision and only framed the scope of the exception under Law No. 57-298 of March 11, 1957,[63] in the hypothesis of the reproduction of the Geode on a postal card.[64]

Concerning software copies, Article L. 122-6-1 in combination with Article L. 122-5, 2°, of the IPC only authorize a single backup copy, carried out by the licensee and made in the event of physical or accidental destruction of the software.

Backup copies are not extended to electronic databases that can only be made with the author's consent.

Articles L. 311-1 et seq. of the IPC[65] deal with the regime of remuneration for private copying, implemented to compensate for the losses suffered by authors and based on the medium, the technical devices used to fix the work of the mind.

---

[57] Paris Court of First Instance of Paris, 5 May 1997.

[58] Paris Court of First Instance, 8 October 1982; Court of Cassation, 1st Civil Chamber, 7 March 1984.

[59] CJEU, case C-572/13, *Hewlett-Packard Belgium SPRL v Reprobel SCRL*, ECLI:EU:C:2015:750.

[60] Law No. 2011-1898 of 20 December 2001 "*relative à la rémunération pour copie privée*".

[61] Despite of the silence of the texts, the case law seems to consider that the benefit of the private copying exception assumes that the matrix from which the copy is made must itself be a copy acquired lawfully, Court of Cassation, Criminal Chamber, 30 May 2006.

[62] Quashing the decision of 20 July 2006 of the "private copy Committee" on the ground that the remuneration for private copying can only take into consideration that the licit copies and including copies made from a source acquired lawfully, Council of State, 11 July 2008.

[63] Law No. 57-298 of 11 March 1957 "*sur la propriété littéraire et artistique*".

[64] Paris Court of First Instance, 23 October 1990.

[65] According to Article L. 311-1 of the IPC:

> The authors and performers of works fixed on phonograms or videograms and the producers of such phonograms or videograms shall be entitled to remuneration for the reproduction of those works made in accordance with item 2 of Article L122-5 and item 2 of Article L211-3.

According to Articles L. 311-3 and -4 and the IPC, the compensation, assessed as a lump sum based on the type of medium and recording time, shall be paid by the manufacturer, the importer, or the person making an intra-Community acquisition of recording mediums that may be used for the reproduction of works for private use, at the time these mediums came into play in France.

Article L. 311-5 of the IPC provides for an *ad hoc* Committee, chaired by a representative of the state and composed of organizations representing the beneficiaries of the right of remuneration, persons designated by the organizations representing the manufacturers or importers of the media, and persons designated by the organizations representing the consumers, in charge of the designation of the media to which compensation is granted and the amount to be collected on the device.

Where administrative courts overruled a decision of the Committee, they shall set the amount of the compensation based on the prejudice suffered by the author with the introduction of the private copying exception.[66]

According to Article L. 311-8, I, of the IPC:

> The remuneration for private copying shall be refunded when the recording medium is acquired for their own use or production by:
>
> 1°. Audiovisual communication enterprises;
>
> 2°. Phonogram or videogram producers and persons who carry out the reproduction of phonograms or videograms on behalf of the producers;
>
> 2° bis. The publishers of works published on digital mediums;
>
> 3°. Legal persons or bodies, of which the list shall be established by the Minister responsible for culture, that use recording mediums for the purpose of assisting persons with sight or hearing disability.

Law No. 2011-1898 of March 1, 2012,[67] partially amended the French compensation system by codifying into French law the decisions of the Court of Justice of the European Union[68] and the Council of State of June 17, 2011,[69] which excluded from compensation private copies acquired for professional purposes.

Law No. 2016-925 of July 7, 2016,[70] introduced under the scope of this exception distance digital recording services proposed by publishers and distributors of television services, the network personal video recorder. This law also modified the regime of compensation for private copying.

---

The authors and publishers of works fixed on any other medium are also entitled to remuneration for the reproduction of those works made in accordance with item 2 of Article L122-5 and item 2 of Article L211-3, on a digital recording medium.

[66] Court of Cassation, 1st Civil Chamber, 17 March 2016.

[67] Law No. 2011-1898 of 20 December 2011 "*relative à la rémunération pour copie privée*".

[68] CJEU, case C-462/09, *Stichting de Thuiskopie v Opus Supplies Deutschland GmbH and Others*, ECLI:EU:C:2011:397.

[69] Council of State, 17 June 2011, No. 324816.

[70] Law No. 2016-925 of 7 July 2016 "*relative à la liberté de la création, à l'architecture et au patrimoine*".

According to Article L. 311-8, II bis, of the IPC, the remuneration for private copying is not due to the persons carrying out the export or the intra-Community supply of recording media marketed in France.

The Act further specifies that 25% of the sums collected can be assigned for sociocultural purposes and not for compensation of authors' prejudices.

Technological protection measures, which right holders can establish and which are forbidden to be circumvented, may interfere with certain users who, in order to benefit from this exception, shall find an agreement with the author.

According to Articles L. 331-8 et seq. of the IPC, the "High Authority for the dissemination of works and the protection of rights on the Internet" (hereinafter "the HADOPI") may alternatively be called to seek for conciliation in respecting the rights of authors and considering the interests of users of works.

Hence, the HADOPI balances the rights of authors with the interests of users even if this authority can only intervene on a subsidiary basis if no agreement could be found.

#### 18.3.3.3 Transient Copies

Article L. 122-5, 6°, of the IPC provides for a specific exception allowing temporary reproduction of work without the authorization of its author.

According to this article, "[o]nce a work has been disclosed, the author may not prohibit (…) the temporary reproduction presenting a transitional or accessory character, when it is an integral and essential part of a technical process and where it is for the sole purpose of enabling the lawful use of the work or its transmission between third parties by way of a network involving an intermediary; however, this temporary reproduction that can only bear on works other than software and databases must not have an own economic value."

This exception is not a general exception dealing with provisional reproductions of works of the mind but rather a specific limit to authors' right, which could be regarded as an exception for *technical copies*.

This exception is limited since the reproduction shall be

- temporary;
- transitional or accessory;
- an integral and essential part of a technical process;
- for the sole purpose of enabling the lawful use of the work or its transmission between third parties by way of a network involving an intermediary.

These principles seem to have been recognized by the Court of Cassation, which ruled that "[t]he reproduction on a hard drive is a technical operation, necessary and accessory to ensure the desired programming and to allow the simultaneous and integral broadcasting of commercial phonograms, since the Multimusic service is lacking interactivity as it does not enable the auditor to precisely select the phonogram he wanted to hear within the program he had chosen (…)."[71]

[71] Court of Cassation, 14 June 2007, No. 02-19833, *Multiradio*.

Software and databases are expressively excluded from the scope of this exception.

The Paris Court of First Instance ruled that the transient acts of reproduction exception cannot be invoked in the hypothesis of a *VCR online* service, which offers to its subscribers the possibility to record television programs and to access their request of records, after decryption of those, since the copy made by the operator can be, once decoded, retained in a definitive manner by its user. The Court noted that the copy has its "own economic value," considering the advertising revenues directly related to the number of users of the service and the volume of copies made for the account of these users.[72]

#### 18.3.3.4 Speeches, Public Lectures, Current Economic, Political or Religious Topics

Article L. 122-5, 3°, c), of the IPC provides for a specific exception allowing the diffusion of works through speeches destined to the public, while Article 122-5, 9°, of the same Code provides for a specific exception for the use of graphic, plastic, or architectural works for information.

According to Article L. 122-5, 3°, c), of the IPC, "[o]nce a work has been disclosed, the author may not prohibit (…) on condition that the name of the author and the source are clearly stated (…) diffusion, even in their entirety, through the press or by broadcasting, as current news, of speeches intended for the public made in political, administrative, judicial or academic gatherings, as well as in public meetings of a political nature and at official ceremonies." Besides the fact case law regularly rules that this exception should be strictly interpreted,[73] this exception is particularly limited for the following reasons:

- Its scope only covers *speech destined to the public*, that is to say, speeches made during political, administrative, judicial, or academic gatherings; speeches of a political nature made in public meetings; and speeches made during official ceremonies.
- The diffusion should only be done "for informatory purpose": if it not the case, the speech is protected by copyright and cannot be reproduced without the consent of the author.
- The diffusion can only be made by "the press or by broadcasting, as current news."

Providing the restrictive approach adopted by French courts, a company may not publish in a brochure of June 1995 the speeches made by the President of the French Republic from 1991 to 1995 since such speeches cannot be qualified as "news" due to the time elapsed and the diversity of the topics covered.[74]

---

[72] Paris Court of First Instance, 3rd Chamber, 25 November 2008.

[73] Court of Cassation, 5 May 1959, Ed. *Nuit et Jour/Cruzeiro*; Paris Court of First Instance, 25 October 1995.

[74] Paris Court of First Instance, 25 October 1995.

Similarly, the publication in a book of the speech of a communist leader, long after its pronunciation and after the death of the author, was not considered as a diffusion of a speech designed to the public since this exception only applied to diffusion by press and broadcasting with information or news purposes. The conditions of the exception being not fulfilled, the author of the speech retains the fullness of its exclusivity rights.[75]

The same solution is applied to pleadings, which can be freely reproduced by the newspapers to account for a trial that has just taken place.[76]

Furthermore, Article L. 122-5, 9°, of the IPC provides for an exception specifically relating to the use for information purposes of a work of graphic, plastic, or architectural art.

According to this article, "[o]nce a work has been disclosed, the author may not prohibit (…):

> The reproduction or representation, complete or partial, of a graphic, plastic or architectural art work, by way of written, audio-visual or online press, in an exclusive purpose of immediate information and in direct relationship with the latter, subject to indicate clearly the name of the author.
>
> The first paragraph of this 9° does not apply to works, including photographic or illustration, which aim themselves to account for the information."

Article L. 122-5, 9°, of the IPC transposes partially Article 5.3 (c) of Directive 2001/29 since it does not encompass "works, including photographic or illustration, which aim themselves to account for the information," and requires that reproductions or representations be "by their number or their format (…) in strict proportion with the exclusive purpose of immediate information" or "in direct relationship with this latter."

Hence, a media company that has reproduced on its website a photograph of a public person cannot benefit from the exception since this photograph was dedicated to graphic, plastic, or architectural art.[77]

The uses not respecting the conditions of application of the exception would give rise to the payment of remuneration based on agreements or tariffs in force in the professional sectors concerned.

#### 18.3.3.5 Freedom of Expression

Article L. 122-5, 4°, of the IPC provides for a specific exception in order to allow freedom of expression of creators. The main category is traditionally the one providing an exception for parody, pastiche, and caricature.

According to this provision, "[o]nce a work has been disclosed, the author may not prohibit (…) parody, pastiche and caricature, observing the rules of the genre."

---

[75] Paris Court of First Instance, 28 May 1986.

[76] Paris Court of First Instance, 25 September 1956.

[77] Paris Court of First instance, 6 June 2008.

This article, if it transposes the provisions of Article 5.3 of Directive 2001/29, adds to the three notions of parody, pastiche, and caricature the reference to the *rules of the genre*, understood as the humorous intention that allows the parody to escape from the monopoly of the author.[78]

This rule allows courts to sanction the excessive denaturation of the parodied work and, even beyond the moral right, to balance the right to entertain and the rights of the personality of the author chosen as the target.[79]

Parody, pastiche, and caricature shall all be for free artistic use. Thus, publicity parodies shall be approved by the copyright owner.

Traditionally, both case law and the doctrine consider that parody, pastiche, and caricature in order to be permitted shall fulfil the two following conditions:

- They shall be done in a humorous way[80] and not to harm the author of the work, by, for example, transposing it in a different context from the one of the original work.[81]
- All risks of confusion between the two works shall be excluded, which is the case when the author of the parody obtains a humorous effect absent from the original work.[82]

Although the Court of Cassation makes a distributive application of the three notions, their legal regime is almost identical. Parody, pastiche, and caricature are all "transformative" works, and the freedom on which the exemption is based arises also from the fact that the persons who "borrow" the protected work bring something personal to the work.

However, since the Court of Justice of the European Union ruled that the notion of "parody" is an "autonomous notion" under European law, French courts shall comply with the following principles when applying this exception:

- The parody shall respect a fair balance between, on the one hand, the interests and the rights of persons referred to and, on the other hand, the freedom of expression of the user of a protected work relying on the exception for parody.
- The parody cannot be used for discriminatory purposes.
- The parody does not necessarily have to have its own originality.
- It is not necessary to mention the source of the work.[83]

[78] Seine Commercial Court, 26 June 1934.

[79] A. Lucas, Fasc. 1248, Droits des auteurs. Exceptions au droit exclusif, 14 April 2010.

[80] It is the humorous intention which allows the parody to escape to the monopoly of the author, Court of First Instance of Seine, 26 June 1934. The critical purpose pursued can also make legitimate the caricature or parody, as for example: the desire to raise the absence of sex and violence in the universe of the characters of the "peanuts," Paris Court of First Instance, 19 January 1977.

[81] The purpose of the parody must not be harmful to others, Court of First Instance of Versailles, 17 March 1994; The caricature must not prejudice to the person of the author, Paris Court of First Instance, 15 October 1985.

[82] Versailles Court of First Instance, 17 March 1994; Paris Court of First Instance, 9 January 1970; Seine Commercial Court, 26 June 1934.

[83] CJEU, case C-201/13, *Johan Deckmyn and Vrijheidsfonds VZW v Helena Vandersteen and Others*, ECLI:EU:C:2014:2132.

#### 18.3.3.6 Reproductions in "Another Work"

Article L. 122-5, 3° a) and b), of the IPC provides for a specific exception for press reviews, analysis, and short quotations.

- Press Review
  According to Article L. 122-5, 3°, b), of the IPC, "[o]nce a work has been disclosed, the author may not prohibit (...), on condition that the name of the author and the source are clearly stated (...) press reviews."
  This exception entails that the reproduction of the work of the mind shall be done to invite readers to take position on a subject matter.
  French law being unclear on what this exception encompasses, case law had to frame its scope. Press reviews shall contain the comparative opinions of different journalists on the same theme or event.[84] Thus excluded from the scope of this exception is the reproduction of works of the mind that cannot be considered as "news."[85]
- Analyses and Short Quotations
  According to Article L. 122-5, 3°, a), of the IPC, "[o]nce a work has been disclosed, the author may not prohibit (...), on condition that the name of the author and the source are clearly stated (...), analyses and short quotations justified by the critical, polemic, educational, scientific or informatory nature of the work in which they are incorporated."
  Analyses and short quotations, justified by the critical, polemic, educational, scientific, or informatory nature of the work of the mind in which they are incorporated, can be admitted only if they

  - pursue educational purposes, which implies that they shall be incorporated into other developments that have a critical, controversial, teaching, scientific, or information aim[86];
  - are brief, which is assessed in absolute terms and in relation to the work of the mind quoted[87]; thus, if the reproduction of a work of the mind in reduced format or during a short period cannot be considered as a quotation,[88] the complete representation of a work of the mind, regardless of its format, cannot be considered as a short quotation[89];
  - do not prejudice the author's moral right.[90]

---

[84] Court of Cassation, 1st Civil Chamber, 30 January 1978; Paris Court of First Instance, 25 March 1982; Seine Court of First Instance, 17 June 1964.

[85] Seine Court of First Instance, 17 June 1964.

[86] Quotations are lawful only if they are used to inform or support a discussion, a development or an argument forming the main subject of the book itself, Paris Court of First Instance, 11 February 1988; Marseille Court of First Instance, 26 June 1979.

[87] Seine Court of First Instance, 17 June 1964; Paris Court of First Instance, 22 September 1988; Paris Court of First Instance, 14 September 1994.

[88] Court of Cassation, 1st Chamber, 10 February 1998.

[89] Court of Cassation, 5 November1993; Court of Cassation, 1st Chamber, 4 July 1995.

[90] The quotation can be prejudicial to the moral rights of the author, when it is inaccurate or gives an idea denaturing of the work: Paris Court of First, 6 June 1986. It was judged that there has been

Concerning quotations, it was judged that the recovery in a television work, for a minute, of elements of dialogs contained in a book without reference to the author of the quotation was constitutive of a counterfeit.[91]

The Court of Cassation made an exception to these requirements once, in a case relating to databases.[92]

Analyses shall include a summary, the sources of the author, and its essential elements, generally accompanied by a critical comment, so that the analysis of the work of the mind is not made for the work itself but to serve as a basis for personal assessments of the analyst. Furthermore, freedom of analysis should pass through the requirement of integration in a work with its own identity due to personal developments added.[93]

#### 18.3.3.7 Teaching and Scientific Research

If lots of the exceptions provided for in Article L. 122-5 of the IPC are relating to teaching and education (such as the abovementioned exception related to citation), the main provisions dealing with this issue are set forth in Article L. 122-5, 3°, e), and 8° of the IPC.

According to Article L. 122-5, 3° e), of the IPC:

> Once a work has been disclosed, the author may not prohibit (…), the representation or the reproduction of excerpts of works, subject that the works are designed for educational purposes and partitions of music, for the exclusive purposes of illustration in the framework of teaching and research, including for the development and dissemination of examination subjects or of competitions organized in the extension of the lessons to the exclusion of any activity playful or recreational, when this representation or this reproduction is intended, in particular by means of a digital work space, to a public composed predominantly of pupils, students, teachers or researchers directly concerned by teaching, training or research activity requiring this representation or reproduction, that it is not the subject of any publication or dissemination to a third party to the public thus constituted, that the use of this representation or this reproduction does not give rise to any commercial exploitation and that it is offset by a negotiated remuneration on a lump sum basis without prejudice of the assignment of the right of reprographic reproduction referred to in article L. 122-10.

Even if the scope of this exception was extended by the Law of 8 July 2013[94] to include online representation or reproduction of works of the mind, it remains precisely circumscribed for the reasons below mentioned:

- It only allows the use of "extracts" of works.
- It only applies to a certain type of works.

a violation of the moral right of the author when, by the withdrawal of multiple quotation of his work, the second work loses its originality: Paris Court of First Instance, 5 December 1997.

[91] Paris Court of First Instance, 5 January 1983.

[92] Court of Cassation, 1st Chamber, 9 November 1983.

[93] Paris Court of First Instance, 25 April 1968.

[94] Law No. 2013-595 of 8 July 2013 "*d'orientation et de programmation pour la refondation de l'école de la République*".

- The representation or the use is lawful only if it intervenes for the "exclusive purposes of illustration in the framework of teaching and research, to the exclusion of any playful or recreational activity."
- The public in question must be composed predominantly of "pupils, students, teachers and researchers directly concerned."
- The legislator requires to consider the economic consequences of the exception. It not only prohibits any "commercial operation," but it also imposes compensation in the form of remuneration.

Article L. 122-5, 3°, e), of the IPC specifies that the remuneration should be negotiated on a flat-rate basis. Two agreements were concluded on December 4, 2009, and published on February 4, 2010. Concluded for a duration of 3 years, they allow teachers, researchers, and students in initial training the use of extracts of audiovisual and musical works.

Also pursuing research and education purposes, Article L. 122-5, 8°, of the IPC provides:

> Once a work has been disclosed, the author may not prohibit (…) the reproduction of a work and its representation made for conservation purposes or intended to preserve the conditions of its consultation for the purposes of research or private study by individuals, in the premises of the establishment and on dedicated terminals by libraries accessible to the public by museums, or by archive services, subject that they seek no economic or commercial benefit.

This exception, enacted in favor of museums, libraries, and archives, is the transposition into French law of Article 5. 2 (c) of Directive 2001/29.

However, it remains circumscribed to "the purposes of conservation or intended to preserve the conditions of its consultation on the spot by libraries accessible to the public," and the absence of an "economic or commercial advantage" is required. It does not apply to works "subject to the conditions in the field of purchase and license" under a concluded convention.[95]

Nevertheless, the Court of Justice of the European Union has given a dynamic vision of this exception contained in Directive 2001/29.

Law No. 2009-669 of June 12, 2009,[96] promoting the dissemination and the protection of creation on the Internet, has extended the scope of the exception to include the representation of the work in the premises of the establishment and on dedicated terminals by libraries. It was stated, at the same time, that the exception only covers the consultation for the purposes of research or private study by individuals.

Finally, Article L. 122-5, 7°, of the IPC provides an exception for people with disabilities, stating that the author may not prohibit the reproduction and the representation "with a view to a consultation strictly personal of the work by persons with one or more disabilities."

---

[95] CJEU, case C-117/13, *Technische Universität Darmstadt v Eugen Ulmer KG*, ECLI:EU:C:2014:2196.

[96] Law No. 2009-669 of 12 June 2009 "*favorisant la diffusion et la protection de la création sur internet*".

The exception benefits establishments open to the public whose professional activity may consist in the design, implementation, and communication of media for the benefit of persons with disabilities. The regime of this exception is further developed in Articles L. 122-5-1 and L. 122-5-2 of the IPC.

#### 18.3.3.8 "Data Mining" and "Data Bases"

Article L. 122-5, 10°, of the IPC, introduced by Law No. 2016-1321 of October 7, 2016,[97] codifies the *text and data mining* exception to the benefit of researchers.

"Text and data mining" *is the process of deriving information from machine-read material.* It consists in using software to analyse a "content," including protected data and work, in order to extract elements of knowledge.

There are four stages to the TDM process. First, potentially relevant documents are identified. They are then turned into a machine-readable format so that structured data can be extracted. The useful information is extracted (Stage 3) and then mined (Stage 4) to discover new knowledge, test hypotheses, and identify new relationships.

According to Article L. 122-5, 10°, of the IPC, "[o]nce a work has been disclosed, the author may not prohibit (…) [t]he copies or digital reproductions made from a lawful source, in view of the exploration of texts and data included in or associated with the scientific literature to the needs of the public research, to the exclusion of any commercial purpose."

This exception is strictly framed to avoid a massive dissemination of copies since authors' scientific works that have been disclosed may not ban

- digital copies or reproductions of works (without limitation of volume or format),
- made from a legal source,
- for the exploration of texts and data included in or associated with scientific literature for public research needs,
- with the exclusion of any commercial purpose.

This exception concerns mainly the upstream work (meeting and search). However, a decree relating to the terms of use of the activity is foreseen to limit the potential risks associated with these operations of digital search on what concerns particularly the downstream work.

About electronic databases, right holders cannot prohibit copies and reproductions made by licensees.

#### 18.3.3.9 The "Panorama Exception"

The *panorama exception*, dealing with the reproduction and representation of architectural and sculptural works, was codified under Article L. 122-5, 11°, of the IPC by Law No. 2016-1321.

[97] Law No. 2016-1321 of 7 October 2016 "*pour une République numérique*".

According to this provision, "[o]nce a work has been disclosed, the author may not prohibit (…) [t]he reproductions and representations of architectural works and sculptures, placed permanently on the public road, carried out by natural persons, to the exclusion of any use of a commercial nature."

The exception is framed by strong requirements limiting its scope since

- the use of architectural and sculptural works shall be devoid of any commercial nature;
- only natural persons can benefit from this exception, with the exclusion of corporations and associations;
- the exception only applies to architectural works or sculptures permanently placed on the public road.

#### 18.3.3.10 Persons with Disabilities

Article L. 122-5, 7°, of the IPC provides for a specific exception to the benefit of disabled people.

According to this provision, "[o]nce a work has been disclosed, the author may not prohibit (…) [t]he reproduction and the representation by legal persons and by the establishments open to the public, such as libraries, archives, documentation centers and cultural spaces multimedia, with a view to a strictly personal consultation of the work by persons with one or more impairments of motor functions, physical, sensory, mental, cognitive or psychic and prevented, the fact of these deficiencies, access to the work in the form in which the author makes it available to the public."

This exception benefits establishments open to the public which professional activity consists in the design, implementation, and communication of media for the benefit of persons with disabilities.

It does not provide for compensation to authors.

#### 18.3.3.11 Libraries, Museums, and Archives

Article L. 122-5, 8°, of the IPC allows "specific acts of reproduction made by publicly accessible libraries, museums or archives, which are not for direct or indirect economic or commercial advantage."

The permitted acts of reproduction should be aimed towards the preservation of works or their onsite consultation. The exception also applies to related rights.

## 18.4 Conclusions: France Is Favorable to Authors and Only Slowly and Progressively Adapts Its Legislation to International and EU Standards

The French lawmaker, due to the personalist tradition of the French copyright, remains reluctant to balance authors' rights with those of users.

Indeed, the late transposition of the dispositions of Directive 2001/29 by Law of 2006—4 years and a half after the deadline for transposition of December 22,

2002—reveals the French legislator's will to favor authors and its reluctance to "balance" authors' rights with those of users.

Furthermore, the current discussion[98] in France about the EU copyright package presented on September 14, 2016, by the European Commission[99] and the new users' exceptions proposed in this context proves the reluctance of the French legislator.

However, the current exceptions seem to strike a balance between authors' rights and fair use of their works of the mind by private individuals and others since the current legislation mainly reproduces the principles set forth in Directive 2001/29, which is itself the representation of a fair balance, and pursues an alignment with European and international standards.

Nevertheless, French courts still adopt an approach favorable to authors, and interpret the exceptions in a very restrictive manner.

In conclusion, it seems that French current legislation should be amended in order to strike a fairer balance between authors and users. Indeed, some authors propose "a flexibilization of the exceptions," in transposing literally all the exceptions provided by Directive 2001/29 or inversing the triple test.[100]

[98] National Assembly, 3 May 2016, Information Report on the protection of copyright in the EU, M. Karamanli and H. Gaymard; http://www.senat.fr/ue/pac/EUR000002607.html; P. Bonnecarrère, Report on the EU copyright reform, 8 February 2017, http://www.senat.fr/espace_presse/actualites/201702/trois_questions_a_philippe_bonnecarrere_sur_son_rapport_sur_la_reforme_du_droit_dauteur.html.

[99] http://europa.eu/rapid/press-release_IP-16-3010_fr.htm.

[100] D. Piatek, « La crise des exceptions en droit d'auteur : étude paradigmatique », 31 May 2017, pp 442 to 447.

# Germany

# 19

Thomas Hoeren

## 19.1 Introduction

During the twentieth century, copyright law has largely been ignored by legal scholars and the judiciary. However, with the start of the digital revolution, copyright became more and more important. Today, questions of copyright are ubiquitous: pictures are shared on social media platforms, streaming begins to displace classic broadcast media like TVs or radios, scientists share their latest results via the Internet and online research platforms. Against that backdrop, the crucial question is whether or not the applicable copyright law meets the requirements of the developing information society. Exceptions to copyright are an important factor in this regard. They have to fairly balance the copyright proprietors' interest in a comprehensive protection of their work on the one hand and the increasing common interest in the free use of works on the other hand.

The first part of this article aims at giving the reader an overview of exclusions and limitations to copyright, as codified in the current German Act on Copyright and Related Rights (hereafter *Urheberrechtsgesetz* or *UrhG*).[1] Presenting each and every limitation and exclusion to copyright is certainly beyond the scope of this article so that only some can be closely examined. This contribution focusses on those crucial to works in the digital society and economy.

[1]An official English translation can be found here: https://www.gesetze-im-internet.de/englisch_urhg/index.html. Accessed 16 May 2017.

T. Hoeren (✉)
Westfälische Wilhelms-Universität, Münster, Germany
e-mail: hoeren@uni-muenster.de



B. Kilpatrick et al. (eds.), *Antitrust Analysis of Online Sales Platforms & Copyright Limitations and Exceptions*, LIDC Contributions on Antitrust Law, Intellectual Property and Unfair Competition,
https://doi.org/10.1007/978-3-319-71419-6_19

## 19.2 Rights of the Copyright Proprietor

The German Urheberrechtsgesetz grants the author of a work certain rights. The law differentiates between moral rights and exploitation rights. The moral rights are laid down in §§ 12–14 UrhG. The author has the right to determine whether and how his work is initially published (§ 12 UrhG), to be identified as the author of the work (§ 13 UrhG) and to prohibit the distortion or any other derogatory treatment of his work that is capable of prejudicing his legitimate intellectual or personal interests in the work (§ 14 UrhG). Following the continental European tradition,[2] the Urheberrechtsgesetz thus emphasises the special relationship between the author and his work that arises from the fact that his personal feelings and experiences are made perceptible.[3]

The exploitation rights by contrast aim at providing the author the possibility to economically benefit from his work. According to § 15 (1) UrhG, the author has the *exclusive right* to exploit his work in material form. § 15 (2) UrhG grants the author the *exclusive right* to communicate the work to the public in non-material form. Both provisions contain a non-exhaustive (*in particular*) list of sub-forms of material and non-material exploitation, which are further specified in §§ 16–22 UrhG. Thus, the German law generally guarantees a broad protection for copyright proprietors. As a consequence, authors are also protected against new forms of exploitation that come up due to technological developments.[4] It is upon the legislator to nevertheless ensure a fair balance between the author's economic interest and the public interest in the free use of the work by codifying new limitations and exceptions to the general rule of protection.[5] Consequently, the copyright proprietor profits from a time advantage.

## 19.3 Limitations and Exceptions to the Protection

The Urheberrechtsgesetz contains numerous limitations and exceptions to the general rule of extensive protection. Some sub-forms of exploitation limitations are laid down in §§ 16–22 UrhG. Special exceptions are made in §§ 44a–63a UrhG (Section VI: Limitations to copyright).

[2] G. Schulze, preface to §§ 12 ff. para. 1. In: Dreier and Schulze (eds), Urheberrechtsgesetz, 5th ed, C.H. Beck 2015.

[3] W. Bullinger, preface to §§ 12 ff. para. 1. In: Wandtke and Bullinger (eds), Praxiskommentar zum Urheberrecht, 4th ed, C.H. Beck 2014.

[4] H. Schack, Urheber- und Urhebervertragsrecht, 7th ed, Mohr Siebeck 2015, para. 410.

[5] Cf. H. Schack, Urheber- und Urhebervertragsrecht, 7th ed, Mohr Siebeck 2015, para. 411.

### 19.3.1 System of Exceptions

The rules laid down in Section VI of the Urheberrechtsgesetz mainly set limits to exploitation rights, whereas the moral rights are unaffected.[6] This again follows the continental European understanding of copyright, which focusses on the author's special relationship to his work. Nonetheless, there is no risk that authors' moral rights can be misused to block the exceptions provided for by the lawmaker. Some legal provisions even restrict the author's right of publication (§ 12 UrhG): § 44a (temporary acts of reproduction), § 45 (administration of justice and public safety), § 53 (1) (private copies) and § 57 (incidental works) UrhG are also applicable to unpublished works.

In contrast to other copyright systems, the German law does not provide for a fair-use exception but makes use of narrowly defined exceptions. The vast majority of exceptions expressively refer to one or more sub-forms of exploitation. For example, § 52a (1) UrhG is only applicable for *making a work available* to the public within the meaning of § 19a UrhG. § 52a (3) UrhG then allows to *reproduce* (§ 16 UrhG) the work needed for that purpose. Due to their exceptional nature, the provisions are subject to a restrictive interpretation by practitioners.[7] The exceptions codified in the Urheberrechtsgesetz are exhaustive (see Sect. 19.2 above).[8] However, in some special cases, a broader interpretation of written exceptions can be necessary to ensure conformity with the Basic Law for the Federal Republic of Germany (*Grundgesetz; hereafter GG*).[9] Although the exceptions are narrowly drawn, some leave room for flexibility. Formulations like '*to the extent that is necessary* for the respective purpose' (§ 52a, cf. § 51, cf. § 53, cf. § 58, § 62 (4) UrhG) or '*justified* for the pursuit of non-commercial aims' (§ 52a UrhG) open the possibility for courts to decide on a case-by-case basis and to take constitutional considerations (see Sect. 19.3.2 below) into account.[10] In regard to § 52a UrhG (making works available to the public for instruction and research), for instance, courts granted teachers and

[6] A. Dustmann, preface to §§ 44a ff. para. 7. In: Fromm and Nordemann (eds), Urheberrecht, 11th ed, Verlag W. Kohlhammer 2014; T. Dreier, preface to §§ 44a ff. para. 19. In: Dreier and Schulze (eds), Urheberrechtsgesetz, 5th ed, C.H. Beck 2015; H. Schack, Urheber- und Urhebervertragsrecht, 7th ed, Mohr Siebeck 2015, para. 513.

[7] Federal Court of Justice, Decision of 3 April 1986, Case No. I ZR 83/66, GRUR 1968, pp. 607–612; Federal Court of Justice, Decision of 11 July 2002, Case No. I ZR 255/00, GRUR 2002, pp. 963–967; A. Dustmann, preface to §§ 44a ff. para. 6. In: Fromm and Nordemann (eds), Urheberrecht, 11th ed, Verlag W. Kohlhammer 2014; S. Lüft, preface to §§ 44a ff. para. 1. In: Wandtke and Bullinger (eds), Praxiskommentar zum Urheberrecht, 4th ed, C.H. Beck 2014.

[8] Federal Court of Justice, Decision of 20 March 2003, Case No. I ZR 117/00, NJW 2003, pp. 3633–3636.

[9] Federal Court of Justice, Decision of 20 March 2003, Case No. I ZR 117/00, NJW 2003, pp. 3633–3636.

[10] W. Schulz and S. Hagemeier, § 52a UrhG, para. 19. In: Ahlberg and Göttig (eds), Beck'scher Online-Kommentar Urheberrecht, 15th ed, C.H. Beck 2017; A. Wiebe, § 52a UrhG para. 3. In: Spindler and Schuster (eds), Recht der elektronischen Medien, 3rd ed, C.H. Beck 2015.

**Table 19.1** Interests protected by limitation to copyright

| | |
|---|---|
| § 45 UrhG | Administration of justice and public safety |
| § 45a UrhG | Persons with disabilities |
| §§ 46, 47, 53 (3) UrhG | Usage in public schools |
| §§ 48–50 UrhG | Freedom of information and freedom of press |
| § 51 UrhG | Quotations |
| § 52 UrhG | Communication of works to the public for non-profit purposes |
| § 52a UrhG | Making works available to the public for instruction and research |
| § 52b UrhG | Communication of works at terminals in public libraries, museums and archives |
| §§ 53 ff. UrhG | Private use |
| §§ 55, 56 UrhG | Interventions due to necessary technical procedures |
| §§ 44a, 57 UrhG | Minor interventions |
| § 58 UrhG | Promotion exception for works in exhibitions, on public sale and in institutions accessible to the public |
| § 59 UrhG | Panorama exception |
| §§ 61–61c UrhG | Use of orphan works (cultural heritage) |

lecturers a margin of discretion in respect to what is necessary to reach the educational goals.[11]

#### 19.3.1.1 Colliding Interests

With each exception, the legislator tries to fairly balance the conflicting interests of the author in profiting from his work and the public interest in freely using the work. The colliding interests acknowledged by the exceptions to copyright are manifold, as Table 19.1 shows.[12]

One can also see that the lawmaker sometimes distinguishes between commercial and non-commercial interests in using the work. By way of example, § 53 (1) UrhG only allows reproductions for private usage 'insofar as they neither directly nor indirectly serve commercial purposes'.[13] On the other hand, the panorama exception (§ 59 UrhG) also includes commercial use like the reproduction and distribution of postcards.[14] The Urheberrechtsgesetz also differentiates between usage by individuals (e.g., § 53 (1) UrhG) and other either private or public entities (e.g., § 45 (2) UrhG for public entities, § 61 UrhG for private and public entities).

[11] Cf. Higher Regional Court Frankfurt a.M., Decision of 24 November 2009, Case No. 11 U 40/09, GRUR 2010, pp. 1–4; Regional Court Stuttgart, Decision of 27 September 2011, Case No. 17 O 671/10, GRUR-RR 2011, pp. 419–423.

[12] Chart based on T. Dreier, preface to §§ 44a ff. para. 3. In: Dreier and Schulze (eds), Urheberrechtsgesetz, 5th ed, C.H. Beck 2015.

[13] For more examples see §§ 45a, 46, 52, 52a, 52b UrhG.

[14] T. Dreier, § 59 para. 7. In: Dreier and Schulze (eds), Urheberrechtsgesetz, 5th ed, C.H. Beck 2015; for more examples see §§ 48, 49, 50, 51, 55, 56, 57, 58, 61 UrhG.

#### 19.3.1.2 Compensation

One can distinguish between exceptions that lead to compensation (e.g., § 54 UrhG for private use within the meaning of § 53 UrhG) and those that do not (e.g., § 55 UrhG). If compensation is provided, the law often claims that remuneration may only be asserted by collecting societies (e.g., § 54h (1) UrhG, § 52a UrhG). These provisions ensure that works can be effectively used while the copyright proprietor adequately benefits from the exploitation of his work. Authors are then paid by the collecting societies according to the society's allocation key.[15]

#### 19.3.1.3 Enforcement of Exceptions

In order to prevent copyright proprietors from circumventing the restrictions to copyright through technical measures, § 95b UrhG entitles beneficiaries to demand access to the work. The provision only applies to some exceptions that are specified therein. The listed exceptions are mostly designed to protect state interests,[16] although parts of the private use exception are also mentioned.

It has to be criticised that the list is rather short. Particularly, neither digital private copies[17] nor exceptions of importance to the media and the shaping of public opinion (§§ 48–51 UrhG)[18] are included. § 95b UrhG has to be examined against the backdrop of § 95a UrhG, which legally protects effective technical protection measures taken by copyright proprietors. Consequently, beneficiaries are not allowed to crack the protection themselves with the aim of benefitting from an exception.[19] Thus, even for the limitations listed in § 95b UrhG, there is a risk that individuals and small entities may fear fighting a lawsuit and are thereby hindered from obtaining the benefit of an exception to copyright protection. A right of self-help for beneficiaries would be more effective in this regard.

#### 19.3.1.4 Impact of Contractual Agreements

The question whether or not exceptions to copyright law can be ruled out by contract is crucial for examining to what extent the public interest in freely using the work was adequately regarded by the legislator. Yet the lawmaker did not finally regulate in this regard. Some provisions explicitly state that exceptions do not apply to cases where a contractual agreement between the proprietor and the user has been reached or a fair agreement is at least possible.[20] On the contrary, the legislator

[15] Some allocation keys have been subject to legal discussions and court decisions recently; e.g. Federal Court of Justice, Decision of 21 April 2016, Case No. I ZR 198/13, GRUR 2016, pp. 596–606.

[16] H. Lindhorst, § 95b UrhG, para. 3. In: Ahlberg and Göttig (eds), Beck'scher Online-Kommentar Urheberrecht, 15th ed, C.H. Beck 2017.

[17] H. Schack, Urheber- und Urhebervertragsrecht, 7th ed, Mohr Siebeck 2015, para. 837.

[18] H. Lindhorst, § 95b UrhG, para. 3. In: Ahlberg and Göttig (eds), Beck'scher Online-Kommentar Urheberrecht, 15th ed, C.H. Beck 2017; H. Schack, Urheber- und Urhebervertragsrecht, 7th ed, Mohr Siebeck 2015, para. 837.

[19] G. Spindler, § 95b UrhG para. 10. In: Spindler and Schuster (eds), Recht der elektronischen Medien, 3rd ed, C.H. Beck 2015.

[20] E.g. §§ 52b, 53a (1) UrhG.

explicitly declares some other exceptions to be mandatory.[21] However, as the latter provisions aim to implement EU directives into national law, one cannot conclude by *argumentum e contrario* that other exceptions are not mandatory.[22]

Copyright law is part of civil law. Consequently, private autonomy and freedom of contract, as guaranteed by Article 2 (1) GG,[23] are leading principles for copyright law as well.[24] Therefore, some legal scholars conclude that each and every exception can be restricted by contract.[25] This approach would of course pull the rug out from under the exceptions that are the result of a careful balance of conflicting interests by the lawmaker.[26] Instead, the answer to the question has to be found on a case-by-case basis.[27] Focus has to be laid especially on the spirit and the purpose of the exception: exceptions aiming at (above all) protecting interests of the public or third parties have to be considered as mandatory.[28] Consequently, at least the exceptions laid down in §§ 45, 45a, 46, 47, 50, 51 UrhG are mandatory. These provisions contain, inter alia, exceptions for the purpose of administration of justice or public security, for persons with disabilities, for reports on current events and for school broadcasting. Moreover, one can cast an eye on the exceptions listed in § 95b UrhG.[29] For these exceptions, the legislator provided legal means for beneficiaries to enforce them and thus made clear that the listed exceptions are of high relevance.

Furthermore, contractual restrictions of non-mandatory exceptions in general terms and conditions have to be in line with §§ 307-309 of the German Civil Code (BGB) as well.[30]

---

[21] E.g. §§ 55a, 69g UrhG.

[22] A. Dustmann, preface to §§ 44a ff. para. 14. In: Fromm and Nordemann (eds), Urheberrecht, 11th ed, Verlag W. Kohlhammer 2014; J. Gräbig, Abdingbarkeit urheberrechtlicher Schranken, GRUR 2012, pp. 331–337.

[23] E.g. Federal Constitutional Court, Decision of 27 July 2005, Case No. 1 BvR 2501/04, GRUR 2005, pp. 880–882.

[24] Federal Court of Justice, Decision of 18 February 1982, Case No. I ZR 81/80, GRUR 1984, pp. 45–52; J. Gräbig, Abdingbarkeit urheberrechtlicher Schranken, GRUR 2012, pp. 331–337.

[25] G. Dreyer, preface to §§ 44a ff. para. 17. In: Dreyer, Kotthoff and Meckel (eds), Urheberrecht, 3rd ed, C.F. Müller 2013; M. Vogel, § 60 para. 5. In: Schricker and Loewenheim (eds), Urheberrecht, 5th ed, C.H. Beck 2017.

[26] J. Gräbig, Abdingbarkeit urheberrechtlicher Schranken, GRUR 2012, pp. 331–337.

[27] T. Dreier, preface to §§ 44a ff. para. 9. In: Dreier and Schulze (eds), Urheberrechtsgesetz, 5th ed, C.H. Beck 2015; H. Schack, Schutz digitaler Werke vor privater Vervielfältigung – zu den Auswirkungen der Digitalisierung auf § 53 UrhG, ZUM 2002, pp. 497–511.

[28] A. Dustmann, preface to §§ 44a ff. para. 14. In: Fromm and Nordemann (eds), Urheberrecht, 11th ed, Verlag W. Kohlhammer 2014; cf. T. Dreier, preface to §§ 44a ff. para. 9. In: Dreier and Schulze (eds), Urheberrechtsgesetz, 5th ed, C.H. Beck 2015; J. Gräbig, Abdingbarkeit urheberrechtlicher Schranken, GRUR 2012, pp. 331–337.

[29] T. Dreier, preface to §§ 44a ff. para. 9. In: Dreier and Schulze (eds), Urheberrechtsgesetz, 5th ed, C.H. Beck 2015; H. Schack, Urheberrechtliche Schranken für Bildung und Wissenschaft, ZUM 2016, pp. 266–283.

[30] See A. Dustmann, preface to §§ 44a ff. para. 15. In: Fromm and Nordemann (eds), Urheberrecht, 11th ed, Verlag W. Kohlhammer 2014; see J. Gräbig, Abdingbarkeit urheberrechtlicher Schranken, GRUR 2012, pp. 331–337.

§ 52b UrhG allows the communication of works at terminals in public libraries, museums and archives as long as, among other criteria, *there are no contractual provisions to the contrary*. The German Federal Court of Justice pointed out in this regard that a fair and reasonable contractual offer of the copyright proprietor was sufficient to rule out the exception because, otherwise, beneficiaries could even reject fair offers in order to profit from the legal exception and thus misuse the law.[31] As § 52b UrhG is based on Article 5 (3) lit. n of Directive 2001/29/EC of the European Parliament and of the Council of 22 May 2001 on the harmonisation of certain aspects of copyright and related rights in the information society (hereafter InfoSoc Directive), it was upon the Court of Justice of the European Union to clarify the legal situation. The court ruled that a mere contractual offer could not be understood as 'purchase and licensing terms' within the meaning of the InfoSoc Directive but that a contract was necessary.[32]

Special regard has to be given to the exception laid down in § 52a UrhG, which allows making works available to the public for instruction and research as long as this use is '*justified* for the pursuit of non-commercial aims'. The German Federal Court of Justice ruled that a fair, reasonable and easily detectable offer for a contractual agreement leads to the result that the usage was not justified within the meaning of the provision.[33] This of course only shifts the problem on to the question what fair and reasonable means in the specific case and thereby hinders beneficiaries from relying on the exception.[34] Yet, after the afore-mentioned judgment of the Court of Justice of the European Union, it is likely that courts will apply the same standard to § 52a UrhG so that mere offers for an agreement will not suffice to make the usage unjustified.[35]

In contrast to this, a contractual offer is sufficient to suppress the exception of § 53a (1) UrhG.[36] The provision allows public libraries to reproduce and to transmit works in electronic form in response to an individual order in cases where, among other criteria, 'it is not made manifestly possible, *upon agreed contractual terms*, for members of the public to access the contributions or small parts of a work from a place and at a time individually chosen by them and on terms which are equitable'.

[31] Federal Court of Justice, Decision of 20 September 2012, Case No. I ZR 69/11, GRUR 2013, pp. 503–507.

[32] CJEU, case C-117/13, *Technische Universität Darmstadt v Eugen Ulmer KG*, ECLI:EU:C:2014:2196; Federal Court of Justice, Decision of 16 April 2015, Case No. I ZR 69/11, NJW 2015, pp. 3511–3517.

[33] Federal Court of Justice, Decision of 28 November 2013, Case No. I ZR 76/12, GRUR 2014, pp. 549–556.

[34] Regional Court Stuttgart, Decision of 27 September 2011, Case No. 17 O 671/10, GRUR-RR 2011, pp. 416–423; A. Dustmann, § 52a para. 15. In: Fromm and Nordemann (eds), Urheberrecht, 11th ed, Verlag W. Kohlhammer 2014; T. Dreier, § 52a para. 12. In: Dreier and Schulze (eds), Urheberrechtsgesetz, 5th ed, C.H. Beck 2015.

[35] M. Grünberger, Vergütungspflicht und Lizenzvorrang in der neuen EU-Bildungsschranke, GRUR 2017, pp. 1–11.

[36] T. Dreier, § 53a para. 15. In: Dreier and Schulze (eds), Urheberrechtsgesetz, 5th ed, C.H. Beck 2015; O. Jani, § 53a para. 30. In: Wandtke and Bullinger (eds), Praxiskommentar zum Urheberrecht, 4th ed, C.H. Beck 2014.

## 19.3.2 Triple Test (and Colliding Interests)

### 19.3.2.1 The Triple Test and Legislative Power

According to Article 13 of the Agreement on Trade-Related Aspects of Intellectual Property Rights (TRIPS), Article 10 (1) and (2) of the WIPO Copyright Treaty (WCT) and Article 16 (2) of the WIPO Performances and Phonograms Treaty (WPPT), national legislators of the contracting parties shall only provide for limitations and exceptions in (1) special cases and as long as they (2) do not conflict with the normal exploitation of the work and (3) do not prejudice the author's legitimate interest in an unreasonable way. This means that the lawmaker is asked to develop a fair balance between the conflicting interests of the right holders on the one and the public on the other hand.[37] However, the German legislator cannot be forced to acknowledge the triple test when passing laws on exceptions to copyright law. According to Article 20 (3) GG, the legislator's power is only limited by the constitution itself. International law is therefore not binding for the lawmaker.[38]

Anyhow, the fundamental rights codified in the German Constitution set limits to the legislator's power to pass laws stating exceptions to the proprietors' rights. According to Article 14 (1) GG, property shall be guaranteed. Property within the meaning of this provision also includes an author's copyright.[39] At the same time, it is laid down in Article 14 (2) of the Constitution that the use of property shall serve the public good. It is upon the legislator to fairly balance these constitutional goals.[40] Each curtailment of proprietors' rights has to be justified by a public interest and has to be proportionate against that backdrop in order to be constitutional. As a result, the German Constitution itself states that protection of an author's work must be the general rule.[41]

For those exploitation rights deriving from the InfoSoc Directive, Article 5 (5) of the Directive repeats that exceptions have to be in line with the same triple test. In contrast to other international treaties, European law is subject to an examination by the Court of Justice of the European Union,[42] and any violation can be sanctioned by the means of the EU treaties.

---

[37] P. Runge, Die Vereinbarkeit einer Content-Flatrate mit dem Drei-Stufen-Test, GRUR Int. 2007, pp. 130–137; M. Senftleben, Grundprobleme des urheberrechtlichen Dreistufentests, GRUR Int. 2004, pp. 200–211.

[38] Federal Constitutional Court, Decision of 15 December 2015, Case No. 2 BvL 1/12, NJW 2016, pp. 1295–1307; Federal Court of Justice, Decision of 25 February 1999, Case No. I ZR 118/96, NJW 1999, pp. 1953–1959.

[39] Federal Constitutional Court, Decision of 15 December 2011, Case No. 1 BvR 1248/11, GRUR 2012, pp. 390–392.

[40] Federal Constitutional Court, Decision of 31 May 2016, Case No. 1 BvR 1585/13, GRUR 2016, pp. 690–697.

[41] H. Schack, Urheber- und Urhebervertragsrecht, 7th ed, Mohr Siebeck 2015, para. 93.

[42] T. Dreier, preface to §§ 44a ff. para. 21. In: Dreier and Schulze (eds), Urheberrechtsgesetz, 5th ed, C.H. Beck 2015.

### 19.3.2.2 The Triple Test and Judicial Power

The triple test is, however, binding for the German courts when interpreting exceptions to copyright law. For exceptions mentioned in Article 5 (5) InfoSoc Directive, this follows from the fact that, according to Article 4 (3) of the Treaty on the European Union, national courts must construe national law in a way that the goals of the EU law are put into effect optimally.[43] For the above-mentioned international treaties, this follows from the constitutional rule that national law has to be construed in conformity with international law.[44]

Given the great number of cases dealing with exceptions to copyright protection, the number of cases in which courts denied to apply an exception on the account of the triple test is very low.[45] In the most recent case, the *Higher Regional Court Stuttgart* had to decide on a case concerning the exception of § 52a UrhG, which allows making works available to the public for purposes of instruction and research. The usage is, among other things, allowed for illustration in teaching at universities as long as only 'small, limited parts of a work' are affected and to an 'extent that is necessary for the respective purpose and [that] is justified for the pursuit of non-commercial aims'. In that case, a distance university made available 91 of 476 pages (19.12%) of a textbook for psychology students. The court pointed out that the decision whether or not the published part still is small and limited within the meaning of the law had to be made on a case-by-case basis, taking into account the economic value of the published parts and the proprietor's corresponding interest in economically benefitting from the work.[46] In order to determine whether the publication's extent was 'necessary', the court explicitly applied the triple test and stated that, as the publication covered each part of the book being relevant to the students' final exam, the publication was not necessary.[47] The university's usage of the work conflicted with the normal exploitation of the work as there was no need for the students to purchase the book. For the same reason, the author's legitimate interests were prejudiced in an unreasonable way. As a consequence, the judges ruled in favour of the plaintiff. The German Federal Court of Justice later overruled the decision but also pointed out that the triple test is decisive for the application of exceptions to

[43] A. von Bogdany and S. Schill. Article 4 EUV para. 99. In: Nettesheim (ed), Das Recht der Europäischen Union, supplement 51, September 2013.

[44] Federal Constitutional Court, Decision of 8 December 2014, Case No. 2 BvR 450/11, NVwZ 2015, pp. 361–367; Federal Constitutional Court, Decision of 4 May 2011, Case No. 2 BvR 2333/08, NJW 2011, pp. 1931–1946; Federal Court of Justice, Decision of 25 February 1999, Case No. I ZR 118/96, NJW 1999, pp. 1953–1959.

[45] T. Dreier, preface to §§ 44a ff. para. 21. In: Dreier and Schulze (eds), Urheberrechtsgesetz, 5th ed, C.H. Beck 2015; the following decision can serve as another example: Federal Court of Justice, Decision of 20 September 2012, Case No. I ZR 69/11, GRUR 2013, pp. 503–507.

[46] Higher Regional Court Stuttgart, Decision of 4 April 2012, Case No. 4 U 171/11, GRUR 2012, pp. 718–727.

[47] Higher Regional Court Stuttgart, Decision of 4 April 2012, Case No. 4 U 171/11, GRUR 2012, pp. 718–727.

copyright.[48] The federal judges decided that the normal exploitation is only endangered when the usage is in direct competition with it. As the textbook was not only created for university use, this was not the case.

### 19.3.3 Examples

#### 19.3.3.1 Exhaustion of the Right of Distribution with Special Regard to Digital Works

The Urheberrechtsgesetz provides the author with the right to determine whether or not his work is distributed (§ 17 (1) UrhG). If this right was unlimited, the proprietor could control the distribution of the work even if it was sold with his consent and he thus economically benefited from the work. In order to protect the freedom of trade,[49] § 17 (2) UrhG therefore determines that 'Where the original or copies of the work have been brought to the market by sale with the consent of the person entitled to distribute them within *the territory of the European Union* or *another state party to the Agreement on the European Economic Area*, their dissemination shall be permissible, except by means of rental'.

With respect to Article 4 (2) of the Directive of the European Union and of the Council of 23 April 2009 on the legal protection of computer programs (hereafter *Computer Programs Directive*), which § 69c No. 3 UrhG implements into national law, the Court of Justice of the European Union decided that the right of distribution for software also exhausts when computer programs have not been sold on data storage devices but the 'buyer' downloaded a copy of the program in order to install the software (UsedSoft judgment).[50] Considering the growth of digital distribution channels (e.g., downloads of music files, video files or e-books), the question whether or not the principle of exhaustion also applies to these situations becomes crucial when examining if the Urheberrechtsgesetz adequately regards the challenges of the digital society. Generally, the right of distribution (§ 17 (1) UrhG) applies to physical works like statues, paintings or CDs/DVDs, whereas the right of making works available to the public (§ 19a UrhG) is affected when works are distributed in a non-material form.[51] Consequently, § 17 (2) UrhG does not directly apply to online distribution of works.[52] The controversial question therefore is

48 Federal Court of Justice, Decision of 28 November 2013, Case No. I ZR 76/12, GRUR 2014, pp. 549–556.

49 Federal Court of Justice, Decision of 6 March 1986, Case No. I ZR 208/83, GRUR 1986, pp. 736–739.

50 CJEU, case C-128/11, *UsedSoft GmbH v Oracle International Corp.*, ECLI:EU:C:2012:407, pt 43.

51 A. Wiebe, § 17 UrhG para. 2. In: Spindler and Schuster (eds), Recht der elektronischen Medien, 3rd ed, C.H. Beck 2015.

52 Higher Regional Court Hamm, Decision of 15 May 2014, Case No. 22 U 60/13, MMR 2014, pp. 689–694; D. Heerma, § 17 para. 26. In: Wandtke and Bullinger (eds), Praxiskommentar zum Urheberrecht, 4th ed, C.H. Beck 2014; T. Hoeren and S. Jakopp, Der Erschöpfungsgrundsatz im digitalen Umfeld, MMR 2014, pp. 646–649.

whether § 17 (2) UrhG can be applied by analogy to cases dealing with digital works (online exhaustion). Analogous application is possible where two requirements are met: Firstly, there has to be a loophole that was unintended by the lawmaker. Secondly, the situations and affected interests in the not-regulated case have to be comparable to the one regulated.

German courts[53] and some legal scholars[54] are of the opinion that these criteria are not fulfilled in cases of digital distribution. They argue that § 19a UrhG (making works available to the public) conclusively regulates the topic and contains no provision comparable to § 17 (2) UrhG.[55] Furthermore, they point out that the CJEU's UsedSoft judgment cannot be transferred to other digital works because the InfoSoc Directive and not the Computer Programs Directive governs these cases. Additionally, it is argued that recital 29 of the InfoSoc Directive explicitly states that 'the question of exhaustion does not arise in the case of services and on-line services in particular'.[56] Finally, the opponents point out that, from an economic point of view, embodied and digital works are not comparable: whereas traditional storage devices like CDs are subject to deterioration, this is not true for files so that works on the primary and secondary markets directly compete with each other without qualitative differences.[57] Furthermore, files could be reproduced without loss and any number of times.[58]

However, each and every argument can be opposed. First of all, recitals of directives are not binding so that they can only influence the construction of the law.[59] As the InfoSoc Directive dates back more than 15 years, it is obvious that the European lawmaker did not imagine how the online distribution of works would develop. The same holds true for the national lawmaker. As the UsedSoft judgment and the current legal discussion show, the question of exhaustion does arise in cases of online

---

[53] Higher Regional Court Hamburg, Decision of 24 March 2015, Case No. 10 U 5/11, ZUM 2015, pp. 503–504; Higher Regional Court Hamm, Decision of 15 May 2014, Case No. 22 U 60/13, NJW 2014, pp. 3659–3667; Higher Regional Court Stuttgart, Decision of 3 November 2011, Case No. 2 U 49/11; GRUR-RR 2012, pp. 243–246; Regional Court Berlin, Decision of 11 March 2014, Case No. 16 O 73/13, GRUR-RR 2014, pp. 490–491.

[54] A. Wiebe, § 17 UrhG para. 8. In: Spindler and Schuster (eds), Recht der elektronischen Medien, 3rd ed, C.H. Beck 2015; H. Schack, Urheber- und Urhebervertragsrecht, 7th ed, Mohr Siebeck 2015, para. 463 f.; S. Apel, Keine Anwendung der "UsedSoft"-Rechtsprechung des EuGH jenseits von Computerprogrammen, ZUM 2015, pp. 640–648; M. Becker, Zur Dogmatik des Erschöpfungsgrundsatzes im digitalen Umfeld, UFITA 2015, pp. 687–708; R. Hauck, Gebrauchthandel mit digitalen Gütern, NJW 2014, pp. 3616–3619.

[55] Higher Regional Court Hamm, Decision of 15 May 2014, Case No. 22 U 60/13, NJW 2014, pp. 3659–3667.

[56] Higher Regional Court Hamburg, Decision of 24 March 2015, Case No. 10 U 5/11, ZUM 2015, pp. 503–504; Higher Regional Court Hamm, Decision of 15 May 2014, Case No. 22 U 60/13, NJW 2014, pp. 3659–3667.

[57] R. Hauck, Gebrauchthandel mit digitalen Gütern, NJW 2014, pp. 3616–3619; G. Schulze, Werkgenuss und Werknutzung in Zeiten des Internets, NJW 2014, pp. 721–726.

[58] K.-I. Wöhrn. In: Wandtke (ed), Urheberrecht, 5th ed, De Gruyter 2012, ch. 3 para. 97.

[59] T. Hartmann, Weiterverkauf und "Verleih" online vertriebener Inhalte, GRUR Int 2012, pp. 980–989.

services. Consequently, the obviously outdated recital cannot serve as an argument in this legal discussion.[60] This also leads to the conclusion that there in fact is an unintended regulatory gap.[61]

The opponents also forget that although the CJEU's judgment cannot be transferred directly, it is possible to draw conclusions for other cases. The CJEU laid emphasis on the purpose of the exhaustion principle and pointed out that the author economically benefited from his work once and that he therefore should not be able to control the secondary market with regard to this work.[62] In line with this, it is not understandable why the traditional book buyer should be able to resell the book, whereas e-book buyers do not have that possibility.[63] The slightly lower price for e-books cannot justify that difference. The CJEU's conclusions can thus be transferred to the question at hand. Any other result would provide copyright proprietors with the possibility to circumvent the principle of exhaustion by only relying on online distribution.[64] At the same time, it is the copyright proprietor's very own risk that digital works do not deteriorate when it decides to open up to the online-distribution market.[65] Additionally, the possibility of numerous reproductions is irrelevant for the right of distribution and the question of exhaustion. The right of reproduction never exhausts so that each and every reproduction has to be covered by another exception to copyright.[66] Finally, any other result would eliminate a functioning digital single market within the European Union.[67]

However, as long as the legal discussion goes on and judgments of the highest courts do not clarify the legal situation, one cannot say that the current copyright law sufficiently acknowledges the challenges of the digital society. The lawmaker is consequently asked to explicitly extend the principle of exhaustion to cases of online distribution.

---

[60] J. Druschel, Die Regelung digitaler Inhalte im Gemeinsamen Europäischen Kaufrecht, GRUR Int 2015, pp. 125–137; T. Hoeren and S. Jakopp, Der Erschöpfungsgrundsatz im digitalen Umfeld, MMR 2014, pp. 646–649.

[61] T. Hoeren and S. Jakopp, Der Erschöpfungsgrundsatz im digitalen Umfeld, MMR 2014, pp. 646–649.

[62] CJEU, case C-128/11, *UsedSoft GmbH v Oracle International Corp.*, ECLI:EU:C:2012:407, pt 43.

[63] T. Hoeren and S. Jakopp, Der Erschöpfungsgrundsatz im digitalen Umfeld, MMR 2014, pp. 646–649.

[64] D. Heerma, § 17 para. 29. In: Wandtke and Bullinger (eds), Praxiskommentar zum Urheberrecht, 4th ed, C.H. Beck 2014; T. Hoeren and S. Jakopp, Der Erschöpfungsgrundsatz im digitalen Umfeld, MMR 2014, pp. 646–649.

[65] D. Heerma, § 17 para. 29. In: Wandtke and Bullinger (eds), Praxiskommentar zum Urheberrecht, 4th ed, C.H. Beck 2014.

[66] D. Heerma, § 17 para. 28. In: Wandtke and Bullinger (eds), Praxiskommentar zum Urheberrecht, 4th ed, C.H. Beck 2014.

[67] T. Hoeren and S. Jakopp, Der Erschöpfungsgrundsatz im digitalen Umfeld, MMR 2014, pp. 646–649.

#### 19.3.3.2 Freedom of Expression and Freedom of Press

The Urheberrechtsgesetz contains a number of provisions relating to the freedom of expression and the freedom of the press.

§ 50 UrhG, e.g., allows the usage (i.e., the reproduction, distribution and communication to the public) of works that become perceivable in the course of current events. Newspapers, periodicals, as well as other data carriers mainly devoted to current events and TV stations can rely on this exception when reporting about current events. The exception is limited to the extent justified by the purpose of the report, which opens the possibility to acknowledge conflicting interests above all the freedom of the press as laid down in Article 5 GG. The provision includes not only traditional newspapers but also digital online media.[68] In these cases, however, the content has to be deleted as soon as a report is outdated.[69] It is thus not allowed to create online news archives under § 50 UrhG.[70]

§ 48 (1) UrhG further allows the press to reproduce and distribute speeches relating to current affairs as long as the speeches were made in public or were published by means of communication to the public.

Moreover, § 49 UrhG even permits the reproduction and distribution of individual broadcast commentaries and individual articles, as well as illustrations published in connection therewith if they concern current political, economic or religious issues and do not contain a statement reserving rights. In these cases, however, the author must be paid equitable remuneration for the reproduction unless the new article only contains short extracts of several commentaries or articles in the form of an overview.

§ 51 s. 1 UrhG allows everyone, not just press representatives, to reproduce and distribute a published work for the purpose of quotation in so far as such exploitation is justified by the particular purpose. § 51 s. 2 UrhG then contains model examples: scientific works, works of language and musical works. Other works like videos can also be covered by § 51 s. 1 UrhG.[71] The purpose of quotation is only met if there is a connection between the user's work and the quoted work.[72] This is, for example, the case, if the reproduction aims at illustrating the new content, at critically analysing the quoted work[73] or at supporting one's own

[68] T. Dreier, § 50 para. 3. In: Dreier and Schulze (eds), Urheberrechtsgesetz, 5th ed, C.H. Beck 2015.

[69] Federal Court of Justice, Decision of 5 October 2010, Case No. I ZR 127/09, NJW 2011, pp. 544–545.

[70] S. Lüft, § 50 para. 3. In: Wandtke and Bullinger (eds), Praxiskommentar zum Urheberrecht, 4th ed, C.H. Beck 2014.

[71] S. Lüft, § 51 para. 17. In: Wandtke and Bullinger (eds), Praxiskommentar zum Urheberrecht, 4th ed, C.H. Beck 2014.

[72] Federal Court of Justice, Decision of 20 December 2007, Case No. I ZR 42/05, GRUR 2008, pp. 693–697; G. Spindler, § 51 UrhG para. 16. In: Schricker and Loewenheim (eds), Urheberrecht, 5th ed, C.H. Beck 2017.

[73] Higher Regional Court Munich, Decision of 14 June 2012, Case No. 29 U 1204/12, ZUM-RD 2012, pp. 479–485.

position.[74] The reproduction of a work without any or with only insignificant 'intellectual' debate is not sufficient.[75]

Besides, it is permissible under § 52 UrhG to communicate a published work to the public if the communication serves a non-profit-making purpose for the organiser, participants are admitted free of charge and, in the case of a lecture or performance of a work, none of the performers (§ 73 UrhG) is paid a special remuneration. The copyright proprietor must be reimbursed adequately for the communication of his work in these cases if none of the exceptions mentioned is applicable (e.g., events organised by the youth welfare service). The exception in § 52 UrhG does not extend to the right of making works available to the public in the sense of § 19a UrhG.[76] Therefore, publishing protected works on a private website does not fall within the scope of § 52 UrhG.

#### 19.3.3.3 Science and Education

The current Urheberrechtsgesetz contains several exceptions to copyright in order to meet the demands of scientific and educational facilities.[77]

*§ 52a UrhG* is applicable if works are made available to the public for instruction and research. According to § 52a (1) No. 1 UrhG, it is 'permissible for published small, limited parts of a work, small scale works, as well as individual articles from newspapers or periodicals for illustration in teaching at schools, universities, non-commercial institutions of education and further education, and at vocational training institutions, exclusively for the specifically limited circle of those taking part in the instruction to be made available to the public, to the extent that this is necessary for the respective purpose and is justified for the pursuit of non-commercial aims'. One of the main problems with this provision is to determine how large 'small, limited parts of a work' may be. The Federal Court of Justice is of the opinion that not more than 12% of the work or 100 of its pages may be made available to the public to meet that criterion.[78] Other courts and legal scholars suggest different limits.[79] On the one hand, it has to be criticised that each and every one of those lines is drawn at random and cannot substitute a case-by-case analysis taking into account the colliding interests.[80] On the other hand, precise numbers, of course, improve

[74] Federal Court of Justice, Decision of 30 November 2011, Case No. I ZR 212/10, GRUR 2012, pp. 819–822.

[75] Federal Court of Justice, Decision of 20 December 2007, Case No. I ZR 42/05, GRUR 2008, pp. 693–697.

[76] T. Dreier, § 52 para. 18. In: Dreier and Schulze (eds), Urheberrechtsgesetz, 5th ed, C.H. Beck 2015.

[77] §§ 46, 47, 52a, 52b, 53 (3), 53a UrhG.

[78] Federal Court of Justice, Decision of 28 November 2013, Case No. I ZR 76/12, GRUR 2014, pp. 549–556.

[79] E.g. more than 10 but less than 20%: U. Loewenheim, § 52a para. 4. In: Schricker and Loewenheim (eds), Urheberrecht, 5th ed, C.H. Beck 2017.

[80] U. Loewenheim, § 52a para. 4. In: Schricker and Loewenheim (eds), Urheberrecht, 5th ed, C.H. Beck 2017; T. Hoeren, Kleine Werke? – Zur Reichweite von § 52a UrhG, ZUM 2011, pp. 369–375.

legal certainty. Distance universities also belong to the beneficiaries.[81] 'For illustration in teaching' means that the usage of the work has to be linked to the educational content. It is sufficient that it deepens or complements the content.[82] Furthermore, teachers and lecturers profit from a margin of discretion in respect to what is necessary to reach the educational goals.[83] To profit from the exception, the beneficiary has to make use of technical protection measures (e.g., passwords for online platforms) in order to make sure that the work is only made accessible to the participants of the instructed group.[84] The provision does not contain an absolute limit in regard to the number of participants so that in the case of a distance university the Federal Court of Justice found that 4000 participants can still be 'a limited circle' within the meaning of § 52a (1) UrhG.[85] The usage has to be 'justified for the pursuit of non-commercial aims'. That opens the doors to a case-by-case examination taking into account the conflicting interests. According to the Federal Court of Justice, a fair, reasonable and easily detectable offer for a contractual agreement leads to the result that the usage is not justified within the meaning of the provision (also see Sect. 19.3.1.4 above).[86]

§ 52a (2) UrhG excludes from the exception works intended for use in instruction in schools and sets special rules for cinematographic works. § 52a (3) UrhG states that also the reproduction of works is allowed as long as the copies are necessary to make the work available (e.g., scans and/or storages on hard drives). According to § 52a (4) UrhG, equitable remuneration has to be paid to a collecting society.

*§ 52b UrhG* covers acts of communication of works at terminals in publicly accessible libraries, museums and archives if the institution neither directly nor indirectly serves an economic or commercial purpose (e.g., university libraries). The exception is limited to the stocks (permanent non-lending collection) of the privileged institution. Reproductions of a work in excess of the number stocked by the institution shall not be made available simultaneously at such terminals. Each and every electronic copy has thus to be ascribed to an analogue one.[87] Consequently, the number of available exemplars can maximally be doubled.

---

[81] Federal Court of Justice, Decision of 28 November 2013, Case No. I ZR 76/12, GRUR 2014, pp. 549–556.

[82] U. Loewenheim, § 52a para. 11. In: Schricker and Loewenheim (eds), Urheberrecht, 5th ed, C.H. Beck 2017.

[83] Cf. Higher Regional Court Frankfurt a.M., Decision of 24 November 2009, Case No. 11 U 40/09, GRUR 2010, pp. 1–4; Regional Court Stuttgart, Decision of 27 September 2011, Case No. 17 O 671/10, GRUR-RR 2011, pp. 419–423.

[84] S. Lüft, § 52a para. 9. In: Wandtke and Bullinger (eds), Praxiskommentar zum Urheberrecht, 4th ed, C.H. Beck 2014.

[85] Federal Court of Justice, Decision of 28 November 2013, Case No. I ZR 76/12, GRUR 2014, pp. 549–556.

[86] Federal Court of Justice, Decision of 28 November 2013, Case No. I ZR 76/12, GRUR 2014, pp. 549–556.

[87] T. Dreier. In: Dreier and Schulze (eds), Urheberrechtsgesetz, 5th ed, C.H. Beck 2015, § 52b para. 9.

Works may only be made available under § 52b UrhG if the terminals are specifically dedicated to the purpose of research and private study. Thus, the ability of library users to download works on private laptops is not covered by the exception.[88] Similarly, it is not allowed to provide computers that can also be used for other purposes (e.g., text processing or Internet research).[89] The terminals have to be located on the premises of the privileged institution. That hinders the institutions from offering their users the possibility to access the works from outside the institution, e.g. via VPN access.[90]

In April 2015, the Federal Court of Justice decided that a university library also profits from the exception if it offers its users the possibility to print the works or to store them on external storage media like USB sticks.[91] The court rightly argued that one has to differentiate between the university's usage (making the work available), which is covered by § 52b UrhG, and the usage of the library users (reproduction), which is often covered by § 53 UrhG (see Sect. 19.3.3.6 below).

The provision explicitly states that the exception can be ruled out by contract. The Federal Court of Justice pointed out that only existing contractual agreements hinder the beneficiary from profiting from the exception, whereas mere offers do not suffice.[92] The author is granted equitable remuneration.

Against the backdrop of a developing information society, the foregoing provisions are an important step to adjust the Urheberrechtsgesetz to the needs of the science and education sector. However, there still is pent-up demand in that regard as the wording of the exceptions is often kept very broad, which necessarily leads to legal uncertainty. In order to eliminate the uncertainties, a government draft bill was published in April 2017.[93] The government plans to reorganise and to extend the exceptions for science and education. Therefore, a new subsection shall be introduced (§§ 60a ff. UrhG). The following text gives a short overview of the most important legal changes suggested in the draft (referred to as § X UrhG draft).

---

[88] G. Dreyer, § 52b para. 8. In: Dreyer, Kotthoff and Meckel (eds), Urheberrecht, 2nd ed, C.F. Müller 2013; J. Heckmann, § 52b UrhG para. 18. In: Spindler and Schuster (eds), Recht der elektronischen Medien, 3rd ed, C.H. Beck 2015.

[89] G. Dreyer, § 52b para. 8. In: Dreyer, Kotthoff and Meckel (eds), Urheberrecht, 2nd ed, C.F. Müller 2013; U. Lowenheim, § 52b para. 8. In: Schricker and Loewenheim (eds), Urheberrecht, 5th ed, C.H. Beck 2017.

[90] J. Heckmann, § 52b UrhG para. 20. In: Spindler and Schuster (eds), Recht der elektronischen Medien, 3rd ed, C.H. Beck 2015.

[91] Federal Court of Justice, Decision of 16 April 2015, Case No. I ZR 69/11, NJW 2015, pp. 3511–3517.

[92] Federal Court of Justice, Decision of 16 April 2015, Case No. I ZR 69/11, NJW 2015, pp. 3511–3517.

[93] https://www.bmjv.de/SharedDocs/Gesetzgebungsverfahren/Dokumente/RegE_Urheber-Wissensgesellschafts-Gesetz.pdf;jsessionid=0A0BA9EF8DE1A18DCEB6104980A80EAA.1_cid324?__blob=publicationFile&v=1. Accessed 16 May 2017; an excerpt of the new core provisions in English language can be found here: https://www.bmjv.de/SharedDocs/Gesetzgebungsverfahren/Dokumente/RegE_UrhWissG_draft.pdf;jsessionid=0A0BA9EF8DE1A18DCEB6104980A80EAA.1_cid324?__blob=publicationFile&v=2. Accessed 16 May 2017.

The provision of § 52a UrhG is basically transferred to § 60a UrhG draft. The government suggests to legally define how large a work's part may be (15%). Besides, the draft explicitly states that the use for preparation and follow-up work is also covered by the exception. Section 60a UrhG draft also regards that new technologies may be developed as it refers to 'other forms of communication to the public'.

The current § 52b UrhG is transferred to § 60e UrhG draft. The government, however, suggests a significant change: the exception would no longer require that each electronic exemplar has to be ascribed to an analogue one so that it would suffice that the privileged institution is in possession of one analogue copy of the work. The draft also answers the question how terminal users may use the work. It explicitly allows, inter alia, the reproduction of 10% of a work per session.

It is further suggested to introduce a new exception for scientific use in § 60c UrhG draft. Section 60c (1) UrhG draft would allow to reproduce, distribute and make available to the public 15% of a protected work for a clearly defined circle of persons. According to § 60c (2) UrhG draft, up to 75% of a work may be reproduced for one's own scientific use.

Section 60g (1) UrhG draft explicitly states that the exceptions provided in this new section are mandatory and that contradictory contractual agreements are void. According to § 60g (2) UrhG draft, this shall not be the case for the exception for terminals in public libraries and for the exception for orders for dispatch of copies.

The suggested changes would create a milestone on the way to a copyright law that sufficiently acknowledges the needs of the science and education sector. The changes would make it significantly easier for laymen to understand and follow the law. However, it is uncertain if the bill will be passed during the current legislative term, which will end in September 2017.

#### 19.3.3.4 Exception for Big Data and Data Mining?

The Urheberrechtsgesetz currently does not provide for an exception that allows data or text mining.[94]

In the above-mentioned draft bill (see Sect. 19.3.3.3 above), the government, however, suggests to implement a text and data mining exception with regard to research and science. The proposed provision (§ 60d UrhG draft) allows to reproduce works even if the reproduction is made automatically and systematically in order to gain evaluable data sets. Furthermore, the provision allows to make works available to a limited circle of persons for joint scientific projects and to third parties in order to make it possible for them to verify the scientific quality. The exceptions will only apply if the user pursues non-commercial purposes. Once the scientific purpose is fulfilled, the data sets have to be deleted. It is, however, possible to transfer the data sets to public libraries, archives, museums and other educational facilities, which then store the data sets as long as these institutions do not pursue a direct

[94] Cf. S. Ott, Die Google Buchsuche – Eine massive Urheberrechtsverletzung?, GRUR Int 2007, pp. 562–569.

or indirect commercial goal. § 60d UrhG draft does not allow to access protected works but assumes that the used work is already accessible for the scientists.

#### 19.3.3.5 Temporary Copies with Special Regard to Streaming

Section 44a UrhG provides an exception to copyright in regard to temporary acts of reproduction:

> Those temporary acts of reproduction shall be permissible which are transient or incidental and constitute an integral and essential part of a technical process and whose sole purpose is to enable
>
> 1. a transmission in a network between third parties by an intermediary, or
>
> 2. a lawful use of a work or other protected subject-matter to be made and which have no independent economic significance.

The provision implements Article 5 (1) InfoSoc Directive into national law[95] and is not mandatory (see Sect. 19.3.1.4 above). The main question in regard to § 44a No. 2 UrhG is whether or not the provision is applicable to streaming situations. While courts have not dealt with the problem in detail yet,[96] it is highly controversial among legal scholars.

In order to understand the legal debate, it is first necessary to understand the technical process of streaming. One has to distinguish between the so-called *true-streaming method* and *progressive downloads*. In the first case, single data packages containing work-pieces are downloaded to the RAM or the hard drive. These data packages are deleted immediately after the part has been played so that the next data package can be saved.[97] The technically well-versed user has the possibility to choose the size of the storage (so-called buffer size) and can thus influence how long the stored movie or audio pieces are.[98] The work as a whole is never stored when using this method.[99] In case of the progressive-download method, the work is completely downloaded to the RAM or the hard drive.[100] Normally, the copy gets deleted automatically after some time (e.g., when the play has ended, the browser is

[95] T. Dreier, § 44a para. 1. In: Dreier and Schulze (eds), Urheberrechtsgesetz, 5th ed, C.H. Beck 2015; C. Galetzka and E. Stamer, Streaming – aktuelle Entwicklungen in Recht und Praxis – Redtube, kinox.to & Co., MMR 2014, pp. 292–298.

[96] Hitherto decisions: Regional Court Cologne, Decision of 24 January 2014, Case No. 209 O 188/13, MMR 2014, pp. 193–194; Regional Court Hamburg, Decision of 19 December 2013, Case No. 310 O 460/13, ZUM 2014, pp. 434–435; Local Court Hanover, Decision of 27 May 2014, Case No. 550 C 13749/13, ZUM-RD 2014, pp. 667–669.

[97] T. Busch, Zur urheberrechtlichen Einordnung der Nutzung von Streamingangeboten, GRUR 2011, pp. 496–503.

[98] A. Wiebe, § 44a UrhG para. 8. In: Spindler and Schuster (eds), Recht der elektronischen Medien, 3rd ed, C.H. Beck 2015; T. Busch, Zur urheberrechtlichen Einordnung der Nutzung von Streamingangeboten, GRUR 2011, pp. 496–503.

[99] J. Heerma, § 16 para. 22. In: Wandtke and Bullinger (eds), Praxiskommentar zum Urheberrecht, 4th ed, C.H. Beck 2014.

[100] T. Busch, Zur urheberrechtlichen Einordnung der Nutzung von Streamingangeboten, GRUR 2011, pp. 496–503.

closed or the computer is shut down),[101] but it is also possible to change these settings or to simply prevent the deletion by not causing the deletion point. For an average user, it is hardly possible to find the data on the hard drive and to replay it.[102] The user often has no influence on the streaming method, as for example streaming via 'flash player' always makes use of the true-streaming method, whereas a progressive download runs every time the 'DivX' format is used.[103]

The vast majority of legal scholars are of the opinion that a reproduction of the work is only given in cases where the reproduced part itself is a protected work within the meaning of § 2 (2) UrhG.[104] Others argue from a more economic point of view that, although parts of the work are often deleted immediately after they have been played, the whole work is eventually reproduced.[105]

§ 44a is only applicable to temporary reproductions. The vast majority of legal scholars for good reasons are of the opinion that in the case of progressive downloads, the copies are not temporary[106] because the data are not deleted immediately after the work has been played.[107] This opinion is also in line with case law of the CJEU.[108] Others point out that the user is not aware of the fact that the data may be stored on the computer even after the work's play[109] and ignore that no subjective criterion can be found in § 44a UrhG. Concerning the true-streaming method, it is

[101] A. Wiebe, § 44a UrhG para. 8. In: Spindler and Schuster (eds), Recht der elektronischen Medien, 3rd ed, C.H. Beck 2015; P. Hilgert and S. Hilgert, Nutzung von Streaming-Portalen – Urheberrechtliche Fragen am Beispiel von Redtube, MMR 2014, pp. 85–88.

[102] J. Ensthaler, Streaming und Urheberrechtsverletzung, NJW 2014, pp. 1553–1558.

[103] C. Galetzka and E. Stamer, Streaming – aktuelle Entwicklungen in Recht und Praxis – Redtube, kinox.to & Co., MMR 2014, pp. 292–298.

[104] Cf. CJEU, case C-403/08, *Football Association Premier League Ltd and Others v Leisure and Others,* ECLI:EU:C:2011:631; T. Dreier, § 44a para. 4. In: Dreier and Schulze (eds), Urheberrechtsgesetz, 5th ed, C.H. Beck 2015; J. Heerma, § 16 para. 6. In: Wandtke and Bullinger (eds), Praxiskommentar zum Urheberrecht, 4th ed, C.H. Beck 2014; C. Galetzka and E. Stamer, Streaming – aktuelle Entwicklungen in Recht und Praxis – Redtube, kinox.to & Co., MMR 2014, pp. 292–298; M. Stieper, Rezeptiver Werkgenuss als rechtmäßige Nutzung, MMR 2012, pp. 12–17.

[105] J. Heerma, § 16 para. 22. In: Wandtke and Bullinger (eds), Praxiskommentar zum Urheberrecht, 4th ed, C.H. Beck 2014; A. Wiebe, § 44a UrhG para. 7. In: Spindler and Schuster (eds), Recht der elektronischen Medien, 3rd ed, C.H. Beck 2015; T. Busch, Zur urheberrechtlichen Einordnung der Nutzung von Streamingangeboten, GRUR 2011, pp. 496–503; J. Ensthaler, Streaming und Urheberrechtsverletzung, NJW 2014, pp. 1553–1558.

[106] T. Dreier, § 44a para. 4. In: Dreier and Schulze (eds), Urheberrechtsgesetz, 5th ed, C.H. Beck 2015; C. Galetzka and E. Stamer, Streaming – aktuelle Entwicklungen in Recht und Praxis – Redtube, kinox.to & Co., MMR 2014, pp. 292–298.

[107] A. Wiebe, § 44a UrhG para. 9. In: Spindler and Schuster (eds), Recht der elektronischen Medien, 3rd ed, C.H. Beck 2015.

[108] Cf. CJEU, case C-558/07, *The Queen, on the application of S.P.C.M. SA, C.H. Erbslöh KG, Lake Chemicals and Minerals Ltd and Hercules Inc. v Secretary of State for the Environment, Food and Rural Affairs*, ECR 2009 I 5783.

[109] T. Busch, Zur urheberrechtlichen Einordnung der Nutzung von Streamingangeboten, GRUR 2011, pp. 496–503.

to say that copies are temporary within the meaning of § 44a UrhG as long as the user does not choose a big buffer size.[110]

The question whether or not a reproduction has *independent economic significance* can be answered in a similar way: if the data are stored for a longer period, there is also an independent economic significance.[111]

A reproduction of a work is only in line with § 44a No. 2 UrhG if its purpose is to enable *lawful use*. If that meant any kind of use that is made legal by copyright law,[112] § 44a UrhG would be useless.[113] Rightly, the sole receptive usage of a work is lawful within the meaning of § 44a UrhG because it is not part of the proprietor's exclusive rights.[114] During the streaming process, temporary copies are necessary to enjoy the work, so they are a dependent process within the scope of the work's utilisation.[115] This interpretation is also in line with the legislator's intention.[116]

The most crucial question is whether the streaming source itself has to be legal to justify the users' reproductions. By uploading the file, the source's provider infringes the proprietor's right of making the work available to the public within the meaning of § 19a UrhG. Therefore, consent is generally necessary to justify such usage. Some argue that streaming is not in line with § 44a UrhG if the source is

---

[110] C. Galetzka and E. Stamer, Streaming – aktuelle Entwicklungen in Recht und Praxis – Redtube, kinox.to & Co., MMR 2014, pp. 292–298.

[111] A. Wiebe, § 44a UrhG para. 9. In: Spindler and Schuster (eds), Recht der elektronischen Medien, 3rd ed, C.H. Beck 2015; M. Stieper, Rezeptiver Werkgenuss als rechtmäßige Nutzung, MMR 2012, pp. 12–17.

[112] T. Dreier, § 44a para. 8. In: Dreier and Schulze (eds), Urheberrechtsgesetz, 5th ed, C.H. Beck 2015; M. v. Welser, § 44a paras. 16 ff. In: Wandtke and Bullinger (eds), Praxiskommentar zum Urheberrecht, 4th ed, C.H. Beck 2014.

[113] Higher Regional Court Berlin, Decision of 30 April 2004, Case No. 5 U 98/02, GRUR-RR 2004, pp. 228–236; A. Wiebe, § 44a UrhG para. 10. In: Spindler and Schuster (eds), Recht der elektronischen Medien, 3rd ed, C.H. Beck 2015; J. Ensthaler, Streaming und Urheberrechtsverletzung, NJW 2014, pp. 1553–1558; K. Fangerow and D. Schulz, Die Nutzung von Angeboten auf kino.to – Eine urheberrechtliche Analyse des Film-Streamings im Internet, GRUR 2010, pp. 677–682; C. Galetzka and E. Stamer, Streaming – aktuelle Entwicklungen in Recht und Praxis – Redtube, kinox.to & Co., MMR 2014, pp. 292–298.

[114] Cf. CJEU, case C-403/08, *Football Association Premier League Ltd and Others v Leisure and Others*, ECLI:EU:C:2011:631; G. Dreier, § 44a para. 12. In: Dreyer, Kotthoff and Meckel (eds), Urheberrecht, 2nd ed, C.F. Müller 2013; W. Schulz, § 44a para. 13. In: Ahlberg and Göttig (eds), Beck'scher Online-Kommentar Urheberrecht, 15th ed, C.H. Beck 2017; K. Fangerow and D. Schulz, Die Nutzung von Angeboten auf kino.to – Eine urheberrechtliche Analyse des Film-Streamings im Internet, GRUR 2010, pp. 677–682; A. Stolz, Rezipient = Rechtsverletzer…? – Keine Urheberrechtsverletzung durch die Nutzung illegaler Streaming-Angebote, MMR 2013, pp. 353–358.

[115] K. Fangerow and D. Schulz, Die Nutzung von Angeboten auf kino.to – Eine urheberrechtliche Analyse des Film-Streamings im Internet, GRUR 2010, pp. 677–682; C. Galetzka and E. Stamer, Streaming – aktuelle Entwicklungen in Recht und Praxis – Redtube, kinox.to & Co., MMR 2014, pp. 292–298.

[116] Bundestag Drucksache 4/270, p. 28.

evidently illegal and thus draw a comparison to § 53 (1) UrhG.[117] Others take the view that even those sources can be streamed in accordance with § 44a UrhG and compare the streaming situation to the reception of other communication channels like pirate radio stations or illegally copied books.[118] In these cases, the reception of the work is never restricted by copyright although the source is illegal. Rightly, the same has to apply in the online context because, otherwise, copyright infringements would be dependent from technical coincidences.[119]

On 26 April 2017, the CJEU came to a long-awaited decision in a case concerning the use of illegal streaming platforms.[120] The court ruled that users of those platforms can at least not rely on the exception of Article 5 (1) InfoSoc Directive if they know that the works were made available illegally. The court first referred to former case law[121] and pointed out that the pure reception of a work that was made available illegally generally has to be considered as lawful use. The case at hand, however, had to be judged differently as it was obvious for the user that the streamed content had been made available without the proprietor's consent. To justify that result, the court made use of the triple test laid down in Article 5 (5) InfoSoc Directive (see Sect. 19.3.2 above). In the CJEU's view, the normal exploitation of the work would have been endangered and authors' rights would have been unreasonably prejudiced if the usage was covered by the exception for temporary reproductions.

Before the judgment of the CJEU, it was hard even for legal experts to keep a clear view of the issues and solutions in this matter. Even after the long-awaited judgment, important questions remain unanswered. The CJEU did, for example, not deal with the question whether the copy was temporary and did not differentiate between true streaming and progressive downloads. Furthermore, the court very much referred to the specific case the Dutch national court had to decide. In that case, due to explicit advertising, it was very clear that the users knew that the source was illegal. The decision thus shifts the problem on to the question which criteria determine if a source is obviously illegal. It is very questionable if the judgment can be transferred to less obvious illegal streaming portals.

---

[117] Regional Court Hamburg, Decision of 19 December 2013, Case No. 310 O 460/13, ZUM 2014, pp. 434–435; W. Schulz, § 44a para. 13. In: Ahlberg and Göttig (eds), Beck'scher Online-Kommentar Urheberrecht, 15th ed, C.H. Beck 2017; A.-A. Wandtke and F.-T. v. Gerlach, Die urheberrechtliche Rechtmäßigkeit von Audio-Video Streaminginhalten im Internet, GRUR 2013, pp. 676–683.

[118] C. Galetzka and E. Stamer, Streaming – aktuelle Entwicklungen in Recht und Praxis – Redtube, kinox.to & Co., MMR 2014, pp. 292–298; A. Stolz, Rezipient = Rechtsverletzer…? – Keine Urheberrechtsverletzung durch die Nutzung illegaler Streaming-Angebote, MMR 2013, pp. 353–358.

[119] A. Stolz, Rezipient = Rechtsverletzer…? – Keine Urheberrechtsverletzung durch die Nutzung illegaler Streaming-Angebote, MMR 2013, pp. 353–358.

[120] CJEU, case C-527/15, *Stichting Brein v Jack Frederik Wullems*, ECLI:EU:C:2017:300.

[121] CJEU, case C-403/08, *Football Association Premier League Ltd and Others v Leisure and Others*, ECLI:EU:C:2011:631.

One also has to criticise that the question whether or not a copy is temporary is dependent on the program used by the Internet user, who often does not understand the technical background of streaming and thus does not see any difference. Against that backdrop, the legal situation in Germany and Europe cannot be considered sufficient and is likely to cause chilling effects for the development of an information society. If the reproductions during the streaming procedure are not in line with § 44a UrhG, they can still be covered by § 53 UrhG on the condition that the source is not evidently illegal (see Sect. 19.3.3.6 below).

#### 19.3.3.6 Private Use

§ 53 UrhG provides for exceptions to copyright law in regard to the private use of works. § 53 (1) UrhG allows natural persons to reproduce works for private use and *on any medium*, as long as the copy neither directly nor indirectly serves commercial purposes and no obviously unlawfully produced model or a model that has been unlawfully made available to the public is used for the reproduction. The question whether the copy indirectly serves a commercial purpose is of course a crucial point when applying the provision in practice. For example, copies made for the purpose of professional education (university students) are not covered.[122]

In line with the legislator's intention, the vast majority of legal scholars are of the opinion that a model is obviously unlawful if the specific user could reckon that the source was illegal.[123] The opposing view argues for an objective understanding of the provision and thus examines whether an average user could reckon that the source was illegal.[124]

§ 53 (1) UrhG also covers reproductions made by others as long as no payment is received therefor or the reproductions are on paper or a similar medium and have been made by the use of any kind of photomechanical technique or by some other process having similar effects. Consequently, both the template and the reproduction have to be in physical form; digitals are not covered by the exception.[125] However, this does not cover the distribution of the work. Therefore, § 53a UrhG (order for dispatch of copies) was created.[126] This provision applies to reproductions of individual contributions released in newspapers and periodicals and small parts of a released work made by public libraries that are transmitted by post or facsimile as long as the orderer's usage is covered by § 53 UrhG. For the reproduction and transmission of works in other electronic form, further criteria have to be fulfilled

122 Federal Court of Justice, Decision of 9 June 1983, Case No. I ZR 70/81, GRUR 1984, pp. 54–56.

123 T. Dreier, § 53 para. 12b. In: Dreier and Schulze (eds), Urheberrechtsgesetz, 5th ed, C.H. Beck 2015; U. Loewenheim, § 53 para. 19. In: Schricker and Loewenheim (eds), Urheberrecht, 5th ed, C.H. Beck 2017.

124 M. Witz, § 53 para. 20. In: Fromm and Nordemann (eds), Urheberrecht, 11th ed, Verlag W. Kohlhammer 2014.

125 Federal Court of Justice, Decision of 2 October 2008, Case No. I ZR 18/09, GRUR 2009, pp. 53–55.

126 Cf. U. Loewenheim, § 53a para. 3. In: Schricker and Loewenheim (eds), Urheberrecht, 5th ed, C.H. Beck 2017.

according to § 53a (1) s. 2 f. (also see Sect. 19.3.1.4). Equitable remuneration has to be paid according to § 53a (2) UrhG.

As opposed to this, § 53 (2) UrhG is applicable to 'one's own use' in certain legally defined cases. The difference between these two sections of the provision is that one's own use can also serve professional and commercial purposes as long as the copies are not passed on to external third parties.[127] Legal entities are also covered by these exceptions.[128] § 53 (2) UrhG is also applicable to reproductions made by others for the privileged purpose. § 53 (3)–(7) UrhG covers further specific cases.

The user does not have to pay compensation to the copyright proprietor for the usage covered by § 53 (1)–(3) UrhG. An indirect compensation is, however, ensured by §§ 54 ff. UrhG. For example, manufacturers of appliances and of storage mediums that are used for reproduction of works (e.g., copying machines or hard drives) have to pay remuneration to a collecting society according to § 54 (1) UrhG.

Parts of the provision have to be considered mandatory as § 95b UrhG refers to them (see Sect. 19.3.1.4 above).

#### 19.3.3.7 Panorama Exception

Another exception to German copyright is stipulated in § 59 UrhG:

> (1) It shall be permissible to reproduce, by painting, drawing, photography or cinematography, works which are permanently located on public ways, streets or places and to distribute and publicly communicate such copies. For works of architecture, this provision shall be applicable only to the external appearance.
>
> (2) Reproductions may not be carried out on a work of architecture.

This so-called panorama exception has been part of the German copyright law since the end of the nineteenth century and is of major importance in the field of architecture. Nonetheless, it is also applicable to artistic works, works of applied art and other types of works listed in § 2 (1) UrhG.[129] According to the provision, it permitted to reproduce works that are permanently located in public places and distribute such copies or make them available to the public. The reproduction is, however, only allowed in two-dimensional ways, e.g. in form of a photo or a video.[130] The replication of a whole building, no matter in which size, is not permitted under § 59 UrhG.

In order to minimise the infringement of the proprietor's rights, the exception does also not encompass works that are not located in the public permanently. This is particularly relevant for artists who only present their work (e.g., a sculpture) in

[127] Federal Court of Justice, Decision of 14 April 1978, Case No. I ZR 111/76, GRUR 1987, pp. 474–477.

[128] T. Dreier, § 53 para. 18. In: Dreier and Schulze (eds), Urheberrechtsgesetz, 5th ed, C.H. Beck 2015.

[129] T. Dreier, § 59 para. 2. In: Dreier and Schulze (eds), Urheberrechtsgesetz, 5th ed, C.H. Beck 2015; A. Wiebe, § 59 UrhG para. 2. In: Spindler and Schuster (eds), Recht der elektronischen Medien, 3rd ed, C.H. Beck 2015.

[130] U. Gruebler, § 59 para. 8. In: Ahlberg and Göttig (eds), Beck'scher Online-Kommentar Urheberrecht, 15th ed, C.H. Beck 2017.

public for a limited period of time. In these cases, a reproduction of the work is not permissible without the consent of the artist.[131] Similarly, reliance on the exception is not possible when the reproduction shows parts of a work that are not visible from public places. Therefore, a photo of a building that was taken, e.g., from a private apartment across the street does not fall under the exception of § 59 UrhG.[132] No compensation is granted for the usage in line with § 59 UrhG.

In 2015, when a harmonisation of the panorama exception was discussed in the European Parliament, the topic became part of a heated discussion in the media and the legal world. French delegates in the European Parliament proposed to adopt the French panorama exception which does not encompass reproductions for commercial purposes. This approach would, however, not only create legal uncertainty for photographers and documentary filmmakers. Problems would also arise when pictures or videos are shared on social media since many platforms require users to agree to a commercial usage of their content. In light of these problems and the harsh criticism, the parliament eventually decided to postpone the harmonisation of the panorama exceptions in the European Union.[133]

## 19.4 Conclusion

As shown above, the question whether the Urheberrechtsgesetz strikes a fair balance between the right of proprietors and the interests of the public to freely use a work is not easy to answer.

German copyright law focusses on the protection of the work and its author and is consequently based on copyright protection as its core principle. A fair balance can thus only be reached by means of the exceptions. In an overall assessment, German copyright law does fairly balance these goals.

The exceptions adequately give regard to the freedom of expression and the freedom of the press, which are the most important factors for a lively and stable democracy.

With respect to the exceptions for science and education, the hitherto steps taken by the lawmaker are in the right direction. The provisions, however, contain openly formulated criteria and thus cause legal uncertainty. The government draft bill of January 2017 would solve these problems and would introduce further exceptions

---

[131] Federal Court of Justice, Decision of 24 January 2002, Case No. I ZR 102/99, GRUR 2002, pp. 605–607; T. Dreier, § 59 para. 5. In: Dreier and Schulze (eds), Urheberrechtsgesetz, 5th ed, C.H. Beck 2015; U. Gruebler, § 59 para. 5. In: Ahlberg and Göttig (eds), Beck'scher Online-Kommentar Urheberrecht, 15th ed, C.H. Beck 2017.

[132] Federal Court of Justice, Decision of 5 June 2003, Case No. I ZR 192/00, GRUR 2003, pp. 1035–1037; A. Wiebe, § 59 UrhG para. 2. In: Spindler and Schuster (eds), Recht der elektronischen Medien, 3rd ed, C.H. Beck 2015.

[133] N. Rauer and L. Kaase, "Reda-Bericht": Ansätze für eine Reform des europäischen Urheberrechts, GRUR-Prax 2015, pp. 364–366.

for the scientific and educational sector. It is yet uncertain whether the lawmaker will pass the law during the current legislative term.

Besides, the German copyright law lags behind technical developments. As the German law relies on specific exceptions, it is upon the lawmaker to again and again pass new exceptions to copyright. The most important factor for an undisturbed development of an information society, of course, is legal certainty. The foregoing examination has shown that German copyright law often does not meet that requirement.

Especially in regard to the exhaustion of the right of distribution for digital works, users are confronted with legal problems that are incomprehensible for legal laymen. This legal uncertainty causes chilling effects in trade in such works. The same is true for the usage of works via streaming. The long-awaited judgment of the CJEU is not likely to clarify the situation. It will take further court decisions or even better a legal initiative to dispel legal uncertainty in that regard.

# Hungary

# 20

Zsófia Lendvai

## 20.1 Introduction

In its Preamble, the Hungarian Copyright Act[1] (hereinafter Copyright Act or Act) not only acknowledges the need for and importance of a modern, technology-friendly copyright regime, but also stresses the relevance of striking a fair balance between the prevailing interests of right holders and those of users. As one of the main tools for achieving this aim, the legislator chose to transpose the triple or three-step test[2] into the Copyright Act[3] by omitting the first step and adding two further conditions. Accordingly, the Hungarian "four-step test" shall be read as follows: "The use under the provisions relating to free use is permitted and not subject to remuneration only so far as it does not conflict with the proper use of the work and does not unreasonably prejudice the legitimate interests of the author, and it is in compliance with the requirements of fairness and is not designed for a purpose incompatible with the intention of free use." With regard to the general standards of legal interpretation, all legal instruments should be interpreted in conformity with European harmonizing measures, and the courts may turn to the relevant international treaties when interpreting the above section.

[1] Act LXXVI of 1999 on Copyright.

[2] See Directive 2001/29 of the European Parliament and of the Council of 22 May 2011 on the harmonization of certain aspects of copyright and related rights in the information society; sec. 5 (5): "The exceptions and limitations provided for in paragraphs 1, 2, 3 and 4 shall only be applied in certain special cases which do not conflict with a normal exploitation of the work or other subject-matter and do not unreasonably prejudice the legitimate interests of the rightholder."

[3] See Subsection 2 of Section 33.

Z. Lendvai (✉)
Hegymegi-Barakonyi and Partner Baker & McKenzie, Budapest, Hungary
e-mail: zsofia.lendvai@bakermckenzie.com



B. Kilpatrick et al. (eds.), *Antitrust Analysis of Online Sales Platforms & Copyright Limitations and Exceptions*, LIDC Contributions on Antitrust Law, Intellectual Property and Unfair Competition,
https://doi.org/10.1007/978-3-319-71419-6_20

To this day, however, judgments handed down in relation to copyright infringement cases concerning free uses fail to explicitly assess, analyze, or indicate the test's merits or applicability. Rather, they generally observe the specific requirements to be met for a certain type of free use through the glass of the "four-step test," as cited above. The courts in Hungary afford scrutiny on a case-by-case basis to the special provisions of each and every instance of free use subject to the test.

## 20.2 Closed List of Exceptions

The Hungarian Copyright Act provides for an exhaustive list of exceptions. The closed nature of the list is being confirmed by Section 33 (3), which strictly prohibits legal interpretation of an inclusive nature. Absent any catch-all exception incorporated in the Act, uses that fail to satisfy both the special criteria pertaining to specific cases of free use and the general standards in Section 33 constitute infringement of the right holders' exclusive rights.

Flowing from the exhaustive list of exceptions and the Hungarian version of the three-step test, as well as from the express provision of the Act that the provisions relating to free use shall be interpreted narrowly, the provisions related to permitted uses allow for very little to no room to exercise judicial discretion. Thereby, the courts lack the statutory leeway necessary to flexibly interpret and adapt the existing rules to the unique circumstances of each case. This rigidity, in part, may be attributed to the "extensive exclusive rights – narrow exceptions" constellation in addition to the prohibition aiming to curtail the extensive interpretation of the test.

The free uses are typically uses for noncommercial purposes and therefore undertaken by private individuals. Based on the concept of the narrow interpretation of the free use exceptions and the exclusive nature of the copyright, uses that even indirectly serve commercial purposes shall not be considered free use. As an example, it was ruled by the court[4] that setting up and operating TV and radio devices in communal areas of a holiday resort, which was open to the defendant's employees only, and the failure to pay the required levies constituted the infringement of the right holders' right to communicate works to the public. All of the defendant's defenses that had aimed to support the lack of commercial nature as the service had been provided during a private event were rejected by the court. Instead, it was affirmed that the factual possibility of guests frequenting the resort was enough to establish commercial nature and was stressed that no private performance of a work (under free use) may serve the pursuit of gainful activities or increasing the establishment's possible turnover.

However, in the recent ruling of the Budapest Court of Appeal,[5] the court held that even the for-profit reutilization of an insubstantial part of a database legally obtained, falling under the scope of free use, without the consent of the right holder

[4] BH 2005.144.

[5] BDT. 2016.3424.

(plaintiff), shall be permitted. This decision was based on the fact that the Act expressly provides for this possibility in Section 84/B by stating that "no consent of the maker of the database shall be required for the repeated or regular extraction or reutilization of an insubstantial part of the content of the database by a person lawfully using the database made public."

As the provisions of the Act are typically mandatory, with the exception of the provisions on the use agreements, the exceptions have to be regarded mandatory as well. However, there are some instances where the Act itself allows that the right holder may exclude or limit the free use, for example, in the case of articles published on current economic or political topics, which may be reproduced and communicated to the public in the press freely, but only if the author has not expressly prohibited such a use.[6]

## 20.3 Exceptions and Fundamental Rights

When stipulating the list of exceptions to the otherwise monopolistic copyright protection, fundamental rights play a main role of consideration.

Under the effective laws of Hungary prior to January 1, 2012, it was not possible to extend the applicability or scope of free use exceptions by reliance on fundamental rights/objectives other than regulated in the Act. From the said date onward, signifying the effective date of the new constitution titled "Fundamental Laws of Hungary," a new obligation has been imposed upon courts by Article 28 declaring that they shall "[…] in principle interpret the laws in light of their purpose and in accordance with the Fundamental Law." In principle, this provision could open the door to the possibility of giving effect to other fundamental rights and interests as incorporated by the constitution in cases concerning copyright law. In practice, however, the restriction of the Copyright Act that the provisions relating to free use shall not be interpreted inclusively[7] would be likely to bar any such extensive interpretation of the test and of the free use exceptions.

Below we summarize the exceptions according to fundamental rights that they aim to safeguard.

### 20.3.1 Education and Research

#### 20.3.1.1 Education

Several exceptions pertaining to educational and research-related purposes have been put in place by the Hungarian legislator. In addition to affording scrutiny to their exact requirements, their adaptability to the effective distance learning programs will be outlined here.

As a preliminary remark, it is noteworthy that educational activities in general, distance learning options in particular, may be liable to conflict with the following

[6] Section 36 (2).

[7] Section 33 (3).

exclusive rights: reproduction (e.g., photocopying or scanning analog documents or multiplying digital ones), communication to the public (e.g., linking or uploading those books, other articles, or photos up to the program's respective online platform), making available to the public on an on-demand basis (i.e., uploading movies in part or in full to such platforms), and public performance (e.g., performing songs in class—see more on the traditional public performance exception in Section 38 (1) b) of the Act).

The clear-cut provisions of Section 34 (2) states that "[p]art of a literary, musical work or film made public, or such entire works of a smaller extent as well as pictures of works of fine art, architectural, applied art and industrial design creations as well as photographic works, may be borrowed for the purposes of illustration for school education and scientific research, with the indication of the source and the author named therein, to the extent justified by the purpose and on the condition that the borrowing work is not used for commercial purposes. Borrowing shall mean the use of a work in another work to an extent that goes beyond quotation." From the foregoing, it is clear that in exchange for honoring authors' right to be designated as such, extensive parts of larger works and the entirety of smaller ones may be borrowed, in line with education's definition expounded by the said question. As to scientific research, uses that entail development of competing works intended for actual for-profit exploitation and those stemming from the execution of R&D agreements concluded by an economic operator cannot be subsumed under this exception.

With respect to making use of the resulting derivative work, Section 34 (3) sets forth that "[t]he non-commercial reproduction and distribution of the borrowing work mentioned in Paragraph (2) shall not be subject to the author's authorization where the borrowing work is, pursuant to the relevant legislation, qualified as a textbook or a reference book and the school education purpose is indicated on its front page." However, in line with the provisions of Section 34 (4), all other methods of commercial utilization are subject to permission granted by the right holder.

Most crucially, exceptions rendered to the right of reproduction are to be scrutinized in more detail. First of all, within the meaning of Section 18 (2), for exclusively nonprofit purposes, even entire copies of works may be reproduced in an analog and a digital way by (amongst others) educational establishments, except for architectural works, technical structures, software, databases, live performances, and sheet music, if one of the following requirements are met. Namely, such reproduction may only be undertaken if "a) if the copy is necessary for academic or scientific research; b) if the copy is made for the purposes […] specified in Subsection (5) of Section 38; c) if the copy is made from a smaller part of a work that has already been published or a newspaper or periodical article for internal purposes; or d) if it is allowed under specific other legislation in justified cases subject to specific conditions."[8] Further, Section 35 (5) exempts partial reproduction of books, newspapers, and periodicals "…for educational purposes with a number of copies that corresponds to the number of students in the class or for high school, college, or university examinations." This

[8] Section 35 (4).

is complemented by the provisions regulating the panorama exception[9] and the reproduction of a given database's content, whereby "[a] copy of even a substantial part of the content of the database may be made – in a manner and to the extent consistent with the purpose involved – for purposes of school education and scientific research, provided that reference to the source is made and the use is not intended for earning or increasing income even in an indirect way."[10]

In reading these provisions related to exempted cases of reproduction in conjunction with those of the legal reproduction of hard copy and digital works,[11] their subsequent intraorganizational lending and making available to the public by repositories such as publicly accessible libraries, educational establishments, museums, archives, it is clear that, regarding distance learning, reproduced digital copies of works (or a link pointing to like content) may only be lawfully communicated (as mentioned, e.g., in the form of uploading e-books or links) or made available to the restricted public (e.g., providing full movies) through computers ("computer terminals," as referred to by the Act) for students and staff members if those devices are operated on the premises of educational institutions. Put another way, the Act in its present form precludes the possibility of providing copyright material for students at remote locations under the free use regime. Also, even if these acts were to be theoretically covered by these exceptions, the very organizational decision to charge tuition fees would render the whole regime inapplicable for not supporting commercial purposes.

In addition, the only remuneration due to right holders, in this case, is reprography fees and blank carrier levies.

#### 20.3.1.2 Research

Fundamentally, free use exceptions implemented to support educational activities shall also be applicable to those concerned with research. Here, the precondition of nonprofit utilization of works has to be emphasized.

Where text mining and big data analytics stand for mass-scale processing of data by virtue of automated algorithms programmed to identify and gather relevant information found, more often than not, in copyrighted materials, there the following questions are prone to arise.

Firstly, how shall the scanning and saving of copyright materials' content be classified? Secondly, how would one categorize the subsequent setting up of databases based on such data? Thirdly, how shall generating summaries by cross-referencing a multitude of works and the ensuing, e.g. the printing thereof, be regarded?

In Infopaq,[12] the ECJ assessed questions similar to the above. There the court basically clarified that data capture processes, involving the above-described logic,

---

[9] Section 68 (2).

[10] Section 84/C (2).

[11] Article 38 (5).

[12] CJEU, case C-5/08 *Infopaq International A/S v Danske Dagblades Forening*, ECLI:EU:C:2009:465.

and the subsequent displaying of five words before and after the keyword looked up as short summaries of articles constituted temporary (auxiliary) reproduction. However, producing physical copies of these summaries frustrated the boundaries of the said exception because of not being essential to executing technical processes.

Having regard to the above, the legal consideration of novel data mining techniques shall be as follows.

Bearing in mind that the effective application of free use exceptions requires the said uses to be of noncommercial nature, mass-scale scanning of works may either be regarded reproducing the mentioned works, thus converting their content into digital format, or merely deemed necessary for running computer programs. Under the former scenario, the right of public collections to make a copy of a work[13] may be applicable only if these actions are being carried out by educational establishments, museums, archives or other like organizations not pursuing primary economic aims. Once the said purpose and/or the person undertaking such reproduction changes, these actions will not benefit from the protection afforded by the Act; therefore, authorization granted by the right holder would have to be furnished.

The temporary reproduction exception[14] would be applicable neither to public collections pursuing commercial data/text mining activities nor to individuals or entities other than public collections engaged in nonprofit (e.g., research oriented) writing of text mining algorithms. This is also supported by the underlying rationale of writing and employing data/text mining algorithms. Namely, reproducing, compiling, and (re)structuring data for and within the frame of such algorithms, more often than not, serve commercial purposes; e.g., they may be utilized in social media platforms or could support advertising mechanisms as well. Hence, without authorization granted by the right holder or the Hungarian Intellectual Property Office with regard to orphan works, such reproduction cannot occur lawfully.

As to setting up databases using the data collected, the Act[15] does not only draw distinction between protection afforded under copyright—as a collective work[16]—and under the sui generis regime, but it implies that permission has to be granted by right holders. Furthermore, given the fact that big data analytics not only draw from various sources but may be potentially used for creating works (summaries or any other novel work) subject to copyright, these would also entail the applicability of the right of adaptation. Accordingly, Section 29 of the Act sets forth that "[a]uthors have the exclusive right to adapt their works and to authorize other persons to do so. Adaptation constitutes… any kind of alteration of a work as a result of which a work that is different from the original is created. [t]he author shall have the exclusive right to adapt his work or to authorize another person therefor. […A]ny other altera-

[13] Section 35 (4).

[14] Section 35 (6).

[15] Section 61 (1) and 84/A.

[16] Section 7.

tion of the work as a result of which another work is derived from the original one shall be regarded to mean adaptation."

From the standpoint of balance of interests, the rise of such technological processes has the potential to call the present status quo into question. Utilization of works in a mass scale could outweigh that of individual ones in importance in the near future. Thus, with regard to the interest of furthering scientific advancement, it would be wise to reconsider the scope and applicability of free use exceptions to accommodate the needs of, e.g., technology based on big data analytics.

#### 20.3.1.3 List of Exceptions Supporting Education and Research

Finally, we shall provide a list of free use of copyrighted works the objective of which is to support education and research:

- borrowing from a number of works already published provided that the resulting work is not to be marketed[17];
- noncommercial reproduction and publication of textbooks and course books that either in part or in full consist of or comprise borrowed works[18];
- adaptations of works created for illustrative purposes by educational institutions[19];
- nonprofit reproduction of works essential to attaining such aims by educational establishments, museums, archives, picture and sound recordings held in public collections[20];
- partial reproductions of literary works published as books, newspapers, and periodicals in an amount commensurate to the number of students attending classes or sitting exams[21];
- public performance, recitation, or presentation of works serving educational purposes[22];
- integrating pictures of fine art, architectural, applied art works, as well as pictures of industrial designs and photographic works into scientific and educational lectures[23];
- extracting most of the content of protected databases.[24]

[17] Section 34 (2).
[18] Section 34 (3).
[19] Section 34 (4).
[20] Section 35 (4).
[21] Section 35 (5).
[22] Section 38 (1) b.
[23] Section 68 (2).
[24] Section 84/C (2).

## 20.3.2 Access to Culture and Knowledge

### 20.3.2.1 List of Exceptions Supporting Access to Culture and Knowledge

Gaining access to culture and knowledge in general is achieved by the following free use exceptions: a natural person acting without the intent to directly or indirectly profit from others' intellectual efforts shall be free to

- produce (partial) copies on the basis of educational, research, archival, and intra-organizational purposes,[25] only if classified as one of the following repositories under specific other legislation: public libraries, educational establishments, museums, archives, picture and sound recordings held in public collections;
- make available works to the public in a restricted manner[26];
- engage in lending copies of works except for software and databases safeguarded by technological protection measures if classified as a national library.[27]

### 20.3.2.2 Panorama Exception

The Act devotes two subsections under Section 68 to address the panorama exception. Accordingly,

> (1) Of a fine art, architectural and applied art creation set up with a permanent character outdoors in a public place, a view may be made and used without the author's consent and paying remuneration to him.
>
> (2) For purposes of scientific educational lectures as well as of school education [Article 33(4)], the picture of a fine art, architectural, applied art and industrial design creation, furthermore photographic works may be used without the author's consent and paying remuneration to him.

As to Section 68 (1), it covers nonprofit methods of utilization of certain specific permanently erected works leaving, for instance, billboard or other traveling exhibitions unobserved. Nevertheless, it provides for leeway flexible enough to include posting and uploading of user (profile) pictures that display perceivable part of copyright protected outdoor works without having to remunerate the right holder(s). Here, too, the author's name shall be designated in order to benefit from the protection afforded by this exception.

With regard to Section 68 (2), photos already taken and reproduced may only be lawfully used without compensation paid if the purpose of such use corresponds to those of research and education. In reality, this provision merely extends to classroom uses or development of strictly nonprofit development of scientific publications.

---

[25] As laid down in Section 35 (4).

[26] In concordance with Section 35 (5).

[27] See Section 39.

### 20.3.3 Freedom of Expression and the Right to Receive and Impart Information

From all the exceptions of the Act, several may be subsumed under these two fundamental rights and freedoms. Quotation, as being one of the first recognized limits to copyright, enables the members of the public to lead informed discussions, to contrast their respective contentions, to bring forth novel theories by indicating the source and the author's name provided that the underlying creation is of a creative, original nature and the length of the part borrowed does not exceed the reasonable limits of proportionality.[28] With a view to fostering public discourse, articles and broadcast works concerning current daily events and political and economic occurrences may be referenced, displayed, or otherwise communicated to the public unless precluded by the right holder in advance.[29] Similarly, sections of public lectures, other similar works, and political speeches may also be used for information services under certain specific purpose—and proportionality-related requirements.[30]

#### 20.3.3.1 Quotation

"Anyone is entitled to quote parts of works – to the extent warranted by the character and purpose of the recipient work – by designating the source and the author specified therein."

This exception has not been considered by the Hungarian courts yet. However, quotation of works is being frequently measured by the courts against the right holder's moral rights by reliance on the author's and the work's integrity, as for example in a reported case[31] revolving around the quotation of certain stills made from the author's movies in the defendant's television program.

#### 20.3.3.2 Permitted Uses of Public Lectures, Similar Works, and Political Speeches

"Sections of public lectures and other similar works as well as political speeches may be used freely for information services to the extent justified for the purpose. In such cases, the source and the name of the author must be indicated unless it proves to be impossible. The author's consent is required for the publication of collections of such works."

Here, too, courts have not been tasked with assessing public lectures' or political speeches' utilization for the purposes of copyright law.

[28] See Section 34 (1).

[29] See Section 36 (2).

[30] See Section 36(1).

[31] BDT2004.1037.

#### 20.3.3.3 Making Use of Articles on Daily Events and Other Current Events of Public Interests

"Articles on daily events and on current economic or political issues and works broadcast on these subjects may be freely quoted in the press and communicated to the public – including making them accessible to the general public[32] – provided that the author has not expressly prohibited such use. In such cases, the source and the name of the author must be indicated."

As regards utilization of such works by the media, their practices have not entailed any actions brought before courts by right holders so far.

#### 20.3.3.4 Exemption from Copyright Protection

The abovementioned free uses shall not be regarded as a closed list but shall be complemented by the general provisions of the Act on copyright protection. Accordingly, "[c]opyright protection does not extend to facts and daily news items underlying announcements released in the printed press" and does not allow for "[i]deas, principles, theories, procedures, operating methods, and mathematical operations"[33] to be protected by exclusive rights. Also, documents produced by specific public bodies, authorities, and those of the government, as well as expressions of folklore, fall outside the scope of copyright protection.[34]

Considering foreign practices and the above provisions stemming from requirements set out in international treaties, they are to be regarded sufficiently effective in safeguarding the balance of interests of different stakeholders.

### 20.3.4 Privacy and Private Use

#### 20.3.4.1 List of Exceptions Supporting Privacy and Private Use

Private use as such within the meaning of the Copyright Act is protected by exceptions pertaining to

- private copying[35];
- performance, recitation, or presentation of works for purposes of private use and occasional private events[36];
- certain acts carried out in relation to software legally acquired according to the license agreement's provisions[37]; and
- the exempted reproduction and translation of source codes necessary for establishing interoperability between different computer programs.[38]

---

[32] Section 26 (8).

[33] Section 1 (5)–(6).

[34] Section 1 (4), Section 1 (7).

[35] Section 35.

[36] Section 38 (1) f).

[37] Section 59.

[38] Section 60.

#### 20.3.4.2 Private Copying

Private copying involves acts of reproductions carried out by natural persons pursuing private purposes.[39]

To specifically define the scope of the right of reproduction, the provisions of Section 18 (1) shall be taken into consideration. The right shall entitle the author to undertake by himself or to authorize "[t]he (direct or indirect) recording of a work on any medium in any manner, whether final or temporary, and [t]he preparation of one or more copies of the recording." In the following subsection of the Act, all possible modalities have been enlisted, including prints, magnetic recordings, recording of live performances, recording of broadcast works, storing of digital contents, and digitization of material works.

Against this backdrop, any natural person may rely on the private copying exception when reproducing the whole or parts of works in a mechanical or digital manner if it "does not serve to generate or increase income in any way or form." However, the Hungarian private copying exception does not encompass the reproduction of architectural works, technical structures, software, (substantial parts of) computer-operated databases, recordings of public performances, sheet music, and complete books', periodicals', and dailies' mechanic or digital duplications. Also, having another person make copies of all possible subject matters by means of any digital or electrical technique is considered to fall outside the scope of this exception.

As far as appropriate remuneration is concerned, right holders shall receive reprography fees and blank data carrier levies on an annual basis, as discussed below in more detail.

### 20.3.5 Needs of People with Disabilities

The Copyright Act[40] aims to safeguard the privileged interests of the handicapped and disabled by establishing that in order to exclusively satisfy their particular needs, to the extent required, noncommercial uses of all kinds of works may be permitted.

### 20.3.6 Preservation of Cultural Heritage

Forming an essential part of numerous European and international initiatives, the preservation of cultural heritage shall also extend to creative intellectual works, regardless of their originators' nationality. Thus, the Copyright Act offers legal field specific tools for preserving works available to future generations. Perhaps the most important exception serving such objective is covered by the reproduction, lending, and making available works to the visitors of public libraries and like institutions

[39] Section 35 (1)–(3).

[40] Section 41 (1).

and the performance of works serving educational purposes.[41] Further, if the performance is of noncommercial nature, works may be communicated to the audience of celebrations held on national holidays. Similarly, ephemeral recordings made by radio or television organizations of works previously licensed for broadcasting purposes need not be deleted within the statutory deadline if they are capable of demonstrating exceptional documentary value.[42]

### 20.3.7 Public Security

The overriding interest of the efficient, unobstructed operation of courts and administrative and other authorities, including the Parliament, often requires copyright works to be used in a variety of ways, which would otherwise infringe upon right holders' exclusive right to prohibit or authorize the exploitation of their works. To alleviate this tension, the Copyright Act limits the uses of works during the course of such proceedings to a manner that is consistent with and proportionate to the objectives pursued.[43]

## 20.4 Free Use and Economic Rights

In Hungarian copyright law, the free use exceptions are not defined along the lines of certain economic rights, but specifically certain uses by certain persons in certain cases are allowed. The provisions on the exceptions do not make any distinction according to reproduction right or right of communication to the public. If these uses may be exercised in either way, then it is allowed—however, in certain cases (for example, private copy exemption), obviously only one right, the right of reproduction, can be exercised. Practically, the majority of exceptions exclusively or additionally are related to the right of reproduction, while only a few of them have been rendered to, for instance, the performance or communication rights.

Below we list certain exemptions and emphasize the economic rights that can be freely exercised when relying on the exemption.

### 20.4.1 Quotation

Virtually almost all types of works—with the exception of works of fine art, photographs, industrial designs, software, and databases—may be freely quoted (i.e., *reproduced*) with additional restraints regarding proportionality, the purpose of the use, and the mandatory indication of source.[44]

---

[41] Section 35.

[42] Section 35 (7).

[43] Section 41 (2) and (3).

[44] Section 34 (1).

### 20.4.2 Borrowing

Parts of a longer work or the entirety of a shorter one—literary, audiovisual, and visual works and phonograms included—may be the subject of *reproduction, distribution, making available to the public or public performance* without authorization, provided that the resulting work is not utilized commercially and the basic requirements indicated at quotation are met. However, borrowing may only serve educational or scientific purposes.[45]

### 20.4.3 Adaptation by Schools

Adaptation of copyright works serving educational and instructional purposes affects right holders' prerogative to exclusively *adapt* and *reproduce* their respective creations.[46]

### 20.4.4 Private Copying by a Natural Person Pursuing Private Purposes

Private copying is obviously an exemption to the author's exclusive *right of reproduction.* The Copyright Act[47] sets out clear boundaries when emphasizing that the reproduction of architectural works, technical structures, software, databases, and sheet music and the rendering of "bootleg" recordings of live performances are being excluded from the scope of the said exception. Further, the Act implicitly prohibits producing analog or digital (photo)copies of complete books, periodicals, and dailies serving even private purposes. Therefrom, the permissibility of other works' analog or digital reproduction may be easily deduced.

### 20.4.5 Permitted Acts Carried Out by Knowledge Repositories as Beneficiaries of Specific Copyright Exceptions

Premised upon the above "general" criteria pertaining to *private reproduction*, the Copyright Act[48] establishes the licit reproduction of hard copy and digital works, their subsequent intraorganizational lending and making available to the public[49] in a similarly restricted manner by such repositories. It shall be noted that software may also be subject to lending.

---

[45] Section 34 (2)–(3).

[46] Section 34 (4).

[47] Section 35 (1); see also Sect. 20.3.4.2 above.

[48] Section 35 (4)–(5) and Section 40.

[49] Section 38 (5).

### 20.4.6 Temporary and Incidental Digital Reproduction of Software and Databases, Permitted Free Uses of Legally Acquired Copies, and Methods of Utilization That Do Not Require Authorization

*Reproduction* of software codes have become indispensable elements of running, operating, and interacting with computer programs in addition to serving as a basis for every kind of online content-delivery method known to this day. On a combined reading, Sections 35 (5), 59, and 60 delineate the room within which lawful users may use, reproduce, reutilize, exploit, study, create backup copies, and reverse engineer the software and database at hand.

### 20.4.7 Free Use of Public Lectures, Political Speeches, Similar Works, and Reports of Current Events

Public lectures, political speeches, other like works, articles, and reports on current events concerning news that are of high interest to either the public in general or a particular segment thereof may be freely used to the extent justified by the given purpose.[50] Consequently, these uses span *all modalities of utilization* included but not limited to reproduction, broadcast, making available to the public. With the exception set out in Section 36 (1), publishing them as a collective work is invariably subject to authorization by the right holder. As to the inherent difference between the articles' permitted utilization[51] and of those that qualify as reports on current events,[52] the level of originality characterizing those works shall be deemed pivotal.

### 20.4.8 Displaying Works as Scenery, Stage Property, and Costumes

Works of visual arts capable of serving such purposes may be displayed or otherwise embedded into audiovisual media services (e.g., TV broadcasting, online broadcasting, etc.) subject to designating the author's name in case of the former two instances.[53] These criteria need not be met with regard to costumes, however.

[50] Section 36 (1)–(2), Section 37.

[51] Section 36 (2).

[52] Section 37.

[53] Section 36 (3)–(4).

### 20.4.9 Reproduction of Visual Works for Advertising Purposes

Referring to public exhibitions and auctions within the ambit of *droit de suite*, Section 36 (5) governs the lawful and indirectly for-profit *reproduction* works of fine art and *distribution* thereof with a view to publicizing the mentioned events. As an additional remark, the introduction of this exception seems to discriminate against statutory free uses of a noncommercial nature (entailing payment of reprography fees and blank carrier levies) and against the broader category of compulsory licenses granted by collective rights management on behalf of the right holders.

### 20.4.10 Public Performance of Works

In abstract, every provision of Section 38 concerning *public performance of works* under free use shall encompass all protectable creations except for software and theatrical works.

### 20.4.11 Temporary Acts of Reproduction

Fulfilling the harmonization requirement laid down by the InfoSoc Directive, the legislator chose to transpose Article 5 (1) in a way sufficiently mirroring its essence by drafting and enacting Section 35 (6) effective from May 1, 2004. As discussed above, this exception is also of mandatory nature and predominantly relied upon in online/digital context.

The said section reads as follows:

> A temporary reproduction that is auxiliary or interim – and is an integral and essential part of a technological process with no independent economic significance – shall be free if its sole purpose is to enable a) the transmission in a network between third parties by an intermediary service provider, or b) the use of the work authorized by the author or permitted pursuant to the provisions of this Act.

Absent any court decision interpreting or even employing the above provision, we shall refer to the expert opinions of the Council of Copyright Experts, where the merits of such temporary reproductions regarded as free use have been discussed on several occasions. On one occasion, the Council was tasked to assess the copyright-related implications of IPTV services, that is, the provision of television "broadcasting" services based on broadband Internet protocols in a digital (encrypted) format.[54] Two main features of such services were identified as being the so-called PVR (personal video recorder) and the method of "time-shifting." The Council essentially held that with regard to both features, the service provider's activities fell within the ambit of Section 28 (2) of the Act, according to which it was making available

[54] Expert Opinion No. 31/07/01.

works on an on-demand bases to its subscribers (by merely enabling access to the said contents stored on its own servers). However, the reproduction of such works by utilizing its own facilities was deemed to fulfill the requirements of the above exception reasoned by the fact that it was necessary for facilitating subscribers' lawful use. It was therefore stressed that such interim reproduction of licensed works had not carried any independent economic significance.

## 20.5 Free Use and Moral Rights

The moral rights of the authors are not assignable and may not be waived by the author under Hungarian copyright law. Consequently, moral rights may not be disregarded when the use of the work is based on a free use exception. From the three moral rights, that is, right of making the work public, right to be named as author, and right of integrity, only the last two shall be considered when it comes to free use exceptions. No work, prior to first publication, may be the subject of lawful utilization. This means, for example, that in cases concerning the lawfulness of private copies made from leaked phonograms via file-sharing applications and protocols, authors (or related right holders) may assert their right of publication successfully.

Section 11 grants the right for authors to validly withdraw their prior permission for the publication of their works and that of enabling them to prohibit any further use of their work already made public on justified grounds. While theoretically after such withdrawal the work should not be subject to free use exceptions either, the enforceability of this, in practice, is highly questionable.

In accordance with Section 12 of the Act, the right to be named as author entitles the author to affix his real or pseudonym name onto his work to the extent made possible by the size and nature thereof. If choosing so, all others intending to rework, adopt, quote, or present it shall be obliged to designate his name except for a small number of free uses. This right is expressly referred to in the provisions on free use where it is relevant. Thus, the Act expressly provides for the necessity that the source and the author is named if (1) some quote from the work; (2) the work is used for educational purposes; (3) parts of publicly presented lectures and other similar works, as well as political speeches, are freely used; (4) the works are used freely for the purpose of providing information on current events. And in one occasion, the Act expressly allows that the name of the author be not mentioned, namely when fine art, photographic, architectural, applied art, or industrial design creations are freely used as scenery in audiovisual media services.

Free use may occur only without the alteration of the work. Therefore, any modification, alteration, or out-of-context use of the work would not only prejudice the self-expression embedded in the work but would also harm the author's right of integrity.[55] That, undeniably, could occur under various free use exceptions such as quotation, public performance, and reproduction of illegally acquired copies.

[55] Section 13.

## 20.6 Technical Protection Measures

The setting up, operation, and consistent development of technical protection measures are quintessential in blocking attempts to unlawfully access and reproduce authors' and related right holders' content. Such measures span various methods from access control TPMs (e.g., password control-, payment-, time access control systems, encryption) to copy control measures (e.g., zone codes of DVDs and DVD players, file and program locks). However, public interest must be safeguarded as well. The question therefore is, how does copyright law allow for lawful free uses to be carried out when there is TPM put in place?

In short, Section 95/A of the Act aims to resolve the above predicament by granting an enforceable right to the beneficiaries of certain specific free use exceptions as against the right holder, with a view to allowing an exception from the TPM in question. This right shall be enforceable only if

- the exempted uses fall under the scope of those specifically listed in Section 95/A, that is, private reproduction by way of reprography carried out by a natural person (Section 35 (1)), borrowing from copyright works for educational and research purposes not including the reproduction and distribution of the resulting work (Section 34 (2)), reproduction of works for nonprofit purposes undertaken by knowledge repositories (Section 35 (4)), ephemeral reproduction of works made by radio or television organizations (Section 35 (7)), free use for serving the needs of the handicapped and the disabled (Section 41 (1)), uses of works in court or other proceedings (Section 41 (2));
- the beneficiary has "legal access" to the copy of the work. This provision shall be translated to mean that the copy must have been made lawfully available to him (or to the public in general) in a manner other than on-demand communication. As a subjective criterion, it does not necessitate that the lawfulness of the source be verified; rather, it simply requires to show diligence and prudence normally expected in assessing the legal nature of the copies;
- the beneficiary has informed the right holder of his demand;
- they commence discussions pursuant to which, e.g., a copy of the work not protected by TPM will be provided to the beneficiary; or
- failing to come to terms, the proceeding of the Arbitration Board operating within the framework of the Council of Copyright Experts has been requested by either party or on their behalf, which resulted in the conclusion of a settlement agreement from within 8 days of the commencement of the procedure[56];
- the proceedings of the aforementioned body have not been successful whereby the beneficiary may bring an action before the Metropolitan Court to enforce his right.

According to available data, however, no such procedure has taken place yet.

[56] Section 105-105/A.

## 20.7 Compensation

By default, the exclusive economic rights afforded to authors and other related right holders could not serve their purpose intended if their exploitation would not result in incurring financial benefits from the various uses permitted by law. Thus, as a starting point, the Copyright Act[57] provides for statutory entitlement to (appropriate) remuneration with regard to, on the one hand, individual authorizations granted in form of license agreements and, on the other hand, certain cases classified either as free use or uses that are impractical and/or impossible to authorize individually. Logically, the latter category is being governed and administered by collective rights management societies.

Further, as a general rule, free use shall not be subject to the payment of any remuneration.[58] There is one exception to this, that is, the private copying exemption, for which fair remuneration shall be due.[59] This is realized by two compulsory copyright levies, namely the reprography fee and the blank data carrier levy.

The competent collective rights management society, the Hungarian Alliance of Reprographic Rights, has been tasked in case of the reprography fee with the calculation, recurrent publication, collection, and administration of the reprographic fee payable by either the manufacturers of the reproduction equipment or their importers and the persons putting them into circulation under joint and several liability. Further reprography fee has to be paid by commercial operators of such machineries.[60] The Alliance's publication provides for a detailed and differentiated list of fees due. For example, copy/print shops operating in Budapest are obliged to pay a monthly sum of HUF 12,300 per machine capable of producing more than 50 copies per minute. In a commercial establishment whose main area of operation is not professional copying, this amount shall be HUF 9000 if seated in the capital, too.

Blank data carrier levies, by contrast, carry greater significance due to the omnipresence of portable and built-in digital storage units, in addition to the classic carriers such as CDs and DVDs. The collecting society ARTISJUS, the Hungarian Bureau for the Protection of Authors' Rights, sets out and publishes its yearly tariffs in a similarly differentiating manner pursuant to the obligation conferred thereupon by the Act.[61] Accordingly, it shall calculate, collect, and administer the levy payable by the importer, the person introducing the device incorporating the storage unit, or the carrier itself to the market for the first time or by the person required by law to pay the customs duty for importing such media. For instance, after each memory card is integrated into cell phones capable of storing and playing audio content, one shall pay 798 HUF up to 1 GByte of storage capacity or 3724 HUF up to 32 GBytes.

Given the whole structure of now available technical solutions and uses, which often deprives the authors of fair compensation, we are of the view that the

---

[57] Section 16 (4)–(5).

[58] Section 33 (1).

[59] Section 20 (1).

[60] Section 21 (1).

[61] Section 20 (2).

above-described systematic and well-regulated apportionment mechanism does not result in overcompensating the right holders.

## 20.8 Exhaustion of Copyright Protection

The concept of exhaustion of rights shall be equated to that of the distribution right over the copy or copies of works put into commerce upon the right holder's consent or on his behalf. Section 23 (1) regulates the right of distribution as follows: "The author shall have the exclusive right to distribute his work and to authorize others therefor. Making accessible to the public of the original copy or the reproduced copies of the work through putting into circulation or offering for putting into circulation shall be regarded as distribution." Here, the term "copies of works" shall refer to tangible objects only, in accordance with the provisions of Article 6 of WCT, Article 8 of WPPT, the Agreed Statements rendered thereto, and the definition of the Hungarian Civil Code.[62]

In sum, over tangible copies incorporating authors' works, the right of distribution is to be exhausted provided that such copies have been lawfully put into EU-wide circulation upon the right holders' consent or on their behalf. The ruling in favor of exhaustion of digital copies in the UsedSoft case[63] has not prompted regulatory (or judicial) response in Hungary to amend the existing framework. In addition to the rather confining and strict legislative background, distribution of electronic copies of works exclusively online shall not be subject to exhaustion as pursuant to the present status quo, they are being regarded as either making available to the public or communication to the public. As a general rule, Hungarian courts have to observe and follow ECJ's interpretation of laws. Therefore, the findings of UsedSoft shall be applied by the courts. However, to date, no published judgment handed down in cases concerning copyright infringement has made reference to this particular case.

Lastly, pursuant to the Act, the applicability of the distribution right's exhaustion cannot be validly ruled out by law with respect to wholesale, retail, lending, rental, and importation of works.

## 20.9 Conclusion

Taking into account the rate with which digital technologies supplant and supersede analog ones, it has to be acknowledged that the present makeup and scope of statutory exceptions has been rendered obsolete in certain cases. Therefore, a comprehensive overhaul concerning both, the general framework of the free use regime and the specific provisions, would be needed so as to accommodate the needs of versatile user groups, such as developers of state-of-art technology and end users.

[62] Section 5:14 (1).

[63] CJEU, case C-128/11, *UsedSoft GmbH v Oracle International Corp.*, ECLI:EU:C:2012:407.

This contention is based on predicaments concerning, among others, the practicality of allowing an entire book to be copied only by hand in an era in which digitization has deeply pervaded our lives, the legality of the so-called sampling techniques used mostly in the music industry that parallel the free use exception of borrowing, or the apparent statutory safeguards provided for the effective economic exploitation and monopolization of communication rights without introducing exceptions thereto. All of these issues may be attributed, in part, to the rigidity of the three-step test and the minimum protection approach undertaken by EU legislative instruments and to the apparent lack of enacted free use exceptions in the Copyright Act.

As to solutions, consensus shall be reached between the various stakeholders. In doing so, reconsidering the introduction and application of the US's three-step test on European level might be instrumental.

# 21 Italy

Marco Francetti

In Italy, the main law regulating copyright is Law n. 633 of April 22, 1941 (Italian Copyright Law, hereinafter "ICL") on the protection of copyright and other rights related to its exercise, which has been amended and supplemented by some subsequent legislative interventions. Other provisions are contained in the Italian Civil Code in Articles 2575–2853.

Furthermore, being a member of the European Union, the Italian legislation is aligned with the provisions of EU legislation, in particular by directives covering the copyright field, which have been implemented in Italy.

In addition, Italy is a member of a number of international treaties concerning copyright law, which set common rules granting a minimum standard of protection, which include the following:

- Berne Convention for the Protection of Literary and Artistic Works of 1971;
- International Convention for the Protection of Performers, Producers of Phonograms and Broadcasting Organization of 1961;
- WIPO Copyright Treaty of 1996;
- WIPO Performances and Phonograms Treaty of 1996;
- Universal Copyright Convention of 1952–1971.

Special thanks go to Camí Garcia i Carreté, associate lawyer, and Maria Tusa, trainee, at Jacobacci Milan for their significant help and fruitful cooperation in the drafting of this publication.

M. Francetti (✉)
Jacobacci & Associati, Milan, Italy
e-mail: mfrancetti@jacobacci-law.com



B. Kilpatrick et al. (eds.), *Antitrust Analysis of Online Sales Platforms & Copyright Limitations and Exceptions*, LIDC Contributions on Antitrust Law, Intellectual Property and Unfair Competition,
https://doi.org/10.1007/978-3-319-71419-6_21

## 21.1 Triple Test Provision

Article 13 of the TRIPS Agreements stipulates that Contracting States may introduce exceptions and limitations to copyright only (a) in certain special cases, provided that (b) such limitations do not conflict with normal exploitation of the work and (c) do not lead to an unjustified prejudice to the legitimate interests of the holder. Article 5.5 of Directive 2001/29 transposed the "Three-step-test" from the requirements of the national legislators to the rules of interpretation to be applied to the detailed catalog of free uses regulated in this law.

With Article 71-*nonies* ICL, introduced by Legislative Decree 68/03 in implementation of Article 5.5 of Directive 2001/29, the national legislator has transposed the "Three-step-test" in its internal order, leaving margins of flexibility in defining the exceptions for interactive communication, introducing a provision applicable to all the goods used and protected materials made available to the public. The major Italian doctrine has interpreted the introduction of the "Three-step-test" in the sense of giving greater emphasis to the balancing and weighing of the interests of all social economic actors and not only to a part of them.

In particular, Article 71-*nonies* provides: "The exceptions and limitations in this Chapter and in any other provision in this Law, when applied to protected works or other subject-matter made available to the public in such a way that members of the public may access them in a time and from a place individually chosen by them, shall (must) not conflict with the normal exploitation of the work or of the other subject-matter and not unreasonably prejudice the right holders."

This represent a general standard for the limitations and exceptions of copyright but in practice is applied to new technologies. Thus, the judicial practical application of the "Three-step-test" is not particularly widespread outside the scope of private copying disputes.

In addition, it should be noted that some exceptions and limitations, confirmed or introduced by Legislative Decree no. 68 of 2003, contain the main requirement of the eligibility test, in particular those that provide that the restriction of the rights does not compete with the normal economic exploitation of the work or the protected material, such as reprography[1] or citations.[2]

## 21.2 Exceptions to Copyright Protection

In order to balance the author's rights in his works with the public's general right to freely access them, the Italian law provides for a number of limitations to the author's rights. Indeed, the reproduction of copyright protected content does not lead to a copyright infringement if the act of copying is justified by legitimate reasons. The "Exceptions and limitations," provided by Chapter V of ICL, are the following:

[1] See Article 68, para 6 ICL.

[2] See Article 70, para 1 ICL.

- Article 65, para 1, relates to articles of current interest of an economic, political, or religious character, published in magazines or newspapers, which may be freely reproduced in other magazines or newspapers or may be broadcast, unless such reproduction is expressly reserved, provided mention is made of the magazine or newspaper from which they are taken, the date and the issue of the magazine or newspaper, and, in the case of a signed article, the name of the author.
- Article 65, para 2, provides that the reproduction or public communication of protected works or material used in current events is permitted as part of freedom of speech and provided it has an informative aim, as long as, unless impossible, the source, including the name of the author, is reported.
- According to Article 66, the speeches upon matters of political or administrative interest given in public assemblies or in any other public manner may be freely reproduced in magazines or newspapers, or broadcast, provided the source is mentioned, together with the name of the author and the date and place in which the speech was given.
- Article 67 states that works or portions of works may be reproduced for use in judicial or administrative proceedings, provided the source or the name of the author is mentioned.
- Article 68, para 1, relates to the reproduction of single works or of portions of works for the personal use of the reader, when made by hand or by a means of reproduction unsuitable for marketing or disseminating the work in public.
- According to Article 68, para 2, permission is given for the free photocopying of works found in public and scholastic libraries, public museums, and public archives, undertaken by these said bodies for their own duties, without any direct or indirect economic or commercial gain.
- Article 68, para 3, concerns sheet music: while the reproduction of sheet music and musical parts remains prohibited, the reproduction for personal use of an intellectual work by means of a photocopier or similar machine is permitted, up to a limit of 15% of each volume or book, excluding advertising.
- Article 68 *bis* states that except for the legal responsibilities of Internet service providers set out in e-commerce law, exemption from the right of reproduction is granted to acts of temporary noncommercial reproduction of a transitory or accessory nature and an integral and essential part of a technological procedure, carried out with the sole aim of allowing the network transmission between third parties by use of an intermediary or the legal use of an intellectual work or material.
- Article 69, para 1, relates to loans from libraries and record libraries belonging to the State or to public authorities, made exclusively for purposes of cultural promotion and personal study, which shall not require authorization by the right holder, to whom no remuneration shall be due, and shall exclusively concern (a) printed copies of the works, except for music scores, and (b) phonograms and videograms containing cinematographic or audiovisual works or sequences of moving images, with or without sound, provided that at least 18 months have elapsed since the first exercise of the right of distribution or, where the right of

distribution has not been exercised, provided that at least 24 months have elapsed since the making of the said works and sequences of moving images.

- Article 69, para 2, regards that the departments of the libraries and record libraries belonging to the State or to public authorities shall be permitted to reproduce a single copy of the phonograms and videograms containing cinematographic or audiovisual works or sequences of moving images, with or without sound, which are held by those same State libraries and record libraries and by the public authorities.
- Article 70, para 1, concerns the abridgment, quotation, or reproduction of fragments or parts of a work for the purpose of criticism or discussion, or for instructional purposes, which shall be permitted within the limits justified for such purposes, provided such acts do not conflict with the commercial exploitation of the work; if they are carried out for educational or research purposes, their use must be illustrative and not for commercial ends.
- Article 70, para 1*bis*, provides that permission is granted for the free publication on the Internet, without restriction, of images and music of low or degraded quality, for educational or scientific use and only if there is no commercial gain.
- According to Article 71, the bands of the armed forces of the State may perform musical pieces or portions of musical works in public without payment of any fees in respect of copyright, provided the performance is not made for profit.
- Article 71*bis* relates to the permission granted for disabled people to reproduce, for their own personal use, protected works or material or their public transmission, as long as this reproduction is directly connected to their handicap, has no commercial ends, and is limited to a use necessitated by the handicap.
- Article 71*ter* refers to the permission granted for the communication or availability to the individual user, for research or private study, on dedicated terminals situated in public libraries, educational establishments, museums, and archives of the works and other materials contained in their collection and not subject to binding transfer or license agreements.
- Article 71*quarter* refers to the reproduction of television broadcasts carried out by public hospitals and penitentiary institutions, solely for internal use, provided that the rights holder receives the fee laid out in a decree of the Ministry for Arts and Culture.
- According to Article 71*quinquies*, technical protection measures must be removed, by public authority request, for public security or to allow the correct course of administrative, parliamentary, or legal proceedings, as well as to allow the exercise of the exceptions provided by the law.
- Lastly, Articles 71*sexies* and 71*octies* concerning private reproduction and personal use, which consists of "private reproduction of phonograms and video grams on any equipment, carried out by an individual exclusively for personal use, provided there is no direct or indirect commercial gain." As a general "closing" regulation on the subject of exceptions and restrictions, Article 71*nonies* provides that all the exceptions/limitations to author's rights "must be interpreted in a way as to not impinge upon the normal use of the work or other material, nor cause an unjustifiable prejudice to the interests of the rights holders."

In addition to the exceptions and restrictions laid out in Chapter V of ICL, further exceptions are regulated in other parts of the copyright law: in particular, regarding databases, the following activities are not subject to the authorization of the rights holder: "access to or consultation of the database for purely teaching or scientific research purposes outside the framework of a company, as long as the source is mentioned and to the extent justified by the non-commercial purpose to be achieved; in the case of access or consultation, however, the permanent reproduction of all or a substantial part of the contents on another medium shall be subject to authorization by the owner of the rights" and "use of a database for public security purposes or for the purposes of an administrative or judicial procedure."[3]

Moreover, Article 15*bis*, para 1, relates to the performance or recitation of works, which takes place on the premises of officially constituted assistance centers or institutions, or benevolent associations, on the condition that they are intended solely for members and guests and that they are not carried out with gainful intent, while Article 51 concerns the performance of radio works by the broadcasting body and the performances of radio works in public. Finally, Article 91 contemplates the exception regarding the reproduction of photographs in anthologies intended for school use and, in general, in scientific or didactic works and the reproduction of photographs published in newspapers or other periodicals, and which concern persons or current events or matters of any public interest.

The Italian law, according to the international and community line, outlined the free uses as limited and specific derogations to the *ius excludendi alios* of the author, aligning with the tradition of the civil law countries and departing from Anglo-Saxon countries that conceive the exception provisions as general clauses. This is an expression of the general principle of the need to balance the author's private interests of exclusivity with the public interest in the dissemination of the results of creative activity.

In the light of the above, we can affirm that the structure of user rights in Italian law seems mainly well balanced with a series of important exceptions to the exclusive rights of the author, which, however, do not undermine the overall body of law in any significant way. It should be considered that Italian judges, used to making judgments in terms exceptions to holders' rights rather than users' rights, class these provisions as exceptional and tend to interpret them in a very restrictive manner.

## 21.3 The Relation Between Fundamental Rights and Exceptions to Copyright Protection

Free uses aim to balance the author's and community's interests. It follows that the constitutional foundations of the exceptions and limitations can be found in the constitutional provisions that protect these interests.

[3]Article 64*sexies* ICL.

According to Italian doctrine, the same rules of free usage explicitly contain a reference to constitutional principles, namely, the right to information,[4] right to health,[5] freedom of research and promotion of the development of culture and teaching, [6] and right of defense.[7] Therefore, it seems that, in compliance with the Italian Constitution, the fundamental rights or objectives appear to be not overlooked or unduly minimized by the current list and its interpretation.

The primary motivation of the exceptions and limitations to the copyright protection arises, therefore, from the requirement that the copyright imply, in addition to the compensatory award function, the incentive function through the encouragement and promotion of the cultural heritage. It is implicitly recognized that the combination of knowledge and expression of creativity depends not only on individual talent or remuneration but also, to a significant and ineradicable extent, on the circulation and the availability of knowledge and ideas as indispensable *humus* for the development of new works.

Restrictions on rights, motivated by reason of public interest, are accompanied by exceptions and limitations based on motivations related to the effects of technology and the functioning of the market, which make necessary and acceptable the substitution in certain cases of the exclusive rights of the owner with compensation for the author, which will be discussed in Sect. 21.11 below.

Alongside the exceptions determined by what can be defined, in the broad sense, as "the public interest," there are increasingly relevant cases where the limitation of rights is generated by the so-called market failure, especially when the impossibility of ensuring the extension of theoretically recognized rights stems from the development of uncontrollable forms of exploitation. The most common examples of these types of right restrictions relate to uses in the private sphere, such as reprography and private copy of phonograms and videograms.

## 21.4 Interpretation of Exceptions to Copyright Protection

One of the major legal issues related to the rules concerning the exceptions to copyright protection is the possibility of an analogy or extensive application. In particular, with regard to the analogous application of the rules on free use or whether the exceptions can be applied beyond the cases expressly mentioned, Italian doctrine and jurisprudence have regard to the legal nature of the rules and, in particular, if those rules must be considered exceptional or not. According to the majority opinion,[8], Article 65 ff. of ICL provide that the list of exception is an exception from

[4] Article 21 of the Constitution and Article 65 of the ICL.

[5] Article 32 of the Constitution and Articles 71a and 71c of the ICL.

[6] Articles 9 and 33 of the Constitution and 71 and 68 of the ICL.

[7] Article 24 of the Constitution and 67 of the ICL.

[8] P. Caselli, Codice del Diritto di Autore – Commentario alla nuova legge 22 aprile 1941 n. 633, Unione Tipografico-Editrice, 1943, pp 453 ff.; 246; Court of Appeal of Milan, 24.11.2010; Corte di Cassazione, n. 11343 of 1996.

the general principle that reserves the author's economic exploitation rights for his work. The abovementioned provisions must therefore only apply to cases expressly provided and are legitimate only insofar as they are justified by legally constitutionally guaranteed interests of equal or greater rank than those that derogate from them.

These rules, given that they are of an exceptional nature and, in particular, derogations from the general principle that reserves the right to use the work of the author, have to be interpreted strictly, and therefore it is excluded to give the words a meaning other than the literal meaning.

The balance of interests underlying the introduction of exceptions and limitations cannot ignore the orientation expressed by the Constitutional Court, nor can it depart from the principles contained in the international agreements signed by Italy and in the relevant EU directives, which provide a framework for the application and interpretation of the exceptions themselves. Due to their nature of special rules, the provisions relating to exceptions and limitations cannot give rise to analogous and extensive interpretations and must only be applied to cases expressly provided for in the law itself.

For the purposes of determining the principles applicable to copyright restrictions and related rights, attention should be paid to the statement of the Constitutional Court in a number of judgments[9] made on various aspects of ICL. The Constitutional Court reiterated that the function of the protection of works through the assignment of exclusive rights governed by law should also be referred to in the implementation of certain constitutional principles. For these reasons, the Constitutional Court ruled that the copyright was prevalent in relation to the economically relevant interests of those who use the intellectual works, in strict correlation with the interest of the whole community in the promotion of culture and its diffusion, which can only be achieved through the adequate protection and remuneration of those who create the works.

## 21.5 Nature and Extension of the Exceptions to Copyright Protection

It is important to emphasize in this context that the Italian doctrine distinguishes between exceptions and limitations: exceptions refer to acts that, while falling within the powers attributed to the author under certain circumstances and conditions, are exempt from the protection conferred to the author's rights and thus give rise to such free use. Exceptions are generally indicated by the Italian Copyright Act but may also result from the application of rules intended to regulate other sectors. On the other hand, limitations relate to restrictions of rights, which derive from different provisions, such as freedom of speech, free circulation of information and competition.

[9] Corte di Cassazione, Section I, 07 March 1997, no. 2089, Il Diritto Industriale 1997, p. 812; and Giurisprudenza Italiana 1998, p. 1191.

The difference between limits and exceptions presents a connection to the legitimacy of contractual clauses containing restrictions on the rights provided for by law. There are doubts as to the validity of contractual agreements in derogation of limitations (for example, the agreements on the assignment of rights are void if they regard products that lack originality and are of public domain). Instead, the contractual waiver may be eligible for an exception, with the effect only relevant to the parties, not being possible therefore to enforce the latter against third parties.

The question of ruling out the exceptions laid down in the law relies, on one hand, on the nature of the rules on copyright and on the grounds on which the exceptions are based and, on the other hand, on the provisions relating to the formation of the will of the parties. In general, with reference to the possibility that copyright or related rights contracts contain waiver clauses in legally defined exceptions, the answer seems positive for general and particular reasons. With Legislative Decree no. 68 of 2003 was introduced a further explicit admission of exception derogations concerning works and materials made available to the public in interactive services. Also, Article 71-*ter* of Law no. 663 of 1941 can be related to the effect of the contract on the exceptions. This article refers, in particular, to the transmission to the public of private research or study activities through terminals having such a single function, located in library premises, instructional studios, museums, and archives.

The derogation of certain exceptions is, however, excluded in cases where the nature of the provisions is mandatory. For example, the freedom of parody—admissible, as distinguishable from the simple drafting of consolidated case law interpretation in accordance with Article 21 of the Constitution—cannot be excluded from contractual agreements. Other exceptions are made for reasons of public interest in relation to fundamental freedoms enshrined in the Constitution, and therefore these exceptions cannot be ruled out from the will of the parties, as in the case of quotation for criticism and discussion or use in the exercise of the right of chronicle. Also, the exceptions for reasons of public order cannot be excluded from contractual agreements (see, for example, Article 67 of ICL, which refers to the copyright exception on uses for public security purposes or during a judicial, administrative, or parliamentary proceeding).

## 21.6 Exceptions Relating to "Reproduction Right" and "Right of Communication to the Public"

The Italian legal system provides for a list of exceptions that refers both to the right of communication to the public and to the right of reproduction.

With regard to the right of communication to the public, the main exceptions refer to "Articles on current interest of an economic, political or religious character, published in magazines or newspapers, as well as articles broadcast or made available to the public, and other subject-matters of the same character shall be freely *reproduced or communicated to the public* in other magazines or newspapers also in broadcast news programs, unless such reproduction or utilization is expressly reserved, provided the source, the date and the author's name, if quoted, are indicated."[10]

In addition, the Italian Copyright Act provides that "Speeches on matters of political or administrative interest delivered in public assemblies or in any other public manner, as well as extracts of public lectures, shall be freely *reproduced or communicated to the public*, to the extent justified by the informatory purpose, in magazines or in newspapers, also if broadcast or in electronic format, provided that the source, the author's name, the date and the place where the speech was delivered, are indicated."[11]

In relation to the reproduction right exception for private use, with Directive 2001/29, Italy has implemented a systematic and substantial reorganization of private copying regulations. Article 71*sexies* explicitly limits the exclusive right of reproduction to certain acts, fixing the conditions and limits within which private reproduction falls within the exemption and is therefore lawful. The first condition applies to those eligible for the exemption, which are exclusively natural persons in compliance with the technological measures referred to in Article 102*quater*. The application of the provisions on private copying to protected materials other than phonograms and videograms is excluded; the only admissible copy for computer programs is allowed by Article 64-*ter*.

The conditions for limiting the right of reproduction and the limits within which the limitation is applicable are defined in detail by Article 71-*sexies*, although compliance with these limits remains to a large extent entrusted to good individual faith, since the application is in practice uncontrollable.

Reproduction for private use must be made directly by the natural person who is using it. Paragraph 1 of Article 71-*sexies* reiterates that such copies must not be for profit and must be without direct or indirect commercial purpose. Personal use does not include copies made on behalf of third parties, thus excluding reproductions made to give it to friends or family members.

## 21.7 Exceptions and Moral Rights of the Author

Exceptions and limitations apply only to the exploitation rights of the author's work with the exclusion, therefore, of moral rights, which are not restricted and which the legislature has been careful to guarantee also in relation to free usage. The paternity right is always protected by the so-called mention of use: in any case, the title of the work and the name of the author always have to be mentioned. The free use, however carried out, is always accompanied by some indications concerning the paternity of the work. The abovementioned indications are different depending on the type of free use considered: for instance, according to Article 65 of the Italian Copyright Act, the reproduction or communication to the public must always be indicated, "unless this is impossible, the source, including the author's name, if

[10] See Article 65, para 1 ICL.

[11] See Article 66 ICL.

reported"; according to Article 66, in addition to the source and the name of the author, the date and place where the speech was held must be specified; and so on.

The right to integrity cannot be compromised by the free use as such because such free use does not include any right to elaborate or adapt the work itself; the work may, in some cases, be reproduced or communicated to the public, but certainly without any modification. The only problem relates to causality (way, place, time) of reproduction, communication, or citation. Under Article 20 of the Italian Copyright Act, the damage may also derive from any other act of damage to the work, which, as confirmed by doctrine and jurisprudence, allows the author to object to the use even in the absence of alterations to the internal or external form of the work, that is, a real modification in the physical sense of the same, but in consideration of the ways of presenting to the public the work imagined and desired by the author. It follows, therefore, that the violation of the right to integrity could, for example, result from the fact that reproduction of works, public disclosure, or quotation is in such a manner as to affect the author's honor and reputation.

## 21.8 Technological Protection Measures

According to Article 71*quinquies* of the Italian Copyright Act, technical protection measures must be removed, by public authority's request, for public security or to allow the correct course of administrative, parliamentary, or legal proceedings, as well as to allow the exercise of the exceptions provided by the law.

Regarding the relationship between technical protection measures and statutory user rights, the reform of the statutory law introduced in the Italian system a specific mechanism of balance of interests between right holders and third parties. Specifically, the right holders can use technical protection measures to prohibit or to limit the unauthorized copying or reproduction of the work. However, right holders are compelled to adopt suitable measures, also by specific agreement with a third party's representative associations or trade unions, to enable the exercise of exceptions and limitations granted by law. In that case, third parties must have come into lawful possession of works or protected material and, if provided, must pay a fair remuneration.

Moreover, Article 71*sexies* establishes permission for private copying of sound and video recordings on any media support, done by a physical person for personal use only, without profit or (directly or indirectly) commercial purpose. To compensate the rights holders for this private copying, Article 71*septies* states that a fee must be paid to them, determined as a proportion of the sales price of suitable equipment to record audio or video. This fee is fixed by a decree of the Ministry of Culture, and it is paid to SIAE (Società Italiana Autori ed Editori—Italian Society of Authors and Editors) by manufacturers or importers of the said equipment.

## 21.9 "Catch All" Exceptions

The Italian legal system, like other European legal systems, does not have anything equivalent to the doctrine of fair use developed by courts in the United States and adopted in several common law jurisdictions. US law limits the subject matter of copyright in a pragmatic way by applying open and flexible evaluation criteria for the judicial definition of unauthorized uses. On the contrary, Italian law strictly defines and limits the extent of free and unauthorized uses.

Consequently, there are no binding or specific rules to prohibit the undermining of statutory user rights, as long as the Italian system does not provide for statutory user rights. In this regard, few provisions, mainly regarding software and databases, explicitly protect the user's position, establishing that any possible agreements with the right holder to exclude or restrict that position are invalid.

In these cases, therefore, the protection guaranteed to the users is consolidated contractually by disability measures, restricting the private autonomous relationship between the parties.

## 21.10 Abstractions of the Copyright Exceptions

As already mentioned, the Italian Copyright Act provides for a list of exceptions, which is limited, specific, and mandatory. Furthermore, the Italian judges classify the exceptions and limitations to copyright as exceptional and tend to interpret them in a very restrictive manner.

For these reasons, it can be said that the Italian legal system is not inclined to creating an abstraction of the copyright exceptions for the purposes of fundamental rights since the latter are the foundations of the exceptions and limitations that can be found in the Italian Copyright Act.

In fact, as stated in Sect. 21.3 above, the provisions of free usage explicitly contain a reference to constitutional principles, namely, the right to information, right to health, freedom of research and promotion of the development of culture and teaching, and right of defense.

## 21.11 Compensation for Exceptions to Copyright Protection

Section V of ICL[12] provides for a list of exceptions to the rights of the owner in the sense that some of the exclusive rights granted to the owner are limited by reasons of public interest and nonprofit use, which are regarded as prevailing on the author's rights.

In particular, Article 68 of ICL, as amended by Legislative Decree n. 68/2003, implementing Article 5 of Directive 29/2001, provides for a list of exceptions, which can be summarized as follows:

[12] Articles 65 to 71*nonies* "Exceptions and Limitations."

- the reproduction of single works or part of them for personal use, made by hands or without means intended for the public spread of the work;
- the reproduction, for personal use, of books or periodical dossiers within the limit of 15% of their content.

In this latter case, compensation for the author will be due from the owner of the reproduction center, and the amount of the compensation will be calculated in accordance with a private agreement between the trade associations and SIAE. In the absence of such an agreement, the amount of the compensation and the way to calculate it are to be decided by a decree of the Prime Minister, after having heard the trade associations and the Authors Society (SIAE) and having collected the opinion of the Copyright Permanent Advisory Committee established according to Article 190 of ICL.

In addition, Article 71*quater* provides that the reproduction of TV programs made by public hospitals and/or prisons for mere internal use is allowed on the condition that the copyright owner is paid an equitable compensation calculated by the Ministry for the Cultural Activities.

Any reproduction likely to compete with the copyright of the author is strictly forbidden.

## 21.12 Exceptions for Temporary Acts of Reproduction

Article 68-*bis*, which has been implemented according to the provision of Legislative Decree n. 68/2003, expressly provides that "Apart from what is stated with respect to the responsibility of the intermediaries in the field of electronic commerce, no right of reproduction is due for the acts of temporary reproduction having no economic value which are transient or subsidiary and essential part of a technological procedure, made with the only aim to allow the transmission in the net among third parties with the intervention of an intermediary, or a legitimate use of a work or other material." The present provision has been introduced in accordance with the provisions of Article 5 of Directive 29/2001, which provides for a hypothesis of mandatory free utilization. According to the EU regulations, this provision states that an act of reproduction is free, namely does not fall within the scope of the copyright protection, on the condition that it is (1) temporary, (2) subsidiary, (3) an essential part of a technological procedure, (4) executed with the only aim to allow the transmission in the net among third parties with the intervention of an intermediary or a legitimate use of a work or other material, and (5) devoid of economic value. In this respect, the EU Court of Justice has stated that the temporariness requisite exists only when its duration is limited to the needs of a good performance of the technical procedure being intended that said procedure must be automatized in such a way to cancel said act in an automatic way, without any human intervention, when the function intended to realize such a procedure is exhausted.[13]

[13] CJEU, case C-5/08, *Infopaq International*, ECLI:EU:C:2009:465, para 64: "In the light of the foregoing, the Court finds that an act can be held to be 'transient' within the meaning of the second

According to part of the authors, the *ratio* of this exemption must be found in the fact that the acts of reproduction mentioned herein are devoid of any economic value and therefore do not compete with the exclusive right of the owner.

## 21.13 The Freedom of Expression

Freedom of expression is expressly ruled by Article 70 of ICL, which provides as follows:

> The summary, quotation, or reproduction of works or part of works and their communication to the public are free if made for purpose of criticism or discussion, within the limits justified by said purposes and on condition that they do not compete with the economical use of the work; if made for teaching purposes or of scientific research their use must be made for explanatory purposes and for non-commercial aims.

The exception of freedom of expression has the purpose of finding a balance between the rights of the owner and the right to the freedom of expression, which—as previously said—is expressly recognized by Article 21 of the Constitution. Needless to say, the exception cannot be granted if the use of the work has any economical purpose.

According to the authors, the list of purposes, which includes for purposes of criticism, discussion, teaching, and scientific research not aimed at a commercial use, is peremptory, while summary, quotation, or reproduction must aim for the criticism or quotation made by the user.[14]

In accordance with this principle, the reproduction of a newspaper article in a press review has been regarded as nonadmissible.[15]

In any case, a lawful quotation must never compete with the rights of the author of the original work, independently of the purposes of the user; in order to appreciate the existence of a competition between the quotation and the original work, it is necessary to consider the impact of the quotation on the economic life of the original work.[16]

---

condition laid down in Article 5(1) of Directive 2001/29 only if its duration is limited to what is necessary for the proper completion of the technological process in question, it being understood that that process must be automated so that it deletes that act automatically, without human intervention, once its function of enabling the completion of such a process has come to an end."

[14] In this sense, Tribunal of Milan, 13 December 2007 and Tribunal of Palermo, 9 May 2003.

[15] Tribunal of Milano, 13 July 2000; Court of Appeal of Milano, 26 March 2002.

[16] Supreme Court n. 2089/1987; Court of Appeal of Milano, 25 January 2002; Tribunal of Milano, 2 April 2003.

## 21.14 Political and News Reporting Exceptions, Other Exceptions Justified by Reasons of Public Interest

According to Article 65 of ICL (as amended by Legislative Decree n. 68/2003), "The news articles having an economic, political or religious content, published in magazines or newspapers, or broadcasted or made available to the public, as well as other material of the same character may be freely reproduced or communicated to the public in other magazines or newspapers, or broadcasted even by radio or television, provided that the reproduction has not been expressly reserved and on condition that the source, the date of publication and the author's name are mentioned. The reproduction or communication to the public of protected works or material which are used during public events is allowed for public information purposes, on condition that the source and the author's name – if known – are mentioned."

The free use provided for by the above provision is an exemption justified by public use and interest, namely, by the character of the reproduced work in the hypothesis of the first paragraph and by the informative purpose pursued by the reproduction, with respect to paragraph 2. The exemption provided for in paragraph 1 expressly refers to works that (1) have been already published with the consent of the author, (2) whose reproduction conforms to the original and (3) on the condition that the magazine/newspaper, the date and place of publication, and the name of the author are mentioned. According to the case law, the reproduction of an article not authorized by the author or without mentioning his name, the source, or the fact that it has already been published in another newspaper is unlawful.[17]

On the other side, with respect to the works mentioned in paragraph 2, their reproduction or communication to the public is made on the condition that (1) the materials have been used on the occasion of current events, (2) their use is justified by the exercise of the right of information, and (3) they are used within the limit of said purpose.

The Italian courts have denied the existence of this justification when the events did not have an actual interest or when their reproduction was not made during the same factual or time context.[18]

Article 65.1 provides the right of the author to expressly reserve the right of reproduction or the use of his works by adding a reservation clause (*Riproduzione riservata*), which limits the scope of the exception with respect to one or more of their works in order to avoid any possible use by the competitors and protect the economic value of the work.

The subsequent Article 66 (as amended by Legislative Decree n. 68/2003) provides that "The speeches having a political or administrative content made in a public assembly, or even publicly made, as well as the extracts of conferences open to the public, can be freely reproduced or communicated to the public, within the

[17] Tribunal of Napoli, 21 March 1994; Pretura of Roma, 19 September 1998 and 3 October 1998.

[18] Court of Appeal of Milano, 26 March 2002; Tribunal of Roma, 22 April 2008; Tribunal of Milano 17 July 2009.

limits of the informative purposes, in magazines, newspapers, even via radio or television as well as by telematics means, provided that the name of the author, the date and the place of the speech are mentioned." The *ratio* of the rule is to protect the higher interest of the public information and of its circulation; its limit is in fact determined by the informative purpose and cannot be applied by analogy.

Finally, Article 67 (as amended by Legislative Decree n. 68/2003) of ICL provides for an exception that most of the authors consider as strictly connected with the right of self-defense provided by Article 24 of the Constitution, allowing the use of works (or part of them) whenever it is necessary in the course of a judicial procedure.

The rule expressly states that "Works or part of them may be reproduced for purposes of public security, during parliamentary, judiciary or administrative procedures, on condition that the source and – if possible – the name of the author are mentioned."

According to the authors, the word "reproduction" is used in a nontechnical meaning, that is, to refer to any possible form of use of the work aimed at achieving the purposes of the rule; in the same sense, the word "procedures" must be read in an extensive sense, including those that take place not only before judicial authorities but also before any kind of administrative court and/or authority.

## 21.15 Exception for Purposes of Education

The exception for education purposes are provided by Article 70 (as amended by Legislative Decree n. 68/2003), whose paragraphs are reported here below:

> 1-bis. It is allowed the publication in internet for free of images and music at low resolution or downgraded, for teaching or scientific purposes and only in case of non-lucrative purposes. By decree of the Ministry for Cultural Activities, after having heard the Ministry for Instruction and the Ministry for the University and Research, after the opinion of the competent parliamentary Commissions, the limits of the teaching and scientific use are defined.
>
> 2. In the anthologies for scholastic use, the reproduction cannot exceed the measure provided for by the regulation, which provides for the fair compensation.
>
> 3. The summary, quotation, or reproduction must be always accompanied by the mention of the title of the work, of works, the names of the author, of the editor and, if case of translation, of the translator, if said indications appear on the reproduced work.

As the above demonstrates, all the exceptions are justified by purposes of teaching and/or research and can be applied not only to works published on the Internet but also to works that can be accessed by users of universal services of telecommunication, even when said access is subject to subscription or registration procedures, with the only exclusion being networks that are not open to all users and subject to access protocols.

The free use is subject to some objective conditions, which can be summarized as follows: (1) the teaching/research purpose, (2) the absence of any lucrative purpose, (3) the deterioration of the published works, (4) the nature of the published works, and (5) the gratuitousness of the publication.

With regard to the anthologies for scholastic use provided for by paragraph 2, the rules mention a fair compensation in favor of the right owner, and said compensation must be paid by the editor of the anthology; the reproduction is not allowed if the anthology is not intended to have an exclusive scholastic destination. There are no limits with respect to the works that may be reproduced in an anthology: literary works, music, photographs, and movies, within the limits provided for by Article 22 of the implementing regulation; the fair compensation due to the rights owner is determined by the Prime Minister with the agreement of the Ministry for the Public Education, upon proposal of the permanent committee for the copyright.

Free uses must respect the moral rights of the author; quotations must report the title of the work and the names of the author, of the editor, and of the translator (if mentioned on the original work). The author cannot require additional indications, but the violation of this provision implies a violation of the moral right of the author and may lead to a reimbursement of the damages.[19]

## 21.16 Exception Supporting Big-Data-Related Activities

Data bank protection is provided for by Article 64*quinquies* and 64*sexies*, as well as by Title 2-*bis* of ICL, which have been respectively added by Articles 4 and 5 of Legislative Decree n. 169 of May 6, 1999, in compliance with the provisions of Directive 1996/09 (Database Directive).

Databases are protected on the condition that they are characterized by a sufficient degree of "creativity" and are the result of the investments borne to create the database. The right owner, as any other author, enjoys the exclusive right to perform any activity connected with the right, as well as to authorize the total or partial or temporary or permanent reproduction, the translation or any other modifications, as well as any form of distribution or reproduction of the work.

According to Article 64-sexies, no authorization is required to access or consult the database for the exclusive purpose of teaching or carrying out scientific research on the condition that said activities are not performed by a commercial company and are performed within the limits of the said activity, not connected with any commercial purpose. Permanent or temporary reproduction of a substantial portion of the content on a different support is in any case subject to the authorization of the right owner. The use of the data bank for purposes of public security or in case of a judicial or administrative procedure is also free. All the activities reserved to the right owner, as described above, do not require authorization if performed by a "lawful user," if said activities are required to access the content of the database or for its normal use; if the "lawful user" access is limited to a part of the database, the "lawful use" is limited to that part only.

[19] Court of Appeal of Milan, 25 January 2002; Tribunal of Milan, 8 July 2009.

According to the authors, anyone who has acquired the data bank whose first circulation has been made with the consent of the right owner must be regarded as a "lawful user." In any case, the "lawful user" will have the right to copy the data bank totally or partially, temporarily or permanently, on any media, as well as its translation, adjustment, or any other modifications as long as they are required to maintain the usefulness of the bank at that time.

## 21.17 Copyright Exhaustion

In Italy, the principle of exhaustion is provided by Article 5 of the Industrial Property Code (Legislative Decree no. 30 of February 10, 2005), which states:

> 1. The exclusive rights attributed by this Code to the owner of an industrial property right are exhausted once the products protected by an industrial property right have been put on the market by the owner or with his consent in the territory of the Country or in the territory of a Member State of the European Union or the European Economic Area.
>
> 2. This limitation on the powers of the owner does not however apply when there are legitimate grounds for the owner himself to oppose further marketing of the goods, in particular when the condition of the same has been modified or altered after being put on the market.
> …

Moreover, Article 17 of ICL specifies:

> 1. The exclusive right of distribution concerns the right to market, place in circulation or make available to the public, by whatever means and for whatever purpose a work or copies thereof and also includes the exclusive right to introduce into the territory of the countries of European Community, for distribution, copies of a work made in countries not members of the European Community.
>
> 2. The distribution right shall not be exhausted within the European Community in respect of the original or copies of the work, except where the first sale or other transfer of ownership in the Community is made by the right holder or with his consent.
>
> 3. What is provided for under paragraph 2, shall not apply to the making available to the public of a work in such a way that members of the public may access it from a place and at a time individually chosen by them, even when the making of copies of the work is permitted.
>
> 4. For the purposes of exhaustion under paragraph 2, the free delivery of copies of a work for promotional purposes or for teaching or scientific research, when carried out or authorized by the right holder, shall not be deemed to be exercise of the exclusive right of distribution.

In the light of the above, the principle of exhaustion, in Italian law, is closely related to the right of distribution of the protected work, which concerns the distribution of the original work and includes the exclusive right of introducing it into a territory. This right runs out, as we have seen above, when the work or the product has been marketed within the territory by the author or by third parties with the consent of the author.

As for the material copies of the work, which are realized by incorporating the work on physical supports that allow it to be used directly or indirectly by means of special technical tools, these, once entered into the distribution network within the European Union by the right holder or with his consent, will no longer be subject to control by the author in respect of the subsequent passages of ownership. In essence, in the latter case, the distribution right is exhausted by the first act of sale or transfer of title to another person in any of the member countries of the EU made directly by the right holder. Exhaustion of the right means that the subsequent transfer or lease of specific copies of the work will no longer be subject to the authorization by the right holder.

Prior to the legislative amendment of 2003, Article 17 of ICL did not propose the special provision contained in the third paragraph, which was made necessary by the emergence of digital technologies as a channel of diffusion of alternative content, often widespread, compared to the traditional one.

With reference to copies originated by downloading the work in digital format, instead, the rights of communication to the public and the right of reproduction must be taken into account. In this case, circulation of the copies made by transferring the work in digital format to a storage media is subject to the right holder's authorization because their transmission through digital channels does not exhaust, as already stated, the distribution right.

## 21.18 Panorama Exception

ICL contains no panorama exception to photographs taken in public places. Therefore, freedom of panorama is not foreseen within the Italian law. However, it is necessary to keep in mind the provisions of the Code of Cultural Heritage and Landscape (Legislative Decree no. 42 of January 22, 2004), in particular Articles 107 (instrumental and precarious use and reproduction of cultural goods), 108 (concession, reproduction fees, bail), and 109 (catalog of photographic images and shooting of cultural goods). Such goods may be reproduced in accordance with and subject to the limits set forth in the aforementioned provisions: authorization by the issuing authority and payment of a fee, unless reproductions are requested for personal or educational purposes or noncommercial purposes.

In relation to public goods in the public domain located indoors, the Code of Cultural Heritage and Landscape provides for the possibility of fixing fees and a consideration in case of commercial use of the photograph that portrays the work; strictly personal or study purposes are made for free.

On the other hand, and in regard to the public domain goods located outdoors, the Italian system suffers from a real gap. In 2008, a parliamentary question was submitted, in response to which the competent Ministry clarified that freedom of the landscape "is recognized in Italy for the well-known principle that behaviour that is not expressly prohibited by a norm must be considered legitimate."[20]

## 21.19 Private Copies

A further important regulation in the field of user rights granted for payment is that concerning the right of private copying: Article 71*sexies* establishes an exception to the exclusive reproduction right in respect of reproductions, on any medium, made by a natural person for private use and for ends that are neither directly nor indirectly commercial, on the condition that right holders receive fair compensation. The payment for this right is, in the case of machines exclusively made for the analog or digital recording of phonograms or videograms, a proportion of the price paid by the final purchaser to the retailer; in the case of audio and video recording devices, analog or digital, and fixed or transferable memory recording devices, the payment is proportional to the amount of memory offered by the device. For distance video recording, the payment is made by the individual offering of the service and is proportionate to the monies earned for the said service (Article 71*septies*).

Compensation takes therefore the form of a private copying levy for equipment, devices, and media suitable for copying protected works and other materials. This levy applies to mobile phones, computers, and other equipment, even though these devices are not designed specifically for the reproduction, recording, and storage of content and is aimed at compensating the opportunity to use these devices to make copies of works protected by copyright. The levy was conceived to allow the digital device owner to make a copy of any copyrightable work that it already legitimately possessed.

There is no *ex ante* exemption to the levy for any equipment acquired for purposes unrelated to private copying, and a request for reimbursement of a levy may only be made by the end user and is subject to private negotiation with SIAE.

The Italian copyright levy system provides for, on one side, individually negotiated agreements—or application protocols—by which SIAE may grant objective and subjective exemptions to manufacturers and importers of certain media and devices and, on the other side, for a reimbursement procedure for copyright levies unduly paid by final purchasers of the relevant media and devices, who are not natural persons.

The Court of Justice of the European Union held,[21] regarding the private copying exception in Article 5.2 b of Directive 2001/29, that a national framework that left the exemption from payment of the private copying levy for devices and media intended for a use clearly unrelated to private copying to the free negotiation of agreements between a collecting society and those liable to pay compensation, or their trade associations, was not consistent with Article 5.2 b of Directive 2001/29.

---

[20] Reply from the Legislative Office of the Ministry for the Cultural Activities, 5 February 2008.

[21] CJEU, case C-110/15, *Microsoft Mobile Sales International Oy*, ECLI:EU:C:2016:717, pt 56.

According to the CJEU, consequently, the ICL and the Decree do not contain generally applicable exemptions since they only promote exemption agreements between SIAE and the producers/distributors and therefore are not consistent with the principle of equal treatment. In the light of the above, the private copying levy system in Italy will be likely subject to some adjustments in order to meet the requisites of the exclusions for professional use.

## 21.20 Conclusions

In conclusion, we can affirm that the structure of user rights in Italian law seems mainly well balanced, with a series of important exceptions to the exclusive rights of the author, which, however, do not undermine the overall protection granted by body of law to copyright authors in any significant way. There are not therefore important imbalances within the national legislation in respect of the EU directives in the matter.

Nevertheless, some adjustments would be necessary—as stated above—in relation to the panorama exception, which, in the future, is likely to be the subject of further regulation. In the same way, the recent rulings of the CJEU may have an incidence on the private copying levy system in Italy, which would need to be adjusted in order to meet the requisites of the exclusions for professional use and the principle of equal treatment.

# Poland

# 22

Maria Obara-Piszewska and Filina Sztandera

## 22.1 Introduction

Polish copyright law, enacted primarily in the Copyright and Neighbouring Rights Act of 4 February 1994 (the 'CNRA' or 'Copyright Act'), follows the requirements of the 'triple' or 'three-step' test.[1] This test is used to check if exploitation of works is within the regime of 'permissible use' (*dozwolony użytek*), i.e. that it (1) involves only specific permitted uses (the permissible use regulation may not be too general or broad), (2) does not breach the normal exploitation requirement and (3) does not prejudice the legitimate interests of the author (or other copyright holder).

These requirements are reflected primarily in Article 35 CNRA, which reads as follows: 'Permissible use may not conflict with the normal exploitation of the work or prejudice the legitimate interests of the author.' As can be seen, the provision covers only two of the three limbs of the three-step test, i.e. the normal exploitation limb and the legitimate interests' limb.

Importantly, the terms 'normal exploitation of the work' and 'legitimate interests of the author' have no statutory definitions. As such, they constitute 'general clauses' and thus leave some leeway for interpretation. Copyright law scholars propose

[1] Internationally, the *triple test* is regulated mainly in Article 13 of the TRIPS Agreement and Article 10 of the WIPO Copyrights Treaty adopted in Geneva on 20 December 1996 (the 'WIPO Copyright Treaty'). In the EU, the applicable regulation is to be found in Article 5(5) of Directive 2001/29 (InfoSec Directive).

M. Obara-Piszewska (✉)
WKB Wierciński, Kwieciński, Baehr Law Office, Warsaw, Poland
e-mail: maria.obara-piszewska@wkb.com.pl

F. Sztandera
WKB Wierciński, Kwieciński, Baehr Law Office, Poznań, Poland
e-mail: biuro@wkb.com.pl



B. Kilpatrick et al. (eds.), *Antitrust Analysis of Online Sales Platforms & Copyright Limitations and Exceptions*, LIDC Contributions on Antitrust Law, Intellectual Property and Unfair Competition,
https://doi.org/10.1007/978-3-319-71419-6_22

different constructions of the terms. For example, there seems to be a fair amount of agreement that 'normal exploitation' includes such uses that the right holder (author) could expect to bring him some income.[2] On the other hand, there is more controversy about the exact meaning of 'legitimate interests of the author'. Here, there are generally two parallel constructions: (1) legitimate interests of the author are about his economic (pecuniary) expectations; or (2) legitimate interests of the author include both economic (pecuniary) and non-economic (non-pecuniary) interests.[3] The first approach prevails so that 'legitimate interests of the author' should be taken to mean the right to fair compensation (equitable remuneration).[4] That naturally does not preclude the existence of charge-free statutory or compulsory licences.[5] On the contrary, it is a rule of Polish law that permissible use is *free of charge* and the author will be entitled to remuneration only if specifically authorised by law. In addition, as much as Article 13 of the TRIPS Agreement and Article 10 of the WIPO Treaty mention the interests of right holders, the third limb of the polish *triple test* is (apparently) narrower as it only mentions the interests of the author (not of the author's legal successors, for example). However, according to legal literature, Article 35 CNRA should apply also to author's legal successors because limiting its application to only the author would unjustifiably and excessively narrow the proper scope of this law.

Article 35 CNRA itself does not fully reflect the triple test. As said above, it omits the first limb, which says that copyright restrictions are allowed only in certain special cases. This omission is said to follow from the lawmaker's view that this requirement is already reflected in the other provisions (Articles 23 to 35[12] CNRA) governing specific instances of permissible use, which are formulated casuistically.

Note also that Polish courts have been very reluctant to rely on Article 35 CNRA in their decisions. For example, the Warsaw Court of Appeals held in a judgement on 18 September 2003[6] that applying the Article 35 CNRA test is moot if the uses to which the work has been actually put do not fall within the limits of the CNRA permissible use regulations in the first place.

## 22.2 List of Exceptions

Permissible use of works is regulated only in the Copyright Act: Articles 23 to 35.[12] These regulations make a closed list of instances where a work is allowed to be exploited under the permissible use regime. Use is permissible for these purposes

[2] J. Marcinkowska, Dozwolony użytek w prawie autorskim, Kraków 2004, p. 252.

[3] W. Machała, Dozwolony użytek, Warszawa 2012, p. 99.

[4] J. Barta, R. Markiewicz, Prawo autorskie, Warszawa 2016, p. 281.

[5] P. Ślęzak, Komentarz do art. 35 Prawa autorskiego, in: Ślęzak (ed.), Ustawa o prawie autorskim i prawach pokrewnych. Komentarz, Legalis 2017.

[6] Case no. VI ACa 23/03.

only to the extent CNRA so provides.[7] Any uses or forms of exploitation that fall outside CNRA must be authorised by the right owner. In particular, there is no purpose in trying to devise any new forms of permissible use on the basis of any laws or regulations other than the Copyright Act.[8]

It is permitted to use works for one's private personal purposes.[9] However, Article 23(2) CNRA specifies that this exception applies to the use of single copies within groups of people who have personal ties to each other, such as ties of affinity or consanguinity or social ties.[10]

It is permitted to communicate certain journalistic works to the public for informative purposes.[11] The reason is that it is in the public interest to ensure access to information. This statutory licence applies to the media: the press, the radio and the television. It covers the following works that have already been disseminated: (1) reports of current events; (2) articles on current political, economic or religious topics, unless such use has been expressly reserved; (3) current statements and photographs in the nature of news reports (*aktualne wypowiedzi i fotografie reporterskie*); (4) short extracts from articles on current political, economic or religious topics; (5) short extracts from reports of current events; (6) reviews of publications or works that have been disseminated; and (7) short summaries of works that have been disseminated. The owners of copyright in articles on current political, economic or religious topics or in current statements or photographs in the nature of news reports are entitled to compensation for such statutorily permitted uses of their works.

It is permitted to use public speeches, exclusive of published collections thereof.[12] This copyright limitation is predicated on the right to information. The regulation applies to (1) political speeches,[13] (2) speeches given during public dissertations or disputations, (3) extracts from public speeches,[14] (4) extracts from lectures, (5) extracts from sermons. The permitted uses of such works are limited to the informatory purpose, and the works may be so used by anyone participating in the relevant event.

It is permitted to use works for teaching or scientific purposes.[15] This limitation is justified by the freedom to use works for education or science so as to bring variety to the teaching process and to support public education. Such use is available to

[7] E. Ostapowicz, Dozwolony użytek chronionych utworów w instytucjach kultury, Legalis 2017.

[8] S. Stanisławska-Kloc, Komentarz do art. 23 Ustawy o prawie autorskim i prawach pokrewnych, in: D. Flisak (ed.), Prawo autorskie i prawa pokrewne. Komentarz Lex, Wolters Kluwer 2015.

[9] Article 23(1) CNRA.

[10] Article 23(2) CNRA.

[11] Article 25 CNRA.

[12] Article 26[1] CNRA.

[13] This means long official speeches delivered by politicians for large audiences (see, e.g., P. Ślęzak, Komentarz do art. 26[1] Prawa autorskiego, in: Ślęzak (ed.), Ustawa o prawie autorskim i prawach pokrewnych. Komentarz, Legalis 2017.

[14] This means eulogies, speeches during public disputations or debates, funeral speeches, speeches during strikes or manifestations (*Ibidem*).

[15] Article 27 CNRA.

educational institutions,[16] schools of tertiary education[17] and scientific organisations[18] and only for the purpose of didactic illustration in the teaching process or for the purpose of scientific research. What is more, teaching or scientific purposes justifying the reproduction of small disseminated works or fragments of larger disseminated works are also covered.

It is also permitted to incorporate small disseminated works or fragments of larger disseminated works in textbooks, collections (*wypisy*) or anthologies for teaching or scientific purposes.[19] This restriction of copyright is justified by the need to safeguard access to education or simply the right to education, as established, for example, in Article 26 of the Universal Declaration of Human Rights; in Article 14 of the International Covenant on Economic, Social and Cultural Rights; and in Article 28 of the Convention on the Rights of the Child.

Educational institutions, schools of tertiary education, research institutes, scientific organisations of the Polish Academy of Sciences, libraries, museums and archives may (1) lend copies of disseminated works to the extent this is in compliance with their charters; (2) reproduce any works that are part of their collections in order to add to, preserve or protect those collections; (3) make their collections available for research or study through terminals on the premises of those institutions. Such acts of those institutions are permitted unless they are done for direct or indirect economic or commercial advantage.[20] The lending by public libraries of works expressed in words and published in print in Polish (including translations) entitles the right holders to compensation, except where the works are lent for use exclusively within library premises. The right holders include authors of original Polish-language works, translators of works originally created in foreign languages, co-authors whose creative contribution involves photographic works or works of visual art and publishers of works expressed in words and published in Polish.

It is permitted for works that are intrinsic wholes to quote fragments of disseminated works or disseminated works of visual arts, photographic works or small works in whole, to the extent justified by the purposes of the quotation, such as explanation, polemical argumentation, critical or scientific review, teaching, or by the principles of the genre concerned.[21] This limitation of copyright (often called the

[16] By CNRA and the System of Education Act of 7 Sep 1991, these include, without limitation, kindergartens, primary schools, middle schools, post-middle schools, schools of art, psychological or educational counselling centres, youth education centres, or continuation training centres for teachers.

[17] The law mentions both public and private schools of tertiary education.

[18] In accordance with the Science Funding Act of 30 April 2010, scientific organisations include: basic organisational units at schools of tertiary education (e.g. departments), scientific organisations of the Polish Academy of Sciences, research institutes, international scientific institutes, and the Polish Academy of Sciences.

[19] Article $27^1$ CNRA.

[20] Article 28 CNRA.

[21] Article 29 CNRA.

'right of quotation') is justified by the need to protect such values as freedom of thought, of information exchange and of expression.

Moreover, you are allowed to unintentionally incorporate one work into another, as long as the incorporated work is irrelevant for the work into which it is incorporated.[22]

It is permitted to use works during religious celebrations or official celebrations organised by public authorities, on the condition that no direct or indirect economic or commercial advantage is achieved.[23] It is permitted to publicly perform, play or display, using media or devices located at the same place as the audience, disseminated works during school or academic events on the condition that no direct or indirect economic or commercial advantage is achieved and that the performing artists or the persons who play or display the works receive no compensation.

Works can be used for the purposes of public security or to ensure the proper performance or reporting of administrative, parliamentary or judicial proceedings.[24] The mere fact that a work becomes evidence, e.g. in judicial or administrative proceedings, does make this work an official publication excluded from copyright protection under Article 4 CNRA. This calls for a dedicated regulation of permissible use in such proceedings. The literal reading of Article $33^2$ CNRA excludes pre-trial criminal proceedings (*karne postępowanie przygotowawcze*), which are conducted by the prosecution service and which naturally precede the judicial proceedings of the criminal court.[25] Such legislative imprecision is unacceptable as it precludes use of copyright works at the stage of pre-trial criminal prosecution. Importantly, the uses mentioned in Article $33^2$ pertain also to works that have not been published or otherwise disseminated before. Article $33^2$ allows for the copying of extracts from scientific expert opinions or studies and for quoting draft legislation.

Another permitted use of works is for the purpose of advertising a public exhibition or sale of works, to the extent necessary to promote the event, excluding any other commercial use.[26] This refers especially to publicly accessible exhibitions in museums, galleries or exhibition halls and involves use of works in advertisements, announcements, brochures or other literature published for the purpose of promotion or sale, as well as exhibiting or otherwise making available copies of works for those purposes.

It is permitted to use works in connection with the demonstration or repair of equipment[27] and to use a work in the form of a building or a drawing or plan of a building for the purposes of reconstructing or refurbishing the building.[28]

[22] Article $29^1$ CNRA.

[23] Article 31 CNRA.

[24] Article $33^2$ CNRA.

[25] K. Gienas, Komentarz do art. 33 ustawy o prawie autorskim i prawach pokrewnych In: Ferenc-Szydełko (ed.), Ustawa o prawie autorskim i prawach pokrewnych. Komentarz, Legalis 2017.

[26] Article $33^3$ CNRA.

[27] Article $33^4$ CNRA.

[28] Article $33^5$ CNRA.

The law regulates the permissible use of orphan works,[29] being works whose authors (right holders) have not been identified or found even though a search has been conducted in accordance with CNRA procedures. The intent behind this regulation is to increase access to culture. The National Library alone has approximately 300 thousand orphan works (e.g., a large part of the Polish underground press from the times of the World War II or the communist regime).[30]

The law also regulates the permissible use of commercially unavailable works.[31] This is intended to ensure that there is an appropriate level of domestic commercial supply of works that were published in print in the past but, due to inaction of the right holders (mainly publishers), are now commercially not available to readers to an extent that would reasonably satisfy their needs.[32]

## 22.3 Strict or Flexible Character of Permissible Use of Works

Some forms of permissible use under the Copyright Act are so strictly regulated as to severely restrict any freedom of interpretation or of practical application. This pertains, for example, to permissible use of orphan works[33] or commercially unavailable works.[34] The definition of the subject matter concerned and the list of those eligible for such uses are very detailed. Also, the law expressly describes the permitted purposes of these forms of exploitation. Orphan works are works whose authors cannot be identified or found despite a search and comprise works published in the form of books, journals, newspapers, magazines or other printed publications; audiovisual works or works ordered or incorporated into audiovisual works or fixed in videograms, with respect to exploitation of the audiovisual work or videogram as a whole; works fixed in phonograms. What is more, these works must be contained in collections held by establishments whose charters make them responsible for such missions as the preservation or renovation of, or the provision of cultural and educational access to, their collections. The establishments in questions are archives, educational institutions, schools of tertiary education, research institutes, scientific organisations of the Polish Academy of Sciences, libraries, museums, institutions of culture, public radio or television broadcasting organisations. The Office for the Harmonization in the Internal Market keeps a database of orphan works.

Commercially unavailable works are works published in books, journals, newspapers, magazines or other printed publications and not commercially available to

[29] Articles $35^5$ to $35^9$ CNRA.

[30] M. Brzozowska, Nowelizacja Prawa autorskiego z 11.9.2015 r., Monitor Prawniczy 2016, Nr 5, Legalis 2017.

[31] Articles $35^{10}$ to $35^{12}$ CNRA.

[32] M. Ożóg, Komentarz do art. $35^{10}$ ustawy o prawie autorskim i prawach pokrewnych, in: Ślęzak (ed.), Ustawa o prawie autorskim i prawach pokrewnych. Komentarz, Legalis 2017.

[33] Articles $35^5$ to $35^9$ CNRA.

[34] Articles $35^{10}$ to $35^{12}$ CNRA.

the readers with the authorisation of the copyright holders, whether as copies distributed in numbers that are sufficient to satisfy reasonable needs of the readers or by being made publicly available in such a way that anybody could have access to them at a time and place of their choosing. The list of unavailable works is kept by the Polish minister competent for culture and heritage protection. A work can find its way onto this list even without any prior search. Commercially unavailable works may be reproduced or made publicly available only by the establishments listed in the law, such as archives, educational institutions, schools of tertiary education, scientific organisations and institutions of culture.[35]

On the other hand, the Copyright Act contains permissible use provisions that are more flexible (less casuistic). See, for example, the private use provision in Article 23 CNRA. Although the list of those entitled to such use is exhaustive, it is also quite a broad one. By Article 23(2) CNRA, personal private use comprises use of single copies within groups of people bound by personal ties, including without limitation ties of affinity or consanguinity or social ties (*więzi towarzyskie*). While there are no issues with construing affinity or consanguinity, the term 'social ties' is given a broad meaning, there being no statutory definition or construal guidelines for it. Accordingly, Article 23 CNRA should be interpreted to take into account also current means of interpersonal communication (e.g., social media) and cannot exclude relationships borne out of the Internet.[36] Therefore, a link to a work published on Facebook and visible to friends is considered as a permissible use for private purposes. In addition, Article 23 CNRA does not prescribe any purpose that private use must have. Therefore, the use could be for such purposes as entertainment, leisure, hobby, relationship maintenance, education. The principal restriction on private use is that the work cannot be disseminated for commercial purposes or gain.

While it is true that some of the permissible use provisions are less casuistic and as such allow some leeway in application, any use covered by the permissible use provisions will always be subject to the *three-step test* under Article 35 CNRA. As permissible use provisions impose limitations on the author's monopoly, they must always be interpreted strictly, and any doubts must be resolved in favour of the right holder. Consequently, Polish copyright law does not endorse the general construal guideline that permissible use cases should be interpreted in favour of free access to information.[37]

Commercial exploitation is expressly excluded in some of the permissible use provisions.[38] But others do allow certain entities to generate revenue in the course of permitted uses of copyright works. For example, educational institutions or scientific organisations may generate revenue in the course of exploiting commercially

[35] These may reproduce or make available to the public commercially unavailable works in their collections under contracts with a collective rights management organisation designated by the minister for culture and national heritage protection.

[36] K. Gienas, Komentarz do art. 23 ustawy o prawie autorskim i prawach pokrewnych, in: Ferenc-Szydełko (ed.), Ustawa o prawie autorskim i prawach pokrewnych. Komentarz, Legalis 2017.

[37] E. Traple, Komentarz do art. 23 ustawy o prawie autorskim i prawach pokrewnych, in: Barta and Markiewicz (ed.), Ustawa o prawie autorskim i prawach pokrewnych. Komentarz, Lex 2011.

[38] See e.g. Article 23 CNRA.

unavailable works as long as these revenues are used exclusively to cover the direct costs of digitising such works and making them available to the public.

The beneficiaries of permissible use are defined according to the criterion of whether this is private use[39] or public use.[40] Private use means that the work may be used only by natural persons. Permitted public use provisions allow the exploitation of works in the service of public-interest missions or to fulfil the cultural or educational needs of the people,[41] so those entitled include not just natural persons but also legal entities and certain categories of institutions, e.g. institutions of culture.

## 22.4 Mandatory or Optional Character of Permissible Use of Works

The character of the law on permissible uses is not clearly stated. However, it has been firmly established that these generally are not mandatory rules so that permissible use may be modified by contract.[42] This is said to be justified by the need to respect one of the fundamental principles of civil law, the freedom of contract, and by the fact that the law does not prohibit the option of permissible use provisions being contractually limited or disapplied.

Importantly, while permissible use law can be modified by contract, any restriction or prohibition of permissible use imposed *unilaterally* by the right holder will be ineffective. Such statements sometimes can appear in practice, such as on book covers ('All rights reserved. This publication may not be reproduced without the consent of the publisher') or during film shows ('This film may not be copied. Copying is piracy'). You can also see physical media 'equipped' with technological protection measures[43] preventing the content from being reproduced. However, these safeguards raise controversies as they sometimes make it impossible for users to put the works to lawful uses that are consistent with permissible use requirements.

## 22.5 The Scope of Permissible Use of Works

Some types of permissible use involve only exploitation, including reproduction, of a work for personal purposes but without making it publicly available.[44] Others involve making the work available to the public but without the right of reproduction.[45] There are also permissible use provisions in the Copyright Act that confer

[39] Articles 23, $23^1$, 34 and 35 CNRA.

[40] Articles 24 to $33^5$ CNRA.

[41] E. Ostapowicz, Dozwolony użytek chronionych utworów w instytucjach kultury, Legalis 2017.

[42] K. Gienas, Komentarz do art. 23 ustawy o prawie autorskim i prawach pokrewnych, in: Ferenc-Szydełko (ed.), Ustawa o prawie autorskim i prawach pokrewnych. Komentarz, Legalis 2017.

[43] *Ibidem.*

[44] See e.g. Article 23 CNRA on private use.

[45] See e.g., Article 24 CNRA on rebroadcasting.

both the right of reproduction and the right to make the works available to the public (e.g., Article 27 CNRA on use by educational institutions, scientific organisations and schools of tertiary education; Article $35^5$ CNRA on permissible use of orphan works; Article $35^{12}$ CNRA on permissible use of commercially unavailable works). This distinction usually hinges on the *purpose* of the use.

For example, it is accepted that the purpose of private use is to satisfy user's *personal needs*. It is thus obvious that private use covers such situations as lending a book to your friend or making a photocopy (for your own uses) of a research paper or a copy of a CD. Private use on the Internet most often involves viewing or downloading a work or uploading files to the Internet.[46] In this sense, it is permitted to listen to music files lawfully uploaded to YouTube. However, private use does not include making the work available *to the public* (meaning anyone other than those close to the user: friends, acquaintances, family). Peer-to-peer networks[47] are considered to go beyond private use.[48] File exchanges in such networks (e.g., in Napster or KazaA) typically involve strangers. A user of such a service downloads a work but also uploads 'own' works to make them available to an unlimited group of other users (strangers).

Permitted public uses serve *public-interest tasks*, such as to ensure a broader access to culture. Such tasks would not be achievable without a statutory right of reproducing certain works and making them available to the public. Such permitted public uses include, for example, borrowing a book from a reading room, quoting fragments of a book in a scientific paper or using political speeches for informatory purposes.

Whoever goes beyond permissible use limits may be held liable under Articles 78 and 79 CNRA. In such a case, the right holder is entitled to demand that (1) the actual or threatened infringement be ceased; (2) the infringement be cured; (3) the damage done to him through the infringement be recompensed either pursuant to the general law of damages or through payment of a sum of money reflecting double the fair compensation, which at the time of the claim would otherwise be due to him if the use had been lawfully licensed; (4) the infringer disgorge the profits of his infringement. In addition, the right holder may seek an order compelling the infringer to publish apologies or admission (once or more times) or to publish the full decision of the court that adjudicated on the infringement. Where it would be disproportionately onerous for the infringer to cease or cure the infringement, the court may—on application of the infringer and with the consent of the right holder—order the infringer to pay an appropriate sum of money to the right holder. When adjudicating on the infringement, the court may, on the right holder's application, make an order as to any items that have been unlawfully produced or any means or materials used for the purpose and, in particular, may order that they be destroyed, recalled from the market or granted to the right holder on account of damages.

---

[46] L. Marcinoska, Dozwolony użytek w praktyce, available at http://www.codozasady.pl/dozwolony-uzytek-w-praktyce/. Access on 05.05.2017.

[47] Currently, the most popular of these include eMule, DirectConnect, Bittorent.

[48] O. Wrzeszcz, Trolling prawnoautorski, in: Zeszyty Naukowe Uniwersytetu Jagiellońskiego 2016, Nr 4, Lex 2017.

## 22.6 The Author's Moral Rights

Article 34 CNRA expressly requires respect for the moral rights of the author during permissible use, i.e. requires that the author's full name be mentioned and the source identified. While this provision admittedly does not specifically refer to the other moral rights, such as the right of artistic integrity (see also Article 16 CNRA), it is said that permissible use must respect also these other moral rights.[49] This was confirmed by the Supreme Court, holding that 'moral rights reflect a personal relationship of the author to their work as well as a rational tie between the two, said tie being protected by the moral rights mentioned in an open-ended list in Article 16 CNRA. But Article 16 is not the only law that specifies such rights and the values protected by them. These include also: (…) the right of the author of a work of visual art to have the last say on the original of his work where its owner wishes to destroy it'.[50] The decision to destroy a work is precisely an example of a permitted use of the work pursuant to Article 32(2) CNRA. That permissible use requires respecting all the moral rights of the author was also held in an early (but still relevant) case before the Supreme Court.[51] In its judgment of 14 March 1928, the court ruled that the publication of a press article that was freely changed (breach of integrity) would go beyond permissible use and as such would require specific authorisation from the author. Absent such authorisation, the article may not be published.

As regards the requirement to identify the author and the source, Article 34 CNRA only mentions that this should be done to the extent possible. It is said that this is about the actual technical possibilities or the very sense of making such identification. For example, in a case before the Warsaw Court of Appeals,[52] the court considered the implications of the failure to identify the author's name on photographs shown in accordance with permissible use provisions. It was held that because (1) the news feed in which the photos were used was very short and (2) the photos themselves were shown for just 1.5–2.5 s, there was indeed no way or even sense to mention the author's name in the circumstances. Generally, a mention of the author must be made if the author himself signed the work or otherwise claimed authorship in an unquestionable manner. Interestingly, a dedication is not considered to be such a signature.[53]

As regards the requirement of identifying the source, it seems that this will be particularly relevant when referring to works available online. Such references should state the home page and the specific location of the resources used.[54]

---

[49] S. Stanisławska-Kloc, Komentarz do art. 23 ustawy o prawie autorskim i prawach pokrewnych, in: Flisak (ed.), Prawo autorskie i prawa pokrewne. Komentarz, Lex 2015.

[50] Supreme Court judgment dated 6 December 2013 r., I CSK 109/13.

[51] Supreme Court judgment dated 14 March 1928 r., Kr 474/27.

[52] Judgment of the Warsaw Court of Appeals dated 28 June 2007, VI ACa 447/07.

[53] Judgment of the Warsaw Court of Appeals dated 24 May 2016, VI ACa 293/15, Legalis 2017.

[54] K. Gienas, Komentarz do art. 34 ustawy o prawie autorskim i prawach pokrewnych, in: Ferenc-Szydełko (ed.), Ustawa o prawie autorskim i prawach pokrewnych. Komentarz, Legalis 2017.

In conclusion, the limits of permissible use are defined by the moral rights of the author. Where these rights are breached, the use is no longer 'fair' or 'permitted'. Some examples of conduct that infringe on the author's right to have his work used properly are as follows: biased choice of quotations to give a false impression of the work,[55] improper translation, showing films in such a bad quality as to hinder the viewing process, breaching the integrity of a film by reducing its on-screen time, changing the physical medium so that cuts ensue, adding sound tracks, putting colour on a black-and-white film, showing news or advertising tickers when screening a film.[56]

It seems that the requirement to identify the author by his full name is a proportionate solution as it does not excessively burden the user or prevent him from using the work.

## 22.7 The Technological Protection Measures

As mentioned in Sect. 22.4, technical protection measures may effectively prevent permissible uses.[57] There are certain software solutions that not only prevent any reproduction of a work but even block access to it. This issue was in the spotlight at the EU level so that the EU legislature inserted Article 6(4) in Directive 2001/29, which reads as follows: 'Notwithstanding the legal protection provided for in paragraph 1, in the absence of voluntary measures taken by rightholders, including agreements between rightholders and other parties concerned, Member States shall take appropriate measures to ensure that rightholders make available to the beneficiary of an exception or limitation provided for in national law in accordance with Article 5(2)(a), (2)(c), (2)(d), (2)(e), (3)(a), (3)(b) or (3)(e) the means of benefiting from that exception or limitation, to the extent necessary to benefit from that exception or limitation and where that beneficiary has legal access to the protected work or subject-matter concerned.' The regulation is an attempt to find a middle way between the interests of users in being able to enjoy permissible use exceptions and the interest of authors in being protected against unlawful use of their creations.

However, the Polish legislature remains passive on this issue. For example, nowhere does the Copyright Act expressly prohibit such protection measures. Indirectly, the matter of protection measures is touched upon in Article $118^1$ CNRA, which imposes criminal liability for the *production, trade or advertising* of equipment or components indented for *unlawfully* removing or circumventing such measures. Apparently, to ensure that the interests of users and of authors are balanced in the spirit of the Copyright Directive, it would be advisable to rework that regulation

[55] Judgment of Kraków Court of Appeals dated 6 December 2016, I ACa 931/16.

[56] Judgment of the Supreme Court (Civil Chamber) dated 6 December 2013, I CSK 109/13.

[57] K. Klafkowska-Waśniowska, Ochrona zabezpieczeń technicznych a granice prawa autorskiego, in: Kępiński, Kępiński, Klafkowska-Waśniowska and Sikorski (ed.), Granice prawa autorskiego, Warszawa 2010, p. 63.

to make it clear that it does not impose criminal liability on users that make lawful use of the work, such as within the limits of the permissible use law.

Issues with technical protection measures that restrict permitted uses are noted and discussed by legal commentators writing about Polish law or Directive 2001/29/WE.[58]

## 22.8 'Catch All' Exception

No permissible use provision in the Copyright Act is general enough to catch any broader range that would comprise many widely different uses. As said, Polish permissible use law is, as a rule, casuistic and inflexible. Permissible uses are exhaustively regulated in Articles 23 to 25 CNRA, which specify the purpose and scope of permissible uses and the categories of eligible entities. In addition, the limits on permissible uses are indirectly provided for in Article 35 CNRA, which lays down the Polish version of the triple test (see above Sect. 22.1).

Polish law does not allow for developing any new 'hybrid' kinds of permissible use. For example, you cannot take different permissible use regulations and pick up selected use requirements from them to form a 'combination' creating a new use category that would also be permissible.[59]

## 22.9 The Fundamental Rights in Permissible Use of Works

The Polish law on permissible use is a broad regulation. Each form of permissible use provided for in the Copyright Act has its own axiological justification in a constitutionally protected value, such as privacy, personal sphere or access to education or culture. However, the statutory regulation of permissible use is exhaustive in that, generally, any use that goes beyond the statutory limits will be unlawful, even if it were justified in the light of any of those constitutional values.

Importantly, though, the Copyright Act does make it possible to invoke Article 5 of the Civil Code,[60] i.e. the law on abuse of rights. This is applicable where the right holder takes action to narrow down uses that are otherwise statutorily permitted. As such, the action would be contrary to the commercial or social intent behind intellectual property rights and would be inequitable (would breach the rules of social coexistence).[61] However, such conflicts would in each case be resolved by the court under the specific circumstances.

[58] Directive 2001/29 of the European Parliament and of the Council of 22 May 2001 on the harmonisation of certain aspects of copyright and related rights in the information society.

[59] S. Stanisławska-Kloc, Komentarz do art. 23 ustawy o prawie autorskim i prawach pokrewnych, in: Flisak (ed.), Prawo autorskie i prawa pokrewne. Komentarz, Lex 2015, p. 334.

[60] The Civil Code Act of 23 April 1964 (Dz. U. 1964, nr 16, poz. 93, as amended).

[61] J. Barta, R. Markiewicz, Prawo autorskie, Warszawa 2010, p. 145.

## 22.10 Compensation for Permissible Use of Works

As said, the Copyright Act distinguishes among various types of permissible use, each of them specifically regulated in Articles 23 to $35^{12}$ CNRA. We have also mentioned that Polish copyright law endorses the principle that permissible use is *free of charge* (with no compensation due to the right holder from the user on that account). Any remuneration for permissible use must always be expressly authorised by specific regulations, such as (1) Article 25(2) CNRA, specifically authorising compensation to right holders for reprints; (2) Article 29 CNRA, specifically authorising compensation to right holders for use of their works in quotations; (3) Article 33(3) CNRA, specifically authorising compensation to right holders for dissemination of photographic works or works of visual art in encyclopaedias and atlases. The compensation element of permissible use is also introduced to some degree in Article $35^{8}$(5) CNRA as it entitles the author of an orphan work to claim what is called 'fair compensation' from research institutes or scientific organisations for using his work.

Importantly, even if the law is silent on any remuneration to authors for permissible use of their works and, therefore, such use is considered to be charge-free, the authors are not left without any compensation at all. They are recompensed indirectly via the blank media and private copying levy, which is imposed under Articles 23 and $23^{1}$ CNRA on manufacturers and importers of blank media and copying devices and on holders of reprographic devices.[62]

The calculation of remuneration due for permissible use is considered to be fully governed by the general guidelines specified in Article 43(2) CNRA. In accordance with these guidelines, the amount of remuneration should always be based on the range of uses and the benefits (profits) associated with such uses. Importantly, while the Copyright Act does not impose any specific calculation model, it is agreed that the remuneration should never be 'overestimated' in that it would exceed the actual market value of the work.[63] Thus, the remuneration should take into account the rates offered in the market for similar works. For these purposes, reference can be made to rates adopted by collective rights management organisations in their rate schedules.[64]

Remuneration for permissible use remains due to the right holders until the expiry of the related copyrights. These in principle expire 70 years after the author's death.

[62] For more on these levies—see Sect. 22.18 below.

[63] Note, however, that if a work's market value is understated (i.e. too low comparing to the actual scope of uses to which it is put and to the benefits for the user), it cannot be relied upon to calculate the remuneration due to the author, at least not without adjustments. See Supreme Court judgment of 4 February 1965 (case no. II CR 536/64), where it was held that it would be improper and contrary to fair practice to calculate such remuneration on the basis of understated market rates.

[64] T. Targosz, Komentarz do art. 43 ustawy o prawie autorskim i prawach pokrewnych, in: Flisak (ed.), Prawo autorskie i prawa pokrewne. Komentarz Lex, Wolters Kluwer, p. 671.

## 22.11 Temporary or Incidental Reproduction of Works

One of the forms of permissible use under the Copyright Act is specified in Article 23[1] CNRA, which reads as follows:

> No authorisation from the author shall be required for temporary acts of reproduction having no independent economic significance which are transient or incidental and an integral and essential part of a technological process and whose sole purpose is to enable:
>
> 1) a transmission in a network between third parties by an intermediary, or
>
> 2) a lawful use.

This regulation, which implements Article 5(1) of Directive 2001/29, successfully fills a legal gap and is fully compatible with the commercial reality that has been changing due to technological progress. Undoubtedly, this law applies above all to *digital* copying as precisely this kind of copying can be temporary (short-lived). The explanatory memorandum in support of the implementing act specifically indicates that Article 23[1] CNRA will be applicable mainly to such uses as caching and browsing. Also, commentaries on this article suggest the following uses to which it would apply: (1) reproduction in a computer's RAM when a CD is being played, (2) making copies during Internet browsing, (3) storage in cache memories, proxy servers or Internet routers.[65]

The test for a permitted use under Article 23[1] CNRA has three limbs: (1) the act of reproduction must be temporary (short-lived) and transient or incidental and must be an integral and essential part of a technological process (the technological limb), (2) the act of reproduction may not have independent economic significance (the economic limb), (3) the sole purpose of the act must be to enable a transmission of the work in a network between third parties by an intermediary or a lawful use of the work (the purpose limb).[66]

The technological limb of Article 23[1] test applies to any category of work that is reproduced in whole or merely in fragments, whether or not already communicated to the public before. The requirement for such reproduction (which must be 'an integral and essential part of a technological process') to be 'temporary' and 'transient' or 'incidental' means that the copies must be *removed automatically* (without user's involvement), while the act itself must be *necessary* for the whole process to run properly. In the economic limb, the most important thing is that the act may not generate any *additional* economic benefit that would be on top of that ordinarily achieved through such reproduction. In other words, the user may not 'make money' on such use. As regards the purpose limb, it applies mainly to reproduction that occurs during the performance of Internet provider's services.

As said, it is possible to restrict or exclude the application of Article 23[1] CNRA to any work through a contract between the right holder and the user.

---

[65] S. Stanisławska-Kloc, Komentarz do art. 23 ustawy o prawie autorskim i prawach pokrewnych, in: Flisak (ed.), Prawo autorskie i prawa pokrewne. Komentarz, Lex 2015, p. 361.

[66] *Ibidem*, p. 362.

## 22.12 The Freedom of Expression: Right of Quotation

Freedom of expression, including artistic expression, is safeguarded primarily through the permissible use provision in Article 29 CNRA, which confers the 'right of quotation':

> It is permitted for works that are intrinsic wholes to quote fragments of disseminated works or disseminated works of visual arts, photographic works or small works in whole, to the extent justified by the purposes of the quotations, such as explanation, polemical argumentation, critical or scientific review, teaching, or by the principles of the genre concerned.

Accordingly, the law lays down the following framework for the right to quote exception. Firstly, somebody else's work may only be quoted in a work that constitutes 'an intrinsic whole', which means that you can make such a quotation only in your own work, which you yourself are creating. Secondly, you can quote fragments of other people's works or whole works if those are 'small', provided the works have already been communicated to the public. Importantly, it is accepted that the right of quotation allows for referring to *any* works of others, whatever their kind or category. In practice, references are most often made to literary, musical or cinematographic works and to works of visual art. It is also permissible to quote co-authored or collective works. Equally important are the following considerations: (1) the quoted work has been communicated to the public (so that there is no breach of the author's moral right of divulgation), and (2) if the work is quoted in whole (and not just in fragments), it is a 'small' work. That last requirement certainly leaves the largest space for controversy. While there is no interpretation guidance in the Copyright Act or the related case law, it is generally accepted that it should be tested against the 'size' of the work, i.e. its volume, duration or physical dimensions. The requirement will be more restrictively construed with respect to architectural and photographic works and works of visual art (miniatures, maquettes and other small-scale models).[67]

There are further, equally important requirements for a permissible quotation: (1) the quoted work or fragment must be in a reasonable proportion to the work in which it is quoted, and (2) the quotation must be justified by its purposes, such as explanation, polemical argumentation, critical or scientific review, teaching, or by the principles of the genre concerned. As much as the first requirement is not surrounded by any larger controversy, the other one (including especially the terms 'explanation' and 'the principles of the genre') calls for interpretation. The purpose of 'explanation' is properly applied where the quoted matter is *necessarily* related to the message or argument of the author of the host work. In other words, the quotation is necessary to better illustrate the author's views or creative output. And the principles of the genre are properly invoked where quotation (reference) is a customary device in the given kind of art, such as in a motto, quotes used to beautify a text, a collage, found footage, photomontage.[68]

[67] S. Stanisławska-Kloc, Komentarz do art. 23 ustawy o prawie autorskim i prawach pokrewnych, in: Flisak (ed.), Prawo autorskie i prawa pokrewne. Komentarz, Lex 2015, p. 450.

[68] K. Gienas, Komentarz do art. 29 ustawy o prawie autorskim i prawach pokrewnych, in: Ferenc-Szydełko (ed.), Ustawa o prawie autorskim i prawach pokrewnych. Komentarz, Legalis 2017.

Also, works may be used for the purpose of pastiche, parody or caricature. This is a separate form of permissible use, which is regulated in Article $29^1$ CNRA as follows:

> It is permitted to use works for the purposes of parody, pastiche or caricature to the extent justified by the principles of such genres.

The three major conditions to be satisfied here are the following: (1) the use is to be made of *works* (unlike in the right of quotation exception, the works need to be ones that have been communicated to the public before); (2) the only allowed purposes of the use are those of *pastiche, parody or caricature*; (3) the works may be so used only to the extent justified *by the principles of such genres* (such use is necessary to create a pastiche, parody or caricature).

Importantly, the right of quotation exception (Article 29 CNRA) and the parody, pastiche or caricature exception (Article $29^1$ CNRA) pertain to any manner of exploitation, and the authors of the works so used are not entitled to compensation.

The manner of use under Article 29 or $29^1$ CNRA may be modified (e.g., restricted or entirely prohibited) by contract between the right holder and the user.

## 22.13 Distribution of Press Content

Under Article 4 CNRA, the following are not copyright works: (1) normative acts and official drafts thereof; (2) public documents or other official materials, signs and symbols; (3) published patent or design descriptions; (4) *simple press news*. This list is closed only prima facie. Some of its items are vague enough to allow the list to cover a whole host of 'works' indeed. The most controversial of these terms is 'simple press news'. It is said to include primarily factual press items without any analysis or commentary by the author, such as exchange rate quotations, stock exchange quotations, weather reports, TV or radio listings, movie or theatre schedules. Importantly, this category can include also more 'complicated' or 'sizeable' news items provided that their only and core benefit is *to give information that some fact(s) occurred* (news of natural catastrophes, poll results, sports results, staff changes in law firms, etc.).[69]

Also, as said above, there are some limitations to the protection of press items enjoying the status of copyright works. In accordance with Article 25 CNRA, it is permissible to communicate the following to the public without authorisation from the author (the right of reprint): (1) reports of current events; (2) articles on current political, economic or religious topics, unless such use has been expressly reserved; (3) current statements and photographs in the nature of news reports (*aktualne wypowiedzi i fotografie reporterskie*); (4) short extracts from articles on current political, economic or religious topics; (5) short extracts from reports of current events; (6) reviews of publications or works that have been disseminated; and (7) short

[69] T. Targosz, Komentarz do art. 43 ustawy o prawie autorskim i prawach pokrewnych, in: Flisak (ed.), Prawo autorskie i prawa pokrewne. Komentarz Lex, Wolters Kluwer, Warsaw 2015, p. 671.

summaries of works that have been disseminated. And under Article 261 CNRA, you can use public speeches, that is, political speeches, speeches given during public dissertations or disputations, extracts from public speeches, extracts from lectures, extracts from sermons. These lists, as the list in Article 4 CNRA, are closed only apparently as they use terms that are similarly vague and leave relatively large room for interpretation.

Article 26 CNRA is even more controversial. It reads that '[r]eports of current events may quote works made available during such events, to the extent justified by the informatory purpose'. Many interpretation issues surround particularly the term 'current events'. It is considered to generally apply to public events and only exceptionally to private events (where news of the private event has been made available to the public). Examples include social events (manifestations, contest results, charitable campaigns), religious events (pilgrimage, anniversary mass), political events (elections, presidential visits), artistic events (concerts, music festivals, film premieres, arts exhibition openings), scholarly events (conferences, conventions). These events must (1) be current (they have occurred recently or lately, which for Internet reports means not more than one or two days ago) and (2) relate principally to the work that is to be used for the report (such as where an extract from a theatre play is quoted in an account of its first night).

## 22.14 Permissible Use for the Purpose of Teaching

Permissible uses for the purpose of ensuring the development of science and education and broadening the access to arts and knowledge are regulated mainly in Article 27 CNRA, which provides as follows:

> 1. Educational institutions, schools of tertiary education and scientific organisations as defined in the Science Funding Act of 30 April 2010 may, for the purpose didactic illustration during the teaching process or for the purpose of scientific research, use the originals or translations of disseminated works or reproduce small disseminated works in whole or fragments of larger works.
>
> 2. Where any such use as referred to in para. 1 involves making the work available to the public so that anyone can have access to it at a time and place of their choosing, the use shall be permitted only for the limited range of people who are engaged in the learning process, the teaching process or the conduct of the scientific research, as identified by the entities referred to in para. 1.

Accordingly, the statutory test here is about the purpose of the use, namely (1) to illustrate what is being taught or (2) for scientific research. The former exception covers, for example, collecting and presenting, whether in whole or in fragments, scientific publications, popular science publications or the like; presenting spoken papers, lectures or similar speeches, including with the use of multimedia; preparing teaching resources/study aids to facilitate the educational process.[70] 'Scientific

[70] K. Gienas, Komentarz do art. 27 ustawy o prawie autorskim i prawach pokrewnych, in: Ferenc-Szydełko (ed.), Ustawa o prawie autorskim i prawach pokrewnych. Komentarz, Legalis 2017.

research' is to be understood in accordance with Article 2(3) of the Science Funding Act as (1) *basic research*, which means original inquiry, whether experimental or theoretical, taken up for the primary purpose of acquiring new knowledge about the basis of phenomena or observable facts, without a direct commercial orientation; (2) *applied research*, which means inquiry taken up for the purpose of acquiring new knowledge and oriented primarily towards practical applications; or (3) *industrial research*, which means inquiry designed to acquire new knowledge and skills for the purpose of developing new products, processes or services or significantly improving existing ones.

The other limbs of the Article 27(1) test are clear and do not require elucidation. For the avoidance of any doubt, the term 'small' work should be given the same meaning as under the right of quotation exception.[71]

The benefit of Article 27(1) CNRA is available to any educational institutions, schools of tertiary education or scientific organisations, whether they are for profit or not for profit.

Article 27 CNRA covers also *distance learning* (e-learning). By Article 27(2) CNRA, it is permitted to make works available to people involved in the learning process, teaching process or scientific research, who have been identified by the given institution. Importantly, however, this law does not permit organising open mass participation online courses, online courses being open to an unlimited number of participants who are not known even to the educational institution that is organising the course. This is a safeguard designed to ensure that the Polish educational use exception, which is broad comparing to many other Member States, is not abused and allows the eligible educational institutions to control the scope within which this exception is made use of in its educational processes.[72]

Also, the law not conferring any express entitlement to any remuneration for such permitted use, it should be assumed to be charge-free.

The manner of use under Article 27 CNRA may be modified (e.g., restricted or entirely prohibited) by contract between the right holder and the user.

As a side note, the exception under Article 29 CNRA (right of quotation, see Sect. 22.12 above) can also be classified as serving educational purposes because the right of quotation is often used in scholarly or scientific endeavours.

## 22.15 Exceptions Supporting Big-Data-Related Activities

Polish copyright law does not offer a catch-all framework to exhaustively regulate use of databases or specific data in those bases. Copyright law is only about works, so if it applies to databases, it will be only those that are works of authorship. Accordingly, pursuant to Article 3 CNRA, a database may be considered a work

[71] See Sect. 22.12 above.

[72] K. Gienas, Komentarz do art. 27 ustawy o prawie autorskim i prawach pokrewnych, in: Ferenc-Szydełko (ed.), Ustawa o prawie autorskim i prawach pokrewnych. Komentarz, Legalis 2017.

only if it is characterised by some degree of 'creativity' in the 'original' selection, layout or structure of its elements.

Obviously, where a database is considered a work, its creator will have all the author's rights to and in (author's monopoly over) that database as a whole. As such, the creator is exclusively entitled to use or dispose of the database in all manners of exploitation and to be remunerated for that. However, as in the case of any author, that is not to say that the monopoly of the creator of a copyright database is unlimited. Article $17^1$ CNRA says this:

> Where a database meets the definition of a work, no authorisation of the database's author shall be required for a lawful user of the database or of a copy thereof to alter or reproduce it if doing so is necessary for the purposes of access to the contents of the database and normal use of the contents. Where the lawful user is authorised to use only part of the database, this provision shall apply only to that part.

This law, which was introduced into the Copyright Act to implement Article 6(1) of the Database Directive, introduces two major requirements: (1) the permitted uses are available only to the 'lawful user' of the database, and (2) the permitted uses include only reproduction or alteration (*opracowanie*). As regards the first requirement, while the Copyright Act does not explain what a 'lawful user' means, it is accepted that this should be taken to include any natural or legal person using or accessing the database in accordance with the law, e.g. pursuant to the permissible use regulations. As regards the other requirement, note that the entitlements conferred by Article $17^1$ CNRA are somewhat narrower than those under Article 6(1) of the Database Directive as the latter also permits communication to the public of the database itself or of the results that its alteration processes.

Article $17^1$ CNRA is a mandatory law, so any contractual term barring these uses to a lawful user will be invalid.

In addition, the monopoly enjoyed by the author of a database may be limited by the permissible use framework, especially by Articles 23 or $23^1$ CNRA, except that Article 23 will not be applicable to electronic databases. Furthermore, electronic and non-electronic databases may be used to exercise the right of reprint (Article 25 CNRA) or by educational institutions or scientific organisations (Article 27 CNRA). It has been noted that these provisions are not mandatory so that such permissible uses may be modified by contract. Also, such uses do not entitle the author of the database to remuneration (except for remuneration pursuant to Article 25(2) CNRA—see Sect. 22.10 above).

## 22.16 Exhaustion of a Right

Currently, the Copyright Act provides for what is called the international 'Community' exhaustion model (Article 51(3) CNRA). Under this model, copyright in a specific copy of a work will be exhausted in Poland when it is distributed, whether in Poland or in any other country of the European Economic Area (EEA).[73] Exhaustion means that the copy concerned may now be freely distributed further (with no control by the original right holder).

Generally, exhaustion as above will occur as a result of distribution of a copy of the work (*wprowadzenie egzemplarza utworu do obrotu*),[74] i.e. whenever the following is the case: (1) there is a transfer of ownership of the physical media in which the work is fixed, and (2) the transfer is by the right holder. To clarify, the term 'transfer of ownership' must be interpreted in accordance with Polish civil law, so it may occur through a contract of sale, of gift or of exchange, whether with or without a consideration. The terms and purposes of the transfer are irrelevant either. As regards point (2), the media may be transferred only by the holder of the right of distribution, i.e. a person specifically entitled to distribute the original or copies of the work. A transfer of ownership without permission of the right holder will not count as 'distribution' and therefore will not result in exhaustion.

Also, as said, under Polish copyright law, exhaustion results from a transfer of ownership of *the physical media* in which the work has been recorded (fixed). For that reason, Polish copyright scholars used to consistently take the view that exhaustion does not occur where the 'sale' involves making the work available over the Internet. It was argued that in such situations, there is no exhaustion because there has been no transfer of ownership of any physical media and that, therefore, if the 'seller' has not given the purchaser any specific right of distribution, the latter will not be authorised to transfer the work any further.

This rather firm approach to the issue of online exhaustion has been somewhat weakened after the case *UsedSoft*.[75] The court ruled in July 2012 that the making available by the right holder of a copy of a computer program in an *intangible form* (e.g., where the right holder allows the user to download it via the Internet) will exhaust the right of distribution. However, exhaustion in this case occurs if the right holder has received payment of a fee for making the copy available to the acquirer so that the transaction becomes similar to a sale. Consequently, the acquirer may freely effect a transfer to a third party even in the absence of any licence from the 'seller' on the condition that the acquirer has deleted his own copy and no longer uses it. Importantly, it has been argued after the court that the requirement to make the copy available in a way that is similar to 'sale' means that there is no exhaustion where the software is provided as a service (e.g., cloud services).

While Polish copyright scholars do share CJEU's conclusions on exhaustion of the distribution right to computer programs, there continue to be doubts whether the court's approach is applicable also to other categories of works (music files, films, e-books). The prevailing view is that the term 'copy' should be given a *liberal*

---

[73] J. Barta, R. Markiewicz, Przejście autorskich praw majątkowych, in: Barta and Markiewicz (ed.), Prawo autorskie i prawa pokrewne. Komentarz, Warsaw 2011, p. 360.

[74] Under Article 6(6) CNRA, distribution of a work means the making available of its original or copies to the public through a transfer of ownership thereof by the right holder or with his consent.

[75] CJEU, case C-128/11, *UsedSoft v. Oracle Iternational Corp*, ECLI:EU:C:2012:407.

construal allowing for online exhaustion, and that is for two principal reasons: (1) because there is no equivalence between computer programs and other works in terms of the purposes of the doctrine of exhaustion and (2) because (anyway) there is the Article 23 CNRA exception, which in most cases permits the further acquirer to use the work without any specific licence.

Polish copyright law has not developed any approach to the issue of whether the 'seller' of a digital copy may in any way restrict the right of the 'purchaser' to transfer the copy further. It seems viable to rely here on CJEU's argument, which runs that any such restrictions imposed at the initiative of the original 'seller' could not apply to any further 'purchaser'.

## 22.17 Panorama Exception

Pursuant to Article 33(1) CNRA, it is permissible to disseminate works that are permanently exhibited on or in generally accessible roads, street, squares or gardens, but such dissemination cannot be for the same purpose. This 'panorama exception' is designed to enable free use, including primarily fixation and dissemination, of the general landscape.[76]

The panorama exception pertains to works 'exhibited permanently', which means that the works must be capable of being seen directly by sight (without the need for any transmission or similar devices) and must be made available permanently (rather than in such situations as temporary exhibitions). Usually, these will be architectural works or works of visual art, such as sculptures or murals.

The panorama exception law does not identify anyone specifically eligible for making use of the exception. Therefore, any natural or legal person may be considered to be eligible. Also, there is no limitation as to purpose, i.e. that it must be non-commercial. Since the law does not confer any express entitlement to any remuneration for such permitted use, it should be assumed to be charge-free.

The manner of use under Article 33 CNRA may be modified (e.g., restricted or entirely prohibited) by contract between the right holder and the user.

## 22.18 Private Copies

As mentioned above, Article 23(1) CNRA provides for the right to exploit a disseminated work for one's personal private uses without the author's permission. Article 23(2) specifies that this involves use of single copies by groups of people who have personal ties to each other, such as ties of affinity or consanguinity or social ties.

The Polish law governing the private use exception allows for *any manner of use*, not just copying. The only thing is that Article 23 CNRA does not apply to erecting

[76] S. Stanisławska-Kloc, Komentarz do art. 23 ustawy o prawie autorskim i prawach pokrewnych, in: Flisak (ed.), Prawo autorskie i prawa pokrewne. Komentarz, Lex 2015, p. 524.

a structure according to somebody else's architectural or urban planning work and to the use of electronic databases that are copyrightable. In practice, the most relevant form of private use is copying, including Internet copying, copying one's own or borrowed copy and broadcast copying.

However, the law restricts private use to (1) only *single copies* (mass copying will never be considered private use) and (2) a *group of people*, which is defined rather broadly and generally comprises persons connected by social ties, i.e. those who maintain mutual relationships for a longer time. It is accepted that a person eligible for the private use exception is permitted to use the services of a third party not belonging to the person's family or acquaintances (e.g., a professional photocopying service) to make the permissible copy(-ies), and this will not be a breach of Article 23 CNRA.

That said, the Copyright Act contains no other limitations on private use. In particular, there is no limitation on the size of the copy, meaning that private copies may be made of whole works and not just their extracts. Other than the issue of architectural or urban planning works or electronic databases (see above), there are no regulations that would ban private use in relation to any categories of works. Accordingly, private use applies to works expressed by words, musical works, works involving a combination of words and music, works of visual art, films, etc. As the law does not impose any specific purpose, private use should be interpreted to have many purposes, such as entertainment, collecting, scholarly pursuits,[77] provided the purposes are not commercial.

Article 23 CNRA clearly says that private use is *charge-free*. However, authors are entitled to remuneration for such uses indirectly pursuant to Articles 20 and $20^1$ CNRA. As mentioned above, these articles provide for a degree of compensation for authors in the form of levies, which are collected by collective rights management organisations from manufacturers and importers of blank media and copying devices and from holders of reprographic devices and are then distributed to authors.

## 22.19 Overall Assessment

Generally, the Polish permissible use framework is not free from defects. Criticism is particularly deserved in relation to (1) the regulation on use of orphan works; (2) the scope of copyright granted to press publishers with respect to collective works; (3) the language of Article 23 CNRA, where it applies to works from 'illegal sources'; and (4) the language of 27 CNRA as it excessively narrows down the range of those eligible for the exception.

As regards the orphan works regulation, the newly introduced Articles $35^5$ to $35^9$ CNRA continue to fail to fully address this issue. The way this law has been formulated makes it unfavourable for both authors and users of these works. The main problem is that it faithfully reflects Directive 2012/28/EU, which endorses a very

[77] E. Traple, Komentarz do art. 23 ustawy o prawie autorskim i prawach pokrewnych, in: D. Flisak (ed.), Prawo autorskie i prawa pokrewne. Komentarz Lex, Wolters Kluwer, p. 239.

narrow approach. Even though a directive is that type of secondary law that only directs the Member States to a certain desired legal configuration and leaves them substantial freedom as to the measures to be used to achieve it, Poland did not use that opportunity and chose not to enact an orphan works framework that would be more comprehensive than Directive 2012/28/EU. Consequently, the Polish framework reproduces all the weaknesses of the EU solutions. In particular, the Polish Copyright Act continues to offer no guidance on use of orphan works of the categories which it does not expressly mention (being works other than works published in print, audiovisual works or works fixed in phonograms, which are part of public collections) or by anyone other than just archives, educational institutions, schools of tertiary education and research institutes. What is more, the Copyright Act is very unclear about the 'diligent search' procedure, which is required before a work may be called orphan. The Copyright Act is even more laconic about 'fair' compensation to the authors. Under Article $35^9(5)$ CNRA, the amount of the compensation should refer to the nature and scope of the use, the amount of revenues generated and any damage done to the author through such use. These being quite general guidelines, it is yet to be seen how the compensation will be assessed in practice.

A host of problems arise due to the rather scant copyright regulation applicable to press publishers. While the publisher has copyright in the published collective work as a whole (see sentence 1 of Article 11 CNRA), he has no copyright in any of the contributing works. One practical consequence is that the publisher, who incurs the principal expenditure of money and effort to produce the publication, does not have any tools to ensure proper copyright protection for the individual creative contributions, e.g. against illegal copying and dissemination of these parts without the publication as a whole (the enforcement rights with respect to these contributions are vested solely in their particular authors). This has had important consequences, including financial, for the publishers, with the advent of the various online journalistic aggregation services using selected press articles or photographs on a mass scale. As this issue is not unknown to a wide range of EU Member States, there has for quite some time been a discussion at the EU level about two proposed measures to be introduced nationally: (1) a presumption that the particular contributing authors have authorised the publisher to enforce also their copyrights to the contributions and (2) specific neighbouring rights for press publishers (akin to those held by publishers of phonograms and videograms). Now that press publishers have been widely complaining of large losses due to aggregation and use of their content on a mass scale, questions have arisen whether the Copyright Act properly regulates the right of re-print (Article 25 CNRA). The largest controversies involve two questions: (1) Isn't the re-print exception too broad? (2) Does the group of those eligible (press, radio, television) also include news aggregators and web browsers? The prevailing answer to the latter question is that use by aggregators and browsers goes beyond the permissible limits of the exception.

There are a number of issues with the interpretation of the private use framework under Article 23 CNRA, especially after CJEU's judgment in *ACI Adam*.[78] The

[78] CJEU, case C-435/12, *ACI Adam BV et al. v. Stichting de Thuiskopie, Stichting Onderhandelingen Thuiskopievergoeding*, ECLI:EU:C:2014:254.

European court held that private use is available only for works that come from lawful sources. On the other hand, the predominant view among Polish copyright scholars has been that the private use exception applies whether the work downloaded from the Internet found its way there lawfully or not.[79] That view is shared by the Polish general public, who believes that one does not infringe copyright where one downloads a work from the Internet or creates a digital copy of a work solely for private purposes, whatever is the origin of the file (the way in which it was first uploaded). The ultimate construal of Article 23 CNRA is important in the context of the current substantial uncertainty among both users and right holders as to the actual scope of the private use exception. It seems that the most reasonable approach is that Article 23 CNRA should be interpreted to mean that the private use exception will apply in each case where the user has an at least reasonable belief that the work he is using was made available in a lawful manner.

Finally, criticism is deserved also with respect to Article 27 CNRA regulating the educational use exception (use for didactic purposes or for scientific research). It is universally argued that this law is formulated in such a way as to prevent its benefits from being claimed by non-governmental organisations while unreasonably privileging only educational institutions, schools of tertiary education and scientific organisations. Such unfortunate formulation of Article 27 CNRA is usually said to be necessary in order to ensure that the educational use exception is available only to organisations that are engaged in non-commercial activities. This is unconvincing because Article 27 CNRA gives the benefit of the exception to, for example, privately owned schools of tertiary education, which are generally for-profit institutions. There are no reasonable arguments to justify the exclusion of NGOs from the group of those eligible to enjoy the benefits of Article 27.

In conclusion, many permissible use provisions in the Copyright Act are too imprecise or, a contrario, too narrow. A number of these provisions are also incompatible with the fast-changing reality and the requirements of technological progress. It seems that the best way to avoid such mistakes in future is to have a public debate before any potential changes are made to the Copyright Act. There is a clear need for a platform for the exchange of views on copyright law among all the stakeholders. We believe that such a platform is necessary to strike a proper balance between the interests of the authors and right holders, on the one hand, and the users of their works, on the other.

[79] Ł. Gołba, W. Rodak, Nowa przesłanka dozwolonego użytku prywatnego? Legalność kopii źródłowej w świetle art. 23 ustawy o prawie autorskim i prawach pokrewnych, Transformacje Prawa Prywatnego, 1/2017 ISSN 1641–1609 – www.transformacje.pl/wp-content/uploads/2017/05/tpp_1-2017_golba_rodak.pdf.

# 23 Romania

Paul-George Buta

## 23.1 Introduction

Law no. 8 of 14 March 1996 on Copyright and Related Rights[1] (hereinafter "Romanian Copyright Law") provides for exceptions and limitations to copyright in chapter VI, entitled "Limitations to the Exercise of Copyright," of part I, entitled "General Provisions," of title I, which is dedicated to copyright, of the law. The chapter includes 6 articles, numbered from 33 to 38, with Article 36 having been repealed by Law no. 285 of 23 June 2004 for the Modification and Amendment of the Romanian Copyright Law.[2]

The provisions of chapter VI do not apply to software, such application being excluded by the provisions of Article 81 of the Romanian Copyright Law. As far as software is concerned, Article 80 indicates that, subject to there being no prejudice to the author or to the normal exploitation of the software, the author's consent is not mandatory for the reproduction and translation of the code for the purpose of insuring interoperability, provided that the additional conditions established by Articles 78 and 79 are also met.

The law provides for a general list of exceptions and limitations (subject to (1) the work having been made known to the public, (2) the use being in accordance with good practice, (3) the condition that it does not affect the normal exploitation of the work, and (4) the condition that it does not prejudice the author or the holders of the exploitation rights) and an additional list, specifically of exceptions and

[1] Law on Copyright and Related Rights, Monitorul Oficial 1996 60.

[2] Law for the Modification and Amendment of the Law on Copyright and Related Rights, Monitorul Oficial 2004 587.

P.-G. Buta (✉)
Muşat & Asociaţii, Bucharest, Romania
e-mail: paul.buta@musat.ro





B. Kilpatrick et al. (eds.), *Antitrust Analysis of Online Sales Platforms & Copyright Limitations and Exceptions*, LIDC Contributions on Antitrust Law, Intellectual Property and Unfair Competition,
https://doi.org/10.1007/978-3-319-71419-6_23

limitations to the right of reproduction, distribution, broadcasting, and communication to the public (subject to the added condition that the use be without direct or indirect commercial or economic advantage). In order to qualify for almost every one of the exceptions or limitations under either of the two lists, the user must give proper attribution whenever possible. In addition to the above, some temporary acts of reproduction that are transient or incidental to other activities are expressly carved out of the scope of the reproduction right.

Other major features of these provisions consist of the specific regulation of the private copy exception (under the condition that a remuneration be paid in consideration of such) and the allowing of the transformation of the work, without the author's consent and without payment of any remuneration, in four given cases: where it is a private transformation, for parody or caricature, where necessary for use permitted by the author and where the result of this is a summary presentation of the works, for teaching (in such case proper attribution being also required).

Less relied-on exceptions and limitations that the law provides for refer to certain reproductions and communications to the public, which may be allowed for, and only as needed for, testing of the functioning of the products on manufacture or sale and the possibility of collective management societies to monitor by any means the use of their catalog, without the authorization or compensation of users, as well as the right to demand that public institutions provide them with information of public interest.

Finally, the law also provides for an implicit license to broadcasting organizations in order to record a work, only once and only for the purpose of making the broadcast. This license is deemed granted upon assignment or license of the broadcasting right for the work to the broadcasting organization. Authorization of the author is needed for any additional broadcast of the recorded work, and such authorization can only be granted for paid consideration (the right to such being unwaivable). The authorization is to be sought within at most 6 months from the making of the recording; otherwise, the recording has to be destroyed. In addition, the law allows "conservation in official archives" of temporary recordings of works made by radio or television broadcasting organizations for their own shows but only where such recordings would have "a special documentary value."

## 23.2 The Triple Test in Romanian Copyright Law

The provisions in chapter VI include a "triple test" provision as a complement to the closed list of exceptions and limitations provided for in Article 33 and as a complement to the private copy exception provided for in Article 34.

Article 33 par. (1) of the law thus reads: "The following uses of a work previously made known to the public shall be permitted without the author's consent and without payment of a remuneration, on condition that these are in accordance with good practice, do not affect the normal exploitation of the work, and do not prejudice the author or the holders of the exploitation rights."

The other provision expressly making use of the "triple test" is Article 34 par. (1) of the law, which reads: "The reproduction of a work without the author's consent, for personal use or for the normal family circle, shall not be an infringement of copyright, for the purposes of the present law, on condition that the work had previously been made known to the public, that the reproduction does not affect the normal exploitation of the work and does not prejudice the author or the holders of the exploitation rights."

In practice, the Romanian courts have generally used the triple test as a supplementary test to confirm the application of the exceptions and limitations provided by Articles 33 and 34 of the Romanian Copyright Law, where the type of use would appear, *per* se, to fall in the scope of the "special cases" provided therein.[3]

The High Court of Cassation and Justice (hereinafter "High Court") established that for a given use of a protected work to fall within the scope of the exceptions and limitations provided by the Romanian Copyright Law, such use need not only be of the type indicated by law but must also fulfill the triple test, as implemented by the Romanian legislator.[4] Thus, the triple test appears to serve as a confirmation test for situations where the special cases in which use of the work without the consent of the author and without payment would appear to apply, and it is, in fact, so used by the Romanian courts.

The Bucharest Court of Appeals indicated that each of the four general conditions provided by paragraph (1) needs to be met in order for any limitation provided therein to apply in addition to the special conditions required to qualify under any of the "special cases" specifically indicated by law.[5] The Bucharest Tribunal held that these special conditions "take into account the type of use of the work, the category of protected work concerned and the place where such use is made, all of which require mentioning the source and author of the work."[6] In practice, the courts tend to verify first whether the special conditions are met and, where satisfied, to check whether the general conditions are met as well.

---

[3] Cf. R. Pârvu and C. R. Romițan, Dreptul de autor și drepturile conexe, All Beck 2005, p. 77.

[4] ICCJ, s. I civ., Decision no. 1109 of 24 April 2015, www.scj.ro. Accessed 25 May 2017: use of a protected work "in accordance with article 33 par. (1) [of the Romanian Copyright Law] is subject to multiple conditions, such use not being allowed in all circumstances (of the type that would fall under the exceptions provided at letters a)–i); these conditions are the following: that the work was made public beforehand, and that the use be one in accordance with good practice, does not affect the normal exploitation of the work and does not prejudice the author or the holders of the exploitation rights. [...] it is by a correct application of the law that the Court of Appeals has dismissed the defendants' arguments referring to the application of art. 33 par. (1) letters a) and e), because the legal conditions set by the premise of art. 33 par. (1), which would have allowed use of the work without the author's consent and without payment of remuneration, were not met and therefore such provisions were inapplicable to the case, as was shown."

[5] Bucharest Court of Appeals, s. IX civ., Decision no. 67A of 25 February 2014, www.rolii.ro. Accessed 25 May 2017.

[6] Bucharest Tribunal, s. IV civ., Decision no. 841 of 8 May 2008, www.rolii.ro. Accessed 25 May 2017.

In a case concerning the use of an identical short excerpt from a book about the Romanian Civil Code by the government in the Explanatory Memorandum for the Proposal of a New Civil Code without attribution and without proper identification of the excerpt as a quote, the courts examined whether such use qualifies as permitted under the exception provided by Article 33 par. (1) letter a) of the Romanian Copyright Law using the triple test.[7]

The Bucharest Tribunal indicated that the notion of "good practice" is to be analyzed by reference to the actual type of reproduction and its purpose, and therefore "reproduction of short fragments is allowed, 'short' being subject to the court's appreciation by reference to the length and complexity of the allegedly counterfeit work. Such condition is satisfied where, as in the present case, the length of the allegedly infringing excerpt is very limited (8 lines), and thus is insignificant by reference to both the Explanatory Memorandum (a public document of approximately 30 pages) and the claimant's work (1052 pages). Moreover, there is no ground for holding that by copying these introductory fragments there was a copying of essential passages that concerned the main part of the claimant's work, such as to prejudice him by an abusive exploitation of his work, the purpose of the reproduction being in the public interest i.e. to inform the public of the need of the legislative amendments brought by the new Civil Code, without any direct or indirect commercial advantage. The reproduction of the challenged excerpt does not prejudice the claimant in any way since the purpose of the citation was solely the information of the public and not the usurpation of the authorship in the claimant's work."[8]

On appeal,[9] the court upheld the Tribunal's decision and in doing so emphasized the fact that the use was in accordance with good practice since the purpose of the copying was not personal but to satisfy the public interest and to fulfill the requirements for an Explanatory Memorandum, as provided by Law no. 24 of 27 March 2000 concerning the Norms of Legislative Technique for the Drafting of Statutes.[10] The appellate court also pointed to the absence of commercial purpose, the sole purpose being the information of the public; to the limited length of the copied fragment; and to the fact that the excerpts were included in the Explanatory Memorandum, held to be a general presentation of the Civil Code, a delineation of its purpose, thus indicating that the copying did not aim to appropriate the ideas or passages of the claimant's work but to inform the public, as elements that confirmed that the use was in accordance with good practice. Still in reference to the "good practice" criterion, the appellate court held that the condition was met also on account of the fact that "the originality of the claimant's work cannot be affected by the copying of some passages, insignificant in number by reference to the length of the claimant's

[7] ICCJ, s. I civ., Decision no. 889 of 18 March 2014, www.scj.ro. Accessed 25 May 2017.

[8] Bucharest Tribunal, s. IV civ., Decision no. 1173 of 29 May 2012, www.rolii.ro. Accessed 25 May 2017.

[9] Bucharest Court of Appeals, s. IX civ., Decision no. 108A of 30 May 2013, www.rolii.ro. Accessed 25 May 2017.

[10] Law concerning the Norms of Legislative Technique for the Drafting of Statutes, Monitorul Oficial 2000 139.

work, more so since the 'philosophy' of this code, as presented by the claimant, contains general statements, not by reference to a given statute but to the general notion of 'code.'" The Court of Appeals also linked the effect on the "normal exploitation of the work" to the "important practical effects that this copying could have" and concluded, without further argument, that there were no such effects in this case. Interestingly, the appellate court established the lack of any prejudice to the author or to the holders of exploitation rights by reference to the fact that the inclusion of the excerpts in the Explanatory Memorandum has not generated a new copyright for its authors (statutory instruments being excluded from copyright protection).

The High Court,[11] in affirming the Court of Appeal's decision, clarified that the limitation provided by law was instituted on account of the "need to protect some general interests, of public order, such as the information of the public with respect to the importance and relevance of legislative intervention in the Civil Code." The court concluded that, given the justification of the limitation, the existence of a commercial purpose is irrelevant in the given case, such purpose being excluded "given the initiative and the justification for the creation of the work in which the challenged reproduction is found." The High Court also indicated that a quantitative evaluation of the copying was not required for the fulfillment of the conditions provided by the "special case" at hand but was used by the lower courts in their evaluation of the use being in accordance with good practice, as was the evaluation of the essentiality of the excerpt as compared to the original work.

With reference to a claim for copyright infringement by use of an excerpt of a press article on the website of a regional newspaper, the Galați Tribunal held that the exception provided for by Article 33 par. (1) letter b) of the Romanian Copyright Law is applicable since the respondent "copied only a short excerpt [of the original article] (11 lines), for illustration, and that the length of the quote is justified on account of the intent to get the reader's attention and determine him to look for the rest of the article, but on the original website (of Tango magazine), and not on the respondent's [and therefore] did not prejudice the author (but on the contrary, benefitted her, by determining readers of the Ziua de Constanța publication to also read Tango magazine)."[12]

There were also cases where the courts found that the use complained of did not meet the conditions required by the triple test and, therefore, such use was not permitted under the limitations and exceptions provided by law. One of these cases involved the making available, online and in full, in the Ministry of Interior's Publishing House virtual library, of a book on terrorism, previously edited in print by the same publisher. The respondent tried to defend this use by claiming that it was a reproduction "specific to those made by libraries accessible to the public" or a reproduction "for purposes of public safety."

[11] ICCJ, s. I civ., Decision no. 889 of 18 March 2014, www.scj.ro. Accessed 25 May 2017.

[12] Galați Tribunal, s. I civ., Decision no. 959 of 12 April 2013, www.rolii.ro. Accessed 25 May 2017.

The Court of Appeals found that the use could not qualify under either of the limitations, given that the use prejudiced the author.[13] In order to so hold, the court made reference to the "wide accessibility to the work that publishing it online allows, both in terms of territory (the place where the users are) and in terms of the lack of any substantial impediment to the use of the work by third parties. Practically, the online publication of the claimant's work deprives of purpose any possible attempt by the author to republish his work, since such has become accessible to any interested party."

In affirming,[14] the High Court held that the fact that the use prevented any possible attempt by the author to republish his work means that the condition that the use does not affect the normal exploitation of the work is also not met, in addition to the condition that the use does not prejudice the author. In addition, the court established that "the online publishing of the whole work, with unlimited access for the public, voids of all content and suppresses any eventual intention of the author or of the right holder to republish the work, which is the equivalent of an exclusive assignment of the right to reproduce the work [...] and, consequently, of the definitive removal of this right from the patrimony of the author or of the right holder, without any agreement to such effect and without the work having fallen in the public domain and the economic rights having been extinguished (at the expiry of the legal duration of protection)."

In another dispute that concerned the use of a 10-second sequence from a movie within a 30-second television commercial advertising a charitable campaign, the Bucharest Court of Appeals held that the exceptions strictly and exhaustively provided for by Article 33 paragraph (1) only apply where certain conditions are met, among them being that the use is in accordance with good practice and that it does not affect the normal exploitation of the work. The court found that the use was a separation of a fragment (sequence) from a cinematographic work, its transformation so as to send a different message than the one sent by the original work, and its communication for a purpose with no connection to that of the original work, and therefore this caused the two conditions mentioned not to be met in the given case. The appeals court stated that "it is inconceivable that, in what concerns a work of intellectual creation, generating specific intellectual property rights for its authors, acts of copying and transformation of a part of the work for the purpose of satisfying needs of third parties upon whom an obligation [...] to abstain from any act such as to infringe on the moral rights of the authors is incumbent, could be held to be in accordance with good practices and/or the normal exploitation of the work."[15]

In a yet different case, the Dolj Tribunal seems to have taken the stance that the copying in full of a work would contravene the provisions of the law relating to the

[13] Bucharest Court of Appeals, s. IX civ., Decision no. 67A of 25 February 2014, www.rolii.ro. Accessed 25 May 2017.

[14] ICCJ, s. I civ., Decision no. 1109 of 24 April 2015, www.scj.ro. Accessed 25 May 2017.

[15] Bucharest Court of Appeals, s. IX civ., Decision no. 51A of 26 February 2009, Buletinul jurisprudenței 2009. Curtea de Apel București, Universul Juridic 2011, p. 492.

triple test.[16] This was a claim, grounded on the provisions of Law no. 544 of 12 October 2001 concerning Free Access to Information of Public Interest[17] and on the provisions concerning the limitations and exceptions to copyright in the Romanian Copyright Law, against the University of Craiova's Faculty of Mathematics and Informatics. The claimant requested that he be sent a copy of a dissertation that had been authored by a third party in a master's program organized by the faculty. The University declined, among others, on account of the fact that making such a copy would infringe the author's copyright in his dissertation. The claimant rebutted this, arguing that such copy would qualify as permitted under the limitations and exceptions provided by Articles 33 (without indicating which special case would apply and apparently suggesting that any use that meets the conditions of the triple test ought to be allowed) and 34 of the Romanian Copyright Law. The court dismissed the claim holding that, *inter alia*, no matter which exception or limitation of the two was claimed under, none would apply since the triple test was not satisfied.

The Arad Tribunal also held in a case concerning a preliminary injunction against the owner of a website that provided links to other sites (scribd.ro, zippyshare.com) inviting visitors to read and download books in pdf format by clicking those links that such use did not comply with the general conditions provided by Article 33 of the Romanian Copyright Law in that "Internet users are allowed to access the works free of charge, thereby discouraging the classic manner of acquiring the works in print, at a price."[18]

## 23.3 The Closed List of Exceptions Under Romanian Copyright Law

As indicated above, the Romanian Copyright Law provides for a closed list of exceptions in Articles 33–35 and 37 of the law, Article 38 paragraph (1) concerning in fact an implied license and not an exception to copyright *per se*. While the exceptions provided for by Articles 33 paragraph (3), 34, 35, and 37 were listed above, we will hereunder only list the exceptions provided for by Article 33 paragraphs (1) and (2).

Paragraph (1) of Article 33 allows, subject to the conditions of the triple test being met (other than the "special case" condition, which requires checking that the use is of the type specifically provided for in the closed list), the following uses:

a) the reproduction of a work in connection with judicial, parliamentary, or administrative proceedings or for the purpose of public safety;

[16] Dolj Tribunal, s. cont. adm., Decision no. 896 of 19 April 2011, www.rolii.ro. Accessed 25 May 2017, confirmed by Craiova Court of Appeals, s. cont. adm., Decision no. 2853 of 13 October 2011, www.rolii.ro. Accessed 25 May 2017.

[17] Law concerning Free Access to Information of Public Interest, Monitorul Oficial 2001 663.

[18] Arad Tribunal, s. I civ., Decision no. 9 of 12 January 2015, www.rolii.ro. Accessed 25 May 2017, confirmed by Timişoara Court of Appeals, s. I civ., Decision no. 33 of 25 February 2015 in Curtea de apel Timişoara, Decizii relevante. Secţia I civilă. Trimestrul I – 2015 (2015), pp. 32–37.

b) the use of brief quotations from a work for the purpose of analysis, commentary, or criticism or for illustration, to the extent such use justifies the length of the quote;
c) the use of isolated articles or brief excerpts from works in publications, television or radio broadcasts, or sound or audiovisual recordings, exclusively intended for teaching purposes and also the reproduction for teaching purposes, within the public education or social welfare institutions, of isolated articles or brief extracts from works, to the extent justified by the intended purpose;
d) the reproduction of brief excerpts from works, for the purpose of information or research, by not-for-profit libraries, museums, film archives, sound archives, archives of cultural or scientific public institutions; the complete reproduction of the support of a work is allowed for the replacement of the sole copy in the permanent collection of a library or archive in the event of the destruction, serious deterioration, or loss thereof;
e) specific acts of reproduction made by publicly accessible libraries, educational establishments, or museums, or by archives that are not for direct or indirect economic or commercial advantage;
f) the reproduction (with the exclusion of any means involving direct contact with the work), distribution, or communication to the public of the image of an architectural work, work of plastic art, photographic work or work of applied art, permanently located in a public place, except where the image of the work is the main subject of such reproduction, distribution, or communication and where it is used for commercial purposes;
g) the representation and execution of a work as part of the activities of educational establishments, exclusively for specific purposes and provided that both the representation or execution and the public's access are free of charge;
h) use of works during religious celebrations or official ceremonies organized by a public authority;
i) use for the purpose of advertising of the images of works presented at exhibitions with public access or public sale, fairs, public auctions of works of art, as a means to promote the event, excluding any commercial use.

Bearing in mind the conditions set forth by the triple test, other than the "special case" condition, as was the case for paragraph (1), and of the additional condition that the use be without direct or indirect commercial or economic advantage, paragraph (2) provides for an additional closed list of exceptions where the reproduction, distribution, broadcasting, or communication to the public of the work is allowed without the author's consent and without any payment. These additional "special cases" refer to the reproduction, distribution, broadcasting, or communication to the public

a) of brief excerpts from press articles and radio or televised reports, for the purpose of informing on current events, with the exception of those for which such a use is expressly reserved;
b) of brief excerpts from lectures, addresses, pleadings, and other similar works that have been orally expressed in public, provided that these uses have the sole purpose of informing on current events;

c) of brief excerpts from works, within information on current events, to the extent justified by the purpose of information;
d) of works, where used exclusively for illustration in teaching or scientific research;
e) of works, for the benefit of people with disabilities, which are directly related to that disability and to the extent required by the specific disability.

Moreover, as indicated above, in order to benefit from any of the exceptions provided by Article 33 paragraph (2) or the ones provided by Article 33 paragraph (1) letters b), c), e), f), or i), proper attribution is required, unless it is impossible. In addition to the requirement for attribution, for works of plastic art, photographic works, and works of architecture, the place where the original of the work is found must also be indicated.

The list of exceptions thus provided by law is a closed one, meaning that in order for any exception to apply, the use must fall within the ones on the list, any other use being subject to the authorization of the author and/or right holder. Specifically, the High Court has expressly indicated,[19] in a case concerning an infringement of copyright in a book on Romanian geography by the publishing of a nearly identical book for use as a course manual and for sale to the students of a university, that "Article 33 of the [Romanian Copyright Law] to which reference is made in the grounds for final appeal, expressly and exhaustively regulates certain limitations to the exercise of the economic prerogatives of the author, i.e. the exercise of the exclusive economic right to decide if, how and when his work is used, including to consent to use of the work by others [cit. omitted], of the right to authorize or forbid use in any of the forms provided by Article 13 of the law, and of the right to an equitable remuneration, when and under the conditions expressly provided by law." The court thus confirms that the closed list of exceptions is in fact an exhaustive list, no other exceptions or limitations being allowed.[20] In another case mentioned above,[21] the High Court confirmed this approach and held that "the appellate court correctly indicated the exceptional character of these provisions, as the rule of strict interpretation of such exceptional provisions, to the effect that the application of such cannot be extended, by means of interpretation, to other situations than those limited situations the legislator had in mind at the time of their adoption."

The Bucharest Court of Appeals held,[22] in a case concerning the alleged infringement of copyright in a ballet choreography organized by the Bucharest National

[19] ICCJ, s. I civ., Decision no. 1067 of 28 March 2014, www.scj.ro. Accessed 25 May 2017.

[20] Other court decisions holding the same are the ones issued in the case concerning the use of a 10-second film sequence in a television commercial – Bucharest Tribunal, s. IV civ., Decision no. 841 of 8 May 2008, www.rolii.ro. Accessed 25 May 2017, affirmed by Bucharest Court of Appeals, s. IX civ., Decision no. 51A of 26 February 2009, Buletinul jurisprudenței 2009. Curtea de Apel București, Universul Juridic 2011, p. 492.

[21] ICCJ, s. I civ., Decision no. 1109 of 24 April 2015, www.scj.ro. Accessed 25 May 2017.

[22] Bucharest Court of Appeals, s. IX civ., Decision no. 190A of 11 November 2013, www.rolii.ro. Accessed 25 May 2017.

Opera, that "the fact that the show promoted the image of Romania is not an exception to the economic rights under copyright as it is not provided for by Article 33 of [the Romanian Copyright Law]," therefore emphasizing the fact that the list of exceptions provided by law is closed and cannot be extended without legislative intervention. Similarly, the same court held that the "humanitarian purpose of the event for the promotion of which the video containing the ball sequence from the movie 'A Dream of January' was created, and the absence of any economic advantage" to the persons involved are not able to place the use outside the remit of infringement as such can only be achieved by cumulatively satisfying the conditions laid out by Article 33 of the Romanian Copyright Law.[23]

As indicated above, there seems to have been one court decision where the possibility of a use not expressly provided for in the closed list of "special cases" might have been considered as potentially allowed under the general condition that it meets the triple-case test.[24] However, the court did not expressly consider this as it merely acknowledged that the triple test was not satisfied, and therefore no exception was held to be applicable.

## 23.4 Fundamental Rights as a Basis for Creating the Exceptions and Limitations

As also mentioned above, the High Court held that the exception provided by Article 33 paragraph (1) letter a) of the Romanian Copyright Law was instituted as necessary on account of the "need to protect some general interests, of public order, such as the information of the public with respect to the importance and relevance of legislative intervention in the Civil Code."[25]

However, in another case mentioned above,[26] the High Court held that in evaluating the exceptions to copyright in light of the purpose for their establishment, it is the immediate and direct purpose that was to be attained by the exception that has to be considered. Thus, the court held that "the appellate court correctly established that the immediate, direct purpose of the online publishing of the work on the Internet, on the publisher's website/Virtual Library was to insure the instruction of the specialized personnel with legal attributions pertaining to the insuring of public safety or of the ones tending to obtain such professional qualification (school children, students, people enrolled in courses for continuous learning etc.), while the indirect and only eventual purpose was the public safety, as only authorities vested by law with such attributions can insure public safety, in the limits set by law." On

[23] Bucharest Court of Appeals, s. IX civ., Decision no. 51A of 26 February 2009, Buletinul jurisprudenței 2009. Curtea de Apel București, Universul Juridic 2011, p. 492.

[24] Dolj Tribunal, s. cont. adm., Decision no. 896 of 19 April 2011, www.rolii.ro. Accessed 25 May 2017, confirmed by Craiova Court of Appeals, s. cont. adm., Decision no. 2853 of 13 October 2011, www.rolii.ro. Accessed 25 May 2017.

[25] ICCJ, s. I civ., Decision no. 889 of 18 March 2014, www.scj.ro. Accessed 25 May 2017.

[26] ICCJ, s. I civ., Decision no. 1109 of 24 April 2015, www.scj.ro. Accessed 25 May 2017.

appeal, in the same case, the Bucharest Court of Appeals indicated that the fulfilling of the purpose envisaged by the legislature upon instituting the exception needs to be proven "beyond the limits of a simple supposition."[27]

In a case concerning the reproduction, on a blog, of photographs from calendars made by a business magazine featuring their female employees, for the purpose of a satirical article, the 4th District Court of Bucharest considered that it fell within the exception provided by Article 33 paragraph (1) letter b) of the Romanian Copyright Law but was made "within the defendant's right to freedom of expression guaranteed to professional journalists by Article 30 of the Romanian Constitution and Article 10 of the European Convention on Human Rights, and the right to access to public information guaranteed by Article 31 of the Romanian Constitution."[28]

The Bucharest Court of Appeals held,[29] in a case concerning football matches highlights made available on the website of a sports newspaper, allegedly infringing the copyright of the broadcaster holding exclusive rights in the broadcast of these matches, that the exception established by Article 33 paragraph (2) letter c) of the Romanian copyright law was so provided for the purpose of informing the public, as can be deducted from the fact that such use is only allowed to the extent needed to so inform the public. The court further held that maintaining the excerpt available to the public for a long period of time has overstepped the limit imposed by the purpose of informing the public of a sporting event. Relatedly, in a different case, the same court held that in order for such limitation to apply, the information must concern current events related to the work itself, so the legal conditions are not met where the work is used to create a new work that, in its turn, has the purpose of promoting a competing event.[30]

The exceptions and limitations are therefore generally assumed to have been introduced to ensure a proper balancing of copyright with the exercise of other rights, most relevant being the freedom of expression, the right to information, the right to education, etc. However, the importance of economic justifications for the implementation of such exceptions and, even more, for properly delimiting their scope has also been highlighted in the literature.[31]

---

[27] Bucharest Court of Appeals, s. IX civ., Decision no. 67A of 25 February 2014, www.rolii.ro. Accessed 25 May 2017.

[28] 4th District Court of Bucharest, s. civ., Decision no. 1314 of 4 February 2016, www.rolii.ro. Accessed 25 May 2017, confirmed by Bucharest Tribunal, s. III civ., Decision no. 3859 of 14 October 2016, www.rolii.ro. Accessed 25 May 2017.

[29] Bucharest Court of Appeals, s. IX civ., Decision no. 178A of 4 December 2012, www.rolii.ro. Accessed 25 May 2017.

[30] Bucharest Court of Appeals, s. IX civ., Decision no. 51A of 26 February 2009, Buletinul jurisprudenţei 2009. Curtea de Apel Bucureşti, Universul Juridic 2011, p. 492.

[31] P. G. Buta and A. Muşat, Limitările în exerciţiul dreptului de autor. Condiţiile în care intervin, Revista Română de Dreptul Proprietăţii Intelectuale 2007(2), pp. 107–119; P. G. Buta, Despre limitările şi excepţiile dreptului de autor. După 10 ani, Revista Română de Dreptul Proprietăţii Intelectuale (forthcoming).

## 23.5 Exceptions and Limitations to Copyright Need to Be Interpreted Narrowly

The courts and literature have indicated that these exceptions and limitations must be narrowly interpreted and applied restrictively due, first and foremost, to their qualifications as exceptional situations carved out of the scope of the generally applicable copyright protection. The need to ensure a high level of protection of copyright, coupled with the granting of copyright protection upon the work fulfilling the minimum criteria provided by law, have limited these situations, which are exhaustively provided for by law, to "special cases" within the meaning of the "triple test" and have therefore imposed, as a rule, a very strict application of the statutory criteria for benefitting from such exceptions and limitations.

In one case, concerning the unauthorized use of panoramic photographs of the city of Brașov on billboards by a retailer, the High Court held that the provisions of Article 33 paragraph (4) need to be abided by in all cases provided therein. Therefore, in order to qualify for the panorama exception to copyright, the user has to give proper attribution and indicate the place where the original is found.[32] The fact that the respondent did not know the information for giving attribution, when selecting the photographs with Google—a fact that was also disproved—was also deemed irrelevant by the court, therefore emphasizing the strictness applied by the courts when dealing with the exceptions to copyright. Such strict approach is also warranted by the qualification of these provisions as exceptions, a fact that requires all interpretations of such to be strict—an approach that has been also confirmed by the High Court in the two cases discussed above.[33] The need to interpret the exceptions restrictively also determined the Bucharest Court of Appeals to hold that "the four general conditions provided by the first thesis of [Article 33 paragraph (1) of the Romanian Copyright Law] are cumulative, therefore not meeting any of them makes the exception inapplicable. Beyond these general conditions, any of the special conditions provided by letters a)–i) must be additionally met, as it is in consideration of those that the limitations to the economic rights were instituted."[34] In the same decision, the court concluded that the fact that a single condition is not fulfilled is sufficient to make the exception inapplicable and to consider that the copyright is infringed.[35]

In one of these abovementioned cases, the High Court additionally held[36] that a defence to a claim of copyright infringement by reference to Government Decision no. 1676 of 10 December 2008 concerning the approval of the National Program for

[32] ICCJ, s. I civ., Decision no. 651 of 12 February 2013, www.scj.ro. Accessed 25 May 2017.

[33] ICCJ, s. I civ., Decision no. 1067 of 28 March 2014, www.scj.ro. Accessed 25 May 2017 and ICCJ, s. I civ., Decision no. 1109 of 24 April 2015, www.rolii.ro. Accessed 25 May 2017.

[34] Bucharest Court of Appeals, s. IX civ., Decision no. 67A of 25 February 2014, www.rolii.ro. Accessed 25 May 2017.

[35] Also held in Bucharest Court of Appeals, s. IX civ., Decision no. 51A of 26 February 2009, Buletinul jurisprudenței 2009. Curtea de Apel București, Universul Juridic 2011, p. 492.

[36] ICCJ, s. I civ., Decision no. 1109 of 24 April 2015, www.scj.ro. Accessed 25 May 2017.

the Digitization of National Cultural Resources and the creation of Romania's Digital Library[37] cannot succeed on account of the fact that all limitations to the exercise of economic rights pertaining to copyright are provided for by chapter VI of the Romanian Copyright Law, and these cannot be supplemented except by means of a statute of equal normative value or by amendment to the Romanian Copyright Law. Moreover, it also indicated that the Government Decision cannot be taken to mean that the digitization process can be made by infringement of copyright but that such process is to take place in full observance of the rights granted by the Romanian Copyright Law.

In the case concerning the abovementioned geography book, the Bucharest Tribunal also held that the use complained of could not fall under the scope of the exception provided for by Article 33 paragraph (1) letter g) of the Romanian Copyright Law since that provision relates solely to the communication to the public of certain works, susceptible of being made public by representation and execution.[38] Moreover, the court held that neither the exception provided by Article 33 paragraph (2) letter d) of the Romanian Copyright Law can be deemed applicable since the use complained of was not made for illustration purposes as in such case, only fragments of the work would have been used to provide ground for the respondent's own arguments and proper attribution given. In affirming, the Bucharest Court of Appeals also indicated that the fact that the respondent gave attribution in respect of some of the fragments copied did not make any exception applicable since all conditions provided by law need to be met cumulatively, and the fact that the respondent copied all of the plaintiff's work for the purpose of distributing the infringing work at a profit causes the exception not to apply.[39] The reverse was also held to be insufficient as the Bucharest Tribunal held that, even if the use did fall in a specific special case provided by Article 33 of the law, lack of proper attribution made the provision inapplicable.[40]

The Neamț Tribunal held, in a claim for infringement by use of a photograph of a painting in an electoral booklet, without attribution, without the author's consent and with no payment, that such use is not excepted by the provisions of Article 33 paragraph (1) letter f) of the Romanian Copyright Law since it is contrary to good practice, it was made without giving attribution and without indicating the location of the original, these conditions being expressly provided for by law.[41] With a

[37] Government Decision concerning the approval of the National Program for the Digitization of National Cultural Resources and the creation of Romania's Digital Library, Monitorul Oficial 2008 855.

[38] Bucharest Tribunal, s. IV civ., Decision no. 1997 of 15 November 2011, www.rolii.ro. Accessed 25 May 2017.

[39] Bucharest Court of Appeals, s. IX civ., Decision no. 158 of 30 October 2012, www.rolii.ro. Accessed 25 May 2017.

[40] Bucharest Tribunal, s. IV civ., Decision no. 841 of 8 May 2008, www.rolii.ro. Accessed 25 May 2017.

[41] Neamț Tribunal, s. I. civ., Decision no. 463/C of 8 April 2013, www.rolii.ro. Accessed 25 May 2017.

similar restrictive interpretation of the panorama exception, the Bucharest Tribunal held that the posting of a photograph online is not equivalent to having the work "located in a public place," the provision being limited to "works specifically created for that purpose: to be a part of the public landscape," whereas in the given case, the photograph was posted to the claimant's own website with an express reservation as to its use.[42]

However, in some instances, some courts adopted a flexible approach in their reading of these exceptions and limitations. In a dispute concerning, inter alia, the alleged infringement of copyright in personal photographs (which had been inserted in a published biography) by use of such in a historical TV show about the person about whom the biography had been written, the Bucharest Tribunal held that even though the exception provided by Article 33 paragraph (1) letter b) of the Romanian Copyright Law refers to "short quotations from a work," the provision can also be extended, by analogy, to the photographs published in the biographical book.[43] The findings of the first instance were upheld on appeal by the Bucharest Court of Appeals, although it had previously held, in a different case, that "the Court is of the opinion that there can be no equivalence between the concept of film sequence and that of a quote – the quote being by definition a fragment of a written work, identically reproduced."[44] On final appeal in the case concerning the use of the personal photographs, the High Court eluded the direct question and held that since the claimed copyright was a copyright in the biographical book (a compilation that included the photographs), the use of some of the photographs was merely use of a fragment of such mixed work, and thus it was similar to a quote made exclusively from a written work.[45]

In contraventional law, the courts generally hold that the burden of proof is reversed; therefore, the sanctioning authority needs to prove, beyond any reasonable doubt, that the alleged offender is guilty. To this effect, the Iaşi District Court held that since the sanctioning authority did not prove, beyond any reasonable doubt, that the exception provided for by Article 37 paragraph (1) of the Romanian Copyright Law did not apply, in the sense that the contravention did not play background music but simply tested the products he offered to his customers, the minutes by which the sanction was imposed were annulled.[46]

[42] Bucharest Tribunal, s. V civ., Decision no. 553 of 28 April 2014, www.rolii.ro. Accessed 25 May 2017.

[43] Bucharest Tribunal, s. III civ., Decision no. 1686 of 1 October 2013, www.rolii.ro. Accessed 25 May 2017.

[44] Bucharest Court of Appeals, s. IX civ., Decision no. 51A of 26 February 2009, Buletinul jurisprudenţei 2009. Curtea de Apel Bucureşti, Universul Juridic 2011, p. 492.

[45] ICCJ, s. I civ., Decision no. 104 of 22 January 2016, www.scj.ro. Accessed 25 May 2017.

[46] Iaşi District Court, s. civ., Decision no. 16245 of 22 December 2014, www.rolii.ro. Accessed 25 May 2017.

## 23.6 Relevance of Noncommercial Purpose and Use by an Individual

As courts tend to follow the rule of narrow interpretation and strict application of the provisions concerning exceptions and limitations, the weight placed on whether the use is commercial or not and whether the use is made by an individual or a legal person is also dependent on whether the criteria provided by the Romanian Copyright Law make such differentiation or not. The focus therefore lies on the cumulative meeting of the conditions provided by law, with the courts relying on additional considerations only in cases where they have found that the "basic" conditions are, or appear to be, met.

In denying that two of the limitations provided for education were applicable in the abovementioned geography manual case, the Bucharest Tribunal held that the limitation under Article 33 paragraph (1) letter g) requires that the communication to the public of the works had to be free, whereas the copying of the claimant's work was made in view of the publishing and distribution for profit.[47] Moreover, the court held that neither the limitation under Article 33 paragraph (2) letter d) was applicable since the use was made for economic advantage since "publishing, by university professors, of a number of scientific papers confers upon them a series of advantages, including economic ones." In affirming, the Bucharest Court of Appeals additionally held that since the reproduction was not made by a library or an archive of a not-for-profit public or scientific institution but in the respondent's work and subsequently by publishing the infringing work with the purpose of distributing it at a price to the students of a private university, the use could not qualify as permitted under Article 33 paragraph (1) letter d) of the Romanian Copyright Law, and the lack of any money being paid to the respondent does not affect such finding.[48] The appellate court also indicated that the fact that the respondent copied all of plaintiff's work for the purpose of distributing the infringing work for a profit causes the exception not to apply.

In a criminal case concerning the usurpation of authorship by copying 90% of a book on the methodology of scientific research and providing the infringing work as a distance learning course and publishing it in print, the Bucharest Court of Appeals held that the fact that the defendants were not paid any money by the publishing house has no effect and no bearing on the application of the exception to copyright provided by Article 33 paragraph (1) letter c) of the Romanian Copyright Law or on the fulfillment of the conditions for applying the sanction for the crime provided by Article 141 of the Romanian Copyright Law.[49]

[47] Bucharest Tribunal, s. IV civ., Decision no. 1997 of 15 November 2011, www.rolii.ro. Accessed 25 May 2017.

[48] Bucharest Court of Appeals, s. IX civ., Decision no. 158 of 30 October 2012, www.rolii.ro. Accessed 25 May 2017.

[49] Bucharest Court of Appeals, s. II pen., Decision no. 136/F of 7 March 2014, www.rolii.ro. Accessed 25 May 2017.

The High Court also held that the use of panoramic photographs on billboards by a retailer cannot qualify under the panorama exception since the purpose of the use was clearly commercial. The court held that "even if an intention to have pursued another purpose – tourism – had existed, it would be irrelevant in respect of the respondent's line of business – a company that, in the given hypermarket, only offers products to its customers and no other services."[50]

In the football matches excerpt case mentioned above, the Bucharest Court of Appeals indicated that "the phrase 'without any direct or indirect commercial or economic advantage' refers to whether access to the particular news item was conditioned upon a payment of a sum of money and not to whether the activity of the respondent is not-for-profit."[51]

Where a hotel is playing background music, the Bucharest Tribunal held that it cannot benefit from the provisions of the private copy exception to copyright since these provisions are to be strictly interpreted as referring solely to private users who make copies for their own personal use or for the normal family circle.[52]

## 23.7 The Mandatory Character of the Exceptions

Under Romanian Copyright Law, all the exceptions provided therein are mandatory and cannot be ruled out by contract. This stems from the fact that the provisions of the law are imperative and binding on every subject, while the contractual provisions are only binding on the contracting parties. As to the possibility that a user contracts away the benefit of the exceptions provided by law, although no decision specifically addressed this question, the answer appears to be in the negative since the High Court held that "the limitation applies and produces full effects for as long as the legal provision confirming it is in force, the validity of such legal provision exceeding the possible scope of current proceedings."[53] Although the specific case concerned the exception provided by Article 33 paragraph (1) letter a) of the Romanian Copyright Law, the same principle should apply equally to all other exceptions as well.

Further confirmation of such conclusion comes by way of a decision by the Bucharest Court of Appeals in a claim for the modification of a methodology for collective management established by means of arbitration within the framework of the Romanian Copyright Office.[54] One of the issues under discussion was that the methodology as approved by the arbitrators provided that the collective management

[50] ICCJ, s. I civ., Decision no. 651 of 12 February 2013, www.scj.ro. Accessed 25 May 2017.

[51] Bucharest Court of Appeals, s. IX civ., Decision no. 178A of 4 December 2012, www.rolii.ro. Accessed 25 May 2017.

[52] Bucharest Tribunal, s. V civ., Decision no. 1130 of 9 June 2011, www.rolii.ro. Accessed 25 May 2017.

[53] ICCJ, s. I civ., Decision no. 889 of 18 March 2014, www.scj.ro. Accessed 25 May 2017.

[54] Bucharest Court of Appeals, s. IX civ., Decision no. 139A of 3 May 2011, Monitorul Oficial 2011 420.

societies can monitor the use of their catalog and, in order to do so, can use audio and/or video recorders wherever musical works are being used, with the user's consent. The Court of Appeals held, upon the collective management societies' claim, that such provision is "evidently contrary" to the provisions of Article 37 paragraph (2) of the Romanian Copyright Law and replaced "with the user's consent" by "with no authorization from the users being necessary and without any payment."

The courts indicated on several occasions that no distinction is to be made between online and offline uses, except where the law provides for such. The 4th District Court of Bucharest made no such distinction when dealing with what it held as a permitted quotation on an online blog of some photographs from calendars issued by a different publication, such calendars being also available on the latter's website.[55] The Bucharest Court of Appeals specifically indicated that the fact that the excerpts of football matches were communicated online in no way affected the court's decision to withhold the application of the exception provided by Article 33 paragraph (2) letter c) of the Romanian Copyright Law.[56] The High Court also made no distinction as to the fact that the unauthorized use was made by means of a digital library in denying the application of the exceptions provided by law.[57]

## 23.8 The Rights Covered by the Exceptions and Limitations

As indicated above, the High Court stated that "Article 33 of the [Romanian Copyright Law] [...], expressly and exhaustively regulates certain limitations to the exercise of the economic prerogatives of the author, i.e. the exercise of the exclusive economic right to decide if, how and when his work is used, including to consent to the use of the work by others [cit. omitted], of the right to authorize or forbid use in any of the forms provided by Article 13 of the law, and of the right to an equitable remuneration, when and under the conditions expressly provided by law."[58]

The decision of the High Court would seem to indicate that all rights provided by law under the general exclusive right of use would be subject to the limitations provided by the law. These rights refer to the reproduction, distribution, importation, rental, lending, communication to the public (including the making available), broadcasting, retransmission by cable, and making of derivative works.

In fact, Article 33 paragraph (1) specifically mentions that the rights in respect of which exceptions are provided refer to the right of reproduction in respect of the limitations provided for by letters a), d), and f); the right of distribution in respect of the limitation provided for by letter f); the right of communication to the public in

[55] 4th District Court of Bucharest, s. civ., Decision no. 1314 of 4 February 2016, www.rolii.ro. Accessed 25 May 2017, confirmed by Bucharest Tribunal, s. III civ., Decision no. 3859 of 14 October 2016, www.rolii.ro. Accessed 25 May 2017.

[56] Bucharest Court of Appeals, s. IX civ., Decision no. 178A of 4 December 2012, www.rolii.ro. Accessed 25 May 2017.

[57] ICCJ, s. I civ., Decision no. 1109 of 24 April 2015, www.scj.ro. Accessed 25 May 2017.

[58] ICCJ, s. I civ., Decision no. 1067 of 28 March 2014, www.scj.ro. Accessed 25 May 2017.

respect of the limitations provided for by letters f) and g). The limitations provided by letters b), c), h), and i) refer to the general notion of "use" and therefore should be considered as covering limitations to all rights derived from the general right of use.

The law expressly indicates that the limitations contained in paragraph (2) of Article 33 cover the rights of reproduction, distribution, broadcasting, and communication to the public, while paragraph (3) clearly provides for an exception to the right of reproduction.

The limitations provided by Articles 34 and 35 primarily refer to, respectively, the right of reproduction and the making of derivative works. However, given the purpose of these limitations, they are to be taken to refer also to use of the private copy thus made and use of the derivative work thus made, a contrary overly restrictive interpretation stripping the limitations of their content.

Paragraph (1) of Article 37 expressly refers to reproduction and presentation of works, with the latter being taken to refer to the communication to the public, while paragraph (2) refers to "monitoring," which could be taken to cover reproduction, distribution, and maybe also communication to the public.

Interestingly, in the football matches excerpts case mentioned above, the Bucharest Court of Appeals held that the online posting of the match excerpts on the newspaper's website is an act of communication to the public (by making available) and that there was no possibility for the users to copy the content since in order to do so, they would have had to take several steps that required an advanced knowledge of informatics, there being no download button on the website.[59] The court's reasoning is interesting even if the court has analyzed this under the conditions for the application of the exception provided by Article 33 paragraph (2) letter c) of the Romanian Copyright Law, which expressly concerns the reproduction, distribution, and communication to the public of the work, which would make the distinction irrelevant for the outcome of the case. The better view would therefore be that the court has made the distinction in light of the fact that it went on to hold that the exception would not apply and that, at first instance, the Bucharest Tribunal held[60] that the respondent had infringed both the communication to the public right (by making available the excerpts) and the distribution right (by allowing the download of the excerpts by the website visitors). In such latter case, the finding of the court meant that there was no infringement of the distribution right.

In consonance with the restrictive interpretation of these exceptions and limitations, the courts have carefully avoided to extend the scope of application of these exceptions. The Bucharest Court of Appeals held that the exceptions provided by Article 33 paragraph (2) of the law exclude uses "aimed at the transformation of the sequence to which claimant holds the moral rights," such activities being related to

[59] Bucharest Court of Appeals, s. IX civ., Decision no. 178A of 4 December 2012, www.rolii.ro. Accessed 25 May 2017.

[60] Bucharest Tribunal, s. III civ., Decision no. 1165 of 13 June 2012, www.rolii.ro. Accessed 25 May 2017.

the making of derivative works, a right that "evidently" exceeds the scope of the provisions of Article 33 paragraph (2) of the Romanian Copyright Law.[61]

## 23.9 Relationship with Moral Rights

The Romanian Copyright Law provides expressly and unequivocally that moral rights cannot be waived and are unassignable (Article 11 paragraph (1) of the law). Moral rights are linked to the person of the author and are inseparable from it. Only the exercise of three of those rights (authorship, right to determine the name under which the wok is made public, and right to integrity of the work) is inherited in perpetuity.

The Romanian High court indicated in clear terms that "however, the limitations provided by Article 33 [of the Romanian Copyright Law] do not cover the moral prerogatives provided by Article 10 of the law, among which the right to claim authorship of the work, the infringement of which was established in this case by both lower courts. Therefore, even if the appellant's arguments on the applicability of the limitations provided by Article 33 paragraph (1) letters d) and g) were upheld, this would still not affect the respondent's liability for infringing the claimant's moral rights."[62]

However, the same court indicated, only 10 days prior to the above decision, that since Article 33 paragraph (4) excludes from its scope the exception provided by Article 33 paragraph (1) letter a), as was the case with both exceptions referred to above—i.e., provided by Article 33 paragraph (1) letters d) and g)—there was no obligation on the beneficiary of the exception to give proper attribution.[63] However, although the aspect of infringement of the moral right to authorship was mentioned on appeal, the High Court did not expressly rule on whether the moral rights of the author had been infringed even where the exception to copyright was applicable.

The above decisions of the High Court show that it is unclear whether the exceptions to copyright affect the moral rights of the author or not. The clear wording of the 28 March decision would appear to have more force and would therefore suggest that moral rights are not impacted by the exceptions but that would make the exclusion of the need to give proper attribution in the case of some limitations completely meaningless since even though the exception would apply, the moral rights of the author would still be infringed and, consequently, the author might have any such use enjoined and the benefit of the exception lost.

We therefore believe that the provisions of Article 33 paragraph (4) ought to be read as implicit limitations or exceptions to the moral right of authorship for the limitations excluded from its scope—i.e. under letters a), d), g), and h). This would also be supported by a decision of the Bucharest Court of Appeals, which held that

---

[61] Bucharest Court of Appeals, s. IX civ., Decision no. 51A of 26 February 2009, Buletinul jurisprudenței 2009. Curtea de Apel București, Universul Juridic 2011, p. 492.

[62] ICCJ, s. I civ., Decision no. 1067 of 28 March 2014, www.scj.ro. Accessed 25 May 2017.

[63] ICCJ, s. I civ., Decision no. 889 of 18 March 2014, www.scj.ro. Accessed 25 May 2017.

"[i]t is in this context, of the respecting of the [moral] right of authorship, that the obligation to indicate the author in the case of quotations and use of short excerpts was imposed, when such acts of use are permitted without the author's consent."[64] This appears to have been the position of the courts in the past as well, the same court having held that "the right to authorship implies an obligation to indicate the author where quoting or using short excerpts, when such uses are permitted without the author's consent."[65]

## 23.10 Technological Protection Measures and the Benefit of the Exceptions and Limitations

Article $138^5$ paragraph (4) of the Romanian Copyright Law provides that "the right holders having instituted technical protection measures have the obligation to provide the beneficiaries of the exceptions provided by Article 33 paragraph (1) letters a), c), and e), Article 33 paragraph (2) letters d) and e), and Article 38 the necessary means to legally access the work or any other protected object. Nevertheless they have the right to limit the number of copies made in the conditions mentioned above." Paragraph (1) of the same article indicated the "right holders" being referred to as "the author of a work, the performing artist, the producer of phonograms or audio-visual recordings, the radio or television broadcasting organization, and the maker of the data base."

Paragraph (5) of the article carves out of the scope of paragraph (4) "protected works, made available to the public in accordance with the contractual provisions agreed by the parties, so that any member of the public might have access to such in any place and at any moment, individually chosen by them."

The Romanian Copyright Law thus excludes from the scope of beneficiaries of exceptions who can demand access, if such is blocked by means of technical measures, those who would benefit from the exceptions relating to the following:

- use of short quotations;
- reproduction of brief excerpts from works, for information or research, by not-for-profit libraries, museums, film archives, sound archives, archives of cultural or scientific public institutions, including replacement of the sole copy;
- the panorama exception;
- representation and execution of a work for specific purposes by educational institutions;
- use of works during religious celebrations or official ceremonies;
- use for advertising of images of works presented at exhibitions;

[64] Bucharest Court of Appeals, s. II pen., Decision no. 136/F of 7 March 2014, www.rolii.ro. Accessed 25 May 2017.

[65] Bucharest Court of Appeals, s. IX civ., Decision no. 51A of 26 February 2009, Buletinul jurisprudenței 2009. Curtea de Apel București, Universul Juridic 2011, p. 492.

- reproduction, distribution, broadcasting, or communication to the public of brief excerpts for the purpose of informing on current events;
- reproduction, distribution, broadcasting, or communication to the public of brief excerpts from works orally expressed in public for informing on current events;
- reproduction, distribution, broadcasting, or communication to the public of brief excerpts from works, within information on current events;
- the private copy exception;
- all permitted transformations of a work;
- certain reproductions and communications for the testing of the functioning of the products on manufacture or sale; and
- the monitoring by collective management societies of the use of their catalog by any means.

The long list of exceptions to the right holder's right to prevent access to the work by technical protection measures is the result of the strict transposition, in the Romanian Copyright Law, of the provisions of Article 6 paragraph (4) of Directive 2001/29 on the Harmonisation of Certain Aspects of Copyright and Related Rights in the Information Society.[66] Although the Romanian Copyright Law does not provide any mechanism to insure that right holders allow private copying as per the limitation in Article 34 paragraph (1) of the Romanian Copyright Law, the Romanian legislator has not provided for this exception to be included in the scope of Article $138^5$ paragraph (4), as Article 6 paragraph (4) subparagraph (2) of Directive 2001/29 would have allowed.

The issue of whether an individual user of a work can enforce an exception has not been resolved by the Romanian courts. Providing an answer to this is even more complicated, given the ambiguous nature of these exceptions or limitations. The ambiguity arises from the fact that the Romanian Copyright Law itself has included the provisions under the marginal title of "limitations to the exercise of copyright," while Article $138^5$ paragraph (4) refers to the "beneficiaries of the exceptions." The courts have also termed these "exceptions," "limitations to copyright," or "limitations to the exercise of copyright." Moreover, the literature on the subject has also used all these notions,[67] sometimes interchangeably. While some authors have

[66] Directive 2001/29 of the European Parliament and of the Council of 22 May 2001 on the Harmonisation of Certain Aspects of Copyright and Related Rights in the Information Society, OJ 2001, L 167, p. 10.

[67] "limitations to the exercise of copyright" – A. Dietz, Dreptul de autor în România şi armonizarea acestuia în baza normelor europene. Evoluţie şi situaţia actuală după aderarea României la Uniunea Europeană, Revista Română de Dreptul Proprietăţii Intelectuale 2009(4), p. 26; N. R. Dominte, Parodia, pastişa şi caricatura – cele trei libertăţi de expresie satirico-umoristice ale transformării unei opere originale, Revista Română de Dreptul Proprietăţii Intelectuale 2014(3), p. 106; "limitations and exceptions to the exercise of copyright" – L. Pop, Autorul între suveranitate şi suzeranitate. Limitele exercitării dreptului de autor, Revista Română de Dreptul Proprietăţii Intelectuale 2009(2), p. 147; "limitations to copyright" – V. Roş, Dreptul de citare, Revista Română de Dreptul Proprietăţii Intelectuale 2009(3), p. 17; I. Macovei and N. R. Dominte, Hermeneutica copiei private în cadrul limitelor dreptului de autor, Revista Română de Dreptul Proprietăţii Intelectuale 2013(1), pp. 22–29; E. G. Olteanu, Copia privată, între interesele utilizatorilor şi cele ale titularilor de drepturi, Revista Română de Dreptul Proprietăţii Intelectuale 2013(3), p. 13; M. Dănilă,

suggested qualifying them as "restrictions to the exercise of copyright,"[68] we are of the opinion[69] that they are in fact limitations to copyright (Article 33 paragraph (1) and (2), Article 35, and Article 37) and exceptions to copyright (Article 33 paragraph (3), Article 34, and Article 38 paragraph (2)), with Article 38 paragraph (1) providing for merely an implicit limited assignment. The importance of correctly qualifying the nature of the provisions is manifold. Most relevant to the issue at hand is the fact that an exception can only be raised as a defence (i.e., without the possibility of being claimed under); the existence or inexistence of a right (with reference to its exact limits and scope) can be the object of a declaratory action, while a limitation of the exercise of a right can only form, at most, the object of a negative declaratory judgment.

There is inconclusive evidence that the limitations can be directly claimed under since, in a case mentioned above, the Dolj Tribunal went on to analyze the merits of a claim that was, in part, grounded on the provisions of Article 33 of the Romanian Copyright Law.[70] However, since neither of the issues has been raised or any claim granted, it would be far-fetched to argue that the court has seriously considered the issue. Similarly, the Constanța Court of Appeals was vested with an administrative claim to issue an authorization allowing the claimant to "copy or make derivative works of national standards, as allowed by Article 33 paragraph (1) letters a), and g), par. (2) letter d), Article 34 paragraph (1), and Article 35 letter (a) of the Romanian Copyright Law." However, the claimant did not pursue the claim, and the court simply acknowledged that it had lapsed.[71]

Considerații privind plagiatul din perspectiva originalității operei și dreptului de citare. Autoplagiatul și protecția ideilor, pledoariilor și a predicilor, Revista Română de Dreptul Proprietății Intelectuale 2015(3), p. 63; both "limitation of the exercise of copyright" and "limitation to copyright" – I. Macovei, Tratat de dreptul proprietății intelectuale, CH Beck 2010, p. 466; N. R. Dominte, Limitele exercitării dreptului de autor în statele membre ale Uniunii Europene, Revista Română de Dreptul Proprietății Intelectuale 2009(3), pp. 106–108; D. Chiroșca, Copia privată – o limită a exercitării dreptului de autor în legislația Republicii Moldova, Revista Română de Dreptul Proprietății Intelectuale 2007(3), pp. 15–16; M. Olariu, Dreptul de citare în cazul operelor de artă plastică și fotografică, Revista Română de Dreptul Proprietății Intelectuale 2014(1), p. 57.

[68] T. Bodoașcă and A. Drăghici, Contribuții la studiul reglementărilor legale referitoare la limitele exercitării dreptului de autor, Revista Română de Dreptul Proprietății Intelectuale 2009(3), p. 75; T. Bodoașcă and L. I. Tarnu, Dreptul proprietății intelectuale, ed. 3, Universul Juridic 2015, pp. 66–67.

[69] P. G. Buta and A. Mușat, Limitările în exercițiul dreptului de autor. Condițiile în care intervin, Revista Română de Dreptul Proprietății Intelectuale 2007(2), pp. 107–119; P. G. Buta, Despre limitările și excepțiile dreptului de autor. După 10 ani, Revista Română de Dreptul Proprietății Intelectuale (forthcoming).

[70] Dolj Tribunal, s. cont. adm., Decision no. 896 of 19 April 2011, www.rolii.ro. Accessed 25 May 2017, confirmed by Craiova Court of Appeals, s. cont. adm., Decision no. 2853 of 13 October 2011, www.rolii.ro. Accessed 25 May 2017.

[71] Constanța Court of Appeals, s. II civ. și cont. adm., Decision no. 26/CA of 12 January 2012, www.rolii.ro. Accessed 25 May 2017.

## 23.11 No "Catch-All" Exception Under Romanian Copyright Law

The Romanian Copyright Law contains a closed list of exceptions, with no alternative "catch all" provisions. As noted above, the courts consistently held that the law provides no flexibility in the restrictive interpretation of such closed list of exceptions and that there can be no extensive reading of such or an enlargement of their scope by means of interpretation.

## 23.12 Relationship with Other Fundamental Rights

As mentioned above, in providing for the exceptions to copyright so as to also balance the exclusivity inherent to copyright protection with other fundamental rights (e.g., freedom of expression, right to information, right to education), the Romanian Copyright Law excluded to a very large extent the situations where, outside the ambit of the exceptions so provided, a balancing exercise between copyright and other fundamental rights ought to be performed. Such possibility is further reduced by the practice of the Romanian courts, indicated above, whereby all situations where copyright is limited are construed against the background of the exceptions provided by the Romanian Copyright Law, with no extension thereof held possible, other than by legislative intervention either by means of another law or by means of an amendment to the Romanian Copyright Law itself.

Courts therefore seem to prefer giving voice to other fundamental rights within the scope of the existing exceptions and not against such. For example, the 4th District Court of Bucharest analyzed the exception provided by Article 33 paragraph (1) letter b) of the Romanian Copyright Law, together with "the defendant professional journalist's right to freedom of expression guaranteed by Article 30 of the Romanian Constitution and Article 10 of the European Convention on Human Rights, being also guaranteed by Article 31 of the Romanian Constitution and the right to access to public information."[72]

Similarly, the Bucharest Tribunal found, in a case concerning a request that the Ministry of Culture be obliged to give to the claimant NGO (whose purpose was the protection of the Roşia Montană site) the documentation filed by a third party gold-mining corporation in order to obtain a certificate of archaeological clearance for the site, that the existence of copyright in the documentation cannot justify the refusal to supply such documentation. This is because the reproduction and distribution of the work to the claimant was "justified under the general interest right to have free and unrestricted access to any information of public interest, which is a fundamental principle of the relationship between individuals and public authorities, according to

[72] 4th District Court of Bucharest, s. civ., Decision no. 1314 of 4 February 2016, www.rolii.ro. Accessed 25 May 2017, confirmed by Bucharest Tribunal, s. III civ., Decision no. 3859 of 14 October 2016, www.rolii.ro. Accessed 25 May 2017.

the Romanian Constitution and the international documents ratified by the Romanian Parliament."[73] However, the court also indicated that, where the documents are under the protection of copyright, the additional conditions provided by Article 33 paragraph (1) letter a) of the Romanian Copyright Law must also be observed.

One case where copyright was held to prevail over other fundamental rights was the case concerning the online publishing of a book within the Ministry of Interior Publishing House's Virtual Library. In that particular case, the publishing house argued that the Government Decision approving the National Program for the Digitization of National Cultural Resources (pursuant to which the respondent claimed that it had published the book online) was meant to insure the freedom of information, the universal access to information, and the necessity of integrating national cultural resources in the European Digital Library—Europeana.eu. The High Court rejected such defence, as mentioned above, reiterating that all exceptions to copyright are provided for in the Romanian Copyright Law, and these cannot be supplemented other than by legislative intervention.[74]

## 23.13 Compensation to Copyright Owner

With respect to the limitations provided by Article 33 paragraphs (1) and (2), the law explicitly provides that these are not subject to the payment of any remuneration. The same is true for the limitations provided by Article 35 and Article 37 paragraph (2).

Article 34 paragraph (2) of the Romanian Copyright Law specifically provides for a "compensatory remuneration established by means of negotiation, according to the provisions of this law" in respect of the exception for private copying.

Article 38 paragraph (1) provides for an implicit limited license for the recording of the work needed for one act of broadcasting and also provides that any subsequent broadcasting of the work thus recorded is subject to the payment of remuneration, which cannot be waived. There is no guidance as to how such remuneration should be calculated, but given the fact that the provision concerns an implicit license within a contract, the additional remuneration could be either agreed by the parties to the contract or, in absence of such agreement, determined by the court in accordance with the general provisions of the law regarding the assignment of copyright (Article 43 paragraph (2) of the Romanian Copyright Law).

The law regarding the exceptions and limitations under Article 33 paragraph (3), Article 37 paragraph (1), and Article 38 paragraph (2) is silent in this respect.

With regard to the exception provided by Article 33 paragraph (3) of the Romanian Copyright Law, the Bucharest Court of Appeals held that since these temporary acts of reproduction are transient or incidental to the streaming of

[73] Bucharest Tribunal, s. IX cont. adm., Decision no. 4222 of 9 December 2011, www.rolii.ro. Accessed 25 May 2017, reversed on different grounds by the Bucharest Court of Appeals, s. VIII cont. adm., Decision no. 3421 of 4 October 2012.

[74] ICCJ, s. I civ., Decision no. 1109 of 24 April 2015, www.scj.ro. Accessed 25 May 2017.

musical works online, the remuneration that is to be paid to the authors and right holders by means of the collective management societies is to be calculated in respect of the right of communication to the public only and not also in respect of the right of reproduction, a higher remuneration being due solely in cases where the download of the works is also permitted.[75] It would appear therefore that the court has come to the conclusion that no separate compensation is due when the exception provided by Article 33 paragraph (3) is applicable.

Insofar as the limitation provided by Article 37 par. (1) is concerned, some limited guidance can be taken from the above-mentioned decision of the Iaşi District Court, where the court indicated that the sanctioning authority did not prove that the relevant limitation did not apply and did not provide any grounds on account of which the claimant ought to have obtained a license (authorization) from the relevant collective management societies.[76] Since it is only on the basis of such license agreement that any compensation could have been paid, we can infer from the decision that where the limitation provided by Article 37 paragraph (1) of the law is applicable, no compensation would be due to the author or right holders. This conclusion is supported by the literature on the subject.[77]

Although there is no specific guidance concerning the application of the limitation provided by Article 38 paragraph (2) of the Romanian Copyright Law, we believe that no compensation would be due in such cases, given the very limited scope of the provision: "conservation in official archives" only of temporary recordings of works made by radio or television broadcasting organizations for their own shows and only where such recordings would have "a special documentary value."

The compensation for the private copy exception is exhaustively dealt with in the law in Articles 107–110. Paragraph (1) of Article 107 confers upon the authors of works "susceptible of being reproduced on any support by means of sound or audiovisual recordings" and of works "susceptible of being reproduced on paper directly or indirectly" as private copies, and upon the editors, producers, and performers (if the case), the right to be compensated for the private copy exception. The right to such remuneration cannot be waived, and the obligation to pay rests with the manufacturers and/or importers of supports on which such copies can be made and of devices meant for the making of such copies, irrespective of whether the process involved is analogic or digital. The list of supports and devices and the quantum of the remuneration can be subject to negotiation every 3 years in two commissions (one for sound and audiovisual copies and one for paper copies) made up of representatives from the relevant collective management societies and the associations representing the persons obliged to pay the remuneration (who need to be registered

[75] Bucharest Court of Appeals, s. IX civ., Decision no. 139A of 3 May 2011, Monitorul Oficial 2011 420.

[76] Iaşi District Court, s. civ., Decision no. 16245 of 22 December 2014, www.rolii.ro. Accessed 25 May 2017.

[77] V. Roş, D. Bogdan and O. S. Matei, Dreptul de autor şi drepturile conexe. Tratat, All Beck 2005, p. 321.

with the Romanian Copyright Office in order to manufacture and/or import such products and/or devices). The negotiations follow the route provided by law for the negotiation of the methodologies for collective management.

The remuneration is calculated as a percentage of the customs value of the goods (for imports) or of the value of the goods upon placement on the market, without VAT (for manufactured supports and/or devices), and is currently at 0.1% for blank A4 paper, 3% for other supports, and 0.5% for devices.

Article 107[1] of the law provides that the remuneration is to be collected by a single collective management society for each of the two types of copy and then distributed to the other collective management societies and then to the beneficiaries of the compensation, according to clear rules, set by Article 107[2] of the Romanian Copyright Law.

There is no compensation due for blank audio, video, or digital supports sold in bulk to phonogram or audiovisual producers or to radio and television broadcasting organizations for their own shows or for supports and devices allowing the making of copies with no commercial purpose, imported in legally permitted hand luggage.

In theory, the fact that the remuneration is subject to negotiation between those who represent the paying parties and those who represent the beneficiaries, all within the rather strict framework of negotiation provided by law (and with a possible final jurisdictional review) should ensure a proper balancing of the compensation. However, skewing is possible due to the fact that the two parties negotiate in light of the total quantity and value of the supports and devices, and therefore it is possible that logrolling might cause individual instances of over-/undercompensation in respect of a given support or device. This risk is, however, remote given the fact that the remuneration is based on wide classes of supports and devices, and therefore there would be little room for such discrimination.

However, in an appeal concerning the payment of remuneration due for private copying, the Bucharest Court of Appeals refused to allow the remuneration to be calculated in respect not of the value of an entire multifunctional device but solely in respect of the value of the subunit effectively allowing copying. The court held that the law was not to be read as allowing such a distinction, and, additionally, such a distinction would allow an arbitrary determination of the value of the remuneration due (and a subcompensation of the right holders), given that there are no legal criteria or provisions to establish which devices are simple and which are complex, which subunits effectively allow the making of copies and which do not.[78]

## 23.14 Temporary Acts of Reproduction

As already indicated, Article 33 par. (3) of the Romanian Copyright Law provides that "temporary acts of reproduction that are transient or incidental and which form an integral and essential part of a technical process and the sole purpose of which is

[78] Bucharest Court of Appeals, s. IX civ., Decision no. 382A of 8 November 2005, O. S. Matei, Proprietate intelectuală. Practică judiciară, Hamangiu 2006, p. 278.

to enable a transmission, in a network between third parties, by an intermediary, or the lawful use of a work or of another protected object and which have no independent economic significance, are exempted from the reproduction right."

The Bucharest Court of Appeals held that "the reproduction of musical works on a computer/server for the purpose of permitting streaming has a temporary character irrespective of the period of time for which such reproduction is made since, at any moment, it is possible that the respective musical work/works can be deleted. Moreover, the reproduction of the musical work on a computer/server for the purpose of permitting the subsequent streaming is incidental and an integral and essential part of a technical process. The purpose of this storage is to allow the lawful use of the musical work by streaming, and without such storage on the computer/server, the on-demand listening [of the work] by a third party would be impossible. Also, the reproduction of the musical work on a computer/server has no independent economic significance since mere storage, not followed by the making available of the work, would trigger application of the provisions [concerning the private copy exception]. Therefore storage does not gain economic significance unless regarded as an integral and essential part of the technical process by which the musical work is made available to the public for listening."[79]

By means of the same decision, the appellate court (sitting as final court) also hinted that the exception is mandatory (as is its interpretation of it) when it dismissed the appellant's arguments that the exception (so interpreted) diverged from the European practice. The court stated that "the interpretation of the provisions of the Romanian law cannot be made by reference to the European practice," and even if the Romanian Copyright Law provides that European practice is to be taken into account when negotiations take place, "negotiations cannot concern the provisions of the law."

The current interpretation of the limitation, as provided by the Bucharest Court of Appeals, seems permissive enough to allow most legitimate online activities, possibly even those activities based on a model of p2p distribution. For example, if, in order to optimize streaming (especially with regard to files requiring a very high use of bandwidth), the lawful provider of a streaming service would want to allow two of its lawful users (who share between them access to more bandwidth than each with the central server) to stream that file simultaneously, with the two users downloading alternative parts of the file from a central server and then sharing the missing parts among themselves (in order to benefit from the higher bandwidth they share), this would qualify under the current definition as a reproduction for the purpose of streaming and therefore could be allowed.

[79] Bucharest Court of Appeals, s. IX civ., Decision no. 139A of 3 May 2011, Monitorul Oficial 2011 420.

## 23.15 Exceptions and Limitations to Copyright and the Freedom of Expression

Although there is no exception or limitation in the Romanian Copyright Law specifically referring to the freedom of expression, the literature on the subject[80] has indicated that the limitations provided by Article 33 paragraph (1) letter b)—use of short quotations—and those provided by Article 35 letters a) and b) were defined, mainly, to ensure that copyright does not unnecessarily stifle this right.

Article 33 paragraph (1) letter b) reads: "The following uses of a work previously made known to the public shall be permitted without the author's consent and without payment of a remuneration, on condition that these are in accordance with good practice, do not affect the normal exploitation of the work, and do not prejudice the author or the holders of the exploitation rights: [...] b) the use of brief quotations from a work for the purpose of analysis, commentary or criticism, or for illustration, to the extent such use justifies the length of the quote."

Article 35 letters a) and b) of the Romanian Copyright Law provide that "the transformation of a work, without the author's consent and without payment of a remuneration, is allowed in the following cases: a) if it is a private transformation, neither intended for nor made available to the public; b) if the result of the transformation is a parody or caricature, provided the result does not cause confusion as to the original work and its author."

Regarding the use of quotations, the special conditions expressly provided by law refer to the purpose of the use (which must be one of the four provided by the law) and the length of the quote, such quantitative condition requiring an evaluation by reference to what is necessary in respect of the purpose being pursued.

The literature on the subject[81] indicates that in order for such use to fall within the limitation, the following conditions need to be met: the quoted work is made available to the public; the excerpt is an identical reproduction; the excerpt is short by reference to both the work from which it is taken and the work where it is used; the use of the excerpt is incidental to the new work; the excerpt is identifiable in the new work by the use of inverted commas; proper attribution is given; the fragment is used for one of the purposes permitted by law, which requires that the new work has a critical, polemical, pedagogical, scientific, or informational character; and the copying does not prejudice the author.

In respect of the transformation allowed by Article 35 letter a), the literature indicates that two special conditions need to be cumulatively met: that the transformation needs to be made in private or individually by a natural or legal person and that the transformation thus made is not made available to the public; i.e., use of the transformation needs to be private as well.[82]

---

[80] V. Roş, Dreptul proprietății intelectuale. Vol. I. Dreptul de autor, drepturile conexe şi drepturile sui-generis, CH Beck 2016, pp. 371–372, 383.

[81] V. Roş, Dreptul de citare, Revista Română de Dreptul Proprietății Intelectuale 2009(3), pp. 19–22.

[82] T. Bodoaşcă and L. I. Tarnu, Dreptul proprietății intelectuale, ed. 3, Universul Juridic 2015, p. 89.

In order for the limitation provided by Article 35 letter b) of the Romanian Copyright Law to apply, the literature indicates that the user ought to have obtained a satirical or caricatural effect, different from that of the original work, and that the result must not create confusion as to the original work and its author.[83]

The limitation for use of quotations was successfully applied in respect of the use of an excerpt of a press article on the website of a regional newspaper, the court having found that the copied passage was short (11 lines), was used for one of the purposes prescribed by law (illustration), and that "the length of the quote is justified on account of the intent to get the reader's attention and determine him to look for the rest of the article, but on the original website (of Tango magazine), and not on the respondent's [and therefore] has not prejudiced the author (but on the contrary, has benefitted her, by determining readers of the Ziua de Constanța publication to also read Tango magazine)."[84]

The 4th District Court of Bucharest also found lawful the use of a selection of 26 photographs from a series of 156, which had been used by a business publication in its yearly calendars and which featured its female employees and had been made publicly available online on the latter publication's website. In order to so find, the court indicated that the photographs had been made available to the public on the claimant's website; that they were part of 14 works—i.e., the 14 yearly calendars, with 12 photographs each—since they were meant to be used as such and not individually; that the 26 photographs were used by the respondent professional journalist in a satirical article that she posted on her blog; that the respondent thus used a part of a photographic work and just for the purpose of being used in the respondent's satirical article; that the article clearly indicated the source of the photographs and also provided a link to the original source and therefore the respondent never claimed authorship of the respective photographs.[85] The court also found that the use was one in accordance with good practice, did not affect the normal exploitation of the work, and did not prejudice the author, even though in this case the claimant legal person was merely the right holder.

Romanian courts considered this limitation applicable also in the case concerning the use of personal photographs inserted in a published biography in a historical TV show about the biography's subject, with the High Court indicating that, given the fact that the claimant did not ground his claim on an infringement of the moral rights (but only on an infringement of economic rights), the fact that there was no proper attribution of the photographs cannot be claimed by way of appeal, and therefore this aspect cannot make the limitation inapplicable.[86]

---

[83] V. Roş, Dreptul proprietății intelectuale. Vol. I. Dreptul de autor, drepturile conexe şi drepturile sui-generis, CH Beck 2016, p. 383.

[84] Galați Tribunal, s. I civ., Decision no. 959 of 12 April 2013, www.rolii.ro. Accessed 25 May 2017.

[85] 4th District Court of Bucharest, s. civ., Decision no. 1314 of 4 February 2016, www.rolii.ro. Accessed 25 May 2017, confirmed by Bucharest Tribunal, s. III civ., Decision no. 3859 of 14 October 2016, www.rolii.ro. Accessed 25 May 2017.

[86] ICCJ, s. I civ., Decision no. 104 of 22 January 2016, www.scj.ro. Accessed 25 May 2017.

However, the Bucharest Court of Appeals found the limitation inapplicable in a case concerning the use of a 10-second sequence of a film for a television commercial on account of the fact that the use was not for one of the purposes indicated by the law and, as indicated above, because "the Court is of the opinion that there can be no equivalence between the concept of film sequence and that of quote – the quote being by definition a fragment of a written work, identically reproduced."[87]

## 23.16 Content Excluded from Copyright Protection

Article 9 of the Romanian Copyright Law contains a list of types of content that are specifically excluded from copyright protection. The provisions reads as follows: "The following cannot benefit from the legal protection of copyright: a) the ideas, theories, concepts, scientific discoveries, processes, methods of functioning or mathematical concepts as such and inventions, contained in a work, whatever the manner of the adoption, writing, explanation or expression thereof; b) official texts of a political, legislative, administrative or judicial nature and official translations thereof; c) official symbols of the State, of the public authorities and organizations, such as: the armorial bearings, the seal, the flag, the emblem, the coat of arms, the insignia, the badge and the medal; d) the means of payment; e) news and press information; f) simple facts and data."

As the list of content excluded from copyright protection is qualified as an exception to the general rule that all content is entitled to copyright protection (provided that the criteria for protection are met),[88] we can consider that the list provided by Article 9 of the Romanian Copyright Law is a closed list. Courts have sometimes struggled to shoehorn some particular content in some category of content provided for by Article 9.

In a case involving the online posting of an excerpt from a press article copied from the website of a magazine, the Galați Tribunal qualified this article (entitled "Adina Alberts and Viorel Cataramă Have Separated") as a simple news or press information. To do so, the court stated that the article contained no original element of intellectual creation, such as to allow the article to be qualified as a literary work on account of the fact that the message of the article is simply that the two former lovers had separated. The court also pointed to the disproportion, within the article, between the claimant's creation (quantified as 11 lines) and the preexisting elements (18 lines, which consisted in statements made by the two persons).[89]

Even if the list of content specifically excluded from copyright protection is a closed list, we believe that it does not need to be extended since courts tend to use it

[87] Bucharest Court of Appeals, s. IX civ., Decision no. 51A of 26 February 2009, Buletinul jurisprudenței 2009. Curtea de Apel București, Universul Juridic 2011, p. 492.

[88] V. Roș, Dreptul proprietății intelectuale. Vol. I. Dreptul de autor, drepturile conexe și drepturile sui-generis, CH Beck 2016, p. 184.

[89] Galați Tribunal, s. I civ., Decision no. 959 of 12 April 2013, www.rolii.ro. Accessed 25 May 2017.

as a complement to the basic criteria for the protection of copyright. As seen from the case law above, courts have tended to anchor the justification for the inclusion, by the legislator, of different items on the list in the fact that such content inherently does not meet the conditions for protection. Therefore, the list tends to be merely a shortcut allowing courts, in specific cases, to bypass verifying the meeting of the criteria for protection in respect of the type of content already on the list.

## 23.17 Uses Permitted in Education

Subject to the work having been made known to the public, the use being in accordance with good practice, the use not affecting the normal exploitation of the work, and it not prejudicing the author or the holders of the exploitation rights, the law allows certain uses for educational purposes. The first of such is the use of isolated articles or brief excerpts from works in publications, television or radio broadcasts, or sound or audiovisual recordings, when such are exclusively intended for teaching purposes. Additionally, the law also allows the reproduction for teaching purposes, within the public education or social welfare institutions, of isolated articles or brief extracts from works, to the extent justified by the intended purpose.

Publicly accessible libraries, educational establishments, museums, and archives are also allowed to perform specific acts of reproduction if such establishments are not for direct or indirect economic or commercial advantage. Educational establishments are also allowed to represent and execute a work if it is part of their activities, it is made exclusively for specific purposes, and both the representation or execution and the public's access to such are free of charge.

Moreover, the reproduction, distribution, broadcasting, or communication to the public of works is allowed if used exclusively for illustration in teaching or scientific research and if there is neither a direct nor an indirect commercial or economic advantage.

For teaching purposes, the law also allows a transformation of the work, without the author's consent and without the payment of remuneration, if the result of the transformation is a summarizing presentation of the works, and proper attribution is given.

With regard to the limitation provided by Article 33 paragraph (2) letter d), in the geography manual case, mentioned above, the Bucharest Tribunal held that the conditions required for the limitation to apply were not met because the respondent had not used the work for illustration purposes as, in such case, only fragments of the work should have been used, and solely for the purpose of illustration of the respondent's own arguments, and proper attribution should have been given. Moreover, as indicated above, the court found that the use was made for economic advantage since "publishing, by university professors, of a number of scientific papers confers upon them a series of advantages, including economic ones."[90]

[90] Bucharest Tribunal, s. IV civ., Decision no. 1997 of 15 November 2011, www.rolii.ro. Accessed 25 May 2017.

In respect of the limitation provided by Article 33 paragraph (1) letter c), in the criminal case concerning the usurpation of authorship in a book on the methodology of scientific research, the Bucharest Court of Appeals held that this limitation was not applicable on account of the fact that the use did not concern use for analysis, commentary, or illustration; the use did not concern short excerpts but almost all of the original work (approximately 90%).[91]

The limitation provided by Article 33 paragraph (1) letter e) was found inapplicable by the High Court in the case concerning the unauthorized making available of a book in the digital library of the Ministry of the Interior. Even if it upheld the finding of the appellate court that the provision would not apply on account of the use affecting the normal exploitation of the work and prejudicing the author, the High Court also indicated that the use did not meet any of the special conditions since neither the Ministry of the Interior nor its publishing house could qualify as publicly accessible libraries, even though the book was made publicly available online through a virtual library.[92] This finding of the High Court contradicts the argument made in the literature that the limitation is applicable if the purpose is met, irrespective of the person doing the reproduction.[93]

Finally, the provisions of letter g) of Article 33 paragraph (1) were found inapplicable by the Bucharest Tribunal in the case concerning the geography manual. The court found that the provision in question relates solely to the communication to the public of certain works, susceptible of being made public by representation and execution, therefore excluding books such as the one allegedly infringed. It also found that such communication to the public ought to be free, while the copying of the claimant's work was made in view of the publishing and distribution for profit.[94]

We have identified two cases that would have a direct bearing on the functioning of distance-learning programs. The first one would be the case concerning the geography manual, where the courts held that no limitation was applicable and the copyright had been infringed. However, there was gross copying of nearly all of the claimant's work, with attribution for only a small part of the copied text, and the work was then distributed (for a fee) to the students of a private university (including those studying in a distance-learning program). The second case concerns a claim by a collective management society for performers against the Timişoara Polytechnic University concerning the remuneration due to performers for use of phonograms in the television broadcasts made by the university's TV station. These were meant to inform the public on the academic and social life related to the university's activities, including distance learning. The High Court, sitting as final court, determined that the respondent university could not benefit from the

[91] Bucharest Court of Appeals, s. II pen., Decision no. 136/F of 7 March 2014, www.rolii.ro. Accessed 25 May 2017.

[92] ICCJ, s. I civ., Decision no. 1109 of 24 April 2015, www.scj.ro. Accessed 25 May 2017.

[93] T. Bodoaşcă and L. I. Tarnu, Dreptul proprietății intelectuale, ed. 3, Universul Juridic 2015, pp. 77.

[94] Bucharest Tribunal, s. IV civ., Decision no. 1997 of 15 November 2011, www.rolii.ro. Accessed 25 May 2017.

limitation provided by Article 33 paragraph (1) letter c) of the Romanian Copyright Law because the channel ought to have used only brief fragments of phonograms in its broadcasts and solely for educational purposes. The court found that the university had not proven that only short excerpts were used and that, since the channel's program structure approved by the National Council for the Audio-Visual indicated that the channel also broadcasts movies, advertising and entertainment shows, the use was not exclusively for educational purposes.[95] The same decision also indicated that the Romanian Copyright Law makes no difference between public and private institutions, even though, as seen above, in other cases a private university was considered to have been under a presumption of commercial gain where its manuals and distance-learning materials were distributed to its students. It was unclear in that case whether the court considered that the distribution was subject to a special fee or just the fee for the educational program with which the students were enrolled.

## 23.18 Uses Permitted in Research

Article 33 paragraph (1) letter d) reads: "The following uses of a work previously made known to the public shall be permitted without the author's consent and without payment of a remuneration, on condition that these are in accordance with good practice, do not affect the normal exploitation of the work, and do not prejudice the author or the holders of the exploitation rights: […] d) the reproduction of brief excerpts from works, for the purpose of information or research, by not-for-profit libraries, museums, film archives, sound archives, archives of cultural or scientific public institutions; the complete reproduction of the support of a work is allowed for the replacement of the sole copy in the permanent collection of a library or archive in the event of the destruction, serious deterioration or loss of thereof."

Article 33 paragraph (2) reads: "Subject to conditions provided for in paragraph (1), the reproduction, distribution, broadcasting or communication to the public, with neither direct nor indirect commercial or economic advantage, are allowed: […] d) of works, where used exclusively for illustration in teaching or scientific research."

There is no limitation or exception to copyright to support big-data-related activities or one that would concern "text and data mining." However, Article $122^3$ paragraph (4) letters b) and c) allow the lawful user of a database to extract or reuse a substantial part of its content, without authorization from the maker of the database, provided that the database is made available to the public in any manner, that the extraction is made solely for use for the purpose of teaching or scientific research—in which case the amount of use must be justified in view of the noncommercial purpose and proper attribution given—or for the purpose of insuring public safety and national security or in administrative or jurisdictional proceedings.

[95] ICCJ, s. I civ., Decision no. 9699 of 27 November 2009, www.scj.ro. Accessed 25 May 2017.

With respect to the limitation under Article 33 paragraph (1) letter d), the Bucharest Tribunal held in the Romanian geography manual case that said limitation was not applicable in the given case because the copying did not cover brief excerpts of the work but covered the entire work. It also found that the copying was made not for information or research but for the distribution of the infringing work for a fee and was not performed by a not-for-profit cultural or scientific public institution.[96] The High Court, on final appeal, additionally held, in respect of the latter point, that the Faculty of Geography of the private university concerned was not a scientific institution. While it acknowledged that universities may conduct scientific research, the court considered that such activities are conducted by means of distinct components of the faculty or university, such as research institutes, and the fact that the work in question potentially represented scientific research (given the fact that it concerned materials for the distance-learning program) did not change the educational character of the faculty into a scientific one.[97] Moreover, the court indicated that the private university was not a "public" institution, although it was "of public utility," since it was not dependent on the state or local budget; therefore, it could not have in any event qualified under the limitation. In addition to this, the court also held that the special conditions were not met since the reproduction did not take place for the archive of an institution but was published and copied in view of it being distributed to the students of the university, for a fee.

## 23.19 Exhaustion of Copyright

Under Romanian law, the distribution right, an economic right under copyright, is exhausted, in respect of each material support, upon that support's first sale or transfer of ownership, on the domestic market. In this respect, Article $14^1$ paragraph (2) of the Romanian Copyright Law provides that "the distribution right is subject to exhaustion upon first sale or with the first transfer of ownership of the original or of the copies of a work, on the domestic market, by the right holder or with his consent."

Distribution is defined by the law as meaning "the sale or any other manner of transmittal, for a consideration or free of charge, of the original or of copies of a work, as well as their offering to the public."

Exhaustion does not occur in respect of the lending right (upon first sale or first assignment of ownership), irrespective of whether it is made or agreed by the right holder or with his consent, and neither does it occur in respect of the right of communication to the public (upon any act of communication to the public or making available), irrespective of whether or not it was made with the right holder's consent.

[96] Bucharest Tribunal, s. IV civ., Decision no. 1997 of 15 November 2011, www.rolii.ro. Accessed 25 May 2017.

[97] ICCJ, s. I civ., Decision no. 1067 of 28 March 2014, www.scj.ro. Accessed 25 May 2017.

However, in respect of software, "the first sale of the copy of a computer program, on the domestic market, by the right holder or with his consent, shall exhaust the exclusive right for the authorization of the distribution of such copy on the domestic market."

The Romanian law therefore expressly excludes exhaustion in respect of the making available right, which would apply to online situations where the work has been made available in a digital format.

Since the provisions of the law concerning exhaustion of rights are mandatory provisions, there can be no contractual derogation. However, given the fact that the exhaustion concerns solely the "domestic market," which is to be interpreted as the internal market of the EU (including the EEA), parties can limit the exports of supports incorporating copyright-protected works outside the EEA but must also observe to this end the application of the provisions of Competition Law no 21 of 10 April 1996,[98] as interpreted by the Romanian Competition Council in *Bayer*.[99] In that case, the authority found that the contractual restriction of parallel exports outside the EEA may have significant effects on the trade between member states of the EU and therefore can constitute a hardcore infringement of EU and Romanian competition law.

## 23.20 The Panorama Exception in Romanian Copyright Law

Article 33 paragraph (1) letter f) reads: "The following uses of a work previously made known to the public shall be permitted without the author's consent and without payment of a remuneration, on condition that these are in accordance with good practice, do not affect the normal exploitation of the work, and do not prejudice the author or the holders of the exploitation rights: […] f) the reproduction, with the exclusion of any means involving direct contact with the work, distribution or communication to the public of the image of an architectural work, work of plastic art, photographic work or work of applied art, permanently located in a public place, except where the image of the work is the main subject of such reproduction, distribution or communication, and if it is used for commercial purposes."

The High Court found the limitation inapplicable in the case of the use of personal photographs taken from a biographical book and inserted in a historical TV short documentary about the subject of the book. In order to so hold, the court has

[98] Competition Law, Monitorul Oficial 1996 88.

[99] Consiliul Concurenței, Decision no. 98 of 27 December 2011 concerning the sanctioning of producers SC Bayer SRL and SC Sintofarm SA, and of the distributors SC Mediplus Exim SRL, SC Polisano SRL, SC Relad International SRL, SC Farmexim SA, SC Farmexpert DCI SA, SC Fildas Trading SRL, SC Montero SA, SC ADM Farm SRL, SC Dita Import Export SRL and SC PharmaFarm SA for the infringement of art. 5 par. (1) of Competition Law no. 21/1996, republished, as amended and modfiide and of art. 101par. (1) TFEU, http://www.consiliulconcurentei.ro/uploads/docs/items/bucket7/id7390/decizie_site.pdf.

considered that the claimant only enjoyed copyright in the book as a whole (as a compilation of materials) and not in the individual photographs themselves.[100]

In the case concerning the use of a photograph of a painting in an electoral leaflet, the Neamț Tribunal took the strange view of considering that the special conditions required by the panorama exception were met on account of the fact that the photograph was not the main subject of the publication (i.e., of the use) as said leaflet instead referred to one of the public figures subject of the painting, one of whom was running for mayor.[101] Although the court found the limitation ultimately inapplicable on account of the fact that the general conditions (i.e., imposed by the "triple test") were not met, the court seems to have misinterpreted the special conditions as these refer to the content of the photograph and not the product where such photograph is used. Instead of asking whether the main subject of the photograph itself was the protected painting (in which case it should have found that the special conditions were not met), the court focused on whether the photograph of the protected painting constituted the main subject of the product where said photograph was used. Given the fact that the photograph was exclusively a photograph of the painting, the court's decision on this point seems incorrect.

Of interest for the application of this particular limitation is the decision of the Bucharest Tribunal in a case concerning the infringement of the copyright in a photograph taken during the June 1990 Mineriad. The photograph was used in a press article regarding the events, which was published both in print and online on 29 July 2012. The publishing newspaper tried to defend the use by claiming that the panorama exception was applicable on account of the fact that the photograph in question had been made available online and was thus "located in a public space." The court disagreed and held that the limitation only concerns "works specifically created for that purpose: to be a part of the public landscape," whereas in the given case the photograph was posted to the claimant's own website with an express reservation as to its use.[102]

Clearly, the wording of Article 33 paragraph (1) letter f) excludes from the scope of its application any use that is made for commercial purposes. The purpose of the use cannot exclude noncommercial use by a for-profit entity. However, the fact that the purpose of that entity is inherently commercial would normally mean that a presumption of commercial purpose would exist, the burden of proof resting with that entity (claiming under the limitation) to show that in the given particular instance, the use was not for a commercial purpose.

[100] ICCJ, s. I civ., Decision no. 104 of 22 January 2016, www.scj.ro. Accessed 25 May 2017.

[101] Neamț Tribunal, s. I. civ., Decision no. 463/C of 8 April 2013, www.rolii.ro. Accessed 25 May 2017.

[102] Bucharest Tribunal, s. V civ., Decision no. 553 of 28 April 2014, www.rolii.ro. Accessed 25 May 2017.

## 23.21 The Private Copy Exception

Article 34 paragraph (1) of the Romanian Copyright Law provides that "[t]he reproduction of a work without the author's consent, for personal use or for the normal family circle, shall not be an infringement of copyright, for the purposes of the present law, on condition that the work had previously been made known to the public, that the reproduction does not affect the normal exploitation of the work and does not prejudice the author or the holders of the exploitation rights."

The literature on the subject indicates that the exception is available if the following conditions are cumulatively met: the copy must be meant for private use, including herein the "family circle"; the work must have been previously made known to the public; the copying must not affect the normal exploitation of the work; and the copying must not prejudice the author or the holder of the rights of use.[103] The condition of not prejudicing the author seems most problematic in the case of the private copy since, at least in theory, any such free and unauthorized copy is a lost sale of an authorized (and revenue-generating) copy. Some authors have argued that the private copy can only be made if the user owns an authorized copy, and only if an authorized copy cannot be acquired can a private copy be lawfully made without the user owning a copy himself.[104]

The Bucharest Tribunal indicated, in *obiter*, in a case concerning a collecting society's claim for, *inter alia*, the communication of data for the distribution of sums collected as remuneration due for private copying, that "the private copy therefore concerns that fact that we, as users of a work, have the right to copy a work only if the right holder grants us such right by means of the license to which we adhere by using said work. If the license agreement 'is silent' with respect to this, we refer back to the general rules, i.e. the ones in [the Romanian Copyright Law]. The provisions of Article 34 are of such nature as to impede a claim filed by the right holder when the conditions provided therein are fulfilled. The user's right to private copying is opposed by the correlative obligation, i.e. the remuneration imposed upon manufacturers and importers of supports and devices used to make a copy, and which is included in the final price of these products. Therefore the private copy is an exception to the right holders' exclusive right to decide and authorize the means of use and reproduction of the work."[105] In relation to the comments made above with respect to the different qualifications of the limitations and exceptions to copyright, we also point out the fact that, even if in the case here discussed the court had clearly qualified the private copy as an exception to copyright, only 6 months before, a different section of the Bucharest Tribunal, had held in a similar case—a claim by a collecting society's claim for the payment of the remuneration due for private

[103] V. Roş, Dreptul proprietăţii intelectuale. Vol. I. Dreptul de autor, drepturile conexe şi drepturile sui-generis, CH Beck 2016, p. 184.

[104] A. P. Seucan, Drepturile morale şi drepturile patrimoniale de autor, ed. 2, Universul Juridic 2015, p. 77.

[105] Bucharest Tribunal, s. IV civ., Decision no. 1689 of 11 October 2011, www.rolii.ro. Accessed 25 May 2017.

copying—that private copying was a limitation to copyright, mentioning however that it is compensated by means of the remuneration due for private copying.[106]

As an exception, the lawful private copying defence is subject to a rigid application by the courts. As a consequence, the party claiming the benefit of the exception has to prove that all conditions are cumulatively met. In the case in which the claimant asked that the respondent university send him a copy of a dissertation authored by a third party, the Dolj Tribunal held that for the exception to apply, the claimant ought to have proven that all the conditions provided by law were met, including the fact that the work had been made known to the public and the envisaged purpose of the use.[107]

The same is true in criminal matters. In a decision of the Bihor Tribunal[108] involving a defendant who reproduced phonograms as mp3s on the personal computer he was using in his office, which was at a music club where unauthorized public communication of phonograms had taken place, the nonguilty verdict was vacated by the Oradea Court of Appeals finding that the exception was not applicable.[109]

## 23.22 Overall Assessment

The regime of exceptions and limitations to copyright under Romanian law is rigid by design, and its qualification as an exception places the burden of proof on the user and only allows application of the defence where all conditions provided by law are cumulatively met. Due to the unclear legal qualification of these exceptions and limitations, claiming the benefit of these provisions is difficult. Moreover, such benefit can only be raised as a defence to a claim of copyright infringement, and since claims of damages for copyright infringement are subject to a very small judicial stamp duty tax, irrespective of the amount claimed, users can only be confirmed in their reading of the law when sued, and facing the risk of high damages. For example, in the case concerning the use of the photograph of the June 1990 Mineriad, the author requested an award of damages in the sum of RON 80,000 (approximately EUR 17,750), while in the 10-second film sequence case the author asked for damages in the sum of EUR 100,000.

A possible solution to this problem would be to clarify the qualification of these provisions in such a way as to grant standing to users in (at least) declaratory claims. Such claims would be subject to a similarly low judicial stamp duty tax and would

[106] Bucharest Tribunal, s. V civ., Decision no. 610 of 24 March 2011, www.rolii.ro. Accessed 25 May 2017.

[107] Dolj Tribunal, s. cont. adm., Decision no. 896 of 19 April 2011, www.rolii.ro. Accessed 25 May 2017, confirmed by Craiova Court of Appeals, s. cont. adm., Decision no. 2853 of 13 October 2011, www.rolii.ro. Accessed 25 May 2017.

[108] Bihor Tribunal, s. pen., Decision no. 132/P of 31 May 2011, www.rolii.ro. Accessed 25 May 2017.

[109] Oradea Court of Appeals, s. pen., Decision no. 9/A of 2 February 2012, www.rolii.ro. Accessed 25 May 2017.

allow users to have a judicial determination of their use before any damages are incurred by the author or right holder. On the other hand, an increase of claims with the Romanian courts would place an additional burden on a system that is already stretched to its limits and could cause severe delays in the resolution of such claims.

The current status quo is reasonable because the Romanian courts (especially the courts in Bucharest, which have specialized panels for intellectual property cases) have kept the balance between the interests of the authors and right holders and those of the users. However, given the fact that there is a tendency at administrative level to reduce the number of specialized panels for intellectual property cases and the specialized division of the Bucharest Court of Appeals was merged into a civil division, there could be more deviations from this balance, and the increased uncertainty for the users will need to be addressed by means of statute.

# Switzerland

# 24

Sevan Antreasyan

## 24.1 Introduction

Through the analysis of the various exceptions enshrined in Swiss copyright law, this report aims to assess whether these exceptions (and the way they are applied by courts) strike a fair balance between the rights of copyright owners and fair use by individuals and others.

Before diving in, it is worth noting that the last substantive changes to the Swiss Federal Act on Copyright and Related Rights ("CopA")[1] entered into effect on July 1, 2008, in order to implement the WIPO Copyright Treaty.[2] These changes include new language to existing provisions aiming at taking into account the use of works in a digital context (e.g., in relation to the private use exception), as well as new exceptions (e.g., temporary/cache reproduction of works). These will be discussed below. Further, a legislative process is currently underway to further modernize the CopA. A predraft of the revised CopA ("CopA Predraft") was circulated to interest groups at the end of 2015. Due to the important number of opinions received (1224 totaling more than 8000 pages), the

[1] An official translation (although only the French, German, and Italian versions are binding) of the CopA is available on the following link: https://www.admin.ch/opc/en/classified-compilation/19920251/index.html. Accessed 31 October 2017.

[2] RO 2008 2421; FF 2006 3263. Another revision of the CopA took place more recently—on January 11, 2011 (RO 2010 1739; FF 2006 6841)—but was limited to adaptations further to the entry into force of the new Federal Codes on Civil and Criminal Procedures.

S. Antreasyan (✉)
Lenz & Staehelin, Geneva, Switzerland
e-mail: sevan.antreasyan@lenzstaehelin.com



B. Kilpatrick et al. (eds.), *Antitrust Analysis of Online Sales Platforms & Copyright Limitations and Exceptions*, LIDC Contributions on Antitrust Law, Intellectual Property and Unfair Competition,
https://doi.org/10.1007/978-3-319-71419-6_24

finalization of the CopA draft can be expected at the end of 2017.[3] The CopA Predraft will be referred to below where relevant.

After laying out the copyright owners' exclusive rights (*infra*, Sect. 24.2), we will provide an overview of the system of exceptions in Swiss copyright law (*infra*, Sect. 24.3). Further, some of the most important exceptions will be discussed (*infra*, Sect. 24.4), and a few thoughts on the exhaustion of copyright under Swiss law will be given (*infra*, Sect. 24.5) before providing some concluding remarks (*infra*, Sect. 24.6).

## 24.2 Exclusive Rights

Article 10(2)(a)–(f) CopA provides an exemplary list of the exclusive commercial rights enjoyed by the copyright owner, i.e.

- to produce copies of the work, such as printed matter, phonograms, audiovisual fixations, or data carriers;
- to offer, transfer, or otherwise distribute copies of the work;
- to recite, perform, or present a work or make it perceptible somewhere else or make it available directly or through any kind of medium in such a way that persons may access it from a place and at a time individually chosen by them;
- to broadcast the work by radio, television, or similar means, including by wire;
- to retransmit works by means of technical equipment, the provider of which is not the original broadcasting organization, in particular including by wire; and
- to make works made available, broadcast, and retransmitted perceptible.

In addition, the CopA sets forth the following moral rights:

- paternity (Article 9 CopA): this includes the right to decide under which name (or pseudonym) a work may be published or not to be named at all;
- divulgation (Article 9(2)–(3) CopA): it includes the right of the author to decide whether and when a work shall, in whole or in part, be made available to the public; and
- integrity (Article 11(1)–(2) CopA): it is debated among scholars whether the right to modify the work (Article 11(1) CopA) is mainly patrimonial or also bears a moral aspect[4]; in our view, it is both patrimonial and moral; in any case, the mandatory right of authors to oppose any distortion of the work that infringes their personal rights (Article 11(2) CopA) is clearly a moral right (such right is referred to in French as the *noyau dur*).

[3] A summary of this process is available in English on the website of the Swiss Intellectual Property Institute ("IPI"): https://www.ige.ch/en/law-and-policy/national-ip-law/copyright-law/modernisation-of-copyright.html. Accessed 31 October 2017.

[4] E. Philippin, Commentaire romand du droit de la propriété intellectuelle, Basel 2013, Art. 11 LDA N 4-5; *see also* the references cited by the author.

## 24.3 System of Copyright Exceptions

In general, the conditions mentioned in the provisions pertaining to copyright exceptions do not appear unduly strict or compelling.[5] However, some exceptions (e.g., private use *stricto sensu* in Article 19(1)(a) CopA) provide more flexibility than others, which are more specific (e.g., temporary copies exception in Article 24*a* CopA).

### 24.3.1 Triple Test

The CopA does not explicitly refer to or include a provision reflecting the "triple test," as set forth in Article 9(2) of the Berne Convention for the Protection of Literary and Artistic Works ("Berne Convention") and Article 13 of the Agreement on Trade-Related Aspects of Intellectual Property Rights (TRIPS).[6] However, it is worth noting that one exception—the decoding of computer programs exception at Article 21 CopA—integrates the second and third steps of the "triple test" as follows:

1. Any person who has the right to use a computer program may obtain, either personally or through a third party, necessary information on the interfaces by decoding the program code using independently developed programs.
2. The interface information obtained by decoding the program code may only be used for the development, maintenance and use of interoperable computer programs **insofar as neither the normal exploitation of the program nor the legitimate interests of the owner of the rights are unreasonably prejudiced**. (emphasis added)

As Switzerland has ratified these international conventions, the copyright exceptions set forth in the CopA must comply with the "triple test," and the latter shall be taken into account by courts when interpreting the CopA. The Swiss Supreme Federal Court (**SFC**) has referred to the "triple test" on several occasions.[7] In one of those cases,[8] the question was whether the tariff applicable to blank media (*support vierge*) mainly used to store works protected by copyright (e.g., memory cards or hard drives integrated in audio recorders or iPods) complied with the triple test.[9] The SFC decided that such was the case.

[5] For example, the right to decode computer programs (Article 21 CopA) shall be interpreted in order also to encompass the use for bugs detection and citation rights for pictures shall be permitted (*see* Question 5 of the report for Switzerland of AIPPI Q216B, available at: http://aippi.org/wp-content/uploads/committees/216B/GR216Bswitzerland.pdf. Accessed 31 October 2017).

[6] The triple test is also set forth in Article 10 of the WIPO Copyright Treaty and Article 16(2) of the WIPO Performances and Phonograms Treaty.

[7] *See e.g.* ATF 133 II 263 c.7.3.2, JdT 2007 I 146; ATF 133 III 473.

[8] ATF 133 II 263 c.7.3.2, JdT 2007 I 146.

[9] On compensation, *see below*, Sect. 24.3.8.

To our knowledge, there is no precedent in Switzerland where a court would have found that the application of an exception conflicts with the normal exploitation of a work and/or unreasonably prejudices the legitimate interests of the author. If such was the case, a court would have to interpret the CopA in a way that would comply with the relevant international convention (Berne Convention, TRIPS, WCT, and/or WPPT), and if no compliant interpretation can be found, the relevant international convention shall take precedence and limit (or exclude) the application of a particular exception.[10]

## 24.3.2 Closed List

The CopA provides a list of exceptions in Chapter 5 of Title 2 (Articles 19 to 28 CopA). In addition, the parody exception is set forth in Article 11(3) CopA, which relates to the moral right of integrity.

Although not an exception *per se*, Article 5(1) CopA excludes certain works that shall not be protected—at all—by copyright, i.e. (a) acts, ordinances, international treaties, and other official enactments; (b) means of payment; (c) decisions, minutes, and reports issued by authorities and public administrations; and (d) patent specifications and published patent applications. Article 5(2) CopA further excludes official or legally required collections and translations of the works referred to in Article 5(1) CopA. Moreover, all these exceptions are applicable by analogy to the rights to which the performers, phonogram and audiovisual fixation producers, and broadcasting organizations are entitled (Article 38 CopA).[11]

The exceptions set forth in the CopA are exhaustive.[12] In this respect, any use that falls outside the list shall in principle not be permitted without authorization from the copyright owner. The exceptions set forth in the CopA are the result of a balance of fundamental rights provided for in the Swiss Federal Constitution ("**Cst.**"): for the copyright owner, the right of ownership (Article 26 Cst.) and for users, various fundamental rights (depending on the exception), such as the freedom of expression (Article 16 Cst.) and of the media (Article 17 Cst.).[13] According to the

[10] *See e.g.* P.-E. Ruedin, Commentaire romand du droit de la propriété intellectuelle, Basel 2013, Introduction aux articles 19 à 28 LDA, N 6.

[11] As Article 38 CopA does not refer specifically to the parody exception (at Article 11(3) CopA), it is debatable whether the exception of parody also applies e.g. to the parody of a performance. This has not been decided by courts. B. Wittweiler, Zu den Schrankenbestimmungen im neuen Urheberrechtsgesetz, AJP 1993, p. 588, argues that it should also apply.

[12] However, *see* the report for Switzerland of AIPPI Q216B (available at http://aippi.org/wp-content/uploads/committees/216B/GR216Bswitzerland.pdf. Accessed 31 October 2017) where the authors refer to "extra-statutory limitations" in Question 5, which in our view shall be construed as broad interpretations of the CopA exceptions.

[13] On the topic of fundamental rights and copyright, *see e.g.* C. P. Rigamonti, Urheberrecht und Grundrechte, ZBJV 153/2017 365.

case law of the SFC, the relevant fundamental rights protected by the Cst. should be taken into account when interpreting a copyright exception but shall, however, not serve as a basis to extend or create a new exception to copyright.[14]

It is also worth mentioning that neither the CopA nor the CopA Predraft provides for a catch-all exception.

### 24.3.3 Mandatory Nature of the Exceptions

Although the SFC seems to have ruled that the copyright exceptions are mandatory,[15] it is debated among scholars whether such is the case due to the general and superficial reasoning of the SFC.[16] The imperative nature is explicitly set forth only for the exception of archive or backup of a computer program (Article 24(2) CopA), which provides:

> Any person entitled to use a computer program may make one backup copy thereof; this right may not be waived by contract.

In our view, all exceptions shall in principle be considered to be mandatory and, therefore, that they cannot be ruled out by contract.[17]

### 24.3.4 Interpretation

As a matter of principle under Swiss law, exceptions provided in an act shall be interpreted restrictively. In addition, according to a general principle of interpretation under Swiss copyright law, in case of doubt, a statute shall be interpreted in favor of the author/copyright owner (*in dubio pro auctore*).

However, legal scholars recommend not applying such principles of interpretation in a schematic way: all circumstances and interpretation methods shall be used in each particular case.[18] It shall further be noted that copyright exceptions shall be interpreted in compliance with the Cst. and international conventions.

---

[14] *See e.g.* ATF 131 III 480, JdT 2005 I 390.

[15] ATF 127 III 26.

[16] P.-E. Ruedin, Introduction aux articles 19 à 28 LDA, N 9 and the cited references.

[17] This would in principle also apply to works made available online. With respect to copyright exhaustion, *see below*, Sect. 24.5.

[18] In this respect, *see* P.-E. Ruedin, Introduction aux articles 19 à 28 LDA, N 7 and the cited references.

### 24.3.5 Scope

#### 24.3.5.1 Commercial/Noncommercial Uses

Three exceptions are (explicitly) subject to the condition that the use be noncommercial:

- Article 19(1) CopA, which includes the following exceptions: private use *stricto sensu* (lit. a), educational use (lit. b), and intraorganization reproduction (lit. c);
- Article 24($1^{bis}$) CopA (archival and backup exception); and
- Article 24*c* CopA (use of works by people with disabilities).

Other exceptions may, by their very nature, be noncommercial—e.g., the archival and backup exception (other than those of publicly available archives) in Article 24 CopA—or allow a commercial use explicitly or implicitly, e.g. Article 11(3) CopA (parody), Article 25 CopA (citations), Article 27 CopA (works on premises open to the public), and Article 28 CopA (reporting of current events).

#### 24.3.5.2 Ratione Personae

In terms of the persons or category of persons who may claim an exception to copyrights, the CopA provides both general exception (applicable to "any person") and specific exceptions (e.g., broadcasting-related exceptions and museum catalogs exceptions). Two exceptions are applicable only to individuals:

- the private use *stricto sensu* exception (Article 19(1)(a) CopA) applies to any individual; and
- the educational exception (Article 19(1)(b) CopA) applies to teachers and their class.

#### 24.3.5.3 Exclusive Rights Concerned

The exceptions provided in the CopA generally refer to the permitted use(s) in an explicit way, which vary depending on the exception.

Some exceptions relate exclusively to the reproduction right, such as intraorganization reproduction (Article 19(1)(c) CopA), archive and backup copies (Article 24 CopA), and temporary copies (Article 24*a* CopA).

Other exceptions allow a broader range of uses. For example:

- the private use *stricto sensu* exception allows any personal use, e.g. reproduction (on tangible media or on a cloud server) and making available of the work, subject of course to the requirements of Article 19(1)(a) CopA;
- the educational exception also allows any use by teachers and their class (Article 19(1)(b) CopA);
- the freedom of panorama exception allows the offer, transfer, broadcast, and distribution of the depiction of the work (Article 27(1) CopA); and

- the reporting of current events exceptions allows the works to be fixed, reproduced, presented, broadcast, distributed, or otherwise made perceptible (Article 28(1) CopA).

It appears that when drafting the exceptions provisions in the CopA, the legislator has taken into account the specificities of each exception. Indeed, distinguishing the permitted use(s) for each exception allows addressing the particular interests of the users.

### 24.3.6 Impact of Exceptions on Moral Rights

Although not explicitly stated in the provisions of the CopA, the exceptions of copyright apply only for works that have been made available by the author (divulgation right).[19]

Some exceptions necessarily have an impact on moral rights.[20] With respect to the right of integrity, for instance, a parody modifies the original work by its very nature. The fact that this exception is structurally provided within Article 11 CopA (on the right of integrity) shows that it is meant also as an exception to the moral right of integrity. In our view, the right of integrity may in principle not be claimed by the author against a user of a work to the extent that a modification of such work is required to benefit from an exception. Nonetheless, the author may always be able to claim the *noyau dur* protection.[21]

As regards the right of paternity, it is less likely to be affected by exceptions to copyright under the CopA. In this respect, Article 25(2) CopA (citation) and Article 28(2) CopA (reporting of current events) explicitly provide that the source shall be referred to.

### 24.3.7 DRMs vs. Exceptions

Article 39*a*(1) CopA provides that "[e]ffective technological measures for the protection of works and other protected subject-matter may not be circumvented." However, the prohibition of such circumvention may not be enforced against those persons who undertake the circumvention exclusively for legally permitted uses (Article 39*a*(4) CopA). Accordingly, circumvention would be authorized in order for a user to benefit from an exception.

There is, however, no obligation for the copyright owner to provide the means of benefitting from an exception to users, which may impede the effectiveness of

[19] P.-E. Ruedin, Introduction aux articles 19 à 28 LDA, N 8.

[20] D. Barrelet/W. Egloff, Le nouveau droit d'auteur, 3rd ed., Bern 2008, p. 118.

[21] *See above*, Sect. 24.2.

exceptions.[22] Rather, Article 39*b* CopA provides grounds to the Federal Council to establish a monitoring office for technological measures,[23] which

a. monitors and reports on the effects of technological measures in accordance with Article 39a paragraph 2 on the exceptions and limitations regulated by Articles 19–28;
b. acts as a liaison between user and consumer groups and the users of technological measures, and encourages cooperative solutions.

Users may report issues to the monitoring office through a web form.[24] The monitoring office also publishes activity reports on its website.

### 24.3.8 Compensation

Compensation in favor of the copyright owner is provided in Article 20 CopA in relation to the exceptions of private use (i.e., private use *stricto sensu*, educational use, intraorganization reproduction) as follows:

- For private use *stricto sensu* (e.g., the reproduction made on a personal computer when downloading a work from the Internet): no compensation is due directly by the users for such exception (Article 20(1) CopA). However, Article 20(3) CopA provides that "[a]ny person who produces or imports blank media suitable for the fixation of works owes remuneration to the author for the use of the works under Article 19." In addition, when a private copy is made by a third party for the user, such copying is subject to compensation (Article 20(2) CopA). There is thus an indirect compensation to the copyright owner for the private use *stricto sensu*.
- For educational use and intraorganization reproduction: compensation is due from educational institutions and from organizations that reproduce works.

Remunerations are collected and claims for remuneration can only be asserted by the authorized collective rights management organizations (Article 20(4) CopA). For the purposes of this provision, (1) ProLitteris[25] collects and distributes remuneration for works of literature and art, and (2) SUISA[26] collects and distributes remuneration for copies made on blank tapes, CD-ROMs, and any other kind of digital or analog data carriers.

The remuneration is based on tariffs that are prepared by the collective rights management organizations, which shall be negotiated with the relevant associations

[22] On this topic, *see* W. Egloff, Das Urheberrecht und der Zugang zu wissenschaftlichen Publikationen, sic! 2007 705.

[23] Available at https://www.btm.admin.ch/btm/fr/home.html. Accessed 31 October 2017. Accessed 31 October 2017.

[24] Available at https://www.btm.admin.ch/btm/fr/home/dienstleistungen/meldung.html. Accessed 31 October 2017.

[25] Available at https://prolitteris.ch/fr/. Accessed 31 October 2017.

[26] Available at https://www.suisa.ch/en/home.html. Accessed 31 October 2017.

of users (Article 46 CopA). The tariffs are approved by the Federal Arbitral Commission and are published (Articles 46 and 55 CopA) and are binding on the courts when finally approved[27] (Article 59(3) CopA). The tariffs shall be fair and reasonable (Article 59(1) CopA). Article 60 CopA further provides the principle of fairness applicable to the tariffs:

1. When determining remuneration, account is taken of:
   a. the proceeds obtained from the use of the work, performance, phonogram or audio-visual fixation or broadcast, or alternatively the costs incurred in such use;
   b. the nature and quantity of the works, performances, phonograms or audio-visual fixations or broadcasts used;
   c. the ratio of protected to unprotected works, performances, phonograms or audio-visual fixations or broadcasts as well as to other services.
2. Remuneration normally amounts to a maximum of ten per cent of the proceeds or costs incurred from the use of the copyright and a maximum of three per cent for related rights; however, it is determined in such a way that entitled persons receive equitable remuneration conditioned upon sound financial management for the administration of rights.
3. The use of the work under Article 19 paragraph 1 letter b is subject to preferential tariffs.

The following are examples of tariffs:

- Tariff 4[28] and 4i[29] on blank media and memory integrated in devices;
- Tariff 7[30] on educational uses;
- Tariffs 8I-VII[31] on intraorganization reproduction; and
- Tariffs 9I-VII[32] on use of works within internal organizations' networks.

The same system applies to the exception pertaining to the use (reproduction and distribution) of works by people with disabilities (Article 24*c*(3)–(4) CopA). Such uses are subject to Tariff 10.[33]

[27] A tariff is finally approved when it has been approved by the Federal Arbitral Commission and cannot anymore be contested before the SFC (*see e.g.* P. Fehlbaum, Commentaire romand du droit de la propriété intellectuelle, Basel 2013, Art. 59 N 14). A court may nonetheless examine the compliance of a finally approved tariff with mandatory law, its application and its interpretation (SFC 4A_203/2015, sic! 2015 639).

[28] Available at https://www.suisa.ch/fileadmin/user_upload/downloadcenter/tarife/Tarife_ab_2017/GT4_2017-2018_FRE.pdf. Accessed 31 October 2017.

[29] Available at https://www.suisa.ch/fileadmin/user_upload/downloadcenter/tarife/Tarife_ab_2017/GT4i_2017-2018_FRE.pdf. Accessed 31 October 2017.

[30] Available at http://www.prolitteris.ch/fileadmin/user_upload/ProLitteris/Dokumente/Tarife_ab_2017/GT_7_F_2 017_2021.pdf. Accessed 31 October 2017.

[31] Available at https://prolitteris.ch/fr/bases/documents/. Accessed 31 October 2017.

[32] Available at https://prolitteris.ch/fr/bases/documents/. Accessed 31 October 2017.

[33] Available at http://www.prolitteris.ch/fileadmin/user_upload/ProLitteris/Dokumente/Tarife_ab_2017/GT10-fr-2013-2017.pdf. Accessed 31 October 2017.

These provisions aim at ensuring that the remuneration does not result in over-compensation in favor of the copyright owners.[34]

It shall further be noted that Article 23 CopA (compulsory license for the manufacture of phonograms) is not a typical restriction as it provides for the right of certain users to obtain a license from the copyright owner under certain conditions.[35] Such compulsory license is subject to compensation, which is due directly by the user to the copyright owner.

## 24.4 Exceptions

### 24.4.1 Private Copy

The exception for private copies is included in the private use *stricto sensu* exception (Article 19(1)(a) CopA).

According to Article 19(2) CopA, individuals who are entitled to make copies for private use may also have them made by third parties, subject to the restrictions set forth in Article 19(3) CopA:

> The following are not permitted outside the private sphere defined in paragraph 1 letter a:
>
> a. the complete or substantial copying of a work obtainable commercially;
> b. the copying of works of art;
> c. the copying of musical scores;
> d. the fixation of recitations, performances or presentations of a work on blank media.

Except with respect to copies that are made by accessing works that are lawfully made available, the private use *stricto sensu* exception is not subject to direct compensation (Articles 19($3^{bis}$) and 20(1) CopA). However, any person that produces or imports blank media suitable for the fixation of works owes remuneration to the author for the use of the works under Article 19 CopA (Article 20(3) CopA).[36]

---

[34] Considering the tariffs that are based on a "tax" on all blank media and that Article 19($3^{bis}$) CopA exempts from compensation for copies made of works made available lawfully, it has been argued that such tariffs result in a double payment by the consumers (once for the legal download and once for the "tax" on the blank media they are using. However, it shall be noted in this respect that Article 19($3^{bis}$) CopA shall be taken into account when fixing the relevant tariffs which results in a lower tariff (*see* e.g. V. Salvadé, Du streaming au cloud computing: quel avenir pour la copie privée en Suisse?, sic! 2016 434, p. 436 s).

[35] On this topic, *see* P. Ling, Commentaire romand du droit de la propriété intellectuelle, Basel 2013, Art. 23 N 1 ss.

[36] For more information on compensation, *see above*, Sect. 24.3.8.

### 24.4.2 Temporary Reproduction

Under Swiss law, the exclusive right of reproduction provided in Article 10(2)(a) CopA applies whether the copy is permanent or temporary.[37] As a result, any use of works in a digital context—which may otherwise be lawful—would in principle infringe on such right as reproduction is technically required, e.g., to browse the Internet, send emails and run a computer program. The adoption of a temporary copy exception was thus necessary to ensure that such uses do not constitute an infringement of the CopA.

Such exception is provided in Article 24*a* CopA. Its wording is based on Article 5(1) of Directive 2001/29/EC of the European Parliament and of the Council of May 22, 2001, on the harmonization of certain aspects of copyright and related rights in the information society. It states:

> The making of temporary copies of a work is permitted if:
>
> a. they are transient or incidental;
> b. they represent an integral and essential part of a technological process;
> c. their sole purpose is to enable a transmission of the work in a network between third parties by an intermediary or a lawful use of the work;
> d. they have no independent economic significance.

These four conditions need to be satisfied cumulatively:

- The reproduction shall be transient or incidental. A reproduction is transient when it is not stored in a lasting way on a medium. In this respect, the relevant test is whether the data remain stored after an electricity interruption: if it is not, then the copy is considered transient. Such is the case, for example, for copies made in RAM when browsing the Internet or segmented copies (part of works) stored in a buffer. A reproduction is considered incidental when its goal is to store data for the purpose of facilitating another use's process. Although such copy shall not be permanent, it can nonetheless be stored for several days. Such is, for example, the case of data stored in the cache memory of a computer.
- The reproduction shall be an integral and essential part of a technological process. This condition implies that the reproduction and deletion of data shall be made automatically. Therefore, the act of downloading content on a hard drive—even if deleted shortly thereafter by the user—cannot satisfy the requirements of Article 24a CopA due to the manual process that is involved.
- The sole purpose of such reproduction shall be to enable either (1) a transmission of the work in a network between third parties by an intermediary or (2) a lawful use of the work. The first purpose amounts to a limitation of liability of intermediaries—such as Internet access and service providers, as well as hosting providers—to the extent that they allow the transfer of data. A transmission within an internal network is not covered by this purpose. The second purpose is met, in

[37] *See* P. Gilliéron, Commentaire romand du droit de la propriété intellectuelle, Basel 2013, Art. 24*a* LDA N 4 and the cited references.

particular, when the reproduction is required to exercise a copyright exception or when the user benefits from an authorization to access a work given by the copyright owner.

- Finally, a temporary reproduction shall not bear an independent economic significance. This fourth condition related to the second and third prongs of the "triple test." It shall therefore be assessed in each particular case whether a temporary reproduction conflicts with a normal exploitation of the work or unreasonably prejudices the legitimate interests of the copyright owner. Such would be the case, in particular, where the copyright owner could generate revenues from such temporary copies, e.g. when the temporary reproduction can be substituted for a permanent copy.[38]

This exception applies in principle to streaming (whether the source is lawful or not). As Article 24*a* CopA is not subject to compensation, it was proposed to the Federal Council in 2014 to amend the CopA in order for streaming to be subject to compensation (as is the case for downloading[39]). The Federal Council has, however, decided not to introduce a compensation for streaming mainly for practical reasons.[40]

Article 24*a* CopA was to our knowledge never applied by Swiss courts. In our view, it strikes a right balance between the interests at stake and is effective to enable the development of legitimate online activities/new business models. It should, however, be suggested to include a compensation for the cases where the temporary reproduction exception is used to serve works from an illegal source (e.g., streaming from unlawful platforms).

### 24.4.3 Freedom-of-Expression Related Exceptions

The CopA provides two mandatory exceptions related to freedom of expression that do not give rise to compensation.

Article 25 CopA (citations) provides:

1. Published works may be quoted if the quotation serves as an explanation, a reference or an illustration, and the extent of the quotation is justified for such purpose.
2. The quotation must be designated as such and the source given. Where the source indicates the name of the author, the name must also be cited.

Article 28 CopA (reporting of current events) provides:

1. Where it is necessary for reporting current events, the works perceived in doing so may be fixed, reproduced, presented, broadcast, distributed or otherwise made perceptible.

[38] P. Gilliéron, Art. 24*a* LDA N 22.

[39] *See above*, Sect. 24.3.8.

[40] On this topic, *see* V. Salvadé, p. 438.

2. For the purposes of information about current affairs, short excerpts from press articles or from radio and television reports may be reproduced, distributed, broadcast or retransmitted; full reference must be made to the relevant excerpt as well as the source. Where the source refers to the name of the author, the name must also be cited.

In a case regarding the citation exception, the SFC has ruled that reproducing an entire press article in another journal—with very limited added original content—is not covered by the citation exception.[41] The facts of this case are interesting: a journal reproduced two articles (discussing the same topic but with opposite views) that were published in another journal, together with a criticism of those articles. The journal argued that it did so to enable its readers to form their own view by getting access to the full and original views expressed in the previous two articles (an argument that relates to the freedom of information and press).

The same case also involved a (short) discussion on Article 28 CopA. The journal, which had reproduced the two previously published articles, argued that such reproduction shall fall within the scope of the reporting of current events exception. The court stated that the publishing of an article shall not be considered as a "current event" pursuant to Article 28 CopA and that, in any case, this article only allows to reproduce short excerpts of works.

### 24.4.4 Educational Exception

The educational exception is part of the private use exception in Article 19 CopA:

1. Published works may be used for private use. Private use means:

[...]
b. any use of a work by a teacher and his class for educational purposes;
[...]

2. Persons entitled to make copies of a work for private use may also have them made by third parties subject to paragraph 3; libraries, other public institutions and businesses that make copying apparatus available to their users are also deemed third parties within the meaning of this paragraph.1
3. The following are not permitted outside the private sphere defined in paragraph 1 letter a:

a. the complete or substantial copying of a work obtainable commercially;
b. the copying of works of art;
c. the copying of musical scores;
d. the fixation of recitations, performances or presentations of a work on blank media.

3bis Copies which are made by accessing works that are lawfully made available are neither subject to the restriction of private use under this Article nor are they included in the claims for remuneration under Article 20.3
4. This Article does not apply to computer programs.

Subject to paragraph 3, works that are related to the taught matter can be used by teachers and their students. All commercial uses are encompassed in this exception

[41] SFC 131 III 480, JdT 2005 I 390.

(e.g., reproduction, performance, and making available). The making available of works over a network is allowed to the extent that only teachers and their students have access to the works.

This exception typically applies at all levels of education (kindergarten, primary school, middle and high school, as well as universities), whether public or private. It is debated whether distance learning is covered by the educational exception.[42] In our view, this exception should apply to distance learning to the extent access controls to the lectures and teaching materials (i.e., providing access only to the teacher and the students) are properly implemented as this would, in principle, satisfy the "triple test."

The law does not explicitly distinguish whether the classes are held within a nonprofit organization or if it pursues a commercial purpose. However, some scholars are of the view that the educational exception should not apply in the context of continuous education, especially when it is organized by a for-profit organization.[43]

This exception gives rise to compensation, as discussed above.[44]

## 24.5 Exhaustion of Copyright

Article 12 CopA sets forth the principle of exhaustion under copyright law:

> 1. Where the author has transferred the rights to a copy of a work or has consented to such a transfer, these rights may subsequently be further transferred or the copy otherwise distributed.
>
> 1^bis^ Copies of audio-visual works may not be further transferred or rented as long as the author is thereby impaired in exercising his right of performance (Art. 10 para. 2 let. c).
>
> 2. Where the author has transferred the rights to a computer program or has consented to such transfer, such a program may subsequently be used or further transferred.
>
> 3. Works of architecture that have been constructed may be altered by the owner; Article 11 paragraph 2 remains reserved.

According to Article 12(1) CopA, only the distribution right (Article 10(2)(b) CopA) is exhausted when the author has transferred such distribution rights or has consented to such transfer. The distribution right implies that a transfer of property of the material incorporating the work be transferred. Since a download on the Internet requires a reproduction on another digital medium, such download should, in principle, not be considered as exhausting the copyright owner's distribution right, and a further transfer should thus not be permitted.

---

[42] *See* P. Gilliéron, Art. 19 N 33 and the cited references. This author suggests that the "triple test" should be applied on a case-by-case basis to assess whether the educational exception applies to distance learning.

[43] *See* P. Gilliéron, Art. 19 N 33 and the cited references.

[44] *See above*, Sect. 24.3.8.

To the extent that the "purchase" of a work by way of download from the Internet is economically similar to the purchase of a material copy of a work, it is debated among scholars whether Article 12(1) CopA should apply in such case.[45]

In our view, this should be the case to the extent that the work has been made available for an unlimited period of time through download (download to own) by or with the consent of the copyright owner. Accordingly, one who has downloaded a copy of a work in the aforementioned context should have the right to further transfer such copy to a third party, it being specified that this should not result in additional copies being made in the process (i.e., the person who transfers to a third party should not keep a copy of the work for himself).[46] Such right has been recognized with respect to software in a cantonal preliminary injunction decision.[47]

Terms and conditions that would prevent a user from further transferring a work that has been made available for an indefinite period of time (download to own) could be considered unenforceable on the basis of consumer protection law to the extent that such prohibition is deemed unusual.[48] However, when the works are made available on the basis of a subscription (e.g., Apple Music or Spotify), such works are not made available for an indefinite period of time. Such agreements correspond economically to the renting of works, which does exhaust the distribution right of the copyright owner. Consequently, the contracts related to such use may prevent the further transfer of works made available in that context.

## 24.6 Conclusion

Overall, it appears that the CopA strikes a satisfactory balance between the rights of copyright owners and users. There is, however, room for improvement, and the following remarks shall be considered in order to refine the status quo.

The fact that the CopA does not provide for a catch-all exception results in a lack of adaptability of the CopA to new uses that would otherwise satisfy the "triple test" and be fair. This has the upside of providing more legal certainty—as the exceptions shall be specifically set forth in the CopA—but has the downside of preventing certain uses, at least until the CopA is amended accordingly.

In our view, a catch-all exception—which should be based on the "triple test," be subsidiary to the other exceptions, and be applied exceptionally and only for

[45] *See* the thorough discussion of that topic in A. Alberini, Switzerland Chapter, in: Compatibility of Transactional Resolutions of Antitrust Proceedings with Due Process and Fundamental Rights & Online Exhaustion of IP Rights, Zurich 2016, p. 633 ss. *See also* H. Böttcher, Die urheberrechtliche Erschöpfung und ihre Bedeutung im digitalen Umfeld, Bern 2013.

[46] *See e.g.* E. Philippin, Art. 12 N 13 LDA.

[47] Zug cantonal tribunal, ES 2010 822 (May 4, 2011), sic! 2012 99.

[48] *See* A. Alberini, p. 650-651 and the cited references.

noncommercial uses—should be included in the CopA.[49] This does not mean that new exceptions should not be added to the CopA. When necessary to provide more legal certainty, new exceptions should be added to the CopA in order not to rely on the catch-all exception.

More specifically, the following exceptions should be considered:

- noncommercial user-generated content that makes use of works to the extent that such use satisfies the "triple test"[50];
- research uses; to a certain extent, the educational exception[51] could be applicable to research in a teaching context. The CopA Predraft includes a new exception (Article 24*d*) for scientific uses, which would authorize the reproduction and adaptation of works when they are necessary for the application of a technical process. This new exception would apply to text and data mining.[52] Such exception would be subject to compensation and would be mandatory. No distinction is made as regards the for-profit or nonprofit organization in Article 24*d* CopA Predraft; and
- A broader educational exception in order to ensure that distance learning is also included.

[49] On this topic, *see* C. P. Rigamonti, p. 391 ss, who suggests a wording for such "catch-all" provision: "*Soweit die Verwendung eines veröffentlichten Werks nicht in den Anwendungsbereich einer Schranke des Urheberrechts fällt, ist sie nur zulässig, wenn sie der Information, der Meinungsäusserung, der Ausbildung, der Wissenschaft, der Forschung, dem Kunstschaffen oder als untergeordnetes Beiwerk dient und keinen kommerziellen Zweck verfolgt. Diese Verwendung darf die normale Verwertung des Werks nicht beeinträchtigen und die berechtigten Interessen des Urhebers, unter Berücksichtigung der berechtigten Interessen Dritter, nicht ungebührlich zurücksetzen.*"

[50] *See e.g.* Article 29.21 of the Canadian Copyright Act (available at http://laws-lois.justice.gc.ca/eng/acts/C-42/page-9.html#h-27. Accessed 31 October 2017).

[51] *See above*, Sect. 24.4.4.

[52] *See* C. P. Rigamonti, p. 391.

# United Kingdom

# 25

Eleonora Rosati

Like all the other Member States of the EU, in general terms, the "acts permitted in relation to copyright works" under the Copyright, Designs and Patents Act 1988 (the "CDPA")[1] follow the closed system of exceptions and limitations envisaged by relevant EU directives, notably Directive 2001/29[2] (the "InfoSoc Directive").[3] However, it should be noted at the outset that, while the InfoSoc Directive is "the" general EU copyright directive, EU legislature has adopted directives relating to specific subject matter, which also provide for sets of exceptions and limitations that

The author is grateful to Michael Browne (Wiggin LLP) and the attendees of the workshop organized by the Competition Law Association at Redd Solicitors (London) on June13, 2017, for their feedback on an earlier version of this report.

[1] Chapter III CDPA refers to "acts permitted in relation to copyright works." For the avoidance of doubt, this report will consider the phrase "acts permitted in relation to copyright works" as synonymous with copyright 'exceptions', 'limitations', 'exclusions', and 'defences'.

[2] Directive 2001/29 of the European Parliament and of the Council of 22 May 2001 on the harmonisation of certain aspects of copyright and related rights in the information society, OJ 2001 L 167, p. 10.

[3] When the CDPA was enacted, UK legislature still enjoyed significant freedom from EU law constraints: the first copyright directive was in fact adopted in 1991 (Council Directive 91/250 of 14 May 1991 on the legal protection of computer programs, OJ 1991 L 122, p. 42).

E. Rosati (✉)
University of Southampton, Southampton, UK
e-mail: eleonora@e-lawnora.com



B. Kilpatrick et al. (eds.), *Antitrust Analysis of Online Sales Platforms & Copyright Limitations and Exceptions*, LIDC Contributions on Antitrust Law, Intellectual Property and Unfair Competition,
https://doi.org/10.1007/978-3-319-71419-6_25

are either optional[4] or mandatory[5] for EU Member States to transpose into their own legal systems.

## 25.1 The System of the InfoSoc Directive

The adoption of the InfoSoft Directive aimed at harmonizing certain aspects of substantive copyright law. Without harmonization at the EU level, diverging levels of protection at national level would have resulted in restrictions on the free movement of products incorporating, or based on, intellectual property.[6] This would also become more acute in light of the challenges posed by technological advancement.[7] Inconsistent national responses needed to be avoided, also "to ensure that competition in the internal market is not distorted as a result of differences in the legislation of Member States."[8]

In parallel with harmonization of the exclusive rights of reproduction (Article 2 InfoSoc Directive), communication and making available to the public[9] (Article 3 InfoSoc Directive), and distribution (Article 4 InfoSoc Directive),[10] the InfoSoc

[4]Article 6(2) of Directive 96/9 of the European Parliament and of the Council of 11 March 1996 on the legal protection of databases, OJ 1996 L 77, p. 20; Article 10 of Directive 2006/115 of the European Parliament and of the Council of 12 December 2006 on rental right and lending right and on certain rights related to copyright in the field of intellectual property, OJ 2006 L 376, p. 28.

[5]Directive 96/9 of the European Parliament and of the Council of 11 March 1996 on the legal protection of databases, OJ 1996 L 77, p. 20, Article 6(1); Directive 2009/24 of the European Parliament and of the Council of 23 April 2009 on the legal protection of computer programs, OJ 2009 L 111, p. 16, Articles 5 and 6; Directive 2012/28 of the European Parliament and of the Council of 25 October 2012 on certain permitted uses of orphan works, OJ 2012 L 299, p. 5, Article 6. See also the recent proposal for a directive of the European Parliament and of the Council on copyright in the Digital Single Market, COM(2016) 593 final, 2016/0280 (COD), contains three new mandatory exceptions at Articles 3 to 6.

[6]Directive 2001/29 of the European Parliament and of the Council of 22 May 2001 on the harmonisation of certain aspects of copyright and related rights in the information society, OJ 2001 L 167, p. 10, Recitals 6 and 7.

[7]*Ibid*, Recital 7.

[8]CJEU, case C-510/10, *DR and TV2 Danmark A/S v NCB – Nordisk Copyright Bureau*, EU:C:2012:244, pt 35, referring to ECJ, case C-479/04, *Laserdisken ApS v Kulturministeriet*, EU:C:2006:549, pts 26 and 31–34.

[9]The rights of communication and making available to the public are distinct and have different scope: "as follows from the wording of Article 3(1) of Directive 2001/29, and in particular from the terms 'any communication to the public of their works, … including the making available to the public', the concept of 'making available to the public', also used in Article 3(2) of that directive, forms part of the wider 'communication to the public'": CJEU, case C-279/13, *C More Entertainment AB v Linus Sandberg*, EU:C:2015:199, pt 24.

[10]As regards exhaustion of the right of distribution, UK law follows the EU approach. With specific regard to digital copies of copyright works, also under UK law it is uncertain whether exhaustion is available as a general principle or only applies to digital copies of computer programs (CJEU, case C-128-11, *UsedSoft GmbH v Oracle International Corp*, EU:C:2012:407). See further E. Rosati, Online Copyright Exhaustion in a Post-*Allposters* World, JIPLP (2015)(9), p. 673.

Directive also harmonized related exceptions and limitations (Article 5). Apart from the exception for temporary copies (Article 5(1) InfoSoc Directive), all the other exceptions and limitations within Article 5 are *optional* for EU Member States to implement. The InfoSoc Directive sought to define exceptions and limitations more harmoniously, but it was felt that their degree of harmonization should be based on their impact on the smooth functioning of the internal market,[11] taking account of the different legal traditions in the various Member States.[12] The outcome of this approach has been criticized by some commentators, who have stated that "the effect is of rough harmonisation only"[13] or even declared (with particular regard to the optional nature of exceptions and limitations in Article 5) that the InfoSoc Directive has been "a total failure, in terms of harmonization."[14]

The exceptions and limitations available under the *exhaustive* list of Article 5 are subject to the three-step test (Article 5(5)): they shall only be applied in certain special cases, which do not conflict with a normal exploitation of the work or other subject matter and do not unreasonably prejudice the legitimate interests of the right holder. Despite precedents in the Berne Convention (Article 9(2)) and the TRIPs Agreement (Article 13), the three-step test in Article 5 of the InfoSoc Directive is derived from the one contained in WIPO Treaties (Article 10 of WIPO Copyright Treaty and Article 16(2) of the WIPO Performances and Phonograms Treaty), which EU legislature sought indeed to implement into the EU legal order by adopting the InfoSoc Directive.[15]

As far as the United Kingdom is concerned, this Member State initially took limited advantage of the possibilities offered by Article 5 of the InfoSoc Directive; the UK approach was criticized in both the Gowers[16] and Hargreaves[17] reviews.

[11] Directive 2001/29 of the European Parliament and of the Council of 22 May 2001 on the harmonisation of certain aspects of copyright and related rights in the information society, OJ 2001 L 167, p. 10, Recital 31.

[12] *Ibid*, Recital 32 and Article 5(3)(o).

[13] W.R. Cornish, D. Llewelyn and T. Aplin., Intellectual Property: Patents, Copyright, Trade Marks and Allied Rights, 8th ed, Sweet&Maxwell 2014, §12.37.

[14] P.B. Hugenholtz, Why the Copyright Directive is Unimportant, and Possibly Invalid, EIPR (2000)(11), p. 501. In the same sense, see M.C. Janssens The Issue of Exceptions: Reshaping the Keys to the Gates in the Territory of Literary, Musical and Artistic Creation. In Derclaye (ed.) Research Handbook on the Future of EU Copyright, Edward Elgar Publishing 2009, p. 332, and bibliography cited in it. For similar criticisms, expressed at the proposal stage, see M. Hart, The Proposed Directive for Copyright in the Information Society: Nice Rights, Shame about the Exceptions, EIPR (1998)(5), pp. 169–170.

[15] Directive 2001/29 of the European Parliament and of the Council of 22 May 2001 on the harmonisation of certain aspects of copyright and related rights in the information society, OJ 2001 L 167, p. 10, Recital 15. For a discussion of the three-step test in the InfoSoc Directive, see R. Arnold and E. Rosati, Are national courts the addressees of the InfoSoc three-step test?, JIPLP (2015)(10), pp. 742–744.

[16] Gowers Review of Intellectual Property (2006) https://www.gov.uk/government/uploads/system/uploads/attachment_data/file/228849/0118404830.pdf. Accessed 15 April 2017.

[17] Digital Opportunity: A Review of Intellectual Property and Growth (2011) https://www.gov.uk/government/uploads/system/uploads/attachment_data/file/32563/ipreview-finalreport.pdf. Accessed 15 April 2017.

Eventually, in 2014, the UK Government chose to implement new exceptions from the Article 5 list (parody, quotation, personal copies for private use, text and data analysis) and to broaden the scope of certain existing exceptions (education, disabilities, libraries and archives, public administration).

## 25.2 UK Exceptions at a Glance: The 2014 Reform

As a reflection of the closed system of exceptions and limitations under Article 5 of the InfoSoc Directive, also the acts permitted in relation to copyright works (Chapter III CDPA) are a *numerous clausus*. Generally speaking, UK exceptions do not differentiate as to the exclusive rights at stake. In addition to a number of general exceptions in sections 28A to 31 CDPA (temporary copies; research and private study; text and data analysis; criticism, review, quotation, and news reporting; caricature, parody, or pastiche; and incidental inclusion of copyright materials), miscellany provisions for specific types of works (sections 57 to 75, including freedom of panorama subsection 62[18]), and an exception to the right of adaptation (section 76), the CDPA provides for a number of exceptions relating to disabilities (sections 31A to 31F), education (including distance learning, sections 32 to 36A), libraries and archives (sections 37 to 44A), orphan works (sections 44B and 76A), public administration (sections 45 to 50), computer programs (sections 50A to 50C), databases (section 50D), designs (sections 51 to 53), typefaces (sections 54 and 55), and works in electronic form (section 56).

As mentioned, the rigidity and narrow scope of UK copyright exceptions has been subject to criticism over time. Both the 2006 Gowers Review and the 2011 Hargreaves Review considered the copyright exceptions to be inadequate. They recommended the introduction of new exceptions (private copying,[19] parody,[20] text and

[18] Section 62 applies to buildings, sculptures, models for buildings and works of artistic craftsmanship, if permanently situated in a public place or in premises open to the public. It provides that copyright in such works is not infringed by: making a graphic work representing it; making a photograph or film of it; or making a broadcast of a visual image of it. Nor is the copyright infringed by the issue to the public of copies, or the communication to the public, of anything whose making was, by virtue of this section, not an infringement of the copyright.

[19] Gowers Review of Intellectual Property (2006) https://www.gov.uk/government/uploads/system/uploads/attachment_data/file/228849/0118404830.pdf. Accessed 15 April 2017, Recommendation 8; Digital Opportunity: A Review of Intellectual Property and Growth (2011) https://www.gov.uk/government/uploads/system/uploads/attachment_data/file/32563/ipreview-finalreport.pdf. Accessed 15 April 2017, §§5.27–5.31.

[20] Gowers Review of Intellectual Property (2006) https://www.gov.uk/government/uploads/system/uploads/attachment_data/file/228849/0118404830.pdf. Accessed 15 April 2017, Recommendation 12; Digital Opportunity: A Review of Intellectual Property and Growth (2011) https://www.gov.uk/government/uploads/system/uploads/attachment_data/file/32563/ipreview-finalreport.pdf. Accessed 15 April 2017, §5.32.

data analysis[21]) or the broadening (education,[22] libraries, and archives[23]) of existing ones. As a follow-up action to the recommendations included in the Hargreaves Review, the UK system of copyright exceptions was reformed in 2014. New exceptions were introduced allowing caricature, parody, or pastiche (section 30A); quotation (section 30(1ZA); the making of personal copies for private use (section 28B); and the making of copies for text and data analysis for noncommercial research (section 29A). The scope of a number of existing exceptions was also broadened: research and private study, education, libraries and archives, disabilities, and public administration.

Section 28B CDPA (personal copies for private use) was quashed in 2015, further to an application for judicial review filed by the British Academy of Songwriters, Composers & Authors (BASCA), the Musicians' Union, and UK Music over lack of a fair compensation mechanism.[24] The High Court of England and Wales (Green J) motivated the decision[25] on the ground that the UK Government had not provided adequate evidence that would justify a new UK private copying exception exempt from the provision of a fair compensation requirement under Article 5(2)(b) of the InfoSoc Directive.[26]

[21] Digital Opportunity: A Review of Intellectual Property and Growth (2011) https://www.gov.uk/government/uploads/system/uploads/attachment_data/file/32563/ipreview-finalreport.pdf. Accessed 15 April 2017, §5.33.

[22] Gowers Review of Intellectual Property (2006) https://www.gov.uk/government/uploads/system/uploads/attachment_data/file/228849/0118404830.pdf. Accessed 15 April 2017, Recommendation 2 (recommending amendments to sections 35 and 36 CDPA to cover distance learning and interactive whiteboards); Digital Opportunity: A Review of Intellectual Property and Growth (2011) https://www.gov.uk/government/uploads/system/uploads/attachment_data/file/32563/ipreview-finalreport.pdf. Accessed 15 April 2017., §5.3.

[23] Gowers Review of Intellectual Property (2006) https://www.gov.uk/government/uploads/system/uploads/attachment_data/file/228849/0118404830.pdf. Accessed 15 April 2017, Recommendations 10a and 10b; Digital Opportunity: A Review of Intellectual Property and Growth (2011) https://www.gov.uk/government/uploads/system/uploads/attachment_data/file/32563/ipreview-finalreport.pdf. Accessed 15 April 2017, Recommendation 5.

[24] Doubts regarding the lawfulness of the new exception for personal copies for private use had been also expressed prior to the application for judicial review: see A. Cameron, Copyright Exceptions for the Digital Age: New Rights of Private Copying, Parody and Quotation, JIPLP (2014)(12), p. 1003; K. Grisse and S. Koroch, The British Private Copying Exception and its Compatibility with the Information Society Directive, JIPLP (2015)(7), pp. 566–569.

[25] *British Academy of Songwriters, Composers and Authors and Others v Secretary of State for Business, Innovation and Skills* [2015] EWHC 1723 (Admin).

[26] However InfoSoc Directive, Recital 35 provides that "[i]n certain situations where the prejudice to the rightholder would be minimal, no obligation for payment may arise." This means that "the notion and level of fair compensation are linked to the harm resulting for the author from the reproduction of his protected work without his authorisation. From that perspective, fair compensation must be regarded as recompense for the harm suffered by that author": CJEU, case C-572/13, *Hewlett-Packard Belgium SPRL v Reprobel SCRL*, EU:C:2015:750, pt 36, referring to CJEU, case C-467/08, *Padawan SL v Sociedad General de Autores y Editores de España* (SGAE), EU:C:2010:620, pt 37. In the same sense, see also CJEU, case C-463/12, *Copydan Båndkopi v Nokia Danmark A/S*, EU:C:2015:144, pt 65.

## 25.3 The (Nonexistent) UK Three-Step Test

Unlike other Member States (eg, France[27]), the UK has not transposed the language of the three-step test within Article 5(5) of the InfoSoc Directive into its copyright law. The reason is that, at the time of implementing the InfoSoc Directive into its own legal system, UK Government took the view that relevant copyright exceptions already complied with the three-step test in the InfoSoc Directive.[28]

It is arguable that lack of a specific provision outlining the three-step test in the CDPA, together with the idea that the three-step test would be akin to the UK concept of "fair dealing,"[29] is the principal reason as to why "[th]ere has been very little judicial consideration"[30] of the three-step test in UK case law. Only the decisions in *England and Wales Cricket Board v Tixdaq* (2016)[31] (*Tixdaq*) and *Services v Chief Constable of West Yorkshire* (2011)[32] provide some meaningful analysis of the InfoSoc three-step test in the UK context.

In particular, *Tixdaq* (also discussed further in Sect. 25.4.4.2 below) was a case concerning whether the unauthorized reproduction and making available of short extracts of television broadcasts of cricket matches would amount to a copyright infringement or whether, instead and among other things, the defense of fair dealing for the purpose of reporting current events within section 30(2) CDPA would apply. The High Court of England and Wales (Arnold J) ruled against the defendants, in that their conduct could not be regarded as fair dealing within such provision. In reaching his conclusion, the court also provided some clarifications on the individual steps of the three-step test. In particular, it noted that "conflict with a normal exploitation of the work or other subject-matter" refers to exploitation of the work by the copyright owner, whether directly or through licensees. This requires

> consideration of potential future ways in which the copyright owner may extract value from the work as well as the ways in which the copyright owner currently does so. On the other hand, it also embraces normative considerations i.e. the extent to which the copyright owner should be able to control exploitation of the kind in question having regard to countervailing interests such as freedom of speech.[33]

---

[27] Article L 122-5 of the French Intellectual Property Code (Code de la propriété intellectuelle, consolidated version as to 17 March 2017).

[28] R. Arnold and E. Rosati, Are National Courts the Addressees of the InfoSoc Three-Step Test?, JIPLP (2015)(10), p. 743, citing DTI, Consultation paper on implementation (August 2002), 11–12, as reported in W.R. Cornish et al., Intellectual Property: Patents, Copyright, Trade Marks and Allied Rights, 8th ed, Sweet&Maxwell 2014, §12.37. See also M. Hart and S. Holmes, Implementation of the Copyright Directive in the United Kingdom, EIPR (2004)(6), p. 255.

[29] *England and Wales Cricket Board Limited and Others v Tixdaq Limited and Another* [2016] EWHC 575 (Ch), pt 89.

[30] *Ibid*, pt 88.

[31] *Ibid*, pts 88–92.

[32] *Services v Chief Constable of West Yorkshire* (2011) [2011] EWHC 2892 (Ch), pt 113.

[33] *England and Wales Cricket Board Limited and Others v Tixdaq Limited and Another* [2016] EWHC 575 (Ch), pt 91.

Considering the third step (that the exception at hand must not "unreasonably prejudice the legitimate interests of the rightholder"), Arnold J found:

> Although this is often treated as a separate and additional requirement to the second step, it has also been forcefully argued that it qualifies the second step. In other words, it indicates that it is not sufficient for an exception not to apply that there is some conflict with the copyright owner's legitimate interests, including the copyright owner's normal exploitation of the work. Rather, the exception can apply unless those interests are unreasonably prejudiced. This requires consideration of proportionality, and a balance to be struck between the copyright owners' legitimate interests and the countervailing interests served by the exception.[34]

## 25.4 Specific Aspects of UK Copyright Exceptions

Determining whether a certain unauthorized use of a work is shielded from liability by means of an exception is not entirely straightforward. The situation may be complicated further if the applicable law is that of a country, eg the UK and all the other EU Member States, that does not have an open-ended fair-use-style exception but rather requires one to, first, *identify* what exception might be applicable to the case at hand and, second, *verify* that all the relevant conditions for the application of that particular exception are satisfied.

As mentioned, the general approach of UK copyright law to copyright exceptions has been overall in line with the approach under Article 5 of the InfoSoc Directive. This means that, with the exclusion of certain subject-specific exceptions (eg, libraries, archives, public administration, educational establishments, or persons with disabilities), the beneficiaries of the principal exceptions are any user of protected works. Thus, the relevant assessment focuses on the type, finality, and modality of the use at issue. More specifically, the following questions are relevant under the UK to determine that the applicability of a certain exception is to address the following questions[35]:

a) Is the exception limited to particular beneficiaries?
b) Is the exception limited to certain subject matter?
c) Are the conditions provided for in the relevant provision respected?
d) Does the relevant provision envisage that the use is for a specified purpose?
e) (If the exception is framed within fair dealing) Must the use at hand be a "fair dealing" with the work in question?
f) Are there other considerations?

[34] *Ibid*, pt 92.

[35] A preliminary checklist was published in E. Rosati, Am I Covered by that UK Copyright Exception? Here's my Checklist, The IPKat, http://ipkitten.blogspot.com/2017/04/am-i-covered-by-that-uk-copyright.html. Accessed 15 April 2017.

Answering questions a) and b) serves to rule out the applicability to the case of exceptions whose beneficiaries are limited (eg, in the case of exceptions for libraries, archives, public administration, educational establishments, persons with disabilities) or only apply to certain types of works (eg, computer programs or databases). In a sense, these are preliminary questions to be considered and addressed. By contrast, questions c) to e) constitute the core of the assessment regarding the applicability of an exception in a specific instance.

Question c) considers whether a certain exception requires a number of conditions to be satisfied. For instance, the new exception for quotation within section 30(1ZA)—introduced in 2014 and yet to be subjected to judicial consideration[36]—requires that (1) the work has been made available to the public, (2) the use of the quotation is fair dealing with the work, (3) the extent of the quotation is no more than is required by the specific purpose for which it is used, and (4) the quotation is accompanied by a sufficient acknowledgement, unless this is impossible for reasons of practicality or otherwise.

Question d) requires one to determine whether the exception considered is only applicable to the use of a work for certain specified purposes. While section 30(1ZA) CDPA does not require the quotation to be made for any particular purposes, the same is not the case for other exceptions, such as criticism or review (section 30(1)), news reporting (section 30(2)), caricature, parody, or pastiche (section 30A CDPA).

Question e) is a crucial one for those exceptions that are framed within fair dealing (see also Sect. 25.4.5 below).

Finally, question f) considers other factors that might have an impact on the actual applicability of a certain exception. For instance, while applicability of the exception for caricature, parody, or pastiche within section 30A CDPA cannot be waived by contract (the exception being mandatory law, such contractual terms would be unenforceable), the exception leaves an author's moral rights unaffected.

A more detailed discussion of the issues underlying these questions is provided below.

## 25.4.1 Beneficiaries of UK Copyright Exceptions

As mentioned, with the exclusion of specific exceptions in favor of, eg, libraries, archives, public administration, educational establishments, and persons with disabilities, relevant CDPA provisions do not seem to restrict the beneficiaries of copyright exceptions. It is worth observing that, recently, the UK Government has legislated to broaden the types of beneficiaries of certain exceptions (eg,

[36] One of the principal decisions to consider will be CJEU, case C-145/10, *Eva-Maria Painer v Standard VerlagsGmbH and Others*, EU:C:2011:798, concerning interpretation of Article 5(3)(d) of the InfoSoc Directive. For a discussion of the international and EU quotation exceptions, see E. Rosati, Neighbouring Rights for Press Publishers: Are National and (Possible) EU Initiatives Lawful?, IIC (2016)(5) 47(5), pp. 588–591.

disabilities), and the UK's position in relation to other exceptions—notably text and data analysis—is generous regarding its beneficiaries.

In relation to the broadening of the type of beneficiaries of certain exceptions, one might recall that with its 2014 reform, the UK altered the scope of the disability exceptions (sections 31A to 31F) so that they would apply to any persons whose disability prevents them from enjoying the work to the same degree as a person who does not have that disability. Previously, the exceptions within sections 31A–F only allowed accessible versions of literary, dramatic, musical, and artistic works to be made for visually impaired persons.[37]

Turning to consideration of UK text and data analysis for noncommercial research (section 29A, also introduced in 2014), the UK Government believed that it could adopt such an exception by taking fuller advantage of the possibilities available under Article 5(3)(a) of the InfoSoc Directive. In particular, the new exception for text and data analysis was framed within a scientific research purpose and was allowed insofar as this remains of a noncommercial character. This was required to comply with the wording of Article 5(3)(a) of the InfoSoc Directive. However, this provision of EU law does not set any particular limitations as regards the beneficiaries of the exception. The UK decided not to impose any restrictions as long the work used to make a copy for text and data analysis research is one to which the relevant person has lawful access. In this sense, the range of beneficiaries of section 29A CDPA is broader than what is currently being considered for introduction at the EU level.

In September 2016, as a follow-up to its Digital Single Market Strategy,[38] the EU Commission released a proposal for a DSM Directive that—among other things and if adopted in the same form—would indeed introduce a new mandatory exception for text and data mining (Article 3 of the draft directive). Although including commercial and noncommercial uses alike (thus differing from section 29A CDPA), the scope of the proposed text and data mining exception would be limited to research organizations and appears to be narrower than the UK exception as regards its catalog of beneficiaries. They would be able to rely on the exception solely to carry out text and data mining of works or other subject matter to which they have lawful access for the purposes of scientific research. In addition, the definition of "research organization" itself is narrow: it only includes universities, research institutes, and nonprofit or public interest research-intensive organizations. In principle, the draft directive does not exclude the applicability of the text and data mining exception to public–private partnerships (Recital 10) but rules out that this could be possible when a commercial undertaking has a decisive influence and control over the research organization in question (Recital 11). At the time of writing, the DSM Directive has not been yet adopted by EU legislature.

---

[37] For doubts concerning the compatibility with EU law of the pre-2014 UK disability exceptions, see E. Rosati, Copyright in the EU: In Search of (In)Flexibilities, JIPLP (2014)(7), pp. 594–596.

[38] European Commission, Communication from the Commission to the European Parliament, the Council, the European Economic and Social Committee and the Committee of the Regions – A Digital Single Market Strategy for Europe, COM/2015/0192 final (2015), http://eur-lex.europa.eu/legal-content/EN/TXT/?qid=1447773803386&uri=CELEX%3A52015DC0192. Accessed 15 April 2017.

### 25.4.2 Subject Matter of Exceptions

The CDPA contains exceptions that are only applicable to certain categories of works. The introduction of subject-matter-specific exceptions has been often the result of implementing relevant provisions in EU directives. This has been, for instance, the case of sections 50A to 50C in relation to Articles 5 and 6 of the Software Directive, section 50D in relation to Article 6 of the Database Directive, and section 44B in relation to Article 6 of the Orphan Works Directive.

### 25.4.3 Conditions of Exceptions

Some CDPA exceptions are subject to a number of conditions. An example is the exception allowing the making of temporary copies (section 28A). Based on Article 5(1) of the InfoSoc Directive (this being the only mandatory exception under that directive), section 28A provides that copyright in a literary work, other than a computer program or a database, or in a dramatic, musical, or artistic work, the typographical arrangement of a published edition, a sound recording or a film, is not infringed by the making of a temporary copy that is transient or incidental, which is an integral and essential part of a technological process and the sole purpose of which is to enable (a) a transmission of the work in a network between third parties by an intermediary or (b) a lawful use of the work and which has no independent economic significance. Following lengthy litigation against media monitoring provider Meltwater,[39] which also included a reference for a preliminary ruling to the CJEU,[40] the UK Supreme Court held that section 29A CDPA would also apply to temporary copies generated by an Internet end user.[41] Recently, the CJEU ruled that the exception within Article 5(1) of the InfoSoc Directive does not apply to viewers of unlawful streams.[42]

A condition that is often found in relation to CDPA exceptions is the one imposing sufficient acknowledgement, unless this would be impossible for reasons of practicality or otherwise. While this aspect is also a factor considered when undertaking the fair dealing assessment,[43] it should be noted that lack of acknowledgment could not only prevent the application of a certain exception (eg, quotation within section 30(1ZA) CDPA) but also amount to an infringement of the author's moral right of attribution

---

[39] *The Newspaper Licensing Agency Ltd and Others v Meltwater Holding BV and Others* [2010] EWHC 3099 (Ch); *The Newspaper Licensing Agency Ltd and Others v Meltwater Holding BV and Others* [2011] EWCA Civ 890.

[40] *Public Relations Consultants Association Ltd v Newspaper Licensing Agency Ltd and Others*, C-360/13, EU:C:2014:1195.

[41] *Public Relations Consultants Association Limited (Appellant) v The Newspaper Licensing Agency Limited and Others (Respondents)* [2013] UKSC 18.

[42] CJEU, case C-527/15, *Stichting Brein v Jack Frederik Wullems, also trading under the name Filmspeler*, EU:C:2017:300, pts 59–70.

[43] L. Bently and B. Sherman, Intellectual Property Law, 4th ed, Oxford University Press 2014, pp. 224–226.

under section 77 CDPA, unless such right does not apply. The moral right of attribution is in fact excluded in relation to section 30, insofar as it relates to the reporting of current events by means of a sound recording, film, or broadcast; section 31 (incidental inclusion of work in an artistic work, sound recording, film, or broadcast); section 45 (parliamentary and judicial proceedings); section 46(1) or (2) (Royal Commissions and statutory inquiries); section 51 (use of design documents and models); sections 57 or 66A (acts permitted on assumptions as to expiry of copyright). The list in subsection 79(4) suggests in any case that the moral right of attribution remains enforceable in relation to exceptions that require acknowledgment.

### 25.4.4 Purpose of the Use

Determining whether the use at hand complies with the purpose allowed by a certain exception has proved challenging. In this sense, instances relating to criticism or review and news reporting are enlightening.

#### 25.4.4.1 Criticism or Review

Section 30(1) CDPA states that fair dealing with a work for the purpose of criticism or review, of that or another work or of a performance of a work, does not infringe any copyright in the work provided that it is accompanied by a sufficient acknowledgement and provided that the work has been made available to the public. Criticism or review of a work has been always permitted and, since the 1911 Copyright Act, has been the subject of a specific statutory provision. Prior to the inclusion of a quotation exception in 2014, formulation of the exception for criticism or review appeared, however, fairly narrow, especially if one compared the UK position to that of other EU Member States, and what is expressly permitted under Article 5(3)(d) of the InfoSoc Directive.

Despite its potential range, this fair dealing defense has not been much elucidated in UK case law.[44] In *Hubbard v Vosper* (a case concerning the publication of a book that criticized the Church of Scientology and allegedly included material copied from works by Scientology founder Ron Hubbard), the Court of Appeal of England and Wales (Lord Denning MR) clarified that the exception applies equally to the ideas expressed in a work and their mode of expression and that overall assessment is a matter of impression.[45] In general terms, it is necessary that the criticism or review relates to the work or another work or a performance of a work. It may concern the work as a whole or a single aspect of a work, the thought or philosophy underpinning a work, or its social and moral implications.[46] Some decisions have suggested that the criti-

---

[44] W.R. Cornish, D. Llewelyn and T. Aplin, Intellectual Property: Patents, Copyright, Trade Marks and Allied Rights, 8th ed, Sweet&Maxwell 2014, p. 494.

[45] *Per* Lord Denning MR, *Hubbard v Vosper* [1972] 2 QB 84, pt 94.

[46] L. Bently and B. Sherman, Intellectual Property Law, 4th ed, Oxford University Press 2014, p. 210; N. Caddick, G. Davies and G. Harbottle, Copinger and Skone James on Copyright, 17th ed Sweet&Maxwell, London, §9.52.

cism or review may not necessarily relate to a work at all.[47] For instance, in *Time Warner v Channel 4*,[48] the Court of Appeal of England and Wales considered whether use in a TV documentary of twelve clips from Kubrick's film *A Clockwork Orange* that varied in length between 10 s and 115 s and amounting in aggregate to about 12.5 min (8% of the film and 40% of the TV program) could be considered fair. The court answered affirmatively because inclusion of parts of Kubrick's work served the aim of illustrating the Kubrick's decision to withdraw the film from circulation in the UK. It was held that, although there is no codified test of fairness under UK law, there are criteria that courts take into account, including (1) to what extent the alleged infringing use competes with exploitation of the copyright work by the owner, including any form or activity that potentially affects the value of the copyright work; (2) the extent of the use and importance of what has been taken; (3) the purpose of the use, *ie* whether the use was necessary at all to make the point in question; and (4) proper acknowledgment of the author of the work.[49] It would appear that *Time Warner v Channel 4* pushed the exception (at least in the pre-2014 context) to the extreme. In another case, *Ashdown v Telegraph*,[50] the Court of Appeal of England and Wales held that the publication of the memorandum of the meeting between UK politicians Paddy Ashdown and Tony Blair was not for criticism of 'the work' but rather for criticism of the political events described/recorded therein. As such, the defense of fair dealing for criticism or review did not apply.

#### 25.4.4.2 News Reporting

Section 30(2)–(3) provides that fair dealing with a work (other than a photograph) for the purpose of reporting current events does not infringe any copyright in the work provided that it is accompanied by sufficient acknowledgement. No acknowledgement is required in connection with the reporting of current events by means of a sound recording, film, or broadcast where this would be impossible for reasons of practicality or otherwise. The applicability of the exception for news reporting was considered in the 2016 decision in *Tixdaq*.[51]

The claimants in this case owned the copyrights in TV broadcasts (and films incorporated therein) of most cricket matches played by the England men's and women's cricket teams. The defendants operated a website, www.fanatix.com, and various apps whose features have changed over time. By using screen capture technology, the defendants, their contractors, and members of the public uploaded clips

[47] But see, critically, T. Aplin and J. Davies, Intellectual Property Law – Text, Cases, and Materials, 3rd ed, Oxford University Press 2017, §4.3.2.3., referring to *Pro Sieben Media AG v Carlton UK Television* [1999] 1 WLR 605.

[48] *Time Warner Entertainment Ltd v Channel 4 Television Corporation Plc* [1994] EMLR 1.

[49] As clarified by section 178 CDPA, "'sufficient acknowledgement' means an acknowledgement identifying the work in question by its title or other description, and identifying the author." *See* also *Express Newspaper Plc v News (UK) Ltd* [1990] FSR 359, pt 367.

[50] *The Right Honourable Paddy Ashdown, MP PC v Telegraph Group Ltd* [2001] EWCA Civ 1142.

[51] *England and Wales Cricket Board Limited and Others v Tixdaq Limited and Another* [2016] EWHC 575 (Ch), pts 88–92.

of the claimants' broadcasts lasting up to 8 s. These clips were also available on their social media accounts. The claimants sued for copyright infringement, with the defendants denying infringement on the ground that their activities were protected—among other things—as fair dealing for the purpose of reporting current events within section 30(2) CDPA.

The High Court of England and Wales (Arnold J) noted at the outset that section 30(2) CDPA must be construed in accordance with Article 5(3)(c) of the InfoSoc Directive.[52] The expression "for the purpose of reporting currents" in section 30(2) is very close to the expression "in connection with the reporting of current events" in Article 5(3)(c), but Article 5(3)(c) permits use "to the extent justified by the informatory purpose." whereas section 30(2) permits use that is "fair dealing." It follows that "an important consideration in the assessment of fair dealing is whether the extent of the use is justified by the informatory purpose."[53] Arnold J considered the various elements of the defense in section 30(2) CDPA and noted that domestic authorities "must be treated with a degree of caution, since they were mostly decided prior to the implementation of the [InfoSoc] Directive and all of them were decided well before the recent jurisprudence of the CJEU concerning the interpretation of that Directive."[54]

The question whether the use was "for the purpose of" reporting current events is to be judged objectively. Arnold J noted that although Recital 34 of the InfoSoc Directive refers to "news reporting," there is no warrant for interpreting "reporting current events" as being restricted to "news reporting." This said, "there has been very little consideration in any of the case law of what amounts to 'reporting' a current event,"[55] although in *BBC v BSB*,[56] the High Court of England and Wales (Scott J) held also that news of a sporting character could fall within the scope of the defense. Arnold J held that a contemporaneous sporting event would amount to a current event for the sake of the defense.[57] The core of the question was, however, whether the reproduction and communication to the public of the clips by the defendants could be considered for the purpose of reporting those events. The judge reviewed relevant evidence and held that the clips were reproduced and communicated for the purposes of (1) sharing the clips with other users and (2) facilitating debate among users about the sporting events depicted.[58] However, (1) was the primary or predominant purpose: users added comments to the clips they uploaded; they did not create a report to which they added clips. Equally, the clips were presented to viewers accompanied by the comments rather than reports being presented to viewers illustrated by clips. As such, use of the claimants' works was not for the purpose of reporting current events: "The clips were not used in

---

[52] *Ibid*, pt 68.

[53] *Ibid*, pt 70.

[54] *Ibid*, pt 74.

[55] *Ibid*, pt 81.

[56] *Ibid*, pt 82.

[57] *Ibid*, pt 106.

[58] *Ibid*, pt 128.

order to inform the audience about a current event, but presented for consumption because of their intrinsic interest and value."[59] The court decided to address nonetheless whether—assuming that the purpose was to report current events—the dealing at hand could be considered fair. It concluded in the negative, also holding that the defendants' activities were commercially damaging to the claimants and conflicted with a normal exploitation of their works and that the amount and importance of the works taken could not be justified by any informatory purpose.

### 25.4.5 Fair Dealing

A substantial number of UK copyright defenses are framed within the concept of "fair dealing." The CDPA does not contain a definition of "fair dealing," nor does it stipulate what factors are to be considered when assessing whether a certain dealing with a work is to be considered fair. The notion of "fair dealing" has been thus developed through case law from the perspective of a "fair-minded and honest person"[60] and has been traditionally considered a matter of degree and impression.[61] A number of considerations may inform the decision whether a certain use of a work is fair, although the relative importance of each of them will vary according to the case in hand and the dealing at issue.[62]

In *Ashdown v Telegraph*, citing with approval a passage from leading UK copyright treatise on *The Modern Law of Copyright and Design* by Laddie, Prescott, and Vitoria, the Court of Appeal of England and Wales (Lord Phillips) noted the impossibility of laying down

> any hard-and-fast definition of what is fair dealing, for it is a matter of fact, degree and impression. However, by far the most important factor is whether the alleged fair dealing is in fact commercially competing with the proprietor's exploitation of the copyright work, a substitute for the probable purchase of authorised copies, and the like … The second most important factor is whether the work has already been published or otherwise exposed to the public … The third most important factor is the amount and importance of the work that has been taken. For, although it is permissible to take a substantial part of the work (if not, there could be no question of infringement in the first place), in some circumstances the taking of an excessive amount, or the taking of even a small amount if on a regular basis, would negative fair dealing.[63]

---

[59] *Ibid*, pt 129.

[60] *Hyde Park Residence Ltd v Yelland and Others* [2001] Ch 143.

[61] *Hubbard v Vosper* [1972] 2 QB 84.

[62] L. Bently and B. Sherman, Intellectual Property Law, 4th ed, Oxford University Press 2014, p. 224. See also R. Arnold and E. Rosati, Are National Courts the Addressees of the InfoSoc Three-Step Test?, JIPLP (2015)(10), p. 748; S. Jacques, Are the New 'Fair Dealing' Provisions an Improvement on the Previous UK Law, and Why?, JIPLP (2015)(9), p. 703.

[63] *The Right Honourable Paddy Ashdown, MP PC v Telegraph Group Ltd* [2001] EWCA Civ 1142, pt 70.

### 25.4.6 Other Considerations

When assessing whether a certain exception would be applicable to the case at hand, a number of considerations other than those addressed above may require to be undertaken. These include, among other things, the issue of contractual override, moral rights, and technological protection measures.

#### 25.4.6.1 Contractual Override

Further to the recommendations included in the Hargreaves Review, the initial position of the UK Government appeared to be in the sense of favoring a broad prohibition of contractual override of exceptions.[64] More explicitly (and subject to the responses to be received by means of a public consultation), the government stated to be committed to introducing "a clause, applying to every exception provided by the [CDPA], which would make clear that any contract term purporting to prohibit or restrict the use of an exception is unenforceable."[65] The government's response in December 2012 excluded the feasibility of a blanket ban on contract overriding copyright, although "the general principle that contracts should not be allowed to erode the benefits of permitted acts is accepted."[66] The result was that only the drafting of exceptions relating to (the now defunct) private copying, education, quotation, text and data analysis, parody, research and private study, disabilities, preservation, public administration, and reporting was accompanied by a clause preventing contractual override.

#### 25.4.6.2 Moral Rights

Moral rights have traditionally failed to receive a particularly strong protection in the UK. Formally acknowledged only since 1988, their scope is arguably narrower than in continental, *droit d'auteur*-like traditions, especially as far as the right of integrity is concerned. While French law apodictically[67] states that the author has the perpetual right "au respect … de son oeuvre,"[68] the UK right of integrity (section 80 CDPA) requires a "treatment" of the work in question. In this sense, section 80 CDPA appears even narrower than what is provided under Article 6*bis* of the Berne Convention,[69]

[64] HM Government, The Government Response to the Hargreaves Review of Intellectual Property and Growth (2011), http://webarchive.nationalarchives.gov.uk/20140603093549/http:/www.ipo.gov.uk/ipresponse-full.pdf. Accessed 15 April 2017, p. 8.

[65] HM Government, Consultation on Copyright (2011), http://webarchive.nationalarchives.gov.uk/20140603093549/http://www.ipo.gov.uk/consult-2011-copyright.pdf. Accessed 15 April 2017, §7.249.

[66] HM Government, Modernising Copyright: A Modern, Robust and Flexible Framework. Government Response to Consultation on Copyright Exceptions and Clarifying Copyright Law (2012), http://www.allpartywritersgroup.co.uk/Documents/PDF/Modernising-copyright.aspx. Accessed 15 April 2017, p. 19.

[67] A. Dietz, The Artist's Right of Integrity under Copyright Law – A Comparative Approach, IIC (1994)25, p. 179.

[68] Code de la propriété intellectuelle, consolidated version as to 17 March 2017), Article L121-1.

[69] J. Griffiths, Not Such a 'Timid Thing': The United Kingdom's Integrity Right and Freedom of Expression. In Griffiths and Suthersanen (eds), Copyright and Free Speech, Oxford University Press 2005, p. 222.

which encompasses not just any distortion, mutilation, or other modifications of a work but also any other derogatory action. Overall, it would seem that UK right of integrity does not protect against nontransformative uses of one's work.[70]

While the UK's understanding of the right of integrity appears narrower than other jurisdictions, UK law currently lacks a statutory defense rooted within freedom of expression.[71] This means that alleged infringers of the right of integrity (but the same also applies to other moral rights) may not be able to rely on defenses like fair dealing for caricature, parody or pastiche, or fair dealing for criticism, review, and news reporting. It is, however, worth recalling that section 171(3) states that the enforcement of copyright can be prevented or restricted on grounds of public interest or otherwise. In *Hyde Park Residence v Yelland*, the Court of Appeal of England and Wales (Aldous LJ) reviewed a number of authorities and concluded that section 171(3) could be used to prohibit the enforcement of copyright in the case of a work that is "(i) immoral, scandalous or contrary to family life; (ii) injurious to public life, public health and safety or the administration of justice; (iii) incites or encourages others to act in a way referred to in (ii)."[72] Having said so—even if the existence of a public interest defense could be inferred from relevant statutory provisions and case law—its relevance would be residual, in the sense that it could only add to statutory exceptions in limited situations.[73]

### The Case of Parody

With particular regard to caricature, parody, and pastiche (section 30A CDPA), the scope of the exception (yet to be applied at the judicial level) may be potentially narrow. The need to introduce a specific exception pursuant to Article 5(3)(k) of the InfoSoc Directive was acknowledged by the Hargreaves Review and, prior to this (unsuccessfully), the Gowers Review. In accepting the recommendation of the Hargreaves Review, the UK Government observed[74] that the InfoSoc Directive does not require framing this exception within fair dealing. However, UK legislature decided not to go for an "unlimited"[75] exception (but no exception would be

[70] E. Adeney, The Moral Rights of Authors and Performers. An International and Comparative Analysis, Oxford University Press 2006, p. 406.

[71] See J. Griffiths, Not Such a 'Timid Thing': The United Kingdom's Integrity Right and Freedom of Expression. In Griffiths and Suthersanen (eds), Copyright and Free Speech, Oxford University Press 2005, pp. 211–244, explaining that omission of a defence based on freedom of expression from the drafting of section 80 CDPA was justified on fear of excessive complexity of the law.

[72] *Hyde Park Residence Ltd v Yelland and Others* [2000] EWCA Civ 37, pt 66. According to Mance LJ, instead, it would not be possible to categorize the possible scenarios that would trigger section 171(3): see pt 83.

[73] In this sense, Laddie et al., The Modern Law of Copyright and Designs, 4th ed, LexisNexis 2011, §21.22.

[74] HM Government, Technical Review of Draft Legislation on Copyright Exceptions: Government Response (2014), http://webarchive.nationalarchives.gov.uk/20140603093549/http://www.ipo.gov.uk/response-copyright-techreview.pdf. Accessed 15 April 2017, p. 9.

[75] HM Government, Copyright Exception for Parody – Impact Assessment (2014), http://webarchive.nationalarchives.gov.uk/20140603093549/http://www.ipo.gov.uk/ia-exception-parody.pdf. Accessed 15 April 2017, p. 1.

unlimited as compliance with the three-step test would be still required, especially if one accepts that Article 5(5) of the InfoSoc Directive is addressed at national legislatures and courts alike[76]). Although using a "minimalistic" wording (eg, without including references to the parodied work being published and receiving sufficient acknowledgement)[77] when drafting section 30A, the government decided to include a reference to the need for a fair dealing with the original work, so to minimize the potential harm to relevant copyright owners. Section 30A CDPA provides that "[f]air dealing with a work for the purposes of caricature, parody or pastiche does not infringe copyright in the work."

Relevant guidance on section 30A released by the UK Intellectual Property Office explains that further to the introduction of this new exception, a comedian may use a few lines from a film or song for a parody sketch, a cartoonist may reference a well-known artwork or illustration for a caricature, an artist may use small fragments from a range of films to compose a larger pastiche artwork.[78] Overall, fair dealing only allows one to make use of a limited, moderate amount of someone else's work. This means that any dealing that is not fair will still require a license or permission from the copyright owner.[79] While this might be acceptable for, say, a literary work, one could wonder whether the same could be possible in relation to a parody of an artistic work that did not reproduce a substantial part—if not the whole—of it. Leading copyright treatise *Copinger & Skone on Copyright* observes that "[a]s parody depends upon recognition of the work being parodied, the substantial part requirement will sometimes be satisfied."[80] If one considers the corresponding exception under French law, Article L 122-5 No 4 of the Code de la Propriété Intellectuelle apodictically states that once a work has been divulged, the author cannot prevent "[l]a parodie, le pastiche et la caricature, compte tenu des lois du genre." At first sight, the wording of the French *right* to parody[81] appears broader than that employed by the new UK exception.

---

[76] In this sense, R. Arnold and E. Rosati, Are National Courts the Addressees of the InfoSoc Three-Step Test?, JIPLP (2015)(10).

[77] J. Griffiths, Fair Dealing after *Deckmyn*: The United Kingdom's Defence for Caricature, Parody and Pastiche. In Richardson and Ricketson (eds) Research Handbook on Intellectual Property in Media and Entertainment, Edward Elgar 2017, p. 69, observing that "[t]he minimalistic drafting of section 30A reflects the text of Article 5(3)(k) of the [InfoSoc] Directive. However, it also recognizes the realities of cultural practice. Parodists do not generally adapt unpublished works, and parodies are rarely accompanied by explicit acknowledgment of source" (footnote omitted).

[78] UK Intellectual Property Office, Exceptions to Copyright: Guidance for Creators and Copyright Owners (2014), https://www.gov.uk/government/uploads/system/uploads/attachment_data/file/448274/Exceptions_to_copyright_-_Guidance_for_creators_and_copyright_owners.pdf. Accessed 15 April 2017, p. 5.

[79] *Ibid*, p. 6.

[80] N. Caddick, G. Davies and G. Harbottle, Copinger and Skone James on Copyright, 17th ed Sweet&Maxwell, London 2016, §9.63.

[81] Speaking of a "droit de parodie," see M. Vivant and J-M. Bruguière, Droit d'Auteur et Droit Visins, 3rd ed, Dalloz 2016, §651, also highlighting that this right is not limitless.

Furthermore, the changes to the CDPA have had no impact on the law or libel or slander, and left unaffected the regulation of UK moral rights, including the right of integrity. More often than not, a caricature, parody, or pastiche involves a treatment of an earlier work. Such treatment might be prejudicial to the honor or reputation of the author of the original work. As expressly recognized by the CJEU in *Deckmyn*,[82] there might a legitimate interest in objecting to a disparaging parody. More specifically, in this reference for a preliminary ruling concerning the understanding of "parody" within the meaning of Article 5(3)(k) of the InfoSoc Directive, the CJEU held that it follows from Recital 31 in the preamble to that directive that freedom of parody as an expression of one's own opinion is not unlimited. A parody that conveys a message that is discriminatory/racist may not be eligible for protection under Article 5(3)(k). To state otherwise would contradict the requirement for a fair balance between the rights and interests of the author of the parodied work and the rights of the parodist. It follows that, in these instances, the person who holds the rights to a work has a "legitimate interest in ensuring that the work protected by copyright is not associated" with the message conveyed by its parody.[83]

Finally, as mentioned, section 80 CDPA is drafted in such a way that there can be no defense based on freedom of expression against a claim brought on integrity grounds.[84]

#### 25.4.6.3 Technological Protection Measures

In line with EU law (Article 6 of the InfoSoc Directive), also UK law allows right holders to implement technological protection measures (TPMs) on their works and represses related circumventions (sections 296 to 296ZD CDPA). At the same time, the presence of a TPM may prevent uses of a work that are instead authorized by the law by means of relevant exceptions. Where the application of any effective technological measure to a copyright work other than a computer program prevents a person from carrying out a permitted act in relation to that work, section 296ZE allows that person or a person being a representative of a class of persons prevented from carrying out a permitted act to issue a notice of complaint to the Secretary of State. To be eligible for the complaints process, it is also required that the person has lawful access to the protected copyright work, or where the complainant is a representative of a class of persons, the class of persons has lawful access to the work (section 296ZE(10)).

[82] CJEU, case C-201/13, *Johan Deckmyn and Vrijheidsfonds VZW v Helena Vandersteen and Others*, EU:C:2014:2132.

[83] *Ibid*, pt 32. For discussion of how such 'legitimate interest' may be qualified, see E. Rosati, Just a Laughing Matter? Why the Decision in *Deckmyn* is Broader than Parody, CMLRev (2015)(52), pp. 523–528.

[84] J. Griffiths, Not Such a 'Timid Thing': The United Kingdom's Integrity Right and Freedom of Expression. In Griffiths and Suthersanen (eds), Copyright and Free Speech, Oxford University Press 2005, p. 223. But see N. Caddick, G. Davies and G. Harbottle, Copinger and Skone James on Copyright, 17th ed Sweet&Maxwell, London 2016, §11.51, suggesting instead a narrow reading of the potential of the right of integrity in relation to caricatures, parodies and pastiches.

## 25.5 Assessment of the UK System of Copyright Exceptions

The 2014 reform has introduced into UK copyright law new exceptions the necessity of which had been long advocated, eg parody and private copying. While the latter was short-lived and the UK Government does not appear intentioned to reintroduce it—even as a modified version—in the near future, the former has yet to be tested in court. However, similarly to the case of quotation (the presence of which is particularly important due to the narrow wording and interpretation of preexisting exceptions, notably criticism or review), also parody is subject to a number of limitations that might reduce its actual scope. In particular, the circumstance that section 30A is framed within "fair dealing" and leaves the laws on libel and slander—as well as the application of moral rights—unaffected might result in a narrow judicial interpretation.

As far as UK copyright is concerned, the forthcoming exit of the UK from the EU (Brexit) might present challenges but also open up opportunities for reform. This might be so, especially in case of "hard" Brexit, ie a scenario in which the UK is part of neither the EU nor the European Economic Area. In such instance, in fact, the UK would be no longer bound by the EU *acquis* in the area of copyright, including the closed system of exceptions and limitations within Article 5 of the InfoSoc Directive. The UK might thus decide to reform its copyright law and inject some additional flexibility into its own system of copyright exceptions. This might be so by means of (1) an open-ended clause in addition to existing exceptions that would encompass uses that could not fall within the scope of the other exceptions and employ the language of the three-step test[85] or even (2) introducing a system of fair use similar to that in place in jurisdictions like the US.[86] The High Court of England and Wales has recently interpreted and applied Section 107 of the US Copyright Act in *Sony/ATV Music Publishing v WPMC*,[87] a case concerning a documentary on the first concert of The Beatles in the US. Among other things, the dispute required the court to determine whether the exploitation of the documentary in the US would be an infringement of the US copyrights in the works of the claimants or whether instead the fair use defense would apply. Besides the US Supreme Court decision in *Campbell*,[88] Arnold J also recalled Pierre Laval's influential article entitled *Toward a Fair Use Standard*[89] and addressed criticisms of the fair use doctrine as being

[85] This is the proposal that the Wittem Group advanced with its model European copyright code: Wittem Group, The Wittem Project – European copyright code (2008), http://copyrightcode.eu/Wittem_European_copyright_code_21%20april%202010.pdf. Accessed 15 April 2017, Article 5(5).

[86] In this sense see also R. Arnold, L. A. F. Bently, E. Derclaye and G. B. Dinwoodie, The Legal Consequences of Brexit through the Lens of IP Law, University of Cambridge – Faculty of Law – Legal Studies Research Paper Series 21/2017, p. 7.

[87] *Sony/ATV Music PublishingLLC & Another v WPMC Ltd & Another* [2015] EWHC 1853 (Ch).

[88] *Campbell v Acuff-Rose Music*, 510 US 569.

[89] P.N. Leval, Toward a Fair Use Standard, HarvLRev (1989)(103), pp. 1111–1112.

"indeterminate and unpredictable."[90] The court noted how "[o]ver the last decade, however, work by scholars such as Pamela Samuelson, Barton Beebe and Matthew Sag has demonstrated that what at first blush may appear to be an amorphous mass of individual decisions can be analyzed and categorized in the same way as other areas of common law (negligence, for example)."[91]

## 25.6 Conclusion

Past application of UK copyright exceptions has not really considered the three-step test and appeared to favor a narrow construction of exceptions. The actual scope of the new UK exceptions is yet to be tested, and the possible opportunities presented by Brexit might result in an overall rethinking of the UK approach to copyright exceptions. In particular, the rigidity of a closed system of copyright exceptions on the model of Article 5 of the InfoSoc Directive might make it arguably difficult to accommodate instances arising out of technological advancement (an instance being the *PRCA* litigation and the question of lawfulness of internet browsing). In addition, with specific regard to the UK, the lack of a defense specifically rooted within freedom of expression and the potentially narrow scope of certain exceptions (including the new ones) might result in an undue compression of fundamental rights other than copyright,[92] including—notably—"users' rights."[93]

[90] *Sony/ATV Music PublishingLLC & Another v WPMC Ltd & Another* [2015] EWHC 1853 (Ch), pt 100.

[91] *Sony/ATV Music PublishingLLC & Another v WPMC Ltd & Another* [2015] EWHC 1853 (Ch), pt 100.

[92] Protection of copyright has been recognized as a fundamental – yet not limitless – right: see ECtHR, *Ashby Donald and Others v France* [2013] 287; ECtHR, *Frederick Neij and Another v Sweden* [2013] 76 (in relation to Article 10 of the European Convention of Human Rights); CJEU, case C-277/10, *Martin Luksan v Petrus van der Let*, EU:C:2012:65; CJEU, case C-314/12, *UPC Telekabel Wien GmbH v Constantin Film Verleih GmbH and Wega Filmproduktionsgesellschaft mbH*, EU:C:2013:781; CJEU, case C-160/15, *GS Media BV v Sanoma Media Netherlands BV and Others*, EU:C:2016:644, pt 31 (in relation to Articles 11, 16 and 17(2) of the Charter of Fundamental Rights of the European Union).

[93] The CJEU itself has referred to exceptions as users' rights in case C-117/13, *Technische Universität Darmstadt v Eugen Ulmer KG*, EU:C:2014:2196, pt 31.

FSC
www.fsc.org
MIX
Papier | Fördert
gute Waldnutzung
FSC® C083411

Kolibri 360 GmbH
Ferdinand-Jühlke-Straße 7
99095 Erfurt, Deutschland
produktsicherheit@kolibri360.de